Calendar Of Treasury Papers, 1556-7--[1728]... 20-1728

Great Britain. Public Record Office, Great Britain. Treasury

Nabu Public Domain Reprints:

You are holding a reproduction of an original work published before 1923 that is in the public domain in the United States of America, and possibly other countries. You may freely copy and distribute this work as no entity (individual or corporate) has a copyright on the body of the work. This book may contain prior copyright references, and library stamps (as most of these works were scanned from library copies). These have been scanned and retained as part of the historical artifact.

This book may have occasional imperfections such as missing or blurred pages, poor pictures, errant marks, etc. that were either part of the original artifact, or were introduced by the scanning process. We believe this work is culturally important, and despite the imperfections, have elected to bring it back into print as part of our continuing commitment to the preservation of printed works worldwide. We appreciate your understanding of the imperfections in the preservation process, and hope you enjoy this valuable book.

CALENDARS.

Instructions to Editors.

The Master of the Rolls desires to call the attention of the Editors of Calendars to the following considerations, with a view to secure uniformity of plan in the important works on which they are engaged:—

He is anxious to extend, as far as is consistent with proper economy and despatch, the utility of the Calendars of State Papers now publishing under his control: 1st. As the most efficient means of making the national archives accessible to all who are interested in historical inquiries; 2nd. As the best justification of the liberality and munificence of the Government in throwing open these papers to the public, and providing proper catalogues of their contents at the national expense.

The greater number of the readers who will consult and value these works can have little or no opportunity of visiting the Public Record Office, in which these papers are deposited. The means for consulting the originals must necessarily be limited when readers live at a distance from the metropolis; still more if they are residents of Scotland, Ireland, distant colonies, or foreign states. Even when such an opportunity does exist, the difficulty of mastering the original hands in which these papers are written will deter many readers from consulting them. Above all, their great variety and number must present formidable obstacles to literary inquirers, however able, sanguine, and energetic, when the information contained in them is not made accessible by satisfactory Calendars.

The Master of the Rolls considers that, without superseding the necessity of consulting the originals, every Editor ought to frame his Calendar in such a manner that it shall present, in as condensed a form as possible, a correct index of the contents of the papers described in it. He considers that the entries should be so minute as to enable the reader to discover not only the general contents of the originals, but also what *they do not* contain. If the information be not sufficiently precise, if facts and names be omitted or concealed under a vague and general description, the reader will be often misled, he will assume that where the abstracts are silent as to information to be found in the documents, such information does not exist; or, he will have to examine every original in detail, and thus one great purpose will have been lost for which these Calendars have been compiled.

As the documents are various, the Master of the Rolls considers that they will demand a corresponding mode of treatment. The following rules are to be observed:—

1st. All formal and official documents, such as letters of credence, warrants, grants, and the like, should be described as briefly as possible.

2nd. Letters and documents referring to one subject only should be catalogued as briefly as is consistent with correctness. But when they contain miscellaneous news, such a description should be given as will enable a reader to form an adequate notion of the variety of their contents.

3rd. Wherever a letter or paper is especially difficult to decipher, or the allusions more than ordinarily obscure, it will be advisable for the Editor to adhere, as closely as is consistent with brevity, to the text of the document. He is to do the same when it contains secret or very rare information.

4th. Where the Editor has deciphered letters in cipher, the decipher may be printed at full length. But when a contemporary or authorised decipher exists it will be sufficient to treat the cipher as an ordinary document.

5th. Striking peculiarities of expression, proverbs, manners, &c. are to be noticed.

6th. Original dates are to be given at the close of each entry, that the reader may know the exact evidence by which the marginal dates are determined.

7th. Where letters are endorsed by the receivers and the date of their delivery specified, these endorsements are to be recorded.

8th. The number of written pages of each document is to be specified, as a security for its integrity, and that readers may know what proportion the abstract bears to the original.

9th. The language of every document is to be specified. If, however, the greater part of the collection be in English, it will be sufficient to denote those only which are in a different tongue.

10th. Where documents have been printed, a reference should be given to the publication.

11th. Each series is to be chronological.

12th. The Prefaces of Editors, in explanation of documents in the volume, are not to exceed fifty pages, unless the written permission of the Master of the Rolls to the contrary be obtained.

*** Editors employed in foreign archives are to transcribe at full length important and secret papers.

CALENDAR

OF

TREASURY PAPERS,

1720—1728.

CALENDAR

OF

TREASURY PAPERS,

1720–1728.

PRESERVED IN

HER MAJESTY'S PUBLIC RECORD OFFICE.

PREPARED BY

JOSEPH REDINGTON, ESQ.,

ONE OF THE ASSISTANT KEEPERS OF THE PUBLIC RECORDS.

PUBLISHED BY THE AUTHORITY OF THE LORDS COMMISSIONERS OF HER MAJESTY'S TREASURY,
UNDER THE DIRECTION OF THE MASTER OF THE ROLLS.

PRESENTED

LONDON:
PRINTED FOR HER MAJESTY'S STATIONERY OFFICE,
BY EYRE AND SPOTTISWOODE,
PRINTERS TO THE QUEEN'S MOST EXCELLENT MAJESTY.

And to be purchased, either directly or through any Bookseller, from
EYRE AND SPOTTISWOODE, EAST HARDING STREET, FLEET STREET, E.C.; or
ADAM AND CHARLES BLACK, 6, NORTH BRIDGE, EDINBURGH; or
HODGES, FIGGIS, & Co., 104, GRAFTON STREET, DUBLIN.

1889.

Printed by
EYRE and SPOTTISWOODE, Her Majesty's Printers.
For Her Majesty's Stationery Office.

CONTENTS OF THIS VOLUME.

PREFACE.

ABSTRACTS of the Treasury Papers, extending from the year 1720 to the year 1728 inclusive, will be found in the present volume (the sixth of its series). Among the subjects which engaged attention, and which have left their mark in these papers, wero the affairs of the South Sea Company, the resistance to the Malt Tax in Scotland (accompanied by riots), and the ferment about the copper coinage in Ireland, known as "Wood's Copper Coinage."

In addition to the domestic matters with which the volume is of course principally concerned, several papers are found which are of some interest in connexion with the Island of St. Christopher. These are specially referred to in this preface. Under the head "Taxation," there is also a paper touching upon the great constitutional question of taxation in relation to Jamaica.

Under the head "Administrative Practice" attention is drawn to much of the information to be found on that subject. The control of the Treasury over other departments, and over individuals, as well as the internal management of those departments, has been kept in view in making the references. Although some of the information may not be new, and some perhaps of not very great importance, it still contributes something to the history of the Government Departments.

Other matters of interest, historical, biographical, social and topographical, are noticed under heads, as in previous volumes.

It is usual to add the minute of the Treasury Board at the end of each entry in the calendar, when the minute can be found; but no Treasury Minute Book is known to exist for the period between 28th April 1722 and 13th January 1724–5, so that where the minutes happen not to be written on the papers for that period the defect cannot be supplied.

Administrative Practice.

The following documents throw light more or less upon administrative practice as connected with Government Departments, viz. :—

A representation of the officers of the receipt of the Exchequer sets forth that the business of the officers of the Exchequer is to receive, direct, register, examine, record, enrol and pay all orders for money, &c. The officers complain of a large increase in their business, and hope their Lordships will not lessen their ancient allowance (CCXXXIII. 10).

A memorial under date 13th March 1720–1 touches upon the method of meeting the charges of prosecution for crimes and the maintenance of public prisoners in Scotland. Before the Union the charges were ordinarily advanced by the Solicitor General, and were refunded at least once a year by the Treasury; but when the prosecutions were more numerous, money was imprested by the Treasury to the Solicitor for that purpose. The Keepers of the prisons, before the Union, advanced what was necessary for the aliment of the prisoners who could not maintain themselves, and "fitted their accounts yearly" in the Treasury. Since the Union the Exchequer in Scotland refused to pass all those accounts, there being no fund for payment. Remedies are proposed (CCXXXIII. 39). The subject is again referred to in Vol. CCXLIII. 5.

A paper of the date 19th July 1721 refers to the management of the revenues in the Province of New York and the refusal to account with the Auditor General.

The Auditor General received a fee or salary of five per cent. upon the King's revenue in the province, which had never exceeded 4,000*l.* per annum (CCXXXIV. 51).

Charles Wither, Surveyor General of Woods, was contesting his right to perform all manner of work in the King's parks. He says Lord Chetwynde would do him a great injustice should he obtain leave to perform the work. It had always been understood to belong to his (the Surveyor's) office (CCXXXV. 56).

An importunate claimant upon the Treasury, who had already received a sum of money in full for his "pretended" service, makes a further effort and gets 10*l.*, upon condition that neither he nor his wife attend nor solicit the Treasury any more; and they sign a promise to that effect (CCXXXVIII. 64).

The Commissioners of Customs, Edinburgh, were of opinion that the salaries of most of the inferior officers were in no way equal to the trust reposed in them, and that the lowness of their salaries subjected them to too much temptation. Nothing was more apparent than that the revenue daily decreased by the corruption of their officers. The Commissioners were to advise as to what increase should be made (CCXXXIX. 12).

Precedents of warrants for cutting down trees in his Majesty's forests (particularly Sherwood Forest) were to be searched for in the Treasury Books, the Verderers of Sherwood Forest being very displeased with being forbidden to cut trees as "fee trees" by their own authority (CCXL. 2).

The Lords of the Treasury were disposed to relax the claim for duties on certain pictures, belonging to the late Ambassador to Berlin, in like manner as had been accustomed to be allowed to other Ambassadors on their return, but the Commissioners of Customs argue the matter with their Lordships, and plead that it has been the constant practice to insist on the payment of the duties, which (they say) are by law appropriated (CCXL. 5).

Their Lordships, by a minute, order a warrant for 500*l.* to Joseph Billers, a citizen of London, who claimed to have been engaged in detecting several public abuses by direction of the Government. A few days later they confirm the minute, on condition that he promises not to trouble them any further on account of "his pretended services." [This seems rather inconsistent of their Lordships, for it may be asked, if the services were pretended, why did they award him 500*l.* for them] (CCXL. 29).

The Collector and Controller of Customs of the town of Glasgow give an account of their method of carrying on business. They kept no other books but "Permit books." There was no order, rule, or precedent for keeping a Ledger or striking a balance; but they had gone in the method of their predecessors. They further add that all their endeavours to keep their books in the manner prescribed will scarce suffice without a sufficient number of hands (CCXL. 91).

Their Lordships make a minute (17th July 1722) on an application by the Lieutenant Governor of Virginia for allowances for his transport to his Government thus:—"All preced[ts] are against such allowances" (CCXLII. 43).

The Commissioners of Customs, Scotland, in reply to the Lords of the Treasury, say they will prosecute fraudulent importers of tobacco, but they have, upon several occasions, attempted to recover the King's duties by English Bills in the Exchequer, without success. Their Lordships' minute is to the effect that they wonder that this has not been reported before, and they are determined to obviate such ineffectual attempts for the future. They direct the Commissioners to transmit the several instances to which they refer, in order that their Lordships may give instructions to prevent the like for the future (CCXLIII. 39). The Barons of the Exchequer of Scotland recommend proceeding by English Bill, but they express the opinion that whenever any prosecutions are carried on that way for duties, if the defendants can cover themselves by any claims of exemption by private rights, the determinations in such causes will, in all probability, go against the Crown (CCXLIII. 46).

John Hamilton had been appointed Head Distributor and Collector of H.M. Stamp Duties of North Britain. He owed his appointment to his having been instrumental in preventing the repeal of the penal statutes against Papists, in the reign of King James, and to his losses of 1,000*l.*, at least, upon that occasion. He was dismissed for non-payment of his balance. He says that this deprived him of 800*l.* which was offered for his post, and precluded him from a similar advantage to Mr. Pitcairn, late under distributor for Edinburgh and Leith, who had his arrears paid for him by his successor (CCXLIV. 62).

Sir R. Raymond, who was one of the Judges of the Court of King's Bench, says in a letter of 2nd March 1723 that he is informed that the Lords of the Treasury generally gave directions for payment of the salary of a succeeding judge from the time his predecessor was last paid. In his case it would be from the previous 28th of November (the last day of Michaelmas term), to which day the Lord Chief Baron Eyre was paid. This had been done in the cases of all the judges lately, and was so when his father was made a judge, nearly 45 years previously. Some instances are recited on the back of the letter, and others might "be found, to make it appear "that ye King is to save nothing by the death or "removal of any [of] the Judges" (CCXLVII. 27).

The Merchants of London complained of the many holidays kept at the Custom House (contrary to law), and that the Officers did not attend at other times. The Searchers likewise took exorbitant fees. They (the Merchants) asked that one Commissioner should attend every morning at 9 o'clock in the Long Room to despatch merchants' business (CCXLVII. 31).

The Commissioners for Salt Duties were censured for remissness in calling for their papers left at the Treasury. In reply they say it was their constant practice to order their messenger to enquire frequently for them, and they were assured that he did so. Upon enquiry for certain of the papers, the messenger was told they could not be found (CCXLVIII. 14).

The Commissioners of Customs (Scotland) proposed, for the better service of the revenue, to revive the practice of refusing employment in the Customs to inhabitants resident in the outports, and their Lordships approved of their presentment (CCXLIX. 6).

There is a letter of the eminent painter Sir James Thornhill to the Commissioners of Works. He says that he is informed that the Commissioners had received instructions to employ some improper person to do the gilding on the wainscot in the Gallery at Kensington, &c. As the gilding had always been done by his predecessors and himself, he thinks it a great encroachment on his office, as well as on his patent. The Lords of the Treasury, by a Minute of 5th October 1725, direct the Vice-Chamberlain to write to the Board of Works that the gilding is to be performed by Sir James Thornhill, the King's painter, whose office it is to perform works of that nature (CCLIII. 46).

A Report of the Commissioners of Excise on the memorial of the Controller, asking for an allowance to himself and clerks, shows how the office was managed. A claim was set up by the Controller in the year 1715, but was disregarded as unreasonable by the then Lords of the Treasury, and the Commissioners conceived that it was because there was no addition of business to the Controller himself, who did not execute the Office in person. The case of the Commissioners of Excise differed from that of the Controller inasmuch as the Commissioners executed their Office in person. They have to observe that the business in the Controller's Office must suffer, since there are clerks employed in it at large salaries that do no business themselves, but hire deputies at small salaries to perform it for them. One who is so employed by the Controller is by no means qualified. The evil has been complained of without redress, and they beg that no clerk be admitted without their (the Commissioners') approbation (CCLIV. 4).

The method of filling up a collectorship in the Customs is discussed in an opinion of the Attorney General [of Barbadoes], the point being whether Mr. Dunbar, Surveyor General of the Island, could lawfully depute Mr. Lascelles, or any other person, to grant a warrant to any officer of the Customs, or, if not, how the post might be filled until Mr. Dunbar could make the appointment (CCLVIII. 28).

The system of conducting the business of the Treasury as regards the issue of money is described in an undated paper [? 1727 or later]. No money was issued without the authority of the Great or Privy Seal. The paper explains the difference between the General Letters of Privy Seal and the General Letters Patent dormant (CCLX. 41).

The Lords of the 'Admiralty, in reply to a communication from the Treasury, say that they did not conceive that the information for which the Treasury had asked could be of any service. There is a very angry letter from the Treasury to them on the subject. In an addition to the Treasury Letter (but scored out) it appears that their Lordships had sent an order to the Comissioners of the Navy to prepare and lay before them the account which they wanted; and they remarked that they hoped they should receive a civil answer. An entry in the Minute Book states that their Lordships resented the treatment they had received (CCLXI. 1).

From a minute entered in the Minute Book, Vol. 25, p. 291 (1727), it appears their Lordships made enquiries of the Postmasters General to ascertain if their Officers, like others in the Revenue, submitted to a deduction from their salaries to make a fund for age and indigency (CCLXIV. 21).

Robert Knaplock and three others who were appointed by the Speaker of the House of Commons to print the reports, "representation," and votes, (mentioned in an account annexed,) apply for payment of their bill. The minute thereon is:—"My Lords understanding that the "votes delivered for the service of the House itself were "not used heretofore to be paid for by the Crown, their "Lordships order that fact to be enquired into and "stated," &c. In the Minute Book of 7th January 1729–30 their Lordships, having reconsidered the petition, agree that they be paid for all extraordinary papers and proceedings that the House may order to be printed; but their Lordships cannot advise that the King should be at the charge for the Votes daily delivered to the House of Commons (CCLXVI. 14).

The whole state and condition of the Office of Great Wardrobe are enquired into, the method of signing the account, and the fees and allowances due to the Keeper and other officers, the manner in which orders were given to the tradesmen, the mode of keeping the accounts, &c. were considered, and recommendations for better management were made (CCLXVI. 26).

AMERICA.—CLAIMS TO CUT TREES IN AMERICA.

The inhabitants set up claims to cut tress of upwards of 24 inches diameter at the butt, maintaining that all lands in townships, before the late charter, were private property. Timber and plank were also exported to Portugal, Spain, &c. (CCXL. 16).

Robert Armstrong's opinion was that the trees (in the province of Maine), whether standing or felled, were the property of his Majesty (CCLV. 22).

BIOGRAPHICAL NOTICES.

FLAMSTEAD, THE EMINENT ASTRONOMER.

From a petition of Margaret, the widow of Mr. John Flamstead, "his Majesty's Astronomer," it appears that 300 copies of the Astronomical Observations made by him, which were comprised in the "*Historia Cœlestis Britannica*," were printed at the expense of the late Prince George of Denmark, for the benefit of the author, but since that time the author had printed 340 copies of another part of the work, to make it perfect, and the petitioner prayed that the remaining 39 copies then at the Treasury should be delivered to her. Their Lordships' minute on the petition is: "9th March 1719–20. Mrs. Flamstead to send to the Treasury 39 copies of *Historia Cœlestis*, corrected by her late husband, and then my

Lords will re-deliver her the 39 copies which she deems uncorrect" (CCXXVII. 23).

THE DUCHESS OF MARLBOROUGH.

The Duchess complained of an encroachment made upon the passage that turned into Marlborough House occasioned by building sheds and cellars and by setting out benches. Besides this the persons concerned let stalls for herbs and stinking things that were a nuisance in the passage to the house. The Duchess desired that the passage should remain as it was without encroachments, according to the plan annexed to her grant from the Crown. She proposed to their Lordships to signify [to the persons concerned] that the leases were forfeited by the encroachment; but that the houses would not be pulled down if the persons referred to would themselves pull down those things by which they have encroached since this reign. The surveyor was to take such measures as might legally be taken to remove the same in case the Crown right was concerned therein (CCLIII. 14).

The Surveyor of His Majesty's Woods reports on a memorandum of the Duchess Dowager of Marlborough, who proposed to plough up certain of the ground in the Great Park at Windsor, without any great expense to the Crown, and with some little advantage to herself. The surveyor was of opinion that if 200 acres of the coarsest ground were annually ploughed and sown with grain in six or more parcels remote from one another, and if after three years of tillage they were laid down with proper grass seed, it would increase and preserve the game (CCLIX. 12).

William Penn, the proprietor of Pennsylvania.

A memorial on behalf of the widow of William Penn shows that at his death in 1718 the power of conveying the province of Pennsylvania to the Government was left vested in his executors, the Earls of Oxford and Powlet, and that his heir-at-law disputed the will. The widow was advised to apply to the Court of Chancery, and to make the Earls parties to the suit, and she prays to be allowed to do so. This was agreed to (CCXXVIII. 18). A report of the Attorney General on this subject is fully abstracted. It contains a history of the negotiations about the conveyance, and shows that the Lords of the Treasury agreed to have their names made use of in the Bill in Chancery (CCXXXIV. 8).

A further petition from the widow shows that she had been since advised to exhibit the bill in the Court of Exchequer, and that it would not be proper for their Lordships to be made parties; but that the Attorney General should be made a party to the bill (CCXXXIV. 9).

The cause was to be heard in the Court of Exchequer after Hilary Term 1725–6, and the widow and four of her children memorialised the Treasury to give instructions on his Majesty's part "against the hearing of the cause" (CCLV. 10).

Crown Jewels and Plate.

A copy of the Order in Council for the preparation of the gold work, jewels, &c. required for the coronation of King George II. is described (CCLIX. 36).

There is also an account of the charges of the coronation (CCLX. 15).

Also an account for the medals (CCLX. 21).

Foreign ministers and others were permitted to have plate from the Jewel Office, and to bespeak the same after what fashion they pleased. A report states that this had always been the case, and if it had introduced extravagance the Office could not help it. A limitation is proposed to this. The Lord Chancellor had 4,000 ozs. of white plate, and had the same liberty given to him as to others of having it made after what fashion he pleased, but not to exceed 1,700*l.* It was feared it would not content the Ambassadors to receive the better half of their warrant in common plate and in dishes (CCLX. 22).

The Goldsmiths Company.

There is an interesting report of the Attorney-General on the petition of the Wardens and Commonalty of the mystery of Goldsmiths of the City of London, who were empowered by Acts of Parliament to assay and mark, at Goldsmith's Hall, all sorts of manufactured plate, to prevent fraud. To defray the expenses of this work they usually took four grains upon every pound weight troy (being about one halfpenny value). For the last seven years, by agreement with a majority of the small workers, they had taken other sums; but there was still a deficiency of about 200*l.* per annum. They complained that they could not support the charge; more particularly as they were prosecuted for receiving these allowances. They asked for a *nolle prosequi* and for further relief. The paper contains a good deal of information as to the manner of their carrying on their business. The silver had to be assayed and marked with the leopard's head. The company was satisfied with the four grains for the large plate, but it was not adequate for the small wares. The artificers were evidently very averse to foreigners sharing their privileges, and they made efforts in the direction of excluding them; but the Attorney General did not conceive that it could be done by law. The Attorney General considered that the fee of four grains was established by prescription or usage, but the increase would be extortion, and would, in some instances, amount to twenty times as much as was taken before. He further says that the public was concerned in the redress of this grievance, for the increase fell on the buyer and lessened the export (CCLIII. 10).

The Heralds.

The Heralds' claim to largesse fees at the coronations of Queens-Consort produce some interesting papers, and a representation by the Heralds as to their claims is printed in full (CCLXV. 19).

Historical Notices

Copper Coinage for Ireland.

There are notices as to the Copper Coinage for Ireland in which Mr. Wood, of Bristol, was concerned. The introduction of this copper coin into Ireland produced a good deal of excitement in that country. The methods taken in respect to this coinage and the comparison of the quality of the copper are referred to in the papers (CCXLVII. 39 and CCXLVIII. 13).

The state of feeling upon the matter is shown in a communication by the Commissioners of Revenue (Ireland) to the Lords of the Treasury. They speak of the disorder the nation was in about "these half pence," declarations having been signed by all sorts of people that they would not receive nor utter them. The whole nation thought they might safely refuse them. The Commissioners say that the uneasiness that people of all ranks were in was greater than could be imagined by any not on the spot (CCXLVIII. 17).

A Messenger to King William III.

Elizabeth Hyde, the wife of the master of a vessel belonging to Pool, in Dorsetshire, being in Holland, at the time of King William's expedition to England, is stated to have had an audience with the Princess of Orange and to have brought certain "packets of the greatest consequence" to the Princess and the States of Holland to be delivered to the Prince. This she effected by having the letters quilted in her clothes, and returning by Rotterdam, arrived at Pool. She went "thro' several of King James's troops" and, about thirty miles from Pool, met the Prince of Orange, and delivered the letters into his own hands. Fifty pounds per annum was settled on her and her husband and the survivor of them. They enjoyed the annuity till the beginning of the reign of King George II. Their son found that the annuity was continued in his mother's name after her death and he was anxious to have it in his own (CCLX. 34).

Scotland.

The State of the Highlands and Islands of Scotland, principally with regard to the multitude of Papists, is set out in an Address of the Commissioners of the late General Assembly of the Church of Scotland dated 12 March 1724. The address asserts that some of the remote Islands are wholly inhabited by Papists, and in divers parishes "on the continent" the greatest part of the people are popish. The parishes are from thirty to forty miles and upwards in length, and one minister and one school for each cannot suffice for instructing the inhabitants. The paper contains other interesting matters (CCXLVII. 29).

The Presbytery of Abertarf addressed the King on the same subject. They asked for an allowance to maintain preachers, catechists, &c. (CCXLVIII. 33).

A copy of a petition (the meaning of which in places is somewhat obscure) of the several Brewers in and about Edinburgh, to the Lords of Sessions, gave violent offence; for the Lords of Sessions found that it was false, scandalous, and seditious, and they ordained a copy of it to be forthwith burnt by the hand of the common hangman at the Market Cross of Edinburgh (CCLIII. 29).

In the previous volumes it has been shown how difficult it was to induce the Scotch to assent to the changes brought about by the Union. As the difficulties had been very great in getting them to pay excise duties on their liquor, so now the difficulty was not less in inducing the Maltsters to pay what was required on the material out of which the liquor was made. The papers have been very fully abstracted, as they are authorities for the history of this time, so far as Scotland is concerned. At Edinburgh the Commissioners of Excise report that they allowed the officers entrance, and made entries of their malt, but paid no duty and gave no security, and if the Justices gave judgment against them, they intimated that they would go to prison and leave off brewing. This would have the effect of distressing the people and disturbing the quiet. The Lords of Session would, however, oblige them to give security to carry on their trade for three months, or go to prison. No more than one brewer complied with the Acts, and he was branded with the name of traitor to his country, and the people he served with drink returned it to him. The other brewers left off brewing. A little later it is stated that by the prudent management of the Lord Hay, the Lord Advocate, and others, the concert of the Brewers was broken up; for a good number of them had begun, or designed to begin, to brew, and the Commissioners of Excise did not doubt that the opposition to the malt tax would decline apace, the whole country seeming to depend on the behaviour of "this place" (Edinburgh). Four or five of the ringleaders were confined in separate prisons.

At many other places they would not allow the officers entrance to their malt houses, and General Wade had to be appealed to for troops to protect the officers (CCLIV. 5). Glasgow, as a result of the riots, appears to have had to pay in damages 6,080*l.* (CCLV. 37).

The perplexed question of the 12 Scots Gallons which by the article of Union was said to amount to 34 gallons English, was not yet settled, for the brewers took the benefit of a sentence of the Justices, and retained 40,800*l.* as the amount of the difference. This the Commissioners of Excise (Scotland) proposed should be allowed them by an Act of Parliament, and further that an impost of 2*s.* a barrel, containing 34 English gallons, should be laid on (CCLV. 27). The Commissioners continue to complain of the Justices who acquit offenders though the proof be never so clear (CCLVIII. 7).

INSURANCE OFFICES.

The Royal Exchange Insurance Company was anxious to extend its business and obtain the "Fire Charter," and was in difficulty as to the payment of 300,000*l.* "for "the debts and expenses of the King's Civil Govern- "ment," which it seems to have been under obligations to pay, and which could no longer be delayed. My Lords in a Minute, which appears to apply to this company, say they will move the King to indulge the "2 Corporations." The Insurances were to extend to Ireland, but the grant extending them to Scotland would require to pass under the seal kept there in lieu of the great seal, &c.

The payment of 189,000*l.* by each of the companies was also delayed (CCXXIX. 1).

The Company again memorialized, as their attempts to raise sufficient money to meet their engagements had not been successful. This failure they say might be owing to the calamity of the times and the low ebb of public credit, &c. (CCXXXIV. 49). They were memorializing for further favour on 17th October 1721 (CCXXXV. 44).

The London Assurance Company was the other Corporation above referred to. There is a memorial from the Company in which they say that they were obliged to pay 300,000*l.* at several times into the Receipt of the Exchequer. They had already paid 100,000*l.* and endeavoured to raise 50,000*l.* more; but such was the pressure of the times, both for money and credit, that they have not any hopes of raising the same within the time. From the Minute above named it seems they obtained an extension of the time (CCXXVIII. 43).

Caveats were entered against the proposed charter to the Royal Exchange Office on the part of the Sun Fire Office and the Hand-in-Hand and Union Fire Offices (CCXXXIII, No. 13).

IRELAND.—THE LORD LIEUTENANT OF IRELAND.

The Lord Lieutenant's salary was paid out of the revenue arising from wool licences, and it was usual for previous sovereigns to make up the salary of 4,000*l.* per annum from the general revenue when the revenue from wool licences was insufficient (CCXXVIII. 7).

Law and Law Reform.

The Attorney and Solicitor General report upon a memorial of the Chief Cashier of the Bank of England in relation to an Act then recently passed. The questions were: (1) whether Trustees could receive the principal, notwithstanding the minority of their wards, and (2) whether such infants as had stocks in their own names might receive the same by their guardians (CCXLIII. 45).

In a copy of a letter of the Lord Chancellor to [? the Lord Chief Justice] the former says his Majesty has declared his desires that advantage should be taken of the yearly meetings of parliament to frame useful laws for the benefit of his subjects in their private property and commerce, for the encouragement of industry, and for the easy redress of fraud and oppression, and he desired that the annual provisions for securing the public peace might be constantly accompanied with one or more of such laws. His Majesty was anxious that the judges should be consulted, and that alterations in the old laws or additions of new ones should be immediately set about (CCXLVIII. 65).

Liability for Loss by Robbery.

The liability for loss by a receiver of revenue in a case of robbery in the receipt of the Exchequer is reported on by the Attorney and Solicitor General, and the Lords of the Treasury agree with those Officers that the loss cannot be made good otherwise than by the aid of the legislature (CCLXV. 11).

The Marshalsea.

It is represented that a prisoner in the Marshalsea prison was most inhumanly treated by the keepers and turnkeys.

He had to wear 30 lb. weight of iron for five months, and was loaded with 150 lb. weight of iron for nine days, was chained to the floor for three days and beaten by the turnkeys and convicts, &c. (Vol. CCXXXIII. 21).

THE NEWFOUNDLAND FISHERY.

Captain William Taverner, who had been employed in 1713 to survey the coasts of Newfoundland, and whose proceedings are noticed in the last volume (*see* preface p. xvii.), was recommended by the Commissioners of Tráde and Plantations to make a survey of the west and north-west parts of the Island. It was said that the survey would greatly contribute to the increase of the cod fishery and to the establishment of the salmon fishery which had been begun there (CCLV. 54).

QUEEN ANNE'S PHYSICIAN.

Sir Richard Blackmore, Knight, Queen Anne's physician, petitions for such a recompense as should seem meet to the Lords of the Treasury for his attendance on Her Majesty, which extended over a very considerable time. It involved visits generally once, twice or three times a day, including consultations, and he attended her Majesty in her last illness at Kensington several days without following any other business. He had received only twenty guineas at her first coming from Newmarket. It is to be hoped his other patients were more prompt in their payments, for his claim was only to be considered when her Majesty's tin was disposed of, and when her other servants were paid (CCXXXV. 38).

WILLIAM PITT, THE KEEPER OF NEWGATE GAOL.

The Attorney General gives his opinion upon the

demands for compensation of the Keeper of Newgate Gaol. Seventy rebel prisoners were committed to the Keeper's custody after the Rebellion, and thirty more were brought from the Tower and Fleet prison, and also committed to his custody. The prisoners spoiled the beds, bedding, and furniture, so that they were of little value. Seven hundred pounds seem to have been awarded to him (CCXXVII. 8).

Post Office.

Much information is given on the subject of franking letters, and its abuse by the Members of Parliament for Ireland. It was complained (29th August 1721) that the revenue was almost entirely sunk, in consequence of the great liberty taken by the members, who not only franked their own but other persons' letters. Statistics are given to show how the revenue was affected. The practice of freeing the letters was also indulged in by the Members of Parliament of Great Britain, who sent and received letters to and from Ireland free. Officials also covered traders' and other persons' letters.

A letter from Mr. Manley, who was a Post Office Official, says, "I beg you to acquaint our Masters that the franking "of letters by our Peers and Commoners increases every "day, as does the anger of 'em all ag'st me for endea- "vouring to put a stop to the extravagant freedome that "is practiced by them in franking letters that are not "their owne," &c. (CCXXXV. 17).

The Records.—The Right to Search Records.

Mr. Auditor Godolphin instructed his Deputy to reply to an applicant, who had asked to be allowed to examine the accounts of the Receiver of Lincoln, "that tho' every

" subject has a right to search for any records in his office, " paying the usual fees, &c.; yet those that come as dis- " coverers for their own advantage he does not think " himself obliged to give such any insight or assistance " therein" (CCXXVII. 16).

The State of the Records:—

The State of the Records at the Chapter House [Westminster] is described by Mr. John Lawton [one of the Deputy Chamberlains of the Exchequer]. The Rolls of the Court of Common Pleas suffered from damp and dust, and were lying on mats on stone floors. Many of the Star Chamber records were also rotting. A suggestion was made that certain of the writs from the Office of the *Custos Brevium* should be received into two rooms appropriated to the old port books. Their Lordships seem to have taken time to consider the matter (CCXLVIII. 26).

Rewards for Apprehensions of Offenders.

Claims for these are somewhat numerous in this volume.

The notorious thief-catcher, Jonathan Wild, is mentioned as being concerned with others in the apprehension of a highway robber (Vol. CCXLVI. 86).

The payments for rewards from 1720 to 1725 had been 5,000*l.*, and there were great demands not then satisfied. The proclamation under which these rewards was given was dated 21st January 1719. As the claims under it were becoming very burdensome the matter was submitted to the Attorney and Solicitor General (CCLV. 7). In their report on the question of what was proper to be done they say it is a question of prudence rather than law, for whilst the proclamation is in force any person performing the service will be entitled to the reward. His Majesty can determine the force of the proclamation by publishing a new one (CCLV. 55).

Scientific Instruments.

Some satisfactory method of ascertaining the longitude at sea had long been desired, and the matter had exercised the powerful minds of Newton, Halley, and others, who were of opinion that expensive experiments might be requisite, and a Bill had passed both Houses of Parliament some years before which provided for the payment of a reward to anyone who should discover a more certain and practicable method of ascertaining the same. Apparently as the result of this measure, William Whiston, clerk, sometime Professor of Mathematics in the University of Cambridge, who was striving to discover, by means of a dipping needle, the longitude at sea, endeavoured to obtain from his Majesty the means to enable him to gain observations at sea in remote countries to complete the "method" (CCXXXIV. 2). He obtained 100*l.* bounty.

Peter Laurans, who was also giving his attention to the same subject, claimed, by long study, to have attained the knowledge of making a machine for the discovery of the "longitude upon sea," and sought their Lordships' assistance to produce "the machine to the world in all its perfection," but my Lords would not pay any money until the machine was produced (CCXL. 19).

Upon a further petition their Lordships would not order him any money (CCXLIV. 33).

John Rowley, Master of the Mechanics to his Majesty, in petitioning for payment for work done by him, says that he had lately repaired the "Great Solar System, and "made several new additions to the same," for which he deserved 500*l.*, and had made for his Majesty's use a curious silver universal pocket dial, valued at 30 guineas (CCXLIII. 69).

St. Christopher, the Island of.

Many materials will be found for the history and topography of the Island of St. Christopher. The documents have been very fully described (CCXXXIX. 37 and CCXL. 3).

The papers (chiefly letters) relating to the sale of that part of the Island of St. Christopher called "Basse Terre" and "Cabeça Terre" arising in the year 1726 are fully abstracted. The proceedings of the Commissioners appointed for negotiating the sale are given. According to the opinion of opponents of the Commissioners the effect of the sale would be the depopulation of Basse Terre. The Commissioners seem to have thought it quite consistent with their duty to propose to purchase some of the lands for their own use. This may in some measure account for the many complaints and clamours that were made against them. His Excellency the Governor also opposed them. He did not like the price set upon the land which was sold to him, and could not forgive being left out of the Commission (CCLVI. 8).

Various letters of the same Commissioners on the same subject in the following year (1727) are also fully abstracted. They speak of the difficulties and disputes in which they were involved as well as improvements which have already taken place in the island in consequence of the sale (CCLXIII. 1). The Commission was renewed to the same Commissioners, with the addition of Lord Londonderry on 1 May 1728, and there are further papers in that year. His Lordship did not approve of the proceedings of the other Commissioners, and, like the Governor, he objected to the validity of the sales. He also expected to have had some of the surplusage (CCLXVIII. 6).

The Skerries Light-house.

Some interesting particulars are given as to the maintenance of this light-house, which was about three leagues from Holyhead. William French, Esq., built the light-house at a cost of 3,000*l.* His son (who was to have superintended the building of the light-house) lost his life at the commencement of the work. Six seamen also lost theirs at the same time (CCXLIV. 23).

The Lords of the Treasury, on 19th September 1723, by warrant directed the Postmaster General to pay Mr. French 200*l.*, as the money contributed from the navigation was not sufficient to support the light-house.

The Rev. Sutton Morgan (son-in-law of the above William French) petitioned the Treasury for consideration. He says he had spent about 400*l.* upon the light-house. He was referred to the Trinity House; but eventually the Lords of the Treasury were acquainted by Mr. Chancellor that the King was pleased to give him 300*l.* in full of all "pretenc̃ons" (CCLX. 25).

The petitioner sent a "supplemental" petition to their Lordships. In this it is stated that the Trinity House had reported in 1712 adversely to the scheme, and to the granting of a right to the profit that might arise from the light-house when erected; but the petitioner's counsel advised that their Lordships might have given him a renewed grant without reference to the Trinity House, with the addition of a halfpenny per ton, and double upon foreigners, &c. (CCLX. 39).

Taxation.

The Attorney and Solicitor General give an opinion to the Commissioners for Trade and Plantations, in their report of 18th May 1724, that "the laying on new taxes "will depend upon the question whether Jamaica is to be "considered merely as a colony of English subjects or as "a conquered country." If a colony of English subjects they cannot be taxed but by the Parliament of Great Britain or by consent of some representative body of the people of the island; but if a conquered country they may be taxed by the authority of the Crown (CCXLVII. 54).

Topography.

Various interesting particulars are set forth in a report of the Commissioners of Customs as to the Borough of Barnstaple and the Port of Bideford and the creek and harbour of Appledore. The Mayor and Aldermen of Barnstaple were apprehensive that Appledore would be annexed to Bideford, which, they say, would be of most fatal consequence to their town (CCXLI. 6, p. 179).

In answer to the above the Mayor, Aldermen, &c. of Bideford memorialize their Lordships, and state that they furnished their late Majesties William and Mary with several thousand men for the Royal Navy and about 50 sail of stout transport ships for the reduction of Ireland when Barnstaple did not send out five. They give particulars as to the state of the river (CCXLIII. 38).

Transportation and Subsistence of Prisoners.

Felons were transported from Newgate to the Plantations in America at the rate of 4*l.* a head. Jonathan Forward of London, merchant, was the person who was anxious to enter into a new contract in connexion therewith (CCXXXIV. 11). He complains that he had sustained a considerable loss by transporting the prisoners and "by the returns which have been made to him in tobacco." He was making further complaint that he should be 3*l.* a head out of pocket through the low price of tobacco. Their Lordships appear to have allowed him 150*l*. (CCXXXV. 22).

There are his articles of agreement to transport to America the prisoners at 5*l*. a head from Newgate and the home counties (CCLX. 9).

Mr. Cracherode reports that an application of the Keeper of the Gaol for the County of Buckingham is the first that has been made for compensation, in respect of the support of convicted felons, to the time of their transportation; and submits whether their Lordships will make a precedent. Their Lordships order a letter to the under-sheriff to ask why the demands are not paid (CCXLIII. 25).

There is the certificate of the Deputy Sheriff as to the subsistence of these prisoners. He says that until the year 1720 no persons were appointed by the Judges to contract for the transportation of felons, and it was not known on the sheriff's last petition for allowances, when the charges of subsisting the convicts would end, the general directions in the Act being found not sufficient. A warrant was ordered for the payment of the claim (CCXLIII. 37).

Warlike Inventions.

Sir Polycarpus Wharton invented a shell to be shot out of three several kinds of cannons, the principal merit of which was that when it pierced the enemies' ship it would burst into 30 or more pieces. He asked to be allowed a trial, but the minute of their Lordships is "My Lords can " do nothing herein (CCXLIV. 35).

Water Supply.

Thomas Acherley, Gentleman, was anxious for the Government to support a scheme he had contrived to supply all the western parts of Westminster and London with water. His first attempt had been to obtain an Act in 1718, 1719, and 1720 to bring water from the River Colne, at St. Albans. A committee reported that the scheme was practicable. The millers of Hertfordshire and others, however, opposed the scheme, and the Bill was laid aside. He now was endeavouring to obtain the supply from the Colne above Rickmansworth, and from the Gultchwell springs, which run into the Colne two miles below the place. He was opposed by Mr. Blackmore and others, who proposed to obtain a supply from the Cowley Stream, which was a branch of the River Colne; but his (Blackmore's) plan was found impracticable, as the level was too low (CCXLVIII. 30).

The supply of Westminster with water was evidently causing perplexity. Sir John Vanbrugh reported on the subject in May 1725. He says the scarcity about Whitehall was occasioned partly by the great failure of the springs in Hyde Park for want of rain, and partly by the proprietors of the New River Water cutting off a branch which served Whitehall for many years. He had endeavoured to recover some of the springs about the Mews and St. Martin's Lane, and believed that the additional quantity would prove sufficient to supply the Cockpit and Whitehall without any further aid (CCLII. 64).

The Surveyor General also reports in June 1725 on a petition of the Governor and Company of Chelsea Waterworks, who had undertaken to supply the City of Westminster and parts adjacent with water, which (by reason of the great increase of new buildings) was much needed. To carry out their scheme they say that they cannot have a proper place to make a reservoir to supply St. James Palace and the middle and lower parts of Westminster unless his Majesty will permit them to use the canal or basin lately made in St. James' Park over against Devonshire House, as well as the old pond adjoining to the Deer Pen Grove. They pray to be allowed to lay their mains to the pond and canal and from thence to the palace and streets adjoining. The question is considered of the resisting power of their mains, which would be of wood of sufficient thickness to be four inches from the bore. The surveyor reports in favour of the scheme, and says that if it were allowed the supply of water would be sufficient for common use, and for a fountain or other waterwork in the garden of the palace; and the canal (then dry) and the old pond would be an ornament to the park. By the minute it seems the report was agreed to (CCLIII. 11).

A further report of the Board of Works on the supply of the palaces of St. James's and Whitehall with water from the Chelsea Company shows that there was a verbal contract in the Treasurer of the Chamber's Office with the New River Company to serve the palace and stables at St. James's three times a week at 36*l.* per annum, but the company had often insisted upon 60*l.* per annum. They had taken off their "two inch main" which supplied Whitehall, and the palace would be almost destitute of water. There were about 104 houses about Whitehall, and the Chelsea Company offered a supply at 100*l.* per annum, which was considered reasonable (CCLV. 25).

THE COMMISSIONERS OF WORKS.

Repairs and alterations were going on or were proposed in connexion with the Painted Chamber, the House of Commons, the equestrial statue at Charing Cross, and the ceiling of the Great Chamber at Kensington. This latter seems to have been very badly executed (CCXLI. 12).

His Majesty commanded the Vice-Chamberlain to treat with Sir James Thornhill for the painting of the above ceiling, which was to be done out of hand (CCXLIII. 20).

ZOOLOGY.—HIS MAJESTY'S WILD ANIMALS.

The cost of keeping various wild animals and birds at Kensington is shown (Vol. CCLIX. 6); the tigers cost 16*d.* a day each. Some of the animals were kept in a paddock there.

The butcher's bill for feeding the leopard, tiger, and lion is reported on. Their allowance was said to be less than Sir John Eyles gave them. In his time each of them had 6 lb. of meat a day (CCLXV. 15).

Mr. C. H. Woodruff, M.A., has prepared the Index, and the Editor is indebted to him for the prevention of some typographical errors in passing the volume through the press.

TREASURY PAPERS.

VOL. CCXXVII. 1720. JANUARY–APRIL.

[1719 or 1720 or perhaps earlier.] 1. "A state of demands made by several foreign Princes, not yet satisfyd by the Crown of Great Brittain, for arreares of subsidies pursuant to Treaties or Conventions made for carrying on the late war against France."

Undated, but claims of this kind were in course of settlement (*see* Vol. CCXXIII. 27.) 1 *page*.

[1720 or later.] 2. Memorial of Alexander Bayne, Esq., to ——— Memorialist has presented a petition to his Majesty, setting forth his case in relation to the estate of Leuchars Forbes, to procure the consent of the King to have his claim tried. The estate being charged with debts "above the value" was sequestered by order of the Lords of Session. Robert Carstairs, deceased, purchased the right of the whole preferable debts, except those belonging to Captain Crichton, deceased. The estate was, in 1719, purchased by memorialist as a further security for the sums due to him by Carstairs. The Act of 5 Geo. [I.] in relation to forfeitures debarred memorialist from having the case tried at common law. Prays relief. 2 *pages*.

[After 1719.] 3. "Copy of instructions prepared by the auditors of the imprests in May 1714 for regulating the office of the Great Wardrobe and passing the accounts thereof."

Some of the instructions were added in 1719.

Docketed :—"Copy of Instructions marked B." 7 *pages*.

[? About 1720.] 4. Report of auditor Harley to the Lords of the Treasury on the state of the account of Col. John Husk of the money received and paid by him, as well for the pay and subsistence of three Dutch and two Swiss battalions belonging to the States General of the United Provinces (which were taken into his Majesty's service in April 1719 on occasion of a sudden invasion, intended to be made from Spain upon his Majesty's dominions, in favour of the Pretender); as for the charges of transporting the said troops from Holland to Great Britain. The accountant had to bring over the troops and to concert with Mr. Whitworth, H.M. Plenipotentiary at the Hague, the proper measures for drawing the troops together and embarking them at Williamstadt. 9 *pages* (*brief size*).

1720. Vol. CCXXVII.

[? 1720.] 5. Petition of Alexander Bland to the King in Council. Petitioner was sworn at Maidstone and "renewed" when made high constable for Ruxley Hundred, in the parish of Farnborough, where he made good improvement for the space of twelve years in the town. Was informed of the buying up of arms in secret, and of the open Rebellion to overturn the government by mobs, &c. By his Majesty's command, backed by those of the Privy Council, an order was sent to petitioner on 9 Feb. 1718–9, whereby he apprehended several of the chief actors and carried them to Rochester Gaol, together with 200 stands of arms; whereby he became a butt to their malice, and, having broken down his shop, they took 418 guineas and other money and goods to the ruin of his trade, which resulted in his committal to prison: prays to be provided for.

Also another brief petition from him to Mr. Walpole. 1¼ *pages.*

[? 1720.] 6. A portion of a series of accounts "of estates of papists as registered pursuant to an Act made in the first year of his Majesties reign" showing total annual rents, &c. arranged opposite the counties. Some of the names of the Popish recusants are given. Probably drawn out about the year 1720. 8 *pages.*

1719–20. 7. "New years guifts or other annual grat[uities] for the Secrÿs."

"New yeares guifts or other annual dues for the Lords," also "for the Clerks." 1719–20. 3 *pages (quarto).*

18 Jan. 8. Report of N. Lechmere, Attorney General, to the Lords of the Treasury, on the petition of William Pitt, Keeper of Newgate, in which petition he sets forth that soon after the late Rebellion there were 70 rebel prisoners committed to his custody, and 30 more brought from the Tower and the Fleet prison and committed also to his custody, by the order of the then Lords of the Council and Secretaries of State; that the common gaol not being large enough to contain the prisoners, the petitioner was obliged to lodge them in the Press yard and other rooms, which stood him in 200*l.* p ann., besides the expense of forty new beds, bedding, and other furniture; all which were so much spoiled that they are of little value. Petitioner was at great expense in paying guards and other "attenders" appointed by the Government, and for a guard-room, fire, and candles for the officer and guards for 15 months, and was at great charge in providing coaches and attendance for conducting the petitioners to be tried at Westminster. Has been at great expense in keeping other State prisoners, and prays for satisfaction. By affidavits it appears that 10*s.* a week has been usually taken by the keepers for lodging and accommodation of all the prisoners lodged in the Press yard; and the commitment fee at their entrance was 3*l.* 6*s.* 8*d.*, or three guineas at least; and when the State prisoners have been unable or refused to pay the keeper, the Government has given the keeper satisfaction. [The affidavits specify some overcharges.] Is of opinion that the petitioner paid for the accommodation of the guards 86*l.* 18*s.*, and for

VOL. CCXXVII.

1720. the conducting the prisoners to their trials 103*l.* 11*s.* 6*d.*; but for the beds, furniture, &c., fees, chamber rent, &c. for which the petitioner claims 1,643*l.* 2*s.* 2*d.*, the accounts appear to be much too high. Dated 18 Jan. 1719.

The petition referred to. The accounts of the charges in which the names of the prisoners are given.

Minuted:—"12th Septr 1721. Prepare a warrt on tres patents dormt for 500li in full of all expences and demands upon this account." Again:—"14 Novr 1721 Wt to be for 700li." 29 *pages or parts of pages.*

[About 27 Jan.] 9. "Charles Harison's report concerning lycences granted by the Court of Exchequer to compound upon penal laws, and from the last day of Trinity term to the last day of Michaelmas term 1719."

"Rs 27th Janry 1719–20. 5 *double pages.*

28 Jan. 10. Lord Stanhope to the Lords of the Treasury. Encloses, by the King's direction, papers in the behalf of William Fariss, Esq.—Whitehall, 28 Jan. 1719–20.

The enclosures are (1) a letter from J. Craggs to the Earl of Stanhope referring to the following. (2.) Letter from the Duke of Bolton to Mr Secretary Craggs touching the mills and weirs of Kilmainham, in the county of Dublin (being the forfeiture of one Macwey in the year 1641), the clear rent of which has been 77*l.* 18*s.* 2*d.* Has caused a *custodium* during the King's pleasure to be issued to William Fariss, Esq., his steward, at that rack rent. The mills are out of repair and must be rebuilt, and the weirs out of repair. If a grant be made to the said Farris for ever, at the same rack rent, he will lay out 1,000*l.* or more for the rebuilding, &c. Requests that the matter may be laid before his Majesty.

Minuted:—"2d May 1720. The survr of Ireland is to make a particular of the mills, weirs, &c. desired by Mr. Farris and to make a return to my Lords as soon as may be." 4½ *pages.*

29 Jan. 11. Report of the Barons of the Exchequer of Scotland to the Lords of the Treasury as to the grant to John Forrest merchant in Edinburgh, of the lands and barony of Tolqution, lying in the county of Aberdeen. Finds that the grant contains "a taxing of the waird holding" of a part of the said lands, but do not find that there are any non-entry duties or casualties and forfeitures by recognition or escheat affecting the lands, which will be discharged by the signature of his Majesty granting the same. The valued rent of the land is 73*l.* 14*s.* 11*d.* Edinburgh, 29 Jan. 1719–20. 1 *page.*

9 Feb. 1719–20. 12. Report of the Comrs of Excise for Scotland to the Lords of the Treasury on the memorial of Sir Patrick Murray and Mr John Drummond for themselves and the other sureties for James Freebairne, late Collector of Excise of Perthshire. There is a balance of 1,103*l.* 1*s.* 2¾*d.* due from Freebairne, the greatest part of

1720. VOL. CCXXVII.

which was money for which he falsely claimed credit in his accounts current without paying the same into the office, soon after which he went into the Rebellion. The case of the Memorialists is truly hard and worthy of consideration.

Minuted :—" 19th Augt 1720. Appropriated mo. May apply to parlt for relief."

Also the memorial. 3 *pages*.

9 Feb. 13. " An accot of the ordinary and extraordinary expence of her late Mats household, Chamber, Chappell, and stables for 7 months, vizt: from the 1st Janry 1713 to the 1st of Augst 1714 excl., being the day of her late Mats demise, as likewise what hath been received and paid since and what remains as yet unsatisfyed." Board of Green Cloth, 9 Feb. 1719. 1 *page*.

[? About 12 Feb.] 14. Petition of George de Lima, Greek merchant, to the King. Petitioner, residing at Port Mahone, in the Island of Minorca, was robbed of a chest of the value of 1,600 dollars by soldiers under command of Col. James O'Hara. Petitioner spent 500 dollars more in prosecuting them: prays reparation.

Minuted :—" 12th Feb. 1719–20. Mr Gascoign, the Recr of the rents of Minorca, to lay a state of his Accounts before my Lords as soon as he can." " Lr̃e writ." 1 *page*.

[? About 13 Feb.] 15. Memorial of the Duchess of " Buccleuch " to the Lords of the Treasury. King Charles II. by letters patent of 21 Sept. 26th year granted to James, late Duke of Monmouth, the manors of Spalding, Holbech, Whaplode, and Moulton, &c., in the co. of Lincoln, for 99 years from the death of Catherine, the Queen Consort. Afterwards the duke was outlawed, and the King by other letters patent of the 36th year granted the same in trust to Sir Stephen Fox, Knt., and Nich. Fen, Esq., together with other lands for a similar term to memorialist: hopes if there is any defect in her (the memorialist's) title that it may be made good, as it was the intention of his late Majesty to grant everything to her which the Duke forfeited.

Minuted :—" Feb. 1719–20. Agreed to." 2 *pages*.

[? About 13 Feb.] 16. Papers connected with the claims of Robert Hewitt for compensation for his own and clerk's labour in making states of Account for the Treasury, &c., and for expenses as Auditor General to the late Queen dowager, &c. Also for satisfaction to be made to him as a discoverer of rents and arrears concealed from the Crown, for which it has been usual to allow three fourths to the discoverer. The papers (which are copies) include the report thereon of the Auditors (S. Godolphin and Tho. Jett). [The last minute on the report is :—" 9th May 1719. My Lords cannot advise making any graunt to him out of ye growing rents ; but as to the demand of 200li and the discovery proposed, my Lords will move the King for a recompence, If he makes a discovery to the Auditors "] : the letter from Mr Lownrds by command of the Lords of the Treasury directing the Auditors to receive from him

VOL. CCXXVII.

1720.

the discovery, and after examination to report their opinion; Robert Hewitt's letter stating what he conceives there is due for the last fourteen years from the manor of Whoplode, in the co. of Lincoln, and the manor of "Moulton Dnor̃ cum Bewsolus," in all 1,811*l.* 10*s.* 10*d.*; letter from the same to Mr Robert Lloyd, deputy to Mr Auditor Godolphin, in which he says he was refused permission to see the Accounts of Mr Rose, the Receiver of Lincolnshire, and hopes he will not deny him what he thinks to be the right of every subject being ready to pay the usual fees. Dated 13 Feb. 1719–20; the reply:—Mr Godolphin ordered him (Mr Lloyd) to return this answer, viz.: "That tho' every subject has a right to search for any records in his office, paying the usuall fees, &c.; yet those that come as discoverers for their owne advantage he does not think himselfe obliged to give such any insight or assistance therein." There is also a copy of the memorial of the Duchess of Buccleuch described in the last entry. 7 *pages.*

24 Feb. 17. A. Cracherode to Charles Stanhope, Esq.: prays him to get his enclosed memorial read to-day to their Lordships, for the Sessions and Assizes approach, and he has an order to pay 56*l.* 14*s.* to the Judge's Clerks for their attendances at the late trials of the rebels, and another from Mr Secretary Craggs to pay 66li 13*s.* 11*d.* to one Mr King, an attorney, of Yorkshire, for prosecuting rioters at Ealand, in Yorkshire. Has already disbursed as much as can be spared. 24 Feb. 1719.

The memorial referred to, which prays payment for 800*l.* balance, and an order for 1,000*l.* on account, and another order for 250*l.* for his salary and allowance to clerks.

Minuted:—"24 Feb. 1719. To be considerd on Wednesda next." 2 *pages.*

2 March. 18. Letter from the "distillers at Bristoll abt running French brandy," to the Lords of the Treasury, enclosing a paper setting forth their real thoughts of the matter that the growing evil may be prevented. Bristol, 2 March 1719. *Signed.*

The paper referred to, which states that "we have no settled commerce with France, and probably never may." 5 *pages.*

5 March. 19. Petition of the Lady Catherine Jones, Administratrix of Richard, late Earl of Ranelagh, deceased, to the King. King William the Third, in consideration of the long and faithful services, and the great losses her father suffered during the war in Ireland, granted him a pension of 300*l.* per ann. upon the Establishment of that Kingdom for 21 years from 25 March 1699. The pension has been paid in Irish money with very great deductions for exchange, taxes, and other charges; prays for the extension of the pension for a further term. 5 Mar. 1719. 1 *page.*

7 March. 20. Two letters signed Will. Yonge, to the Secretary-at-War, as to the sums alleged to be due to the troops of his Majesty as Elector of Brunswick Lunebourg from the States General, no vouchers for which have been produced. Dorset Court, Mar. 7, 1719.

1720. VOL. CCXXVII.

Minuted:—"7th March 1719. Audrs of Imprest to prepare a sign manual to stop the sum of [ ] due to the Scots regimts and the sum of [ ] to the King as Elector of Hannover upon accot of pay to his troops in the State's service and to the Crown of England for naval stores furnished since the commencement of the last war out of the money certifyd by the comon to be due to them from G. Britain." 3½ *pages, quarto.*

8 March. 21. "Navy Office, March the 8th, 1719. An account of the value of the stores supplyd and workmanship performed to the ships of the States General, as also of pylotage paid for them the last two wars and which are still owing for, to his Majestie's navy." 8 March 1719. 9 *pages.*

8 March. 22. Memorial of Francis Nicholson to the Lords of the Treasury. Had a Commission to make sundry enquiries in North America. On his return attended the Board of Ordnance to make out what he had transmitted thither in relation to Col. Vetches' accounts. Draws attention to these accounts as well as to Mr John Bordland's connexion with the same. Dated 8 March 1719–20.

Also copies of her Majesty's Commission, caveat against Col. Vetch, and Col. Vetch's account. 9 *pages.*

[? About 9 March.] 23. Petition of Margaret Flamstead to the Lords of the Treasury. His Majesty in the year 1715 bestowed on petitioner's husband, Mr John Flamstead, his Majesty's Astronomer, 300 copies of the astronomical observations made by him, and comprised in a book entitled *Historia Cœlestis*, which was printed at the expense of the late Prince George of Denmark, and were designed by his Royal Highness for the benefit of the author. Mr Flamstead has since that time been at a very great expense in printing 340 copies of another part, to perfect the afore-mentioned book, without which the petitioner is of opinion it ought not to go abroad as a performance of her deceased husband: prays that the remaining thirty-nine copies now in the Treasury may be delivered to her.

Minuted:—"9th March 1719-20. Mrs Flamstead to send to the Treasury 39 copys of Historia Cœlestis corrected by her late husband, and then my Lords will re-deliver her the 39 copys which she terms uncorrect."

Accompanied by a list of persons who received copies of the above work. There is also a memorandum showing the number of "Rymers Fœdera" remaining at the Treasury, &c. 3 *pages.*

15 March. 24. Memorial of the Commrs of Customs and Salt duties in North Britain to the Lords of the Treasury; respecting illegal practices carried on by several merchants in running and re-landing salt and fish shipped for exportation. Had advertised the Comrs of Excise to stop payment of all debentures until further enquiry, and had appointed Mr Legrand, one of the Inspectors General, to enquire and report on the ports of Kirkaldy and Anstruther. Enclose his report and accounts, from which it appears the revenue has been defrauded of 59,393*l.* 17*s.* 11*d.* Have laid before the Deputy Advocate, for his

VOL. CCXXVII.

1720.

opinion, a state of the frauds, of which they enclose a copy, together with his answer. Will refuse to make out or pay debentures for salt re-delivered to [? by] their officers to such merchants as appear to have been guilty of any of these frauds. The Advocate doubts if by law they can justify such a step. Pray their Lordships' directions. Dated 15 March 1719–20.

Accompanied by all the papers referred to. 26 *pages.*

18 March. 25. Report of A. Cracherode to the Lords of the Treasury on (1) the petition of William Rhett, junior, showing that Col. Wm Rhett was appointed by Robert Johnson, Esq., Governor of South Carolina, as commander of two sloops fitted out to take certain pirates who infested the coast, and that the said Col. captured the ship Revenge, alias the Royal James, and brought her into Charlestown harbour, the crew amounting to 35, whereof eight were officers; (2) on the certificate of the Lieut.-Governor and Commander-in-Chief of the colony of Virginia, which states that two sloops were furnished and manned at his expense to destroy Edward Thach, a notorious pirate, with his crew; (3) on the certificate of Woodes Rogers, Esq., Governor of the Bahama Islands, who states that 13 persons were taken in piracy and brought into the port of New Providence, whereby the captors were entitled to 380*l.* reward; (4) on an instrument under the hands of two inhabitants of Harbour Island in New Providence, claiming 200*l.* for having delivered to the Governor of the Bahama Islands five pirates: giving his opinion upon these claims. Dated 18 March 1719.

Minuted:—"Wt prepared for 750li out of pyrates' effects in Lascells' hands." 8 *pages.*

24 March. 26. Draft of articles of agreement *docketed*:—"Contract with the Bank for circulating Exchr Bills." Dated 24 March 1719. 4 *pages (brief size).*

25 March. 27. Copy of resolutions of the House of Commons as to notice to be given to the Bank of England of the redemption of annuities of 88,751*l.* 7*s.* 10½*d.* and 100,000*l.* 25 March 1720. ½ *page.*

26 March. 28. Translation of the Swedish Envoy's letter (signed "Sparre") to Mr. Secretary Craggs. Touching the subsidies stipulated by the treaty of defensive alliance concluded with the King of Great Britain, deprecating the abatement of the value of the subsidies in the manner hitherto done by reckoning no more than 3*s.* 8*d.* of English money for a crown. London, 26 March 1720.

Also copy of the letter in French. 5 *pages and* 2 *halves.*

28 March. 29. "Auditors of the Imprests certificate [E. Harley and T. Foley] how far accotants have passed their accots." 28 March 1720. 16 *pages.*

[? About 9 April or perhaps May.] 30. Memorial of James Bogdani to the Lords of the Treasury enclosing the full state of his case touching the mills and manor of Hitchin in the co. of Hertford, which he found out by accident had been leased to one George Draper. Apprising their Lps that Draper was his intimate acquaintance and was ordered by him (Brogdani) to solicit their Lordships for a renewal of the lease of the premises. To his surprise found that Draper had obtained a warrant for a lease to himself. Prays that the Surveyor General's report and consent of the Duke of Newcastle in his (Brogdani's) favour may be called for, that Draper's wicked practices may be discountenanced, and that a renewal of the lease for 31 years may be granted to memorialist.

The "case" above referred to. [The pickage, stallage, tolls, and mills of Hitchin were demised by Catherine, the late Queen dowager, to Samuel Hemming, Gent., deceased, and by marriage settlement Bogdani was entitled through his wife (who was Hemming's daughter) to the premises]. April 9, 1720.

Testimonial of the Duke of St Albans in his favour. George Draper's answer; in which he says that Shotling Mill was burnt down in the year 1694, when Mr Hemming had 26 years to come therein, and that the same has not been rebuilt. These mills were then in the possession of Mr Hemming and not of the Duke of Newcastle. Portmill was suffered to run to decay by Mr Hemming and Mr Bugdani, and not by the Duke of Newcastle, who had no other interest therein than a yearly rent of 13*l.* 2*s.* 6*d.* Denies that he undertook to solicit for Mr Bugdani.

Two affidavits and two other papers.

Besides the above there are two other petitions and a previous report, and on the back of one is this *minute*:—"12 Augst 1720, Bogdani to have this lease; but my Lords will give Mr Farrer's man leave to resign his place of Landwaiter as desired." 17 *pages or parts of pages.*

12 April. 31. Report of Sir Isaac Newton to the Lords of the Treasury "on the value of Imperial dollars both intrinsically and by way of Exchange with Sweden." The difficulty is to know whether by the Imperial dollar be meant the common dollar, or the Rix dollar. If any payments have been made to Sweden since the Treaty of $\frac{6}{16}$ January 1700, the precedent is to be followed as the best interpreter of the treaty. If none; is told that the Imperial dollar is sometimes taken for the common dollar, but more usually for the Rix dollar, and that the word reichs or rycks thalere signifies Imperial dollar; but is not skilled in the German language. Mint Office, 12 April 1720.

Also extract from the Treaty between Great Britain and Sweden. 2 *pages.*

12 April. 32. Report of the Surveyor General (Cholmley) to the Lords of the Treasury, on the memorial of the Rt Hon. the Lord Aylmer, setting forth that Robert Osbolston, Esq., by his will gave to the Royal Hospital at Greenwich two light houses standing on the North and South Forelands, in the county of Kent, which he held by grants from the Crown at a rent of 20*l.* per annum. Has perused the letters patent of Queen Anne of 1 June in her 3rd year, reciting letters patent of 13 Feb., 12 Car. I., whereby the King granted to Sir John Meldrum two light houses erected on the North and

1720. VOL. CCXXVII.

South Forelands, and ordained 1d per ton to be paid of all laden ships and vessels of subjects or strangers passing from port to port, or "cross the seas by the Goodwin Sands"; half by the master of the ship and half by the merchant or owner of the goods; and 2d per ton by all strangers not trading in our ports, but coming in of necessity; to support the Light Houses: and granted to the said Sir John the power to erect and continue the light houses, and receive the dues for fifty years, at 20*l.* a year rent: reciting also that King Charles II. by similar letters of 21 July, in his 23rd year, granted a power to maintain, continue, and alter the Light Houses and the duties of 1d and 2d per ton to John Smith, Esq.; for 30 years from the surrender, forfeiture, or other determination of the term of 50 years, reserving a like rent; and by the letters patent of Queen Anne the light houses are granted to the said Robert Osbolston, Esq., with the same powers and clauses for the term of 17 years, ending 13 Feb. 1734. The clear profits may be estimated at 1,000*l.* per annum, and as this estate is a branch of the Civil list, and the surplus thereof is appropriated, cannot advise the granting of any term in reversion in trust for the Hospital, except a full consideration be paid to his Majesty for the additional term to be granted. April 12, 1720.

Also the application for the reversion to be made over to the Hospital, and the reference thereon to the Surveyor General. 3½ *pages.*

12 April. 33. "Report of the Right Honble the Earl of Lincoln and Mr Treby upon demands of Col. John Moody [late Lieut.-Governor of Placentia] for reimbursement of his expences for support of ye Garrison of Placentia." Dated 12 April 1720.

Minuted:—"5th March 172[1]-2. My Lords agree to the report . . order the ballance to be [p]aid out of the savings of the respective years upon . . pay of the garrison." "See in whose hands these savings are."

Col. Moody's demands are placed in one column and the "observations" opposite, and the report is signed. 10 *pages.*

14 April. 34. "State of the case concerning the Auditor General of the plantations right to audit the account of the four and half p cent. ariseing in the Leeward Charibbee Islands." April 14, 1720. Signed "J. Walpole," who is described as "the present Auditor General of the American Revenues."

There is also "Copy of Mr Secretary Guy's letter to Mr Auditor Blathwayt, dated the 16th of June 1680," as to the auditing previous similar accounts. 2 *pages and* 2 *halves.*

30 April. 35. Lord Lieut. of Ireland (Bolton) to the Lords of the Treasury. Encloses the address of the House of Lords of Ireland in behalf of the officers and servants attending their house, that they may receive the allowances therein mentioned, for their services during the Session. If his Majesty approve the augmentations, has to observe that the Gentleman Usher of the Black Rod may as reasonably have his allowance doubled. Dated, Dover St, 30 April 1720.

1720. Vol. CCXXVII.

The address referred to: besides which there is a list of allowances to them for the Session of 1717. 3 *pages.*

30 April. 36. The same to the same. Transmits lists of payments made by *Concordatum* in the years 1718 and 1719, for the necessary services of the Government of Ireland, together with the Lords Justices representation thereon. Asks for the usual warrant to ease the Concordatum of the said payments, by placing them on the revenue at large. 30 April 1720. Also the papers referred to. 5 *pages.*

30 April. 37. The same to the same. Encloses a letter from the Lords Justices, relating to the allowances to the Clerk of the Privy Council, and the Clerk of the Hanaper, and to several officers in Great Britain for services during the last Sessions; together with a list of the particular sums to be paid: asks for a warrant for payment. Also the papers referred to. 3 *pages.*

30 April. 38. The same to same. Has received a letter, &c. from the Lords Justices relating to a debt to the clothiers of certain regiments, for which a provision has been made by the Parliament of Ireland. These he encloses. The Rebellion of 1715 having occasioned the raising of eight regiments of foot and five of dragoons in Ireland, those regiments were placed on that establishment on 16 Feb. 1715 and clothed there, upon credit of their off-reckonings for two years forward, as was the practice at that time; but the regiments having been all disbanded in June 1717, the off-reckonings fell short of answering the whole charge of their clothing, whereupon the clothiers appealed to the House of Commons to be relieved; who voted 8,983*l.* 4*s.* 11½*d.* to pay the balance. Further represents that six regiments of foot and two of dragoons having been disbanded in the year 1718, to make room for the like number of regiments transferred thither from the English establishment, and not having subsisted long enough for their off-reckonings to satisfy the full demand for the last clothing, the House of Commons provided 4,450*l.* 2*s.* 7½*d.* in satisfaction of the debt. Asks for his Majesty's warrant to direct the payment of these sums. Dover Street, 30 Apr. 1720. 2½ *pages.*

VOL. CCXXVIII., 1720. May–September.

4 May. 1. A paper *docketed*:—"A. Cracherode's [Treasury Solicitor] state of causes under prosecution for Easter term, 1720. 4 May 1720." Lower down is:—"Some of these states are read and minutes set on the side." Dated 4 May 1720. 13 *pages.*

VOL. CCXXVIII.

1720.

7 May. 2. Com[rs] of Revenue, Ireland, to the Lords of the Treasury. Have been directed by their L[ps] to use all possible endeavours to detect and prevent agents from France from buying up wool in Ireland to be carried to France. State what they have done to prevent this "pernicious practice." Their endeavours have been so successful that there have been more than double the convictions, both for wool and ships, since the King's Accession, to what there had been in the previous fourteen years. By the measures they have taken they have reason to hope that any agents who shall be sent over for this purpose will be detected and prevented. Custom House, Dublin, 7 May 1720. 2 *pages.*

12 May. 3. Duke of Bolton to the Lords of the Treasury. Encloses petition of Major General Wynne praying for an allowance of 310*l.* 5*s.* per ann. on the establishment till a troop shall be given to him; which allowance is equal to the pay of a captain of horse in Ireland and which his predecessor General Davenport enjoyed in lieu thereof. As the Major-General would be a sufferer by having the regiment of horse, late Major-General Davenport's, conferred on him, without this allowance, desires that his Majesty's warrant may be obtained for the same. Dover S[t], 12 May 1720.

The petition referred to. 2¼ *pages.*

[? About 18 May.] 4. Petition of Captain Francis Stevens to the Lords of the Treasury. Petitioner was appointed by Sir Solomon de Medina in the year 1711 to solicit and obtain for him his several demands for bread and bread waggons, &c. due in the late war. Has brought these affairs to a conclusion, and Sir Solomon refuses to pay what he contracted for. Hopes to have his demand adjusted by the Com[rs] of the Army debt out of the 2,880*l.* in the hands of the Duke of Chandos. Prays their L[ps] to order petitioner's accounts to be laid before the Com[rs] to prevent his utter ruin.

Minuted:—"18th May 1720. This matter is not before my Lords."

Also a letter and five certificates in favour of the petitioner's claim. 7 *pages.*

19 May. 5. Copy of the Resolutions of the Court of Directors of the South Sea Company sent to the Lords of the Treasury, relating to the terms and prices to be allowed to the proprietors of the Long Annuities, 9 per cents, and tickets of Lottery, 1710. The Court was held 19 May 1720. 1 *page.*

25 May. 6. Report of Hugh Cholmley, Esq., Surveyor General to the Lords of the Treasury, on the state of repair of the gaol and Court House of the Manor of S[t] Mary's without the walls of the city of York. Has caused an estimate of the repairs to be made. The jurisdiction of the manor is very extensive and the repairs necessary. May 25, 1720.

Also the memorial of the Steward and Bailiff on which the report was made, and the estimate. 4 *pages.*

1720. VOL. CCXXVIII.

31 May. 7. Duke of Bolton to the Lords of the Treasury. Representing the deficiency of the wool licences from which he derived his revenue as Lieut.-General and Governor General of Ireland, and that it was usual for his Majesty's predecessors to make up the deficiency out of the revenue at large in case it fell short of 4,000*l.* per ann. Obtained his Majesty's warrant for the deficiency of the last year. Asks now that his Majesty's warrant may be obtained for the present deficiency, and that a clause may be inserted empowering him whenever the wool licences fell short to make it up whilst he continued Governor. 31 May 1720.

Abstract of the produce of the wool licences from 27 April 1719 to 26 April 1720. 3 *pages.*

31 May. 8. The same to the same, advocating an increase for five years of 300*l.* per ann. of Lord Blainey's pension, which was 182*l.* 10*s.* a year, as he had conducted himself with a becoming zeal and a firm attachment to his Majesty's interest, and was at present in circumstances too low to live suitably to his quality, or to exert his endeavours for the public service so far as he was desirous. 31 May 1720. 1 *page.*

3 June. 9. Report of A. Cracherode to the Lords of the Treasury on the petition of Benjamin Mence of the city of Worcester; in which he sets forth that he expended a considerable sum in proclaiming his Majesty in the city, of which he was sheriff; and in the following year, when mayor, was active in suppressing many rebellious mobs in the city, and in assisting Col. Newton in raising his regiment of dragoons in Worcester; for which services he was frequently insulted by the enemies of his Majesty and was put by, at the end of his mayoralty, from being an Alderman, contrary to the common practice; and has been ever since a great sufferer in his trade as a glover, on account of his known zeal for his Majesty and Government. Is of opinion that he might well deserve 200*l.* as his Majesty's bounty.

The petition and an affidavit. 2 *pages and* 2 *halves.*

3 June. 10. Duke of Bolton to the Lords of the Treasury. Sends memorial of Lieut.-Col. Richard Cole, lately presented to his Majesty, together with a copy of letter from the Secretary-at-War, signifying his Majesty's pleasure that he should find out some expedient to make up the Colonel's half pay to whole pay, till he is otherwise provided for. Also another copy of a letter. Has no other expedient to propose, than that he should be placed on the Military Establishment of Ireland by way of pension, at an allowance of 16*s.* 6*d.* a day.

The papers referred to. 5 *pages and* 2 *halves.*

9 June. 11. J. Craggs to the Lords of the Treasury. Transmits copy of an anonymous letter received by his Majesty concerning some fee-farm rents belonging to the Crown for consideration and report.

The letter referred to, which concerns property granted in fee in divers counties to William Berriff and others. 2 *pages.*

Vol. CCXXVIII.

1720.

16 June. 12. *Docketed*:—"Duke of Bucks' case as to alienacion fine on subscribing annuities settled on his wife." Copy of a memorial on behalf of the Duke of Buckingham. His grace and the duchess have agreed "to write into the South Sea 1,000[li] per ann. of the long annuities, part of her Grace's Jointure." They are advised to levy a fine, and the Com[rs] of the Alienations insist on 2[s] in the pound. If mitigated to 6[d] in the pound it will prevent him and others from bringing an amicable bill into Chancery, which will be a less expense and answer the end as well. Also copies of a report of the Com[rs] of Alienations, an opinion of the Attorney General thereon, and the Report of the Lords of the Treasury advising that the lowest fine ought to be accepted, viz., 25*l.* for the pre-fine, and 37*l.* 10*s.* for the post fine. The last dated 16 June 1720. 2 *pages.*

17 June. 13. "A particular of the causes now under prosecution with states thereof." *Docketed*:—"A state of the causes under prosecution for Trinity Term 1720. 17 June 1720.
Signed:—"A. Crachcrode." 5½ *pages.*

22 June. 14. A paper *docketed*:—"A memorandum, with the Prince's Attorney and Solicitor General's opinion thereupon." As to an allowance of taxes claimed by the farmers of the *pre* and *post* fines. The opinion was that they ought not to have the same allowed for the rents reserved upon their several grants, &c. Dated 22 June 1720. It is a copy. 2 *pages.*

23 June. 15. Warrant of the Duke of Newcastle to the Treasurer of the Chamber for the payment of 292*l.* 19*s.* 7*d.* to M[r] John Howard, joiner, of the Privy Chamber, for carved gilded frames and cases provided for pictures of her late Majesty and for gilded frames for several other pictures, &c. Dated 23 June 1720.

The allowance for her Majesty's pictures (which were whole length) was 12*l.* each, and they were for the following persons:—Charles Cesar, Esq., Treasury of the Navy, Lord Pagett, the Duke of Buckingham, Lord Bingley, Mons. Pless, and the Earl of Strafford.

The list of pictures is curious.

Minuted:—"Warr[t] signd 15th Sept[r]. 11 *pages.*

[11 July 1720.] 16. Petition of George Tushingham, Gent., to the Lords of the Treasury. King Will. III., on 18 Aug. 1696, demised to petitioner certain lead mines in Grinton and Fremington (co. York) for 31 years at 40*s.* per ann. and $\frac{1}{10}$th of the profits. The mines have been for several years very poor and in decay. Petitioner has been at great expense to improve them. Prays for a further term to make up his present term to 31 years, as his lease has eight years to run, under the old rent.

Undated, but by comparison with an entry in a *Register of Treasury papers read at the Board* on 1 July 1720 the date is fixed. 1 *page.*

[? About 5 July.] 17. (*Docket*):—Petition of the Heralds for their Largesses for creations of peers and for their waiting at festivals.

On the back of a "List of Nobility created."

1720. VOL. CCXXVIII.

Minuted:—" 5 July 1720. To be read when Lord Sunderland is here." "Respited." *Again*:—" 9th Feb. 1721–2. Enquire if this has at any time been allowed.

Allowed them by warrt under his Mats Royal Sign Manual, dated 30th Septr 1715. Several sums in the paper annexed, amounting to 632li."

On another paper annexed is:—" Allowed them by warrt under his Mats Royal sign manual, dated the 30th Septr 1715, vizt.:—

For Peer on his Mats Coronacon - - -	100li
For sevl scarlet robes at the same time - -	167
For Peer upon his Mats assuming his seat as sovereign of the most noble order of the garter -	40
For Largesses upon ye creation of his royal highness ye prince of Wales - - - -	10
For do on ye creation of 63 noblemen, 5l each -	315
	632 "

1 *page and two parts.*

[? About 5 July.] 18. Memorial of Simon Clement in behalf of Mrs Penn, the widow of Wm Penn, Esq., late Proprietor and Governor of the Province of Pennsylvania. Represents that Mr Penn whilst he was in treaty for the sale of his powers of Government to her late Majesty, being taken sick, made his will and devised the government to the Earls of Oxford and Powlet in trust, and with intent that in case of his death they might be able to complete the sale and convey the same; but Mr Penn recovering, afterwards in the year 1712 finished the contract himself, and agreed to resign his powers of Government to the Crown for 12,000*l*., whereof 1,000*l*. was then paid in part, but before the conveyances were perfected he was again seized with an apoplectic fit, so that he was never capable of executing the same before his death in 1718. The power of conveying the government seems now to be vested in the before-mentioned Earls. But William Penn, Esq., heir-at-law to the deceased, disputes this will, and the Earls are unwilling to act in the trust without a decree in Chancery, so that Mrs Penn, the widow and executrix, is advised to bring a bill to have the determination of that court thereon, and is advised that their Lordships must be parties: prays permission for the same.

Minuted:—" 5th July 1720. Agreed to." 1 *page, quarto.*

[? About 5 July.] 19*a*. "The case of Katherine Roos, relict and adminx of John Roos, Esq., late Engraver of his Maties. seals."

A bill for 788*l*. 15*s*. 8½*d*. was laid before the Lords of the Treasury in 1716 by John Roos, Esq. (since deceased), for furnishing silver and engraving several public seals, including the great seal and privy seal for Ireland, amounting to 240*l*. The Lords of the Treasury thought these should be paid for by the Treasury for Ireland, and ordered the bill to be paid with this exception. The widow petitioned the [English] Treasury thereon, stating that the seals for Ireland were always paid out of the treasury of this Kingdom. Their Lordships thereupon referred the petition to the

1720. VOL. CCXXVIII.

officers of the Mint, who made their report, now in the hands of Mr Frecker, one of the Clerks of the Treasury. Undated.

Minuted:—"To be p̄d here."

The Report referred to, dated 5 July 1720. Also the petition. 3 *pages*.

[? About 5 July.] 19*b*. Petition of Captain Charles Morgan to the King. Petitioner's father, Major Thomas Morgan, being Major of the Marquis De Montandre's Regiment and captain of a company in the same, in the year 1711 obtained leave to resign his company to petitioner, who accordingly had a Commission and served as Captain till the year 1712, when being dangerously ill he had leave to give back the company to his father, who was again commissioned thereto. In 1713, the regiment "being broke," petitioner, with his father's consent, was put upon half pay as Captain, his father contenting himself with half pay as Major, and the Captain's half pay was continued to petitioner upon the two establishments made for Ireland since H.M. accession, but received no pay since Christmas last, and is struck off the Establishment because he was not "actually broke" with the regiment. Petitioner has been nineteen years a commissioned officer, and was a sufferer by being taken prisoner at the battle of Almanza. His family are reduced to great straits. Prays for a royal letter to the Lord Lieut. to restore him to half pay or for other provision.

Minuted:—"5 July 1720. To Lord Lieut[t] of Ireland." 1 *page*.

20 July. 20. Report of A. Cracherode to the Lords of the Treasury on the petition of William Harper, printer, whereby he sets forth that since the execution of "young Matthews" he has been insulted after the most barbarous manner imaginable for discharging his duty, in giving a full and impartial evidence against the said Matthews for printing a treasonable pamphlet called *Vox populi vox Dei*. By the disaffected parties' interest the petitioner has lost all hopes of getting his bread in his business, and prays to be provided for. Certifies that the petitioner was a material evidence and had a reward of 200*l*. Is of opinion that it will be a great goodness of their Lordships to bestow on the petitioner some small employment. 20 July 1720.

Minuted:—"11th Aug[st] 1720. To be provided for by some small employm[t] when a vacancy happens."

The petition referred to and an affidavit. 3½ *pages*.

20 July. 21. Report of the same to the Lords of the Treasury on the petition of John Derby, Keeper of the Marshalsea prison in Southwark, Alexander Bowler, George Halfhyde, Lewis Snagg, and Anne his wife, and Katherine, widow of Thomas Nightingale, deceased, setting forth that pursuant to his Majesty's proclamation, dated 5 May 1716, the petitioners, with the said Thomas Nightingale, discovered and apprehended John Mackintosh, one of the persons in the proclamation named, after which he was committed to Newgate, where he remains, and praying that they may receive their shares of the 500*l*. in the proclamation mentioned. Certifying that on the

1720. VOL. CCXXVIII.

5th of May 1716 his Majesty issued a proclamation reciting that William Mackintosh, Charles Wogan, James Talbot, Robert Hepburn, William Delmahoy, John Tasker, and John Mackintosh, lately committed to Newgate for high treason in levying war against his Majesty, had on the 4th of May escaped, and offering a reward of 1,000*l.* for the apprehension of the first-named, and 500*l.* for each of the others. Is of opinion that the whole merit of discovering the said John Mackintosh, and even of forming the stratagem by means of which he was taken, was owing to Philip Reeve, who has been since tried, condemned, and executed for robbing on the high way, and that the petitioners Derby, Bowler, Halfhyde, Snagg, Ann his wife, Katherine Nightingale, Daniel Molloy, and Daniel Chandler do not deserve above 10*l.* a piece for their respective shares, in case their Lordships are of opinion that the reward ought to be paid at all, and that the intention of his Majesty's proclamation was answered by the apprehending of the said John Mackintosh about three years and three quarters of a year after the issuing of the proclamation; and at a time when he could not by law be brought to justice for his treason. 20 July 1720.

The petition referred to, 3 affidavits, a further memorial and copy of the proclamation. 10 *pages.*

[? About 21 July.] 22. Petition of Harcourt Goodrick, Esq., brother and administrator to Richard Goodrick, Esq., deceased, for a lease for 50 years of premises at Richmond, late in lease to John Lauze, Gent., under a due proportion of the rent of 10*l.* per ann., and for the like term for another tenement adjoining; and a barge-house, parcel of the manor of Richmond, together with an addition of 4 feet of ground in length and six feet in breadth, to be added to the ground whereon the barge-house stood, to build coach houses or stables, under the old rent.

Minuted:—"21 July 1720. To Survr Generall." 1 *page.*

21 July. 23. Comrs for Forfeitures (Pat. Haldane, Arthur Ingram, W. Hoghton and Robert Munro) to the Lords of the Treasury. Transmit an account of moneys paid into the Exchequer out of the forfeited estates; also an account of the precepts issued by them requiring further payments, for making of which effectual they have ordered the prosecutions in the Exchequer, &c. Edinburgh, 21 July 1720.

Minuted:—"19 Augt 1720. Read."

[? About 21 July.] 24. Petition of John Annis, master of the "London Hope," attorney of John Kay, of Philadelphia, Assignee of Captain Matthew Wooton; as to a claim of the latter for 36*l.* 10*s.* 7½*d.* for provisions supplied to Woodes Rogers, Esq., Captain General, Governor and Vice-Admiral of the Bahama Islands, "during the Invasion from the Spaniards against the Island of Providence," when the Inhabitants and others of that place were forced to continue under arms for a considerable time, and the governor was obliged to be at Extraordinary charge to support near 500 men exclusive of his Majesty's garrison: praying payment.

Also copies of two documents relating thereto; the second is dated 21 July 1720. 3 *pages.*

VOL. CCXXVIII.

1720.

[? About 21 July.] 25. Memorial of Mary Murray, widow of George Murray, Esq., deceased, late Paymaster of the 1,400,000*l.* Lottery, 1714, to the Lords of the Treasury. Has paid 4,215*l.* 18*s.* to Robert Murray, Esq., the present paymaster, but as the time allowed has been so short she has not been able to recover several debts. Has good reason to believe that some part of her late husband's effects were at his death in the South Sea Company, of which she has not yet any account. Gives a statement as to which of the accounts had been passed by the Auditor; prays further time to discover her husband's effects.

Minuted:—"21 July 1720. Enlarge the time for 3/m further." Also copy of warrant. 5 *pages.*

26 July. 26. Order in Council referring to the Lords of the Treasury the petition of Samuel Slatford to report thereon. The petitioner states that he was an inhabitant of Oxford at the late Rebellion, and was instrumental in detecting many dangerous practices carried on there: in particular by discovering a great quantity of arms designed by the rebels for the use of the Pretender, as appears by the order for apprehending Col. Owen and other dangerous persons. For his zeal had to quit his habitation and livelihood: prays to be allowed a pension or otherwise to be provided for.

Also copy of a certificate of the citizens and inhabitants in his favour.

Minuted:—"19th Jan^ry 1720–21, 20li p Mr Lowther." 3 *pages.*

26 July. 27. Report of the Barons of the Exchequer of Scotland to the Lords of the Treasury. Have examined the warrant prepared for his Majesty's signature for granting the lands and Barony of Phantillunds, lying in the Lordship of Lochow and county of Argyle, to John, Duke of Argyle and Greenwich: find that this signature contains a "de novo domus and taxing of the waird holding," &c. The valued rent is 37*l.* 2*s.* 5*d.* yearly. Exchequer, Edinburgh, 26 July 1720.

Minuted:—"28th March 1721. My Lords order this to be given to Ld Sunderland for his Ma^ts signature: signd, 30th March 1721." 1 *page.*

27 July. 28. Report of the same to the same on the petition of Æmilia, Lady Lovat. Are of opinion that the petitioner's distressed condition, and that of her numerous family, make them very proper objects of the King's bounty; and think it very reasonable and fit that the arrears of the annuity of 300*l.* per ann. should be paid her presently, and that so much should be secured out of the rents and sale of the forfeited estates as would answer the payment thereof for the future; but are at present not in a position to lay before the King and their Lordships any proper forms by which his Majesty's intention may be carried out. Edinburgh, Exchequer Chamber, 27 July 1720.

Also the petition referred to. 2½ *pages.*

28 July. 29. "Copy of Mr Walpole's memorial to the R^t Honble ye Lords Comm^rs of his Ma^ts Treasury with a proposal for letting ye French

1720. VOL. CCXXVIII.

part of St Christophers, at 20s. p acre on his Maties account. Dated July the 28th 1720." 2½ *pages*.

28 July. 30*a*. "Mr Audr Walpole's memorial relating to the casual revenues in the Leeward Charibbee Islands." Offers to prepare letters for the signature of the Lords of the Treasury to General Hamilton, the Governor of those Islands, to pay to the receiver the balance of the casual revenues which he at present refuses to do. Signed. Dated 28 July 1720.

Minuted:—"28 July 1720. Mr Walpole to prepe lre accordly." 2 *pages*.

28 July. 30*b*. "Mr Audr Walpole's memorial relating to an act of the Assembly of Barbadoes, directing a 100li to be pd out of the casual revenue towds the charge of the Grand Sessions there."

The Auditor remarks that instead of answering the expense out of the public Treasury, the Assembly would lay it upon his Majesty's casual revenue, which is already in a very low state. Proposes that the Board of Trade should give the Lords of the Treasury a full account of that matter, and that the latter should instruct the Board of Trade not to present any acts or papers to the King and Council for his Majesty's approbation until such clauses as relate to the revenue of the plantations be first laid before them (the Lords of the Treasury). 28 July 1720. 1 *page*.

28 July. 31. Report of the Barons of the Exchequer of Scotland to the Lords of the Treasury on the petition of Alexander Ross, the Deputy Clerk to the Court of Justiciary, and of the three Macers thereof, as to the additional salaries asked for by them. Edinburgh, Exchequer Chamber, 28 July 1720.

With this are three petitions, an extract from the "books of adjournall," "an acct of the Inditemts, Criminall Libells, &c. served on criminalls by the Macers of the Court of Justiciary for his Majty's Advocate." Also another petition of the Macers. 10½ *pages*.

28 July. 32. Barons of the Exchequer of Scotland to the Lords of the Treasury. Transmit a certificate of all moneys paid to the Receiver General from the rents of the forfeited estates; to which is subjoined a list of some estates sold by the Comrs and Trustees of the forfeited estates, with the values thereof. 28 July 1720. 5 *pages*.

29 July. 33. An estimate of the charge of the present for the Dey of Algier desired by Mr Charles Hudson, Consul at Algier. Signed:—S. Thomson. July 29, 1720.

With this are:—(1) Letter from Ch. Delafaye to the Lords of the Treasury; (2) another letter from R. Powys to Mr Thompson on the same subject; and (3) a list of his Majesty's present sent in Augt 1715 to the Dey of Algier; and (4) "an extract out of a letter sent by Charles Hudson, Esq., his Majesties consul at Algier." He says the Governor has not received any compliment from the King since his being made Dey, which he seems to take something amiss. The French in two years have sent two ministers, one of which, Monsr Duscault, has brought the Governor a present from the King of upwards of 1,000*l*. sterling value, besides others for the leading

1720. VOL. CCXXVIII.

people in the King's house and marine, which may enable them to carry some points very prejudicial to the trade of our nation, except his Majesty thinks proper to continue the usual presents (which generally come every two or three years at farthest) to support the interests of his subjects.

On the back of the letter from Delafaye is :—" Orderd as usual. 29th July 1721. Warrt signd." *6 pages.*

There are also five invoices and another estimate, which appear connected with this business. *6 parts of pages.*

2 Aug. 34. " Mr Audr Walpole's Report upon the petition of Mrs Thomas relating to the accots of her deceased father, late receiver of the Casual revenue [and prize officer] in Barbadoes." August 2, 1720.

The report recommends the acceptance of the composition of 2*s.* 6*d.* in the pound on the debt of 1,457*l.* 0*s.* 10¾*d.* owed by her father, which Susannah Thomas, the daughter, offered as a means to bring Benjamin Bullard, her father's executor, to account.

Minuted :—" 4 Augt 1720. Accepted and agreed to, and let a warrt be prepared." *4½ pages.*

2 Aug. 35*a.* " Comptroller's report on Mr Missing's three lists and one certificate for victualling the garrison of Gibraltar." There is due to the Contractor 2,680*l.* 8*s.* 9⅝*d.* 2 Aug. 1720.

Also " a state of provisions laid into the victling store-houses at Gibraltar." *2 pages.*

9 Aug. 35*b.* J. Burchett to the Secretaries of the Lords of the Treasury. Sends by command of the Lords of the Admiralty copy of a letter of Mr Bridger, late Surveyor General of H.M. woods in America, relating to the abuses in cutting woods there.

The copy of letter referred to. Amongst other things he says :— " The people are come to that boldness, nay the agent to Mr Taylor agreed with people here to cut such a quantity of mast trees, as should load six ships, without ever giving me any notice, or ever shewing me his order or power to this day for doing so ; and here are three ships arrived, and the other three are expected every day to load these trees." *3 pages.*

17 Aug. 36. Petition of Sir Bibye Lake, Bart., in behalf of himself and the other creditors of Robert Peter, formerly Receiver General of the Taxes for the co. of Hertford, to the Lords of the Treasury, praying directions to be given for assigning Peter's estate to him, on condition of his (Lake's) paying the sum of 10,000*l.* to the Crown, that being the debt due by Peter to the Crown.

Minuted :—" 20 Augt 1720. Look out the repts and paps relating to this case." *1 page.*

[? About 17 Aug.] 37. " Petition of several tradesman " addressed to the Lords of the Treasury. Supplied her late Majesty's stables then under the direction of the Hon. Conyers Darcy and George Feilding, Esq., Comrs for the office of Master of the Horse. On her Majesty's death 10,030*l.* were due to them. No part thereof has been paid but about 1,900*l.*, most of which was paid to one or two persons. Pray for relief.

At the end is a petition in their favour by the above Darcy and Feilding.

Minuted:—"17 Augt 1720. To be read again w^{n} any m^{o} in Ex^{r} applicable to these arrears." 2 *pages*.

19 Aug. 38. Petition of Edward Bealing, of Penryn, in the county of Cornwall, merchant, to the Lords of the Treasury, praying that directions may be given that no further prosecution be had against petitioner for a supposed fraud in relation to certain salt for the pilchard fishery, landed "at the Parr within the port of Toy," in the county of Cornwall, about the end of November 1716.

Petitioner in July 1715, some time before the Rebellion, being in France, and zealous for the present establishment, with hazard of his life and much expence, discovered the designs then hatching there against his Majesty and Government, and sailed from France and brought over the Pretender's Declaration and Parson Lesly's letter, which were forthwith by a Justice of the Peace for the borough of Penryn transmitted to a Privy Councillor, &c. 19 Aug. 1720.

Also at the foot a certificate of the truth of the petition, with several signatures. 1 *large page*.

[? About 19 Aug.] 39. A memorandum as to the appointment of John Ashley and John Caswell as Collectors General, Receivers General, or Managers of the Duty of 4½ per cent. in Barbadoes and the Leeward Islands. They offer to pay down 5,000*l.*, the half of the sum agreed upon, and the other half the following Midsummer.

Minuted:—"19 Augt 1720. Enq^{e} if Mr Walpole has made any report."

Also copies of letter from H. Walpole to the above Ashley and Caswell, in respect to their proposal to farm the duty of 4½ per cent., and their reply thereto; and a second letter on the same subject. 6½ *pages*.

15 Sept. 40. The Attorney General (Robert Raymond) to the Lords of the Treasury. Has prepared the draft of a warrant to be transmitted to the King, to authorize the preparation of bills for the Royal signature, for Charters to pass the Great Seal in favour of the Royal Exchange Assurance for Insuring houses and goods from fire and Assurances upon lives. Dated 15 Sept. 1720. ½ *page*.

27 Sept. 41. "An accompt of the debt that will [be] due on the pensions payable in the office of Walter Chetwynd, Esq., between Michaelmas last, 1719, and Michaelmas next, 1720." 27 September 1720.

A List of pensions added in the office of Walter Chetwynd, Esq., since his Majesty's establishment, dated the 25th of August 1718.

A List of persons dead and determined since his Majesty's establishment, dated the 25th of August 1718.

Pensions increased other than those taken notice of in the foregoing List. 7¼ *pages*.

VOL. CCXXVIII.

1720. 29 Sept. 42. Account showing (as near as can be computed) the debt due to his Majesty's foreign ministers to Michaelmas, 1720, during one year.

The account shows the names of all the ambassadors, &c., places where residing, rates of allowance, &c. The total was 38,980*l.* 5*s.* 7*d.* 2 *pages.*

Sept. 43. Memorial of the Court of Directors of the Corporation of the London Assurance to the Lords of the Treasury. The King in pursuance of an Act of Parliament erected the Corporation by his Royal Charter, and in consideration of the benefits thereof the Corporation was obliged to pay 300,000*l.* at several times into the Receipt of the Exchequer towards the debts of his Majesty's Civil Government. Have already paid 100,000*l.* and endeavoured to raise 50,000*l.* more; but such is the pressure of the times, both for money and credit, that they have not any hopes of raising the same before the 22nd instant; but in lieu thereof offer their Lps 11,000*l.* in money and 39,000*l.* in tallies upon the plate Act; or to deposit the 39,000*l.* in the tallies as security: pray for a favourable representation to his Majesty that a longer time may be granted them. Signed:—" Wm Chapman, Sub-Governor."

In the *Minute Book*, vol. 22, p. 312, 16 Oct. 1720 is:—"Sir Wm Chapman calld in. He acquaints my Lords that he hath brought the tallys for annuitys on plate amounting to 39,000, according to agreement, to remain as a deposit or security for the 4th paymt to the public. He says he is ready to pay 11,000li in money to compleat the 50,000li, the amount of their 2d payment, which was due the 22d Septr last. Mr Chancellour admonishes him to redeem the tallys so deposited by small paymts, vizt: 5,000li at a time, as the Company shall be able, till the whole be redeemed."

The following *minutes* are on a separate sheet:—

"16 Oct. 1720. My Lds order 6,956*l.* 17*s.* 4*d.*, resd of the contri. for us on the plate, but in the hands of the Trer of the Navy, to be applyed towards 14,300li demanded for the course of the vict. for [the year ?] 1719."

Again:—" Directors of the Corp. for the Lond. Assurance attend my Lords wth a rep. in writing, whereby they propose to pay 11,000 in mo into the Exchr, and to make a deposit of tallys for 39,000 struck for their plate, 3d paymt of the contrib. for annuitys on the Plate Act, both which to secure the 50,000 wch was due to be pd from them the 22d Septr last for his Mats Civil List. My Lords in this time of difficulty are enclined to indulge them to the utmost of their power, and leave it to Mr Lowndes to treat with them in order to make the proposal practicable." 2½ *pages.*

[This is also in the *Minute Bk*, vol. 22, p. 312.]

1720.

VOL. CCXXIX., 1720. OCTOBER–DECEMBER.

5 Oct. 1. John Williams, Sub-Governor, and Rand. Knipe, Deputy Governor of the Royal Exchange Insurance Office, to the Lords of the Treasury. Have laid before their Directors their L^ps order to delay no longer the second payment of 300,000*l.* for the debts and expenses of the King's Civil Government. Will do what they can to comply therewith, but apprehend they will not be able to do it without the assistance of the Fire Charter, which they, as well as the several proprietors, always looked upon as the best part of their agreement, and doubt not, if that were in their possession, they should be quickly enabled to perform their contract. Thank their Lordships for the notice given them of the warrant for the charter being sent to his Majesty, by order of the Lords Justices, and beg that it may be dispatched. It will be the only means to extricate them out of the difficulties from the necessity of the times and other unexpected disappointments, and lay a lasting obligation on the Royal Exchange Assurance Company. Royal Exchange, Oct. 5, 1720.

Minuted :—" 6 Oct. 1720. Read at ye Board." 1 *page.*

In the *Minute Book*, vol. 22, p. 310, 13 Oct. 1720, is:—

" Sir J. Williams, Mr London, and Mr Cole are call'd in: a lrẽ sent in by them on the behalf of the Comp^a is read, praying that the Fire Charter may be prepar'd in the interim of the warr^t, and that the grant of Assurance may be made to extend to *all* his Ma^ts dominions. As to the first, Mr Chancellour says they may attend the Attor. Gen^ll and talk to him about it, but as to the 2^d nothing can be inserted in the charter which is not specifyd in the warr^t. Sir J. Williams proposes in lieu of the next paym^t to deposite in my Lords' hands the tallys for the Plate Act till they shall be able to raise the money. Mr Chancellour recommends to them the disposing of those annuitys, that they make their paym^ts at the time appointed and in the manner prescribed by the Act."

Again, in vol. 23, p. 5, 18 Nov. 1720:—

" The Deputy Gov^rs of the 2 Assurance Companys are call'd in. Mr Chancellour says the Earl of Sunderland has acquainted the King with their petition to have the Grant of Insurance on lives, houses, &c. to extend to Ireland: who has been graciously pleas'd to grant their request; and as to its extending to Scotland, the difference of the forms of law, in that Kingdom and this, will require that such grant do pass under the seal kept there; in lieu of the Great Seal: and the draught must be approved of by the King's Counsel there.

My Lords will also move the King to indulge the 2 Corporations by giving them further days for payment of the sum of 189,000*l.*

VOL. CCXXIX.

1720. remaining unpaid by each of them, to wit:—One third part on the 25th March 1721; one third, 25th May 1721; the remaining ⅓ on the 25th July 1721."

15 Oct. 2. Comrs of Forfeitures, Scotland, to the Lords of the Treasury, enclose account of moneys which have arisen by forfeitures, with the amount of the claims on the four estates sold last year, and the balance remaining to the public. There is due from the purchasers of principal and interest (exclusive of what they are allowed to retain in respect of the annuities granted to the ladies of the forfeiting persons) about 7,000*l.* There remains to be paid in, upon their precepts, about 9,000*l.* more. Give reasons for the produce of the forfeitures being so small. When the claims of property are determined considerable sums will arise to the public. Have sold seven of the forfeited estates this week, viz.:—

The estate of Stirling, late of Keir, at twenty-one years' purchase.

That of David Threapland, late of Fingask, at about twenty.

That of Pitcairn at twenty.

That of the late Earl of Southesque at nineteen.

That of Hugh Paterson, late of Bannockburn, at twenty.

That of Rob Roy at about twenty-five.

That of the late Earl Marischall at nineteen years' purchase.

The whole amounting to 134,279*l.* Will expose the estate of the late Earl of Linlithgow on Monday, which at twenty years' purchase will add about 20,000*l.* Will have to leave this country shortly to give attendance in Parliament and beg payment of the two last quarters' salaries. Edinburgh, 15 Oct. 1720.

Minuted:—"25th Octr. My Lords order a. quars salary to Midsr 1720 with the incidts. Wt signd." 3 *pages.*

25 Aug. and 17 Oct. 3. Two certificates of the Comrs for the forfeited estates and estates given to superstitious uses, viz.: that Richard Grantham, Esq., had on two occasions absented himself from the office to which he was appointed, as one of the Commissioners, without the consent of the others, for three weeks and more, and thereby incurred a forfeiture of 500*l.* Dated 25 Aug. and 17 Oct. 1720. 3 *pages* and 2 *halves.*

20 Oct. 4. The Barons of the Exchequer of Scotland to the Secretary of the Treasury. Have received a warrant from the Lords Justices requiring them to cause the Receiver General to send up the money in his hands, on account of forfeitures for treason, and pay the same into the Exchequer at London. Have ordered the Officers belonging to the Comrs of Enquiry to certify what sum remains above the payment of Creditors. Are informed by Brigadier Preston, the Commander-in-Chief here, that though he is ready to give a sufficient guard for the safe-conduct of the money to Berwick, yet unless there be a party here empowered to receive it, the money will be returned here; which has obliged them to send an express to Berwick to see if it can be conveyed under safe conduct. If they find there is no order to receive the same at Berwick, they will be obliged to wait further orders. Exchequer Chamber, Edinburgh, 20 Oct. 1720. 2 *pages.*

1720. VOL. CCXXIX.

20 Oct. 5. Agents (Richard Thomlinson and Jonas Alstrom) for receiving the subsidies to the King of Sweden, to the Lords of the Treasury. Apply for payment of such part of the subsidies as their Lordships shall direct, to enable them to discharge the bills drawn and execute other commissions for his Swedish Majesty's immediate and pressing occasions. Baron Sparre has despatched the necessary orders for the payment of these subsidies, the sum payable being 280,000 imperial Rix-dollars granted by treaty at Stockholm in 1719. October 20, 1720. 2 *pages.*

22 Oct. 6. Report of the Com[rs] of Taxes to the Lords of the Treasury upon the case of Sir Bilbye Lake. M[r] Peter's debt appears to amount to 10,892*l.* 5*s.* 9*d.* The real and personal estate at the time of his failure were estimated at about 24,000*l.* The board closed with the offer of Sir Bibye Lake to discharge the debts, and he paid 2,257*l.* 4*s.* 10*d.* What money has accrued from the estates is in the hands of the Sheriffs and Trustees for the use of the creditors.

Also "the case."

Minuted:—"21st Nov[r] 1720." Sir Bibye Lake to attend the Attor. and Sol[r] Gen[ll] with the copies of all the proceedings in the Courts of Law and Equity when M[r] Wills may attend with his state of the case and objections, and thereupon my Lords desire their report." 3 *pages.*

24 Oct. 7. Report of A. Cracherode to the Lords of the Treasury. According to instructions attended the Com[rs] of Forfeitures to hasten the bringing in of 200,737*l.* 14*s.* $9\frac{1}{4}$*d.* granted in the last Parliament to his Majesty. The Com[rs] gave orders to their Solicitor, M[r] Samuel Allen, to give a state of the prosecutions under his management, who has delivered the same. 24 Oct. 1720.

The state referred to, and two other papers. 9 *pages.*

26 Oct. 8. Barons of the Exchequer of Scotland to [the Secretary of the Treasury]. Have received from the Com[rs] and Trustees of the forfeited estates in Scotland an account of the moneys arising from the forfeitures (above the debts and claims thereon), amounting to 46,616*l.* 11*s.* $\frac{1}{6}$th. By another account there are in the hands of the purchasers 18,881*l.* 8*s.* $8\frac{5}{12}$*d.*, so that there are only 7,735*l.* 2*s.* $3\frac{3}{4}$*d.* in the Receiver General's hands. Have issued their warrant for the amount to be transmitted. 26 Oct. 1720.

Accompanied by copies of the two accounts.

In the *Minute Book*, Vol. 22, p. 320, 4 Nov. 1720, is:—

"To Comm[rs] Forfeitures in Scotland to acquaint my L[ds] how it comes to pass that the sum of 18,881[li] 8s. $8\frac{1}{5}$*d.* remains still in the hands of the purchasers of certain estates in Scotl., and to inform their Lordp̃s in what time they think the said sum may be received, and likewise desire them pressingly to solicite the paym[t] of it, and to inform my Lords when the appeals will be adjusted." 5 *pages.*

4 Nov. 9. Memorial of Sir Bibye Lake, Bart., to the Lords of the Treasury. The Com[rs] for Taxes having certified the state of Mr. Peter's debt, prays for their warrant for vesting in his (memorialist's) hands the

VOL. CCXXIX.

1720.

estates and the bonds of him and his sureties to the Crown for the use of memorialist and other creditors. 1 *page*.

7 Nov. 10. Report of the Auditor (S. Godolphin) to the Lords of the Treasury. Has considered the discovery of concealed rents and arrears thereof. The substance is as follows:—Upon the demise of Katherine, Queen dowager, there was due to his Majesty out of the manor of Whapload, in the co. of Lincoln, 38*l.* 6*s.* 5½*d.* per ann., and out of the Manor of Moulton Dnoř cum Bewsolus, 78*l.* 5*s.* 0½*d.*, in all amounting to 116*l.* 11*s.* 6*d.* per ann., which for fourteen years, ending at Michaelmas, is 1,632*l.* 1*s.*, and which were charged in the declaration of the accounts of Richard Rose, the receiver, ending at Mich. 1707, and the same ending at Mich. 1710, were exonerated by grant of 36 Charles II. to Sir Stephen Fox, in trust for the Duchess of Monmouth and her children for 99 years; whereas there is no more granted than the Manor of Spalding and Holbech, amounting to 474*l.* 19*s.* 11¾*d.*; the residue whereof, being 116*l.* 11*s.* 6*d.*, issues out of the manor of Whapload and Moulton cum Bewsolus, remaining still in the crown and which ought to be charged from the demise of the late Queen.

In his answer says that the later grant to the Duchess (reciting the former grant to the Duke) appearing to be so very extensive as to comprehend the Manors of Spalding and Holbech, besides the Manors of Whapload and Moulton, and the duchess being in possession when he entered on his office in June 1705 might be the reason his clerk, one Bolton (formerly clerk to the Petitioner Hewitt), discharged the sum in the account. If it should happen to be otherwise than a mistake, has good reason to suspect that it was done by contrivance between Mr Hewitt and his former clerk, with a further view of making such discovery for his private advantage. It manifestly appears that the petitioner's whole view in all these transactions was to impose on their Lordships, and to carve out more for his own benefit than for the advantage of the crown; besides, in case my lady Duchess should not have a title to the premises, she is answerable for the arrears. Had his report ready long ago to lay before their Lordships, but was prevented by their Order until her Grace the Duchess of "Buchleaur" had consulted with her counsel relating to her title to the premises, &c. Now sends it in, at the importunity of Mr Hewitt. Nov. 7, 1720.

Accompanied by copies of clauses from the grants referred to, and the memorial of Robert Hewitt, dated 17 Sept. 1720, a petition, Auditor's Report, and a state of the case, "Pro Rege." Dated 14 Sept. 1720. 19 *pages*.

10 Nov. 11. Report of the Attorney and Solicitor General to the Lords of the Treasury on an annexed draft which they "apprehend to be intended to make the first payment of 39,000*l.* paid in by Sir John Williams and Sir Randolph Knipe in Trust for the company of the Royal Exchange, Assurance," &c. Are of opinion that the day fixed by the Act for making the second payment being already past, the company are, in point of law, liable to the penalties; but in

1720. Vol. CCXXIX.

case their Lordships have authority by their Privy Seal to grant forbearance or give further day of payment, then the existence of this security will amount to a suspending of those penalties for the time thereby given. But in case their privy seal does not extend to give them such power, then this agreement will not defeat or suspend any of these penalties, but only amount to a collateral security, which will not affect the provisions made by the act of parliament to enforce the payment. Have made some alterations on the draft. 10 Nov. 1720.

The draft referred to. 7 *pages.*

15 Nov. 12. Copy of representation of David, Earl of Wemyss, to the Lords of the Treasury, and copy of the report thereon by the Barons of the Exchequer of Scotland, and of three other documents touching certain salt shipped from the Earl's harbour of Methel without entry and payment of duty. One is a certificate of the correctness of the copies, and is dated 15 Nov. 1720. 6¼ *pages.*

18 Nov. 13. Lord Lieut. of Ireland (Grafton) to the Lords of the Treasury. Has enclosed a copy of a letter received from the Lords Justices of Ireland, with a report of a Committee of Council relating to the means for the better performance of "Quarantain" there; by which their Lps will see that it is thought advisable that several armed wherries and sloops should be disposed in different bays and stations for that purpose. The Lords Justices must have the requisite power to issue such money as is requisite for this service. Asks for the proper warrant to be prepared. Bond Street, 18 Nov. 1720.

Minuted:—"19th Novr 1720. Prepare the proper warrt."

The copies of the letters referred to, also a list of quarantine ships. 8½ *pages.*

24 Nov. 14. E. Pauncefort to Mr Lowndes. Lord Coventry tells him that his brother is joined with him (Mr Pauncefort) in the room of Mr Charlton, deceased. This will, if not prevented, oblige him to procure fresh security which he could not trouble his friends to give. Besides people will be more cautious of entering into security, and the rather because it is too well known that he has been forced to pay 10,000*l.* for a person acting under him, who had been in the office a great many years, and was recommended to him by the Comrs as a person of approved honesty and integrity. Desires that a way may be found to let Mr Coventry have a share with him of the salary as cashier. November 24, 1720.

Minuted:—"Read." 1½ *pages.*

26 Nov. 15. Report of the Controllers of the accounts of the army to the Lords of the Treasury on a memorial of Mr Thomas Missing craving payment of 998*l.* 4*s.* on account of victualling the garrisons of Annapolis Royal and Placentia, 998*l.* 4*s.* is due to him by the contract. 26 Nov. 1720.

Minuted:—"26th Novr 1720. Order'd out of the money voted by parlt for this service now in Lord Lincoln's hands. The Secry-at-War to write to the commanding officers in Annapolis and

1720. VOL. CCXXIX.

Placentia to send duplicates of their effective numbers, &c. pursuant to the desire of the Comptrollers." 2 *pages.*

29 Nov. 16. Report of the Lord Lieut. of Ireland (Grafton) to the Lords of the Treasury on the petition of Capt Wm Hamilton, wherein it is set forth that the petitioner and several other officers were struck off the half pay list, upon a false information of their refusal to go to the West Indies, but that in the year 1712 upon an Address of the House of Commons the petitioner with Lieut. Gunter was restored. The petitioner is thought to have been wrongfully struck off, and Lieut. Gunter obtained his Majesty's warrant for his arrear of half pay upon the very same reasons as the petitioner offers. Thinks that the petitioner should be recommended for his Majesty's bounty. Bond Street, 29 Nov. 1720.

Accompanied by the petition, report of the Lords Justices, and report of the Deputy Muster-Master-General. There is also a letter signed:—"Ja. Hamilton" pressing for payment of these arrears, as that Gentleman's circumstances are brought to a very low ebb. Dated 4 May 1721.

Minuted:—"Prepare a warrt upon the report." 1 *page.*

[? About 8 Dec.] 17. Petition of Thomas Madox, Esq., his Majesty's historiographer, to the Lords of the Treasury. At the time of the death of her Majesty there was and still is due to the petitioner 120*l.* 2*s.* 9*d.* from Christmas 1713 to Aug. 1714. Prays payment.

Certificate to the same effect. Dated 8 Dec. 1720. 1½ *pages.*

14 Dec. 18. Report of Charles Withers, Esq., Surveyor-General of his Majesty's woods, on the memorial of Charles Frampton, Esq., Lieut. Col. in the first regiment of foot guards, who three months since purchased the place of Keeper of the Goose green Lodge in his Majesty's Forest of Alice Holt, and now asks allowance of timber to do the necessary repairs. The late King William granted the office of Ranger in Chief of the forests of Alice Holt and Woolmer to Emanuel Howe, Esq., with power to appoint underkeepers, upon condition to maintain all the lodges in repair, &c. for 45 years. His relict granted to James Pendlebury, Esq., the office of keeper of the above lodge, &c. for the residue of the term, viz., 29 years; who assigned the same to the memorialist. The repairs will require about 80 loads of timber. It has been customary for the keepers of this forest, by direction of the chief ranger, to fell great quantities of timber for repairs. And the memorialist caused 15 oaks to be felled for the repairs, although his (the surveyors) deputy marked them with the broad arrow. 14 Dec. 1720.

Minuted:—"29th Decr 1720. My Lords direct the survr to cause the broad arrow to be marked upon such trees as are felled for the repairs of his lodge." 3½ *pages.*

22 Dec. 19. J. King to the Lords of the Treasury. Her late Majesty in her 12th year granted to Edward Harley, commonly called Lord

1720. Vol. CCXXIX.

Harley, all wrecks between 26 and 40 degrees N. lat. in the West Indies, and which should be taken up before 24 June 1734: reserving $\frac{1}{10}$ to her Majesty, with a provision for the attendance of a person or persons to be appointed to inspect the fishing for and taking up the said wrecks.

As great riches have been wrecked within the limits of the grant, the ships "Foresight and Assurance" are fitting out to take up the same, and all possible accommodations will be made on board of these ships for the person or persons appointed. 22 Dec. 1720.

Also an affidavit as to a Spanish Galleon which had been lost near the Island of Bermudas. 1½ *pages.*

26 Dec. 20. Robert Armstrong, Collector of Customs, to Charles Burniston, Esq., Surveyor General of his Majesty's woods in America. By the copies of reports formerly made, it would appear that the collector of New Hampshire was the most proper person to take care of his Majesty's woods, &c. Is under great surprise that his friend Dummer should join with Mr Bridger against him. The Lords of Trade have wonderfully forgotten themselves, since by their own reports they approved of him and ordered their Secretary to thank him, and desired that he should continue to give their Lps the best information as to the production of naval stores in America. Sends a duplicate of letter previously sent as to the preservation of the masts and timber. Only adds in this duplicate what was not in the first, the advantage it would be to the Crown to raise and produce hemp in the province of New Hampshire. Prays that the quantity of hemp seed he wrote for may be sent New Hampshire, New England, 26 Dec. 1720. 3 *pages.*

[? About 1720.] 21. Petition of the "creditors of the late Duke of Ormond on the butlerage and prizage of wines" in Ireland to the Lords of the Treasury. The Duke in the year 1707 assigned for ten years, from 1711, 3,500*l.* a year out of the butlerage and prizage of wines to the petitioners until his debts were paid. Before the Duke's attainder they received certain sums; but since that time the butlerage, &c. having vested in Comrs for estates of Traitors, they have received nothing. The Comrs have decreed their claims to be just, and have issued debentures for 5,639*l.* 16*s.* 5*d.*: pray for payment of the debentures. Undated. 1 *page (brief size).*

22. "Abstract of a scheme for raising a sum of money for the use of the government, approv'd by the late Mr. Lownds and deliver'd into his hand in ye year 1720." 2½ *pages.*

23. "A List of extra Clerks [employed in the subscriptions] who had money imprest to Christmas 1720." 1 *large page.*

24. Petition of the noblemen, gentlemen, &c. of the Western Shires of Scotland to the King. By several laudable and standing laws the importation of oat-meal and cattle is forbidden; but vast quantities are notwithstanding imported, to the discouragement of tillage and pasturage, and the ruin of the landed interest.

VOL. CCXXIX.

1720. The excessive running of French brandies without payment of duties is also a heavy grievance: pray that the laws may be put in force.

Signed. Undated except in a more modern hand, 1720.

Copy of the same. 2 *pages.*

25. Certificate of the Auditors (Harley and Foley) to the Lords of the Treasury as to how far the several accountants have passed their accounts. [Undated, but after 1719.] 13 *pages.*

VOL. CCXXX. Classified. 1720. Part I.

1. Letters from Mr Burchett to the Secretaries of the Lords of the Treasury (1) touching two fields purchased by the Government and required by the Chatham Yard; (2) the destruction of woods in New England; [*Minuted:*—"30th June 1720. To the Lords of the Admty that if they think it necessary for the preservation of the woods in America that another officer be appointed, Mr Brydger may be nominated, wth such allowance of salary as they shall think proper to be charged upon the ordinary of the navy."] (3.) On the same subject; (4) the difficulties of making contracts for flesh for the navy; (5) as to a convoy for two vessels laden with provisions for the garrison of Gibraltar; (6) the arrears of the artificers working in the Yard at Chatham. 29 *pages.*

2. Papers relating to the affairs of the Treasurer of the Chamber, viz., as to the necessities of persons in his Majesty's service who have been obliged to sell and pawn their goods. Accounts of what is owing and as to what will be required to clear the Messengers' bill. 23 *pages.*

3. Reports and memorials of the Comrs of Customs to the Lords of the Treasury, touching (1) a complaint of misbehaviour of Mr John Hilden, Collector of Customs at St Christophers; (2) vexatious suits against officers of Customs; (3) as to unrated goods; (4) as to a ship stranded near Bridgewater; (5) clauses to be offered to Parliament to prevent fraud; (6) seizure of uncustomed goods; (7) as to the amount of tare to be allowed on goods; (8) drawback on cider and perry; (9) on the dismissal of Mr Gravenor, late Collector of Customs at Ipswich; (10) frauds carried on in the Isle of Man by smugglers; (11) as to "sinking" two land surveyors as they die or are removed (London); (12) as to the prosecution of E. Carll, bookseller, for reflecting on the board. They are willing, upon his submission, to drop the prosecution. *Minuted:*—"Agreed to." 12 *sets of papers.*

1720. Vol. CCXXX.

4. Reports and two or three other papers of the Commissioners for stating the debts due to the army: viz., on demands for disbursements for victualling the Garrison of Annapolis Royal; on allowance for subsistence of non-commissioned officers and privates at Alicant; on demands of the States General for bread and forage furnished by them; on demands of the officers of Lord Galway's regiment of foot, and M[rs] Baccalan's demand for an allowance for her husband's service as paymaster to prisoners; on claims for clothing, &c.; on demand for mules furnished for the forces under the command of the Earl of Galway in 1708; on demands for the pay of divers officers; on demand of the regiment of horse under the command of Lord Londonderry; on demands of several regiments that served in Spain and Portugal; on demand of contractors for forage delivered to the Hanover Dragoons. 13 *papers or sets of papers.*

5. Reports of the Com[rs] of Excise to the Lords of the Treasury on (1) memorial for repayment of 2,500*l.* advanced by the Com[rs] of Excise in North Britain to Major-Gen[l] Whetham; (2) on the memorial and account of drawbacks for hops exported to Ireland; (3) on the memorial concerning the prosecutions against Caleb Powell and William Vaston, tanners at Leominster. Also letter and account touching the produce of the duties on malt, mumm, cider, and perry, and another letter and papers as to the auditing of the accounts of the duties on hides by Sir Basill Dixwell. 28 *pages.*

6. Various papers relating to financial matters, such as estimates, propositions for paying the debts of the civil list, memoranda as to Exchequer Bills, lotteries, &c. 28 *papers.*

VOL. CCXXXI. Classified. Part II.

---

1. Letters of the Com[rs] of the Navy to the Secretary of the Treasury respecting deeds relating to houses occupied in right of their offices, about the Chest at Chatham, about the state of the late Treasurer's accounts, and about the debt of the Navy. 10½ *pages.*

2. Various papers connected with the affairs of the paymaster of the guards, garrisons, and other his Majesty's land forces, including estimates. 29 *papers.*

3. Numerous papers, most of them arising out of two acts of parliament, the one entitled:—an Act for enabling the South Sea Company to increase their present capital stock and fund by redeeming such public debts and incumbrances as are therein men-

1720. VOL. CCXXXI.

tioned, and for raising money to be applied for lessening several of the public debts and incumbrances, and for calling in the present Exchequer Bills remaining uncancelled, and for making forth new bills in lieu thereof to be circulated upon demand at or near the Exchequer: the other entitled:—an Act for making forth new Exchequer Bills, not exceeding one million, at a certain interest, and for lending the same to the South Sea Company at any higher interest upon security of repaying the same and such high interest into the Exchequer for uses to which the fund for lessening the public debts, called the Sinking Fund, is applicable, and for circulating and exchanging, upon demand, the said bills at or near the Exchequer. [*See* one of the papers dated 26 May 1720.]

There are also proposals by the Governor and Company of the Bank of England to add to their stock, and comparisons of the proposals of the two companies. Also accounts and memorials of moneys due to the persons employed.

The last paper is entitled:—"Appendix No. IIII. Copies of the resolutions of the South Sea Company relating to loans and the particulars in which the said rules have been exceeded."

4. Reports, &c. of the Officers of Works to the Lords of the Treasury on various claims arising in that department.

One of them relates to the carvings in the palace of Windsor. Mr Gibbons, his Majesty's carver, had a warrant for cleaning and repairing the same from King Charles II., which was continued in the succeeding reigns. *Minuted*:—"7th Decr 1720. See what Mr Gibbons was allow'd and where he was paid." "100^li p ann. by the hands of the payma^r of the works at Windsor by warrant under her late Ma^ts signe manual, dated the 8th July 1702." Another is as to the accommodation of the "young princesses" with stables and coach-houses in the Mews at Charing Cross. 9 *pages*.

VOL. CCXXXII. 1720.

Date.	Description of Document.	From	To	Purport.
—	1. Estimate	—	—	Of the charge of his Majesty's Ordnance for the year 1720. 1 *page*.
1719–20	2. Account	Ciryl Wich, Esq., appointed resident.	—	Receipts and expenditure. 2 *parts of pages*.

1720. VOL. CCXXXII.

Date.	Description of Document.	From	To	Purport.
—	3. Account	—	—	Arrears due to the tradesmen of her late Majesty's stables under the direction of Mr. Darcy and Mr. Feilding. 2 *pages.*
9 Jan.	4. Letter -	Allan Boresele Vander Hooghe.	"My Lord" -	Respecting a Dutch ship wrecked at Orkney, a great part of the cargo being saved: asking for speedy justice in giving possession of the goods to the owners. (French.) *Minuted*:—"2nd Febry. 1719-20. See if any directions have been given to the Commrs. of Customes. 2 *pages.*
1 Feb.	5. Do. -	John Clayton -	—	Reasons offered by the Judge of ye Court of Vice-Admiralty in Virginia in support of his decree (of 13 March 1718) on the sloop Adventure and goods piratically taken.
1 Feb.	6. Do. -	Charles Carkesse -	William Lowndes, Esq.	Respecting the insolence of the smugglers who defended their illegal practices by force of arms. 1 *page.*
5 Feb.	7. Do. -	Lord Stanhope -	Lords of the Treasury.	Sends letter from the Lords of Trade as to building of two new rooms. 2 *pages.*
6 Feb.	8. Do. -	George Gordon -	William Lowndes, Esq., Secretary to the Treasury.	Sends letter as to injustice suffered by Capt. Brand, late Commander of H.M. Ship "Lyme," and by Capt. Pearse and himself from custom house officers. 1 *page.*
9 Feb.	9. Do. -	Comrs. of Ordnance	Lords of the Treasury.	Send copy of the security taken on the appointment of Mr. John Lansdell as Paymaster. 2 *pages.*
11 Feb.	10. Representation	—	—	About "insupers" of the Clerk of the Pipe. 1 *page.*
18 Feb.	11. Letter -	Lord Stanhope -	Lords of the Treasury.	For payment of 200*l.* to Capt. Corner, who was sent hither with the instruments of His Catholic Majesty's Accession to the Convention made at Paris, and to the Treaty of London. 1 *page.* *Minuted*:—"20th Feb. 1719-20. Prepare a sign manual." 1 *page.*

1720. VOL. CCXXXII.

Date.	Description of Document.	From	To	Purport.
24 Feb.	12. Report and Warrant (Copies).	—	—	For payment of 600*l.* to John Mulcaster, late Agent to the Garrison of Annapoles Royal, from the Paymaster General. 2½ *pages.*
29 Feb.	13. Letter - -	William Yonge, for himself and other Commissioners.	Secretary-at-War	Not authorised to examine the accounts in the enclosed memorial, and have no authority to make any stoppage from the States General. Dorset Court, Feb. 29, 1719–20. *Minuted* :—"When the Comm[rs] send a farther account of this matter to my Lords, they will determine upon it." 1 *page.*
[? about 24 Mar.]	14. Memorial -	The Duke of Montagu. [Wardrobe.]	Lords of the Treasury.	As to the great debt due to the tradesmen. *Minuted* :—"24th March 1719–20. Issue 2,000 li. to the Duke of Montagu for furniture of the apartments at Kensington over and above the establishmt of 13,000 li. per ann." 1 *page.*
25 Mar.	15. Account -	—	—	Of what is due and in arrear from her late Majesty to the Public Ministers to the day of her decease. 1 *page.*
25 Mar.	16. Do. - -	—	—	Arrears due at Midsummer 1714 to her late Majesty, Queen Ann, annual pensioners, and charities established by her late Majesty. Examined "per Edw. Godfrey, March 25, 1720." 1 *page.*
25 Mar.	17. Do. - -	—	—	A state of the debt unpaid on account of the late Queen's Civil List. 1 *large page.*
—	Duplicate of the same.	—	—	1 do. [It has an entry additional at the foot.]
4 Apr.	18. Letter - -	J. Craggs -	Lords of the Treasury.	Encloses two extracts of letters from Mr. Pulteney concerning the present state of our gold and silver coin. 6 *pages.*
4 Apr.	19. Do. - -	Lords Justices -	Lord Lieutenant of Ireland.	Sends petition, &c on behalf of the clothiers of Dublin for his Majesty to be moved for a warrant to discharge the debt. 1 *page.*

Date.	Description of Document.	From	To	Purport.
5 Apr.	20. Report - -	Comrs. of Customs, Scotland.	Lords of the Treasury.	On the petition of Hendrick Smith, vinegar maker a Leith. The petitioner can be only relieved by Act of Parliament. Also the petition. *Minuted*:—"Read 6 July 1720. They may apply to Parlt." 5 *pages or parts.*
6 Apr.	21. Do. - -	Controller of Army Accounts (Medows).	Do. - -	On memorial of Viscount Irwin, Col. of his Majesty's own regiment of horse, as to clothing of the "Kettle-drum and nine trumpeters," and as to claim to have colours and liveries for trumpeters, hautboys, and drums. Also two other papers. 3 *pages.*
22 Apr.	22. Letter - -	J. Burchett (Admiralty).	Wm. Lowndes, Esq.	Forwards copy of letter from Capt. Brand of H.M. Ship "Lyme," as to the Custom House Officers corresponding with the pirates abroad. Also the letter. 2 *pages.*
[? About 10 May.]	23. Petition -	Clifford William Phillips and others.	Lords of the Treasury.	For a reward of 100li. for apprehending and convicting one William Joans, alias Charles Campbel, of robbery within five miles of London Dated 10 May 1720. Also a certificate. 2 *pages.*
13 May	24. Account -	—	—	Money requisite for the immediate service of the office of ordnance. *Minuted*:—"4 June 1720. 16,000 ordered." 1 *page.*
9 June	25. Letter - -	Mr. Secretary Craggs	Lords of the Treauy.	For directions to be given for payment of 300*l.* for services of Mr. John Bermingham in the late expedition to Spain under Lord Cobham. 1 *page.*
9 June	26. Do. - -	F. Osborne .. -	William Lowndes, Esq., att his house i[n] Duke Street.	Is kept in bed by a severe hit "got by a fall." 1 *page.*
15 June	27. List - -	—	—	Of H.M. Ships, &c. in Sea pay with an estimate of wages. 6 *pages.*

Date.	Description of Document.	From	To	Purport.
20 June	28. Balance sheet	—	—	Income by forfeitures in England. 2 *pages*.
[? About 30 June.]	29. Petition -	William Cobbe, Receiver General of Taxes, Chester.	Lords of the Treasury.	For an allowance of 521*l*. 14*s*. for remitting the money collected. Has never kept an exact account of the charges he was at, an affidavit having never been required from receivers of Wales, to which this country was formerly joined. *Minuted:*—"30 June 1720. Commrs. Taxes to report to my Lords of the Treasury their reasons for not making report on ye petition of Mr. Cobbe for allowances." 1 *page*.
1 July	30. Lease - -	—	—	"An English copy of the Exchequer lease to the D[uke of S[omerse]t of ground, &c. at Newmarkett. July the 1st, 1720." 4 *pages*.
28 July	31. Report (Copy)	Barons of the Exchequer (Scotland).	Lords of the Treasury.	On the petition of the Deputy Clerk of the Court of Justiciary and the three Macers as to additional salaries. Also the petition of the Macers. 2 *pages*.
8 Aug.	32. Report - -	Secretary - at - War (Treby).	Do. - -	On the case of the drummers, hautbois, and trumpeters' liveries. *Minuted :*—"19 Augt. 1720. Respited." 1 *page*.
[? About 10 Aug.]	33. Memorial -	James Chase, Esq., Apothecary in Ordinary to King Will. III. and Queen Anne.	Do. - -	For payment of arrears. Also certificate. *Minuted :*—"10 Aug. 1720. To be paid out of the 1st money coming in upon these arrears." 2 *pages*.
20 Aug.	34. Letter - -	Comrs. for Forfeitures, Scotland.	[? Secretary of the Treasury.]	For payment of their salaries. *Minuted :* —"25th Oct. Orderd." 1 *page*.
25 Aug.	35. Do. - -	Chr. Delafaye - -	Lords of the Treasury.	The Lords Justices recommend William Nost (who suffered by detection of treasonable practices) for a tidesman's place for London. 1 *page*.

Date.	Description of Document.	From	To	Purport.
10 Sept.	36. Letter - -	Comrs. for Forfeiture in Scotland.	[? Secretary to the Treasury.]	Enclose certificate of the absence of Mr. Grantham, one of their number. 1 *page.*
13 Sept.	37. Do. - -	G. Bridges - -	The Hon. Richard Edgecomb, one of the Lords of the Treasury.	For 40 or 50*l.* and some timber for the repair of his Lodge, "Lady-cross Lodge, in the New Forest. 7ber ye 13th, 1720." *Minuted:* — "21st Sept. 1720. My Lords adhere to their order (viz., not to allow any repairs to persons who have lodges for the future"). 1 *page.*
21 Sept.	38. Report - -	A. Cracherode -	Lords of the Treasury.	On the petition of Thomas Middleton and others, setting forth that John Potter was robbed on the highway, near Kennington (Surrey), by Thomas Metterick and Nicholas Henshaw, whom they apprehended. Is of opinion they ought to receive 200*l.* Also the petition. 3 *pages.*
28 Sept.	39. Opinion (copy).	—	—	The Attorney and Solicitor Generals' opinion on extraordinary allowances to Receivers General of Taxes. Dated 28 Sept. 1720. Also copy of letter of W. Lowndes to the Comrs. of Taxes. 2 *pages.*
29 Sept.	40. List - -	—	—	Of Extra Clerks who had 3*l.* per month imprested to them to the 29th September 1720. 1 *large page.*
29 Sept.	41. Account -	—	—	"Of arrears of taxes set off for the aggregate fond" at Michaelmas 1720, and the issues that have been made out of the same. 1 *page.*
30 Sept.	42. Letter - -	Ch. Delafaye -	Lords of the Treasury.	Expressing their "Excellencies' the Lords Justices'" approval of the list of presents to be given by Governor Nicholson to the Indians, bordering on Carolina, to regain some and preserve others in the interest of the British Nation: for orders to be given thereon. *Minuted:*—"28 Octr. 1720. Lrẽ signd." 1 *page.*

Date.	Description of Document.	From	To	Purport.
6 Oct.	43. Letter - -	Ch. Delafaye - -	Lords of the Treasury.	For repayment of 13*l.* 13*s.* to Mr. Wace to reimburse him that sum paid by order of the Lords Justices to 12 Algerines. 1 *page.*
11 Oct.	44. Do. - -	Do. - - -	Do. - -	Has enclosed copy of a letter from Mons. de Castro, Envoy from the King of Portugal, for leave to export to Holland (custom free) some plate of Dn. Luis d'Acuntra, formerly Envoy here, and now Ambassador at the Congress at Cambray. In favour thereof. Also the letter. 2 *pages.*
13 Oct.	45. Certificate -	Officers of Alienations	Do. - -	As to the gross produce of the Office of Alienations for the year ended Mich. 1720. Dated 13 Oct. 1720. 1 *page.*
14 Oct.	46. Representation	Comrs. of Excise (Scotland).	Do. - -	Praying the assistance of the military force to prevent smuggling. 1 *page.*
18 Oct.	47. Letter - -	Ch. Delafaye - -	Do. - -	For the Lords Justices that order be given for payment of 63*l.* to William Harper for services. 1 *page.*
24 Oct.	48. Estimate -	—	—	Of the debt of his Majesty's Navy as it stood on 30 Sept. 1720. Also the amount of money and tallies to satisfy the same. 2 *large pages.*
25 Oct.	49. Report - -	Officers of Works -	Lords of the Treasury.	For building a new charcoal house at St. James. Dated "Board of Green Cloth," 25 Oct. 1720. *Minuted* : — "26th Octr. 1720. My Lds. agree to this, provided it be within the rules." 2 *pages.*
Oct.	50. Petition -	George Ingoldsby, son and administrator of Col. Richard Ingoldsby, deceased.	Do. - -	The respits on his father's company amounted to 1,083*l.* 0*s.* 8*d.*; prays for consideration. *Minuted* :—"See if there is any money to pay this." 1 *page.*

1720. VOL. CCXXXII.

Date.	Description of Document.	From	To	Purport.
[? About Oct.]	51. Petition -	Jane Stuart, widow -	Lords of the Treasury.	For continuance of his Majesty's bounty, her husband having served as drum-major 25 years, partly in Flanders, where he was dangerously wounded, and afterwards in Portugal, where he was mortally wounded. Also copy of certificates of his services, one of which is dated 25 Oct. 1720. 2 *pages*.
3 Nov.	52. Estimate -	—	—	Of the debt for Transport service as it stood on 30 Sept. 1720. 1 *page*.
16 Nov.	53. Memorial -	Thomas Missing, contractor for victualling the Garrison of Gibraltar.	Lords of the Treasury.	As to the supply of 600 men under Col. Kane arrived at Gibraltar. 1 *page*.
22 Nov.	54. Letter - -	Mr. Secretary Craggs	Do. -	For payment of 500*l*. as a mark of H.M. special favour to Signior Claudio Ró, Secretary to the Duke of Parma, recalled home. 1 *page*.
23 Nov.	55. Do. - -	James Craggs -	Do. - -	Transmits the gross and net produce of the revenue of the Post Office. 1 *page*. [Enclosure not now with it.]
20 Dec.	56. Do. - -	George Treby - -	Secretaries of the Treasury.	For their Lps. to give directions to the Contractor for provisions at Gibraltar, that there may be always four months' provisions in advance. *Minuted*: — "22 Dec. 1720. Write to Mr. Missing accordingly." 1 *page*.
25 Dec.	57. Account -	—	—	Salaries and incidents of the Comrs. and Trustees for sale of forfeited estates and of their officers. Mich. to Christmas 1720. 2 *pages*.
1720.	58. Do. - -	—	—	Of presents bought by the Hon. Charles Stewart, Esq., on account of his Majesty, for the Emperor of Morocco. Together with the Invoices. 14 *pages or parts of pages*.

1720. VOL. CCXXXII.

Date.	Description of Document.	From	To	Purport.
[? In or after 1720.]	59. Memorial -	Lord Killmaine, Col. Archibald Hamilton, and Col. Wentworth.	Lords of the Treasury.	For the difference of pay due to their men for the time they served on board the fleet until their landing in Ireland, to be included in the demand to be laid before Parliament. 1 *page*.

VOL. CCXXXIII. 1721.

[? About 1721.] 1. Shorthand notes, some of them apparently respecting subsidies having some notes in the margin in a hand resembling Mr Lowndes'. 6 *pages*.

[? 1721.] 2. "An account of all money granted by parliament for the service of the navy, from the 1st day of January 1710; and how far the said money has been issued for that purpose." Continued to 1721. Probably one of a series. 3 *pages*.

1721. 3. Petition of Lieut. Matthew Sempile to the Duke of Grafton, Lieut. General and Governor General of Ireland. Served twenty-eight years as commissioned officer in the late regiment of Col. William Carr, till it was broke. His Majesty in consideration of the hardships that the regiment had met with, &c., granted on Aug. 22, 1715, commissions *en seconde* to seven of them, &c.: but petitioner had not received one farthing since the date of the Commission, having lost his half pay by the same. Was ordered from Edinburgh to Col. Sidney's regiment, on which he has his Commission. Earl Galway found his commission good, but said he had no fund for his pay. The Duke of Bolton referred the case to the board of General officers, who reported that he should receive full pay. The Duke promised that he should be restored to his half pay, seeing there was no precedent for *seconde* officers to receive full pay in Ireland; and ordered Mr Webster to take petitioner's papers to England, that he might be restored. Notwithstanding which, he was left out of the list: prays for present relief and to be restored to his half pay from the date of his Commission.

The copy of the papers referred to.

[He had served 22 years in 1715, and now had served 28 years, so that the date appears to be 1721.] 2 *pages*.

1721. VOL. CCXXXIII.

1720-1. 4. New year's gifts or other annual gratuities for the Secretaries. Also for the Clerks. 6 *pages.*

[Probably after 1720.] 5. "The case of Mr Jeronimy Clifford, merchant and sugar planter of the Dutch Colony of Surinam, in America, now in London, humbly presented to the Rt Honoble Lords of his Majties Treasury at Whitehall." Concerning the strengthening the Colony, a gold mine there, &c. Undated. *The first leaf only.*

[After 1720.] 6. An account of the several sums of money paid into the Exchequer on account of the late Duke of Ormond. 2 *pages.*

[? After 1720.] 7. Representation of the Royal Burghs and Merchants in Scotland to the Lords of the Treasury. The Comrs of Customs of Scotland and the magistrates of Edinburgh in behalf of the Royal Burghs, on 10 June 1716, agreed upon a table of fees and on general rules to which the taking of fees should be restricted. The reports thereon of the Attorney General and the Comrs of Customs have laid several years before the Lords of the Treasury: pray for their Lps directions. 1 *page.*

[? After 1720.] 8. "Petition of Captain Margaritte for reward for apprehending and convicting ye commander of a pyrate ship."

The "commander" was one Charles Vane, who at a Court of Admiralty held at St Jago de la Vega in the Island of Jamaica was tried on 22 March 1720 and convicted of piracy and executed, as certified by Nicholas Lawes, Esq., then Governor. 1 *page.*

[After 1720.] 9. Notes with references to the page of some larger book or report of a Company having large stocks, some of the transactions in which were fictitious. Probably the South Sea Company. The following note is for p. 115 "Janssen pressing Knight to discover all. Who answered if he should disclose all he knew it would open such a scene as the world would be surprised at." 4 *pages.*

[After 1720.] 10. Representation to the Lords of the Treasury of the officers of the Receipt of the Exchequer, relating to their allowances for the annuities.

The officers of the "Receipt" are informed that their Lordships have under their consideration the settling the further allowances for the charges of management to be given to the South Sea Company pursuant to the Act 6 Geo. [I.]. The officers give their version of the Act as it affects the Receipt of the Exchequer. They remark that "the business of the officers of the Exchequer is to receive, direct, register, examine, record, enrol, and pay all orders for money, &c. None of which words nor any words meaning or importing the same thing (except paying) being used in the Act of Parliament, the business of the officers of the Exchequer is not described, and consequently they are not included." As the Act has led to a considerable increase in their business, hope their Lordships will not lessen their ancient allowance. Remind their Lordships that since the making of the Act the officers of the Exchequer have had a considerable increase in their business by other annuities,

1721. Vol. CCXXXIII.

viz., the 4 per cent. annuities granted for the service of the year 1720; the Army-debenture annuities and the Nevis and St Christopher's debenture annuities. 5¼ *pages.*

1720–1. 11. Memorial of Edward Harley, Esq., one of the Auditors of his Majesty Imprests, to the Lords of the Treasury. The account of Col. Clement Neville, Paymaster of the Prisoners in British pay (who were taken at Brihuega, in Spain, from 24 Dec. 1710 to 3 Apr. 1713), was examined and prepared for declaration by him; the payments and receipts were examined by the Auditor: prays a warrant for an allowance for auditing the same; also prays consideration for other services rendered by him. Undated, but the present year, 1720–1, mentioned.

Encloses:—A representation of the nature of the services performed in his office, pursuant to the precepts of the Comrs for stating the debts of the Army, in the course of five years and a half. 4 *pages.*

[After 1720.] 12. Memorial of Fotherley Baker, executor of Nicholas Baker, Esq., deceased, to the Lords of the Treasury. Mr Nicholas Baker was Solicitor to the Treasury from 1695 to 1700, and a state of his account had lain before their Lps since 1718, but process had issued against memorialist, which, however, was stayed in July 1720: prays that as process has again been issued, the account may be called for and read. 1 *page.*

12 Jan. 13. Report of the Attorney and Solicitor General to the Lords of the Treasury, on the draft of a Charter intended to be granted to the corporation called the Royal Exchange Assurance. Certifying that caveats have been entered on behalf of the Trustees of the Sun Fire Office and the Hand-in-Hand and Union Fire Offices against the passing of any Charter of this kind. Counsel had also attended them and raised objections. The parties concerned in interest decline to accept the same "upon the present scheme," and desire it may be sent back to give them liberty to make a further application. Have returned the same to their Lordships without any alteration. 12 Jany 1720, *i.e.*, 1720–1.

The draft of the Charter above referred to and a copy of it, together with a Royal warrant for a bill to pass the Great Seal. The date not filled in, but probably a little later. 49½ *pages.*

[? About the same date.] 14. Draft of a warrant for a further Charter for insuring lives, houses, &c. in favour of the Corporation of the London Assurance. Undated, but probably about the same time as the last named. 1½ *pages.*

14 Jan. 15. Report of the Comrs of Revenue in Ireland to the Lords of the Treasury on the memorial of Sir John Eccles, late collector of the port of Dublin, praying that, as he has put into their (the Comrs) hands an estate of 1,800*l.* per ann. to answer any debt due to the crown, he may be restored to his employment, also for time to pay what was due from him. Had remarked some "manage-

1721. VOL. CCXXXIII.

ments" in his office which they did not approve, and ordered him to pass his accounts, which he neglected to do, and they dismissed him. Finding a much larger balance in his hands than he had charged himself with, they insisted that he should immediately convey his estate to his Majesty. Know not whether his clerk has deceived him, nor whether the cash has been employed in the South Sea Stock or other stocks. As to there being some connivance in some clerks of the Treasury or too much indulgence (having examined all the parties) find the suggestion entirely false and groundless. The accounts are now passed, and the balance amounts to 26,782*l.* 11*s.* 3½*d.*, and the memorialist has promised to pay in a considerable sum in a few days, or they would by "public cant" be obliged to dispose of memorialist's estate so conveyed to his Majesty, that so great a sum may not lie out, which in this time of scarcity and want of trade would be highly detrimental to his Majesty's affairs. Advise against his further employment, or the giving him time. Custom House, Dublin, 14 Jan. 1720.

A testimonial with numerous signatures highly in his favour. It states that, in the latter end of the reign of Queen Anne, when he was Lord Mayor of Dublin, he distinguished himself for the House of Hanover and the protestant interest by opposing the Duke of Ormonde and his adherents in all their measures against the liberties of the protestant citizens of Dublin. He was also one of the three Aldermen in 1714 sent to London by their bretheren to defend the rights and liberties of the protestants of the city of Dublin at the hazard of their fortunes. He was also an eminent trading merchant.

Also an affidavit of the memorialist. 4 *pages and* 2 *halves.*

14 Jan. 16. Memorial and recommendation by Adam Cockburn, of Ormistoun, Lord Justice Clerk, Sir Alexander Ogilvie, of Forglan, Bart., Sir Francis Grant, of Cullen, Bart., Sir Andrew Hume, of Kimmergham, Sir Walter Pringle, of Newhall, Knights, Lords Delegates of Scotland, in favour of their officers, to the Lords of the Treasury, announcing the appointment of Thomas Fordyce to be their principal clerk and register, and Alexander Pitcarn the second and assistant clerk and register, also a housekeeper at certain salaries mentioned, asking for directions to be given to the Barons of the Exchequer to pay their salaries. "Att the Court of Delegats Office in Edinburgh, 14 January 1721."

Minuted:—"Septbr. 20, 1721. Agreed." 2 *pages.*

17 Jan. 17. Representation of the Directors of the South Sea Company to the Lords of the Treasury on the memorial of Matthew Barton and Robert Murray, Esq[res], Comptroller and Paymaster of the 1,400,000*l.* Lottery, 1714, which asked for instructions as to the payment of interest due at Michaelmas last, on the unsubscribed orders lying in the Controller's office, and as to whether the principal may not be discharged on such orders as remain unsubscribed into the capital stock of the South Sea Company. The Directors have no objection to the payment of the interest due at Michaelmas last,

1721. Vol. CCXXXIII.

but ask for their Lordships' directions, as to the application of the 26,180*l.* for payment of the principal. South Sea House, 17 Jan. 1720.

Minuted:—"18th Janry 1720. My Lords direct the paymt of the int. due at Michas last." 2 *pages.*

22 Jan. 18. Fr[ancis] Nicholson to [? Mr Lowndes]. This is designed to be presented by Mr Thomas Moor (one of the Officers to the Society for Propagation of the Gospel in Foreign parts) in the behalf of Messrs —— Clark and Francis Merry, who are going over as missionaries to South Carolina. Desires to obtain the Royal bounty of 20*l.* for each of them. Hoped to have the Royal Commission for trying pirates. Saw by the public prints that the Treasury had a great deal of business to do in Parliament, but had very great satisfaction in seeing also that the house of Commons (of which the person addressed was a member) had voted all the sums, &c., and had agreed to the scheme for restoring public credit. Congratulates him on the share he had in it, both at the Treasury and in the House. Begs that the Commission, if not already passed, may be promoted and sent to him by the first opportunity. Plymouth, Jan. 22, 1720. 1 *page, quarto.*

[? About 25 Jan.] 19. Petition of Timothy Goodwin, Jacob Tonson, William Taylor, and Bernard Lintot, to the Lords of the Treasury, for payment of 162*l.* 10*s.* for printing the special report from the Committee to enquire into several subscriptions for fisheries, insurances, &c. The work was done by order of the Speaker of the House of Commons.

Docketed:—"Booksellers petition for allowance for printing the report of the Comtee of Bubbles."

Minuted:—"25th Janry 1720. See what has been done in cases of the like kind."

The following is the report on that minute:—"30th July 1719. 240li was issued to Timothy Goodwin for printed reports of the Commrs. and Trustees for forfeitures in Scotland, and for Reports relating to the equivalent delivered to the House of Commons. His Mats Printers are paid for all printed papers delivered to both Houses of Parliament."

Minuted again:—"20th Decr 1721. Order'd." 1 *page.*

[? About 25 Jan.] 20. Petition of John Haynes, Gent., to the Lords of the Treasury. In 1698, Mr. Whitley, Receiver General of Taxes, of Chester and North Wales, failed, being indebted 90,000*l.* The Treasury was empowered to compound with his security, and the composition money reduced the debt to about 37,800*l.*, and Whitley had effects to have cleared the debt, but concealed them. Petitioner can "discover" a large sum, and the 8,000*l.* may be recovered by his pains, if he has three quarters of what he shall recover. If he does not succeed, the Crown will be at no charge: prays for a warrant for three quarters of the money recovered.

1721. Vol. CCXXXIII.

Minuted:—"25th Janry 1720. It being appropriated money, my Lords cannot make such grant as is desired." 1 *page*.

28 Jan. 21. Report of A. Cracherode to the Lords of the Treasury. Has considered the annexed petition of Edward Mackmanus setting forth that in 1714 the petitioner made a discovery to the Lords of the Treasury of divers frauds and abuses against the Royal Hospital, near Chelsea; whereby the government was saved in one payment to the pensioners 76,741*l.* 5*s.*, besides yearly pensions of 5,046 persons, who were discharged and struck out of the books as disqualified; several of whom were evidence to prove petitioner's discovery before the Comrs appointed to examine these abuses. The petitioner spent a good deal of time and money in the discovery of these frauds and abuses, besides others committed by persons who were established on half-pay as officers, under colour of forged commissions, and by infamous women under pretence of being officers' widows. By these means petitioner created abundance of implacable enemies, who have since that time, to screen themselves from justice, oppressed the petitioner, who has been several times tried for his life by their malicious revenge, and hurried from one gaol to another; where he underwent very barbarous usage, and must have perished had not the Court of King's Bench relieved him. He therefore prayed either to be admitted to make out the truth before their Lordships, or for compensation and relief. Certifies that petitioner produced two affidavits, a certificate, and a commission, as to the truth of the allegations (the purport of which documents he sets out). A joint affidavit of Elizabeth Atterbury and others states, "that the said petr Mackmanus hath for 5 or 6 years past been continually a prisoner, having been scarcely out of prison in all that time above a month or six weeks together, and hath been several times try'd for his life, on indictmts maliciously preferr'd against him, by John Le Mater, and others, his accomplices. That the Petr being a prisoner for twelve months together in the Marshalsea, the depont Atterbury carried him linnen, victuals, and other necessaries, but often received very ill-usage from the turnkeys and others, being often denyed entrance, and when she was admitted to defendt she was always abused, and sometimes beaten by the turnkeys; that the Petr Mackmanus during his imprisonmt in the Marshalsea was most inhumanly treated by the keeper, turnkeys, and others by wearing 30li weight of iron for five months, and being loaded for nine days with 150li weight of iron (vizt) with two pair of fetters, a pair of shears, and handcuffs, and being chained to the floor for the space of three days, and by being often barbarously beaten by the turnkeys and convicts, who were hired (as believed) by the said Le Mater and his accomplices so to do, in order to murder him, wch was near effected; the said Petr Mackmanus being once so barbarously beaten, that by all the means his surgeons could use they could not stop his bleeding for nine days together."

Mr Cracherode certifies further, that on 21 Sept. then last past, he made a report to their Lordships, upon a petition of Peter Villeneuve

1721.

and four others, concerning the frauds, &c. in Chelsea Hospital; by which it appeared how much money Mackmanus had received as one of the witnesses, and that neither the Com[rs] for the affairs of the Hospital, nor the Lords of the Treasury, had made any distinction between Mackmanus and the other witnesses. Takes exception to Mackmanus claiming the whole merit of the discovery, as he was joined by four others in giving information: to prove which, sends copy of all the minutes of the Com[rs] for the hospital relating to the subject. (The copy is embodied in the report.) Further certifies that M[r] Stanwix, solicitor for the affairs of the Hospital, had delivered to him various papers on the subject. (These are also given.)

Thinks it his duty to lay before their Lordships several other papers brought to him by other witnesses as to these abuses, and against Mackmanus's pretentions. (The titles and substance of the papers then follow.)

As to the allegation of petitioner having been frequently thrown into prison and prosecuted, certifies that it is fully made out. (The evidence for which he supplies.) Submits it to their Lordships what further reward petitioner deserves, having received 106*l.* 16*s.* as his share.

Minuted:—"9th Feb. 1720–1. My Lords adhere to their minute of the 18th May 1720, which is as followeth, viz[t]: "My Lords direct M[r] Lowther to pay y[e] witnesses for frauds committed in Chelsea Hospital the money for their subsistence due on Fryday next (being y[e] 20th May 1720), and to acquaint them with their Lordships' resolučon, that this is the last money they are to expect from the Crown on acco[t] of their being witnesses." 8½ *pages.*

28 Jan. 22. Report of the same to the same. Has considered the petition of Major Henry Irwin, of the colony of Virginia, setting forth that under two proclamations for suppressing piracy, he discovered and apprehended, in the Colony and dominion of Virginia, Tobias Butler, Daniel Degatt, William Lake, and Thomas Hall; who were at a Court of Admiralty sentenced to death; and by him the material evidence was procured, and a considerable sum secured for his Majesty's use; and that he (the petitioner) prays payment of 80*l.* or such sum as he is entitled to by the proclamations. Has further considered a certificate annexed, under the seal of the Colony of Virginia, signed by Alexander Spotswood, Esq., his Majesty's Lieut.-Governor, Vice-Admiral, and Commander-in-Chief of the Colony testifying to the same. Certifies what the effect of the proclamations was, viz.: offers of pardon to those who surrendered before a certain day, and 20*l.* reward for each private person arrested. Is of opinion that the Major is entitled to 80*l.*, and that a warrant for the issue of that sum should be issued. 28 Jan. 1720.

The petition and certificate referred to. 3½ *pages.*

28 Jan. 23. Similar report of the same to the same on the petition of Benjamin Bartholomew, who made a similar claim for the arrest of John Law and George Gaddis, who were convicted of running away with a merchant ship called "the Beginning."

1721. Vol. CCXXXIII.

Is of opinion that he should receive 40*l.* 28 Jan. 1720.

The petition referred to and a certificate of Sir Henry Penrice, Kn[t], LL.D., Lieut. Commissary in the High Court of Admiralty and Judge and President of that Court, on the same subject. 2½ *pages and a piece of parchment.*

31 Jan. 24. Report of the Attorney General to the same, on the memorial of the Duchess of Buccleuch, to the King. The memorial sets forth that on her marriage with the late Duke of Monmouth, King Charles II. agreed to make a settlement on them in Scotland, to the value of 40,000*l.*, which was not done. Afterwards the King granted the manor of Spalding, and other manors in the county of Lincoln, said to be of the yearly value of 566*l.* 10*s.* 1⅜*d.*, for 99 years, from the decease of the late Queen Dowager. On the outlawry of the Duke, the manors were granted to trustees, for the use of the Duchess. On the demise of the Queen Dowager, the Duchess came into possession, and received the rents. By an error of the Clerk, who made out the schedule by which the first grant was formed, the rents of the Manor of Whaplode (37*l.* 17*s.* 4½*d.*) and those of the Manors of Moulton, Bowesllas (75*l.* 13*s.* 8½*d.*) were not inserted, though the manors were granted and the advowsons to the livings were reserved to the crown. This shows the intention, and as the Duchess is advised, would have been good in law, if made by a private person; but may be disputable by the Crown. Memorialist prayed to be discharged from the rents which she had received from these manors, and for a lease for 31 years at the above rents. Certifies the effect of various grants (which he sets out) touching those manors, and is of opinion that the manors of Whaplode and Moulton, Bowsellas, and the premises, which make up the rents of 37*l.* 17*s.* 4½*d.* and 75*l.* 13*s.* 8½*d.* did not pass to the Trustees of the Duchess; but that the yearly rents of those manors and premises, from the death of the Queen Dowager, belonged to the late Queen during her life and ever since her death to his Majesty. It is in his Majesty's power to discharge the Duchess of those rents, by a proper instrument, if he please to do so. His Majesty may grant such parts of the premises as are not in lease, for a term of 31 years, under certain conditions (which are specified). Jan. 31, 1720.

Minuted:—"April 1, 1721. The King consents that the Duchess be discharged of the arrears and that a new lease pass as is desired." 6 *pages.*

31 Jan. 25. Report of the Barons of the Exchequer of Scotland to the Lords of the Treasury on a warrant for the Royal signature for granting to William Hall, Esq., one of the Clerks of Session, the lands of Churnside, Spence mains, and other lands lying in the county of Berwick, "proceeding on the resignations of M[r] James Hume, Advocate, John Carmichaell, writer in Edinburgh, and John Dunce. The signature contains a *De novo damus*, but the

1721. VOL. CCXXXIII.

Barons do not find that there are any non-entry duties or casualties and forfeitures, by recognition or escheat, affecting the lands, which will be affected by the grant. It also contains an erection of the lands into a Barony. "Edin^{r}, 31 January 1720–21."

Minuted:—"17 Feb. 1720. To be layd before the King for his signature." The warrant is not with it. 1 *page.*

2 Feb. 26. Report of the Barons of the Exchequer of Scotland to the Lords of the Treasury, on the question whether 1,000*l.* would be sufficient for the needful repairs of the palace of Holyrood House. Find that it is in much worse condition than when they had it inspected, and will rapidly run into ruin unless prevented. It will take at least 1,000*l.* to do what is necessary. Edinb^{r}, Exchequer Chamber, 2 Feb. 1721.

Minuted:—"August 2^{d}, 1721. Agreed out of ye mony of Scotland. Warr^{t} sign'd 31st Augt 1721." 2 *pages.*

6 Feb. 27. Report of R. Powys to the Lords of the Treasury on the state of the demand made by Martin Bladen, Esq., in a memorial annexed, praying to be paid his allowances, as far as had been paid to Daniel Pulteney, Esq., as he was joint Commissary with Mr Pulteney for transacting certain matters with the Court of France. Certifies that the memorialist was to have had 3*l.* a day, but it was to cease on 26 Dec. 1720. It would amount to 1,140*l.* after deducting 273*l.* advanced to him. Feb. 6, 1720–1.

Minuted:—"11th May 1721. Prepare a warrant."

The memorial and copy of the Commission to Daniel Pulteney and the memorialist. 5½ *pages.*

9 Feb. 28. Report of the Barons of the Exchequer of Scotland to the Lords of the Treasury, on the memorial of John, Earl of Stair. Certify that the Earl and his family appear to be heritably entitled to the office of baily of the Regality of Glenluce, in the county of Wigtoun, with a yearly fee or salary of three "chalders" of meal, and that King William granted two tacks or leases to the Earl's father of all the lands, few and teind duties and others "payable out of the regality and 'parochine' of Glenluce to the Crown, as come in place of the bishop of Galloway," the first for seven and the second for nineteen years. Both the leases are expressed to be in satisfaction of the fee of the three chalders of meal, and for relieving the crown of the stipends payable to the ministers of the old and new church of Glenluce. If his Majesty grants a further lease or tack of the few and teind duties to the Earl, it ought to be on the same conditions as are contained in the former tacks. Edinb^{r}, Excheq^{r} Chamb^{r}, 9th February 1721.

Minuted:—"20th Feb. 1720–1. The signature to be layd before the King for his signing. 21st D^{o}. Warr^{t} signd."

The memorial and copies of the two tacks. 8 *pages.*

[After 10 Feb.] 29. "State of money issued to Sir Luke Schaub since his being employed at Paris."

1721. VOL. CCXXXIII.

It includes "the allowance which would have been due in case he had gone with the character of Envoy." 1 *page.*

16 Feb. 30. Two accounts of disbursements, the 1st by Mr Rot Dundass, the younger, of Arnistoun, the King's Advocate for Scotland, on account of the government during the time he was solicitor and since; and 2nd by Walter Stewart, the King's Solicitor General for Scotland. Sworn 16 Feb. 1720-1. 5½ *pages.*

[? About 18 Feb.] 31. Petition of Peter Hartop, merchant, for himself and others, to the Lords of the Treasury. Windsor Sandys, Esq., obtained a grant from his present Majesty "for fishing upon all wrecks lost in and between the latitudes of 12 and 17 degrees North Latitude in the West Indies for a term yet unexpired." Petitioner and several merchants have, at great expense, fitted out several vessels to fish for wrecks within the same latitudes. Is informed another grant is applied for. Prays to be heard by counsel before a grant is made.

Minuted:—"18th Feb. 1720. Sir Thos Mackworth and the petr may be heard at the same time. Lre writ accordingly." 1 *page.*

? About 18 Feb. 32. Memorial to the Lords of the Treasury from Charles Delafaye in behalf of the proprietors of Mr Rowe's diving engine, and of the grant to Lord Harley and others to fish upon wrecks, praying a short day for hearing applications for the grant.

Minuted:—"18th Feb. 1720. My Lords appoint Tuesday next."

Another memorial and a note signed "Jno Ward" to Charles Delafaye on the same subject.

Also "copy of a grant unto Edward Harley, Esq., commonly called Ld Harley, of all wrecks, &c., wch before the 24th June 1713 have been cast away, &c., or wch before the 24th June 1724 shall be cast away, in or between ye latitude of 26 and 40 degrees of No lat., in ye West Indies, with ye variations in ye grants to Morgan Randyll, Windsor Sandys, Andrew Becker, being ye only grants whose terms are not ended." With various notes. 8½ *pages, besides short notes written on divers other pages.*

[? About 24 Feb.] 33. Petition of Anthony Roig and John Colomer, citizens of Barcelona, contractors for bread and forage for the army of the High Allies in Spain during the late war. Furnished the army in 1707. For this there remained due for what was taken by the enemy, viz., 111,226 dollars; whereof Great Britain's proportion was 32,506, for which the petitioners have obtained the King's warrant; but the Comrs for stating the debts due to the Army are directed to compute each dollar at the current price of exchange, which is 3*s.* 10½*d.*; whereas they hoped to have had 4*s.* 9*d.*, for so the exchange was when the contract was to have been paid: viz., about thirteen years ago. By the 12th article of the contract it is expressly agreed that the powers in alliance should bear the loss of exchange. Pray a suitable alteration to be made in the warrant; otherwise by this loss and the great discount now on debentures they and their families must be ruined. Besides their effects have already been seized and their persons

1721. Vol. CCXXXIII.

imprisoned, because they displeased the King of Spain in serving the allies and afterwards the Emperor.

Minuted:—"24th Feb. 1720–1. To be considered when the Comm^rs army debts are here to-morrow." 1 *page*.

2 March. 34. Memorial of Charles Wither, Esq., Surveyor General of the Woods, &c., to the Lords of the Treasury. Receives daily informations of spoil in all his Majesty's forests. The only way to deal with wood spoilers will be to exhibit informations in the Exchequer against the most notorious offenders, some few examples of which would be sufficient to terrify them in each forest. Nothing has been done to punish them lately, and they have become unreasonably bold. Submits that directions be given to Mr Cracherode to exhibit informations against such "offenders in Vert" and to prosecute them. 2 March 1720–1.

Minuted:—"2 March 1720–1. Lrẽ signed." 1 *page*.

4 March. 35. Report of the Attorney General (Raymond) to the Lords of the Treasury on the petition of Abraham Gerard Borsholt, under prosecution for subornation of perjury by the Com^rs of Customs. The petitioner came over hither eight years ago, and has exercised the trade of a merchant, and by the prosecution has been put to 100*l*. charges. The crime charged against the petitioner he (the Attorney General) takes to be of a high nature, but whether he is guilty must depend upon the event of the trial. The Com^rs strongly oppose granting a *nolle prosequi*, but it is in his Majesty's power to grant it. March 4, 1720.

Also an affidavit.

Minuted:—"5 May 1721. My Lords cannot advise the King to extend his Royall favour." 5 *pages*.

[? About 4 March.] 36. Petition of Jane Robson, of North Shields, in the county of Northumberland, widow, "aged 75 years," to the Lords of the Treasury. Had complained to their Lordships of the great losses she sustained by the prosecution of Mongoe Chrisop and William Williams, of North Shields, for receiving and collecting from the inhabitants of that town above 100*l*. more than they had warrant to do, or than was paid the Crown for the land tax. Prays repayment of what she had lost by the prosecution.

Also a letter signed by various of the inhabitants agreeing that petitioner should receive their shares of what had been wrongfully charged. Dated 4 March 1720. 2 *pages*.

8 March. 37. Report of the Board of Works to the Lords of the Treasury relating to the appointment of an engine keeper at Windsor. Conceive it absolutely necessary to have an engine keeper, and being informed that the engine was out of order, Sir Thomas Hewett, the present surveyor, and Mr Gibbons went down to Windsor to view it, and found that the pipe that conveys the water to the castle was not more than 2 inches diameter, and in some places less, and was not wide enough to receive the water of so great an engine. The pipe ought to have been 4 inches diameter.

1721. VOL. CCXXXIII.

Therefore ordered that one of the two forcers belonging to the engine should not work, for if both were employed they would either burst the pipe or break the engine. [The appointment seems to have laid between Mr John Rowley, who made the engine, and Mr Thomas Rowland, clerks of the works at Windsor, both of whom claim to have taken care of it.] 8 March 1720.

Copy of two subordinate documents. 2 *pages*.

11 March. 38. Report of A. Cracherode to the Lords of the Treasury on the petition of Robert Linass, who had prosecuted Michael Idle, of Broughton, in the parish of Appleton-in-the Street, in the county of York, yeoman, for a debt of 198*l*., who was thereupon outlawed. The goods of Idle were appraised at 85*l*. Their Lordships may very properly grant their warrant to the Attorney General, empowering him to consent (on his Majesty's behalf) that the 85*l*. in the hands of the Sheriff of Yorkshire may, by the Court of Exchequer, be ordered to be paid to the petitioner. 11 Mar. 1720.

The petition and two affidavits. 5 *pages*.

[13 March.] 39. "Memorial concerning the charges of prosecutions for crimes, and the maintenance of public prisoners in Scotland." Before the Union the charges of prosecutions for crimes, carried on at the suit of the King's Advocate, were ordinarily advanced by the Solicitor General, and were refunded at least once a year by the Treasury upon demand; but when there were more numerous prosecutions, money was imprested by the Treasury into the hands of the Solicitor for that purpose. The Keepers of the Prisons in Scotland, before the Union, advanced what was necessary for the aliment of public prisoners who could not maintain themselves, and "fitted their accounts yearly" in the Treasury, and had the money allowed without any charge or difficulty. Since the Union, the Exchequer in Scotland refuses to pass all those accounts, there being no fund for payment. This is a very great prejudice to the public service, for since the King's Accession, there having been frequent disorders committed, and insults against the Government in "different corners," a vigorous execution of the laws would necessarily have demanded a considerable advance of money for defraying such expense, which none would take upon them where they saw no way of reimbursement. Public prisoners have in effect starved, having no fund of maintenance but what they received in charity; which makes Justices of the Peace very unwilling to commit persons to prison for crimes, though the keeping of the peace seems necessarily to require it; and the magistrates of Burghs do, as in law they can, refuse to receive criminals into their prisons where they see there is no fund for their maintenance till trial. The Memorialist [whose name is not mentioned] proposes that the Solicitor to the Exchequer in Scotland (Mr Bowles) and his successor in office should be empowered, by the direction of the Advocate or Solicitor General in Scotland, to defray the charges of prosecutions at the instance of the Crown, whether in criminal matters before the Court of Justiciary, or in civil cases before the session, where the interest of the Crown is concerned, and that the Exchequer should be directed to pass his accounts, or else that a sum of money should be impresled yearly into the hands of the Solicitor General for defraying those charges, and that he should "fit an account for it yearly" in the Exchequer: and that the Exchequer be likewise directed once a year to receive and fit the accounts of the Keepers of the Prisons for maintenance of public prisoners. If no method be fixed as to these things, the public service must suffer and the quiet of the country cannot be preserved.

Referred to the Lords of the Treasury for their report. Mar. 13, 1720–21. 3 *pages.*

17 March. 40. Petition of the Noblemen, Gentlemen, &c. of the Western Shires of Scotland to the King, showing "that by several laudable and standing laws the importation of oatmeal and cattle from Ireland is forbidden under severe penalties. That notwithstanding the said laws vast quantities of oatmeal and cattle are yearly imported to this country, to the manifest discouragement of tillage and pasturage, and consequently to the ruin of the landed interest. That the excessive and unrestrained running in of French brandy, without paying the legal duties and excise, contrary to many good laws made against the same, is a heavy grievance which this country groans under: for thereby money is carried out of the kingdom, the fair trader is "prejdged," and the profitable art of distilling spirits from corns and sugar is absolutely discouraged." Petitioners pray that his Majesty would order the laws to be put in execution against the same.

Referred on 17 Mar. 1720–1 to the Lords of the Treasury to consider and report. There are twenty-four signatures. 1 *large page.*

[? About 23 March.] 41. Memorial of Edward Harley, Esq., one of the Auditors of Imprests, to the Lords of the Treasury, respecting the account of Col. Clement Nevil, paymaster of the prisoners taken at the action at Brihuega, in Spain. The account consists of the payments made every two months to the officers and privates of the British troops and the officers and privates of the Imperial, Spanish, Portuguese, and Palatine troops in British pay. States how the same were audited. Prays a warrant to pay him an allowance for auditing the same. Also states other services for which he seeks consideration.

Minuted:—"23^d March 1720–1. Ref. to Mr Baillie and to Mr Lowndes." 2 *pages.*

23 March. 42. Memorial of John Ward, one of the persons concerned in the ships fitted out by Lord Harley and others under a grant for fishing upon wrecks, to the Lords of the Treasury. Their Lordships appointed Mr Phillip Lascells, Agent, to take care of his Majesty's tenths that might be recovered under this grant. He was to give 2,000*l.* security. This he could then have done; but owing to the delay, &c. the persons he proposed now refuse to give bonds. The ships are ready to sail at Gravesend, and if their Lordships would appoint Capt. Crawcroft, who goes pilot, to be Agent for his Majesty, without security, he would effectually discharge the trust.

1721. VOL. CCXXXIII.

The ships would give all proper accommodation to any one appointed. March 23, 1720. 1 *page.*

25 March. 43. An account of the debt of the Great Wardrobe to Ladyday 1721. Signed :—Tho. Dummer. 2 *large double pages.*

25 March. 44. "An acco[t] of what was wanting at Ladyday 1721 to clear all fees and salaries payable at the Exchequer." 3 *pages* (*brief size*).

[? About 25 March.] 45. A paper indorsed "Westminster Abbey, &c.," but which contains notes of various Acts of Parliament relating to the funds for building churches, Greenwich Hospital, &c., propositions for taking loans, &c. [The date is inferred from an entry stating that the duties were deficient in answering the payments charged on them at Ladyday 1721. 7,151*l.* 9*s.* 8½*d.*] 3 *pages.*

28 March. 46. A representation of the nature of the services performed by Auditor Harley, in preparing acco[ts], making searches for papers, and copies of vouchers for the use of the Commis[rs] for the debts of the Army, since their appointment in September 1715; being now five years and a half. 28 March 1721.

The docket states that the service was required of him by precepts or orders from the Com[rs] and for making up Col. Nevill's account of prisoners in Spain. 4 *pages.*

31 March. 47. Letter of William Popple, on behalf of the Com[rs] of Trade and Plantations, to Charles Stanhope, Esq., on the case and petition hereafter described. The Com[rs] have no objection to the petitioners being relieved as desired. Whitehall, 31 March 1721.

Encloses copy of an extract of a letter from Col. Spotswood to the Hon. M[r] Secretary Craggs thereon, and :—

"The case of Francis Stevens, Abell Grant, Thomas Melton, and Samuel Allen and Samuel Fry, merchants and owners of the ship 'Callabar-Merchant,' of Bristol."

The ship was fitted out with a cargo proper to purchase negroes and carry them from Guinea to Virginia. The ship was attacked by pirates, was captured, and the master and men kept prisoners for nine weeks, the cargo being made use of or taken away; but at last the master was allowed to depart with his ship, and, at the parting, twenty-one negroes were given him as a satisfaction for the damage. On arriving at Virginia the master gave information to the Hon. Alexander Spotswood, Esq., the Governor, who seized the negroes for his Majesty's use, and only allowed 126*l.* for the same, which is not one fourth of their value, whereas the owners sustained the damage of 1,200*l.*

At the foot is the petition of the owners to have the negroes delivered up or satisfaction for them.

Minuted :—" Warr[t] signed, 15th May." 4 *pages.*

VOL. CCXXXIV. April–July.

[About 4 April.] 1. "Charles Harison's report concerning lycences granted by the Court of Exchequer to compound upon penal laws, &c. from the last day of Trinity term to the last day of Michaelmas term 1721 inclusive."

With this note also on the back "R. 4 Apr. 1721." 4 *double pages.*

[? About 12 April.] 2. Petition of William Whiston, Clerk, sometime Professor of Mathematics in the University of Cambridge, to the King. By an Act of the 12th year of her late Majesty's reign a public reward is provided for such person or persons as shall discover the longitude at sea. Petitioner has been at a great deal of pains and expense in finding out a method for discovering the same by means of a dipping needle, and that with great hopes of success, and is not able by his poverty to go on with that discovery, as it will require a considerable sum for gaining a sufficient number of observations at sea and in remote countries to complete the "method": prays his Majesty to bestow such a sum on him, for this work, as to his "wisdom shall seem meet."

Minuted:—"100li bounty. Pp̄are a wart. 12 Ap. 1721. Warrt signd 18th." 1 *page.*

13 April. 3. The Lords of the Admiralty to the Lords of the Treasury The Directors of the Royal Hospital at Greenwich have represented that the collection of the sixpences from merchant seamen within the kingdom of Ireland produces annually little more than 200*l.*, and that the chief cause is from want of power in the collectors to stop the ships in port till the duty is paid, as the Act directs, and as is practiced in England. Lay this matter before their Lordships, conceiving that the only remedy for the abuse will be, that their Lordships send directions to the Comrs of revenue in Ireland to order the proper officers, in the ports of that kingdom, not to suffer any ships to clear out till they have paid the sixpences due. It is further represented that very great damages are committed on his Majesty's manor of Greenwich, and encroachments made therein: and as these abuses are only cognizable at the Courts to be held within the Manor, where the homage ought to present and fine the offenders, it is desired that a steward may be constituted, so that the Courts may be regularly held to support the King's rights and redress grievances. Admiralty Office, 13 April 1721. 2 *pages.*

13 April. 4. J. Burchett to the Lords of the Treasury. Sends copy of the letter hereafter described giving an account of the havock made in the woods in New England. Admiralty Office, 13 April 1721.

In a postscript he says he sends another letter from Mr Wentworth, Governor of New Hampshire, on the same subject.

1721. VOL. CCXXXIV.

Copy of letter of Robert Armstrong to Charles Burniston, Esq., Surveyor General of his Majesty's woods in America. The people elude the force of the Act of 9 Anne in reference to masts. They have taken in thousands of acres of the woodland, wherein the best timber grows, and formed the same into their township, though the thousandth part is not under any immediate improvement. 14 or 15 years since they petitioned to have their town grants confirmed; but the King and Council repealed the grants to keep them from destroying and encroaching his Majesty's timber and waste lands. Still they continue to make townships and take tracts of land without any title: and the inhabitants cut and fell all trees at will. There will shortly be no occasion for a King's Surveyor of Woods. Therefore this must be corrected by an explanatory Act, or otherwise: and then there must be an alteration in the penalty, which is 100*l.* sterl. This is impossible to be obtained. The qualification should be "100*l.* or the value in Province bills of credit." There are other defects of the Act, whereby all trees under 24 inches are destroyed at pleasure. As the people are much more numerous now than formerly, the saw mills are increased in proportion; and what they generally destroy is between 18 and 24 inches. It is a great abuse to send ship timber from New Hampshire to Portugal. Notwithstanding his checks as collector this trade has been carried on; there being no law against exporting timber to foreign parts. It is by no means prudent to suffer ship timber to be carried to any foreign prince or state; first because it furnishes our enemies, and secondly, it disfurnishes the King of such a nursery of noble timber in New Hampshire as he has not in all his dominions. New Hampshire, New England, November 20, 1720. 8 *pages.*

14 April. 5. Order in Council on the petition of John Winn, Commander of the ship "Bristol Merchant," and of John Bennett, Commander of the "Turkey Merchant," whose ships (having come from infected places) were to be destroyed. Praying to be allowed their wages, provisions, &c. from the time they came into Standgate Creek till the ships were destroyed: referring the matter to the Treasury to state the *quantum* and value, and what was reasonable to be allowed. 14 April 1721.

The petition and another petition of the seamen. 2 *pages.*

17 April. 6. An account of the debt due on the pensions payable in the office of Walter Chetwynd, Esq., between Michaelmas 1719 and Ladyday 1721. Signed:—"Walt. Chetwynd." 17 April 1721. 7 *pages and* 2 *halves.*

[? About 20 April.] 7. Memorial of Henry Sully and others appointed to distribute his Majesty's Royal bounty to the poor manufacturers lately brought over from France. Have received 2,000*l.* out of the 3,000*l.* granted by the King in Council, and have distributed the same, but have been much interrupted by designing, ill-intentioned persons, who misrepresent them: pray to have a proper person appointed to examine their past conduct.

1721. VOL. CCXXXIV.

Minuted:—"20th April 1721. Mr Stanyan to desire the Secr$\tilde{y}$ to lay the papers relating to this matter before my Lords." 2 *pages*.

25 April 1721. 8. Report of the Attorney General (Robert Raymond) to the Lords of the Treasury on the petition (referred 21 May 1720) of Hannah Penn, widow of William Penn, Esq., deceased, late proprietor and Governor of the province of Pennsylvania. The petition states "that ye s^{d} Mr Penn being in treaty wth her late Matie for ye sale of his powers of Governm^{t} of ye s^{d} province, was taken sick and made his will, whereby he devised his s^{d} governm^{t} to ye Earl of Oxford and Earl Poulet in trust, wth intent that in case of his death they might be enabled to compleat ye sale and effectually convey ye same; but recovering from that sickness he did afterwards in ye year 1712 finish ye contract himself, and agreed to resign his powers of Governm^{t} to ye crown in consideration of ye sum of 12,000^{li}, whereof one thousand pounds was then paid him in part, but before ye requisite conveyances were perfected he was again seiz'd with an apoplectic fit, wch so disabled him that he was never afterwards capable of executing ye same to ye time of his death in ye year 1718, so that ye power of conveying ye s^{d} governm^{t}, whenever his Matie shall think fit to require ye same, seems now to be vested in ye s^{d} Earles. But Wm Penn, Esqr, heir-at-law to ye deceased, disputes this will, and the s^{d} Earls are unwilling to act in their trust wthout a decree of ye Court of Chancery, so that y^{r} petition^{r}, being executrix to her s^{d} husband, is advised to bring a bill to have ye determination of that Court touching ye s^{d} Governm^{t}, as well to compleat ye s^{d} sale to ye crown, as wth respect to ye s^{d} Mr Penn ye heir, and is advis'd that it will be requisit to make y^{r} Lord^{ps} parties, wch she cannot presume to do without first acquainting y^{r} Lord^{ps} therewith:" prays the permission to insert the same.

The report sets out the grants that had been made to William Penn and the terms of the will and of a draft of surrender of the powers of Government, and that the will was disputed by Wm Penn, the son and heir, who insisted that he was entitled to the Government or money for which it should be sold. Until the contract with the Crown is determined the family affairs will be in great confusion, and if it be his Majesty's pleasure to proceed on this contract, the money cannot be safely paid without the directions of a court of equity. Is of opinion that their L^{ps} may permit their names to be inserted in the Bill. Dated 25 Apr. 1721.

United is the petition. *Minuted*:—"21st July 1721. My Lords give leave that their names be made use of in a bill ꝑsuant to the desire of the pet^{r}." 4½ *pages*.

[After 25 April.] 9. Another petition from the same Hannah Penn to the Lords of the Treasury referring to the foregoing, and stating that she has since been advised to exhibit such bill in the Court of Exchequer, and that it would be most proper not to make their Lordships, but his Majesty's Attorney General, a party thereto, for the purpose aforesaid, which she had done: prays their Lordships to give

1721. Vol. CCXXXIV.

directions to the Attorney General to put in such answer as may be agreeable to the King's pleasure.

To the petition is added a copy of the preceding report. Besides which is a copy of the warrant for the payment of the 1,000*l.* above referred to. 4½ *pages.*

26 April. 10. Order in Council made on reading the report of the Com[rs] of the Admiralty upon the petition of Andrew Duncan and others of H.M. ship "Scarborough," touching a pirate ship they had taken in June 1718 named "the Blanco," which they represented was afterwards seized by M[r] Lowther, then Governor of Barbados. The value of the ship was to be forthwith paid into the High Court of Admiralty and granted to Captain Hume and the officers and men of the same ship at the time of the capture, and to be divided as was done in the last war.. 26 April 1721.

With it is an account of the loss of time and money paid by Francis Kirby, Quarter-Master, and others, mariners of the above ship, concerning the "Blanco" prize.

Minuted:—"August y[e] 29, 1721. Agreed that a warrant be prepared for allowing to y[e] ship's crew of y[e] Scarborough concerned in taking the pyratical vessel called y[e] Blanco 400[li] in liew of all demands to be payd out of y[e] pyraticall effects in M[r] Lascelles y[e] collector of Barbados' hands, or M[r] Carter's, his deputy. Warr[t] signd 12th Sept[r] 1721." 4 *pages.*

[? About 29 April.] 11. Representation of Jonathan Forward, of London, merchant, to the Lords of the Treasury, offering to enter into a new contract to transport the felons from Newgate and the other prisons (the old one having expired). Proposes that he may have 4*l.* per head for the malefactors to be transported from Newgate, which he hopes will be considered reasonable in regard he has sustained a considerable loss, not only by transporting them, but by the returns which have been made to him in tobacco, which will not sell for more than will defray the charge of freight and custom. Prays for the allowance of 4*l.* per head for the malefactors from the prisons in the home circuit and for such others as he shall transport from Newgate to the plantations in America.

Minuted:—"29 Apr. 1721. Agreed upon the former foot."

Another proposal from him (perhaps of a little later date) at the former allowance for the country gaols and at 5*l.* a head for those from Newgate. Upon a petition the aldermen had appointed a committee to recommend an additional allowance of 20[s] per head for 97 persons:- prays payment thereof as well as of 84*l.* for the like additional allowance for 84 persons since transported. 2 *pages.*

April. 12. "Memorial of Tho. Cornwallis et al. concern[g] y[e] paym[t] of half a y[rs] int[st] due Mich[s] 1720 to the prop[rs] of y[e] fortunate tickets in each of y[e] Lotteryes anno 1719."

The above persons had been employed by the Treasury and offered their services again. Banqueting House, April 1721.

Minuted:—"10th July 1721. Agreed to if agreable to y[e] act." 1 *page*

VOL. CCXXXIV.

1721.
7 May. 13. Order in Council on a presentment to the Lords of the Treasury from the Com[rs] of Customs of 21 April respecting the insolent gangs of smugglers in Kent and Sussex which proposed the quartering of such a number of dragoons as his Majesty should see fit, to assist the Civil Magistrates or officers in hindering the exportation of wool and importation of prohibited and unaccustomed goods, &c., approving of the quartering the same, &c. 7 May 1721. 1½ *pages.*

7 May. 14. Similar order on a presentment of the same Com[rs] of 8 March then last: approving the appointment of armed sloops on the same coast, from the Isle of Wight eastward to the North Foreland, to stop the traffick in brandy, &c. as well by barter between ships, as by carrying the goods ashore. 7 May 1721. 1 *page.*

8 May. 15. Lord Townshend to the Lords of the Treasury. His Majesty has been pleased to comply with the address of the House of Peers, and his pleasure is, that the Lords of the Treasury prepare a state or estimate of the debt of the nation unprovided for by Act of Parliament, exclusive of the debt of the navy already laid before that House. Whitehall, 8 May 1721.

The copy of the address. 2 *pages.*

10 May. 16. Memorandum of a request on the behalf of the Barons of the Exchequer to consult M[r] Horatio Walpole in respect to the working of an Act of parliament, which gave them power to administer interrogatories concerning money carried to Holland supposed to belong to the late South Sea Directors, but did not appoint any person to attend and expend the money necessary to put the Act in execution. 10 May 1721.

Minuted:—"11th May 1721. Mr. Cracherode to attend the Barons in all matters relating to the execution of the act for vesting the Directors' estates, &c. But my Lords at the same time order Mr. Lowndes to prepare a clause to be inserted in the bill now depending, directing that the charges attending such service shall be born out of the money arising by the said estates, and to be replaced to the Civil List." 1 *page.*

[? About 15 May.] 17. Petition of Col. Charles Frampton to the Lords of the Treasury, praying their Lordships to direct M[rs] Ruperta Howe, who is entitled to "house boot" and "fire boot," to allow him the same. Their Lordships had ordered that the wood felled by the petitioner for the repairs of his lodge should be sold for his Majesty's use, and that no other wood should be felled for the future on pretence of repairs.

Minuted:—"15th May 1721. The pet[r] may settle this matter with M[rs] Howe, my Lords not thinking fit to interpose." 1 *page.*

15 May. 18. Report of the Surveyor General (Cholmley) to the same, on the petition of the Right Hon. George, Earl of Kinnoull, who prayed to have a lease of a house called Little Wallingford House, situate on the Great Street leading from Charing Cross to Westminster.

1721. VOL. CCXXXIV.

King William and Queen Mary in the second year of their reign granted to William Blathwaite, Esq., two tenements called Little Wallingford House and Pickering House, in the parish of St. Martins in the Fields, for 31 years, at a rent of 31*s.* 4*d.* The premises consist of an old brick building formerly two tenements. They extend from St James' Park wall on the west, to the High Street leading from Charing Cross towards Westminster, east, and adjoin the ground on which Wallingford House stood, north, and to the house formerly Sir Robert Holmes's, and another in the possession of the Earl of Ranelagh, now in the possession of petitioner, south; with a yard or passage and a small garden plot thereto belonging, the whole containing in breadth at the East end towards the street 59 f. 9 in., and at the West end by the Park wall 77 f. 5 in., and in length from East to West 94 f. or thereabouts. The premises are much out of repair, but considering the situation they may be well worth 150*l.* per ann. in the state they are. Is of opinion that a fine of 700*l.* to his Majesty (reserving the old rent of 13*s.* 4*d.* and an increased rent of 18*l.* per ann.) may be a valuable consideration for a lease of 31 years. 15 May 1721.

Minuted:—"20th June 1721. Warrt signed."

The petition. 2½ *pages.*

17 May. 19. Representation and petition of Joseph Billers, citizen of London, to the Lords of the Treasury. His case had been referred to Anthony Cracherode, Esq., to examine and report thereon, and in May 1719 he was ordered to bring it into Parliament. He printed the case (copy annexed), but upon the overtures made by John Aislabie, Esq., then one of the Lords of the Treasury and Chancellor of the Exchequer, to allow him 1,000*l.*, and to recommend him for a place, he made no application to parliament as directed. Neither of those offers had been complied with by Mr Aislabie: prays relief. London, 17 May 1721.

At the foot is a recommendation of his case, signed by the Mayor and twenty others.

Minuted:—"7th July 1721. Mr Chancr will speak to Sir J. Ward about this." 3 *pages.*

18 May. 20. Petition of John, Lord Viscount Lisburne, in the Kingdom of Ireland, to the same, praying that he may be constituted Steward and Court Keeper of the King's Manors of Mevenneth, Croythyn, Heninnoch, Caerwedros, and Perveth, in the county of Cardigan, which office his father held. The office was of very little profit, but the manors were contiguous to, and intermixed with, petitioner's estate.

Minuted:—"18th May 1721. See in what manner these were granted to his father." 1 *page.*

20 May. 21. Report of the Attorney and Solicitor General to the Lords of the Treasury on the affairs of Sir Biby Lake (often previously referred to in this Calendar) in connexion with the debts of Mr Peter, Receiver General of taxes for the county of Hertford, who failed and was indebted to the crown 13,149*l* 10*s.* 7½*d.* Upon the

whole matter conceive that it might be for the benefit of the crown to receive the 10,892*l.* 5*s.* 9¼*d.* (as proposed by Sir Bibye) in present discharge of the debt, instead of waiting the delay of raising the same by receipt of the profits. See no objection to the assigning all the extended estate of the said Peter to the said Sir Bibye, in trust and for the benefit of the latter and other persons interested. General Wills will not be prejudiced thereby. May 20, 1721.

Minuted:—"5th September 1721. My Lords agree to the report. The Attor. and Solr Genll are desired to make a draught of a proper warrt hereupon, and to transmit it to their Lordships." 5½ *pages.*

27 May. 22. Draft of a report to the King unsigned [of the Lords of the Treasury], the corrections apparently being in Mr Lowndes handwriting, concerning the erection of a Bank in Ireland, the necessity for which called "aloud for an immediate relief." Their opinion was that the authority of Parliament would be required to carry out the rules, &c. which they proposed. Treasury Chambers, 27 May 1721. 4 *pages.*

28 May. 23. Order in Council, viz., that a charter for setting up a Bank in Ireland be passed pursuant to the foregoing report, and the Lords of the Treasury are to prepare the draught of the Charter together with a warrant thereupon for his Majesty's signature, empowering the Lord Lieutenant (Grafton) to pass the same under the Great Seal of Ireland. 28 May 1721. 5 *pages.*

[About May.] 24. An account of several things proper for Governor Nicholson to carry with him, in order to make presents to the head men of the Indians in Carolina.

The last item is:—"2 dozn prints of his Maty and ye Royll family in small gilt frames, prints of his Matys arms. A few new guineas, half guineas, crowns, half-crowns, and shillings to be strung on red ribbons and wore by the Chiefs."

[Nicholson was appointed Governor in May 1721.] 1 *page.*

1 June. 25. Copy of report of A. Cracherode to the Lords of the Treasury on the petition of Sarah Read in behalf of herself and eight others, setting forth that the petitioner was assaulted and robbed in the Haymarket, in the parish of St. James's, Westminster, by two men, one of whom was taken by the petitioner and convicted thereof at the Old Bailey, and lay under sentence of death. Prays for payment of the 100*l.* reward offered by proclamation for taking highwaymen. Is of opinion that they are well entitled to have the reward of 100*l.* divided amongst them in the proportions that 40*l.* was awarded by the Lord Mayor and Deputy Recorder. 1 June 1721. 2 *pages.*

[? About 9 June.] 26. Petition of Sir Patrick Johnston to the King. For twenty years has devoted himself entirely to the public service, during which time he represented the city of Edinburgh in the Scots Parliament, and struggled for the protestant succession, and his endeavours united their zeal for so good a cause. Nor was he less serviceable as a Commissioner for the Treaty of Union, and as a member in

1721. VOL. CCXXXIV.

several British Parliaments; which services are well known to the Duke of Roxborough, the Earl of Sunderland, Viscount Townshend, and George Baillie, Esq., a Com^{r} of the Treasury. For these services his life, and those of his family, had often been attempted and he thereby lost one of his sons. And by his firm, opposition to the Pretender, he impaired his circumstances much. Prays to be appointed a Commissioner of Customs or Excise in North Britain.

Minuted:—"Read 9 Jun. 1721. The next vacancys are disposed." 1 *page*.

9 June. 27. "A. Cracherode's [Treasury Solicitor], particular of cases now under prosecution with states thereof. 9° Junii 1721."

Minuted:—"12th D^{o}. Read, and the directions set against each state." 7½ *pages*.

10 June. 28. An account of all the salaries and allowances payable at the receipt of his Majesty's Exchequer.

Giving the names of the persons, and in many cases how much per day as well as per annum.

Salaries payable out of 4^{li} 10^{s} p cent. to the Governors of Barbados and other Islands, and to the Auditor General of the Revenues in America.

Salaries payable out of the public funds at the Exchequer. Exchequer, 10 June 1721. 8 *pages and* 2 *halves*.

11 June. 29. Order in Council on the report of the Com^{rs} of Customs, concerning the value of the ships "Bristol Merchant" and the "Turkey Merchant," both from Cyprus and other parts of Turkey; and on a petition of the Commanders praying to be allowed their extraordinary expenses, seamen's wages, &c., refering the same to the Lords of the Treasury. 11 June 1721.

The petition named, and an account of the men's wages (totals) 7 *pages*.

12 June. 30. Petition of Isaac Escot, late Chaplain of the French Regiment of Col. Labarthe, to the Lords of the Treasury, praying to be put on the half pay of the Irish Establishment, as well as the Officers of the regiment, whereof he was chaplain, having the very same title by his commission.

Minuted:—"12th June 1721. See the warr^{t} for placing the other officers and chaplains on the half pay of Ireland." 1 *page*.

17 June. 31. Copy of notes of various resolutions and proceedings in the House of Commons "relating to the Bill 7 Geo. I.," which appears to have touched the trade with the East Indies. The last date is 17 June 1721, but the copy probably was made later. 5 *pages*.

20 June. 32. Wm Popple to William Lowndes, Esq., transmitting copy of a letter from Mr Francis Harrison, Surveyor of Customs at New York, to the Com^{rs} of Customs, relating to copper shipped from New Jersey for Holland As there is no law to prevent the carrying of ore from the plantations, the Lords of the Treasury think that this practice may be of such consequence to the revenue that it deserves to be considered in parliament. Whitehall, 20 June 1721.

1721. Vol. CCXXXIV.

The letter referred to.

Minuted:—"21st June 1721. My Lords will consider this when they have any leisure." 2½ *pages*.

[? About 20 June.] 33. Memorial to William Lowndes, Esq., of poor artificers, who were seduced into France and had attended the Treasury for 1,000*l.* ordered by the King, as contained in Lord Carteret's letter, which had been before the Board for the last month: praying the business might be expedited.

Minuted:—"20th June 1721. My Lords will order the remaining 1,000li when there is money sufficient after the payment of the King's servants." 1 *page*.

[? About 20 June.] 34. Petition of the United Company of Merchants of England trading to the East Indies, to the Lords of the Treasury. Have frequently represented their hardships and sufferings by the deficiencies of the fund of 160,000*l.* a year, to which they are entitled by Act of Parliament of 9 & 10 Will. [III.]. The interest amounts to near 40,000*l.* At Mich. 1720, when there was a surplus arising by the Fund, they were told it could not be paid to them, but must be applied to other uses. Petitioners being indebted for Customs to very near the same amount, pray that in consideration of their hard case the arrears may be paid to them.

Minuted:—"20th June 1721. Read: *vide* Min. Book."

[Vol. 23, p. 74.] "Several Directors of the E. India Company attend with a memll, setting forth the deficiency of their fond, praying paymt of their arrears, and that a future provision may be made for them to prevent the like inconveniencys hereafter; to which my Lords are pleased to answer that the E. India Company's Fond being deficient and no provision being made by Parlt to make good the said deficiency, and the produce of the sinking fond for the time past and time to come, being appropriated as a fond and security for circulating Exchr Bills, they are not able to give any directions for the paymt of it; nor do they know any method for providing for it this year, especially the session being advanced so near to a conclusion." 1 *page*.

22 June. 35. Lord Carteret to the Lords of the Treasury. His Majesty has considered the useful knowledge which Mr Charles Holzendorff has acquired at the Court of Spain as Secretary to Mr Stanhope, his Majesty's Ambassador there, together with his good services. His Majesty's pleasure is that directions be given to pay him 400*l.* a year from 23 May last during pleasure. Whitehall, 22 June 1721.

Minuted:—"17th Octr 1721. Warrt sign'd." 1 *page*.

23 June. 36. John, Bishop of London, to the same. The Bishop of London was by King Charles II. entrusted with providing and sending ministers to the Colonies and Islands in America, and was directed by King William to apply to the Treasury for 20*l.* to each missionary to defray his passage. This bounty was readily paid. Afterwards it was oft-times delayed, and many of the missionaries

1721. Vol. CCXXXIV.

were reduced to great straits. At present the answer given them is that several to whom the bounty has been given, did not proceed on the mission, and therefore their Lordships make a difficulty to grant the same any longer. Hopes there was little ground for the remark in his predecessor's time. Although he once lost 20*l.* of his own money, he has not lost any of his Majesty's, except in one instance, where the party fell into madness and was not suffered to go. Two persons who lately had the 20*l.* did not proceed, but after their despatch at the Treasury they got preferment at home, and one of them refunded the 20*l.*, which he (the Bishop) applied to another missionary without troubling their Lordships; the other has paid back one half and the remainder is daily expected, and he would apply it in the same way. But if (as there seems some reason to apprehend) their Lordships think it not fit to trust him any longer with this "Dispensation," presumes they will move his Majesty to employ some other person, for if this bounty were retrenched it would be impossible to get those Colonies supplied. In that case shall willingly acquiesce in the conviction that he has faithfully and honestly done his duty. This comfortable reflection has hitherto relieved him against malicious slanders, and will continue to do so, especially as he shall be freed from a great and vexatious trouble which has no connexion with the duty of a Bishop of London. June 23, 1721. 3 *pages.*

[? About 27 June.] 37. Memorial of Samuel Edwin, Usher at the Receipt of the Exchequer, to the same. Entreats their Lordships' direction for payment of an order drawn for 1,663*l.* 16*s.* 5½*d.* for necessaries by him delivered to the Treasury, and the old officers of the Exchequer, and for money advanced to watchmen, porters, and others attending the Exchequer, being two years in arrear.

Minuted:—"To be payd 1,663*l.* 16*s.* 5½*d.* pursuant to an order drawn June the 27, 1721."

Also a previous memorial of his of the 15th of May 1721 for payment of the arrears. 2 *pages.*

29 June. 38. Lord Carteret to the same. Captain Charles Stewart, Plenipotentiary for negotiating a peace with the Emperor of Morocco, having concluded a treaty for the redemption of some hundreds of the King's subjects now in slavery (which treaty has been ratified by the King), his Majesty's pleasure is that their Lordships order the purchase of 125 pieces of coarse cloths and 75 half pieces of fine d°; to be sent forthwith to Captain Stewart at Gibraltar: and further, that their Lps give directions for the issue of 4,020*l.* to the Board of Ordnance, to enable them to replace 1,200 barrels of powder, which the King has ordered the Storekeeper at Gibraltar to deliver to Captain Stewart; also for completing the supply of 13,500 gun locks agreed to be given towards the redemption of the captives. Whitehall, 29 June 1721. 1½ *pages.*

[After June.] 39. Two copies of Representations of the Commissioners appointed for visiting the Colleges and Schools of Aberdeen, addressed to his Majesty the King, as to the low and mean condition of the College.

Vol. CCXXXIV.

1721. The first (Aug. 1718) states that the New Edifice, undertaken and considerably advanced in the reign of King William, has been in great danger of ruin for many years for want of money to finish it, and the old fabrick cannot subsist unless a considerable sum is speedily allowed for its repair. The College revenue has been much impaired by new erections and augmentations of ministers' stipends "evicted" by law, so that their debts are increased. The provisions of the Masters are very small, and their share of Queen Anne's bounty has been discontinued for want of a privy seal for its distribution. By former enquiries the Com[rs] found that the revenue was burthened with about 900*l.* debt, and they are fully satisfied of the very low condition of the College. Considering that this ancient Seminary of learning was erected and has been supported by his Majesty's predecessors for nearly three hundred years, and that his Majesty has lately provided well qualified Masters, they recommend the same to the Royal favour; being very hopeful that the supporting and encouraging this society will be very subservient to the training up of the youth in the most remote and disaffected corners of this land in sound principles and useful literature. The Second (June 1721) is a further memorial from the same Commissioners, stating that his Majesty referred the former memorial to the Lords of the Treasury, who directed the "Master of Work in Scotland" to make an estimate for the repairs, which he did. No further progress was made therein, and the Rector, Principal, and the other Masters have again represented the miserable state of their affairs. They have been obliged to expend large sums towards the support of the College Steeple and "Copula," the threatening fall whereof would have completed the ruin of their most valuable buildings, such as their Church, Library, and public Schools. The Commissioners considering that a special care has been taken of this ancient University by the King's predecessors (because of its situation upon the borders of the North Highlands, and where Popery most prevailed), and that if care were now taken, it might be most useful in extirpating these disloyal and pernicious principles, which of late have taken deep root in these remote corners, recommend the University and its members to the Royal favour for competent supplies to be granted.

These copies were probably prepared for a report to be made on them. 2½ *pages.*

[? About 1 July.] 40. Copies of Orders under the sign manual to be observed for the better service of the Office of Works.

The first of these consists of 27 clauses, and was dated 29 April 1715.

Various additional orders follow, and the last is a copy of a Treasury letter, dated 1 July 1721. 20 *pages* (*brief size*).

4 July. 41. Petition of the Com[rs] of Supply and Heritors, in the shire of East Lothian, to the King. By the laws of Scotland the Com[rs] in each county are empowered to tax the heritors to the extent of 10*s.* for every hundred pounds of their valued rent, and no further, for

1721. VOL. CCXXXIV.

reparation of bridges, highways, and such like incidents within the county. The Bridge called Linton Bridge over the River Tyne (East Lothian) is very much damnified by the impetuosity of the river and in danger of falling. The Bridge lies upon the post road between London and Edinburgh, and is the common passage from Edinburgh to a great deal of the east and south-east parts of Scotland. If the bridge should fall, all communication would frequently be stopped by the swelling of the river. The Bridge cannot be repaired for less than 250*l.*, which is far beyond what the Com^rs^ are empowered to tax the heritors; besides which there are several other high ways within the county, which require considerable expense to maintain them. Are informed that there are "few duties" payable to the Crown out of the Lordship of Dunbar, whereof 2,300*l.* (Scots) yearly at least are not already granted: pray for an allowance out of these "few duties" for the repair of the bridge. 4 July 1721.

With a note at the foot that it is referred to the Lords of the Treasury to consider and report. 2 *pages.*

6 July. 42. Certificate of Evelyn, Duke of Kingston, Lord Privy Seal, and Hugh, Earl of Loudoun, testifying that Lieut. Alexander Raitt, of Brigadier Grant's late regiment of foot, has been employed by them for several years, and still continues to be so, and was on their business in Scotland when taken off from half pay in Ireland. 6 July 1721.

United are Rait's petition, a reference thereof to the Muster Master General, and copy of a report on the same. 4½ *pages.*

7 July. 43. Memorial of the Trustees for circulating Exchequer Bills, to the Lords of the Treasury. On first entering upon their business, enquired as to the cash remaining with Mr Collyer, cashier to the late Trustees. The [late] Trustees have been faithful stewards of the money, for by their care in having it locked up under different keys it has prevented embezzlement by the cashier, at a time when views of immense gain might have tempted him; they have been careful to frame their books to answer the intents of the Acts of parliament; they (the late Trustees) appointed officers and clerks (a list of whom is given), and this was laid before the Lords of the Treasury; but the late sudden and noxious turn of affairs and the disqualification by act of parliament of three Trustees prevented further application. The present Trustees to save money discharged their Cashier, and are to take the cash into their own custody, at a saving of 630*l.* per ann. There is a demand (bill enclosed) upon them of 377*l.* 5*s.* 11½*d.* from tradesmen, &c.: ask for payment. 7 July 1721. Signed.

Minuted:—"200^li^ p ann. to be allowed to the present Trustees for their care, &c., 150^li^ p ann. to their Secry. The other inferiour officers' salarys to stand as they do in the draught made by the Trustees."

The Bill referred to, and a copy of the above memorial, but minuted somewhat differently. 5 *pages.*

VOL. CCXXXIV.

1721.

8 July. 44. Jean Hanet [Tutor to Prince Frederick] to———. The kindness he had experienced since he came to Hanover led him to hope for a continuance of the same. Asks the person addressed to speak in his favour to Mr Walpole to order the arrears of his pension, of which three quarters were due. Lord Sunderland paid the pension regularly, but he (Mons. Hanet) is not known to Mr Walpole. Hanover, 8 July 1721. (French.)

Docketed:—"From Mr Hanet, Tutor to Prince Frederick."

Minuted:—"12th July 1721. To be paid 6 months upon his pension." 2 *pages*.

8 July. 45. Report of the Attorney General (Raymond) to the Lords of the Treasury, on the petition of James Reith, watchmaker, which states that the petitioner on the previous 22 March by a petition set forth the hardships of his case with regard to the seizure of some of his effects, and the prosecution of him in the Court of Exchequer for landing them without entry, which petition was transmitted to their Lordships by a letter from Lord Carteret, one of the principal Secretaries of State, signifying the King's pleasure for his relief. A warrant for *nolle prosequi* was thereupon entered upon his paying the duties and satisfying the officers. The petitioner satisfied the officers, but the goods, being French, are charged 65*l.* per cent., which, being added, will be more than they are worth. The petitioner returned from France upon an agreement with Sir Robert Sutton, his Majesty's Minister at that Court, who engaged for the safety of the effects. Petitioner after this agreement paid all the workmen's debts and maintained them till their passes could be got ready at an expence of upwards of 900*l.*, and had never received any consideration. The Attorney General certifies that by the petition referred to (of 22 March) the petitioner was lately a director and afterwards master of a manufactory of watchmaking set up [at Versailles] in France, and that he applied to the Ambassador, who undertook for the safety of the effects. The goods are all made by Englishmen and not purchased by way of merchandise, but certain of the King's Officers carried away the goods, and petitioner prayed relief, as well as to be allowed to bring such other of his effects into his Majesty's dominions as were still in France. His Majesty, by letter of Lord Carteret, one of his principal Secretaries of State, referred his case to their Lordships for their report. Their Lordships transmitted the same to the Comrs of Customs, who reported that in the year 1718 several artificers withdrew to France, and amongst them the petitioner. In the 5th year of his Majesty's reign an act passed to prevent artificers from being seduced into foreign parts. The goods were seized by officers of the port of London, having been made in France and clandestinely landed without paying duty, and were appraised at 557*l.*, being under prosecution in the Court of Exchequer, but the Comrs submitted whether his Majesty would order a *nolle prosequi*, &c. The Attorney General advises that his Majesty may grant a *nolle prosequi* for his part of the forfeiture, but the goods in France are subject to duty, if customable. 8 July 1721.

1721. VOL. CCXXXIV.

The petition and six other papers.

The petition has the following minute on the back :—"21st July 1721. My Lords agree to a *nolle prosequi* as to the King's part psuant to the report. Warrt signd 4th Augt." 17 *pages and* 2 *parts of pages.*

9 July. 46. Order in Council on the petition of John Bennet, Captain of the "Turkey Merchant," and John Winne, Captain of the "Bristol Merchant," referring to the Lords of the Treasury the allowance for damage to them by quarantine. 9 July 1721.

Also the petition. 2½ *pages.*

10 July. 47. Lord Carteret to the "Rt Honble Mr Walpole," introducing the bearer as the person appointed by the Earl of Coventry to receive the 500*l.* which his Majesty had granted to the Earl "to be disposed of by him for his Majesty's service." Whitehall, July 10, 1721. 1 *page.*

12 July. 48. Francis, Bishop of Rochester, to —— Was forced to leave town without thanking him for his favour to the Church of Westminster, being seized with the gout in his right hand. Prays him to accept his acknowledgments for the 1,000*l.*, and doubts not he will give orders for perfecting what he further intended in relation to the 4,000*l.* more. Would be far from importuning him if the poor workmen could well subsist without it: but they cannot, being already some of them half ruined, by taking up money at great interest, and in very considerable sums, in order to pay their underworkmen. And even after the fictitious tallies struck for the 4,000*l.* intended them "there will still be an arrear of 5,000*l.* more at Midsummer last," and for that they must wait with patience until the fund will admit of a new loan upon it. Bromley, 12 July 1721. 2½ *pages.*

15 July. 49. Memorial of the Court of Directors of the Royal Exchange Assurance to the Lords of the Treasury. Have advanced 150,000*l.* by way of loan at 4 per cent. on the Plate Act. Have paid 111,250*l.* for the Civil Government, and 188,750*l.* still remains to be paid. Their attempts to raise sufficient money to meet their engagements have not been successful, which may be owing to the calamity of the times and the low ebb of public credit, but more especially from a general opinion that it is impossible for the Corporation from the uses of their Charter to pay to the Government the 300,000*l.* stipulated, "without interest," so that they are utterly unable to make any further payment. Notwithstanding the additional grant which his Majesty has conferred on the Corporation for assurance from fire and upon lives, they find the price of their stock much less than the money paid in, and it is to be feared their credit will daily decrease, to the utter ruin of the Corporation and loss to the public (especially the trading part) of so useful and beneficial an undertaking, unless his Majesty remits the above sum, which is unpaid and unsecured by a deposit at the Treasury. A late instance of his Majesty's and the Legislators'

VOL. CCXXXIV.

1721.

tenderness has been compassionately shown to the proprietors of the South Sea Stock. Pray relief.

Minuted:—"15th July 1721. Read. To be layd before the King." 1 *page*.

17 July. 50. Draft of a Commission for taking in subscriptions for erecting and establishing a Bank in Ireland, which was referred by the Lords of the Treasury to the Attorney and Solicitor General for their consideration, with the following report at the foot: "We have perused the aforegoing draught of a Comission for taking in subscriptions and the schedule thereunto annex'd, purporting [to be] the draught of a charter for erecting a Bank in Ireland, and have no objection to the same as now amended. Rob. Raymond, Phi. Yorke, July 17, 1722."

The schedule is not now with it. 36 *pages* (*brief size*).

19 July. 51. A certified copy *docketed*:—"Representation of the Assembly of New York abt ye Auditor of the Plantations." Addressed to William Burret, Esq., Captain General and Governor-in-Chief of the Province of New York, New Jersey, and territories thereon depending, and Vice-Admiral of the same.

Find that the Lords of the Treasury are of opinion that the neglecting or refusing to account with the Auditor General will be looked upon as a contempt of his Majesty's authority. Suspect that artful representations from hence have prevailed, but they have nothing more at heart than to approve themselves his Majesty's faithful subjects Think no one thing would be of greater service to the province than for his Majesty to be truly and thoroughly informed of the "disposition of every penny" of the revenue. If this had been done they would not have laboured under their great body of debt, which was manifestly owing to the misapplication and squandering of public money. Her late Majesty gave them a Treasurer of their own, which made it practicable to retrieve the public credit. Among the extravagances was the allowing to the Auditor General a fee or salary of 5 per cent. upon the King's revenue in the province. His Majesty's Commission appointed a salary of 500*l*. per ann. as a reward for auditing all the accounts in his Majesty's plantations in America. By what authority he could take to himself a twentieth of the King's revenue here, they are "yet to seek." The disposition of the public money, it is true, is in the governor, by the advice and consent of the Council. This, they suppose, gave rise to the demand for it as a fee or perquisite; though they do not find it was ever allowed by the Treasury, and whether ever received by himself there is some reason to doubt. [Give their reasons]. State that the revenue of the province had never exceeded 4,000*l*. per ann. The Treasurer refusing to account with the Auditor General (if so he did) could not proceed from any intention to hinder his Majesty or his ministers from a knowledge of the disposal of his revenue, as he was of the Council and could not be ignorant that no act could be passed here for raising or levying any money, whereby the same should be made liable to be accounted for to his Majesty or his ministers. Fair

1721. VOL. CCXXXIV.

accounts have also to be kept and transmitted to the Treasury. It was before the Treasurer received their Lordships' order to account that he refused (if so he did) to account with the Deputy Auditor; and as soon as their Lordships signified their pleasure, he readily promised to obey their commands. How hearty and ready the Assembly has been to support his Majesty's Government is not unknown to his Excellency. There are few branches of our imports (except European goods) but what are loaded as much as the trade will bear, and the revenue is as yet insufficient to pay officers and incidents. What then must be the consequence if the dead weight of 5 per cent. on the whole revenue for several years be added? Heartily wish that, without ruining the trade, they could make the revenue ample for the handsome support of the Government and enable His Majesty to extend his Royal bounty to fit objects of it. Beg their Lordships to disallow the demand. Certified 19 July 1721. 7½ *pages.*

25 July. 52. "Extract of the minutes of the General Court of the South Sea Company relating to the allowing stock for the redeemables and the several money subscriptions." Certified by E. Welcomb, Secretary. South Sea House, 25 July 1721. 5 *pages.*

26 July. 53. Report of the Barons of the Exchequer, Scotland, to the Lords of the Treasury, on the petition of James Stephen, Deputy Usher to the Court of Exchequer Chamber (Scotland). As Mace Bearer to the Court he discharges the office of Serjeant-at-Arms, and has diligently discharged his duties. Advise that he receive 50*l.* yearly for the same. Edinburgh, Exchequer Chamber, 26 July 1721.

The petition referred to. *Minuted*:—"20th Decr 1721. My Lords agree to the Barons' rept. Warrt signed 17 Janry 1721." 2 *pages.*

26 July. 54. Report of the same to the same on the petition of David, Earl of Leven. It appears by the certificate of the Treasurer's Remembrancer that there is chargeable on the petitioner "as the non-entry, blench, few, taxtward, and relief duties of the lands contained in the infeftment given to him 215*l.* 18*s.* 9⅔*d.* sterling." The sovereign has sometimes discharged such casualties to his vassals, and if his Majesty is inclined to remit what is due by the Earl, yet the sum of 17*l.* 19*s.* 2*d.* due on account of his relief, must be answered to the Crown, being discharged by law from being compounded or granted away. Same date.

With it is what appears to be the petition, but it is in a very faded condition. It was referred to the Lords of the Treasury for their report on 15 June 1720, and they referred it to the Barons on the 1st of July following. 2 *pages.*

26 July. 55. Report of the same to the same on the memorial of Patrick, Earl of Marchmont, the representative of George Home, deceased, late of Kimmergham; David, Earl of Glasgow, Sir Robert Anstruther, Sir John Swinton, George Home, the representative of Sir George Ho. . . late of Kello, deceased; Sir John Home, of Blackadder, the representative of Sir John Home, Bart., deceased

1721. VOL. CCXXXIV.

Sir William Gordon Ba. . ., the representative of Sir Adam Gordon, deceased; Sir John Steuart, of Allanbank, the representative of Sir Robert Steuart, his father; Sir Robert Dickson, the representative of Sir Robert Dickson, of Sornbeg, his father; and Alexander Cunynghame, Esq., the representative of Sir Hugh Cunynghame, late of Craegend, his father, certifying that it appears the Lords of the Treasury and Exchequer of Scotland did, by lease of 15 Aug. 1696, "set or farm" to several of the above persons the customs and foreign excise of Scotland for five years from 1 Nov. then next following, unless the then war with France should cease, in which case they reserved a power to turn the farm into a collection, from the term next preceding the peace to the term next following, and thereafter to set a new farm or to continue that for the year then running.

The lessees or farmers were obliged to pay a yearly rent of 27,000*l.*, and produce their accounts for a moiety of the increasing net profit over and above the 27,000*l.*, &c.

The lessees only managed the Customs and Excise for one year. Proceedings were taken thereafter in respect to their account, and the production of their books. His Majesty's Advocate and the Solicitor General reported that 1,914*l.* 7*s.* were due to the farmers. The Barons further state that the affair was under examination before the Union, and nothing further is to be expected from it, and they think the lessees should be discharged by the Crown. Same date.

Minuted:—"Sep^tr^ 20, 1721. The Lords agree that upon the farmers releasing ye surplusage and all other demands upon ye crown relating to that account, the King may grant them a release of all further demands from ye crown upon them relating thereto."

The memorial referred to. 6 *pages.*

[? About 27 July.] 56. Petition of Robert Hewitt to the Lords of the Treasury showing that by his petition to the late Lords he prayed to be reimbursed 130*l.* expended in H.M. service, and for recompense of his own trouble, and by memorial to Lord Stanhope he prayed to be admitted as a discoverer of concealed rents and arrears, for which it was usual to be allowed ¾ths to the discoverer. This was referred to the Auditors of Land Revenue, who reported that he deserved 200*l.*, and that ¾ths of the arrears were not unreasonable, and a letter was sent to the Auditors to receive the discovery. Petitioner on 27 Nov. 1719 laid his papers before the Auditors. Petitioner's papers showed that there was due to his Majesty for annual rents, besides profits of Courts, &c. of the manor of Whaplode, in the county of Lincoln, 38*l.* 6*s.* 5½*d.* per ann., and from the manor of Molton Dñoř cum Bewsolus, in the same county, 78*l.* 7*s.* 0½*d.* per ann. for 14 years ended at Mich. 1719, making 1,633*l.* 9*s.* 0*d.*, and from the profits of courts at 12*l.* 14*s.* 5*d.* per ann., 178*l.* 1*s.* 10*d.* In all 1,811*l.* 10*s.* 10*d.*, and that the improvements on the demesne lands were of more considerable value. Further, that the rents of these manors had been discharged out of the Receiver's accounts as granted by King Charles II. on 28 Jan., in his 36th year, to trustees for the Duchess of Buccleuch and others; whereas they were never

1721. VOL. CCXXXIV.

so granted: nor were they by the former letters patent of 21 Sept. 1674 to the Duke of Monmouth, before his outlawry, as is set forth in her grace's memorial (a copy whereof and other proceedings are annexed).

With this are copies of the papers previously abstracted under date, "about 13 Feb. 1719–20," relating to the claims of Robert Hewitt.

There is also a letter (of 13 Feb. 1719) in addition from him to William Lowndes, Esq., Secretary to the Treasury, recapitulating what is above stated, and asking to have an order to allow him to have recourse to the accounts and records in Mr Auditor Godolphin's office.

On the last paper is the following *minute*:—"27th July 1721. My Lords have given directions to the Attor. Gen^ll concerning the Dutchess of Buçleuch." 9½ *pages*.

28 July. 57. Petition of John Chaffey, Thomas Hopps, Anthony Watson, and John Andrews to the Lords of the Treasury, praying for a day to be appointed for them to make their several claims for a reward for the apprehension of Robert Jackson, convicted of a robbery on the highway near Tyburn, in the parish of Paddington.

Referred to Anthony Cracherode, Esq., for his report. His report, which is not now with the petition, was dated 28 July 1721, as appears by the docket.

There are also two certificates and an affidavit. 5 *pages*.

29 July. 58. Account of the charge of 200 men with their officers levied by the Provost of Edinburgh for the defence of that city.

Also copies of three letters touching the employment and pay of these 200 men, who were employed for reinforcing the Castle of Edinburgh. In the first, on behalf of his Majesty, Viscount Townshend thanks the Provost and Magistrates for their zeal and diligence on the occasion of the attempt to surprise the Castle.

Minuted:—"29th July 1721. Prepare a warr^t." *Again*:—"Warr^t signd 4th Aug^t." 2½ *pages*.

VOL. CCXXXV. AUGUST–DECEMBER.

[? About 2 Aug.] 1. Five papers touching disputes between the Crown and the Sugar Houses in Scotland as to the rights claimed by the proprietors of exemption from customs and excise. One of them is headed:—

"Articles agreed on betwixt the Lords Comm^rs of his Mat^s Treasury and the proprietors of the four sugar manufactories in Scotland."

The last of them is *minuted*:—

"August 2^d, 1721. The Lords agree to stay all proceedings against ye sugar manufacturers of Scotland untill ye end of ye next sessions of Parl^t, and to a clause to be then brought in, to discharge

1721. VOL. CCXXXV.

all demands of ye Governm^t upon them for customs and excise; the said proprietors agreeing to surrender and disclaim all right of exemption for custom and excise for ye future.

Mr Lowndes and Mr Danl Campbell to meet and settle ye time for wch such discharge and allowance is to be made to ye s^d proprietors; as also all particulars of an agreement to be made wth them." 6½ *pages.*

2 Aug. 2. Representation to the Lords of the Treasury by the Managers and Directors appointed to bring up and perfect "what remained to be brought up and perfected on the act of the 6th of the King, for encreasing the Capital Stock of the South Sea Company by the late Managers and Directors appointed for executing that Act." They point out certain mistakes in the accounts, by means whereof the Company "have had less additional stock and additional annuity declared" than they ought to have had; that is to say, 67,831*l.* 6*s.* 10*d.* in Stock and 3,391*l.* 11*s.* 4*d.* less "in additional annuity." Recommend the case to their Lordships' consideration. Lottery Office, 2 Aug. 1721.

This is accompanied by a large paper book or document entitled "Supplemental Duplicate, South Sea House, 15th October 1720," containing a list of subscriptions for which an annuity of 5 per cent. was payable at the Bank of England, commonly called Lottery Annuities. The sums amounted to 67,831*l.* 6*s.* 10*d.* 11 *large pages.*

[? About 7 Aug.] 3. Petition of Patrick Brown to the Lords of the Treasury. When the Spanish Fleet was in the Road of Barcelona in July 1717, preparing to surprise Minorca, Mr Bub, his Majesty's Ambassador at Madrid, and Mr Crowe, his Majesty's Consul at Barcelona (but at that time at Madrid) apprehending such a design, and believing it absolutely necessary that Lord Forbes, the Governor and Commander-in-Chief of H.M. forces on that Island, should have timely notice of those preparations, recommended it to Mr Shellat (who acted in the absence of Consul Crowe as Consul at Barcelona) to get some fit person to carry their letters immediately to his Lordship. Petitioner being mate of an English ship at Barcelona voluntarily undertook to carry the letters, and performed the service in the ship's yaul with two men, when an embargo was laid on all ships, &c. in the harbour, by which means his Lordship put the Island in a posture of defence. Petitioner returned and went a second time to his Lordship, when the Spanish fleet was within a mile of the Island: prays for an allowance.

Also copies of three certificates in his favour.

Minuted:—"7th Augt 1721. 150^{li}. S. Manual." 3 *pages.*

[? About 9 Aug.] 4. Memorial of Sir Robert Sinclair, Receiver General of his Majesty's land rents and casualties of North Britain, to the Lords of the Treasury. Was authorised by warrant to send up the money in his hands amounting to 27,735*l.* 2*s.* 3¾*d.* His deputy knowing that the sending up as much as he could in English bank

1721. VOL. CCXXXV.

notes would be the speediest way of returning money, sent up 19,825*l.*, which is now paid into the Exchequer. The remainder (7,910*l.* 2*s.* 3¾*d.*) could be remitted by bills of Exchange. The Exchange on the 7,910*l.* 2*s.* 3¾*d.* amounts to 118*l.* 13*s.*, which he prays may be allowed him.

Minuted:—5 Xbr. 1720. When the rest of the 27,735*l.* 2*s.* 3¾*d.* is p̃d into the Excheq[r] my Lords will move the K. for a warr[t] to allow 118*l.* 13*s.* upon the Rec[r] Gen[ll's] acco[t]." Warr[t] sign'd 12th D[o]."

The business was probably completed about 9 Aug. 1721, as the memorial is accompanied by a certificate of that date that the remaining sum had then been paid into the receipt of the Exchequer. 2 *pages.*

10 Aug. 5. Report of Charles Wither, Esq., Surveyor of His Majesty's Woods, to the Lords of the Treasury, on the memorial of Joseph Banks, Esq., as to his claim of fee trees as Clerk or Steward of Sherwood Forest. No authority is anywhere given by the forest laws to officers to take fee trees by their own warrant, so that where any such are due, by custom or prescription, they ought to be set out and assigned by their Lordships' directions. Has examined the old rolls, Court books, and records of Sherwood Forest, which are in M[r] Banks's custody, and finds that the Clerk and Steward have been allowed two fee trees annually to their respective offices, time out of mind. From his first appointment M[r] Banks is entitled to 30 trees. An order was made at a Court in Eyre held in Sherwood Forest in 1670, that no person claiming fee trees should presume to take them without the assignment of the proper officer; notwithstanding which, the Verderers have constantly taken, and continue to take them, by their own warrant, to the great detriment of the vert of the forest; for it is notorious that they always cut the best trees they can find, and it is a merit in M[r] Banks, that he has not followed so unjustifiable a precedent. Presumes that it was on account of this spoil that the order of Treasury was obtained, about the 9th of King William, for allowing 5*l.* out of the First Fruits and Tenths to each officer in lieu of his fee tree, which at that time was judged an equivalent for the best tree in the forest; "and now, when the woods have been so often picked and culled is much more so." Conceives M[r] Banks has the right to the fee trees demanded. Submits that the Verderers should be forbidden to fell any fee trees by their own warrant, and that the order should be in part revived by directing that the sum their Lordships shall allot, in lieu of fee trees, shall be raised by the sale of dotard trees; by which the largest and most beautiful oaks in the forest will be saved. Is no competent judge of the recompence to M[r] Banks for his trouble about the windfalls in 1714 Hall, Aug. 10, 1721.

Minuted:—" 25th Aug[t] 1721. My Lords agree to the report." Also the memorial. 4½ *pages, and a few lines.*

VOL. CCXXXV.

1721.

12 Aug. 6. Report of the Lord Lieut. of Ireland (Grafton) to the Lords of the Treasury on a report of the late Lord Lieut. upon a petition of John O'Hara, town Major of Galway, the question being whether the petitioner should be placed on the Military Establishment of Ireland at an allowance of 4^s a day. His Majesty appointed the petitioner on 15 Aug. 1715, and by the reports of Lord St George, Governor of Galway, and of Major-General Wynn, who resided there in 1719, to put the town into a posture of defence, it appears that he had behaved well, and that such an officer is as necessary in that garrison as in any other of the kingdom, and the rather because the province wherein it is situate is chiefly inhabited by persons disaffected to the Government. For these reasons recommends the replacing of the petitioner. Bond Street, 12 Aug 1721.

Seven other documents connected therewith. 11 *pages.*

15 Aug. 7. Charles Carkesse to Mr Powys. Gives an account of an outrage committed by the crew of two gallies "above bridge" by flinging stones and shooting at officers of the customs (one Lamb employed on a Custom House boat being shot). Custom House, 15 Aug. 1721.

Three other papers. 5½ *pages.*

[18 ? July or Aug.] 8. *Docket*:—" Westminster Sessions. Certificate from the Sessions for the City and Liberty of $Westm^r$, concerning the common road or highway leading to Hide Park Corner from the Lord Cadogan's House."

The certificate relates to the want of repair of the road, "occasioned by the constant and extraordinary number of coaches, wagons, and carts that daily pass and repass," which made the road so "bad that divers coaches and waggons have been overset and several persons greatly damaged." The Court of Quarter Sessions was of opinion "that that part of the said common road or highway under his Maties said park wall, extending eighteen foot into the road as aforesaid, from the Lord Cadogan's house to Hidepark corner, ought to be paved with stone and gravel or otherwise sufficiently repaired; and that some proper application ought to be made for that purpose, to such of his Maties offices as it may concern; and whensoever that part of the said way shall be duly amended, the court declared that they would oblige the surveyors of the highways of the parish of St Martin-in-the-Fields, and also the inhabitants of the houses and ground on the other side of the said common highway, to pave with stone, or otherwise well and sufficiently to repair and make good, the other part of the said way, according to their respective rights and interests therein as the law requires." 18 [July or August] 1721.

Minuted:—" 21 Augt 1721. To $Surv^r$." 1 *page.*

23 Aug. 9. Report of Edward Godfrey to the Lords of the Treasury on the petition of Dame Mary, Baroness of Mordington. Finds that she had a pension of 40*l.* per ann. from Queen Anne, which was

1721. VOL. CCXXXV.

afterwards discontinued. The Queen subsequently ordered her 10*l.* as a free gift. On the 16th of Sept. 1715 he (Godfrey) paid her 20*l.* for one year's pension by virtue of his Majesty's Establishment.

The petition was referred for report on 23 Aug. 1721.

Minuted:—"12th Septr 1721. To stand as she do's." 2 *pages.*

23 Aug. 10. Report of James Brudenell to the Lords of the Treasury containing a brief account of the debt in his Majesty's Jewel Office. 23 Aug. 1721. 1 *page.*

24 Aug. 11. Order in Council on the petition of Barbara and Elizabeth Collingwood, setting forth their having a lease from the Crown of Holy Island, in the counties of Northumberland and Durham, which lease was about to expire and was not to be renewed, and praying to be heard by Counsel, "whereby they will discover a great scene of injustice done them." Referring the petition and an affidavit to the Lords of the Treasury for their report.

The petition and affidavit:—

In their petition they state that the Surveyor General had put a new covenant into the proposed lease, viz., that at their proper costs and charges, they were "to erect and build good and sufficient sea banks and sea walls in such convenient places as are necessary, to preserve the sd Island, or any part, from being overflowed by the sea," &c., which they conceived was only designed to hinder them having a new lease. The auditor certified that they had forfeited penalties amounting to 29,838*l.* 15*s.* for non-payment of rent, although they had duly paid the same to the Crown Receiver.

Minuted:—"15th Septr 1721. His Maty hath thought fitt to grant this lease to Colo Middleton." *Again:*—"23d April 1722. Mrs Collingwood to have copys." 4 *pages.*

[? About 24 Aug.] 12. Petition of James Moodie, Esq. [M.P.], to the Lords of the Treasury. The petitioner having obtained a warrant for releasing him from payment of a rent of 150*l.* per ann., and the Barons not thinking fit to let a privy seal pass, prays their Lordships' warrant "conformable to the directions of the Barons of North Britain."

Minuted:—"Read. 24 Augt 1721. Warrt originall delivd the petr."

With the above is a previous petition from him in which he states that in the year 1708 he was encouraged to present a memorial "holding forth the ruinous condition of the Bishoprick of Orkney, occasioned by it's being for many years tossed from hand to hand, none enjoying [it] above 3 or 4 years." By which and other means the "whole property lands have been for many years waste and the houses totally ruined." Petitioner desired a lease of the Bishopric might be granted to him for 15 years, for the payment of 150*l.* per ann. Their Lordships ordered the Barons of the Exchequer of Scotland to pass a lease for ten years; but they delayed it till 1719, and then only granted it for five years, three years thus being lost, and during these three years no person had power to collect the rents. Should a new lease be granted to him, he would

1721. VOL. CCXXXV.

be obliged to prosecute the tenants yet remaining, in such a manner, that instead of retrieving and improving the rent roll of that Bishopric, it would entirely lay it waste. Since 1689, when the Bishopric fell to the Crown, it has never produced one shilling to the Crown. And before the Union, when farmed out, the highest ever offered for it was 100*l.* per ann. In 1711 two decrees of the Lords of Session passed against that Bishopric, whereby 1,000 marks Scots, or 55*l.* 11*s.* sterling, per ann. is to be paid in all time coming, to the Ministers of Kirkwall and Lerwick, to complete their stipends; which reduces the value of the Bishopric to a very mean thing. Upon the whole Mr Moodie's case is this: The first three years of his lease has run, the whole rents of the property lands are lost to him, because these rents consist of tithes (parsonage and vicarage) to be drawn in kind annually upon the ground. The other rents, by the avarice and cunning of the Collectors for above 20 years, have been turned to a payment of each third sheaf of all sorts of corn. This made a large profit to them, when at the same time they brought into the Exchequer annual accounts bearing the property lands almost waste. And this vouched from each parish by the very persons concerned with them in that practice. It is now impossible to recover any part of the tithes in kind, nor the several other casual rents, because the property lands lie scattered in 12 parishes, in many very remote islands. By these means, out of the first three years, petitioner has not been able to recover any more than serves to pay the ministers' stipends of that whole Bishopric, which he has actually done. But the land tax is all unpaid, no fund being for it, nor for the 150*l.* per ann. due to the Exchequer. Prays to be excused from the 150*l.* per ann. and for his lease to be continued for five years. 3½ *pages.*

[? About 25 Aug.] 13. Petition of the Minister and Churchwardens on behalf of themselves and the whole Lutheran Protestant Congregation in the Savoy. They petitioned for a lease of a chapel, with a dwelling-house for the minister, a small piece of ground belonging to it, with a vestry room and small house upon it, and that the passage to the chapel at one end of the barracks, for the convenience of coaches and chairs, might be opened again. The petition was rejected. As they had nothing on which to subsist but what came from the generosity of "good disposed people," they prayed for the grant of the passage they formerly had, with the Jesuit ground for the convenience of coaches, as appears by the Surveyor General's Report annexed, or they should be deprived of the benefit of Divine Service.

The copy of the report referred to. Dated 20 Feb. 1720.

Minuted:—"25th Augt 1721. The Clerk of the Works for the Savoy to attend about this." 2 *pages.*

[? About 25 Aug.] 14. Memorial of Thomas Lowther to the Lords of the Treasury stating that the Officers of the Exchequer demand 6^d^ in the pound "for 6,000*l.* issued to William Stanhope, Esq., and for 1,200*l.* secret service money in pursuance of the late Act of Parliament," praying their Lordships' directions thereon.

Minuted:—"25th Augt 1721. Orderd." 1 *page.*

1721. VOL. CCXXXV.

26 Aug. 15. Report of the Attorney General to the Lords of the Treasury on the petition of George Johnston, of London, certifying that Thomas Warcope was outlawed at the suit of the petitioner, and that a special *capias utlagatum* was issued out of the Court of King's Bench, by virtue of which the Sheriff of London seized his goods, which were valued at 35*l.* 10*s.*; that the said writ and inquisition being transcribed into his Majesty's Court of Exchequer at Westminster a writ of *vendicioni exponas* issued out of the Exchequer directing the Sheriff to sell the goods, which was accordingly done. As petitioner's suit was carried on against the said Warcope for a debt due to the petitioner on his own private account, and the money is not sufficient to discharge the petitioner, is of opinion that authority should be given to the Attorney General to consent on his Majesty's behalf that the 35*l.* 10*s.* should be paid over to the petitioner as has been frequently done in cases of this nature. The proper method of doing this will be by warrant signed by his Majesty, and countersigned by their Lordships, commanding the Attorney General to consent to the payment.

Minuted :—" 9th April 1722. Agreed to."

The petition and an affidavit. 4 *pages.*

28 Aug. 16. " Mr Auditor Walpole's memorial relating to ye casual revenue of Barbadoes."

His Majesty having signed a Commission appointing John Ashley, Esq., Receiver General of the casual revenue in Barbadoes, in the room of Samuel Berwick, Esq., who had executed the office since the year 1706, but never could be brought to render any account but what has been very irregular and confused; memorialist now lays before their Lordships a state of the revenue (which was formerly very valuable to the Crown) and the reasons of its being likely to be lost. These are:—

1. The casual revenue of Barbadoes consists not only of fines, forfeitures, amercements and escheats recovered in the respective courts of the Island, but also of all moneys arising by sale of ships forfeited for unlawful and prohibited trade, pirate ships, and piratical effects. These were paid into the hands of the Receiver: yet of late years, the Collectors of customs in Barbadoes and others have pretended to receive, and have secured his Majesty's share of, the effects arising from ships confiscated for unlawful trade, as well as from piratical vessels.

2. The courts have not of late years been duly summoned.

3. The said Berwick has charged the Crown with the payment of several sums not allowable by any warrant of the Treasury or any law or custom of the Island; particularly with the expenses of writs in suits and prosecutions where the Crown has been plaintiff, without giving credit to the Crown for the costs that have been awarded and paid by the defendants.

4. The officers concerned in issuing writs, &c. relating to fines, forfeitures, &c. have negligently performed their duty, making it difficult for the Receiver to recover what was due, &c.

1721. VOL. CCXXXV.

Lastly, several *noli prosequis* have been entered and fines and forfeitures of considerable value belonging to the Crown, together with the costs given against the defendants, have been often remitted by the Governors.

To remedy which, proposes that proper orders, &c. should be laid before his Majesty for his signature. These should be observed by the Receiver General of the casual revenue and the other officers concerned for the managing, recovering, and improving thereof.

These proposals he then sets out. 28 Aug. 1721.

The above memorial or report is accompanied by extracts of items in the accounts of Col. Stede, Receiver General of the casual revenue in Barbadoes, from 4 Aug. 1683 to 28 June 1687, and Mr Thomas's account of the same in 1696–1697. 7 *pages.*

29 Aug. 17. Representation of the Postmaster General to the Lords of the Treasury, respecting that branch of the revenue of their office which arose from Ireland. Observes that during the sitting and continuance of the privilege of Parliament of that kingdom, the inland revenue of the Post Office is almost entirely sunk, by the great liberty taken by the members in freeing letters, which, as Mr Manley their deputy observes, must be their freeing not only their own, but other persons' letters. Compares the produce of the letters in 1718 (when there was a session of three months) with 1719 (when there was a session of nine months). The former was 14,592*l.* 9*s.* 8*d.*, and the charge of management, members' letters, &c., was 11,526*l.* 2*s.* 2*d.*, the net produce being 3,066*l.* 7*s.* 6*d.* The latter year was 19,522*l.* 7*s.* 7*d.*, the charge of management, members' letters, &c., was 18,768*l.* 9*s.* 3*d.*, the net produce being 753*l.* 18*s.* 4*d.*, which is 2,312*l.* 9*s.* 2*d.* less than the net produce of the preceding year. Their Lps would see the true state of the matter by a letter enclosed, which they had received from Mr Manley. Recommends that a warrant should be prepared expressly for Ireland with restrictions. If their Lps are of that opinion, he prays to have the King's warrant. [*Minuted in the margin:* "29th Augt 1721, Orderd."] Observes further that the revenue is much lessened by the members of Parliament of Great Britain freeing letters to Ireland, and by their having their letters come free from thence. There is further liberty taken by persons in office in Ireland, in covering traders' and other persons' letters. General Post Office, London, 29 August 1721.

Accompanied by (1.) Mr Manley's letter (of 10 Aug. 1721) to Edward Parsons, Esq., Secretary to the Postmaster General, showing the abuses of the franking of letters. It commences thus :—

"I beg you to acquaint our Masters that the franking of letters by our Peers and Cōmoners increases every day, as does the anger of 'em all agst me for endeavouring to put any stop to the extravagant freedome that is practiced by them in franking letters that are not their owne.

I am dayly told that a party is forming to address the King in the next sessions to remove me for taxing their letters. How far

1721. Vol. CCXXXV.

they'le go in this I know not, but I verily believe that they will do all that is in their power as to expell me the House of Commons and cōmitt me to their sergeant, or the castle."

(2.) Another letter from him of 19 July 1721 on the same subject, in which he says: "It is a common maxim and is layd down as a fundamental by many members, and they do openly avow it, that the preventing money to go out of the country is a public good, and therefore they conclude that the franking letters is a virtuus action. For as all the nett produce of the Post Office is sent into England they profess to prevent it as much as they can, and therefore some do declare that they will frank all letters that are brought to them, and we have too much reason to believe that they are as good as their words." 7½ *pages.*

[About 30 Aug.] 18. Copy of petition of Edward Shafto to the Lords of the Treasury. Is father of John Shafto, one of the four gentlemen shot at Preston. Was by his unfortunate son seduced and drawn into the Rebellion, and being conscious of the heinousness thereof, after the town was taken offered himself to Sir Henry Houghton, Thomas Molyneux, Esq., and Mr Maisterman as a witness for his Majesty against the rebels, and to prove the Rebellion in the English joining the Scots and proclaiming the Pretender in all the market towns through which they marched. Petitioner, with Mr Calderwode, did [this] upon every trial at Liverpool and elsewhere. Mr Calderwode has been rewarded by a good sum of money and a pension of 40 or 50 pounds per annum, but petitioner has had no other reward but a subsistence for meat and drink during the time of all the trials, and was discharged with only forty shillings. By being an evidence petitioner has drawn upon himself the hatred and malice of all his friends and relations, &c. Prays relief by a pension or place in some hospital.

A postscript is added that the petition was certified and signed by Sir Henry Hawhton, Bart., Tho. Molyneux, and William Shaw, Justices of the Peace, the Rev. Mr Paploe, Rector of Preston, and Mr Maisterman, solicitor, sent down by Lord Townsend.

Minuted: "August 30, 1721. Refer'd to Mr Cracherode or his Deputy, Mr Plaxton, to certify what they know of ye merits of ye petitioner." 1 *page.*

31 Aug. 19. An estimate or calculation of what the expense of the Treasurer of the Chamber's Office may amount to in all particulars for one year from Michaelmas 1721 to Michaelmas 1722; particularizing all additions that have been made to, or reducements from, the establishment of that office, since the same was at first signed by his Majesty. Signed: "Fairfax." Treasurer of the Chamber's Office, 31 Aug. 1721. 3 *pages.*

[7 Sept.] 20. [Pensions.] An account of the debt that will be due in the office of Walter Chetwynd, Esq., between Christmas 1719 and Michaelmas 1721. 12 *pages or parts of pages.*

8 Sept. 21. "Extract of a representation from the Right Honble the Lords Commissioners for Trade and Plantations to his Majesty, dated the 8 of Sepr 1721; relating to rice in Carolina."

Vol. CCXXXV.

1721.

They state that rice is the staple commodity of the province. The merchants trading to Carolina have complained that the advantage formerly reaped, of supplying Portugal with rice, has been entirely lost since the Act of 3 & 4 Anne, whereby the importation is restrained to Great Britain. Before the production of rice in Carolina, Portugal was supplied with very great quantities from Italy. The free exportation of it thither induced the people of Carolina to plant and propagate it. Being deprived of the freedom of export direct, the additional freight and other charges would amount to about one third of its value. The quantity of rice imported and re-exported; for five years ending at Christmas 1717, was 28,323 cwt. per annum. The exportation from Great Britain to the northward is very considerable, but to the southward is very small, and the double freight is the cause; the rice of Carolina being esteemed the best in the world. The Italians, being near, have almost beaten the King's subjects out of the trade, which proves very detrimental to the navigation of Great Britain. The Italians without this vent would hardly be able to carry on a trade to Portugal and Spain, they having no other gross goods but rice and paper, sufficient to furnish a lading for great ships, and not daring to adventure in any others for fear of the Algerines. Submit that it would be for the advantage of the plantations to allow rice to be carried from Carolina direct to Portugal, or any other part of Europe to the southward of Cape Finisterre, upon giving security that the vessels shall touch in Great Britain before they return to the West Indies. 8 Sept. 1721. 4 *pages and 3 lines.*

9 Sept. 22. Report of Sir William Thomson to the Lords of the Treasury concerning a fact suggested in the representation of Mr Forward. Finds that tobacco, which is the usual produce of the felons transported by Mr Forward, has been at a very low price for some time, so that it is probable he may be a loser by his bargain at 3*l.* per head for those felons from Newgate. It is true that he complained that he could not serve the public any longer by transporting the felons upon the terms of his present contract. There being a great number of prisoners lying in gaol in the midst of the summer he (Sir William) pressed Mr Forward to take them away, and promised to recommend his case to their Lordships' consideration. Thinks he deserves encouragement. If their Lordships granted him what he asked (about 150*l.*) it would induce him to continue his care. 9 Sept. 1721.

Minuted:—"12th September 1721. To be paid the sum reported and to attend in order to the renewal of the contract." 2 *pages.*

12 Sept. 23. Memorial of the Four Tellers of the Receipt of the Exchequer to the Lords of the Treasury. There seems some doubt whether the deductions of sixpence in the pound (pursuant to an Act of Parliament) are to be made out of the issues made and to be made in certain cases. Asks the question whether any money payable out of the Receipt of H.M. Exchequer is subject to that deduction other than what is paid out of the Civil List revenues. Exchequer, 12 Sept. 1721. 1 *page.*

1721. VOL. CCXXXV.

[About 13 Sept.] 24. Petition of Richard Score, late Collector of Customs and other duties at Penzance, to the same Petitioner detected the great abuse committed at the Custom House, London, relating to the duties payable for unrated East India goods, as set forth in a former petition reported on by the Attorney General. Their Lordships, on that report, ordered petitioner 500*l.*, which he received, and assurances were given to him that he should very soon be put into one of the best employments in that revenue. He is still without employment and the reward was vastly short of his expense in attending the prosecution of the cause. Prays recompense.

Minuted:—"13th Septr 1721. My Lords will move the King for 200*l.* to the petitioner in reward of his attendance since the discovery made by him, and will take care when the money adjudged to be paid by the E. I. Compa for the Customes for unrated E. I. goods shall be settled, that the petitioner have a suitable reward for his service in discovering, and the assistance given by him in the prosecution." *Again:*—"Warrt signd, 15th Septr."

The copy of the petition and report refered to. 4 *pages.*

14 Sept. 25. An account of all his Majesty's plate in any of his Majesty's palaces or elsewhere; together with the respective denominations and weights of each piece or parcel: as also of all plate now remaining in his Majesty's Jewel Office. Jewel Office, 14 Sept. 1721. 6½ *pages.*

14 Sept. 26. The King's receipt for 15,000*l.* given to Henry Kelsall by Robert Walpole, Esq., first Commissioner of the Treasury, the same sum being paid into the Bank of England on a subscription of 100,000*l.* for the support of public credit and for a further sum of 3,000*l.* for the premium of 3*l.* per cent. upon the said subscription and 704*l.* 5*s.* for interest at 5 per cent. for the money so paid amounting in all to 18,704*l.* 5*s.* Under the sign manual and countersigned by Walpole. 14 Sept. 1721. 1 *page.*

15 Sept. 27. "Copy. Receiver General. Instructions of the casual revenue in the Leeward Island[s]." Dated 15 Sept. 1721.

This is probably an enclosure to some later paper. It is numbered 5. 2 *pages.*

[? About 15 Sept.] 28. Petition to the Rt Hon. Robert Walpole, Esq., First Lord Comr. of the Treasury, of Catherine Rycaut, daughter of Captain Rycaut, who was killed at the attack of Fort Monjuick in Spain. Soon after his Majesty's Accession he granted to petitioner's mother, Charlotte Rycaut, a pension of 40*l.* per ann. for the loss of her husband and for the distinguished services of her family; particularly by her uncle, the late Earl of Macclesfield, whom King William honoured with carrying the Act of Succession to the House of Hanover, and by her husband's uncle, Sir Paul Rycaut, who lent King Charles the second 40,000*l.* "when the whole city of London refused him the loan of thirty," for which and other distinguished services he never received the least consideration.

Vol. CCXXXV.

1721.

Minuted:—"15th Septr 1721. Read. My Lords cannot advise the King to revive a pencōn that is expired." *Again*:—"19th. Read again. My Lords will move the K. to give her 10li p. anñ." 1 *page*.

[? About 15 Sept.] 29. Memorial of Viscount Gage, one of the Verderers of the Forest of Dean (Gloucestershire), to the Lords of the Treasury. In his double capacity as a verderer and an inhabitant represents that the highways in the forest are so much out of repair that they have in several places become "unpassable," and in others dangerous. The whole forest is extra-parochial and within the hundred of "St Brevialls." It has always been incumbent on the crown to repair the Roads, and the Lords of the Treasury have usually, upon application, directed the Surveyor General of Woods to perform the same.

Minuted:—"15th Septr 1721. Read." 1 *page*.

20 Sept. 30. Report of the Attorney and Solicitor General to the same, on the petition of the Governor and Company of Copper Miners in the principality of Wales, the question referred to them being whether the offence upon which there is a prosecution against the Company, is pardoned by the Act of Oblivion: and if not, whether the King can grant a *noli prosequi*, offences of this kind being (as was apprehended) declared public nuisances by the Act of 6 George? Are of opinion that the prosecution against this Company, being by *scire facias* for the supposed forfeiture of a franchise, the same is excepted out of the late act of general pardon; but his Majesty may order a *nolle prosequi*, his Majesty's prerogative of pardoning or discharging prosecutions extending to cases of public nuisance as well as other offences. 20 Sept. 1721.

The petition with the minute authorising the above report. 2¼ *pages*.

25 Sept. 31. Representation of the Comrs of Salt (John Campbell, Ja. Campbell, and H. Brent) to the same. Received their Lps warrant to appoint John Crauford as Surveyor General of the duties on Salt in Scotland, formerly enjoyed by John Cosnan until appointed their Secretary. Had represented that the business of supervisor would be better done by two persons than by one, and had presented William Meinzies and John Smith, two of the best experienced of their officers, to be supervisors at a salary of 50*l*. a year each, whereupon they received a warrant for placing them on the establishment. Pray their Lordships' directions as to their intentions. Salt Office, Edinburgh, 25 September 1721.

Also copies of the former presentment and warrant.

Minuted:—"Octbr 26, 1721. The Lords, when they issued their warrant appointing Mr Crawford to be Supervisor Genll of ye duty upon salt, were apprised that there were two particular Supervisors of yt duty of ye salary of 50*l*. [? per annum], but were upon due consideration, of opinion, yt ye constituting a Supervisor Genll

1721. VOL. CCXXXV.

of y[t] duty was necessary as a farther security and care of y[t] duty, and a letter to be wrote accordingly to y[e] Comm[rs] w[t] directions to them to execute their Lrdp̃s warrant." 2¼ *pages.*

[About 26 Sept.] 32. Petition of Sir George Byng to the Lords of the Treasury praying for the grant of a lease for 31 years of a small piece of waste ground between Whitehall Court and "the house that M[r] Hanbury is building."

Minuted:—26 7[br] 1721. Ref. to Surv[r]."

Accompanied by a ground plan showing the dimensions and adjoining owners. 2 *pages.*

2 Oct. 33. Order in Council made upon reading two petitions of the United Company of Merchants trading to the East Indies, setting forth that ships have frequently been sent out from Great Britain and from the British plantations in America, under pretence of trading to Guinea for slaves, which have carried great quantities of arms and ammunition, stores and provisions to Madagascar within the limits of the petitioner's charter; where the pirates often make their rendevouz, and thereby supply the pirates, enabling them to continue longer in those seas than otherwise they could: that they exchange such ammunition and stores with the pirates at very high rates for Indian goods, which the pirates having no occasion for, part with for little; these goods they dispose of at good prices in H.M. Colonies in the West Indies: that they have also an opportunity of purchasing slaves at Madagascar which they sell to great profit in the West Indies, although the legislature did not think fit to allow the company to send slaves thither, for fear of filling the plantations with Indian goods: that the petitioners have likewise received advices of an Ostend ship from the East Indies selling at Barbadoes, in March last, considerable quantities of China and India goods at such cheap rates, that they drained the Island of a great parcel of money: that by the laws no ships ought to be allowed to trade to any of H.M. American Colonies, except those of H.M. subjects; nor to carry goods for sale except from Great Britain: that the admission of foreigners to trade in those Colonies is very detrimental to the navigation, to his Majesty's revenue, and to the British subjects trading thither, as well as to the petitioners: that unless some effectual remedy be speedily applied the mischief will spread to others of the Colonies, to the enriching of foreigners and impoverishing H.M. subjects. Pray for relief therein. His Majesty orders that the Com[rs] of Trade prepare an Instruction, to be laid before H.M. in Council for approval, strictly requiring all Governors and Commanders-in-Chief to observe the laws in force regulating trade and navigation, &c. [Reference to various Acts follow, and the pains and penalties which H.M. subjects are to suffer for disobedience therein.] The Com[rs] are to insert in their instructions various other clauses in order to the better execution of the laws, and the Governors and Commanders-in-Chief are to report to the Secretaries of State and Com[rs] for Trade exact accounts of their proceedings. The Lords of the Treasury are to

1721. Vol. CCXXXV.

give proper instructions to the Com^{rs} of Customs for the strict observance of the laws above mentioned. 2 Oct. 1721.

Minuted:—"Oct^{br} 4, 1721. Orderd a copy to be sent to the Com^{rs} of y^{e} customs to take care that y^{e} said rules be observed." $4\frac{1}{2}$ *pages.*

2 Oct. 34. Order in Council made upon receipt of information that several places in the southern parts of France continue to be afflicted with the plague, and that the infection has of late extended itself further within that kingdom; viz.: that all masters, &c. of vessels coming from any port or place on the coast of France, northward of the Bay of Biscay, not by former order put under quarantine, shall bring certificates of health signed by the Chief Magistrate of the port from whence they come, &c. The officers of customs to use their utmost diligence to see the orders enforced. 2 Oct. 1721.

Minuted:—"Oct^{br} 4, 1721. Copy to be sent to y^{e} Comm^{rs} of y^{e} customs to take care that y^{e} s^{d} order be observed." $2\frac{1}{4}$ *pages.*

[? About 4 Oct.] 35. Memorial of Patrick Macky, attorney for the Hon. Captain Charles Stewart, to the Lords of the Treasury. When Captain Stewart was ordered on his present station to the coast of Barbary to treat of a peace with the Emperor of Morocco he advanced 1,131*l.* for presents, on the promise of Mr Secretary Craggs that he should be presently repaid. The Captain procured 1,000*l.* of it at interest, which he had ever since paid. Prays payment.

Minuted:—"The accounts of the money expended by Captain Stewart to be layd before my Lords for their consideration. *Again:* —"4th Octr 1721. Prepare a warr^{t}." *Further:*—"17th Octr 1721. Warr^{t} sign'd."

Also copy of a letter from Mr Secretary Craggs to the Lords of the Treasury, on the same subject. 3 *pages.*

5 Oct. 36. The Lord Lieut. of Ireland (Grafton) to the Lords of the Treasury. Viscount Shannon having resigned his allowance as a Lieut. General on the Establishment of Ireland, amounting to 970*l.* per ann., upon his being appointed Commander-in-Chief of H.M forces under the government of Ireland, his Majesty directed, the day before he (the Lord Lieut.) left London, that some alterations should be made in the Establishment of General officers, and that the 970*l.* should be distributed as follows, viz.: 260*l.* per ann. to be added to the pay of the Commander-in-Chief to make it up to 1,460*l.* per ann., which was the ancient and usual allowance for that employment; that James Dormer, Esq., be placed on this Establishment as Brigadier General, with the usual allowance of 365*l.* per ann., and that Major General Joseph Wightman be also placed on this Establishment as Major General, with an allowance of 345*l.* per ann. His Majesty, some time ago, nominated Philip Honywood, Esqre., to be placed on this Establishment as Brigadier General, with the usual allowance of 365*l.* per ann., in the room of

1721 VOL. CCXXXV.

Brigadier Phineas Bowles. Their Lordships are to obtain the proper warrants for the purposes aforesaid. Dublin Castle, 5 Oct. 1721.

Minuted:—"12th Octr 1721. Prepare a warrt." *Again*:—Warrt signd, 19th Do." 2 *pages*.

5 Oct. 37. Memorial of Brigadier Robert Hunter to the Lords of the Treasury. The Auditors of Imprests scruple to pass the accounts of the expedition to Canada for want of the original vouchers. The Brigadier has given in to them a very particular account of that expense, made out from the original vouchers at New York, by Mr James Dupré, Mr George Clarke, secretary of the Province of New York and Deputy to the Auditor of the Plantations, who is charged with the management of the expenses of the Brigadier. Scruples to send over his original vouchers without an order from the Treasury. If necessary for the vouchers to be sent, petitioner begs their Lordships' orders to Dr Clark to send the same, and that he should keep authentic copies. London, 5 Oct. 1721.

Minuted:—"10th Octr 1721. Orderd accordingly." 1¼ *pages*.

[? About 5 Oct.] 38. Petition of Sir Richard Blackmore, Knt., Doctor of Physic, to the Lords of the Treasury in the following terms:—"That whereas your peticoñer was sent for by the late Queen's order to give his advice for the recovery of her health, when in the eighth year of her reign, she came much indisposed from Newmarket, and your petr attended her Maty then and a year and a half after that time generally once a day, often twice, sometimes three times a day, and assisted at all consultations for her Matty during the aforesaid term; and whereas your peticoñer was sent for to attend the late Queen in her last illness at Kensington, where he attended several days without following any other business. And whereas your petr never received any gratuity or reward for such attendance, excepting only twenty guineas at her Mats first coming from Newmarket as aforesaid, Your petr humbly prays your Lordps to take the premises into your consideration and to appoint him such a recompence for his said services as to your Lordp̃s shall seem meet."

Minuted:—"5th Octr 1721. To be considered when the Queen's tyn is dispos'd of and a distribution made thereof to her servants." 1 *page*.

6 Oct. 39. Resolution of the House of Commons of 6 Oct. 1721, upon the petition of the Provost, Fellows, and Scholars of Trinity College, near Dublin, which states that the sums granted for finishing the College Library are insufficient. The Resolution is, that the House address the Lord Lieut. to lay before the King the desire of the House, that his Majesty, out of his bounty, give to the Provost, Fellows, and Scholars such sums, not exceeding 5,000*l*., as shall be necessary for finishińg the Library. *Minuted*:—"Warrt signd, 12th Feb. 1721–2."

Also the petition. 3 *pages*.

Vol. CCXXXV.

1721.

10 Oct. 40. Copy of warrant of the Lords of the Treasury to the Com^{rs} of Customs, "and also for the management of his Majesty's revenue arising by 4½ per cent. in Barbadoes and other the Caribbee Islands in America," directing them to order the Collectors, Receivers, and other officers employed in the management of those duties to transmit accounts, &c. thereof, together with duplicates of the same, to Horatio Walpole, Esq., Surveyor and Auditor General of H.M. revenues in America, to be audited. 10 Oct. 1721.

Also "Extract of the Comp^{r} General's patent relating to the acc^{ts} of ye 4½ per cent." 4½ *pages.*

16 Oct. 41. "Copy of the report and estimate from the Board of Works relating to the building Lazaretts for preventing the plague." State that they had consulted Sir Hans Sloan, Doctor Mead, and Doctor Arbuthnot, who had reported on the subject, and they were still of opinion that the five places mentioned in their report are the most convenient places, provided a sufficient quantity of water can be had. Recommend the buildings to be of timber covered with tarpawlings encompassed with ditches and strong pallisadoes. The cost would be about 9,867*l.* 12*s.* each. 16 Oct. 1721. 2 *pages.*

17 Oct. 42. Ambrose Warren to "the Lord Bishop of Glocester at Westminster Abby." Asks for his assistance with the Lords of the Treasury in bringing before them the deplorable condition of Mr William Lenham, a lunatic, only son of Major Lenham, who, in 1688, brought over the then prince of Orange's Declaration, to the great hazard of his life, which was afterwards lost in the service of the Boyne in 1690. This son was placed by the late Archbishop of Canterbury with the writer in 1696, who "paid for him by the Secretarys of State til 1700, when he was placed with Mr Fearn at the Custom house til about 1706, when Lady Auverquerque took care of him some time, at the late Queen's expence of 40^{li} per ann., til the death of that lady, when Ld Grantham, her ladyship's son, paid all due for him to Mrs Tollet, until April 1720." Lord Grantham then discharged himself from any further care or charge of him. States what he (the writer) had subsequently done for the lunatic, and that the Treasury ordered 20*l.* for him, the writer being still 14*l.* out of pocket; prays for payment and for directions as to what should be done. 17 Oct. 1721. 1 *page.*

17 Oct. 43. J. Wilkins to the R^{t} Hon. Mr. Walpole. Waits for his Lordship's determination and order for the money due to him, and as he has never been wanting in his duty and diligence for the service and ran all risks in time of war, so hopes Mr Walpole will not be so hard as to cut him off 365*l.*, and that he may be allowed his loss in the French bank bills, amounting to 300*l.*, as Lord Stair could fully inform him.

Minuted:—"17th Octr 1721. 800^{li} bounty and is to be understood in full of all pretensions and demands. Warr^{t} signd 26th Oct^{r}." 1 *page.*

1721. VOL. CCXXXV.

17 Oct. 44. Memorial of the Directors of the Royal Exchange Assurance, to the Lords of the Treasury. The Corporation had paid into the Exchequer 156,000*l.* on an annuity at 4 per cent. pursuant to an Act of 7th Geo. I. On this advance they were entitled to issue bonds to the same value at 5 per cent., and they thus hoped to have raised money to that value, but by the turn of affairs they had not been able to issue any of their bonds. Have no other means of raising money, but by the sale of orders and tallies, and this, under the present bad state of credit, they cannot effect. Beg permission to give 28,750*l.* in the said tallies and orders, in payment for that sum, which remains due to the Civil Government. This would enable them to go on prosperously. 17 Oct. 1721. 1½ *pages.*

[? About 17 Oct.] 45. "State of the demand of James Scot, Esq., his Mats Envoy in Poland."

The account states that he was entrusted with 250,000*l.* for concerting measures against the designs of Sweden, and that he took leave of "his Majesty" on 10 Dec. 1719, and that 1,200*l.* were due to him at Christmas 1720.

Minuted:—"10th October 1721. This demand of 1,200*l.* to be satisfyd out of the remainder of the 250,000li granted to hinder the designs of Sweden." *Again*:—"Warrt signd, 17th Octr." 1 *page.*

[? About 19 Oct.] 46. "An acct of stags, hinds and bucks killed by his Majesty's stag hounds between the first of October 1714 and 30th of September 1721, for which the under-keepers of the several walks in Windsor Forest and Epping Forest crave a fee of 40*s.* for each stag, 20*s.* for each hind, and 10 shillings for each buck."

Minuted:—"19th Octr 1721. Prepare a warrant. Warrt signd, 25th Octr." 1 *page.*

20 Oct. 47. Report of Sir Isaac Newton to the Lords of the Treasury on the memorial of the Rt Hon. the Earl of Lauderdale, "General of his Mats Mint in Scotland." By the last renewal of the Coinage Act his Lordship has been Treasurer of the Mint since 1 March 1714, and has received various sums amounting to 5,415*l.* By warrant of 17 Nov. 1718 he was to pay the following salaries, viz.:—"the General 300*l.*, the Master 200*l.*, the Warden 150*l.*, the Counter-warden 60*l.*, the Assayer 100*l.*, the Engraver 50*l.*, the King's Clerk 40*l.*, the Smith 30*l.*, being in all 930*l.* The charges of coinage and keeping the coining tools in repair are paid by the pound weight of the moneys coined; and there has been no coinage. The charges of keeping the offices in repair may amount to 80*l.* or 100*l.* per ann. The annual charges and salaries amount to about 1,020*l.* and from 1714 to 1721 will amount to about 6,885*l.*, whereof 5,415*l.* is already imprested. Hears that his Lordship is ready to make up the account. Mint Office. Octob. 20, 1721.

Minuted:—"27th 9br. 1722. Agreed to."

The memorial referred to. 2 *pages.*

20 Oct. 48. Robert Armstrong to Charles Burniston, Esq., Surveyor General of his Majesty's woods in America. Refers to his former

1721. VOL. CCXXXV.

letter (*see* 20 Nov. 1720) when he had not made a survey of the woods. Upon his surveying the woods, finds in the province of New Hampshire that there were upwards of 25,000 logs cut, about a year before he entered upon his post, and that two thirds of them were from upwards of 24 inches to above 30, and 20 feet long; all cut into suitable lengths and brought down to mills in New Hampshire to be sawn into planks, boards, and other timber. Is sensible how many of these trees might have been fit for the Royal Navy, and asserts that for twenty years past, where one mast was sent home by contract for his Majesty's service, there were 500 cut or destroyed, all, or for the most part, out of New Hampshire. There are likewise some thousands of logs cut in the above woods of the same dimensions for the above mills. On the 2nd of May last, seized 300 pine trees "near the first pond in Lampareel River" cut in his Majesty's woods in New Hampshire, designed to have been converted into logs. Two thirds of these when standing would have made masts for the Royal Navy and are now rotting. There is a great abuse in the manner in which the Acts for the preservation of the woods are construed. The destruction of the King's timber, for years past, has been greatly owing to the Surveyor receiving money from the loggers. Had issued several notifications that he would not receive such sums. The spot of land at Lampareel River, being about five or six miles square, is the most capable place to supply the Crown with masts, for notwithstanding the waste, there are several thousands of pine trees now fit, or will be in a few years, to almost supply the Navy. The inhabitants of this province still continue to take in thousands of acres of the best wood land and form them into their townships, although they have no power to make such townships. Nothing can prevent this, except a special order from the Crown. In respect to those who destroy the King's masts, the *onus probandi* lies on the part of the King, and this can seldom be made out, such is the behaviour of the people: whereas the proof ought to be with the people. Presses that these abuses may be remedied by Acts of Parliament. Portsmouth, New Hampshire, New England. 8br 20, 1721.

P.S.—According to instructions has marked 200 trees upon the spot in Lampareel River and elsewhere for the Navy.

Accompanying the above are (1) one of the notifications above referred to entitled:—"Mr Armstrong's Publication, dated Octbr 10th, 1721," and (2) a testimonial signed by three persons of the diligence and care of the above Robert Armstrong. *5 pages.*

[? About 21 Oct.] 49. Petition of Woodes Rogers, Esq., late Governor of the Bahama Islands, to the Lords of the Treasury. In the year 1717, in pursuance of an undertaking for making a settlement in the Bahama Islands, then possessed by the pirates to the great annoyance of all the American trade, he had a Commission as Governor of those Islands, and went over with an independent company of one hundred private men, raised by himself, for the command of whom he had his Majesty's Commission. Parliament voted one year's

1721. Vol. CCXXXV.

subsistence only for the same. It was supposed in that time there would have been a settlement, the inhabitants of which could subsist the company as at Jamaica. Met with many disappointments amongst a miserable set of people that he found there. Half those he carried with him died in less than four months. Recruited the company there, and could raise no money from the inhabitants. Was obliged to return to Great Britain in a very ill state of health, and on his way stopped at South Carolina and dispatched to Providence provisions for the company till Christmas; but in preserving those Islands from destruction by the Spaniards, or from again being possessed by the pirates, he has disbursed his whole fortune, and his credit stands engaged for large sums: prays for an allowance of victualling for the last three years.

Minuted:—"21st Octr 1721. See copies of his Instructions, Commission, and all powers given him by the Crown, and any other powers given him by the Co-partners." 2 *pages*.

24 Oct. 50. Memorial of Henry Cocksedge, Attorney at Law, and Agent to the Rt Hon. Charles, Duke of Grafton, to the Lords of the Treasury. In 1718 petitioner was employed by the Duke of Grafton to defend two causes brought by the Corporation of Yarmouth against the Vice-Admiral of Suffolk, and expended for fees, &c., 295*l*. The Lords of the Admiralty represented that the said sum ought to be paid out of the perquisites of the Admiralty in the hands of Henry Lascells, Esq., "of the Customs in Barbadoes." His Majesty had ordered this to be paid: prays that Mr. Lascells (who was gone to Barbadoes) might be compelled to pay the same. 24 Oct. 1721.

Minuted:—"To enquire who is Mr Lascelles' security." 1 *page*.

10 & 24 Oct. 51. Report of R. Powys to the Lords of the Treasury on the petition of William Sanderson, yeoman, Usher of the Black Rod, attending the house of Peers, who says that he constantly attended the house and had no salary or allowance and but very small fees. Further, that the place [previously ?] had a salary of 119*l*. 10*s*. per ann., and he prayed for a suitable reward for his services. Mr Powys reports that the salary payable to this office was formerly placed on the establishment of the Treasurer of the Chamber's Office at 109*l*. 10*s*. per ann. and not 119*l*. 10*s*. This salary was paid to Mr Benjamin Coling to the 6th of Dec. 1700, the day of his death. The son of Mr Coling had a reversionary patent under the great seal to succeed his father, but this was disputed by Sir David Mitchell, then Gentleman Usher of the Black Rod, who claimed to present a person for that office, and presented Captain Phillips. Mr Coling petitioned King William in Council thereon, and the King referred the matter to the House of Peers. They ordered the right to be tried at Common Law, where it was determined in favour of the Black Rod, who had ever since presented to that office without interposition, but the salary had not been paid since the decease of Benjamin Coling. 10 Oct. 1721.

1721. VOL. CCXXXV.

A second report follows, in which he specifies the payments which he finds have been made to the office. Encloses copy of a warrant relating thereto.

There are three *minutes* on the back, the last of which is:—" 7th Novr 1721. To have 100^{li} p añ to be paid by ye Trea͞rer of ye Cha^{r} from Mic͞has last." 3½ *pages.*

28 Oct. 52. John Sydenham to the Hon. William Lowndes, Esq. The gentlemen proprietors of the treasure taken up by Captain Jacob Rowe's engines, are resolved to sell their part of the same, and desire their Lordships' commands how to dispose of his Majesty's $\frac{1}{10}$th part. The Gentlemen have given five per cent. to the officers and ship's company out of the treasure, and hope their Lordships will suffer the same deduction out of his Majesty's share as an encouragement to future expeditions. 28 Oct. 1721.

Also an Invoice of the 27 chests of treasure, &c. 2 *pages.*

28 Oct. 53. Memorial of John Adams to the Lords of the Treasury, desiring their Lordships' orders as to shipping the cloth and gunlocks for a present to the Emperor of Morocco; recommends a ship and says that the articles may be insured for 1½ per cent. by substantial merchants "on our Exchange."

Minuted:—" 28th Octr 1721. To the Adm^{ty} to inform my L^{ds} if any of his Ma^{ts} ships are going to Gibraltar who may conveniently take these presents on board." *Again*:—" Lr͞e is writ." 1 page.

31 Oct. 54. Report of Mr. Christopher Tilson to the Lords of the Treasury on the subject of the grant of the office of Ranger of St James's Park and the emoluments thereof during the late Queen's and the present King's reign. The report finishes:—" The Surveyor of the woods, parks, &c. had always the performing of these works in King William's reign, and for the most part found means to defray the charge thereof by wood sales, notwithstanding the great grants out of wood sales y^{n} subsisting. The present Surv^{r} is a very knowing and judicious officer, and will give your Lordships a just and true information with respect to the reasonableness of my Ld Chetwnd's demands, in case they be referred to him, and may propose a way of raising money to bear this expense, without loading ye King's Civil List therewith; for it is but reasonable to expect that ye King's forrests and parks should produce sufficient to maintain themselves." 31 October 1721.

Minuted:—" 2^{d} Novr 1721. Read. See the clause in the patent of the Surv^{r} of the Woods, whereby he claims the performing all repairs in his Ma^{ts} woods, parks, and forests." 1 *page.*

[? About 2 Nov.] 55. Petition of the United Company of Merchants of England trading to the East Indies, to the Lords of the Treasury. Petitioners in 1698 advanced to the Government 2,000,000*l.* sterling on the assurance of Parliament that they should receive out of the Fund appropriated for that purpose 160,000*l.* yearly, the deficiencies to be made up by Parliament. In 1708 they paid into the Exchequer the further sum of 1,200,000*l.* for the service of the Government. The sums falling short, their Lordships paid them 191,029*l.* 2*s.* 10*d.*,

1721. VOL. CCXXXV.

and there yet remained due 40,021*l.* 6*s.* 7*d.* When they have been in arrear for customs, &c. the Com[rs] have always obliged them to pay interest for such arrears. Praying for allowance of the interest on deficiencies.

Minuted:—"Nov[br] ye 2[d] 1721. Read y[e] petition of y[e] United Company of Merch[ts] trading to ye E. Indies, praying that y[e] interest amounting to 40,021*l.* 6*s.* 7*d.* from ye 29th Sep[tbr] 1714 to 29th Sep[tbr] 1719 upon the principall sum of 191,028*l.* 16*s.* 6½*d.*, being the deficiency of their fund to Mich[s] 1719, directed to be payd them by an Act passed last sessions of Parl[t]. The Lords upon considering y[e] same, and finding by y[e] express words of ye clause of y[e] s[d] Act relating to this deficiency, that ye s[d] sum 191,028*l.* 16*s.* 6½*d.* thereby directed to be issued to ye s[d] E. India Company, was in full satisfaction of y[e] deficiency before mentioned, and y[e] company having accordingly received y[t] sum; their L[rd]ps are[e] of opinion that y[e] deficiency of their fund to Mich[s] 1719 is fully satisfyed, there having been no demand to, nor provision made by Parliament, for answering ye pretended interest due thereon."

United is an "Account of interest due on the deficiency of the Company's funds from the under-mentioned times to the 16th September 1721." 2 *pages.*

7 Nov. 56. Ch. Wither, Surveyor General of Woods, to Christopher Tilson. Sends so much of his patent as entitles him to the right of performing all manner of work in the King's parks. Lord Chetwynde would do him a great injustice should he obtain leave to perform a work that has always been understood to belong to his (the Surveyor's) office, and thereby deprive him of some small fees which former surveyors have always received. Gives such proofs as he has been able to pick up, that these works have been constantly performed by his predecessors. Hall, near Basingstoke, Hants, 9[br] 7th, 1721.

Also copy of a large portion of his patent. 4 *pages.*

[? About 8 Nov.] 57. Memorial of Jos. Carpenter to the Lords of the Treasury. There is still due, above what their Lordships have ordered, 60*l.* 19*s.* 2*d.* for alteration and repair of road in Hyde Park, and 47*l.* 7*s.* 6*d.* for the Fulham Road, and for his Majesty's private roads. 115*l.* 5*s.* 6*d.* for various necessary works: praying payment.

Minuted:—"8th Nov[r] 1721. Order'd."

Also a bill of the work done for the 115*l.* 5*s.* 6*d.* Signed: W[m] Watkins, sur[r]. 2 *pages.*

[? About 8 Nov.] 58. Memorial of Joseph Cortizes to the Lords of the Treasury. Praying that his claims on Portugal might be referred to the Com[rs] of Public Accounts, and that the 37,500*l.* still due to Portugal might be ordered to be paid to him. He and the late John Mead, Esq., in the year 1706 provided forage and bread to the King of Portugal's forces, when the army of the allies retired from Madrid "into the Kingdom of Valentia, in Spain;" and his claim had been recommended to be paid out of the subsidies payable to Portugal.

VOL. CCXXXV.

1721. *Minuted:*—" 8th Novr 1721. The Com^{rs} Army's power relating to all forage demands being determined by parl^{t}, the power given to the present Comm^{rs} is confined to demands of the subjects of England on the Crown of England only; so that my Lords can give no directions in this case. 3 *pages.*

17 Nov. 59. Representation of the Com^{rs} of Customs in North Britain to the Lords of the Treasury. To prevent the bringing of "the contagion" into Britain, think it incumbent on them to represent that one of his Majesty's ships of war cruising on each side of this coast will conduce very much to the compelling of ships to the proper places for quarentine and the prevention of smugglers. They had already been at considerable expense for matters of a similar nature. Custom House, Edinburgh, 17 Nov. 1721. 1 *page.*

[? About 21 Nov.] 60. Petition of Elizabeth Carr, widow, relict of Wm Carr, Esq., late one of the Commissioners of Excise. Petitioner's husband quitted his post that he might continue qualified to serve in Parliment. He had served in several Parliaments, and was active in the Revolution in 1688. In the late Rebellion he was engaged in preventing the rebels from seizing New Castle, and was at no small expense. His fortune, by his continuing out of business and by the elections, was so reduced that he had to sell part of his estate: prays for the Royal compassion and bounty for herself and infant son.

Minuted:—" Novbr. 21, 1721. A warrant for 200*l.* p^{r} an. to commence next Mich^{s}." 2 *pages.*

[? About Nov.] 61. Petition of Elizabeth Bye, John Scruton, and Richard Howard, to the Lords of the Treasury, praying payment of the reward of 100*l.* for apprehending Nicholas Fury, convicted of highway robbery, as directed by the King's proclamation.

Also an affidavit and a certificate on the same subject, dated 2 and 4 Nov. 1721. 3 *pages.*

5 Dec. 62. Representation of the Barons of the Exchequer in Scotland to the Lords of the Treasury, on a memorial annexed, "relating to Lord Sutherland's Grant of Ross, &c." The grant intended him was of the office of Chamberlain of Ross, &c. The Barons lay before their Lordships an account of some proceedings relating to this matter "before the said grant; which do not seem very consistent with the facts set forth in the first part of the said memorial." The principal of these were—(1) that in the beginning of June last, a warrant under the Royal sign manual was presented to the Court, for granting the said office of Chamberlain, and also the pention of five hundred pounds per ann. to the said noble Earl during his own life." The Court cannot but think it strange that any of his Majesty's lawyers should advise a grant in those terms, since by the laws of Scotland relating to the annexed property, or land revenues belonging to the Crown, nothing is more plain, than that the Sovereign can make no grant thereof for any longer time than

1721. Vol. CCXXXV.

during his own life. When the Earl's agent attended the Court he was acquainted with this objection, and seemed to acquiesce in it; (2) that at the end of July a warrant was presented to the Court for granting the office of Chamberlain, and a pension of 500*l.* per ann. to the Earl, his heirs and assigns, for 21 years, if his Majesty should so long live. The majority of the Court are of opinion that it cannot legally be passed, &c. Edinburgh, 5th December 1721.

Minuted:—" 1st Feb. 17[21]. My Lords direct a draught of a signature to be made out for the joint lives of the King and the Earl of Sutherland, for the term of 21 years, and determinable upon the death of either of them." " Warrant signd, 12th Feb. 1721."

The memorial referred to. 4 *pages*.

7 Dec. 63. Memorial of the Managers and Directors of the Lottery, anno 1721, to the Lords of the Treasury. Represent their fidelity and care in receiving and paying into the Exchequer 293,700li. The expense of their work has been 1,433*l.* (of which part had been issued): pray for a suitable reward, and for 361*l.* to be issued to clear the expenses.

Minuted:—" 150li each."

Also the account of the expenses. 2 *pages*.

15 Dec. 64. Lord Delawarr to the Lords of the Treasury. The arrears due to the servants of the late Queen Anne and others, payable in the Treasurer of the Chamber's office, amounted, on 1 Aug. 1714, to 22,711*l.* 0*s.* 4½*d.* What remained unpaid of the late Queen's arrears due to her servants from Christmas 1713 to 1 Aug. 1714 (the day of her decease) is contained in the annexed account. It has always been the custom on the death of any King or Queen of England, that the arrears due to the royal servants of the deceased monarch, in all offices of the household, be issued and paid by the " Receive Officers," who were in those offices at the time of the King or Queen's demise. The rule was observed on the death of King Charles II. and King William: prays that the arrears may be issued through the hands of Lord Delawarr.

United is the account. Dated 15 Dec. 1721.

Another memorial from the same on the same subject. Dated 15 Dec. 1721. 24 *pages*.

16 Dec. 65. Memorial of John Burnett, Lieutenant in the Hon. Brigadier General Grove's regiment, to the Lords of the Treasury. Part of his regiment was quartered at Battle, in Sussex, to hinder the smuggling trade. Memorialist apprehended Jacob Walter, the chief and most notorious of the gang of smugglers, and brought him to London under guard of twenty men, when they designed to have rescued him. At great expense he had the smuggler and all the men quartered in one room, every night, from Battle to London. Memorialist also found " several large quantities of brandy and horses": prays for consideration.

Minuted:—"16th Decr 1721. Prepare a warrt for 200li in reward." " Warrt sign'd, 19th Decr 1721." 1 *page*.

VOL. CCXXXV.

1721.

[? About 19 Dec.] 66. Representation by Sir Isaac Newton, Master and Worker of the Mint, and of John Sydenham, to the Lords of the Treasury. Went to the house of Mr Andr Drummond, goldsmith at Charing Cross, where, in the presence of the agent for the proprietors of the patent granted to Jacob Rowe, Esq., for fishing on wrecks, the silver was weighed for the use of his Majesty, viz., $\frac{1}{10}$th part thereof. The same was converted into current coin, which was paid to Casper Frederick Henning, Esq., pursuant to warrant.

Annexed is the account. The treasure was taken from a wreck in the sea near the Isle of Mayo.

Minuted:—" 19th Dec. 1721. Read." 2 *pages.*

19 Dec. 67. Representation of the Com^rs^ of Stamp Duties to the Lords of the Treasury of the difficulties arising by the Act of the last Sessions for deducting 6^d^ in the pound from salaries, fees, and wages derived from the Crown, and upon all other payments from the Crown whatsoever. They relate to the Distributors of Stamped Vellum, parchment and paper; "carriage of stamp goods"; post letters for remitting his Majesty's money, &c.; for fees; the public officers of the Law and the Registers of the two Universities; the contracts with stationers; rewards for detecting frauds, travelling charges, &c. There are separate minutes in the margin as to what should be done in the cases referred to. Stamp Office, Lincoln's Inn, Dec. 19, 1721.

Minuted on the back:—" August ye 22, 1702. A warrant according to ye report by the minutes in the margin. Warr^t^ signd, 4th 8 br., 1722." 2 *pages.*

21 Dec. 68. Report of the Barons of the Exchequer of Scotland to the Lords of the Treasury, on the petition of Katherine, the wife of John Walkinshaw, of Burrowfield, who was by a sentence of the Court of Justiciary in Scotland declared to have forfeited his single and life rent escheat, and to have incurred the penalty of 500*l.* for his disobedience in not appearing before the Court in pursuance of the Act of the 1st year of his Majesty's reign (entitled an Act for encouraging all superiors, vassals, &c.). The report sets out what proceedings had been taken, and finishes by stating that the petitioner has a great many children, and that they are in necessitous circumstances, and that they (the Barons) had nothing to object to the grant of the forfeiture for their relief, and have prepared the draft of a "signature" for that purpose, whereby the rights of all creditors are secured. Edinburgh, 21 December 1721.

Also the petition and the draft referred to, and the reference of the case to the Barons, which has this second minute on it. " Warr^t^ signd, 2^d^ March 1721–2."

In addition to which there is another paper on the same subject. 10 *pages.*

22 Dec. 69. Report of the Attorney General to the Lords of the Treasury on the petition of George Dean, Esq. Taking the facts to be true, is of opinion that if Mr Dyke, in the petition mentioned, was an illegitimate son, his Majesty is entitled to that part of his

1721. VOL. CCXXXV.

personal estate not disposed of by his will, and therefore his Majesty may grant a release by a privy seal of the right he has thereto. 10br 22, 1721.

Minuted:—"Warrt signd, 17th Janry 1721." 2 *pages.*

22 Dec. 70. Duke of Grafton to the Lords of the Treasury. The house of Commons of Ireland having recommended to him the petition of the Provost, Fellows, and Scholars of Trinity College, near Dublin (praying their favourable assistance towards obtaining a further supply for the finishing of their Library, which they have been before enabled to carry on by his Majesty's bounty), his Grace cannot but think they should be encouraged, and asks their Lordships to lay the petition before the King, to obtain a warrant for him to issue 5,000*l.* to them.

Also lays before them the petition of the Hon. Richard Stewart and Thomas Burgh, Esqres for themselves and others concerned in the colliery of Bally Castle, in the county of Antrim, together with the resolution of the house of Commons thereon, whose opinion was that the effectual working of the colliery would be of great benefit to the kingdom, that the petitioners merited 1,000*l.* and a further encouragement of 1,000*l.* when they shall have landed in the port of Dublin 5,000 tons of coals out of the colliery. Asks their Lordships to obtain an authorization for him (the Duke) to issue 1,000*l.* and 1,000*l.* more on performance of the conditions mentioned. Also transmits the petition of Stephen Costilloe, Gent., with the resolution of the House of Commons thereupon desiring his Majesty to order 500*l.* to be given to the petitioner for services performed by him in the river Liffey, which flows to this city: and for having now undertaken to make a navigable communication from the inland country to the sea ports of that kingdom; recommends the same. Also lays before their Lordships resolutions of the House of Lords (Ireland) in behalf of the officers and servants attending the house, recommending that they should be allowed 1,846*l.*: prays their Lps to obtain the proper warrant. Dublin Castle, 22 Dec. 1721.

Minuted:—"Read Janry ye 8, 1721–2. Ye proper warrants to be prepared according to what is desired." Warrt signd, 12th Feb. 1721–2." 4 *pages.*

[After 25 Dec.] 71. Two papers showing the various items of the estates of Mr Craggs and Mr Aislabie. The landed estates of Mr Craggs were at Lewisham and Greenwich. The last date is 25 Dec. 1721. 2 *pages.*

27 Dec. 72. Three affidavits of persons who had traded to, or had lived in, Virginia, as to the purchase by Scotchmen of tobacco in large quantities at greater prices than others. The casks were more weighty than those of English merchants. Their object was to get the trade into their own hands. One of the affidavits states how the running of the tobacco was managed in Scotland, viz., they have a sloop to meet them at the mouth of the river, and there take in the tobacco after they had cleared with the naval officer and collector. 27 Dec. 1721. 3 *pages.*

1721. VOL. CCXXXV.

1721. 73. "Petition to the Lords of Treasury by Mr Alexr MacBean, minister of the Gospell at Inverness 1721." King William authorized the treasury of Scotland, out of the Bishop's rents, to pay to the Governor of Fort William 30*l.* to erect and maintain a school at that fort. Petitioner served as schoolmaster to the same for eight years, and only received two years of his salary from the Treasury of Scotland. Is informed that there are in the hands of the Receiver General of Scotland moneys from the rents of the Bishopric of Ross, amounting to 180*l.* Prays their Lps recommendation for a warrant to pay him out of this fund. 2 *pages.*

[? 1721.] 74. A paper entitled: "Constats made out by the Surveyor General without ye Auditor." It consists of a list of persons to whom houses, &c. were probably granted, or about to be granted. The last but one has the date "1721 May 23" in the margin, and the last has "June 6," so that the paper probably belongs to the year 1721. 1 *page.*

[? About 1721.] 75. Memoranda relating to the grant of the office of Chirographer of the Court of Common Pleas, tracing the same from 1679, when Francis Lawe, of the Inner Temple, London, Esq., was appointed, to 7 Geo. I., when Mountague Garrard Drake, Esq., was appointed.

At the foot is :—" Mr Drake, at Shardeloe, near Agmondesham." 1 *page.*

[? About 1721.] 76. "A particular of the inventories and allowances of Parliament to the late Directors of the South Sea Company, the remainders after such allowances 15*l.* p ct on the said remainders for prompt payment and the sums which will then remain payable to the Company."

[This is probably one of a series, as it is numbered on the back "23."] 1 *page.*

1721. 77. Draft of a notice or advertisement of the chief cashier of the Bank of England (apparently with the sanction of the Lords of the Treasury) that he was ready to receive sums not exceeding 500,000*l.* for purchase of annuities under the Act of 7 Geo. I., at 5*l.* per cent., to commence at 24 June last. Undated, but ? 1721. See *Historical Account of all Taxes,* printed 1725, p. 368 1 *page.*

1721. 78. Estimates of the charge of his Majesty's forces in the Plantations of Minorca and Gibraltar, and in Great Britain. Anno 1721. 5 *pages.*

[? 1721 or 1722. 79. Petition of Major James Cunninghame, Lieut.-Governor of Fort William, to the Lords of the Treasury. In the posts where he commanded, was obliged to advance money, of which 200*l.* remains unpaid. Had he resided in North Britain after the Union, he would have recovered that money; but by his attendance on his post in Flanders that was impossible. Hopes he will not be a sufferer thereby, especially when their Lps consider the known share he had in preserving the quiet of Scotland at the time of making the Union. In 1718–9 received his Majesty's orders that as there was an invasion speedily intended from Spain, he

1721. VOL. CCXXXV.

should have a watchful eye to prevent any attempts to disturb the peace of the Government. Spared no pains, nor money, for the intelligence of the movements and designs of the enemy and the rebels. Has the principal Secretary of State's (Roxburgh's) letter, wherein he owns that petitioner's advices were full and distinct, and other letters to the same effect. [Sent] provisions at his own risk to Island Donald . . . . [Wrote letter] to Sir Robert Pollock, Governor of Fort William, wherein he told Sir Robert that he wished he had sent 100 men to join Major-General Wightman, also that he had sent the ship and provisions, without which neither the wounded men could have been saved, nor the troops subsisted. Col. Clayton, an eye witness, told the Secretary-at-War the same. Has his Majesty's approval of his conduct in the affair of the Camerons. Maintained two prisoners of that importance that they were sent to him by the Lords Justices of Ireland, with the high sheriff of the county attending them, and a sergeant and six men to guard them. In his 34 years' service has neither spared his person, purse, nor credit. His attendance on Major-General Wightman at Glenshiel was by the Major-General's orders. Petitioner commanded a detachment of 340 men from the regiments of Major-General Wightman, Montague, and Cholmley for enquiring into the murder of 12 men of Wightman's regiment by the Camerons. In which case there is, as their Lps well know, allowances for camp equipage, &c. In these conjunctions can safely assert that he laid out twice the sum charged in the account.

The account referred to, the last date on which is 24 July 1721.

It is indorsed: "The petition of Major James Graham." 2 *pages*.

1721. 80. Representation and petition of the persons subscribed, for themselves and other Importers and Dealers in tar made in the British Plantations in America, to the Lords of the Treasury, asking them to recommend to parliament that the methods which are practicable, may be made use of for making tar in our plantations, and that the rewards or premiums granted and continued, by former Acts of Parliament, may be further continued, for promoting and carrying on so useful and beneficial a work, without which there is great danger of its being entirely lost.

It is mentioned that the method prescribed for making tar was when the trees were fit to bark, the bark was stripped 8 feet or thereabouts from the root of the tree, a slip of the bark about four inches in breadth having been left on one side of the tree, and each tree having been so barked stood one year at the least, and was not before that time cut down for making the tar: but this method rendered it altogether impracticable to make tar in the plantations in America; for when the trees so managed came to the kiln, they would not produce any sap whereby tar could be made from them.

47 signatures, to one of which is added the year 1721, which appears to be the date of the document. 1 *large page*.

1721.

VOL. CCXXXVI. 1721. Classified. Part I.

1. Letters from the Secretary of the Admiralty to the Secretaries of the Treasury, as to remission of taxes to the clerks, and as to abuses committed in embezzling goods belonging to the Turkey ships lately burnt and sunk near the Red Sands (affidavits therewith); remission of taxes to the clerks. 4 *papers, one with enclosures.*

2. Reports of the Controllers of the Army Accounts (Medows and Bruce) to the Lords of the Treasury upon (1) Mr. Mulcaster's demand for 600*l.* due from the late Agent of the Garrison of Annapolis Royal [*Minuted:*—21st Jan^ry^ 1720–1. Agreed to]; on Mr Bealing's memorial for 10^s^ a day out of contingencies, &c., and to be put on the establishment (In favour of the memorialist); and on several memorials of Mr Missing for allowances for victualling Gibraltar, Annapolis Royal. 8 *papers, with some enclosures.*

3. Reports of the Com^rs^ for examining debts due to the Army, addressed to the King on the following subjects:—(1.) A demand on behalf of 27 lieutenants to complete their full pay for their service in America. (2.) and (3.) On several articles for which the accountants ought to have credit. (4.) On the pay of Lieut. Joseph Snellis and for his pay as Adjutant, also on the pay of Simon Parry, Esq., Captain. (5.) On the pay of Commissioned Officers (Brigadier Lepell's dragoons), of Oliver Arthur as Supernumerary Ensign, and of Lieut. Matthew Swinney (when taken prisoner at Brihuega in Spain). (6.) On the demand of the Officers of the late Major-General Edward Pearce's late regiment of dragoons, for horses lost in action in the late war in Spain. 6 *papers.*

4. Reports of the Com^rs^ of Customs to the Lords of the Treasury, on the following subjects:—Imports of goods by men-of-war; allowance for leakage or damage; as to two persons lately gone to Calais, one of whom was supposed to be Mr Robert Knight, late cashier to the South Sea Company (two letters); the prohibition of the wearing of printed calicoes, and the difficulties of carrying on the trade of the East India Company; his Majesty's thirds of the forfeiture of a ship seized by the Collector in the lower district of James River, Virginia, condemned by the Admiralty; the gross and net produce of the duty on tea and pepper; complaints of Captain Brand and others against Mr Tobias Knight, Collector of Customs in North Carolina, and against Mr Fitzwilliams, collector of the lower district of James River, in Virginia; on bonds in the hands of the Receiver General and Cashier of Customs, which ought to be delivered to the present Receiver General; the memorial of Sir Robert Davers and others interested in the Island of Barbadoes, charging Mr Henry Lascelles, Collector of Bridge Town in Barbadoes, with fraud and exactions

1721. VOL. CCXXXVI.

connected with the duty of 4½ per cent. on sugar; proposal to prevent the clandestine importation of brandy, spirits, &c.; on two Turkey ships to be destroyed and the cost of their cargoes; proposal for alteration in the Wine Act; a ship from China with the Emperor's Commission, which had brought great quantities of silks and sold them at Barbadoes, &c.; money due from Francis Hawes, Esq., Receiver General and Cashier of the Customs, when he was succeeded by John Selwyn, Esq., or since, and as to the recovery thereof; seizure of brandy from an inn-holder at Guildford, Surrey; seizure of bombs and utensils of war; salaries of the Com^rs and other officers, &c.; gallies built for smuggling; additional salaries paid here or in the plantations; as to commissions granted to persons in the plantations empowering them to receive fines and forfeitures, so far as they relate to trade and navigation; petition of the Mayor and Jurats of Folkstone on behalf of the inhabitants under prosecution in the Court of Exchequer; on an affidavit of John Upton and that of John Richardson, relating to goods taken out of two Turkey ships called "the Bristol Merchant" and "the Turkey Merchant," before and after they were burnt; snuff, a brass mortar, and damaged gunpowder taken in the Mediterranean; 11 vessels belonging to smugglers, taken by Captain James Wyndham; liberty to carry coals and lime on the river Eden, free of duty; as to North Bergen in Norway being infested with a pestilential distemper; a ship plundered and burnt near Mullion in Cornwall; proposed discovery to be made by one Gabriel Tomkin, a notorious smuggler, then in the Fleet Prison under sentence of transportation; petition of merchants of Bristol concerned in the importation of tobacco, and memorial of the Mayor, Aldermen, and Merchants of Liverpool in relation to the tobacco trade. 30 *papers or sets of papers.*

5. Four papers connected with the business of the Trustees for Circulating Exchequer Bills relating to the salaries of the officers, expenses, &c. 5 *pages.*

6. Reports of the Com^rs of Excise to the Lords of the Treasury on petition of the manufacturers of knives and cutlery wares in and about Sheffield for relief by Parliament; on the running of brandy by smugglers; on charge of management; on auditing the accounts of duties on hides; on frauds committed by Mr Benjamin Le Gross, accountant for the duties on soap, paper, and callicoes; on deduction of 6^d in the pound on pensions, annuities, and salaries derived from the Crown. 6 *papers and enclosures.*

7. Papers relating to the financial affairs of the country, such as money paid into the Exchequer, estimates, &c. 9 *papers.*

1721.

VOL. CCXXXVII, 1721, Classified. Part II.

1. Several papers connected with lottery affairs for the year 1721, or about that period (some being undated are perhaps later).

One of them is docketed:—"Scheme for a lottery of 50,000*l.* for Greenwich Hospital, 1721." 15 *papers, with one or two enclosures.*

2. Letters of the Com[rs] of Ordnance to the Lords of the Treasury relating to salaries, powder, &c. Also two estimates. 6 *papers.*

3. Memorials of Robert Jacomb, Deputy of Sir Robert Walpole, Paymaster General; with one or two from Sir Robert Walpole and the Earl of Lincoln addressed to the Lords of the Treasury for issues of money for subsistence, pay, &c. Horse Guards. 30 *papers and some enclosures.*

4. Various papers relating to the late Queen's debts, including a list of salaries in arrear, and an account of the income and issues of his Majesty's Civil List revenues. 11 *papers.*

5. Scotland. Accounts of salaries and incident charges of the Commissioners and Trustees for the forfeited estates and their officers. One of the papers contains a list of the persons and the yearly value of their estates remaining to be sold. 4 *papers.*

6. Papers relating to the affairs of the South Sea Company, including a return to the House of Commons. There are two memorials of contracts between the Company and the Governor and Company of the Bank of England. Dated 28 and 30 October 1721, and a paper *docketed*:—"For the Bill for the relief of the unhappy sufferers in the South Sea Company." This last consists of a series of resolutions, the first of which is:—"That the late Sub-Governor and Directors of the South Sea Company, and their officers, and their aiders and abettors, in lending out the Company's money upon stock and subscriptions, without taking sufficient security for repaym[t] thereof, have been guilty of a notorious breach of trust and have thereby occasioned great loss to the Company, for which they ought to make satisfaction out of their own estates."

Some of the papers are *docketed*:—"For M[r] Lowndes," and they were probably under his consideration. 21 *papers (one with enclosures).*

7. A few papers touching expenses of his Majesty's stables and stud. One relates to the "debt in the stables, whilst the Duke of Somerset was Master of the Horse to her [late] Majesty." 7 *papers.*

8. Reports of the Com[rs] of Taxes to the Lords of the Treasury on claims made by Receivers General of Taxes, &c. 5 *papers and enclosures.*

9. Two estimates of the debt for the Transport Service. 3 *pages.*

1721. VOL. CCXXXVII.

10. Various reports and papers connected with business of the Board of Works, relating to repairs of "the guard rooms, officers and sutlers at St James, Tilt Yard, and Whitehall; works at the Bird Cage house in St James's Park; extraordinary work performed by direction of the Lords of the Treasury; proposed lazarettes in case the plague should break out; stables for the service of the young princesses; also the debt of the office, &c. 10 *papers (one or two with enclosures).*

11. Warrants of the Lord Chamberlain to the Master of the Great Wardrobe for the delivery of various articles. (Part of a series.) 4 *pages.*

VOL. CCXXXVIII. 1721.

DOCUMENTS for which a brief description suffices.

Date.	Description of Document.	From	To	Purport.
Between 1718&1821.	1. Receipt -	—	William Lowndes, Esq.	For 1,862*l.* 10*s.* for secret services. (Unsigned.) 1 *page.*
2 Jan.	2. Letter - -	Mr. Auditor Walpole	The Lords of the Treasury.	The accounts of Samuel Berwick, Esq., Receiver General of Casual Revenue in Barbadoes, are insufficient, &c., asks for a proper person to be appointed in his stead. 1 *page.*
4 Jan.	3. Abstract -	—	—	Return of number of men borne and mustered aboard H.M. ships in sea pay. 1 *page.*
11 Jan.	4. Report - -	R. Powys - -	—	On the claim of Thomas Harley, Esq., for moneys paid by special command of her late Majesty Queen Anne. 1 *page.*
15 Jan.	5. Account -	—	—	Money due to the Hon. Geo. Feilding, Esq., to the time of the demise of her late Majesty. 1 *page.*
17 Jan.	6. Letter - -	Lord Lieut. of Ireland (Grafton).	The Lords of the Treasury.	For 820*l.* to be issued to defray the expense of new clothing for the State officers in Ireland. (Two enclosures.) 3½ *pages.*

Date.	Description of Document.	From	To	Purport.
[? About 27 Jan.]	7. Petition -	James King, on behalf of the Hon. Lord Harley himself, and others.	The Lords of the Treasury.	Asks to be heard by counsel against any grant to fish for "wracks" within the latitudes of 26 and 40 north in the West Indies; the same being prejudicial to Lord Harley's grant. *Minuted*:—"27th Jany. 1720–21. My Lords will hear my Lord Harley's councill upon this matter at any time, provided he gives Mr. Rowe notice to attend at ye same time." 1 *page*.
[? About 28 Jan.]	8. Account -	—	—	Of service and extra service performed by clerks to Christmas, 1720, connected with the South Sea Company. 3 *pages*.
3 Feb.	9. Memorial -	Earl of Cadogan -	The Lords of the Treasury.	For payment of balances due to him as Governor of the Isle of Wight. (One enclosure.) 2 *pages*.
22 Feb.	10. Do. - -	Lord Townshend -	Do. - -	For payment of 34*l*. 14*s*. for seizing Robert Clark, a distributor of stamped paper, late of Norwich, and bringing him to England, the same having gone off with a considerable sum of H.M. money. 1 *page*.
[? About 11 March.]	11. Do. - -	Col. John Fane and Col. Berkeley.	Do. - -	For grant of a warrant for new clothing to the drummers and hautbois of the two troops of Grenadier Guards under their command. *Minuted*:—"11th March 1720–1. The Secretary at War may obtain his Majesty's Warrt. for this cloathing to be paid out of the contingencies if he thinks proper." 1 *page*.
18 March	12. Report - -	Lord Lieut. of Ireland (Grafton).	Do. - -	On the petition of Captain Charles Morgan to be restored to half-pay as captain of foot. Recommending his case. *Minuted*:—"5 Apr. 1721. Agreed to." 2 *pages*.

1721. Vol. CCXXXVIII.

Date.	Description of Document.	From	To	Purport.
[About 20 March.]	13. Petition -	Marmaduke Bealing	The Lords of the Treasury.	For a warrant for an allowance of 10*s.* a day as Secretary to the Board of General Officers for inspecting the clothing of the army. Also copy of a certificate and another paper. 3 *pages.*
22 March	14. Certificate -	Robert Sedgwick, clerk.	—	As to plate delivered to the Rt. Hon. the Lord Carterett, ambassador extraordinary and plenipotentiary to the Court of Sweden. 1 *page.*
[After 25 March.]	15. Memorial -	Duke of Bolton -	The Lords of the Treasury.	For a warrant for paying the salaries due to the officers of the New Forest. 1 *page.*
31 March	16. Account -	—	—	Debt due upon the extraordinaries of his Majesty's stables. Signed Fr. Negus. 2 *pages.*
[? About 5 April.]	17. Memorial -	Sir John Eccles -	The Rt. Hon. Robert Walpole, Esq., First Commissioner of the Treasury.	Praying for an order to stop the sale of his estate in Ireland during "the badness of the present times." *Minuted:*—" 5th April 1721. My Lords adhere to the report of ye Commrs. Revenue in Ireland, dated 14th Janry. 1720." 2 *pages.*
[? About 9 April.]	18. Petition -	Seven officers and clerks of the Tally Court in the receipt of H.M. Exchequer.	The Lords of the Treasury.	For payment of 195*l.* 8*s.*, being the same encouragement they formerly had, as they had received no fees from Mich. 1720 to Easter last. Also certificate. 2 *parts of pages.*
11 April	19. Letter -	Lord Carteret - -	Do. - -	For the issue of 1,500*l.* to the Board of Ordnance, to enable them to replace 300 barrels of powder of that value, which they are about to send to the Emperor of Morocco from Gibraltar. 1 *page.*
13 April	20. Certificate -	Robert Sedgwick, clerk.	—	Of delivery of plate from the Jewel office to the Rt. Hon. the Lord Carterett, one of his Majesty's Principal Secretaries of State. 1 *page.*
16 April	21. Bill - -	Mr. Manning, his Majesty's Resident with the 13 Canons of Switzerland, and the "Three leagues of the Grisons."	—	For incidental expenses. Dated Berne. With note allowing the amount. Signed "Carterett." 1 *page.*

Date.	Description of Document.	From	To	Purport.
18 April	22. Letter - -	Comrs. of Ordnance	Lord Lieut. of Ireland (Grafton).	For restoration of Captain John Seliok to half pay. 1 *page.*
24 April	23. Memorial -	P. Medows - -	—	For half-a-year's salary due to his father, who was a Commissioner for Trade, to whom he was executor. *Minuted* :—"25th April 1721. To be paid in proportion as the rest have been." 1 *page.*
26 April	24. Balance Sheet	Comrs. of Forfeitures	—	"Account of money paid by, and due from, the York Building Company." *Parts of* 2 *pages.*
[? About 1 May.]	25. Petition -	Edward Bangham, Esq., Receiver General of Taxes for the county of Hereford.	The Lords of the Treasury.	Asks to be heard, before their Lordships appoint another Receiver. *Minuted* :—"1 May 1721. Read. My Lord's resolve to appoint Mr. Robert Clayton, Recr. Genl. of ye Taxes for Herefordshr," 1 *page.*
[? About 1 May.]	26. Memorial -	Col. George Feilding	—	For payment of 178*l.* 14*s.* 6¼*d.* due in her late Majesty's reign out of the Cofferer's office. *Minuted*:—"1 May 1721. To be considered when the state of the Queen's debt is layd before my Lords." Again "4 May 1721. My Lords order ⅘ths." 1 *page.*
2 May	27. Do. - -	Comrs. of Excise -	The Lords of the Treasury.	"Relating to accounts of excise, &c., at the Treary., which are refused to be delivered to the Secretary of Excise, though Mr. King, a late clerk belonging to the Treary., recd. the fees due for passing the same." 2 May 1721. *Minuted*:—"18 May 1721. The accot. to be issued." Two enclosures. 3 *pages.*
[? About 19 May.]	28. Account -	—	—	"Money disbursed in entertaining grenadiers for the King of Prussia's service and sending them to Hamburgh." *Minuted*:—"19 May 1721. Prepare a S.Manual. 25th do. Warrt. signd." 2 *pages.*

1721. Vol. CCXXXVIII.

Date.	Description of Document.	From	To	Purport.
22 May	29. Memorial -	Earl of Cadogan -	The Lords of the Treasury.	For 1,200*l*. to be impresed on account of robes for mournings and other uses. *Second Minute*:—"25th May 1721. Warrt. signd." Also an abstract of the moneys due. 2 *pages*.
25 May	30. Letter - -	J. Burchett (Admiralty).	Do. - -	Encloses petition of Mr. John Bridger, late surveyor of H.M. woods in America; also a certificate: prays payment of his salary. The Lords of the Admiralty think his case very hard and recommend the payment. The petition is *minuted*:—"28th June 1721. Prepare a S. Manual to the Trea'rer Navy to pay Bridger to the time Burniston's Depty. came over." *Again*:—"Warrt. signd. 2nd Aug." 5 *pages*.
26 May	31. Do. -	Lord Townshend	Lords of the Treasury.	For 1,000*l*. to be lodged with the Treasurer of the Chamber for the expenses of the Messengers abroad. *Minuted*:—"12th June 1721. Order'd." 1 *page*.
May	32. Memoranda -	—	—	As to sums due to Mr. Peter La Roche and Mr. Daniel Crohare. *Docketed*:—"Queen's arreares." 4 *pages*.
2 June	33. Letter - -	Commrs. of Victualling.	Mr. Walpole -	Send an account of the salaries payable to themselves and their officers. Also the account. 2 *pages*.
2 June	34. Account -	Commrs. for Hackney Coaches and Chairs.	—	The charges of the office. 1 *page*.
17 June	35. "Memorial & Caveat."	Charles Cox on behalf of Samuel Cox, president and Commander-in-Chief of Barbadoes.	Lords of the Treasury.	John Frere, Esq., took the administration contrary to his Majesty's express commands. Objects to the salary being paid to him. *Minuted*:—"21st July 1721. To be considered when Mr. Frere applys to the Trea'ry for his salary." 1 *page*.

Date.	Description of Document.	From	To	Purport.
17 June	36. Account -	—	—	"Of the produce of wool licences to his Grace, Charles, Duke of Grafton, Lord Lieut. Genl. and Genl. Governor of Ireland from the 18th day of June 1720 to the 17th of June 1721." 1 *page.*
20 June	37. Letter - -	John Delafaye -	—	As to a warrant for 1,000*l.* per ann. to the Duke of Newcastle during the joint lives of the King and the Duke. Also a brief note on the same subject. 3 *pages.*
[? About 24 June.]	38. Scheme -	—	—	Entitled :—" A distribution of money and annuity tallys towards payment of the debts of the Civil List." 1 *large page.*
25 June	39. [Petition] -	Andrew Shields -	"My Lord" -	For speedy payment of balance due to him for subsistence. *Minuted :* — "26th June 1721. Prepare a warrt. for 212*l.* ꝑsuant to this petition. Warrt. signd 24th August." 1 *page.*
26 June	40. Bond and counterpart.	—	—	"Bank of England. Security for their Cashiers as Receivers of the Lottery, A°. 1721." 2 *large pages.*
26 June	41. Certificate -	—	—	"Of plate delivered out of his Ma'ties Jewell Office to the late Mr. Secretary Craggs." *Minuted :*—" 3rd August 1721. Prepare a warrt. for a P. Seal for the discha. of this plate." 1 *page.*
29 June	42. Letter - -	Edward Southwell -	Mr. Walpole -	Asking for payment of the salary of the four clerks of the Council. *Minuted :*—"29 June 1721. To be paid up equall with the Board of Trade." 1 *page.*
[? June]	43. Petition -	Peter Voyer Richaussee.	The Rt. Hon. Robert Walpole, Esq., first Lord Commissr. of H.M. Treasury and Chancellor of the Exchequer.	For arrears of his pay for taking care of her late Majesty's saddle horses. Also certificate. 2 *pages.*

1721. Vol. CCXXXVIII.

Date.	Description of Document.	From	To	Purport.
8 July	44. Certificate -	Comrs. for Alienations	Lords of the Treasury.	Of the charges of the Alienation Office. 1 *page.*
9 July	45. Order in Council.	—	—	Referring the case of William Gratwick and Elizabeth his wife to the Lords of the Treasury. Elizabeth Gratwick having a claim on the government as executrix of Ph. Warwick, Esq., envoy to the Crown of Sweden at the end of the reign of King Charles [II.], King William gave directions that (since money could not be spared) her husband should be employed, and he was afterwards employed as Customer of Chester until 1718, when he was deprived, and thought he ought to be restored. *Minuted:*—"9 July 1721. My Lords can do nothing in this." Five enclosures. 7 *pages.*
10 July	46. Petition -	Cornelius Cayley -	Lords of the Treasury.	Asks that William Cayley, Gent., may be appointed his deputy as Commr. for Alienations during his absence from London. Also a letter from the petitioner to Sir Charles Turner, one of the Lords of the Treasury, on the same subject. *Minuted:* — "10th July 1721. Agreed to." 2 *pages.*
11 July	47. Letter - -	Lord Townshend -	Do. - -	For payment of 200*l.* forthwith to Mons. Carrard, who lately came from Vienna with despatches of great importance. 1 *page.*
12 July	48. Memorial -	The Judges - -	Do. - -	For payment of their salaries for last Trinity term, they having suddenly to go their circuits. *Minuted:* — "12th July 1721. 6,370*l.* to be paid to them for Trinity term last past." ½ *page.*
13 July	49. Letter - -	S. Percivall - -	Chr. Tilson, Esq.	Stating the amount of the salaries and pensions under 100*l.* a year. Navy Office. 1 *page.*
13 July	50. Do. - -	Wm. Jessop -	Lords of the Treasury.	Similar letter as to salaries in the Alienation Office. 1 *page.*
13 July	51. Do. - -	Tho. Holdip -	Chr. Tilson, Esq.	Similar letter as to salaries in the Salt Office. 1 *page.*

Date.	Description of Document.	From	To	Export.
13 July	52. Certified copy		—	Of Minute of Council at New York for allowing Mr. Blathwayt 5 p. c. as Auditor-General of their Majesty's revenues arising in America. 1 *page.*
13 July	53. Memorial -	Managers and Directors of the Lottery for 700,000*l.*	Lords of the Treasury.	Asking for 1,000*l.* to be paid to Mr. Christopher Rhodes (one of the managers) to pay wages to clerks, &c. Banqueting house. (30 signatures.) *Minuted:* — "14th July 1721. 1,000li to be imprested to Mr. Rhodes for the purposes in the memll. mentioned." 1 *page.*
14 July	54. Petition -	William Watkins, Surveyor of H.M. Private Roads.	Do -	Asks for payment of his salary of 200*l.* per ann. Sir Thomas Hewet, the Surveyor of the works, takes upon himself to set aside the royal sign manual, &c. *Minuted:* — "21st July 1721. Read. Sir Thomas Hewett and Brigadier Watkins to attend on Monday morning next." *Again:*—"24th July 1721. Upon a hearing, my Lords direct that the salary of 200li p. ann. granted to Mr. Watkins as Survr. Roads be paid quarterly to him out of the 14,000li (the sum allowed for the ordinary) as it usually has been.' Also copy of a letter on the same subject. 2½ *pages.*
14 July	55. Letter - -	S. Manesty - -	—	Sends account of salaries in the Victualling Office under 100*l.* per ann. Also the account. 2 *pages.*
14 July	56. Account -	—	—	Salaries payable in the Wine Licence Office under 100*l.* per ann. 1 *page.*
14 July	57. Letter - -	Lord Townshend -	Lords of the Treasury.	For payment of 200*l.* to Captain Charles Briemer sent hither with despatches of importance from H.M. minister at Stockholm. *Minuted:* — "17th July 1721. Order'd. Warrt. signd 24th July 1721." 1 *page.*

Date.	Description of Document.	From	To	Purport.
14 July	58. Report - -	"Fairfax" -	The Lords of the Treasury.	View of the salaries and pensions payable in the Office of Treasurer of the Chamber. 1 *page*.
28 July	59. Memorial -	Rice William, a poor Knight of Windsor.	Do. -	For directions to be given for the repair of his house in Windsor Castle. *Minuted*: — "30th Augt. 1721. See the report of the Board of Works." 1 *page*.
3 August	60. Letter - -	Lord Townshend -	Do. - -	For the reimbursement of 92*l*. 16*s*. 7¾*d*. disbursed by Mr. Joshua Kenworthy, the King's agent at Dantzick. *Minuted*: — "24th Augt. 1721. Order'd." 1 *page*.
11 August	61. Do. - -	Lord Chamberlain (Newcastle).	Do. - -	For 30*l*. to be paid to Mr. George Cook as a gift from his Majesty at the christening of his child. 1 *page*.
21 August	62. Do. - -	Lord Townshend -	Do. - -	For accounts of the duties on the exports of English manufactures, and of the duties on unwrought silk and dying materials imported. 1 *page*.
24 August	63. Return - -	—	—	Debts due to the King from the late collectors of the duties on Scots salt, &c. 1 *page*.
[? About 30 Aug.]	64. Petition -	John Maddocks -	Rt. Hon. Robert Walpole, Esq., Lord Commr. of the Treasury.	Is in fear of arrest for debt and of losing his serjeant's place in the guards: prays relief. *Minuted*:—"30th Augst. 1721. He has already rece'd a sume of money in full of his pretended service." *Again*: "10th Novr. 1721. My Lords agree to give him ye sume of 10ll. by Mr. Lowther upon condition that neither he nor his wife attend or sollicit the Treasury any more." There is also a promise signed by them not to trouble the Treasury any more for the above consideration. 2 *pages*.
[? About the same date.]	65. Do. -	Do. - -	The Rt. Honble. Esq. Bayley, one of the Lords of his Maties. Treasury.	If he grants his last request he will never be any more troublesome. It has the same minute on it as that above given, viz., on 30th Aug. 1 *page*.

Date.	Description of Document.	From	To	Purport.
August	66. Memorial -	John Gore - -	Lords of the Treasury.	Relating to the tin at Hamburgh. There is due to him 21,600*l*.
	Do. -	Charles Gore - -	Do. -	The first is *minuted*:—"29th Augt. 1721. The memorialist and his brother Charles Gore to attend my Lords on Thursday morn. next." 2 *pages*.
1 Sept.	67. Letter - -	Lord Cobham - -	[? Do.] -	For payment of 40*l*. to defray the expenses of the swainemote Court of the forest of Windsor. *Minuted*:—"10th Octr. 1721. Orderd." ½ *page*.
5 Sept.	68. Bonds - -	Governor & Co. of the Bank of England and Thomas Madockes, of London, gent., chief clerk of the Bank of England.	The King - -	To pay 100,000*l*. in money received into the Receipt of the Exchequer under the act of the last session for raising 500,000*l*. upon the Civil List Revenues. 2 *pages*.
[? About 6 Sept.]	69. Memorial -	Joseph Carpenter -	Lords of the Treasury.	For an advance of money for repair of H.M. private Road leading to Fulham. *Minuted*:—"6th Septr. 1721. 600li to be issued to the paymr. upon accot. of these works now in hand." 1 *page*.
[About 12 Sept.].	70. Petition	Henry Villiers - -	Do. -	A year and ¾ is due upon the King's bounty of 100*l*. a year. Has nothing else to depend on, and by the death of his brother, the Earl of Jersey, and the growing charges of his education at the University, is put to great distress. Prays for the arrears. *Minuted*:—"12th Septr. 1721. To be paid the arrear due to him." There is also a memorandum that there was granted in 1708 to the widow and children of Col. Henry Villiers (late Governor of Tinemouth Castle) a pension of 300*l*. vested in the Earl of Jersey. The widow afterwards, with her youngest son, had 100*l*. of it apart. As she is dead it is hoped the 100*l*. may be again joined to the 200*l*. and vested in the Countess of Orkney for the children's use. 2 *pages*.

1721. Vol. CCXXXVIII.

Date.	Description of Document.	From	To	Purport.
12 Sept.	71. Memorial -	Cofferer of the Household.	Lords of the Treasury.	For 70,619*l.* 8*s.* 5¾*d.* to clear the household expenses for a year. Two other papers on the same subject. 4 *pages.*
[? About 13 Sept.]	72. Petition -	James Merest, one of the clerks attending the service of the House of Lords.	Do. -	For recompence of his labours. *Minuted:* — "13th 7br. 1721. Augment his usual allowance to 100li p. an." 1 *page.*
19 and 26 Sept.	73. Letter - -	Lord Carterett -	Do. -	For payment to be made to Francis Smart, gunmaker, of 500*l.* for 2,500 gun locks to be shipped to Barbary to Captain Stewart upon his conclusion of the treaty with the Emperor of Morocco. Another paper on the same subject of 26th Sept. *Minuted:* — "4th Novr. 1721. Prepare a warrt. for 1,000li upon account for these locks. Warrt. sign'd 19th Decr. 1721." 2 *pages.*
20 Sept.	74. Memorial -	Samuel Edwin, Usher of the Receipt of the Exchequer.	Do. -	For warrant to the Auditor of the Exchequer to examine, rate, and allow his accounts. *Minuted:* — "10th Octr. 1721. Order'd." ½ *page.*
23 Sept.	75. Letter - -	Board of Greencloth	Do. -	Have made disposition of the 4,000*l.* tallies assigned in part payment of the household, &c. 1 *page.*
26 Sept.	76. Petition -	Ann Powell, widow of William Powell, deceased.	The Rt. Hon. Robert Walpole, Esq., First Commr. of the Treasury.	Her husband served King William as prime huntsman to the stag hounds forty years. The present King granted him a pension of 40*l.* per ann., which had ceased at his death: prays for its continuance. *Minuted:* —"Septr. 26, 1721. A warrant 30 pr. an." 1 *page.*

Date.	Description of Document.	From	To	Purport.
27 Sept.	77. Memorial -	Comrs. of Excise -	Lords of the Treasury.	As to proposed surrender of himself by Francis Norwood, a notorious smuggler. *Minuted:* — "28 7br. 1721. Read to his Maty. In case Norwood surrendrs and do any service, his Maty. will grant him a pardon and reward his service as ye Comrs. of Excise shall think reasonable. Lre. writ." Encloses letter from the Supervisor of Ewell giving the conditions. 2 *pages.*
[About 27 Sept.]	78. Petition -	Daniel Owen -	Do. -	For appointment to an office in the Custom house. With letter from him to the Hon. Wm. Lowndes, Esq., in which he says that at the last election for Westminster, notwithstanding he was severely bruised and beaten, he voted in his honour's interest, and created what votes he could, whereby he lost many customers. 2 *pages.*
29 Sept.	79. Letter - -	Mayor and [Bailiffs or Jurats] of Yarmouth.	The Rt. Hon. Charles Turner, Knt., one of the Comrs. of the Treasury.	For their interposition in favour of three tide-waiters discharged through Mr. Negus, a land surveyor. *Minuted:* — "4th Octr. 1721. Send a copie of this lre and the 2 affidts. annexed to the Commrs. Customes, who are to state the cause of the dismission of the 3 tide-waiters as it appeared to them." Also two affidavits. 3 *pages.*
[29 Sept.]	80. Account -	—	—	Debt due to the extraordinary expense of H.M. stables and stud, payable by Francis Negus, Esq., Commr. for executing the office of Master of the Horse. 3 *pages.*
[After 29 Sept.]	81. Memorial -	Andrew Drummond, Attorney, to the Rt. Hon. the Earl of Lauderdale, Genl. of H.M. Mint, North Britain.	Lords of the Treasury.	For payment of arrears connected with the mint. 1 *page.*

Date.	Description of Document.	From	To	Purport.
2 Oct.	82. Letter - -	Lord Townshend -	Lords of the Treasury.	As to informations received, connected with the suppression of the gang of smugglers who resorted to Horsham in Sussex. Also eight informations and a letter. 11¼ *pages.*
3 Oct.	83. Certificate -	Commrs. of Alienations (Wm. Ashburnham and Cor. Cayley).	Do. -	Of the produce of the office. The post fines are collected by the Sheriffs and accounted for to the Pipe. 1 *page.*
3 Oct.	84. Salary bill -	[? Commrs. of Customs.]	—	List of extra clerks employed in the "Company's service," with their salaries. 25th Dec. 1720 to 28th Sept. 1721. Numbered 10 and 17. They are probably two of a series. 2 *large pages.*
13 Oct.	85. Letter - -	Lord Carteret - -	Lords of the Treasury.	For payment of a bill for 12,900 dollars to Mr. Moses Beranger who had given a credit to Captain Charles Stewart, H.M. Plenipotentiary for negotiating a peace with the Emperor of Morocco. *Minuted* :—"19th October 1721. Prepare the proper warrt. Warrt. signd 25th Octr." 1 *page.*
16 Oct.	86. Do. - -	Do. - -	Do. -	For payment of a bill of 300*l.* drawn by Sir Luke Schaub, for money expended by him at Paris for H.M. particular service. Also a schedule of sums issued to the above Schaub. 2 *pages.*
20 Oct.	87. Report -	Secretary of the South Sea Company.	H. Walpole, Esq., Secretary to the Lords of the Treasury.	Relating to a subscribed annuity in the name of Brand H. Schilden. Also another report, a memorial, and "the case." *Minuted* :—"21st Oct. 1721. Read. Make a copie of this rept." 7 *pages.*
24 Oct.	88. Letter - -	Lord Townshend -	Lords of the Treasury.	Encloses copies of affidavits taken before Mr. Eversfield, connected with the affairs of the smugglers at Horsham. Also a letter signed :—"M. Tupper," connected with the same affairs. 9 *pages and* 3 *halves.*

1721. VOL. CCXXXVIII.

Date.	Description of Document.	From	To	Purport.
24 Oct.	89. Letter - -	Lord Cartret - -	Lords of the Treasury.	For arrears to be paid to Mr. Davenant, Mr. Burges, and Mr. Manning, the King's Ministers abroad, whom he had recalled. *Minuted:* — "Warrants drawn and signed. 7 Novembr 1721." 1 *page.*
31 Oct.	90. Memorial -	Thomas Lyndford, Sub-Almoner.	Do. - -	For sums due to the Lord Almoner and others. *Minuted:*—"Orderd." 1 *page.*
[? About 31 Oct.]	91. Case - -	—	—	Of the creditors of the office of Ordnance: pray payment of their debt. (Printed.) It is stated that the creditors consisted of above 500 families. *Minuted:*—"31st October 1721. Read. There is no provision made by Parliament for this debt, therefore my Lords can do nothing in it. 2 *pages.*
[After 1 Nov.]	92. Petition -	Elizabeth Frere, widow and administratrix of John Frere, Esq., deceased.	Lords of the Treasury.	Prays payment of a moiety of the salary of the Governor of Barbadoes. Also a certificate. Dated 1 Nov. 1721. 2 *pages, much decayed.*
4 Nov.	93. Letter - -	Lord Carteret - -	Do. -	For directions to be given for payment of the allowance of 1,000*l.* per ann., granted by the King to Col. Charles Du Bourgay, Lieut. Governor of Jamaica. *Minuted:* — "9th April 1722. Prepare a p. seal for paying 1,000li. ꝑ ann. to Colo. Du Bourgay, as Lieut. Govr. of Jamaica, out of the revenues of that Island, in the form and manner as hath been before used." 1 *page.*
6 Nov.	94. Account -	—	—	Produce of the several branches of the Civil List revenues.—Exchequer, Auditor's Office. 1 *page.*

1721. VOL. CCXXXVIII.

Date.	Description of Document.	From	To	Purport.
14 Nov.	95. Memorial -	Anthony Cracherode	Lords of the Treasury.	For 500*l.* to be impressed to him. *Minuted:* — "500 to Mr. Cracherode, and to deliver in an account of ye law suits depending, and a state of them." 1 *page.*
[? About 18 Nov.]	96. Order - -	Lords of the Treasury	Mr. Cracherode -	To pay Mr. West, one of H.M. counsel, his fees for his attendance at the Board of Trade twice a week, about H.M. affairs, at the rate of 3 guineas for every attendance. *Minuted:* — "18th Novr. 1721. Order'd. Lrẽ writ." 1 *page.*
27 Nov.	97. Account -	T. Fauquier - -	—	Various particulars as to her late Majesty's tin unsold. Mint Office, 27 Nov. 1721. Another paper on the same subject. 2 *pages.*
2 Dec.	98. Report - -	Comrs. for the debts due to the Army.	The King - -	In favour of allowances being made to certain regiments which served in Portugal in the late war; for the maintenance of mules. *Minuted:*—"Warrt. signd 19th Jan. 1721-2." 1 *page.*
4 Dec.	99. Petition -	Richard Payn, of Wallingford, Berks, gent.	Lords of the Treasury.	For further stay of process to enable him and his fellow securities to discharge the debt of Robert Payne. *Minuted:* — "Warrt. for stay of process for 6 months, is sign'd 19th Decr. 1721." 1 *page.*
5 Dec.	100. Letter - -	Lord Carteret - -	Do. - -	Transmits report from the Comrs. appointed to determine the debts due to the army. The report is not now with the letter, and there is nothing to show to what they related. *Minuted:* — "10th Janry. 1721. To Audrs. Imprest to prepare a S. Manual." ½ *page.*

1721. Vol. CCXXXVIII.

Date.	Description of Document.	From	To	Purport.
9 Dec.	101. Letter - -	Lord Carteret - -	Lords of the Treasury.	For directions to be given to pay Mr. Chirac, jeweller, 500*l.* for a diamond ring by his Majesty's order sent to Spain. *Minuted:* — "15 Decr. 1721. Warrt. sign'd accordingly." 1 *page.*
11 Dec.	102. Do. - -	Comrs. for the debts due to the Army.	Do. - -	For directions to be given to issue to each of them 125*l.* for his allowance. 1 *page.*
11 Dec.	103. Do. - -	Do. - -	Do. - -	For payment of 750*l.* in part of his allowance to Mr. James Moody. 1 *page.*
14 Dec.	104. Do. - -	F. Osborne - -	William Lowndes, Esq.	For arrears of wages (in the Queen's time) due to Mr. Osborne, to whom he was executor. Is at his son Digby's. He says, "if you knew the tenth part this family hath suffered by the Crown you would think they had hard measure. Sr. John Digby was prisoner in the Fleet several years for money borrowed for the King's service in those unhappy times." 1 *page.*
[? About 14 Dec.]	105. Petition -	Robert White, grandson and executor of Robert White, deceased, coroner of the verge, &c.	Lords of the Treasury.	For a warrant for salary due to the late coroner (during King William's time). *Minuted:* — "14th Dec. 1721. Order'd accordingly." 1 *page.*
14 Dec.	106. Letter - -	Charles Carkesse (Customs).	Mr. Lowndes -	Sends copy of a letter from the Collector of Falmouth, announcing that a tide surveyor had given leave to the master of a ship under quarantine to sail; for which he was suspended. The letter referred to. There is also another paper which appears to have been sent by the Collector of Falmouth, relating to the manufacture of copper and brass, and complaining of the importation, under fallacious titles, of metals from abroad. $6\frac{1}{2}$ *pages.*

1721. VOL. CCXXXVIII.

Date.	Description of Document.	From	To	Purport.
11 and 16 Dec.	107. Two letters -	Lord Falmouth	Mr. Lowndes -	On the above quarantine business, also two other letters and an extract from another on the same subject. 6½ *pages.*
18 Dec.	108. Letter - -	Ja. Hilhouse -	Daniel Campbell, Esq., M.P.	Gives a long account of the tobacco trade carried on at Bristol, Scotland, Liverpool, &c. Dated at Bristol. 1 *page.*
[? About 19 Dec.]	109. Do. - -	William Norris -	The Hon. Robert Walpole, Esq.	For a letter in his favour to the Comrs. for Hackney Coach Licences, he being anxious to obtain a licence. *Minuted:* — "19th Decr. 1721. Enquire if Pugh, lately recommended by the Chancr. to the Comrs. for the like favour, be made a coachman." 1 *page.*
19 Dec.	110. Representation	Comrs. for Stamp Duties.	Lords of the Treasury.	Setting forth the hardships arising out of the deduction of 6*d.* in the pound, the difficulty of renewing their contracts with the stationers, &c.: asking for directions. 2 *pages.*
25 Dec.	111. Account -	—	—	"Extraordinary payments made by concordatum from 25 Dec. 1719 to the 25th of December 1721." 3 *pages.*
[? 1721 or 1722.].	112. Petition -	Noah Regnaut -	Lord Lieut. of Ireland (Grafton).	Prays to be put upon the half-pay list again, having been employed by the Crown from 1689.
[? About 1721.]	113. Draft -	—	—	Of part of Act of Parliament entitling persons holding debentures to an annuity at 4 per cent. in lieu thereof. 3 *pages.*

VOL. CCXXXIX., 1722. JANUARY–JUNE.

1. New year's gifts or other annual gratuities for the secretaries and clerks; also for the Lords. Three papers. 5 *pages.*

11 Jan. 2. Draft of minute of 11 Jan. 1721. Commencing: "The Merchants of Bristol, Liverpool, Whitehaven, and Liverpool attend, and Serjeant Pengelly on behalf of those of Whiteh[aven] and Cockerm[outh].

1722. VOL. CCXXXIX.

The Com^rs of Customs are also present. Their petitions [? are read] complaining of great frauds committed by the importation of tobacco from Scotland into several parts of England and sold at a lower rate that [? than] tobacco of equal goodness can be sold by ye English importers of tobacco in those parts, or than could be sold, considering ye charge of land carriage, if ye dutys upon ye sayd tobacco imported were regularly and duely payd, wch fraud it is apprehended arises chiefly upon ye short weighing of ye tobacco for ye payment of ye dutys when imported."

The minute refers also to the Com^rs report thereon and proposed remedies, &c.

The commencement of the above minute is only entered in the *Minute Book*, vol. 23, p. 125, space being left of several pages.

Three other papers relating to this business, entitled :—(1.) "Answers of the merchants of Glasgow to the memoriall of the merchants of Whitehaven, relating to the lessening the duties on tobacco." (2.) "Answers of the merchants of Glasgow to the petition of sundrie merchants of Bristoll, &c." Both with numerous signatures, and both have on the back, "Lect. 11 Jan^ry 1721–2." (3.) Various notes of what was testified by witnesses on the same subject. 15½ *pages*.

15 Jan. 3. The Earl of Rothes to ——. About six years ago, when Lord Townshend was Secretary of State, his Lordship procured for the Earl his Majesty's Commission as Chamberlain of Fife and Strathern, with a yearly salary of 320*l*. There is about 200*l*. more of the few duties payable to the Crown which used to be allowed to his predecessors in that office, and his L^p assured him that he should be in no worse case than they. Had memorialized the Treasury for a discharge of that small surplus. There is also a small balance due by him to the Exchequer as Sheriff Principal of Fife and Aberdeenshire, for which he asks a discharge. It bears a very small portion to the expense he laid out on the country for his Majesty's service during the Rebellion. Leslie, Jan. 15, 1722. [*i.e.* 1721–2.]

Minuted:—"24th Jan. 1721–2. Ordered." 2 *pages*.

23 Jan. 4. "A particular of the causes now under prosecution with the states thereof." Signed:—"A. Cracherode, 23° Jan^rii 1721." 9 *pages*.

25 Jan. 5. Four memorials from the South Sea Company to the Lords of the Treasury for certain stock to be created, for allowances to be made to the Company, &c. 4 *pages*.

26 Jan. 6. "Representation of the Deputy Receivers General of the Post Office relating to the deduction of 6^d per lb." Setting out various items of expense on which they press for a remittance of the tax. Jan. 26, 1721.

Minuted:—"26th June 1722. The articles marked to be excepted, those not marked are to be paid and placed to the account of incid^ts.

1722. VOL. CCXXXIX.

Again:—"26 July 1722. The pencons charged on the Post Office before his Ma^ts Accession to the Crown to be excepted. Warr^t signd 8th Augt 1722." 2 *pages*.

26 Jan. 7. Report of the Com^rs of the Navy to Mr Lowndes, on the petition of the Com^rs of the Navy. By an Act of 7 & 8 Will. III. the Navy board was directed to buy English, in preference to foreign made sail cloth, and to allow the makers 2^d a yard above what would be paid for foreign. The act expired in 1702, since which time very great improvements have been made therein; so that it is in all respects equal, if not superior, to the best foreign, and no foreign cloth is bought. As to the encouragement to be given to the manufacturers, they submit that to their Lordships. 26 Jan. 1721.

The report is written on the back of the petition.

Minuted:—"16th Feb. 1721–2. My Lords think they should apply to parl^t for such reward as the house shall think fit." 2 *pages*.

29 Jan. 8. Com^rs of Ordnance to the Lords of the Treasury. A declaration of ejectment having been delivered by the Trustees of Sir John Morden's charity, in order to recover possession of some lands belonging to the Armoury Mills, that are under the care of the Com^rs, they desire their Lordships will order the Auditor of the county of Kent, and the surveyor of the King's lands, to search for the title deeds and surveys of all lands that now do, or formerly did, belong to the Crown, in the parishes of Greenwich and Lewisham; and that they let the Com^rs' solicitor peruse the same and have copies thereof, to defend the King's title now in dispute; and to make discovery of other lands belonging to the Crown. Jan. 29, 1721.

Minuted:—"31 Jan. 1721–2. To the Surv^r Lands and the Aud^r of Kent to transmit the papers, deeds, and surveys to the Board of Ordnance according to their desire. Lrẽ writ 1 Feb. 1721." 1 *page*.

31 Jan. 9. Report of A. Cracherode to the Lords of the Treasury on the memorial of Col. Adam Williamson, which related to the case of Thomas Davis, a soldier, who had been fined ten pounds, and committed to prison until it was paid, the offence was only giving Mary Ward "a slap in the face." He had already suffered almost a year's imprisonment, and is described as a poor honest fellow. Recommending the remission of the fine and the discharge of the prisoner. 31 Jan. 1721.

Minuted:—"12th March 1721–2. Approved."

The memorial, a certificate, and an affidavit. 4¼ *pages*.

— Jan. 10. William Popple, on behalf of the Lords of Trade, to Horatio Walpole, Esq., asking for the dispatch of presents to the Indians, Mr. Burnett, Governor of H. M. province of New York, has been successful in his negotiations with the five nations of Indians inhabiting the frontiers of the province, but it is absolutely necessary that they should be as well treated as formerly to prevent them joining the French, who are daily endeavouring to gain them over. Whitehall, Jan. 1721–2. 1½ *pages*.

1722. VOL. CCXXXIX.

[? About 1 Feb.] 11. Memorial of Daniel Campble, Esq., to the Lords of the Treasury. Katherine, the wife of John Walkinshaw, of Borrowfield, had petitioned the King to grant the benefit of her husband's forfeiture to some person in trust for her and her children. Memorialist represents that he is a very considerable creditor upon the estate, and if the rents and profits were granted to the petitioner and her children, without restriction, memorialist would be deprived of principal and interest, &c. Prays that he may be heard by counsel, or that the grant may be limited.

Minuted:—"1st Feb. 1721–2. Read. Mr Campbell and Mr Hamilton present." 1½ *pages*.

1 Feb. 12. Report of the Comrs of Customs, Edinburgh, to the Lords of the Treasury, on the petition of Mr Lane Whitehall. Are of opinion that the salaries of most of the inferior officers in Scotland are no ways equal to the trust reposed in them. The Comrs could therefore wish that better rewards were afforded them, because they think that the lowness of the salaries subjects the officers too much to temptation, and nothing is more apparent than that the revenue daily decreases by the corruption of the officers. "Custom House, Edinburgh, 1 February 1721–2."

The petition referred to, and "An account of seizures made and condemned in his Majesties Court of Excheqr at Edinburgh, by Lane Whitehall, commander of the Royal George 'Yatch.'"

Minuted:—"28th June 1722. The Commrs to advise what increase of salary they think Mr Whitehall deserves, and what addition the inferior officers ought to have for their encouragement." 4 *pages*.

3 Feb. 13. "Copy of Mr Robert Sutton's letter to Mr Secry Craggs in favour of Mr Reith," described as "director of the late manufactory at Versailles, a man of good parentage and of a very good character for probity and fair dealing." He was applying for protection and liberty to carry home, free from duty, his effects, which consisted chiefly of work unfinished to a considerable value. Paris, 3 Feb. 1721. 1 *page*.

3 Feb. 14. Report of A. Cracherode to the Lords of the Treasury, on the petition of Elizabeth Hopton, widow, who was induced to sell several small pieces of plate and some other things in a method which was against the laws for suppressing unlawful lotteries, for which she was prosecuted by the Attorney General in the court of Exchequer. Prays to have the proceedings stopped. Is of opinion that the petitioner, if convicted, is utterly unable to pay the fines. 3 Feb. 1721.

The petition referred to. Also warrant to stay the proceedings. Dated 8 Feb. 1721. 3 *pages*.

1722. VOL. CCXXXIX.

[About 8 Feb.] 15. Memorial of Col. Charles Lanoe to the Lords of the Treasury; asking for the grant of a "letter" to the Lord Lieut. of Ireland, as the Irish Government would not receive a warrant (copy annexed) which memorialist had, authorising him to reserve the clothing then ready till the year 1722, whereby the off reckonings would be saved to be employed in furnishing the arms and accoutrements wanting.

Minuted:—"8 Feb. 1721–2. Prepare a warr^t according to the prayer of the petition."

Copy of the warrant. 2 *pages.*

10 Feb. 16. Report of A. Cracherode to the Lords of the Treasury, on petition of Elizabeth Askew, who had been fined 20 marks, and had ever since lain in the common side of Newgate. The sheriffs of London would have discharged her if the fine had belonged to them, "but the fact being in Middlesex, it belonged to his Majesty." She was convicted of a misdemeanour and fined 20 marks, and ordered to stand upon the pillory for an hour with a paper fixed upon her head denoting her offence, and to be kept in gaol until she should pay the fine. She has stood in the pillory, and has suffered eight months' imprisonment, and is utterly unable to pay the fine: recommending her discharge.

Minuted:—"12th March 1721–2. Ordered."

The petition, letter from George Caswell to William Billers, Esq., an order for her discharge, also a copy of her sentence (Latin). 3 *pages and* 2 *halves.*

12 Feb. 17. Certificate signed "Halifax" of the payment out of "Loans on Coals," 7,936*l.* 13*s.* There remained 15,063*l.* 7*s.* to be paid to John Leacroft, Esq., for purchase of lands, &c. and building new churches. Exchequer, 12 Feb. 1721. 1 *page.*

[? About 12 Feb.] 18. Resolutions of the House of Commons of 13 Oct. 1721, on the petition of the Hon. Richard Stewart and Thomas Burgh, Esquires, on behalf of themselves and others concerned in the colliery of Ballycastle in the county of Antrim (Ireland). The principal resolution is "that it is the opinion of this committee that the petitioners have fully proved the allegations of their petition, have merited the reward of a thousand pounds in their petition mentioned, and such further encouragement as this Honble House shall think fit." The House was further of opinion that the petitioners would deserve a further sum of 1,000*l.* when they should have landed in the port of Dublin 5,000 tons of coals taken out of the colliery.

Minuted:—"Warr^t sign^d 12 Feb. 1721–2."

Also the petition. 3 *pages.*

[? About 12 Feb.] 19. Resolution of the House of Commons of 25 Oct. 1721, on the petition of Stephen Costilloe, Gent., in favour of addressing the Lord Lieut. of Ireland, that he would lay before his Majesty the desire of the House that his Majesty would order 5,000*l.* to be given to the petitioner for the many services performed by him to the public. The petitioner had been for thirteen years successively

1722. VOL. CCXXXIX.

employed in making a "survey and estimate" of the most considerable rivers of Ireland, in order to a navigable communication from the midland country to the principal sea ports, and from one port to another throughout the kingdom.

Minuted:—"Warr[t] sign'd 12th Feb. 1721–2. 2 *pages*.

13 Feb. 20. John Plumptre (Board of Ordnance) to the Lords of the Treasury. Asking for a reconsideration of the Memorial of the Board of Ordnance, in which they had applied for 65,359*l*. 18*s*. 10*d*., and for an issue to be made to them out of the supplies granted for the year 1722. 13 Feb. 1721–2. 1½ *pages*.

16 Feb. 21. Memorial of the Royal Academy of Music to the Lords of the Treasury. The King having ordered 1,000*l*. per ann. for seven years, to be paid out of the Bounty Office, to the Royal Academy, they pray for a warrant for payment of 500*l*. Opera House in the Hay Market. 16 Feb. 1721–22. 1 *page*.

16 Feb. 22. Representation of Walter Stubbs on behalf of Sir Jonathan Cope, Bart., to the Lords of the Treasury. Petitioner is entitled to a perpetual rent of 274*l*. per ann., payable to him for the Custom House, London. Finds the same is charged with the tax of 3*s*. in the pound under the Land Tax Act, and with 6*d*. in the pound under the late Act. Is advised that he ought not to be so charged under the terms (there given) of the deeds relating to the property in question. 16 Feb. 1721.

Minuted:—"26th June 1722. The 6[d] ꝑ lb. to be stoppd, but to be repayd and placed to the head of incid[ts]." 1 *page*.

25 Feb. 23. Memorial of Ch. Wither, Esq., Surveyor of H.M. Woods, &c., to the Lords of the Treasury. Finds he must repeat what he had already stated, viz., the forest [of Dean] contains 23,600 acres of land; that 11,000 acres of the best woodland of the forest were enclosed pursuant to Stat. 20 Charles II. These enclosures were to remain in severalty in the possession of the Crown for ever, and to be reputed a nursery for wood and timber only, for the future benefit of the kingdom. For several years after the enclosures were made, great care was taken in preserving them, insomuch that they produced a considerable annual revenue, "but of late years they have been all slighted and thrown common," and when any part has been felled it has not been fenced and secured from cattle, so that the spring thereof has been cropped and spoiled. The soil of the forest of Dean is naturally so kind for wood and timber that the enclosures might easily be restored to a flourishing condition by being cut in orderly and reasonable proportions, and kept carefully fenced from the injuries of cattle: proposes an annual warrant for cutting and fencing. "Hall, Feb. 25th, 1721–2." 2½ *pages*.

26 Feb. 24. Report of the [Auditor of Plantations] to the Lords of the Treasury, on the petition of George Newport, of London, merchant, in behalf of Joshua Byrch and other merchants at Barbadoes, late owners of the ship "Conrade," of Barbadoes, which was taken by

1722. VOL. CCXXXIX.

pirates, and, together with the cargo, by them given to Capt. Thomas Hill, who delivered the same up at Barbadoes as piratical effects. The petitioner prayed that the produce of that portion which was sold might be given up. Finds that the ship and cargo cost 6,500*l.* (Barbadoes money). Specifies the owners. There were on board "160 negroes, besides many other goods." Gives other particulars. The petitioners are justly entitled to receive the produce of the ship. London, 26 Feb. 1721.

Also the petition. 5 *pages.*

[? About 3 March.] 25. Memorial of the Com^rs and Trustees appointed for Forfeited Estates in England and elsewhere, except Scotland, to the Lords of the Treasury. Besides a considerable part of the 200,737*l.* 14*s.* 9¼*d.*, applied by their L^ps directions, a great part of the expense of executing the trusts reposed in the Com^rs for Scotland, has been borne out of the produce of the Estates in England. There remains due to memorialists from the York Buildings Company 31,526*l.* 14*s.* 8¾*d.* for principal and interest, part of the purchase money for the late Lord Widdrington's estate in Northumberland, which is not yet paid into the Exchequer: pray that the 23,000*l.* issued to the Com^rs in Scotland may be replaced out of the forfeited estates in Scotland; and that directions may be given for the money due from the York Buildings Company to be forthwith paid into the Exchequer.

Minuted:—"3^d March 1721–2. Send a copie of this mem^ll to the York Build^s Company. Write to the Com^rs for Scotl. to send my Lords an account of what money arisen from sale of forfeited estates, receipts of rents, fines, &c. in England, has been issued to them or their inferior officers for sala[ries] or incid^ts; and that they send my Lords an exact state of what money is to be expected from the estates remaining unsold in Scotl. either arrears of rents or purchase money unpaid."

Lre signed 6th Mar. 1721. 2 *pages.*

4 Mar. 26. Order in Council on a representation from the principal officers of H.M. Ordnance relating to the changing the time prefixed by the instructions for the Treasurer of the Ordnance to make up his accounts, the same having been found to be inconvenient: referring the matter to the Lords of the Treasury for their opinion. 4 Mar. 1721.

Minuted:—"12th March 1721–2. Prepare a draught of a rep^t to the King in Council upon this reference agreeing to it.

30th March 1722. Rep^t read, approved of and sign'd."

[The report is not now with the above, but the representation and instructions above referred to are enclosed.] 5 *pages.*

[? About 5 March.] 27. Memorial of the Lords and other Commissioners for the affairs of Chelsea Hospital, to the Lords of the Treasury. Mr Alexander Inglis, surgeon to the Hospital, had represented to them that Dr Thomas Rentone had found out a means for curing ruptures, hitherto unknown, and ruptures are very common among pensioners, especially the cavalry. The Com^rs think it much for the advantage

1722. VOL. CCXXXIX.

of the pensioners to encourage the doctor, but no additional salary can be made without his Majesty's or their Lordships' consent. The Com[rs] desire their L[ps]' warrant for such an increase of salary to the doctor as they think fit.

Minuted:—"5th March 1721–2. Prepare a warr[t] with the allowance of 50[li] p ann. out of the money voted for Chelsea Hospital." 1 *page*.

6 March. 28. Lord Townshend to the Lords of the Treasury. John Mitchell having apprehended Charles M'Caw, one of those principally concerned in the riot in Play House Passage, Drury Lane, in December last, their Lordships are to order that he be paid the reward of 50*l.* as advertised in the Gazette of the 6th of last month. 6 March 1721–2.

Minuted:—"12th March 1721–2. Order'd."

A certificate and the Gazette relating thereto. 4 *pages*.

[? About 10 March.] 29. A memorial detailing the services rendered by Edward Harley, Esq., Auditor of H.M. Imprests, to the Lords of the Treasury, including the examination of the account of Col. Clement Neville, as paymaster of the prisoners in British pay, which were taken at the action of Brihuega in Spain. The account consisted of payments to officers and privates of the British troops, and the Imperial, Spanish, Portuguese, and Palatine troops in British pay that were prisoners: prays for consideration of his services. The employment was to the 10th of March 1721–22.

Representation of the nature of the services performed by the Auditor in preparing accounts, making searches for papers and copies of vouchers for the Com[rs] of the debts of the army from the year 1715, viz., for six years and a half.

Also a schedule of the salary of clerks and other disbursements about the same business. 8½ *pages*.

10 March. 30. Lord Lieut. of Ireland (Grafton) to the Lords of the Treasury. The fees of the licences for exporting wool from Ireland to Great Britain having fallen short of the annual income of 4,000*l.*, whereby his revenue as Lieutenant and Governor General was much impaired, prays that he may have a warrant for 1,429*l.* 10*s.* (the amount of the deficiency) out of the revenue of Ireland, as had been allowed to preceding Lords Lieutenant. Bond Street, 10 March 1721–2. 1½ *pages*.

[About 12 March.] 31. Memorial of the R[t] Hon. John, Lord Ballenden, Baron of Broughton [? to the King]. Memorialist is possessed of the post of Usher of the Exchequer in Scotland, which before the Union was a post of honour and considerable profit, insomuch that his Deputy Usher has now settled on him 200*l.* per ann. on the establishment in Scotland: prays that his losses may be compensated by the establishment of such a heritable salary upon his office of Usher of the Exchequer, as his Majesty shall think fitting.

Referred to the Lords of the Treasury, 12 March 1721–2. 1¼ *pages*.

1722. Vol. CCXXXIX.

[? About 12 March.] 32. Report of Thomas Jett, Esq., auditor, to the Lords of the Treasury, on the case of Elizabeth Smart and other almswomen in his Majesty's almshouses in Lady Alley in St. Margaret's, Westminster; setting forth that their houses were ready to fall for want of repair. Finds they are most hazardous for any one to dwell in, and to pull them down and rebuild them will cost 139*l.* 11*s.* 7*d.*, which might be defrayed by the Receiver General of the land revenue for the county of Middlesex.

At the foot is a warrant for the pulling down and rebuilding of the same.

Also the "case" and an estimate.

Minuted:—"12th March 1721–2. Agree to, taking care the charge do not exceed the estimate." 3 *pages.*

13 March. 33. Report of the same, to the same, on the memorial of the Right Hon. George, Lord Newburgh, praying their Lps' warrant for a new patent of the offices of steward and keeper of the Courts Leet and View of Frank Pledge, within the manor and lordship of Sheen *alias* Richmond, in the county of Surrey. If it were granted, it should be under covenant to account before the auditor in some reasonable time, for the whole time that he hath been steward thereof, and once a year for the time to come, &c. Mar. 13th 1721.

Minuted:—"16th March 1721–2. My Lords will consider further of this."

Again:—"13 7br. 1722. My Lords agree to this report. The acco[unt] for the time past to be rendred in one year's time or the patent to be void. See how the last patent of ye stewardship past."

The memorial referred to. 2 *pages.*

14 Mar. 34. Report of Sir Isaac Newton to the Lords of the Treasury, on the bill of Mr James Girard for engraving seals. Certifies that the work is good and the prices reasonable, and that the seals are of the weight expressed in the bill. Mint Office, 14 March 1721.

Minuted:—"25th June 22. Agreed to."

The bill and a petition of James Girard.

The bill describes the several seals and their inscriptions. 4½ *pages.*

[? About 24 March.] 35. Petition of Lieut. Edward Scattergood, of the Hon. Col. John Cholmley's regiment of foot, to the King. Petitioner commanded a detachment of forces sent to Cromarty to cause quarantine to be performed by ships coming from infected places abroad. A ship came into the Road of Cromarty from the Bay of Biscay with wine and brandy, a considerable portion of the cargo was unladen, and an officer of customs seized part of the same in plain contradiction of the proclamation, and suffered the men to escape to the danger of the plague being brought in. By the sheriff's direction petitioner seized the ship and the goods as a legal forfeiture. The Custom House officers notwithstanding lay claim to the seizure: asks for directions in relation thereto.

Referred to the Lords of the Treasury on 24 Mar. 1721. 1 *page.*

VOL. CCXXXIX.

1722.

[? About 29 March.] 36. Petition of Richard Osgood, statuary to the Lords of the Treasury. Was employed by the Office of Works to model and cast in hard mettle, two large sea horses, and two large tritons, to spout the water in the great bason or fountain in Bushey Park, at Hampton Court, the bills for which were entered and passed for 180*l*. The figures were set up and finished eight or nine months after the King's Accession to play the water against the King's coming to Hampton Court, but the bills remain unpaid to this day.

Minuted:—"29th March 1722. To be paid 180li." 1 *page*.

4 April. 37. The Governor of St Christopher's (Jo. Hart) to Horatio Walpole Esq. Being obliged to remain at Antigua until he had executed the King's commands, has not sooner answered the Instructions of the Lords of the Treasury; but has lost no time in gaining the best information on them, which he has communicated in an enclosure. Will only add to what he has said in relation to his encouraging and countenancing the Receiver of the Casual Revenue and the Deputy Auditor. As these officers are not personally known to him (Mr Walpole), it may not be improper that he should be better acquainted with their characters. Col. Crooke, receiver of the casual revenue, is a very honest man, of good substance, in great esteem in these parts, is Speaker of the Assembly of St Christopher's, in which station he has done the writer good service, and will answer the trust reposed in him. Mr Jones, the Deputy Auditor, is an old but active man, of very litigious and peevish disposition, busy in his nature, therefore equal to the employment he has. He (the Governor) will make proper use of his talents to do justice to, and promote the revenue. There are very large demands made on the estates of his predecessors, Codrington, Parkes, Douglass, and Hamilton, which could not be recovered but in the Court of Exchequer: but must say, however their estates may suffer, the casual revenue was formerly esteemed as a perquisite of this Government, and if it were not for the provision that has been made for him (the Governor), the Government would not be worth 200*l*. more than the salary paid out of the 4½ per cent. Has mentioned the trade with the Dutch at Eustatia, as a great cause of the decrease of the duty of 4½ per cent., but besides this, these Islands have been almost reduced to famine for want of rain for these four years; since his arrival, however, they have had seasonable weather so they may expect that account to amount to as much as it has done in three years past, provided there be ships sufficient to carry the sugars to Great Britain. There is a most pernicious and unlawful trade carried on between these Islands and the French Islands, which could not [otherwise] be supplied with provisions, materials for shipbuilding, horses, and sugar works. By our indiscretion the French are grown so formidable, "that in case of a war, it will be no vast difficulty to destroy these Colonies." Our purchasing sugars from the French increases our duties, employs our ships, and has other advantages; but submits whether a present conveniency shall outweigh the strong probability of a future ruin. This trade could not be carried on without the conni-

1722. VOL. CCXXXIX.

vance of the Custom House officers, who are reputed to be deeply concerned in it themselves. Has produced his Majesty's instructions to them prohibiting that trade, and has told them in plain terms what they may expect from him, if they persist or permit it in others. Suggests a reprimand from the Treasury or Com^rs^ of Customs. Must do Mr Man the justice to say he is very exact in his duty, and he (the Governor) has not heard that he is concerned in trade, but is in the esteem of all men. Has given their L^ps^ general information of the French lands, but in addition finds his predecessors, especially Messrs. Douglass and Hamilton, have given themselves grants of very large tracts of land, and have also made a very partial distribution to such as were their favourites, or to those that gave them most for such grants, without making any provision for the poor inhabitants that were before settled upon the lands. By these means many of them have left this island, and others, since his coming, have made such crying complaints of their oppressions by the possessors of these great tracts, as not only moves his compassion, but gives him an alarm that in case of a war with the French, this dis-peopled Colony would become an easy prey to our formidable neighbours of that nation in the Islands of Martinique and Guadaloupe. It is high time that these lands were disposed of, for the present possessors have paid no acknowledgment to the Crown for them, and think it very hard that they should not be indulged as tenants at will for ever, though they have already grown very wealthy by the cultivation of those lands. Many of the present possessors think they have a just claim to his Majesty's bounty for grants for their services, tho' in his sentiments they are amply rewarded by so long free enjoyment of their grants. The list enclosed of the present possessors, showing the number of acres held of the French lands, was taken by a surveyor appointed by Mr Hamilton, but he (the Governor) has good reason to think it is not a just return, and that a re-survey is wanting to do the public justice. Holds to his former opinion that the French lands should be leased out for a certain term of years, rather than disposed of in fee for ready money: for there are very few purchasers that can make an immediate payment in specie, and the custom of this country is to sell lands for five years' purchase. The reason of so low a purchase is that the expense of settling a plantation is four times more than the real value of the land: the charge of building is excessively high, both of dwelling houses and sugar works. The number of negroes is great which they are obliged to keep upon these lands to make sugar, which is the staple commodity of this Island. Is waiting a few days longer to inform himself further of the condition of these lands, and then intends to publish the Instructions given him by the Lords of the Treasury, and shall give orders to all persons possessed of any of these lands to produce their grants, and so will get a further light into the real value of those lands, in order to form a scheme, either for their speedy disposal by sale or lease, for the benefit of the Crown, that it may no longer lose 8,000*l.* or 10,000*l.* sterling per ann. All the advantage he proposes to himself for his services is the grant of 200 acres (as mentioned in

1722. VOL. CCXXXIX.

his memorial). It is the utmost number that ought to be granted to any one person, if the preservation of this colony in time of war from an enemy be duly considered. Gives reasons for complying with the grant. Does not propose to touch one shilling of the profit accruing from these lands; for by his scheme the money is to be transmitted to the Treasury. Besides the instructions received from the Lords of the Treasury, in relation to Mr Hamilton, has observed his (Mr Walpole's) verbal instructions. Had almost forgotten to let him know that a French war would scarce be more terrible to the inhabitants of this Island, than that any merchant should have the purchasing of these lands in gross, in Great Britain. Is truly of opinion that in a little time it would dispeople the Island, "for the inhabitants must then expect to sit at a rack rent, and be made mere merchandise of." St Christopher's, 4 April 1722.

The following is an abstract of the enclosure above referred to:—

The Governor of St Christopher's (Jo. Hart) to the Lords of the Treasury. On his arrival sent for Clement Crooke, Esq., Receiver of H.M. rents, revenues, &c. in the Leeward Islands, and communicated their Lps orders. Found there were several matters which the Receiver was at a loss to prosecute, and for which there was no remedy but by erecting a Court of Exchequer, which he has done at Antigua. A Court of Exchequer has been long disused in these Islands, but as he has appointed persons of the most liberal education and best fortunes in these parts to preside in it, hopes the revenue will be much increased and many evil practices brought to light. The revenue of 4½ per cent. falls short of what might be expected from the trade of the Leeward Islands. One of the causes of the decrease is the pernicious trade carried on with the Dutch settlement at the Island of Eustatia, within two leagues of St Christopher's. It is a small barren Island belonging to the Dutch West India Company, producing nothing of itself that is merchantable, though from thence that company carries on a vast commerce to the British Islands, by importing there great quantities of East India and other wares, and by sending eight or ten ships of burthen freighted with slaves from Africa, which are disposed of at a rate under what the English can afford them, they having returns not only of the current coin of these Islands, but also their ships are freighted home with sugars and other produce. By this means his Majesty loses much of the duty of 4½ per cent. and the duty of 3*s.* 6*d.* per hundred paid in England for customs there. This is not only a prejudice to our navigation, a great detriment to the Royal African Company and other lawful traders; but also by the avarice and want of judgment in the planters and others, the Hollanders become more and more our rivals in the sugar trade, though of the growth and produce of our own plantations. Will apply all remedies to suppress that unlawful trade. Communicated their Lps orders relating to the demands of the Crown on Walter Hamilton, Esq., late Governor of the Leeward Islands, and required him to render a true and ample account of the casual revenue arising in these Islands, and a state of the money received by him during his government, and to cause the balances to be paid into the Receiver's hands.

1722. VOL. CCXXXIX.

Mr Hamilton answered that he would always obey their Lordships' commands, and would immediately account, and this he is doing. Will transmit the account before Mr Hamilton leaves, which will be in a month. Arrived on the 26th of March at St Christopher's, and has made enquiry into the condition of the French lands surrendered to his Majesty by the treaty of Utrecht, and finds them of considerable value; but no benefit has been made of them as yet to the Crown or the public, and a very unequal and partial distribution has hitherto been made of those lands, which has in no wise corresponded with the intentions of his Majesty for the better peopling of this Island, these lands having been granted gratis for that purpose; whereas the present possessors have had no other view but to make the most of the soil, without adding any considerable improvements on the plantations so granted. On the contrary, they have cut down the fine trees planted in all the roads by the French, which were the produce of four score years. The soil of the French lands is the finest in the West Indies, and produces great quantities of sugar with very little labour and without manuring, and is now most of it under canes; but if the present possessors are permitted to work the land out of heart, it will much impair the value thereof in a few years.

The number of the French acres in the two divisions called Basseterre and Capisterre amounts to 11,161, exclusive of those that are patented under the great seal of Great Britain, as will be seen by the list sent, &c.

There is also one continued tract of mountainous land commonly called the Salt Ponds, as yet unsurveyed, but supposed to contain about 2,000 acres. This land is also given in patents for pasturage, without any benefit or advantage to the Crown; though formerly this tract (when in possession of the French) supported 200 families, who subsisted by making cotton and indigo, and by raising cattle and sheep, which were sold in this and the adjacent islands. Estimates the yield of the 11,161 acres to the revenue at from 8,000*l*. to 10,000*l*. per ann. Intends to remain on the Island until he can procure a more certain account of the real value of these lands, &c., and asks their Lordships to prevent the grant of them until they shall know their true value; for many of the possessors, who are grown wealthy out of the produce of these lands, are mightily alarmed at his enquiry into the value of them. St Christopher's, 4 April 1722.

Minuted:—"17th Augt 1722. My Lords will humbly advise the King not to make any grants of land in this Island till their Lordp̃s are more fully informed, by exact surveys and other informations, of the full value thereof." 14 *pages*.

[? About 6 April.] 38. Petition of Frances Wyndham to the King. King Charles II. in consideration of the good services performed by Sir Francis Wyndham, Bart. (petitioner's father), in being instrumental to his Majesty's preservation after the battle of Worcester, granted him and his heirs male an annuity or pension of 600*l*. per ann. and an annuity of 400*l*. per ann. to Ann Wyndham, his wife. At the

1722. VOL. CCXXXIX.

request of the latter his Majesty, in the 34th year of his reign, accepted a surrender of his letters patent, and granted in lieu thereof, to Rachel and Frances Wyndham (the petitioner), her daughters, an annuity or pension of 200*l.* per ann. each for life. These pensions were in arrear, in 1714, 2,550*l.*, besides 675*l.* more due to the said Rachel (to whom petitioner is executrix) for wages as bedchamber woman to Queen Mary, Consort of King William. Prays an order for payment of the arrears.

Minuted:—"6th April 1722. There is no money provided by parliamt for the debts of K. William, and for the claim upon her late Matie, she will be consider'd in proportion with the rest of Her Maties' creditors."

A similar petition to the Lords of the Treasury. 2 *pages.*

9 April. 39. Certificate of Francis Neale, Deputy Clerk of the Pipe, to the Lords of the Treasury as to claims of the Crown to rent from the Corporation of Dunwich, in the county of Suffolk. Observes that the ancient rent of 65*l.* per ann. being reduced by letters patent of King Charles II. only during pleasure, determined on his death, and that 60*l.* per ann. was due to the Crown from that time to the death of Catherine, late Queen dowager, and from her death the whole rent of 65*l.* became due to the Crown. The Queen died in December 1705. Pipe Office, 9 April 1722. 1 *page.*

11 April. 40. "A particular of the causes now under prosecution, with states thereof," returned by the Treasury Solicitor, "A. Cracherode." 11 April 1722.

Minuted:—"13 April 1722. Read." In the margin there are brief directions in most cases as to what was to be done. 10 *pages.*

[? About 12 April.] 41. Petition of John Sydenham, Agent for his Majesty to inspect into the wreck fishing, by virtue of a grant to Jacob Rowe, Esq., to the Lords of the Treasury. Went on board the "Audery," merchantman bound to the Isle of Mayo. Paid to the Privy Purse 1,840*l.* as his Majesty's part of the treasure. Afterwards went into Sussex and subsequently to the Lizard Point to inspect the fishing for treasure: prays for an allowance.

Minuted:—"12th April 1722. To apply for an allowce for these 2 voyages upon the next successfull expedition." 1 *page.*

12 April. 42. Thomas Woolley, Secretary to the East India Company, apologizing for the non-attendance of the Directors in answer to a summons from the Lords of the Treasury to attend them on the previous Tuesday. The votes for the new election were not brought in till the 4th inst., and it was not till yesterday that a Chairman or Deputy Chairman was appointed. In the absence of the Court or Chairman, no letters to the Court are to be opened. Pray that their Lps will appoint a day for their attendance. East India House, 12 April 1722.

Minuted:—"12th April 1722. The directors or a Committee of them to attend on Thursday next at 12." 1 *page.*

1722. VOL. CCXXXIX.

14 April. 43. Lord Carteret to the Lords of the Treasury. Certain arrears of the royal patrimony in the Island of Minorca were claimed by the Emperor, when the Island was yielded up to the Crown, as well as since. Don Domingo Roca, a Spaniard, demanded these arrears by the Emperor's authority. The King in 1716 allowed Roca to receive the part thereof in the Receiver's hands. He now demanded the remainder. Their Lps were to enquire into the case and report. Sends copy of the letter received by him from Col. Kane, Lieut.-Governor of Minorca, on this subject, and an extract of the late Lord Stanhope's letter to Col. Kane. Whitehall, 14 April 1722.

Minuted:—"16th April 1722. Send copies of these lres to Mr Gascoign, who is to inform my Lords if any of these arrears are collected and paid and whether in his hands." 6 *pages*.

15 April. 44. Report of Mr Christopher Tilson to the Lords of the Treasury "on the proportions to be allowed to the South Sea Company for additional charges of management in respect to the increase of their capital by virtue of the Act 6o Georgii." 15 April 1722.

Accompanied by two accounts. 5 *pages*.

16 April. 45. Order in Council on a report from the Lords of the Committee of the Privy Council, which was made upon a memorial from the Comrs for executing the office of Lord High Admiral. The memorial related to a petition of the seamen who served some years before, in the Mediterranean, under Viscount Torrington, praying to receive their proportions of prizes taken from the Spaniards. The report recommended that they should receive the value of the ships, which were by treaty to be restored to the Spaniards, and the Order in Council directs the Lords of the Treasury to issue the value of the ships, &c. 16 April 1722.

Minuted:—"Warrt signd 18th Ap. 1722.

Also a schedule of the value of the ships, &c. 4 *pages*.

18 April. 46. Report of A. Cracherode to the Lords of the Treasury on a memorial of Richard Rigby, Esq., wherein he set forth that there was a debt of 2,800*l*. due from the estate of Sir Alexander Rigby to Captain Edward Rigby (who had for many years been outlawed). The amount was the penalty of a bond. Represents that Capt. Charles Gibson attended their Lordships and declared that Capt. Rigby, who was outlawed, owed him a sum of money, and that a part of his personal estate (which by his outlawry was vested in the Crown) he was willing to discover, if their Lps would allow him a proportionable reward. Subsequently Mr. Lowndes agreed with Gibson, that the latter should have ⅓ of the money recovered by his discovery. Captain Gibson attended him and discovered to him that Sir Alexander Rigby was indebted to Capt. Rigby 1,400*l*. principal money by bond. The estate of the said Alexander was vested in trustees to pay his debts. Caused a *caveat* to be entered with the trustees giving them notice of the Crown's title, &c. The Attorney General directed an English bill or information to be exhibited in the Exchequer against Richard Rigby, to compel him

1722 Vol. CCXXXIX.

to deliver up the bond, and against the trustees to compel them to pay the debt. Prays directions whether he shall apply to Richard Rigby for the further discovery, or rest upon the prior discovery made by Charles Gibson. 18 April 1722.

The memorial referred to and another memorial from him *minuted*:—"12th June 1722. The memorialist to attend his Mats Attor. Genll to give him full information of this matter & that he prosecute the same at his own expence, when my Lords will move his Maty to allow him one half of what shall be recover'd to the Crown by his means free of charges." 4¼ *pages*.

19 April. 47. Lord Carteret to the Lords of the Treasury. It having been represented to his Majesty that the laws of Jamaica will expire in the year 1724, and the Duke of Portland desiring to be instructed upon that head, before his departure for the Island, the consideration thereof has been referred to the Lords for Trade and Plantations. Their representation and instructions are enclosed and are hereafter described. As the revenue act ought to be settled upon some more certain foot than it seems to be at present, His Majesty thinks that part of the instruction very fit for the consideration of the Lords of the Treasury. The Duke of Portland is empowered by the Instruction, as it now stands, to signify His Majesty's consent to the renewing of the laws of the Island, either making them perpetual or for 21 years, according as the revenue act shall be made perpetual or for that term. The principal condition is, that a revenue be provided, equal to the present; but as it does not appear what the present expenses and contingent charges are, these must be particularly specified. The necessity of affairs in Jamaica requires that the Duke should forthwith repair thither, and in case the state of the revenue there cannot be duly considered by their Lps before his departure, it is his Majesty's instruction that for the present his Grace should only propose this matter to the Council and Assembly, by acquainting them that his Majesty is willing to renew the laws of the Island some time before their expiration; provided they are ready to make a due provision for the expenses of his Majesty's government there, and that his Grace should transmit an account to his Majesty how he finds the Council and Assembly disposed thereupon. Whitehall, 19 April 1722.

Copy of the representation referred to, of the Board of Trade, on the memorial of the Duke of Portland. The laws would expire in the year 1724, and the Duke of Portland asked for the King's Instructions for renewing the same. The laws would have expired in 1703, but her then Majesty gave instructions to the Governor to acquaint the Assembly that, in case they agreed to a new revenue act with a provision for the support of the Government there, she would continue the laws for 21 years more, &c. A new revenue act was thereupon prepared for the term of 21 years, which would expire in 1724; and by the same, the laws of Jamaica were further confirmed during the continuance of that act. Think it desirable to procure a new act of the Assembly. The renewal of the laws is a grace which the people of Jamaica cannot reasonably expect without a suitable return. The Attorney and Solicitor General apprehend that His Majesty's revenue will likewise expire at the same time with the laws; whereas, before the last confirmation, the revenue of the Crown would have subsisted by virtue of one or both of the acts passed in 1683 and 1688, although the laws of Jamaica had expired at the time prefixed for their continuance by King Charles the 2d. Persuaded themselves that the people of Jamaica would be induced, on a renewal thereof, to grant a settled perpetual revenue equal to the present expenses, or at least for a term of 21 years. Advise that the Duke of Portland should be instructed to acquaint the Council and Assembly that his Majesty will continue their laws for a further term upon the above conditions. Whitehall, 28 March 1722.

Also "additional Instruction" to the Duke of Portland in accordance with the above recommendation. 11 *pages and* 2 *lines.*

20 April. 48. Memorial of the Directors of the London Assurance Company to the Lords of the Treasury. Assigned annuity orders and tallies for 38,750*l.* paid in on the Plate Fund, for so much remaining due from the Corporation for their Charter. Have since paid into the Exchequer 30,000*l.* in money, as part of the 38,750*l.* Their Lps in November last ordered an allowance of 1,250*l.* to be made them, for payments in money, in lieu of plate tallies. Are ready to pay the remaining 7,500*l.* and pray their Lps to accept the 1,250*l.* in part payment.

Minuted:—"Aprill ye 23d 1722. The London Assurance Company to pay into ye Exchequer ye remaining 8750 and to take a Tally in discharge of their whole Debt, and ye Lords will direct a warrant for ye 1250 to be payd them pursuant to ye agreement for that purpose."

A duplicate of the above memorial, with the date 20 April 1722 at the foot. 2 *pages.*

[? About 23 April.] 49. Memorial of the Six Clerks of the Court of Chancery to the Lords of the Treasury. On the 4th of Feb. 1718 the two senior Six Clerks were ordered, by the Lords Committee, to whom the matter was referred by the House of Peers, to view the Records of the Court of Chancery, &c., to attend their Lordships, and to give an account of the condition of the Records of that Court, and what conveniency there was at their office for keeping them for the future. It appeared to their Lps, upon examination of the said six clerks, that there were vast quantities of bills, answers, depositions of witnesses and other pleadings from the reign of Charles I., to which it was very difficult to have recourse, being for want of room crowded into very inconvenient places. They had not then received any damage, but lay very much exposed thereto. About six years before that time they were carefully bundled up and put into a regular and proper method and condition to be transmitted to the Tower of London, but the Record rooms there, were not capable of receiving any of them, being already full.

VOL. CCXXXIX.

1722.

Their Lps, being informed of the great difficulties and delays which had for several years obstructed the obtaining of a new room for the reception of these Records, repaired to the Tower of London, and were of opinion that a large room on the east side of the White Tower, adjoining to Cæsar's Chapel, should be allotted for that purpose, and ordered a plan and estimate, which amounted to 350*l.* On 17 April 1719, the report of the Lords Committees being approved of by the House of Peers, an address was presented to his Majesty, desiring that he would give directions thereon. His Majesty replied that he would give proper directions thereupon. As the Records will unavoidably receive damage from their present position, besides the difficulty and almost impossibility of having due recourse to them, and as they daily very much increase, memorialists apply to their Lps to lay the affair before his Majesty to obtain his directions for the issue of the money necessary for the work.

Minuted:—"23 April 1722. See the Rept from ye Board of Works concerning all the rooms for records. Ordnance writ to." 1 *large page.*

24 April. 50. "Report of Joseph Gascoigne Esq. Recr Genl of the Island of Minorca on a demand made by Domingo Roca, of arrears due to his Impl Maty as King of Spain." Spring Garden, 24 April 1722.

Encloses an "Account of moneys due to his Imperial Majesty wch was to be collected by Dn Jos. de Vigo after the English collours were mounted," and a receipt. (Both are copies.) 4 *pages.*

25 April. 51. Certificate of Richard Hays and Humphrey Fowle, Esqres, two of H.M. Justices of the Peace for Sussex, to the Lords of the Treasury, that they had arrested Gibb Jarvis *alias* Tompkin, who was concerned in rescuing Jacob Walter, a notorious smuggler and owler; and that Thomas Jarrett the elder and Thomas Jarrett the younger, both of Rotherfield, and Thomas Marchant, a constable, arrested the said Gibb Jarvis. A reward of 40*l.* was offered in the Gazette on conviction to each person who was concerned in the arrest. The justices hope the reward will be paid. 25 April 1722.

Minuted:—"6th Decr 1723. To Commrs cust. to pay these sums & to place them to the head of incidts." *Again:*—"A wart was signed for this, 23 August last, and is gone to the custos." 1 *page.*

28 April. 52. John King and two other Bristol merchants to William Lowndes, Esq. The good order they obtained of their Lps of the Treasury, in January last, they hoped would, in some measure, have prevented the clandestine trade carried on by the Glasgow men, in reference to the tobacco trade; but, to their great surprise, and the utter ruin of the trade, they find that more has been "put hither" since Michaelmas last than in any one year; and it is sold at such low rates that they can carry on that trade no longer, without ruining themselves. Enclose an account, to be laid before the Lords of the Treasury, of what has been imported from Glasgow since the last account. Have been informed that the order obtained in January has not been put in execution. Bristol, 28 April 1722.

The account referred to. 2 *pages.*

1722. VOL. CCXXXIX.

5 May. 53. Report of R. Powys to the Lords of the Treasury on the prices set down by John Baskett, his Majesty's printer. The charges were for "Fast prayer," inventories of the estates of the late Directors of the South Sea Company, and Plantation laws. 5 May 1722.

Minuted:—"18th May 1722. To be paid p Tallys of Pro." 1 *page*.

5 May. 54. Order in Council on the report from Sir Nathaniel Lloyd, H.M. Advocate General, on the petition of Luke Knott, late master of the ship "West River Merchant," which was taken by pirates in her passage to Virginia in January 1719, and plundered of a considerable value, and after a detention of two days was set at liberty, upon a constrained promise the master made to them, to land eight of their crew at Virginia, and to serve them upon his arrival there as much as lay in his power; they having desired to be discharged from their gang, and having put themselves voluntarily on board his ship. When petitioner arrived in Virginia, he informed the Governor as to the pirates he had brought, who were thereupon tried and convicted, and six of them executed, and petitioner delivered up to the Governor all their effects. These amounted to about 800*l*. Petitioner will be obliged to quit the merchants service, as the pirates threaten to torture him to death if he falls into their hands. Prayed for the reward promised for their apprehension, although not strictly entitled to it, the pirates having voluntarily put themselves on board. Ordered that the petitioner be allowed the reward, but the order is not to be made a precedent. 5 May 1722.

List of the pirates' names and sums for their apprehension.

Minuted:—"19th June 1722. Respited till the powers relating to the disposal of piratical goods are known and adjusted. *Again*:—19th July 1722. Prepare a warr^t to the Govr, Rec^r and all others who have the effects of these men in their hands, to pay to Luke Knott the sum of 230*l*., being after the rate of the reward promised by proclamation; but as this case is different (as p this order in Council) the said 230^li is to be esteemed and accepted as bounty."

Warr^t signd 8th Augt 1722. 3½ *pages*.

8 May. 55. Comm^rs for forfeiture, to the Lords of the Treasury. There have been 1,728 claims entered before them on the estates of the forfeiting persons in England and elsewhere (except Scotland), exclusive of the claims made by the sufferers at Preston. These have all been heard and determined. Have also examined into the truth of the claims entered before them, for losses sustained in the borough and parish of Preston, amounting to 226, and in value to 6,481*l*. 10*s*. 10¾*d*. It appears to them that there is due to the claimants, the sufferers at Preston, 4,680*l*. 7*s*. 6*d*. Send an account of the money due for principal and interest from the York Buildings Company on 25 April last, amounting to 32,217*l*. 5*s*. 1¼*d*. There also remains due from Croft Corles, the remainder of the purchase money due for the estate late of John Leyburne, 425*l*.; and from

Vol. CCXXXIX.

1722.

Robert Stoddart for the remainder of the purchase money due from some lead mines, late the estate of Thomas Foster, 5,360*l.*; making in the whole 38,102*l.* 5*s.* 1¼*d.*; being the whole of the purchase money due from the several purchasers. Essex House, 8 May 1722. 2 *pages.*

9 May. 56. The information and complaint of Robert Armstrong, Esq., Deputy Surveyor of H.M. Woods in America to William Pepperell, Esq., one of H.M. Justices of the Peace for the county of York [America], and several other documents, relating to cutting of woods contrary to the Act of 1710 in the colonies of New Hampshire, Massachusetts Bay, Province of Maine, &c. The information charges Benjamin Libby and William Lord, both of Barwick, in the co. of York, in the province of Maine, yeomen, with cutting 43 pine trees of 24 inches diameter and above, for masts and bowsprits. They were tried and acquitted, but it did not appear that the trees mentioned were the same as those named in the complaint. The information prays that Libby and Lord may appear before the justices of the peace, to answer in the premises, and that witnesses named may be summoned thereon. The last dated of the documents is 9 May 1722. 8¼ *pages.*

10 May. 57. Report of the Com[rs] of Trade to the Lords of the Treasury on the waste in his Majesty's woods on the continent of America. It is apprehended that the Act of last session, giving further encouragement for the importation of naval stores, &c., duty free, will, unless prevented, induce the inhabitants in several provinces to cut down and convert into lumber such of H.M. woods as may be fit for the Royal Navy. Remind their L[ps] of the necessity of sending a proper person as Surveyor General of Woods in America (the present Surveyor residing in England) and the Deputy is a Custom House Officer residing in New Hampshire, whose duty cannot admit of his visiting the woods in other parts. Whitehall, 10 May 1722.

Minuted:—"18th May 1722. To be read on Tuesday morn., & Mr. Bridger to attend."

With it is a petition from John Bridger, late Surveyor of the Woods in America, for restoration to his former employment of Surveyor of Woods. 3 *pages.*

11 May. 58. Report of A. Cracherode to the Lords of the Treasury. On the petition of Richard Johnson, who had lent 800*l.* to Elizabeth Somner, widow, and Henry Somner, Esq., her son, secured by mortgages of a close of pasture called Putlowe Close, in Fleet Marston, in the co. of Bucks, containing 135 acres; and since the lending the money, Elizabeth and Henry Somner had sold the close to Richard Hampden, Esq., who had since conveyed it, or was then conveying it, to some persons in trust to satisfy a debt due to his Majesty. There is 80*l.* due to the petitioner for two years' interest. Certifies that the conveyance had been made to Hampden, the consideration being 6,360*l.*, and that the mortgage is prior to Mr. Hampden's purchase, and is a legal incumbrance. It ought to

1722. VOL. CCXXXIX.

be discharged out of moneys raised by sale of the estate, and the interest ought to be paid out of the rents, &c. 11 May 1722.

Minuted:—"14th June 1722. Approved and directions are to be given accordingly." *Again*:—"24 July 1723. Mr Hampden will order the tenant to pay the interest already become due."

The petition. 3 *pages*.

16 May. 59. James Payzant to the Rt Hon. Robert Walpole, Esq. In relation to a bill of 1,046*l*. 10*s*. 3*d*. drawn upon him by Mons. St Saphorin, and payable to the Lord Forbes. 16 May 1722.

Minuted:—"16th May. 1,046l 10s 3d with ye fees added to James Payzant to answer a bill of excha drawn by St Saphorin for money expended by him at Vienna for his Mats special service."

"Warrt signd 19th May 1722." 1 *page*.

[? About 18 May.] 60. "Accot of the charges on His Majesty's birth day distributed by his Maties almoner for Scotland for 1721 & 1722."

Minuted:—"18th May 1722. Prepare a warrt. Wt signd." 1 *page*.

21 May. 61. Lord Carteret to the Lords of the Treasury. The Dutch, Envoy having represented that the ship "St Peter" of Amsterdam when stranded on the 14th of Nov. last, near Penzance, was plundered and burnt by the people there, his Lordship, by the King's command, wrote to the Comrs of Customs to direct their officers in those parts to give the best information they could thereon, in order that justice might be done. The Comrs in answer, have acquainted him, that the Collector of Penzance had informed them of the whole state of the matter, and that they (the Comrs) had transmitted to their Lps the several letters, affidavits, &c. relating thereto. Transmits extract of the letter from the Comrs. His Majesty directs the Comrs to give orders thereon, and his Lordship desires them to acquaint him therewith, that he may make a proper answer to the Dutch minister. Whitehall, 21 May 1722.

The extract referred to. 3½ *pages*.

21 May. 62. The same to the same. Transmits for consideration a representation from the Lords of the Admiralty on the necessity of appointing some experienced person to inspect and preserve H.M. woods in New England, and to advise and assist in the further growth and improvement of naval stores in those parts; together with a memorial of Mr Bridger, who was many years surveyor of those woods, and copies of two letters from the Navy Board. 21 May 1722.

The documents referred to are with it (except Mr Bridger's memorial) and one of the letters is in duplicate, and there is a covering letter from Mr Burchett. 13 *pages*.

23 May. 63. "An accompt of the debt due and owing on the pensions payable in the office of Walter Chetwynd, Esq., from Midsummer 1721 to Lady day 1722." 23 May 1722. 6 *pages*.

Vol. CCXXXIX.

1722.
25 May. 64. "A. Cracherode's particular of causes now under prosecution, with states thereof." 25° Maij 1722.

Minuted on the back:—"Read. Directions are set on the sides of each leaf."

Among the causes for prosecution are: (1) for a seditious libel entitled the Freeholder's Journal; (2) for another seditious libel entitled "A Supplement to the Freeholders' Journal"; (3) A seditious libel entitled "An Historical Account of the advantages that have accrued to England by the predecessors in the illustrious House of Hanover;" (4) for a seditious libel entitled "The Saturday's Post or Weekly Journal," and (5) a most villainous and traitorous libel entitled "The second part of the Historical Account of the advantages that have accru'd to England by the Succession in the illustrious House of Hanover." 6½ *pages.*

[? About 26 May.] 65. Memorial of Captain William Clarke, first Adjutant to his Majesty's third Regiment of Foot Guards, to the Lords of the Treasury. Had expended 250*l.* in making a house habitable, the same being necessary for him to reside in to take charge of certain companies. His Majesty had lately granted the use thereof for a place of public worship to his subjects of Hanover attending his royal person, and memorialist was commanded to leave. Presumes it is not his Majesty's intention that memorialist should entirely leave the Savoy, and that such a great number of soldiers should be left without control of a commissioned officer; when in all H.M. garrisons in Great Britain there are several houses allotted to officers. Upon a late application to their L^ps their pleasure was that he "should pitch upon another convenient habitation" in the Savoy, in the room of that from which he is to remove. Has viewed a house in the Strand next to the Quakers' meeting, which is held by one Mrs Briggins during pleasure; prays that the house may be granted to him, and that it may be made tenantable, or for [another held] by one Miller fronting the Thames; and that the 250*l.* may be reimbursed to him.

Minuted:—"26th May 1722. 250^li to be paid to him by the paym^r workes, to reimburse him the like sum laid out in fitting up a lodging in the Savoy, lately delivered up to the Lutheran Minister." "Lrē sign'd." 1 *page (gnawed by vermin).*

30 May. 66. Memorial of Walter Lord Chetwynd, Ranger of St James's Park, to the Lords of the Treasury. Has pressed on the works at St James's Park with all possible despatch, and finds that the 1,200*l.* issued to the Paymaster of the works is quite expended. Prays for directions to be given for 1,000*l.* more to be paid to the Paymaster, which he hopes will be sufficient to build the lodges, the Island Keeper's house, and "grainary," and to dig a reservoir on the upper side of the park, to which pipes may be laid to serve St James's house and Whitehall with water, in case of fire or other necessary uses; and also will be a means of filling up the great gravel-pit lately dug for the service of the park.

Minuted:—"5th June 1722. Orderd." 1 *page.*

VOL. CCXXXIX.

1722.
30 May. 67. Memorial of Sir John Vanbrugh, Knt., Surveyor of H.M. gardens and waters. As the great engine lately erected at Windsor is of a power to raise more water than the old pipe that goes up to the Castle will receive without often bursting and straining the engine, it seems absolutely necessary to take up the present pipe and to place one of larger bore in the room of it, by which means the Castle will be plentifully supplied with water for the future. Whitehall, May 30, 1722. 1 *page.*

? [About 31 May.] 68. Petition of Richard Oglethorp, late Deputy Provost Marshal of the Island of Antigua and Messenger to the Council there, to the Lords of the Treasury. Was ordered by the Government to repair to Great Britain as the most material witness to the barbarous murder of Col. Parke, Governor of the Leeward Carribbee Islands, and waited [in England] three years and eleven months, for which the government ordered him to be paid 5*s.* a day, notwithstanding which he had received but for two years and odd months, and 100*l.* for his voyage. Contracted more debts than the money would pay. Petitioner could not return without danger to his life from the parties concerned in the murder. Mr Cracherode had reported on his case, and whilst he (petitioner) was waiting for their Lordships' order thereon he was arrested for debt, and has been confined for 15 months in a starving condition. Prays further payment.

Minuted:—"31 May 1722. My Lords are of opinion nothing is due." 1 *page.*

[Before June.] 69. Petition of John Duke of Montagu to the Lords of the Treasury. By petition to his Majesty the duke has set forth that the Islands of St Lucia and St Vincent have not hitherto been settled, and if they were settled, it might be an advantage to Great Britain. This would be expensive, but petitioner was willing to undertake it at his own cost, and prayed for the grant of the Islands to him and his heirs, and to be appointed Governor. The Board of Trade, to whom the matter was referred, reported that these two Islands were at present comprehended in the Commission of the Governor of Barbadoes, but as neither of them have been settled they produce no revenue to the Crown. They thought that it would undoubtedly be for his Majesty's service that they should be settled and planted, and so much the rather because the French had heretofore made several attempts to possess them. Petitioner says, if subjected to the restrictions proposed, it will render the whole undertaking impracticable by the little encouragement people will have to settle in the Islands, and the revenue will be less than without the restrictions. Prays for an absolute grant from his Majesty, the Government being absolutely reserved to his Majesty. The petitioner will be obliged to send over 500 white people at the least, to make a settlement in the Island of St Lucia, within three years, and to settle one-fourth part of the Island within thirteen years, one other fourth in ten years more. Petitioner will be answerable for a quitrent at the rate of 2*s.* 6*d.* for every hundred acres of land as leased out. [There are also some other provisions.] And after ten years the grantees shall be obliged to pay to his Majesty the duty of 4½ per cent. as in Barbadoes and the Leeward Charibbee Islands. But inasmuch as the Island of St Vincent is at present possessed by Indians and Negro slaves, who have made their escape thither from the neighbouring Islands, and are armed and very numerous, petitioner hopes to be indulged for a further time for the settling thereof, &c.

[The Duke of Montague obtained a grant of these Islands on June 22, 1722.] 4 *pages.*

70. Copy or draft of Minutes of the Treasury Board for 1 June 1722. 1½ *pages.*

4 June. 71. Report of Charles Wither, Esq., Surveyor General of H.M. woods, to the Lords of the Treasury on the memorial of Brigadier Munden, Out Ranger of H.M. forest of Windsor "in the Baliwic of Surrey," praying them to grant to him the same power of felling the three little groves called Fan Grove, Knowl Grove, and Stubbridge, lying in his bailiwick as was granted to his predecessor Mr Onslow. Advising that they should be felled and better fenced. June 4th, 1722.

Also the memorial.

Minuted:—"Brig^r Munden is to perform this work according to the advice of the Surv^r in this report." 2 *pages.*

4 June. 72. Lord Townshend to the Lords of the Treasury. Sends papers enclosed relating to a dispute between Major Bealing and Mr Paunceforth, in order that their L^ps might give such directions as would prevent persons in his Majesty's service in the revenue from permitting their servants to contribute, by their behaviour, to the stirring up of riots and seditions, and to affront the civil magistrates in the execution of their office. June 4, 1722.

Three enclosures. The first is a copy of a letter signed Marmaduke Bealing, to Edwd Pauncefort, Esq., stating that two servants of the family had appeared in the town (Highgate) with cockades of green boughs, intermixed with white roses (the mark of those disaffected to his Majesty's Government). He thought it his duty to call them to account, and commanded them to surrender, and be examined, and further dealt with for their insolent offence; but the Lady Moyer's butler not only refused to do so, but had the impudence to lift up his stick at the writer, as he attempted to seize him; upon which he "stroke him one blow" with his cane when both ran away. Upon the grant of a warrant to apprehend them, the rest of the family opposed the constable in the execution of his duty, &c. Insists upon their being delivered to the constable directly. May 31, 1722. (2.) Mr Pauncefort's letter in reply excusing the servants on the plea that they had done what every body in the town had done. Would wait upon the Lord Chief Justice and see wherein the transgression lay. If they had done wrong, would make them answer for it. Highgate, May 31, 1722. (3.) The examination of the constable. 4¼ *pages.*

1722. Vol. CCXXXIX.

[? About 5 June.] 73. Petition to the Lords of the Treasury, of the Receivers appointed to take in such of the orders, tickets, affidavits, and affirmations as were not received or taken in by the former Receivers "on the Act 6° Georgii for taking subscriptions to the South Sea Company." Have performed their trusts with great exactness and frugality, and send a specification of their labours. Pray for the issue of 139*l.* 10*s.* to their Secretary to pay him and three clerks, and for consideration of themselves (being six in number) for twelve months.

Minuted:—"5th June 1722. To be paid 150li each for this service & 139li 10s to be paid to the Secry, clerks, &ca psuant to this petition."

Also the "Specification" referred to. 2 *pages.*

8 June. 74. Lord Carteret to the Lords of the Treasury. There being great reason to apprehend that the plague has broken out in Barbary, the King of Spain has prohibited all commerce with that country. The King thinks it necessary that the like precautions should be taken with regard to Gibraltar. Inquiry is to be made as to the state of the provision there, and as to whether the contractors have fulfilled their contract. Whitehall, 8 June 1722.

Minuted:—"13th June 1722. Write to the contractor for an exact account of the amount of all the species of provisions delivered by him into the store-houses at Gibraltar, & now remaining there, & that 3 months' provisions, over & above what is now there, may be immediately sent thither."

"Lre sent." 1 *page.*

8 June. 75. Petition of Robert Dalyell, late Earl of Carnwath, to the King. By his attainder, has forfeited all his real and personal estate, and for six years has been destitute of all manner of subsistence, except what he has received from the charity of his nigh relations, who can no longer contribute to his support. Since his enlargement from the Tower has been obliged to contract many debts for the maintenance of himself and family whereby his liberty is rendered precarious, which with his life he owes to his Majesty. Prays relief.

Referred to the Lords of the Treasury.

Minuted:—"26th June 1722. Prepare a S. Manual for 600li bounty. Warrt signd 28th June 1722." 2 *pages, quarto.*

12 June. 76. Memorial of the Surveyor of the woods (Wither) to the Lords of the Treasury. The repairs done about Boldrewood Lodge in the New Forest are not to exceed 491*l.* 17*s.* 6*d.* Memorialist is authorized to pay the same out of moneys from wood sales. There are great numbers of dead and decaying trees in the above forest. Asks that he may raise the money from them, and that he may fell 120 loads of timber to be used about the repairs. June 12, 1722. 1 *page.*

14 June. 77. Lord Carteret to the Lords of the Treasury. It had been represented to the King that Othniel Beale, master of a ship from New

1722. VOL. CCXXXIX.

England was taken in the channel by an Algerine cruizer. The captors took out all the crew from the ship, except the master and a man and boy, and put on board 14 Algerines to take her to Algiers. After prosecuting their voyage for seven days, the master found means of conducting back the ship with the cargo and the Algerines into the river Thames. To encourage the master, his Majesty's pleasure is that their Lps direct 100*l.* to be paid to him as special bounty. Whitehall, June 14, 1722.

Minuted:—"20th June 1722. Prepare a warrt.—"Warrt signd 26th June 1722." 1½ *pages.*

[After 19 June.] 78. The enclosures to a report of Mr Auditor Jett referred to him on 19 June 1722. They consist of (1) a petition signed by the mayor of the town of Glaston, in the co. of Somerset, and a large number of others addressed to the Lords of the Treasury, asking for a warrant to pay for the repairs of certain houses and chapels which have been previously repaired by his Majesty's predecessors; (2) estimate of artificers for their repair; (3) testimonial to the competency of the persons giving the estimate.

The report is not now with it.

The following is the minute outside the papers:—"12th Sept. 1722. My Lords agree to the report. Wt signd 19 Sep. 1722." 3 *pages.*

22 June. 79. "An accot of the moneys paid into the Exchequer, arisen by the late Duke of Ormond's forfeited Estates." Exchequer, 22d June 1722.

On another page of the paper is an epitome of what appear to be various clauses of the Act 7 Geo. [I.] for enabling the Earl of Arran to purchase the late Duke of Ormond's forfeited estate.

Also another paper of about the same date, entitled:—"The claims decreed out of forfeitures unsatisfyed for want of sufficient money in the Exchequer for that purpose." 3 *pages.*

[About 23 June.] 80. Memorial of James Graham, Esq., Judge of the High Court of Admiralty in Scotland, to the King. Before the Union, memorialist had an "appointment" for his salary out of the duties of tonnage, &c. By the Articles of Union this became ineffectual. His Majesty's love of justice has caused suitable settlements to be made on other judges. Hopes he will not altogether disregard the High Court of Admiralty in Scotland. Prays for a suitable salary.

Referred to the Lords of the Treasury, 23 June 1722. 1 *page.*

24 June. 81. "Scotland. Accompt of salarys and incident charges of the Commissioners and Trustees of the forfeited Estates and their officers from 24th March 1721–2 to 24th June 1722 being one quarter."

Minuted:—"14th Decr 1722. Prepare a warrt. Wt signd 19th Decr 1722." 1 *page.*

[? About 25 June.] 82. Petition of Daniel Warford to the Lords of the Treasury. Has, for the last eight years, rented several parcels of land in Essex through which his Majesty hath a road leading to Newmarket,

1722. VOL. CCXXXIX.

called his Majesty's private road. His Majesty was to pay petitioner 20*l.* per ann. for the use of the road. This rent is now eight years in arrear, and the rent of the farm was proportionably raised. Their L^ps^ had ordered that the same should be paid upon his Majesty having a good title; but as petitioner is a tenant for years, and rents of two different persons, Mr Lindsey being one, who refused to grant such a private road to his Majesty, the title cannot be made secure. Prays payment of the arrears and the rent as it shall become due during his term.

Minuted:—"25th June 1722. To Mr Negus & Brig^r^ Watkins." 1 *page*.

26 June. 83. Memorial of the Master Worker (Newton) and the Controller of the Mint (Bladen) to the Lords of the Treasury. The salaries of the Clerks of the Mint which were settled about sixty years ago being insufficient for their maintenance, memorialists pray that they may be augmented by about a quarter. Mint Office, June 26, 1722.

Minuted:—"19th July 1722. Agreed to. Warr^t^ signd 8th Augt 1722." 1 *page*.

27 June. 84. Memorial of A. Cracherode to the Lords of the Treasury, *docketed*:—"A. Cracherode's memorial praying their Lordships' directions whether he must proceed in his Maj^ties^ cause ag^t^ the Bp̃p of Chester at the next Lancaster assizes." 27 June 1722.

The cause was a refusal to institute Mr Samuel Peploe into the wardenship of Manchester College, to which he was presented by his Majesty. The point being whether the degree of Bachelor of Divinity, conferred upon him by the Archbishop of Canterbury, was a sufficient qualification for the wardenship, or whether the degree ought to have been taken at one of the Universities.

Minuted:—"28th June 1722. The Attor. Genl to proceed in the King's name." 2 *pages*.

VOL. CCXL. JULY–DECEMBER.

[About 6 July.] 1. Memorial of Mr Robert Gray, Minister of the Gospel at Brichen, to the King. In the time of Episcopacy the Bishop of Brichen by himself and his chaplain officiated as one of the ministers of the burgh and parish, and after the Revolution another minister was needful and a stipend was settled for him, and Mr Gray and his predecessors possessed the Bishop's house, not having any manse. The burgh and parish plead that they are not bound to furnish another manse, whereby memorialist has been put to much charges in keeping up the Bishop's house, or it would have fallen to the ground. It will take 1,590*l.* 17*s.* Scots money to make it sufficient. Prays for orders for payment of such a sum as will be sufficient to repair the house.

Referred on 6 July 1722 to the Lords of the Treasury. 1 *page*.

VOL. CCXL.

1722.

6 July. 2. Report of Ch. Wither to the Lords of the Treasury, on the representation of two of the verderers of Sherwood Forest, complaining of the method of felling trees there, by the King's sign manual. Has observed the same course in cutting wood there, as in other places, and nothing has been done without the privity of these gentlemen. His deputy waited on them, as well to inform them of his Majesty's pleasure, forbidding the officers of the forest to mark or fell any wood under pretence of fee trees, and allowing them 5*l.* a piece annually in lieu thereof, as to let them know that there were several dead trees in his Majesty's hayes of Birkland and Billhaigh that were neither of use nor ornament to the forest, which were directed to be sold, to raise the arrears to be paid to several forest officers, &c. Approved of what had been done in this respect by his deputy. Would be at a loss to find a cause for their complaint, but that the verderers of Sherwood Forest are very displeased with being forbidden to cut trees by their own authority, as fee trees, and are not satisfied with the King's allowance of 5*l.* a piece annually in lieu thereof, and have endeavoured to obstruct the execution of the sign manual, which they say has deprived them of a privilege, they having commonly made 7*l.* or 8*l.* per ann. of their pretended fee tree, which they might do, when they had the liberty of picking the best trees in the forest. For a further proof of what he has advanced, informs their L^ps^ that Mr Digby, Mr Chappel, and Mr Mollineux, three of the verderers, have, in direct disobedience to the King's will and pleasure, marked and caused their fee trees to be felled, having first refused 5*l.* allowed them in lieu thereof, though tendered by his deputy. And when his deputy marked the trees with the broad arrow for his Majesty's use, according to the directions of the sign manual, the gentlemen declared they would not regard it, but ordered the men to work them up and promised to hold them harmless. Begs directions as to how he is to proceed with the verderers who have acted so directly in contempt of his Majesty. July 6, 1722.

Minuted:—" 18th July 1722. Inspect the Treāry Books for precedents of warrants for cutting down trees in any of his Mā^ts^ forests, & particularly of Sherwood, & what regard has been had to the verderers therein; when my Lords will give further directions herein."

The representation referred to which was addressed to the Lords of the Treasury. 4 *pages.*

7 July. 3. Report of General Hart, Governor of the Leeward Islands, to the Lords of the Treasury. Has done his utmost to prevent the illegal trade carried on with the French and Dutch in the adjacent islands, by which means, and more especially by the great quantities of sugars made here this year, the revenue of 4½ per cent. is greatly increased, " the sugar colonies having suffered very much by dry weather for three years past." Could never prevail on Mr Hamilton, the late Governor, to deliver an account of the casual revenue, although he used menaces to oblige him to comply. He assured the General, a few days before his death (which happened at

1722. VOL. CCXL.

the latter end of April last) that he made out his account but never delivered it to the Receiver, who since his death, has petitioned for a Court of Exchequer to be erected at St Christophers in order to inquire into the affair, &c. As Mr Hamilton died possessed of a considerable estate, doubts not, but their Lps will have a good account from the executrix of what is due to the Crown. During the three months that he resided at St Christophers, was chiefly employed in inquiry into what disposition has hitherto been made, of that part of the French lands surrendered to His Majesty, by the Treaty of Utrecht, but does not find that any benefit accrued to the Crown except the 4½ per cent. paid here, and the duty of 3*s.* 6*d.* per hundred on sugars landed in England. Transmitted an account of the number of acres, and present possessors of the lands in the two quarters of Bass-terre and Capisterre, which amounted to 11,161; but upon further inquiry finds it amounts only to 11,142 acres (as appears by enclosure No. 1), exclusive of patent land granted by Her late, and by his present, Majesty, to French protestants who were formerly possessors of those lands under the French, and exclusive of that tract of land called the Salt Ponds, containing about 2,000 acres, only fit for pasture. This was given by the French when in their possession to poor people gratis, in order to strengthen the Island by their numbers, and it is the most proper use it can be applied to. For his better information to procure a particular account of the real value of the French lands, and how they have been, and are now managed, ordered the publication enclosed (No. 2) to be affixed in the most public places of St Christophers, requiring all persons possessed of French lands to produce their grants, &c., which most of them complied with. Found those grants had been given in a very irregular and confused manner, which has occasioned a number of law suits, there having been many grants given to several persons for one and the same tract of land: all which disputes he has determined in Council, and quieted their minds by giving new grants to such as desired it during His Majesty's pleasure only. In the same publication he made proposals to all persons concerned in the French lands, to know upon what terms they were willing to hold the same of His Majesty. The answer of many of the possessors is enclosed (No. 3). They are willing to lease or purchase upon any reasonable terms His Majesty shall think fit, but expect that a price should be first put upon those lands, and further expect His Majesty's favour not to require the extreme value from the present possessors. These gentlemen have endeavoured to keep him in the dark as to the real value of the lands, though he is credibly informed that most of them have made very good fortunes out of the lands, and having possessed them so long without any acknowledgment to the Crown, they take it for granted that they are still to retain them on the same terms, or for very slight consideration. Presumes that their Lps will admit that the revenue has been improved, and the value of the lands highly advanced by the industry, and at the expense of the present possessors, at the same time the profits have amply rewarded their labour. Submits whether it is not high time that the Crown should

1722. Vol. CCXL.

have, for the future, a valuable consideration for those lands. Therefore, in obedience to their Lps' commands, lays the proposals (No. 4) before them. By these means the revenue will be advanced, and the purchaser or lessee have a much better bargain than if the lands were in the English quarter. This would be a convenient season for the disposal of these lands for they are now all employed in sugar canes, which very much impoverishes the ground; nor is the soil capable of a greater improvement, and in case of a rumour of war it will much abate the value, having been so often ruined by the French. Should the present possessors refuse to purchase or lease the lands at the price mentioned in the proposals, if their Lps give him authority, he will make publication in the Islands of Barbadoes and Antigua and numbers of people will readily take them. Antigua, 7 July 1722.

Minuted:—"Mr Lowndes & Mr Walpole to collect all orders, minutes & other directions which have been given at any time in relation to these lands."

The first enclosure is not now with the report; the others, however, are with it. 12 *pages*.

10 July. 4. "Memorial from ye Board of Works relating to new buildings &ca that are carrying on in St. James's parke" without the sanction or control of the Board, sending "the plan and upright" which were sent to their Clerk after the houses were far advanced. Whitehall, Office of Works, July 10, 1722.

Minuted:—"24 July 1722. To the workes taking notice their meml dated the 10th was recd but ye 19th." 1 *page and the plan, which is of an ordinary dwelling-house.*

13 July. 5. Memorial of the Comrs of Customs to the Lords of the Treasury. Their Lps having given directions that some pictures belonging to Lord Whitworth (His Majesty's late Ambassador at Berlin), which he has had a great while, and are now under stop here, may be delivered in like manner as has been accustomed to be done to other Ambassadors on their return. Acquaint their Lps that by several laws certain duties are laid on pictures imported. The proper officers have certified that the duties on these 23 pictures amount to 66*l*. The present Bishop of London on his return from being Envoy in Sweden paid custom for a considerable quantity of plate, pursuant to directions from the Treasury. The Earl of Strafford, when Ambassador from his late Majesty to the States of Holland, paid duties upon his pictures, under a report to the Treasury in 1712, and it has been the constant practice ever since to insist on the payment of the duties of pictures, &c. Are, therefore, of opinion that the duties in question ought to be paid, the same being by law appropriated. Custom Ho, London, 13 July 1722. 2 *pages*.

[Between 16 and 26 July.] 6. Messrs H. Holt Henley and John Burridge to the Rt Hon. Robert Walpole, Esq. Ask that orders may be issued for payment of the annuities due to the town of Lyme Regis for the repair of the Cob.

1722. VOL. CCXL.

Minuted:—"July 26, 1722. Order'd. Warr^{t} signd 8th Augt 1722."

Also letter from Robert Burridge to his son, "Mr John Burridge, Memb^{r} of Parliam^{t}," urging him in conjunction with his brother member to press for payment of the annuities amounting to 250*l.*, in order that the corporation may be provided with funds to carry on the work before winter. Lyme, 16 July 1722. 2 *pages*.

[About 16 July.] 7. Memorial of James Carstairs to the King. His Majesty had granted the estate of Kilconquhar to James Carstairs, subject to payment of the debts affecting it, reserving power to revoke the grant. The debts on it amounted to two thirds of the value, and a sale could not be accomplished if the estate were subject to the revocation; whereupon memorialist and others in the like case had prayed for relief. This was referred to the Lord Advocate, who had reported that the power of revocation would disappoint the intention of the grant, and suggested an alteration in the Act vesting the forfeited estates, or that his Majesty should discharge the power of revocation. Memorialist has found a purchaser who is satisfied with the title, if his Majesty will discharge the power of revocation by privy seal. Prays that this may be done.

Referred to the L^{ds} of the Treasury on 16 July 1722.

Minuted:—"2^{d} Augt. It being a rule to all, my Lords will not advise the King to alter it." 3 *pages*.

16 July. 8. Lord Carteret to the Lords of the Treasury. The Sieur D'Hiriberij in the year 1719 made a voyage to the Isle of Canceau in America, by order of the late Lords Justices for the purpose of obtaining restitution of his effects seized there in 1718. The order proved ineffectual, and the case was referred to the Lords of the Privy Council, who ordered Captain Smart, the commander of H.M. ship "Squirrel," to give an account of his proceedings in relation thereto, and he attended the Privy Council, but neither D'Hiriberij attended, nor anyone for him, and their L^{ps} were of opinion that the captain should be dismissed from further attendance, and this was approved by the King; but his Majesty, out of special grace, commands that directions be given to pay the Sieur D'Hiriberij 800*l.*

Minuted:—"17th July 1722. My Lords will take the King's pleasure upon this." *Again*:—"24 July 1722. Ordered. Warr^{t} signd 8th Augt 1722." 3 *pages*.

[About 16 July.] 9. Memorial of Lord Balmerino to the King. Her late Majesty granted to memorialist the feu and blench duties of the lordships of Balmerino and Coupar "for the yearly payment of a small elusory duty for her Majesty's lifetime and 38 years after her decease"; but, as it was countersigned by the Secretary of State, the Barons of the Exchequer in Scotland refuse to pass it, insisting that it ought to be countersigned by the Com^{rs} of the Treasury. Prays for a new gift to be passed in the usual way.

Referred to the Lords of the Treasury, 16 July 1722.

Minuted:—"8th Augt 1722. Prepare a warr^{t}." 1 *page*.

VOL. CCXL.

1722.

[? About 19 July.] 10. Memorial of Brigadier General Thomas Stanwix, Esq., to the Lords of the Treasury. Has no opportunity of subsisting the regiment of foot under his command (now in camp near Hungerford) without the expense of a guard to Bristol. Hopes for the same indulgence that Col. Montague lately received, viz., by having an order from their Lps to the Comrs of Excise to send to the collectors to supply the regiment with 600*l.* monthly, taking the commanding officer's bills upon the agent.

Minuted:—"July 19, 1722 Order'd. Lře signed." 1 *page*.

21 July. 11. Lord Lieut. of Ireland (Grafton) to the Lords of the Treasury. The House of Commons of Ireland has recommended the enclosed petition of Alderman Edward Surdeville, of Dublin (in behalf of himself and Mrs Joanna Bradshaw, &c.) desiring that 600*l.* might be granted the alderman and the executors of Thomas Bradshaw, deceased, for their loss and expense in maintaining the ancient rights and liberties of Dublin in 1713, "when they were sheriffs of that city." Their conduct at that juncture was of great service to the protestant interest of Ireland. Desires their Lps to lay the enclosed address before his Majesty. 21 July 1722.

Minuted:—"26 July 1722. Ordered. Warrt signd 8th Augt 1722." 1 *page*.

21 July. 12. The same to the same. Has lately received the enclosed representation from the Board of General Officers in Ireland setting forth that the arms and accoutrements of the several regiments of foot in Ireland are unfit for service, and proposing that the Colonels (as in Great Britain) may be empowered by his Majesty's warrant to provide a new set of arms and accoutrements out of their off reckonings, by allowing them to clothe their respective regiments but twice in the three years next to come, instead of annually, by which the expense may be defrayed. Thinks it is expedient that the arms should speedily be provided, and recommends this method, &c., and that it be left to the discretion of the Colonels (where any regiment included in the list of regiments given, is not in immediate want of new arms) to continue their assignments for clothing as usual. Bond Street, 21 July 1722.

Minuted:—"26th July 1722. Agreed to. Warrt sign'd 8th Augt 1722."

The representation above mentioned. 4 *pages*.

21 July. 13. The same to the same. Has considered the pretensions of the persons hereafter named who formerly enjoyed half pay, viz.: (1.) Of Captain William Browning, of Col. Abraham Creighton's regiment of foot, who was by mistake omitted in transcribing a new establishment of half pay. He, with others, was recommended by an address of the House of Commons of Ireland to be restored, and was found to be qualified by the Commrs appointed to enquire into the pretensions of half pay officers. (2.) Of Lieut. George Cashell, of the same regiment, recommended by the same address and by a similar certificate. (3.) Of Cornet William Stewart, of the Lord Viscount Mountjoy's late regiment of dragoons, who was about the year

1722. VOL. CCXL.

1718 struck off the half pay for disaffection to the Government. Is informed that it was rather an accidental act of intemperance than any settled disloyalty. The enclosed certificate from some persons of distinction inclines him to recommend him to his Majesty. Same date.

Minuted:—" Warr^{t} signd 8th Augt 1722." 3 *pages*.

[? About 24 July.] 14. Petition of Ambrose Warren, of the parish of St James, Westminster, clerk, to the Lords of the Treasury, showing that Major Lenham, who brought over the Prince of Orange's declaration in 1688, was put into Newgate, but escaped death by the arrival of the Prince and by King James's abdication, but lost his life at the Boyne in 1690. He had one son, William Lenham, who was brought into England about 1695, and placed with petitioner, "Dr. Tenison, then Bishop of Lincoln, late Archbishop of Canterbury, the several Secretaries of State in succession paying for him until Michs. 1700, when he was placed clark to Mr Fearn at the Custom House," but became disordered in his mind, and was removed about 1706, and was by the late Lady Auverquerque settled with Mr Tollit, reader of King St Chapel, the late Queen Anne allowing 40*l.* per ann. for his maintenance. From her Majesty's death Lady Auverquerque advanced the 40*l.* per ann. until her death, and it was continued by her heirs till 1720; all which remained unpaid by the Crown. The widow Tollet with whom Lenham then was being reduced to necessity, and the naked hungry lunatic being chained in the dark and fed only by some few neighbours, petitioner presented a memorial of his case in July 1720 to the Lords of the Treasury, who in August following ordered 20*l.* for his support, and he was removed to the parish beadle's at 10*s.* per week. When that sum was expended, petitioner in April 1721 presented another petition to their L^{ps}, and continued the weekly expenses until he could bear it no longer, and had spent 19*l.* 15*s.* Mr Ellis put the lunatic on the parish charge at 2*s.* 6*d.* per week, but his illness requiring a strict attendance, the parish allowance falls short of what is necessary for his relief. Prays for reimbursement and for further relief of the sufferer.

Minuted:—" 24 July 1722. Send this to St James Vestry to be further considered out of the King's b^{o} to the parish."

Another petition from him, probably that above referred to as of April 1721. 2 *pages*.

[? About 24 July.] 15. "Report of Comm^{rs} of forfeited estates on the acc^{ts} and observations delivered by Mr Cotton." The report encloses an account of all moneys paid into the Exchequer from the forfeited estates of James, late Duke of Ormond, and of all moneys issued from the Exchequer out of the money so paid, to creditors whose claims have been allowed and debentures already issued by the Commissioners.

It will be observed that there remains in the Exchequer from the forfeited estate in Ireland (above the 5,691*l.* 1*s.* 8*d.* issued for payment of creditors) 12,277*l.* 16*s.* 5*d.*, and from the English

1722. Vol. CCXL.

part of the estate (above 10,063*l.* 10*s.* for payment of creditors) 4,533*l.* 16*s.* 7*d.*

Lord Arran was the purchaser of the estate, and there were complications arising out of his purchase.

The account referred to.

Minuted:—"July 24th 1722. Read, Order'd by the Lords that a copy be given to Mr Coton for his answer & observations upon it, & that ye Commrs for forfeited estates, & the said Mr Cotton doe attend on Fryday ye 27th 1722." 9 *pages.*

25 July. 16. Robert Armstrong to Charles Burniston, Esq., Surveyor General of his Majesty's Woods in America. The inhabitants have presumed to cut down several trees contrary to the Act of Parliament and the reservation in the Royal Charter. Brought the case to two trials, in which it was made apparent by affidavits, that 43 pine trees seized were all upwards of 24 inches at the butt, and most of them from that measurement to near 30 inches; and that the land on which they were grown lies in the township of Barwick, three miles within the woods, and could not be called a private property; but the inhabitants claim a private property in all lands granted into townships before the late charter, and will not allow of any reservation for the Crown, but in such townships as were granted since the late charter, which reserves all trees of 24 inches, not heretofore granted to any private person. "Quere wither within any of ye townships the inhabitants therein can cutt any trees of ye dimensions reserved without licence, upon pretence that they grow within ye bounds of their townships." Sends the letter home by the master of the vessel on board of which are the 43 trees seized. Has marked in the several townships about 400 trees for his Majesty's service with the broad arrow, which the inhabitants do not regard, notwithstanding the penalty of 5*l.* a tree.

Has pressed for several years to obtain an act against exportation of timber, plank, &c. to Portugal, Spain, &c., but nothing is done. Portsmouth, New Hampshire, July 25, 1722." 2 *pages.*

[? About 25 July.] 17. Petition of "Rachael Armstrong, born at Yarmouth, and the widow of Mr Farrer Armstrong, of Hexham, in Northumberland, attorney at law, to the Lords of the Treasury. Petitioner's husband during three years attended the trustees of the forfeited estates in Great Britain and Ireland, and made several useful discoveries to those gentlemen without reward. Petitioner and her husband whilst they lived at Hexham, in Northumberland, received officers of note in the Army, when no other place could be found to entertain them. Is left with two children in very deplorable circumstances. The eldest is a midshipman of H.M. ship Leopard and the other, John Armstrong, is a writer in the Examiner's Office. Prays that Robert, the elder, may be recommended to the Lords of the Admiralty for a Lieutenancy, and that they would provide for the younger son in the Stamp Office, and that petitioner may receive his Majesty's bounty.

Copy of certificate in corroboration of the petition. 1½ *pages.*

VOL. CCXL.

1722. [? About 26 July.] 18. Petition of Thomas Baldwin to the Lords of the Treasury. To be allowed 1,422*l.* 2*s.* 9*d.*, being the difference between what was allowed on certain claims for supplies to the allies in Spain, and what ought to have been allowed. The original claim was for 7,020*l.* 3*s.* 6*d.*, and the petitioner received but 6,298*l.* 0*s.* 1½*d.*, the difference being in the computation of the Spanish dollar.

Minuted:—"26th July 1722. This allowance was pursuant to the report of the Comrs whose power is now determined; therefore, my Lords can do nothing in it." 1 *page*.

27 July. 19. Peter Laurans to [? the Secretary of the Treasury] enclosing the following petition. Dated "Att Mr Williams in Salisbury Street in the Strand," July 27, 1722.

Petition of the same to the Lords of the Treasury. Has by long study attained to the knowledge of making a machine for the discovery of the "longitude upon sea," but has "thereby throw'd himself in low circumstances," which renders him incapable of producing the machine to the world in all its perfection. Is informed that there is a "piece of money" lodged in their Lps' hands for the encouragement of any person that shall produce such a machine. Prays their Lps' assistance that he may produce this thing to the world.

The petition is *minuted*:—"Read 27 July 1722. My Lords canot pay any of the mony prescribed by the Act until the machine be produced to the Trustees named in the Act and approved by them." 3 *pages*.

27 July. 20. "Petition & affidt of Robt Thompson, of Aberdeen, concerning frauds & abuses committed in that port." Addressed to the Lords of the Treasury. London, July 27, 1722.

Minuted:—"3d Augt 1722. The petr to attend the Commrs customs in order to make good his allegations.

He charges Mr Gorden, collector of Aberdeen, with conniving at the running of goods and with seizing a few hogsheads of wine for a sham. Mr Ogellby, controller, was also privy to the same. He also charges Mr "Elphaston," surveyor, with refusing his assistance or use of his boat to prevent the running of goods on another occasion and with having an interest in the cargo. The collector and superior officers also refused to search for the goods though he offered to take them where they lay. He further makes one or two other similar charges. 4 *pages*.

28 July. 21. W. Palmer, Usher of the Council Chamber, to John Whichcote, Esq., Secretary to the Duke of Grafton, "Lord Lieut. of Ireland, in Dover Street, London. Respecting a dispute in paying his fee upon Public Bills. He says, "why you don't see a precedent of its being paid me is, because I kept a Deputy since the 2d year of the late Queen's reign, who only had a salary from me, so that he entirely neglected collecting my fees." "Those who got Private Bills this last session, paid the fee without disputeing it, and I hope I shall not be put to the necessity of applying to the Government, either here or in England, for the recovery of it, wch I must do if

1722. VOL. CCXL.

not allow'd it, because 'tis the best perquisite I have." Dublin, July 28, 1722. 2 *pages.*

31 July. 22. Lord Lieut. of Ireland to the Lords [of the Treasury] on the petition of William Caulfield, Esq., one of the Judges of the Court of King's Bench in Ireland, setting forth that it is his province as second Judge of that Court to give the charge to the Grand Jury of the county of the city of Dublin, and to pronounce the judgment of the law against such criminals as are convicted in that court; that for this service a fee of 10*l.* a term has been allowed to his predecessors, and usually paid them out of the fines of that court, but there is not a sufficient authority extant for this application; that the like allowance is granted in Great Britain. Moreover that the Judges of the Court of King's Bench "in this Kingdom" are empowered to pay a third part of such fines, and likewise to order 10*l.* a year to the coroner of that Court for passing the accounts of the fines in the Court of Exchequer. His Majesty is pleased to consent that the like allowances should be established in Ireland. Asks their L^{ds} to obtain a proper warrant to empower the Judges of the King's Bench in Ireland, to apply a proportion of the fines to discharge the allowance of 10*l.* a term to the petitioner. Bond Street, 31 July 1722.

Minuted:—"15th August 1722. Approved."

The petition or memorial referred to and a copy of a privy seal relating to the same fines. 7 *pages.*

[? About 3 Aug.] 23. Memorial setting forth the causes of the meanness and diminution of the revenue of the King's College and University of Aberdeen. King James the Fourth, with a special view to civilise the north Highlands of Scotland, which lie adjacent to Aberdeen, erected the University with most ample and honourable privileges. Private persons gave donations for the maintenance of bursars, and for new buildings; and magnificent and large structures were built. Sundry Kings and private persons also made donations of "teiths" to the college. The heritors, out of whose lands the teiths were payable, raised processes of valuation, putting the University to considerable charges, and the revenue was much diminished. Besides which, new erections of parishes were made, and ministers obtained augmentations of their stipends out of the teiths: "for by the laws of Scotland, the teiths are so far the patrimony of the church, that the parochial ministers are preferred to their stipends and maintenance out of them." By these means, notwithstanding donations by King Charles II., King William and Queen Ann, the revenues are diminished about two thirds; and by law suits they have contracted debts, and the college scarcely receives sufficient to pay the masters' salaries, &c., and cannot pay for the repair of the fabric. The principal's salary is very little better than 100*l.* per ann., the professor of Divinity's is under that sum, the professors of Law, Medicine, and Humanity, also the sub-principal's, does not exceed 40*l.* per ann., and the professors of Philosophy and Greek have only about 30*l.*, "and which is worse, after payment of the 'carents' of debts, which are daily increasing, the college revenue is not by farr

1722. Vol. CCXL.

sufficient for payment of those salaries." After the Rebellion was suppressed, His Majesty appointed Commissioners to visit the University, and they deposed several of the old masters as accessory to the Rebellion, and their places were, by his Majesty, supplied with gentlemen of known abilities and affection to the present happy establishment in Church and State, and who in conjunction with the other masters have used their utmost endeavours to inculcate true protestant principles in the youth under their care. This has exposed the University to several law suits commenced by disaffected persons; all which the masters have borne patiently, but unless his Majesty speedily take the matter into consideration, it will not be safe for them to struggle any longer.

Referred to the Lords of the Treasury, 3 Aug. 1722. 1 *large page.*

[? About 3 Aug.] 24. "The managers memorial to be employed in exchanging the tickets in this year's lottery as they were in the last year."

The following were the persons who sent in the memorial:—Christopher Tilson, Thomas Cornwallis, Nehemiah Arnold, John Duncombe, Christopher Rhodes, and Robert Manning.

Minuted:—"3 Augt 1722. Agreed to, adding Mr Nelson to ye number." 1 *page.*

8 Aug. 25. Report of J. Pulteney, Surveyor General, to the Lords of the Treasury, concerning a grant passed in 1689 to Henry Lord Delamer, of lands, &c., in the counties of Monmouth and Hereford, of the yearly value of 459*l.* for 31 years, since elapsed at a rent of 5*l.*; which estates had been, by inquisitions, found to be forfeited to the crown by being given to Popish and superstitious uses. Wrote to the present Earl of Warrington, who was executor to his father, the late grantee of the premises; and who did not think it advisable to proceed to the recovery of those estates. His L^{p} says he never had any benefit from that grant, nor does he find that his father had any; that he does not know the yearly value of them or in whose possession they now are. Mr. Booth, of Gray's Inn, informed him that he had heard the Lord Delamer say, that not long before, he had a trial with the Duke of Beaufort in the Common Pleas, for some of those lands, and obtained a verdict. The grant to Lord Delamer having determined, and as no other grant has been made of the premises, if his Majesty please to make a further grant thereof, it may pass for any term not exceeding 31 years, or three lives, &c. Soon after the late happy Revolution several such grants were obtained from the Crown, and afterwards some of them appeared to have been procured, with no other view than of raising money by sales to the best bidders, who, becoming purchasers, very often obliged the possessors of these estates to compound for sums of money which they paid rather than be disturbed, &c. 8 Aug. 1722.

This is said on the back to be a copy. It seems doubtful if that is the case; but there is another copy of the report with trifling variations which is *minuted:*—"5 Aug. 1723. Rep^{t} agreed to & w^{t} to be prepared." 10 *pages and* 2 *halves.*

VOL. CCXL.

1722.

[? About 8 Aug.] 26. Memorial of Anthony Balam, Inspector General of Imports and Exports, to the Lords of the Treasury. The Inspector General's Office was erected to keep a Register of all species of goods exported from, and imported into England, specifying the places from whence imported and whereto exported; that from thence some judgment might be made of the increase or decrease of our several foreign trades at distinct times: and that a balance of trade in general or any particular branches of it might at any time be calculated tolerably near the truth; which before, for want of such a regular register, was altogether impracticable. Offers suggestions for the improvement of the office. Recommends Mr John Oxenford to be appointed as First Clerk in the Inspector General's office with a salary of 120*l.* per ann. and the addition of 80*l.* to salaries of other clerks.

Minuted:—" 8th Augt 1722. Prepare a warrt for the additions craved in the memll." 2 *pages.*

8 Aug. 27. Memorial of Sir David Nairne to the Rt Hon. Robert Walpole, Esq. In the year 1703 was made Secretary to the most ancient and most noble Order of the Thistle, with a salary or pension of 300*l.* per ann. for life, by commission and grant, as the laws of Scotland required before the Union. Was paid on the Civil List until the Union, then the payments on the Civil List being precarious, the Earl of Godolphin procured him a privy seal for payment of his salary in England, on which he was paid till Feb. 1712–13. During the Earl of Oxford's administration could obtain no payment. Did not know until lately, that he should have had his privy seal renewed at the King's Accession. Has received no part of his salary since that time. Has suffered much by the general calamity which has of late years happened, besides other losses. Prays payment of arrears.

On the back is a report thereon signed R. Powys corroborating the facts in the petition. 8 Aug. 1722.

Minuted:—" 15th Augst 1722. Read." 2 *pages.*

[? About 8 Aug.] 28. Petition of John Hill and John Jephson the surviving assignees of the Commission of Bankrupt awarded and now in prosecution against Robert Peter or Peters late Receiver General of the county of Hertford, and other his creditors, to the Lords of the Treasury. Setting forth many of the particulars referred to in a previous entry in this calendar (vol. ccxxii. 45). Petitioners had not been able to get in any part of the estate, the debtors pretending they were liable to the extents, and would pay to the Crown, or to Sir Biby Lake (one of the creditors), who refused to receive or get in the same, whereby great part of the debts are become desperate. Sir Bibye Lake on divers pretences, still neglects to pay the 10,892*l.* 5*s.* 9½*d.* according to his undertaking. Pray that he may be ordered by a short day, to pay the same, or that process may issue to compel him. [*See* various references to Peters affairs in previous volume of calendar.]

Minuted:—" 8th Augt 1722. Send a copie of this to Sir Bibye Lake directing him to return to my Lords a speedy answer." " A

1722. VOL. CCXL.

copy sent." 19 7br 1722 A lre from Sr Biby Lake in answer." 1 *page.*

10 Aug. 29. Joseph Billers to the Rt Hon. Robert Walpole, Esq., on the 20th ult. troubled their honours with a letter praying for relief. Continues his request for a speedy supply. Encloses "An estimate of what the estate of Joseph Billers, citizen of London, might probably have been if he had not been engaged in detecting several public abuses by direction of the government." The total of which comes to 23,553*l.* 8*s.*

Minuted:—"10th Augt 1722. My Lords order a warrt for 500li in full of all his services and demands." *Again*:—"15th Augst 1722. My Lords confirm ye above Minute on condicōn he promisses to trouble the Treasury no farther on accot of his ꝑtended services." 2 *pages.*

[About 10 Aug.] 30. Petition of Richard Lloyd, late collector of the land tax of St James and Whitehall, to the Lords of the Treasury. Their Lordships had answered his former petition (annexed) that they had no objection to the composition therein proposed, in case the debt to the Crown was secured. The auditor's certificate (annexed) would show the debt was fully paid. The petitioner's friends are ready to pay to the Comrs of Taxes, for the use of the inhabitants, the sum agreed on (1,700*l.*) upon the Lords of the Treasury granting their warrant to the Attorney General for discharging the extent. The Attorney General has given his opinion (also annexed) that their Lps may grant their warrant to him for discharging the extent, and and that thereupon it may be discharged. Prays the warrant accordingly.

Minuted:—"10th Aug. 1722. Agreed to."

The papers above referred to, and a draft of the warrant prayed for, ordering a *nolle prosequi*, in which it appears that an extent was awarded out of the Exchequer against the said Lloyd who was collector of land tax for the palaces of St James's and Whitehall, for 4,900*l.*, by him received and embezzled, and that his effects amounted to no more than 598*l.* 8*s.* His friends offered 1,700*l.*, provided the extent were discharged and the effects seized were restored. This the Comrs advised should be accepted. 7 *pages.*

15 Aug. 31. Robert Jacomb to Horatio Walpole, Esq. Troubles him again in the affair of the money due from Ireland, to the Earl of Lincoln and Mr Walpole's brother, for the pay of the Irish regiment that was here, during the time they were paymasters of the forces. Notwithstanding his (Mr Walpole's) letter to Mr Secretary Hopkins, there remains upwards of 6,000*l.* of Lord Lincoln's warrant unpaid, besides which, the warrant to Mr Walpole's brother is for upwards of 17,000*l.*, and there is another warrant to Lord Cornwallis for 4,550*l.* 18*s.* 4*d.* still unpaid, the whole amounting to 38,000*l.* The slow remittances hinder the clearing of the forces for Lord Cornwallis's time, and prevent Mr Walpole's brother from passing his accounts. Asks him to consider what further can be done. Horse Guards, 15 Aug. 1722.

1722. VOL. CCXL.

Minuted:—August 16, 1722; a letter to be writt in the strongest terms to L[rd] Leut. to be sign'd by y[e] Lords." 2 *pages*.

[? About 17 Aug.] 32. Memorial of Charles King, late Chamber Keeper to the Treasury, to the Lords of the Treasury. By order of the Earl of Sunderland, when first Lord of the Treasury, memorialist printed and sent into each of the Corporations of Great Britain, which send members to parliament, and to each of the colleges and halls in the universities, one set of the "British Merchant" for the use of the inhabitants, being 331 sets. Prays payment of 1,117*l*. 2*s*. 6*d*. for the same.

Minuted:—"17th Aug[t] 1722. Prepare a warr[t]." 1 *page*.

The receipts given by the recipients of the volumes. 60 *parts of pages*.

17 Aug. 33. The Lord Lieut. of Ireland (Grafton) to the Lord of the Treasury. Sends petition of Captain Henry D'Albenaj with other papers relating thereto, praying for restoration of his pension on the establishment of Ireland, it having been omitted on the framing of the new establishment in 1704 when he was at Geneva. The petitioner served as Captain of horse during the war in Piedmont, which began in 1690, and at the conclusion King William granted him a pension of 4*s*. a day; advises the restoration of his pension.

Minuted:—"August ye 22, 1722. Prepare a warrant accordingly Warr[t] signed 3 8[br] 1722." 2 *pages*.

[? About 17 Aug.] 34. Petition of Robert Weemyss collector of customs at Anstruther, to the Lords of the Treasury. Was appointed in 1714. The port was at first a member port, subject to the port of Kirkaldy, but business increasing, especially in the importation of foreign salt, it was declared independent. Was obliged to have a clerk. Has but a salary of 30*l*., which is inferior to many of the Land-waiters, and little more than that of the boatmen. In the year 1715, when the Rebellion broke out in Scotland, parties came down from the rebel camp to Anstruther, which lay removed from the assistance of his Majesty's troops, and plundered petitioner's house, laid waste his small estate in that country, scattered his family and carried himself to Perth; where he was kept close prisoner for many weeks; and all because he would not deliver up the public money nor own their pretended government.

Referred to the Com[rs] of Customs, Scotland, 17 Aug. 1722. Also five affidavits in corroboration of the above. 3½ *pages*.

[? About 17 Aug.] 35. Part of a petition of "Her Majesty's mesne tenants of the manor of Bray in the County of Berks" in which it is stated that the common, bridges and pounds belonging to the manor of Bray, about the year 1700, were repaired at the charge of the King as lord of the manor, and in 1718, the bridges and pounds being out of repair, as presented at the Courts Leet and Court Baron, the tenants petitioned the Lords of the Treasury to have the same repaired. The Surveyor General reported thereon, that the expense of the same would be 206*l*. The Receiver General of the co. of Berks

1722. VOL. CCXL.

was empowered by warrant to pay the charge. The surveyor received 50*l.* but never disbursed any money thereon. About the year 1721, the tenants lodged another petition embodying the same particulars as to the warrant, and stating that the bridges, &c., were still ruinous. Pray that the warrant may be vacated, and that direction may be given for payment of the 206*l.* out of the Exchequer.

Minuted:—" 17th Aug. 1722. When Mr Lowndes is . . . ." 1 *page*.

21 Aug. 36. Denis Bond, Esq., to the Lords of the Treasury. Lays before their Lps an abstract of the acts to oblige Papists to register their names and real estates with his "opinion wherein the same is defective," and also the value of the estates registered in each county, where the estates are valued in the registries; but there are also several estates of very great value in the possession of the persons registering, the value whereof cannot be ascertained. Essex House, Aug. 21, 1722.

The abstract is not with it. 1 *page*.

27 Aug. 37. Comrs of the Navy to the Secretaries of the Treasury. Laying before them three lists of salaries and pensions above 50*l.* per ann. liable to the deduction of 6*d.* in the pound. Give some names and particulars of persons who they think ought to be excepted.

There are minutes against most of these not approving of the exceptions.

On the dorse is:—" Warrt signed 28th 7br 1722." 3 *pages*.

27 Aug. 38. Copy of divers petitions to the Lords of the Treasury and to his Majesty, together with several other documents relating to the affairs of Captain John Webbe, a prisoner in the King's Bench. He complains that he has been ruined by numerous sham actions commenced against him for having made discoveries of the fraudulent sinking of ships, to obtain the insurances upon them. By these discoveries he is upwards of 2,000*l.* out of pocket. The persons he principally singles out for complaint are William Adye, a packer, living at "Blackwell Hall," and Nicholas Mandell, the Swedish secretary. The latter, he says, had often solicited him to endeavour the burning of the British squadron under command of Sir George Bing, then in the Mediterranean, and to destroy his own and other ships, to obtain the insurance. Another person who he says conspired against him, was Mr Edward Morgan, a Roman Catholic living in Bloomsbury Square, "who was round the Globe" with Captain William Dampiere and was the death of him, by turning him on shore at the Island of St Jago, where he ended his days with hunger and grief. He was afterwards the ruin of the expedition, and now endeavours to ruin the petitioner. States that he (the petitioner) sailed round the Globe with Dampiere in the years 1703, 4, 5, and 6. He claims to be able to make discoveries in the South Seas, and is anxious to be examined by the Comrs of Trade as to the establishment of a company by charter, for carrying on a trade to "*Terra Australis.*" His reasons for the establishment of this company are given in one of the papers.

1722. Vol. CCXL.

In one of his petitions to his Majesty he says that if the treasonable and felonious practices complained of, are encouraged, and his Majesty's subjects suffered to be ruined for discovery of the same, the protestant interest and the balance of Europe cannot long be maintained, neither can his Majesty and his illustrious line expect long to sit upon the British throne; but Popery and arbitrary government must ensue.

In the last paper of the collection dated 21 Aug. 1722, the Captain says he encloses "a Treatise of Philosophy proveing the possibility of regeneration and transmutation called the Philosopher's Stone," which he wrote since his confinement in the King's Bench. Begs that he may have some relief till the parliament meets. The paper finishes thus:—"In consideration of the consequence of my proposals (viz.) one hundred millions sterling which I will engage my life to maintain before the House of Commons whenever I can be admitted." Dated on the back:—Aug 27. 34½ *pages*.

29 Aug. 39. Report of the Com^rs^ of Customs, Scotland, to the Lords of the Treasury in respect to the salaries of the inferior officers. Find it a work of time to adjust their merits and allowances. In the mean time think the salary of Mr Lane Whitehall, (*See* 1 Feb. 1721–22) should be augmented to 100*l.* per ann., and that it would be no unreasonable reward for his fidelity and services. Custom House, Edinburgh, 29 August 1722. 1 *page*.

30 Aug. 40. Report of the Surveyor General (J. Pulteney), to the Lords of the Treasury. Has examined the annexed petition of the minister, churchwardens and overseers of the German Reformed Protestant church in the Savoy, in behalf of themselves and the whole congregation, wherein is set forth that the King of Prussia allowed a pension of 120*l.* per ann. to their late minister, Doctor Cæsar, but that since his death (in the year 1719) it had been discontinued, as proved by an affidavit annexed. The petitioners allege that they had a promise of the late Queen Anne of 1,000*l.* for the building of a church, and that the Lord Treasurer had orders to pay that sum; in proof of which they produce a memorial of the Consistory of the Prussian church, and an affidavit. As his Majesty has lately bestowed his favours on their brethren of the Lutheran church, petitioners hope they may be extended to them, and they pray for a lease of the place they now use for public worship, and for an apartment or house for the minister. Finds that the place mentioned has been in their possession since 1697, and a report in 1715 states that it was held at a rent of 16*l.* per ann., which has been paid to Mich. 1721. The house adjoining, which they desire for their minister, is held at a rent of 16*l.* per ann. and for the reasons given, he cannot advise the dispossession of the tenant. The other house, which petitioners desire is called the Master's house, is valued at 30*l.* per ann. and is in possession of Dr. Pratt, but he has paid no rent on pretence of having been burnt out at Whitehall; though his son says the house was given to his father by the late Queen, in consideration of his having been outed of his lodgings in St James's House, when the council chamber was built in that Palace.

1722. VOL. CCXL.

Petitioners ask, that as the house is large and beyond the tenant's requirements, a dwelling may be made out of it for the minister. As to what was bestowed on their brethren in the Savoy, finds that a constat was made in order to a lease for 50 years of the chapel in use by the High German Protestants and several rooms or lodgings for their minister, at a rent of 5*l.* per ann., which lease was never perfected, but in Sept. 1721, they obtained a sign manual for continuance during pleasure, of their possession. Takes leave to acquaint their Lps that in 1702, upon the Lord Keeper Wright's visitation, the hospital was declared dissolved for want of members, agreeable to the intent of the founder King Henry the seventh, whereby the revenue has been in the hands of the Crown, and leases have been, and may be granted. Therefore the premises may be surveyed in order for a lease to be granted to such person or persons as their Lps think fit, in trust for the petitioners, for such term of years and at such rent as will be agreeable to the Civil List Act, or the last-mentioned premises might be held by the sign manual during pleasure. 30 Aug. 1722.

Minuted:—"21st August 1723. Prepare a S.M."

The petitions, two affidavits, and the memorial referred to, also a copy of the above report. 15 *pages.*

30 Aug. 41. Memorial of the managers and directors of the Lottery, 1722, to the Lords of the Treasury. By their care and diligence the expenses of their work have been defrayed for 1,569*l.* Pray that their Lps would direct the sum of 430*l.* 6*s.* 2*d.* to clear their expenses and for a suitable reward. Lottery Office, 30 Aug. 1722.

Minuted:—"The Comrs to have 150li a piece. Where 2 dyed and 2 came in then to be p'd ꝑ rata and the 430*l.* 6*s.* 2*d.* is orderd."

Also the detailed account of the 1,560*l.* expended. 3 *pages.*

31 Aug. 42. Lord Lieut. of Ireland (Grafton) to the Lords of the Treasury. It being customary for the crown to grant to several persons in England and Ireland, through whose hands the Bills of every session of Parliament in Ireland pass, certain allowances for their trouble in dispatching them, transmits a list of the allowances due on account of the last session, and of the several "offices" to which they are to be paid. Asks that his Majesty's warrant might be obtained for payments of the same. Bond Street, 31 Aug. 1722.

Also the list of the allowances. 2 *pages.*

4 Sept. 43. Proposal of John Gore to the Lords of the Treasury, in relation to the tin at Hamborough. The Trustees for the South Sea Company are desirous to receive the debt due to his estate "in a pawn of tin at Hamburgh, being about 18,000*l.*" London, 4 Sepr 1722.

Minuted:—"5th Septr 1722. Read and agreed to." 1 *page.*

[? About 5 Sept.] 44. Petition of John Fearne and four others, to the First Comr of the Treasury. Are entitled to several houses in the bailiwick of St James's, Westminster, which they hold from the Crown for eleven years to come. Three or four years since petitioners

VOL. CCXL.

1722.

applied to the Com^rs of the Treasury for a renewal to make up their term to 50 years, to enable them to rebuild. Pray that the warrants which are signed may be ordered to be delivered to them.

Minuted:—"5 7^br 1722. Look out these warr^ts to be layd before my Lords as soon [as] the report concerning such leases comes from Mr Attorny & Mr Soll^r." 1 *page*.

10 Sept. 45. Lord Carteret to the Lords of the Treasury. George Lambe, Robert Thompson, Philip Howell and Daniel Douglas, having applied themselves to his office and voluntarily given their information upon oath concerning the seditious and treasonable behaviour of several officers of the customs, and others at Aberdeen and other ports of Scotland, has laid the same before his Majesty, who has commanded that they should be transmitted to their L^ps for their consideration. Whitehall, 10 Sept. 1722.

Minuted:—"12th Sept. 1722. To Lord Carteret wth a copie of a report from the Com^rs Cust. in Scotl. of the 13th Augt 1722, wherein the sev^ll informations of Lamb, &c., relating to frauds committed in the Scots revenue of customs are declared by the s^d Comm^rs, upon the most strict examinations, to be false and malicious. Mr Chanc^r will speak to Ld Carteret touching the informations sent hither by his Lord^p."

The report of the Com^rs of Customs above referred to, on the informations, declarations and affidavits of George Lamb, Philip Howell, John Pagan and Danl Douglas, of many illegal practices connived at by the officers of the Customs, to the great prejudice of the revenue. It states that George Lamb informing them that he could make discoveries of frauds carried on, to the prejudice of the revenue, they made trial of him. The collector and surveyor of Aberdeen were ordered to confer with him. The former says in a letter, that no credit was to be given to his informations; but they gave him letters to the officers in their district, to give him assistance, but no service was likely to be rendered by him. He publicly exposed the officers' letters, whereby the merchants would guard against him. By another letter he is accused of taking a bribe, and this appears by a letter under his own hand to Mr Paterson, land surveyor, wherein he acknowledges to taking four guineas. He had been prosecuted for frauds, and fined 100*l*. and absconded. The pretended frauds were to protect himself.

Philip Howell, late tidesman of Aberdeen, connived at running a cargo, and was dismissed. After which he calumniated the officers. Upon a hearing, he was found to prevaricate and contradict himself, &c.

The complainant, Pagan, was suspended upon suspicion that he had not dealt fairly in his trust, but they found cause to restore him.

Daniel Douglas' information never came to their knowledge in the manner set forth to their Lordships. Were of opinion that the complainants were in no way able to serve the revenue, and that they wanted employment or money before they did anything to deserve it. Custom house, Edinburgh, 13 Aug. 1722.

1722. VOL. CCXL.

Also the "Information and Declaration of George Lamb" and the "Declaration of Daniel Douglas."

George Lamb's paper contains a very wordy account of smuggling transactions, one of which was at the Laird of Troup's house between Banff and Fraserburgh, and he says that the Laird of Troup and Col. John Buchan, Justices of the peace, and the family of the laird were concerned in it, the lady having made the guard of soldiers all drunk. $10\frac{1}{4}$ *pages.*

12 Sept. 46. Com^rs of Victualling to Mr Walpole. Send lists of salaries liable to pay the 6^d in the pound. Give certain exceptions which they have not inserted in the lists, conceiving them not liable to the deductions, &c. Victualling Office, 12 Sept. 1722.

Minuted:—"20th 7^br 1722. My Lords make the same orders in this as the Navy l̃re when the cases are the same." 4 *pages.*

17 Sept. 47. Report of the Attorney and Solicitor General to the Lords of the Treasury on the memorial of the proprietors of the Equivalent debentures, and on the draft of a charter, for incorporating the proprietors. Have heard Counsel as well for the Bank of England, as for the proprietors. On behalf of the Bank it was insisted, that it was not conformable to the Act of the fifth year of the present King, and that the draft far exceeds the purposes of the Act, and creates a general corporation as large and extensive as possible; further, that in the subsequent clause they may set up any trade, or even erect themselves into a Bank of credit, and this would be an infringement of the privileges of the Bank, and that letters patent passed in this form would be illegal, &c. On the other side, on behalf of the proprietors of the Equivalent debentures, it was admitted that they could not by law, claim or exercise any exclusive rights granted to the Bank. But it was insisted that it was not the intention of Parliament that they should be strictly confined to the receiving and distributing the annual sum of 10,000*l.*, and that for this purpose there could have been no occasion for a body corporate, or an allowance of 600*l.* per ann. for management. The agents for the Proprietors of the Equivalent debentures attended them a second time, to explain the particular powers they desired to have granted by the charter, that were not expressed in the Act. They insisted that, as the debt from the Government to them was made the capital stock of the Company, they ought to have the liberty of making use of the capital in any lawful way for their advantage; and that the particular use they desired to make of it was, to be enabled to borrow money on their bonds, payable at a certain distance of time, upon the security of, and to, the value of that capital. Having considered the act and the arguments of counsel, are of opinion that the corporation is to be erected for the purposes expressly declared in the act; which are the receiving, recovering, and distributing of the sums received of the government on account of the Equivalent debt. Are also of opinion that, in the present letters patent, it is not advisable to add such further privileges as were proposed "for that a charter to be passed pursuant to an Act of parliament ought properly to be made conformable to the Act, which is its foundation."

1722. VOL. CCXL.

The draft as sent down to them is not proper to pass, and they have made such alterations in it as are necessary. 17 Sept. 1722.

The petition and the draft with the amendments. 28½ *pages.*

18 Sept. 48. An accompt of the debt that will be due and owing on the pensions payable in the office of Walter Chetwynd, Esqre, from Michaelmas 1721 to Michaelmas 1722. 18 Sept. 1722. 7 *pages.*

[After Sept. 18.] 49. Copies of A. Cracherode's report and letters relating to James Gartside. The report of A. Cracherode to Viscount Townshend, his Majesty's Principal Secretary of State, contains a state of the case of James Gartside, who had given information against James Leonard, commonly called Captain Leonard, of high Treason committed by him in Calais, in the month of December 1716, by being himself paid as a soldier in the Pretender's service, and paying others in the same service. In Trinity Term, 1718, a bill of Indictment was found for the above foreign treason in the Court of King's Bench, upon the evidence of Gartside and three others. Leonard was tried at Lancaster for High Treason, for being in the Rebellion at Preston and acquitted; and Gartside gave evidence, and the latter was subsisted for a long term, but on Leonard being pardoned, there was no further occasion for the evidence of Gartside, and his subsistence was stopped. Believes he is very poor and an object of charity.

There are copies of four documents in all. The last is dated 18 Sept. 1722. 2½ *pages.*

19 Sept. 50. Com^rs of Revenue, Ireland, to the Lords of the Treasury. Mr French, their agent in England, has presented to their L^ps a memorial relating to a patent, said to be passing in England, to empower persons to coin half pence and farthings for the use of Ireland. Persons of rank and fortune, and merchants and traders, apprehend such a patent will be highly prejudicial to the trade and welfare of this kingdom. It will be more particularly detrimental to the revenue. As the matter has made a great noise here, the mischiefs and inconveniences which must attend it may be prejudicial to his Majesty's affairs in the ensuing parliament here, there not appearing, at present, the least want of such small coins for change. Would have had no knowledge of the matter, but from the public newspapers, and if their agent had not sent an account of it. Custom House, Dublin, Sept. 19, 1722.

Minuted:—"28th 7^br 1722. The patent hath been long since passed." 1 *page.*

19 Sept. 51. Sir Bibye Lake to the Lords [of the Treasury]. In reply to their L^ps' commands to answer the petition of Mr Peter's creditors, wherein they set forth that he has neglected to make good his proposal relating to Mr Peter's debt to the Crown. This representation of theirs is extremely unhandsome. They know that in 1713 he undertook to discharge that debt, with no other view than to serve them (having himself at that time much more than sufficient securities to discharge the debt Mr Peters owed him). They know that he or his agents, almost every day, have solicited the

1722. VOL. CCXL.

finishing of this affair. His present misfortune is that Mr Turner, who has had the business in hand, has the papers, and is, during the vacation, in Derbyshire. Prays that it may be deferred until next month. 19 Sept. 1722. 1 *page.*

25 Sept. 52. Draft of a Treasury Minute of 25 Sept. 1722, as to the charging of 43,629*l.* 17*s.* 9*d.* upon Sir John Shaw's account, that sum being the difference of the duties upon unrated goods of the East India Company, and deposited by that company, &c. 1 *page.*

26 Sept. 53. Lord Carteret to the Lords of the Treasury for directions to be given to pay 300*l.* a year for life out of the revenues of Ireland to Edward Hopkins, Esq., to whom the King had granted the office of Master of the Revels and Masks in Ireland. Whitehall, 26 Sept. 1722.

Minuted:—"26th 7br 1722. Orderd. Wart signd 28th." 1¼ *pages.*

26 Sept. 54. Petition of Thomas Wells to the Lords of the Treasury in relation to frauds and impositions in the Wine Licence Office, where he says they give receipts for the rents received, and tell the tenants they are busy, and if they want new licences they must call again, but there is no occasion, they being safe in the receipts only. By this means the Crown has been defrauded of about 800*l.* per ann. Believes that the Comrs for Stamp Duties sent their inspectors to the Wine Licence Office to inspect their books, and they found the number paid for was 38,890, and the petitioner is well assured that one half of that number has not been paid for at the Stamp Office. Is informed one Harbin (a person through whom a great part of the frauds was committed) has laid an information in order to deprive petitioner of his reasonable reward. Prays to be allowed to search the books, and that he may not be deprived by the artful management of others of his reward.

Minuted:—"28th 7br 1722. To Commrs Wine Licences to state the facts." 1 *page.*

26 Sept. 55. Lord Carteret to the Lords of the Treasury. Encloses for their Lps' consideration copy of memorial to the King by the Countess Dowager of Seaforth, who complains that she has not received any part of her jointure upon the late Earl of Seaforth's estate, and alleges that the Government is likewise deprived of what advantage might accrue by the forfeiture of the estate. 26 Sept. 1722.

The memorial.

Minuted:—"28th 7br 1722. This is not a matter before the Lords of the Treasury." 2 *pages.*

[? About 28 Sept.] 56. Memorial of George Luellain, Chamberlain of the City of London, to the Lords of the Treasury. About December last, his Majesty acquainted the Lord Mayor that he had ordered the Bishop of London to receive 1,000*l.* out of the Treasury, to be distributed by him and the Bishop, to the poor of London and Westminster, and parts adjacent, together with what should be collected in the several parishes. The collections have been made, and are

VOL. CCXL.

1722. ready as soon as the 1,000*l.* shall be paid. The time of the Lord Mayor being very short, unless speedily done, it cannot be distributed according to his Majesty's directions. Prays an order to be made thereon.

Minuted:—"Order'd. Warr[t] signd 28th 7[br] 1722." 1 *page, quarto.*

1 Oct. 57. Certificate to the Treasury of the Com[rs] of Alienations (W. Ashburnham and W. Jessop) of the gross and net produce of writs of entry, and writs of covenant, in the Alienation Office, for the year ended at Michaelmas 1722. Alienation Office, Oct. 1, 1722.

With this note at the foot:—"The post fines are always collected by y[e] sheriffs & accounted for in y[e] Pipe, & therefore are not included in this account." 1 *page.*

3 Oct. 58. J. Burchett to Horrace Walpole, Esq. Has to reply to his letter that the Navy Board are preparing the usual Naval estimates, but they cannot be finished until it is known what number of men will be appointed for the next year. Their L[ps] have sent a memorial to be considered by his Majesty in Council. When his Majesty's pleasure is known, the estimates will be laid before the Lords of the Treasury. Adm[y] Office, 3 Oct. 1722.

On the back is:—"L[rd] president to be reminded of fixing y[e] number of men for sea service in Council."

Minuted:—"5th 8[br] 1722. M[r] Chanc[r] hath reminded L[d] Presid[t]." 1 *page.*

10 Oct. 59. Memorial of the Trustees for circulating Exchequer Bills to the Lords of the Treasury. Have examined the computations upon all the Exchequer Loan Bills (a[o] 6 Geo. I.) that have been cancelled at the Exchequer to 28 Sept. 1722. Have, according to the abstract annexed (out of money in their hands on the South Sea Account) paid into the receipt of the Exchequer, upon the account of that company, for interest on Exchequer Bills, 15,041*l.* 3*s.* 11*d.* Send the account of the salaries for executing their trust. Pray for a warrant to pay the same. Trustee's Office, 10 Oct. 1722.

Minuted:—"7th 9[br] 1722. Read & orderd."

The abstract referred to. 3 *pages.*

12 Oct. 60. J. Burchett to Horatio Walpole, Esq. In respect to the claim of Doctor Hawkshaw, Judge of the Admiralty of Ireland, to be reimbursed 124*l.* 7*s.* 8*d.*, expended by him in a suit against the Corporation of Galway, relating to Admiralty jurisdiction. The Lords of the Admiralty had desired that, since the Receiver of the Rights and perquisities of Admiralty had not any money in his hands, to defray the expense, the sum might be paid out of such perquisites of Admiralty as have been accounted for to the Crown; there being no other fund for services of this nature. M[r] Walpole had represented, that possibly the Receiver might now have sufficient to defray the expense, and the Lords of the Treasury conceived that to be the only fund for satisfying the doctor's demand He (M[r] Burchett) has to reply that the Receiver has not where

1722. VOL. CCXL.

withal to reimburse the doctor, and cannot see when sufficient money will be in his hands, and their Lps (of the Admiralty) are of opinion that the perquisites of Admiralty, and particularly the effects of pirates, may better answer the contingencies which the Lords of the Treasury may think necessary to defray out of them, if due care be taken in collecting the same.

The Lords of the Admiralty are sensible that the perquisites of the Admiralty are to be disposed of as the Lords of the Treasury shall judge most for his Majesty's service. But the collecting the perquisites, is expressly allotted to such persons as they (the Lords of the Admiralty) shall authorize.

The Lords of the Admiralty would be very far from interfering with the Lords of the Treasury in anything that does not properly belong to them; and even in this case, they have no other view than to represent to their Lps the obligation they are under (by the clause in the patent) of acting in the manner they have done, and to show the difficulties which arise from the appointment of two receivers for collecting the perquisites. Admiralty Office, 12 Oct. 1722.

Another letter and three other papers on the same subject. 9 *pages and* 2 *halves.*

[Between 18 and 31 Oct.] 61. Memorial of Charles Dartiquenave, Paymaster of H.M. Works, to the Lords of the Treasury. In the annexed "state" is set forth the reason why Mr Auditor Foley cannot proceed in passing the accounts without a royal warrant. Prays for a warrant.

The "state" or certificate referred to, by which it appears that the sum of the expenses was 18,612*l.* 2*s.* 4½*d.*, which was 4,212*l.* 2*s.* 4½*d.* in excess of the yearly allowance of 14,400*l.* limited by his Majesty's instructions. Certified 18 Oct. 1722.

Minuted:—"31st 8br 1722. Prepare a warrt to the Audr for allowing these articles in the Paymrs accounts." 3½ *pages.*

18 Oct. 62. J. Burchett to the Secretaries of the Treasury. The Comrs for Victualling had represented to the Comrs of the Admiralty the bad condition of their storehouses, &c., and proposed several works to be done, amounting to 34,377*l.* Asks that their letter, which he encloses, may be laid before the Lords of the Treasury, that they may see how needful it is that the money may be supplied. Admiralty Office, 18 Oct. 1722.

The copy of the letter referred to, in which the Commrs of Victualling say "neither ought the present shattered condition of the buildings to appear strange, when it is considered that they are no other than what were allotted for the victualling service, long before the Revolution, when the business bore no manner of proportion with what it has been since; so that time itself might be said to have wore them out, and the rather, as no money has been ever given by Parliament, either for supporting them, or making those additions which the increase of the service has necessarily called for." 10 *pages.*

18 Oct. 63. Lord Lieut. of Ireland (Grafton) to the Lords of the Treasury asks them to obtain a warrant from the King for placing Mr Vernon

1722. Vol. CCXL.

Hawly, Major of the Royal Hospital, on the Irish Establishment of Half-pay, as Lieut. of Foot, in the room of Mr Ambrose Burroughs, a reduced Lieutenant of Brigadier Creichton's late regiment of foot. It is stated that the Major had become unfit for his duties, and desired to exchange with Mr Burroughs. Bond Street, 18 Oct. 1722. 2 *pages*.

19 Oct. 64. The same to the same. His Majesty has declared that a new warrant shall be granted to supply the defect of the warrant for placing on the establishment of Ireland the pension of 2,600*l*. per ann., intended to be granted to the Countess Dowager Stanhope, for the term of 31 years. Sends the draft thereof. 19 Oct. 1722.

The draft is not now with it. 2 *pages, quarto*.

23 Oct. 65. Report of the Surveyor General (Pulteney) to the Lords of the Treasury, on the petition of Sir John Vanbruge, who prayed for a lease of the wharf belonging to Somerset House, with the shed thereon, for 31 years. By an Act passed in the 1st year of the present reign, for settling a revenue on her Royal Highness the Princess (in case she shall survive the Prince of Wales) a power was given to his Majesty, at any time before the 25th of March 1716, to grant that palace to her Royal Highness for life, in case she survived his Royal Highness the Prince; which power having been exercised, he conceives that any lease of the wharf, to be granted for a term, will be determinable upon the contingency in the Act mentioned. Would not have advised the granting of the lease if the Act had not been made, as Somerset House may come to be a residence for some of the Royal Family, and then the wharf will be necessary. Gives also other reasons. Has forborne to lay before their Lps a state and value of the premises until he receives their Lps pleasure thereon. 23 Oct. 1722.

The petition referred to. 3 *pages*.

23 Oct. 66. "A. Cracherode's particular of causes under prosecution wth states thereof. 23° Octbr 1722."

[The causes have no minutes against them.] 10 *pages*.

24 Oct. 67. Certificate of the Deputy-Auditors of Imprest to the Lords of the Treasury, in reply to their Lordships' enquiry whether any accounts had been rendered to them by Thomas Missing, Esq., as Contractor for Victualling the garrisons of Gibraltar and Placentia, and in what manner the same are to be passed. Mr Missing has not rendered any account. Give reasons why he should render a General account. Oct. 24, 1722.

Minuted:—"1st 9br. 1722. Mr Missing to render an accot from the commencemt of his sevll contracts psuant to their report. Send a copie of this to the Comptrs Army, acquainting them that, as it appears to my Lords, the passing of the Contractors' accots will take up a considerable time, they do proceed to report upon the Lists & Certificates to them referr'd as formerly, & that my Lords have directed Mr Missing to lay his vo[u]chers before the Audrs, that there may be no delay in passing his accots." 1½ *pages*.

1722. VOL. CCXL.

31 July– 68. Three letters of Lord Carterett to the Lords of the Treasury,
25 Oct. touching payment of bills of Exchange, for money expended at Paris by Sir Luke Schaub, for his Majesty's immediate service.

In the Minute Book, Vol. 23, p. 164, on 28 April 1722, is the following:—"400^{li} to Sir L. Schaub expended for his Majesty's service at Paris pursuant to his Ma^{ts} commands." 4 *pages.*

31 Oct. 69. Memorial of Anthony Vezian, late Agent to the Garrison of Placentia, on behalf of the several Officers of the Garrison and Four Independent Companies there. Praying payment of their demands. Is daily pressed by the Officers and merchants who have given credit for the support of the garrison. Several of the officers are reduced to great necessities for want of their pay, due from 25 Aug. 1717. Praying for directions to be given thereon. 1 *page.*

1 Nov. 70. Memorial of Thomas Missing, contractor for Victualling the Garrisons of Gibraltar, Anapolis, and Placentia. Finds that the passing his accounts by the Auditors will take too long for the contractors to support so great a credit. Prays their L^{ps} orders to the Controllers, that in the mean time they go on reporting as usual, that payments may be obtained according to contracts.

Also the state of the Account.

Minuted:—"1st 9b^{r} 1722. *See* the minute on the Aud^{rs} Rep^{t} ab^{t} the manner of the Contractors passing his Accounts." [The Minute referred is given to the paper of 24 Oct. 1722.] 2 *pages.*

3 Nov. 71. "Commissioners' presentment relating to the six pence in the pound [for salaries, fees, and wages] to be deducted out of all payments that shall be made out of the duties on salt."

A memorial thus docketed from the Salt Com^{rs} to the Lords of the Treasury.

Doubts having arisen, whether the deduction is to be made out of the incident expenses and charges in the receipt and management of the duties, the Com^{rs} pray their L^{ps} directions, whether any, and which of the payments therein specified, are subject to the deduction. Salt Office, 3 Nov. 1722. 2½ *pages.*

[About 72. Petition of Kingsmil Eyre, Esq., Agent to General Nicholson,
6 Nov.] Governor of South Carolina, in America, to the King. The Lords Justices, finding it necessary for his Majesty's service, that new fortifications should be erected in South Carolina, and barracks built there, directed (by warrant) the employment of as many of "the Company" as could be spared in the fortifications and barracks, for which they were to be paid 6*d.* a day each. Pursuant thereto, a number of those soldiers were employed in building the same. Pray that the Board of Ordnance may be ordered to reimburse the petitioner the 960*l.* 8*s.* expended. Referred 6 Nov. 1722.

Another petition to the Lords Justices, copy of the warrant of the Lords Justices, and copy of an account of the charge. 4 *pages.*

8 Nov. 73. Copy of Report of the Lords of the Treasury to the King, on a petition of Bernard Cooke, gent., praying further relief for having attended in England, to prosecute some complaints against M^{r}

1722. VOL. CCXL.

Lowther, late Governor of Barbadoes, and some of the Council, Judges, and Justices of that Island. Their Lordships had referred the examination thereof to Mr Cracherode the Solicitor for affairs of the Treasury, who was of opinion that the petitioner ought not to expect any further reward, than the 100*l.* he had received, until he should have made good his complaints (which it appeared he had failed in proving) or until he should have been able to do some further service. In this opinion they concurred. 8 Nov. 1722.

The Report referred to on Cooke's petition, in which he complained of illegal proceedings against himself and his wife, who gave evidence of traitorous speeches against James Grazett, of Barbadoes. The wife was sentenced to stand in the pillory several times, though ill, and big with child, which usage is said to have caused her death. Grazett was indicted for uttering the following seditious words, viz., "God damn King George and all his family. He is a Dutch dog and son of a whore," and further, "Here is King James the third's health, right and lawful heir to the Crown." He was, however, acquitted. An indictment was found against the wife of the petitioner for having pronounced the following words:—"God damn King George and all his country," and also for having uttered (kneeling) the words following, viz., "Here is King James the third's health." She was found guilty of the last part of the indictment only, and for this was sentenced as above to the pillory. The petitioner's complaint against the Governor was, that to gratify his private resentment against petitioner, he pretended that he had uttered words reflecting on the modesty of Robert Warren's wife, and had caused him to be bound over to a Petty Sessions of the Peace to punish him, and that the Justices refused him a trial by Jury, and condemned him to be publicly whipped, and to have twice thirty-nine lashes; which order was barbarously executed in open Court by the common whipper of slaves. Petitioner offered no proof against the Governor, as to his being illegally whipped, and the petition against him was dismissed, but the Justices and two of the Council were removed for acting arbitrarily and cruelly. 11 *pages.*

9 Nov. 74. Order in Council referring a report of the Comrs of Trade on the petition of Col. Moody, to the Lords of the Treasury, for their report thereon. The petitioner set forth that during the time he was Governor of Placentia, in Newfoundland, he had purchased some houses and lands which were afterwards seized [for his Majesty's use to erect forts upon. He prayed that he, and his tenants, might be reimbursed. The Comrs of Trade were of opinion that satisfaction ought to be made to him. 9 Nov. 1722. 2½ *pages.*

[? About 13 Nov.] 75. Petition of several merchants trading to Virginia and Maryland, in behalf of themselves and others, complaining that since the Union with Scotland, that nation was let into the Plantation trade, and they import into Scotland vast quantities of tobacco from Virginia and Maryland, and bring large quantities thereof into England, and there is just ground to suspect that the duties charge-

1722. VOL. CCXL.

able on tobacco, brought into this kingdom, are not paid by the traders of Scotland upon the arrival of their tobaccos there. The merchants here find a great decay in their trade, and cannot sell the tobacco at any tolerable rates so as to pay the duties to the crown; pray their Lps to recommend this affair to Parliament, that some method may be taken to settle the tobacco trade upon a just and honest foundation. With 35 signatures.

Minuted:—"13th 9br 1722. Read. Mr Brent to attend with his report, concerning the frauds complained of in Scotland to morrow morning. Make an extract of all the directions that were given in pursuance of the hearing of the Merchants at this Board the last year, & what returns have been made to such directions." 1 *large page.*

[? About 13 Nov.] 76. Petition of Frances Wyndham to the Lords of the Treasury, setting out the same particulars as are contained in her petition previously noticed under 6 April 1722, and praying that order may be given to pay her arrears.

Minuted:—"13th 9br. 1722. To be read when Mr Chancr is here." 1 *page.*

17 Nov. 77. Three reports of the Surveyors General to the Lords of the Treasury upon petitions of William Van Hulls, Esq., who in the last of these reports is described as lately deceased, and who was seeking to obtain the grant of a lease of some ground adjoining the Cockpit, Whitehall. He says, in one of his petitions, that soon after the fire at Whitehall, he obtained King William's promise of a piece of ground in the Privy Garden, to rebuild that part of his lodgings which he lost by the fire, and that a lease was granted him in Queen Anne's time, and he expended 2,500*l.* in repairs and new building; yet he had been obliged to quit the best part thereof, whereby the remainder is rendered entirely useless. The report, last in date, gives several particulars as to the situation of two of the pieces of land desired, and refers to a plan annexed, and advises a grant of the lease for 31 years (petitioner surrendering the lease in being), and for the first piece that a fine of 18*l.* 16*s.* 8*d.* should be paid, reserving to the Crown the present rent of 6*s.* 8*d.* per ann. during the first 22 years, and 13*l.* 16*s.* 8*d.* per ann. during the remainder of the term; and for the second piece, a fine of 50*l.*, reserving to the crown a rent of 5*l.* per ann. during the whole term. The petitioner waived his application for a third piece of ground whereon the Battery stands. These petitions are the first of the kind which have fallen under his consideration for a lease of ground within the precincts of Whitehall. The dates of the reports are 13 April 1720, 15 Jan. 1721, and 17 Nov. 1722.

Minuted:—"23d March 1722-3. The Petr must be content with his present intst in ye premisses, for my Lords cannot permit the leasing out that ground, now ye way is to be widened for the conveniency of both houses of Parlt."

Besides the three reports are two ground plans, two petitions, and three letters. 19 *pages and* 2 *halves.*

1722. VOL. CCXL.

22 Nov. 78. Memorial of the Directors of the United East India Company (by Tho. Woolley their secretary) to the Lords the Treasury. By the two million Act there is a clause for the better securing the trade to the East Indies, that three fourths of the forfeitures should be given to the Company and the other fourth to the Crown. By the last act ⅓ of the forfeitures for breach thereof was given to the Crown, ⅓ to the Company, and ⅓ to the officers of the Customs. The Directors have had, and may have, the first information of clandestine and illegal trade, contrary to the acts, and it would be very hard to oblige them to go to a Custom House officer and give him information, which would intitle him to the third of the forfeiture. This they ought to have, who receive the first information and are willing to prosecute. Pray for deputations to two persons named to be Custom House officers for this purpose. East India House, 22 Nov. 1722.

Minuted:—"6th Decr 1722. Mr Chancellour directs deputations to be made out accordingly. Deputations signd." 1 *page*.

24 Nov. 79. Governor, &c. of Greenwich Hospital to the Secretaries of the Treasury. Have received information that several persons are now building and applying for leases of ground on Blackheath, and in Greenwich, within H.M. manor of East Greenwich, wherein are several aqueducts, conduits, and pipes for conveying water to the Hospital, which, by such buildings, may be greatly obstructed, to the damage of the hospital and of several houses of the town of Greenwich that rent their water from the hospital. Desire that the Lords of the Treasury would order a *caveat* to be entered in their office; that no such lease or grant be issued without notice to the Governor. Royal Hospital for Seamen at Greenwich, 24 Nov. 1722.

Minuted:—"9th April 1723. Read." 1 *page*.

27 Nov. 80. Report of the Surveyor General of Woods (Ch. Wither) to the Lords of the Treasury on the memorial of Mr Norton, Warden of his Majesty's forest of East, alias South Bere, alias Beir, in the county of Southampton, praying payment of three years' arrears of salary due to two keepers of Bere Forest, and for some establishment for the future payment thereof, in lieu of an allowance of cordwood, which they had had time immemorial, but of which there is now no more left. The Surveyor confirms the statement as to the arrears, and the mode in which the keepers were paid. There is now due to the two keepers 150*l*. As they have nothing to subsist upon except their wages, thinks it reasonable they should be paid as other keepers of Forests are, and as there is no timber that can be felled with good husbandry, submits that they should be paid out of the Exchequer. 27 Nov. 1722.

Minuted:—"Warrt signd 14 Decr 1722."

Also the memorial. 3 *pages*.

28 Nov. 81. "Petition and memorial" of Robert Bonell to the Lords of the Treasury. Petitioner sent an anonymous letter to their Lps offering to make great discoveries of frauds in the revenue. In answer to advertisement, petitioner waited on the Hon. Horatio Walpole, Esq., and made a full discovery of the frauds and abuses, an

1722. VOL. CCXL.

account of which he now annexed. Petitioner since attended the Com[rs] of Customs several times, and the Com[rs] ordered prosecutions to be commenced against a great number of persons, who have raised considerable estates by such corrupt practices. The consequence would be the immediate recovery of at least 100,000*l.*, and a certain prospect of increasing the revenue 100,000*l.* per ann. Petitioner accepted several gratuities from the runners, but his whole design in so doing was the service of his Majesty, and his expenses have far surpassed his gains. At first, when he could not be brought to give his seeming consent to these corruptions, he was once attempted to be poisoned, and was actually so another time; so that he apprehends himself to be in danger of his life if his name shall be discovered. Prays for encouragement and protection, and that the Com[rs] of Customs may make a report upon his services. November 28, 1722.

Minuted:—"Dec[br] 19, 1722. 200 to be payd out of incidents of y[e] customs."

On the next page to the petition is a warrant from the Lords of the Treasury for the payment of 200*l.* in full satisfaction and reward for his services. Dated 17 Jan. 1722.

Then follow two schedules entitled:—(1) "The officers of the Customs, together with the smuglers, did agree with the merchants, captains of ships, supercargoes and others, importing goods into this port, to run them at the prices following." (2) "An account of monys paid to the officers of the Customs and others, for running of goods out of the following ships according to y[e] s[d] prices." 3½ *pages*.

28 Nov. 82. Petition of Josias Thompson and Elias Barnes, to the Lords of the Treasury. Part of the many services which petitioners have rendered his Majesty, in various kingdoms, may appear by the papers which are recommended to their L[ps] by the Com[rs] of Trade and Plantations, and by letters under the hands of the Com[rs] for Ireland, which the petitioners are ready to produce, &c.; pray for some small subsistence.

Minuted:—"28th 9[br] 1722. Their papers are sent to Ireland, whither they ought to go to attend the Comm[rs], but my L[ds] do not think it reasonable to allow them any thing to carry over" (*sic*). 1 *page*.

29 Nov. 83. Lord Lieut. of Ireland (Grafton) to the Lords of the Treasury. Transmits a memorial of the Lieutenants of Killmain's regiment, together with a memorial in their behalf, of Lord Killmain, their Colonel, representing the loss they have suffered in their pay and in the value of their Commissions, since they were removed from the establishment of Great Britain, to that of Ireland. These memorials set forth that this regiment has been raised near forty years, and had always two lieutenants to each company, who received pay as such, till sent to Ireland in 1718; that from that time, the nine youngest lieutenants have received no more than ensign's pay, though all of them who purchased before that time, paid the price of lieutenancies, and their Commissions give them that rank; that the nine eldest lieutenants likewise partake of this

1722. hardship, not being able, at any time, to dispose of their Commissions in order to their preferment, but at the price of ensigncies; by which means several of them have lost opportunities of advancing themselves according to his Majesty's regulation; moreover, that some of them who were Lieutenants in other regiments, and came into the Royal Fusiliers by exchange, to relieve the Garrison of Minorca, from whence the regiment was sent home, do now receive no more than ensign's pay, though they parted with Lieutenancies in other regiments, in exchange. Desires that their Lps will obtain his Majesty's warrant for allowing the nine youngest lieutenants the same pay, as all other regiments of foot, on the establishment of Ireland, have. Bond Street, 29 Nov. 1722.

Minuted:—" 6th Decr 1722. Prepare a warrt."

Also the petitions referred to. 5 *pages.*

[About Nov.] 84. Memorial of Col. George Douglas, Sir William Hope, Col. George Somerville, William Stuart, Physician General, and George Preston, surgeon, to the Lords of the Treasury. Were paid out of the Treasury of Scotland before the Union, but upon the Union, were placed upon the contingencies of the forces allowed upon the Establishment of Great Britain. State further how they have been paid since, and that they are now two years and a half in arrear, amounting to 2,087*l.* 8*s.* 3*d.*, as appears by certificate annexed. Pray that they may be paid.

Copy of a warrant and the certificate referred to. Dated 16 Nov. 1722. 3 *pages.*

3 Dec. 85. Representation by the Commrs for Hackney Coaches and Chairs, to the Lords of the Treasury on the memorial from Francis Burton, Esq., Receiver General of the Deductions. Apprehended that the deduction of 6d *per libr.* was to be made only upon salaries, fees, &c., but not upon the rent of their office, or upon tradesmen's bills, &c.; and hitherto they have not made such deductions; but as the memorial alleges that other offices have been directed to make such deductions, they pray for directions. 3 Dec. 1722.

Minuted:—" In this as in other Revenue offices."

Also the memorial. 2 *pages.*

4 Dec. 86. Report of Sir Robert Raymond, Attorney General, to the Lords of the Treasury, on the report of Charles Withers, Esq., Surveyor General of H.M. Woods on the memorial of the Duke of Kingston, praying the royal licence to enlarge his park at Thoresby (Notts) by taking in some barren closes and lands of inheritance belonging to the Duke, which lie within the Rangership of Sherwood Forest, and to have free chase and free warren therein. Is of opinion, that since the lands desired to be enclosed are the Duke's inheritance, and that as the Crown has no other rights thereto, than their lying within the Rangership of the Forest, his Majesty may lawfully gratify the Duke therein. 4 Dec. 1722.

The intended enclosure consisted of 1,217 acres 3 r. 30 p.

Also the report and memorial referred to. 3 *pages.*

1722. VOL. CCXL.

5 Dec. 87. "Auditor Harley's report on the demands of the Bank of England for the charges of the annuity offices there, for two years, ending at Michās 1719." 5 Dec. 1722.

The demands fall under the following heads:—

(1) The charge of building offices at the Bank for the transferable annuities, (2) the incident charges of the said offices, (3) the wages or salaries of the officers and clerks employed therein, and (4) a consideration for the pains and service of the persons appointed to take in the Lottery orders at the Bank.

Minuted:—"Wts signed on ye Bills reported." 5 *pages*.

12 Dec. 88. Robert Armstrong to Charles Burniston, Esq., Surveyor General of his Majesty's woods in America. Reiterates much that is previously set out in another letter of 25 July 1722 (*see* vol. ccxl., 16), on the subject of the unlawful cutting of trees claimed to belong to townships. If the inhabitants claim of properties within the townships be good, "then the reservations made by his Majesty for supplying the Royal Navy will only extend to the land lying without the townships, where it is impossible for the crown to be furnished with masts, but at six times the charge, being so great a distance." New Hampshire in New England, 12 Dec. 1722. 2 *pages*.

16 Dec. 89. C. Sibourg to ——. Begs him to remember his favourable promise made about seven months ago, to add so much to his small salary of the Lieutenant Governorship of Nevis, as would make it 400*l*. per ann. As his fate depends upon one who never forfeits his word, his (Mr Sibourg's) hopes are, that his friend, General Harvey, will have such a definitive answer as may set him (Mr Sibourg) above the fears of starving. Bowney in Oxfordshire, December 16 [1722].

Minuted:—"An addll 100li p ann. upon the same foot as his salary as Govr." *Again*:—Warrt signd 7th Feb. 1722–3. 2 *pages*.

20 Dec. 90. Petition of Edward Young, Esq., late Surveyor of the Woods, to the Lords of the Treasury, for payment of 25*l*. 11*s*., being the costs of a suit which Pitman Blanchard, a carpenter, brought against petitioner for work pretended to be done for his Majesty's service in the New Forest, but which the Jury gave against the petitioner. 20 Dec. 1722. 1 *page*.

26 Dec. 91. Representation and memorial of James Loudoun, collector, and Alexander Kennedy, comptroller of his Majesty's Customs at "Glasgow toun" to the Lords of the Treasury. Having seen a copy of a report concerning frauds in the tobacco trade, laid before their Lps in November last, by Humphrey Brent, Esq., one of the Comrs of the Customs in Scotland, and finding that the permits issued out of this office, either for exportation from the principal port of Port Glasgow (whereof this is only a wharf), Greenock, or other ports of the Kingdom, or for home consumption mentioned in that report, as one proof for such alleged frauds, they (the memorialists) offer various considerations for their vindication; though considering they neither have, nor had, any concern in the entries or receipt of duties for tobacco or any other goods, their

1722. Vol. CCXL.

Lps would perceive, that any frauds that have been, or may be, discovered, cannot be justly charged upon them, being capable of drawing no advantage from them. Represent that since the Union, no other books have been kept in this Custom house but Permit books, where all permits outwards are fairly recorded and numbered. "But there don't remain the least foot steps of any order, rule, or precedent for keeping a Leiger either for tobacco or any other goods, or strikeing a balance between the permits for tobacco inwards, and the permits issued out, especially for home consumption," &c. Have gone on in the method of their predecessors, and had never had any distinct rules given them for their conduct till June last, when Mr Brent came thither and called for the books, when the system of carrying on the business was explained. Memorialists give various other particulars in connexion with their method of procedure in their business, and think they have given sufficient evidences that none of the tobacco frauds can be imputed to them. All their endeavours to keep their books in the manner prescribed, will scarce suffice, without a sufficient number of hands. Have sometimes been obliged to keep one or two clerks, which their small salaries can very little afford (the Collector having only 30*l.* per ann. and the Controller 25*l.*) unless, in answer to their petition, they have an augmentation of their salaries. "Custom ho, Glasgow town, December 26, 1722." 3 *large pages*.

[? 1722.] 92. Petition of Nathaniel Kinderley, of Lynn Regis, Norfolk, gentleman, to the King. "Petitioner being one of the Commrs of Sewers for the hundred of Wisbeach, in the Isle of Ely, and also one of the Conservators of the Corporation of the Great Level of the fens, called Bedford Level, and by the said Corporation directed to proceed in finishing a work by them begun for the relief of part of the Fen Country under their care," the rest of the Commrs for that hundred "taking umbrage thereat, under pretence that the Navigation of the River of Wisbeach under their care, would be prejudiced thereby, did at a sessions of sewers by them held at Wisbeach, on Wednesday the thirteenth day of June 1722, set a fine of five hundred pounds" upon the petitioner for proceeding with the work and estreated the fine into the Exchequer. These proceedings of the Comrs of Sewers were occasioned from a clashing of Jurisdiction between them and the Corporation, the merits whereof have been heard in the Court of Chancery, and satisfaction has been decreed to be made to the Comrs of Sewers, by the Corporation, and as the petitioner only acted in obedience to the Corporation, the proceedings (as against petitioner) were dismissed. Prays that the fine may be remitted. Undated. 1 *page*.

[In or after 1722.] 93. "The claims decreed out of forfeitures, unsatisfyed for want of sufficient money in the Exchequer for that purpose."

The claims amounted to 9,548*l.* 8*s.* 9*d.*, and the money in the Exchequer to meet them was 3,984*l.* 7*s.* 11*d.* 1 *page*.

[? 1722.] 94. A printed paper with various notes (? in Lownde's hand) in the margin, and continued on the back, entitled :—"Proposals for an

1722. VOL. CCXL.

agreement between the South Sea Company and the Bank of England as settled by the Courts of Directors of each Company." $1\frac{1}{4}$ *pages.*

[? 1722.] "95. Distribution of the 500,000*l.* raised by an Act 7 Geo[ii] for the debt of his Ma[ts] Civil List."

"List of the Warrants signed for applying the 500,000[li] granted 7[o] G[ii] R[s] for the Civil List." 4 *pages.*

[? 1722.] 96. Petition of Thomas Lechmere, Surveyor General of the Northern continent of America, to the Lords of the Treasury. Was appointed on 1 May 1721, and arrived in New England in September. His salary, &c. are ordered to be paid from 12 Sept. when he was sworn in. Others were paid from the date of the warrant. Prays an order to be paid from the date of the warrant. 2 *pages.*

[? About 1722.] 97. The case of Thomas Corbin late Virginia merchant. Showing the amounts, &c. for which persons had failed who were indebted to him. Corbin was indebted considerably to the crown. "Since the failure of Lee and Corbin the Crown has received by Corbin's means, out of their effects, no less than 32,000*l.*, which is more than ever was recovered (in the memory of man) from any persons whatsoever in the like circumstances." "It appears Corbin has concealed nothing; but on the contrary used his utmost endeavours to serve the crowne. Therefore in a very particular manner merits favour and relief from the Government." 2 *pages.*

[? 1722.] 98. Report, unsigned, but? of the Lords of the Treasury or Board of Trade, to the King, on the petition of the Duke of Montagu, setting forth that the Islands of S[t] Lucia and S[t] Vincent, being part of his Majesty's territories in America, have not hitherto been settled, and that if they were settled it might be an advantage to Great Britain; and praying to have a grant of the same, as well as to be appointed Governor, with power to appoint a Deputy. These are two of the Windward Carribbee Islands comprehended in the Commission of the Governor of Barbadoes; but as neither of them have been settled, they produce no revenue to the Crown, nor advantage to these kingdoms. It would undoubtedly be an advantage that they should be effectually settled and planted, and so much the rather, because the French have heretofore made several attempts to possess them, to the manifest prejudice of the King's title. The petitioner proposes, in consideration of an absolute grant (the Government with all royal and sovereign authority being reserved to his Majesty) to send over five hundred white people at the least, to make a settlement on the Island of S[t] Lucia, within three years. The Duke proposes to be accountable for a quit rent for a third part of the Island at the rate of 2*s.* 6*d.* for every 100 acres of land within 13 years; for one other third within 10 years; and for the remaining third, as it shall be leased out or taken up. As the Island of S[t] Vincent is at present possessed by indians, or negro slaves, who have escaped thither from the neighbouring islands, who are armed and very numerous, he hopes for a further term in settling that Island, and that he may be allowed ten years for making such a

VOL. CCXL.

1722. settlement as may be sufficient to secure the possession thereof, to his Majesty, and that the quit rent shall not commence, but in proportion as the land shall be taken up; that is to say, within three years after the date of each respective lease or grant to be made by his Grace. These proposals are for his Majesty's service, and for the advantage of Great Britain, and tend to open a new branch of trade. When the settlement of Tobago was under consideration, certain rules and restrictions were passed by the writers of the report, to be observed by the Governor of Barbadoes, in the disposition of that Island, which were approved by his Majesty in Council, and if the grant be made, his Grace should be enjoined to observe the same rules in the distribution of these lands; for which reason, they have annexed restrictions of the same nature, which they would make the condition upon which the grant should be made.

Also the restrictions referred to. 4½ *pages.*

[? Circa 1722 or later.] 99. "Reasons offer'd why his Grace ye Duke of Montagu ought not to be restrain'd from planting sugar canes in settling the Island of St Lucia."

The paper finishes thus in respect to the restriction in planting sugar:—It is "not more reasonable that it should be confin'd to one spot of ground, than that one parish in England should be restrained from plowing their lands, least it should lower the price of corn; and all the King's subjects ought to enjoy their propertys in an equall manner, and have an equall liberty of making ye best advantage of it they can."

Also another paper containing some memoranda. 4 *pages.*

1722. 100. "Petition and case" of William Atkinson on behalf of himself, Mary his wife, Agmondesham Atkinson their son, and the rest of their children, to the Lords of the Treasury, showing that Agmondesham Pickayes, the elder, of London, was by letters patent, goldsmith to King James I. and Charles I., and had two privy seals for work done for 4,206*l.* 12*s.*, and Agmondesham Pickayes, the younger, grandfather to petitioner's wife, had a privy seal for work done for King Charles II., for 1,345*l.* 13*s.* Petitioner prays for 40*l.* a year and arrears for nine years and a half's interest on the 1,345*l.* 13*s.* due at Midsummer 1722 (380*l.*).

Also copy of the privy seal of Charles II. 2 *pages.*

[? End of 1722.] 101. Petition of Capt. George Gordon, late Commander of H.M. ship Pearl, in behalf of the officers and company of the ship, and those of H.M. ship Lime, lately commanded by Capt. Ellis Brand, to the King. In November 1718 these ships' companies took a pirate vessel, commanded by Captain Thatch (commonly called Blackbeard), in which engagement, several men were killed on both sides. The pirate vessel and cargo were condemned in Virginia, and the money lodged with the Lieut. Governor for his Majesty's use. By an order in Council the money was directed to be paid to the Court of Admiralty here, and to be granted to the officers and company who belonged to the ships Pearl and Lyme. By

1722. VOL. CCXLI.

another order in Council his Majesty directed the royal bounty or head money, published in his proclamation, to be paid, and by warrant ordered the same, amounting to 710*l.*, to be paid by the Lieut. Governor out of the effects. Prays for the grant of the remainder of the pirate's effects.

Also the Copy of the Order in Council of 23 Oct. 1721. [After 19 Sept., 9 Geo. I., as the warrant referred to is dated on that day. See *King's Warrant Books*, vol. 25, *pages* 194–196.] 3 *pages.*

[? 1722 or 1723.] 102. Memorial of several Officers of the regiment formerly commanded by Lieut. General Macartney, Brigadier Sutton, and the late Col. Leigh, to the Lords of the Treasury. Several months after the regiment was "broke," it appeared that the Government was overpaid. The Com^rs for stating and determining the debts of the Army in Jan. 1721–22 ordered certificates to be prepared upon the overpaid officers, for the payment of others who had balances due; but no certificates were issued, and the Commission had expired: pray for a clause to be inserted in some Act of Parliament to empower the issue of proper certificates. 1 *page.*

[? End of 1722 or in 1723.] 103. "The case of John Lucas, gent., Receiver General of his Majesty's Land revenue in the counties of Worcester, Hereford, Salop, and Stafford. Executed the office of Mr John Digby who was the Receiver from 1689 to 1709–10, and on his decease made up the accounts. Petitioned the Chancellor of the Exchequer and prayed to be appointed, but Mr Robert Hewit was appointed. On the demise of her late Majesty, the receivership determined, and he (Lucas) again petitioned, and was constituted receiver and delivered in his accounts to Mich. 1722; when there was a surplus of 48*l.* 7*s.* 0¾*d.*, but as Hewit's accounts are not yet declared he (Lucas) is incapable of getting his accounts declared, and has petitioned the Chancellor of the Exchequer for a special order for declaring his accounts. 1 *page.*

[After 1722.] 104. "The exact form and method that all ministers have ever gone on an Embassy to the Emperor of Morocco from George Delaval Esq., in 1707, to Charles Stewart, Esq., in 1722." Undated.

Showing the number of persons who went with embassies and their equipage. It is mentioned that there are no inns or entertainment whatever in all Barbary. 1 *small page.*

[? About 1722.] 105. "State of the case upon several acts of Parliament relating to army debentures."

Giving the effect of various Acts between 1 and 8 George I. as respects army debentures.

It is stated at the end that Mr Serjeant Pengelly, Mr Attorney General, and Mr Solicitor General, are of opinion, that the alteration of certain debentures by Captain Pakenham is not felony, because the debentures so altered by him, appear on the face of them, not to have been made out in pursuance of any Act of Parliament. 2½ *pages.*

1722.

VOL. CCXLI. 1722. CLASSIFIED. PART I.

1. Reports of the Commissioners for examining debts due to the Army addressed to the King on the following subjects :—the extraordinary charges of the office of Anthony Hammond, Esq., late Deputy to the Duke of Chandos, late Paymaster General of the forces abroad at Barcelona and Minorca. [*Minuted* :—"24th Janry 1721–2. To Audrs Imprests to prepare a Sign Manual. Warrt signd 12 Feb. 1721–2.] Charge of provisions from the marine and other regiments in Garrison at Annapolis Royal in 1710 and 1711. [*Minuted* :—"8th Feb. 1721–2. To Audrs Imprests to prepare a S. Manual."] Allowance of mule money for regiments in Spain for the years 1707, 1708, and 1709. After the battle of Almanza the officers (Sir Charles Hotham and Col. Fredrick Sibourg) were obliged to maintain the beasts of carriage to protect the adjacent country. Both regiments sustained several losses by being besieged, and their horses, mules, and baggage were taken by the enemy on being forced to retire to defend themselves in the castle of Alicante. [*Minuted* :—"12th Feb. 1721–2. To Audrs Impts to prepare a S. Manual."] Levy money for horses raised by the officers of the regiment of dragoons under the successive command of Lieut. Col. Green, Count Nassau, and the late Earl Stanhope. [*Minuted* as above.] Horses lost in action in the late war in Spain. [*Minuted* as above.] Demand of pay of Captain George Carleton as engineer in Spain. The Earl of Peterborough "commanded him to serve in that capacity at the Siege of Barcelona, Raquina, and Cuenca, and he acted as engineer at the Sieges of Barcelona, Alicant, and Denia where he was taken prisoner. [*Minuted* :—16th Feb. 1721–2. To Audrs imprests to prepare a S.M.] Demand of Mr Vincent Chabanes for his services and disbursements as Commissary of provisions in Spain amounting to 19,311*l.* 8*s.* 6½*d.* [*Minuted* as above.] Demand of officers of regiments of dragoons commanded by Major General John Pepper placed on the Establishment of Ireland. [*Minuted* as above.] Demand of Doctor John le Cane for his disbursements as director of the British Hospital in Spain. [*Minuted* :—"To Audrs Imprests to prepare a wt.] Claim for mule purchase and mule maintenance by Lieut. Genl Wills and officers under his command. [*Minuted* as above.] Demand for subsistence of the supernumerary men of Col. Charles Churchill's regiment of marines. [*Minuted* as above.] Claim of several officers of the late regiment of foot commanded by Col. Constantine de Magny. They were made prisoners at the battle of Almanza. Their application is for completing their full pay. Also a demand made by Mr Thomas Sydenham appointed in England to pay and subsist sundry invalid soldiers, discharged from the service in Flanders and Spain, and further a demand of Lieut. Charles Hutchinson, of Col. Edward Stanhope's late regiment of foot, being respited 64 days. [*Minuted*

1722. Vol. CCXLI.

as above.] Demand for half pay to invalid officers of three companies that did duty at the Tower of London, of four companies quartered at Brentford, and of the officers of eight companies that were to be formed out of Chelsea. Dated between 17 Jan. and 7 March 1721–2. 22 *pages and* 4 *halves.*

2. Various papers connected with the Treasurer of the Chamber's Department, consisting of accounts, an estimate, &c. One is a certificate of what was due to Sir Godfrey Kneller, Bart., principal painter in ordinary to his Majesty; another is an application for an imprest of 500*l.* for his Majesty's intended progress to Salisbury and Portsmouth. 14½ *pages.*

3. Lord Chamberlain's warrants to the Master of the Great Wardrobe, the Master of the Jewel Office, &c., for the delivery of articles of furniture, plate, &c. Besides which there are two certificates of the admission to the place of Gentleman of the Bedchamber, and a request to the Lords of the Treasury to pay 350*l.* to Mons. von Borssele, Envoy Extraordinary from the States General, on his taking leave. 7 *pages.*

4. Reports of the Controllers of Army Accounts (Medows and Bruce) to the Lords of the Treasury, on the accounts of persons victualled, and on payments to be made to the contractors in connexion with the garrisons of Gibraltar, Placentia, and Annapolis Royal; on the allowance to Edward Hughes, Esq., Judge Advocate General; on the case of the Col. and Captains of the regiment of the late Earl of Donegal's regiment, who were charged with an additional company and six men, for the time when most of the officers of that regiment were made prisoners at Almanza, and detained in France two years. Some of the reports have minutes on the back similar to the following:—"Prepare warrant," &c. Dated Controller's Office, Privy Garden. There are also the enclosures to the reports. 33 *pages or parts of pages.*

5. Five Orders in Council, four of which relate to ships arriving, the sanitary condition of which required consideration, as to whether they should perform quarantine, and one relates to the seizure of a pirate ship at Barbadoes called the Royal James. 11 *pages.*

6. Reports (with enclosures) of the Com^rs^ of Customs to the Lords of the Treasury on petitions relating to the following subjects, also some memorials of the Com^rs^ of Customs:—(1) on a composition with the Crown by a merchant indebted for tobacco duties. (The petitioner and his sureties held the manor of Uxendon with divers lands in and near Harrow-on-the-Hill. He had also possessions in London, Guernsey, and lands called Goodwins in Essex; (2) on certain bales of silk in which bags of stones were found for which duty had been paid. (The Com^rs^ say "that admitting the

VOL. CCXLI.

1722.

case to be as represented in the petition, yet the repaying duties of goods as over entered, after they are out of the possession of the officers, is contrary to the constant practice of the Customs, and may be of dangerous consequence to this revenue by opening a way to many frauds"); (2) on the sale of the estates of Cornelius Denne, late of London, merchant, under extent for a considerable debt to the Crown. The estates were at Hemingford Greys and Hemingford Abbots, and difficulties had arisen in making a title to them. As to that at Hemingford Abbots, Capt. Keyser claimed a title under a mortgage made by Mr Denne for 2,000*l.* and part of the estate was copyhold, and was not liable to the extents. Mrs Judith Wonnocott had also a mortgage of 500*l.*, besides a large sum for interest due on both estates. The purchase money for both estates was 9,600*l.*, of which there was due to the Receiver General of Customs, 4,642*l.* 11*s.* 7*d.*; pray their L^ps^ to be a means for passing the grant of the estates to Mr Mitchell, the purchaser. [*Minuted* :—" Warr^t^ sign'd 19th May 1722"]; (4) on what was due to the Crown by Mr Hawes, late Receiver General and Cashier of the Customs' revenue (66,240*l.* 15*s.* 4½*d.*). [*Minuted* :—" 21 Aug. 1722."] Write to the Trustees (for the sale of the Estates of the late Directors of the South Sea Company) to know what money is in the hands of the cashier applicable to this debt; (5) on a deposit for duties on unrated East India goods until the dispute thereon could be adjusted. [*Minuted* :—April 25, 1722]. "The Lords agree that ye sum of 43,629*l.* 19*s.* 9*d.* payd by ye E. India Company by way of deposit, be charged to Sr John Shaw's account, & that ye warrant for deposits be recalled, & ye payments be made & accounted frequently for ye future"; (6) on arrival and seizure of goods from Ostend, when the post announcing the shipment only arrived four days after; whereby the petitioner could not be privy to the running of the goods; (7) on the repayment of land tax to the inferior officers of the Customs, whose salaries do not exceed 60*l.* per ann.; (8) "For the sign manual for deducting 6^d^ in the pound to be explained." [*Minuted* :—Warr^t^ signd 4th 8br 1722.] (9) On the additional business occasioned by the quarantine. (10) On the allowance of duties paid on goods burnt in a ship. The report states that the Commissioners are of opinion the petitioner cannot be relieved, "for that by law the duties of all goods are due and payable on their importation into this Kingdom, that the appropriation of the duties takes place from the time they are legally charged in the King's books, and that ye revenue cannot be affected by any subsequent hazard to the goods"; and if any such indulgence should be brought into practice, it would put the management under many difficulties, and expose the revenue to great hazards. (11) On the gross and neat produce of the revenue [the account not now with it]. (12) On the petition of the Mayor, Aldermen, and burgesses, merchants and traders of the borough and parish of Barnstaple. They represent that the borough formerly comprehended the port of Bideford and all the creeks and harbours within the bar of Barnstaple, the duties of keyage whereof belonged

1720. Vol. CCXXXII.

to that Corporation. Upon the erection of the port of Bideford, the creek or harbour of Appledore was left, as it ever was, to the port of Barnstaple. The dismembering and annexation of it to the port of Bideford would be of the most fatal consequence to the port of Barnstaple, and the revenues and privileges of the latter town. Long since the erection of the port of Bideford the limits and bounds thereof have been visited by virtue of a writ or commission from the Court of Exchequer [of Easter term 29 Car. II.], and by the return to the same, Appledore is limited to be, as it always was, within the port of Barnstaple. Of late the officers of customs at Bideford, have granted warrants for the delivery and shipment of goods imported and exported at Appledore, which will favour clandestine trade, &c., and will be a notorious infringement of the revenues and privileges of the Corporation of Barnstaple. The Com^rs report that it appears that the limits of the port of Barnstaple, by virtue of the above Commission, extend to the Bar of Barnstaple, unto a Rock called Whipplestone, or Hubbastone, in the parish of Northan in the river of Bideford, and that the port of Bideford extends from the said rock, on both sides the river, to Bideford Bridge "and Appledore lying between the said Rock and the Bar of Barnstaple," and they are of opinion that the despatches for the shipping and unshipping goods at Appledore should legally be granted by the proper officers of the port of Barnstaple only. There are also several enclosures including two plans. One of the enclosures is a copy of certificate of the Inhabitants in, and near, the port of Bideford, in which they state that having often viewed the river and port of Bideford and keys thereof, "the 'Lyer' before the Key in the West side of the s^d River is choaked up with sand, mudd, & stones, that ships of eighty tons & upwards, laden with goods, cannot come near the Key, unless on the heigth of a spring tide; and even then are in great danger of damaging both ships & goods by the sands washing away from under their bottoms, as has been often found by experience; and that no part of the ground, near the same key is so safe for any ships, as the ground on the East side of the said River. That for several years last past the river has alter'd its course, and now runs on the East side, as it formerly did on the West side, which has scoured off the sand & mud, and made the ground on the East side, free & safe for ships or galleys of burthen to lie upon with safety, without danger of taking any damage." They further "certifie that on low tides, the boats from Apledore, with passengers, are forced to land them on the East side, not having water to come near the key on the West side." [The report is *minuted* 7th Feb. 1722–3. Make a copie of this report for Mr Whetham, 8th April 1723. Read."] Also (13) copy of memorial of the Com^rs of Customs for additional building to the Custom house, Thames S^t, with Warr^t for the same annex^d, dated 30th March 1722. Mentions that the estate belonging to the Trustees of the Free School at Sevenoaks, Kent, adjoining the East End of the Custom House, is now vested in the Crown. 72 *pages* or parts of *pages*.

Vol. CCXLI.

722.

7. Report and three memorials of the Com[rs] of Excise to the Lords of the Treasury, relating to (1) "duties upon printed linens *ad valorem*"; (2) the insolence of the runners on the Coast near Battle, who are headed by persons for whom rewards have been offered in the Gazette, also as to the quantities of foreign brandy brought in by the Portsmouth dealers by fraud [*Minuted*:—"12th July 1722. My Lords will move his Ma[tie] to send two companies to this Coast as desired"]; (3) the runners of brandy on the coasts of Sussex and Southampton and the attempts to kill the customs officers [*Minuted* like the last]; (4) the gross and net produce of the several branches of his Majesty's Civil List revenues under the management of the Com[rs] of Excise. 13 *pages or parts of pages.*

8. Various financial papers consisting of (1) Estimates of the debt of the Navy; (2) Estimates of the debt for Transport Service; (3) Accounts of debt of the Civil List and declaration of the expense of the same; (4) Accounts of what is wanting to clear the Foreign Ministers (names given); (5) Estimate of charge of the office of Ordnance; (6) State of the sinking fund; (7) Rough draft of contract for circulating Exchequer Bills; (8) Sums voted for the public service; (9) Abstracts of the produce of the revenue in Ireland; (10) Account of the produce of the Excise; (11) Papers as to the South Sea Company's capital, &c; (12) Papers as to Exchequer Bills; (13) Accounts of produce, &c. of the "Aggregate Fond into the Exchequer"; (14) State of the produce of the duty of 4½ per cent. 37 *pages.*

9. A broken series of similar papers numbered on the back. There were originally 59 or more papers. Amongst them are three papers of estimates of the charge of the guards, garrisons and other his Majesty's Land forces in Great Britain; of the out pensioners of Chelsea Hospital; and of the forces in the Plantations, Minorca and Gibraltar. 31 *pages.*

10. Several papers relating to Lottery affairs. 13 *pages.*

11. Memorials from the office of Paymaster of the forces to the Lords of the Treasury, asking for the issue of moneys for remittance to Minorca, Gibraltar, Port Mahon, &c., and in payment of various other services. One relates to Captain John Kelly, who whilst ill of a fever was superseded. His company was serving at Tinmouth Castle. Another relates to fees paid at the Exchequer at 1½*d.* per pound on upwards of two million pounds. [*Minuted*:—"Agreed to make a standing warr[t] for the time to come."] 26 *pages or parts of pages.*

12. Representations of the Com[rs] of Works to the Lords of the Treasury on the following subjects: (1) the upper story of the New Buildings at Kensington; (2) the Court of Requests and the passage

1722. VOL. CCXLII.

between the House of Commons and the Painted Chamber. Recommend that the walls of the former be raised and the roof pulled down and rebuilt, and that the passage Gallery between the House of Commons and the Painted Chamber be made new, the stairs more commodious for the Members, and rooms over the passage for the Clerk of the Parliament; (3) the "condition of the fine equestral statue at Charing Cross which is very much out of repair, the reines of the bridle being broke and wasted small" &c.; (4) the condition of the work of painting the ceiling of the Great Chamber at Kensington. A report by Messrs Nesbott (or Nesbitt) and Rambour is enclosed, which states the work is better than half done; but the perspective is not just. The principal of the work, which consists of ornaments and architecture, is not done as such a place requires. "Mr Nesbott adds, that the boys, masks, mouldings, &c. far from being well, he has seen very few worse for such a place," and Mr. Rambour affirms that the sd work far from being done in the best manner," is not so much as tolerably well performed. They cannot say whether the blue used in the work is true ultramarine, because it does not look fine enough; but Mr Nesbot's opinion is, that it is nothing but Prussian blue, in which perhaps there may be some ultramarine mixed, and (5) the debt due in the office. 6 *pages.*

VOL. CCXLII. 1722.

DOCUMENTS for which a brief description suffices.

Date.	Description of Document.	From	To	Purport.
5 Jan.	1. Report -	Board of General Officers.	The Lord Lieut. of Ireland.	On petition of Ensign George Scot who had not attended an examination, and lost his half pay as a reduced ensign. 2 *pages.*
8 Jan.	2. Account -	—	—	Of bills of lading, vouchers, &c., for provisions for Annapolis Royal and Placentia. 1 *page.*
[? About 26 Jan.]	3. Account -	—	—	Of warrants of Her late Majesty to several persons for whom no money was ordered before the demise of Her Majesty. 1½ *pages.*
5 Feb.	4. Certificate -	His Majesty's Jewel Office.	—	Of 1,066 ounces of gilt plate delivered out to His Excellency, Sir Robert Sutton, Ambassador Extraordinary to France. 1 *page.*

1722. VOL. CCXLII.

Date.	Description of Document.	From	To	Purport.
[? About 12 Feb.]	5. Memorial	Mrs. Anne Hyde	The Lords of the Treasury.	For a bill for chocolate due from the late Queen Anne. *Minuted* :—" 12th Feb. 1721–22. My Lords are come to a resolution already to see what the Queen's tyn will amount to, and then will pay all her mats. servts. in proportion as far as her effects will reach." 1 *page*.
13 Feb.	6. Representation	Comrs. of Excise, Scotland.	Do.	As to allowance of the price of stationery wares. Also copy of the representation, and of the petition. The last has a minute on it of 25 May 1722, agreeing to the report (or representation). 7 *pages*.
14 Feb.	7. Report	Postmaster's General	Do.	The case of Mr. John Luddington, late postmaster at Canterbury, who was indebted to the office, 828*l*. 16*s*. 11*d*. 1½ *pages*.
16 Feb.	8. Letter	Mos Beranger	?	Tin in Holland under his management. 1 *page*.
16 Feb.	9. Petition	" Nath. Rich "	Lords of the Treasury.	For 20*l*. above the 40*l*. " the usual pension." [Nothing to show for what service.] *Minuted* :—" My Lords will make no further allowance." 1 *page*.
22 Feb.	10. Letter	Thomas Madockes and John Monteage.	Do.	As to entering " tallies of Pro " in the Bank books. 1 *page*
23 Feb.	11. Memorial	A. Cracherode	Do.	For 500*l*. on account for conducting causes for his Majesty. 1 *page*.
28 Feb.	12. Letter	Lord Townshend	Do.	Mr. Kenworthy to be reimbursed 126*l*. 9*s*. 3*d*.
[? About 5 March.]	13. Memorial	Thomas Louther	Do.	For a warrant to be signed for some fees for secret service, and for money advanced. *Minuted* :—" 5th March 1721. My Lords have signd the warrt." 1 *page*.
8 March	14. Do.	J. Hancock	Do.	For 200*l*. to be issued for supplying mourning to twenty officers, to whom it was customary to give the same when the Court went into mourning. *Minuted* :—" 9th March 1721–22. Order'd." 1 *page*.

1722. Vol. CCXLII.

Date.	Description of Document.	From	To	Purport.
[? About 12 March.]	15. Petition -	Eight door-keepers of the House of Lords.	Lords of the Treasury.	For a further allowance, they only receiving 50*l.* amongst them for each session. The public business in Parliament has of late years very much increased. *Minuted* :—" 12th March 1721–22. 80li. to be given amongst them." 1 *page.*
[? About 12 March.]	16. Memorial -	Charles Stanhope, Esq.	Do. - -	For repayment of 156*l.* 8*s.* 6*d.* for customs, &c. on certain plate consigned to William Stanhope, Esq., his Majesty's Ambassador Extraordinary at Madrid, which plate was exported by His Majesty's command to be disposed of there, and not for the Ambassador's use. *Minuted* :—" 12th March 1721–22. P'pare a wt. (including ye fees) to be signed by the King." 1 *page.*
[? About 12 March.]	17. Petition -	Robert Bedoe -	Do. - -	For a like allowance to that which he had for the previous sessions of Parliament, for keeping the gates leading from the Privy Garden into Cannons Row, Westminster, for the conveniency of the members of Parliament. *Minuted* :—" 12th March 1721–22. Read. *Qu.* whether the 40li. last paid him was for a yeare's service, or in full of all former demands. The 40li. was paid him by warrt. dated 4th May 1721 in reward for his extry. service, and attendce. on committee nights during ye session of Parlt. begun the 23d of Novr. 1719, & ended ye 11th of June 1720. 11th Septr. 1723. My Lords think he ought to be paid (if any thing is due) by Mr. Kirke." ½ *page.*
[? About 17 March.]	18. Memorial -	William Earl of Dartmouth.	Do. -	For payment of 650*l.* due to him as keeper of her late Majesty's Privy Seal at 5*l.* a day. *Minuted* :—" 17th March 1721–22. Orderd." 1 *page.*

1722. VOL. CCXLII.

Date.	Description of Document.	From	To	Purport.
27 March	19. Memorial -	Thomas Lynford, sub-almoner.	Lords of the Treasury.	For sums for the poor at the gate, for Lady Frances Keightley, and for private pensions, and for two Arabic professors. 1 *page.*
[? About 30 March.]	20. Do. -	John Tooker on behalf of Arthur Collins, late of London, bookseller.	Do. - -	For provision and support, he having been promised employment in the Customs, which was given to others. This so affected his senses that he was unfit for business. *Minuted*:—"30th March 1722. Prepare a warrt. for 200li. bounty to John Tooker in consideration of the facts alleged in the memll. paper annexed. Warrt. signd 5th Ap. 1722." Also an enclosure. 2 *pages.*
2 April	21. Letter -	Lord Carteret -	Do. - -	For payment of 50*l.* as of H.M. special bounty to Capt. John Corso, a subject of the King of Spain. Whitehall. *Minuted*:—"11th April 1722; prepare a warrt. Warrt. signd 18th." 1 *page.*
[? About 4 April.]	22. Petition -	Col. Henry Hawley, Equerry, and Col. John Chudleigh, Page of Honor to the late Prince George of Denmark.	Do. - -	For sums due to them, her Majesty having continued their salaries from the time of the death of the Prince to that of Her Majesty. *Minuted*: — "4 Aprill 1722. A moiety orderd. 12th. Do. Warrt. sign'd." 1 *page.*
10 April	23. Letter -	Mr. George Tilson -	"R. H. Mr. Chancr. of ye Exchr."	Encloses "the charge of the patents for the two Ladys" (648*l.* 10*s.* each). The ladies were (1) Sophia Charlotta, Countess of Leinster, Baroness of Brentford, and Countess of Darlington, (2) Melosina, Baroness of Schulenbourgh, Baroness of Aldborough and Countess of Walsingham. Whitehall. *Minuted*:—"30th April 1722. Prepare a warrt. for 1297 [*l.*] psuant to the accot. annexed in the name of Mr. Geo. Tilson. 12th Do. Warrt. signd." 2 *pages.*

1722. VOL. CCXLII.

Date.	Description of Document.	From	To	Purport.
10 April	24. Letter -	Lord Lieutenant of Ireland (Grafton).	Lords of the Treasury.	For the usual grant of reward of 500*l.* each, to the speakers of the two houses of Parliament in Ireland, viz., to the Rt. Hon. Viscount Middleton, as Speaker of the House of Lords, and the Rt. Hon. William Conolly, Esq., as Speaker of the House of Commons. *Minuted:*—"Warrt. signd. 18th Ap. 1722." 1 *page.*
[? About 14 April.]	25. Memorial -	Col. Charles Du Bourgay.	Lords of the Treasury.	Praying for the settling of the payment of his salary of 1,000*l.* per annum as Lieut. Governor of Jamaica. *Minuted:*—"14th April 1722. Order'd." 1 *page.*
16 April	26. Report -	Brook Plukenet, Deputy Muster Master General.	Lords Justices of Ireland.	On the petition and case of Ensign Charles Turner, advising that he should be replaced on the establishment of half-pay. Also the petition. 2 *pages.*
[About 17 April.]	27. Petition -	Thomas Wyth, gent., and four others of the Colony of Virginia	Lords of the Treasury.	For a warrant to the Receiver of Customs of the Colony of Virginia for payment to them of 120*l.* for the apprehension of pirates. *Minuted:*—"(1.) 1 May 1722. See out of what moneys the stated demands of apprehenders of pirates have been paid. (2.) These rewards being for pyrates convicted in Virginia, have been paid out of pyratical effects or other unappropriated revenues in Virginia, now in ye hands of the Admrs. of Jas. Roscow, decd., late Genl. there. (3.) Mr. Dalrymple the Casual Recr. at Berbadoes has also some pyratical effects in his hands. (4.) 19th do. Prepare a warrt. to pay this out of pyratical effects &c. in the hands of the said administrators." Also a certificate. 2 *pages.*

Date.	Description of Document.	From	To	Purport.
28 April	28. Letter -	Lord Townshend -	Lords of the Treasury.	For 1,000*l.* to be lodged with the Treasurer of the Chamber to defray expenses of messengers sent abroad. Whitehall. *Minuted:* — "7th May 1722. Order'd. Lre signd 9th May 1722." 1 *page.*
[? About 28 April.]	29. Petition -	John le Maitre -	Do. - -	Prays to be put on the establishment of Chelsea Hospital at 12*d.* a day. "Says that in 1717, when at Calais, he discovered a parcel of rebels forming a design to assasinate his Majesty." He further demonstrated the clandestine practices of the smugglers. *Minuted:* — "28 April 1722. My Lords will issue no more money on accot. of any of these ptended services." 1 *page.*
7 May	30. Certified copy of inrolment.	King William and Queen Mary.	Joseph Herne, Knt., and others.	"For coyning copper halfepence & farthings. Anno 1694." *Minuted:* — "7th May 1722. Mr. Lowther is to pay to Mr. Burroughs 4li. for this copie of a patent taken from the Rolls Chapell." The reference to the Patent Roll at the head is:—"11ma pars Pat. de a° rñi Rs. Gul. et Rne. Marie 6to." 9 *pages, brief size.*
17 May	31. Representation or memorial.	Comrs. of Taxes -	Lords of the Treasury.	For an advertisement to be inserted in the Gazette for the estates of Benjamin Blundell, junr., Esq., late Receiver General of the county of Leicester, and of Benjamin Blundell, senior, his security, to be sold to satisfy a debt to the Crown. *Minuted:* — "18 May 1722. Ks. Rembrr. to advertise ye sale of these estates and report ye best bidder." *Again:* — "19th Decr. 1722. Agreed to, *vide* minutes on the Ks. Rembrr. certificates of the best bidders." 1 *page.*

1722. VOL. CCXLII.

Date.	Description of Document.	From	To	Purport.
[? About 18 May.]	32. Letter -	Claudius Amyand -	The Right Hon. the Chancellor of the Exchequer.	To remind the Chancellor. *Minuted* :—"18th May 1722. 200li. ꝑ ann. pension to commence from Lady day last ꝑ Mr. Chetwynd." 1 *page* (4to).
1 June	33. Letter -	John Balaguier -	The Rt. Hon. Mr. Walpole.	For his signature to an order for 100*l.* payable to Mr. Lambert. Encloses also copy of another bill of exchange for 100*l.* payable to him. Also as to arrears on Sir William Gostwycke's pension. Also an enclosure. 2 *pages.*
1 June	34. Memorial -	Mr. Robert Jacomb -	The Lords of [the Treasury].	As to redemption of a loan of 100,000*l.* borrowed from the Bank at 4*l.* 10*s.* per cent. Horse Guards. *Minuted* :—"1 June 1722. Ordered." 1 *page.*
8 June	35. Letter -	Lord Lieut. of Ireland (Grafton).	Do. - -	On petition of Viscount Boyn for transferring his pension of 10*s.* a day to his son Henry Hamilton, Esq. *Minuted* :—"12th June 1722. Prepare the proper warrt." 1 *page.*
[After 13 June.]	36. Account -	—	—	Of persons indebted to the Revenue on salt, and the proceedings against them, and what has been recovered. 7 *pages.*
[? About 19 June.]	37. Petition -	John Baskett, H.M. Printer.	Lords of the Treasury.	3,475*l.* 13*s.* 3*d.* was due for printing Acts of Parliament, &c., in the last year of King William, and 1,502*l.* 0*s.* 8*d.* for the last year of Queen Anne, besides for the last year's service for the present King. Prays payment for the arrears of Queen Anne. *Minuted* :—"19th June 1722. Read." 1 *page.*
21 June	38. Report -	Comrs. for Taxes -	Do. - -	On petition of John Manby, Esq., Recr. General of Land Taxes and Duties on Houses for part of the co. of Lincoln. Recommending an allowance to him of 240*l.* The petition and two other documents. 5 *pages.*

1722. VOL. CCXLII.

Date.	Description of Document.	From	To	Purport.
26 June	39. Memorial -	Royal Academy of Music.	Lords of the Treasury.	For a warrant for 500*l.* for six months bounty due to them. *Minuted:* — "26th June 1722. Orderd." 1 *page.*
[? About 26 June.]	40. Do. -	Officers of H.M. Yards.	The Rt. Hon. Robert Walpole, Esq.	Praying discharge from the 6*d.* tax. *Minuted:* — "26th June 1722. Agreed to." 1 *page.*
30 June	41. Account -	—	—	Of charges paid by the Bank upon account of subscriptions for the support of public credit. 1 *page.*
[? About 17 July.]	42. Do. -	—	—	Scotland ? Of salaries and incidental charges of the Comrs. and Trustees of Forfeited Estates. *Minuted:* — "17th July 1722. Prepare a warrt. Wt. signd." 2 *pages.*
[? About 17 July.]	43. Memorial -	Hugh Drysdale, Esq., Lieut.-Governor of Virginia.	Lords of the Treasury.	For allowance for his transport to his Government. *Minuted:* — "17th July 1722. All precedts. are against such allowances." 1 *page.*
[? About 18 July.]	44. Petition -	Edward Peet -	Do. - -	For payment of 100*l.*, he having apprehended William Fletcher *alias* Fellowes, a highwayman, who robbed Richard Skingle, Esq., in the parish of St. Bride's, London. *Minuted:*—"18 July 1722. My Lords are of opinion that such roberies were not within the meaning of the proclamation." Also copy of certificate. 2 *pages.*
31 July	45. Letter - -	Lord Carteret -	Do. - -	For directions to be given for payment of a pension of 300*l.* per ann. during pleasure to Elizeus Burges late Resident in the Republic of Venice. *Minuted:*—"10th Augt. 1722. Orderd." 1 *page.*
31 July	46. Account -	—	—	Of payments in the Treasurer of the Chambers Office, also what was still due. Signed, C. Stanhope. *Minuted:* — "15 Augt. 1722. Ordered." 3 *pages.*

1722. VOL. CCXLII.

Date.	Description of Document.	From	To	Purport.
[? About – July.]	47. Memorial -	Andrew Shields, page of his Majesty's bed-chamber extraordinary.	The Rt. Hon. Robert Walpole, Esq., First Commr. of the Treasury.	For a Treasury warrant for his half-year's salary due at Midsummer 1722. 1 *page.*
[? About 2 Aug.]	48. Petition -	Edward Peet -	Lords of the Treasury.	In nearly the same terms as that above described. Under date 18th July. Also copy of certificate. *Minuted :* — "2 Augt. 1722. Rejected." 2 *pages.*
[? About 2 Aug.]	49. Do. -	Mary Speke, wife of Hugh Speke, Esq.	Do. - -	The family suffered in King James's reign, being imprisoned and ruined. The late Queen granted her a pension of four score pounds per annum. Had received but 20*l.* since his Majesty's accession: prays their Lps'. favour. *Minuted:* — "2d Augt. 1722. My Lords cannot advise his Matie. to create new pensions." 1 *page.* 4to.
3 Aug.	50. Account -	—	—	Of the duty on wine licences from the commencement of the duty until 3 Aug. 1722. 1 *page.*
[? About 3 Aug.]	51. Memorial -	W. Wood - -	Lords of the Treasury.	For licence to coin the copper money "for Ireland at the city of Bristol." *Minuted :* — "3d August 1722. Prepare a constitution appointing Sir Isaac Newton, Comptr. of this coynage and that for the West Indies; to act by himself or deputy; & then my Lords will give the proper directions & powers to the petr. to coin a certain quantity of copper money at Bristol according to his request. 1 *page.*
14 Aug.	52. Report -	Comrs. of Stamps -	Do. - -	On the petition of Wm. Adderly who asked that the warrant for his dismission might be stopped. The report sets out his great neglect of duties. *Minuted* · — "5th Augst. 1722. My Lords, upon consideration of ye Commrs. Report do not think fitt to restore Wm. Adderly. 2 *pages.*

1722. VOL. CCXLII.

Date.	Description of Document.	From	To	Purport.
[After the middle of Aug.]	53. Petition -	Joseph Bayley, of St. Andrews, Holborn, Coachman,	Lords of the Treasury.	For forgiveness, he having unfortunately misbehaved himself at the Duke of Marlborough's funeral. With certificate at the foot in his favour, with several signatures. 1 *page.*
[? About 15 Aug.]	54. Memorial -	Brigadier-General Bowles and Brigadier General Munden.	Do. - -	For money paid by them for their officers and men whilst detained in England when the regiment was transferred to the Irish Establishment (viz., from 11 Nov. 1718). *Minuted* :—" 15th Augst. 1722. Read & respited." 1 *page.*
17 Aug.	5. Petition -	John Elliott -	Do. - -	Representing seizures made by him in the port of Exeter, and asking for a tidesman's place in " Topsham Pringe." *Minuted* :—" 17th Augt. 1722. Read." 2 *pages.*
[? About 30 Aug.]	56. Do. -	Henry Raingill -	Do. - -	For a tide-waiter's place. Also a letter in his favour. Signed, Richard Abell. Dated 30 Aug. 1722. 2 *pages.*
5 Sept.	57. Letter -	Lord Lieut. of Ireland (Grafton).	Do. - -	For orders for payment for the new furniture for the Dublin yacht, refitting at Portsmouth. 1½ *pages.*
7 Sept.	58. Do. -	Thomas Madockes -	William Lowndes, Esq.	Encloses account of charges in erecting the several annuity offices at the Bank, together with incident charges, wages, and salaries. Also gives the state of the annuities after the subscriptions were made into the South Sea Company. Bank, 7 September 1722. 7 *pages.*
11 Sept.	59. Memorial -	J. Hancock, Yeoman of the Robes for the Rt. Hon. the Earl of Cadogan.	Lords of the Treasury.	For a warrant to allow and pass his account. 1 *page.*
Aug. to 25 Sept.	60. Lists -	—	—	Of persons in the Navy Office, whose salaries exceed 50*l.* per ann., supposed to be chargeable to 6*d.* in the pound. 7 *pages.*
25 Sept.	61. Estimate -	—	—	Expense of H.M. Household for a year. Board of Greencloth. 1 *page.*

1722. Vol. CCXLII.

Date.	Description of Document.	From	To	Purport.
26 Sept.	62. Petition -	Three Inspectors for Gaming Houses, Cards, &c. (Stamp Office).	Lords of the Treasury.	For an addition to their salaries. *Minuted:* — "28th 7br. 1722. Read & rejected." 1 *page.*
29 Sept.	63. Account -	—	—	State of the debt of H.M. stables and stud (Master of the Horse's department) at Mich. 1722. 3 *pages.*
6 Oct.	64. Warrant -	Lords of the Treasury	Thomas Spence, Esq., and Thomas Burton, Esq., Officers connected with Standing Orders (Lottery).	"For paying principal standing orders in Lottery unsubscribed." 2 *pages.*
16 Oct.	65. Account -	—	—	Debt of the Great Wardrobe at Lady-day and Mich. 1722. 2 *large pages.*
16 Oct.	66. Letter -	R. Prosser - -	Hon. Sir Charles Turner, Bart., one of the Commrs. of the Treasury.	For an appointment to a vacancy at the port of Whitehaven. *Minuted:* — "18th 8br. Agreed to." 1 *page.*
17 Oct.	67. Do. -	Mr. Fr. Negus -	—	For direction to be given to let him have 2,000*l.* for the extraordinaries of H.M. stables. *Minuted:* — "20 Oct. 1722. Ordered. Lre writ eod. die." 1 *page.*
18 Oct.	68. Memorial -	Sir Isaac Newton -	Lords of the Treasury.	For a trial of the pixes of the copper coinage to be appointed. *Minuted:* — "18th 8br. 1722. Mr. Powys to be present on the part of the Treary at this Tryal." ½ *page.*
18 Oct.	69. Letter -	Commrs. of Forfeitures.	William Lowndes, Esq.	For orders to the Exchequer to pay their salaries and those of their inferior officers and incident charges. Inner Temple. *Minuted:*—"25 Oct. 538li. is in the Exchr. 28 Nov. 1722. Wt. & order to be signed." 1 *page.*
18 Oct.	70. Do. -	Do. - -	Lords of the Treasury.	To the same effect. 1 *page*

1722. VOL. CCXLII.

Date.	Description of Document.	From	To	Purport.
22 Oct.	71. Letter - -	P. Whichcote, Secretary to the Lord Lieut. of Ireland.	Mr. Powys -	Returns the address of the House of Lords of Ireland, in behalf of their officers, in respect to the allowance to them. 2 *pages*. 4to.
[? About 7 Nov.]	72. Petition -	" Merchant Sympson."	The Rt. Hon. Robt. Walpole, First Lord of the Treasury.	For a stamper's place. 1 *page*.
8 Nov.	73. Account -	[Commrs.] for Wine Licences.	Lords of the Treasury.	Gross and net produce of wine licences. 1 *page*.
13 Nov.	74. Representation	Do. - -	Do. - -	Asking directions in respect to deductions from incident expenses and charges under Act 7 Geo. I. 2 *pages*.
20 Nov.	75. Memorial -	Tho. Lynford, Subalmoner.	Do. - -	" For his Mats. daily alms and poor at the gate, &c." *Minuted:* — " 30th 9br. 1722. Orderd. Lre signed." 1 *page*. 4to.
25 May–24 Nov.	76. Presentments	Comrs. of Customs, North Britain.	Do. - -	Of tide-waiters, &c. for Scotch Ports. 6 *pages*.
30 Nov.	77. Letter -	Lord Carteret -	Do. - -	For directions to be given for payment of 300*l*. per ann., to Mr. Francis Manning, his Majesty's late resident with the cantons of Switzerland. *Minuted:*—" 19th Decr. 1722. Prepare a warrt." 1 *page*.
[? About 6 Dec.]	78. Petition -	Peter Gally De Gaujac, Minister of the French Chapel at Wapping.	Do. - -	For payment of his salary of 40*l*. per ann. for the last year of her late Majesty's reign. He was appointed to minister to a considerable number of her Majesty's subjects from Jersey, Guernsey, and other islands, who were settled at Wapping. He says, " it would be very hard for him to have preached a whole year for nothing, and paid nine pounds out of his own pocket for the rent of the chapel." *Minuted:* — " 6th Decr. 1722. To have 20li. out of the Queen's arrears." Also a certificate. 2 *pages*.
[? About 11 Dec.]	79. Do. -	Richard Andrews, Esq., Recr. General for the co. of Essex.	Do. - -	For an allowance of 270*l*., for bringing to London the money received by him. Also an affidavit, dated 11 Dec. 1722. 2 *pages*.

Date.	Description of Document.	From	To	Purport.
17 Dec.	80. Letter -	A. Carleton - -	[Horatio Walpole.]	Asks him to speak to his brother (the Chancellor) to grant him his petition for [60*l.* bounty]. The previous year he had received but 40*l.*, when the Chancellor ordered him 50*l.* Wokingham in Berks. 1 *page.*
17 Dec.	81. Petition -	The same - -	Lords of the Treasury.	Has been 23 years applying for his debt of 1,778*l.* for brass and iron goods. Money had been advanced to him for bounty. Is "a younger brother of a gent. family, bred to no trade, nor has any dependence but his wife's fortune." He says he slipped his left shoulder, and by the unskilfulness of the surgeon his arm bone was 36 days out of the cup in the shoulder, but two other surgeons reduced it to its place with exquisite pain and torture. Prays that he may be ordered 60*l.* of H.M. bounty. Also a letter on the same subject [to the Secretary of the Treasury.] 2 *pages.*
17 Dec.	82. Memorial -	Sir Basil Dixwell, Bart., Auditor of Excise.	Do. - -	For a warrant for 100*l.* per ann., being the same as was allowed to the Controller of Excise for the increase of business by auditing the additional duties on wrought plate. 1 *page.*
[After 1721.]	83. Petition -	Hugh Hughes, gent.	Do. - -	For a warrant granting him 50*l.* a year to be ratified, the same being stopped, "being most unjustly ill-willed by a great person." 1 *page.*
After 1722.	84. Memorandum	—	—	Of the amounts received for stone raised in the Island of Portland, on which the King was entitled to 3*d.* per ton. 1 *page.*

VOL. CCXLIII., 1723. JANUARY TO JUNE.

[? Beginning of 1723.] 1. New year's gifts or other annual gratuities for the Clerks, also for the Secretaries, and further new year's gifts or other annual dues for the Lords, 1722–3. Four papers, one being in duplicate, and the other also to a large extent. 6 *pages*.

Do. 2. An estimate of the charge of the office of Ordnance for the year 1723. Signed.

Also another similar estimate. 2 *pages*.

11 Jan. 3. Report of the Com[rs] of Revenue, Ireland, to the Lords of the Treasury, on the truth of the matters contained in certain papers "offered by one Josias Thompson and one Elias Barnes" to the Com[rs] of Trade, and from them transmitted to the Lords of the Treasury. They (the Com[rs]) were preparing a full and particular answer to show the malice and falsehood of almost every assertion in the papers, but finding it grew to a great bulk, and to relate to facts pretended to have been transacted near eight years since, they were unwilling to trouble their Lordships with so voluminous a reply, except they pleased to signify their further commands therein; especially as they were put on the task by the bare information of Thompson, who was an officer of the revenue, and dismissed about six years before, by a full board. He was a person of vile character, and affected to be zealous in seizing wool, but never brought any seizure to condemnation, and they believed used his commission to extort money, &c. They suspect that he and M[r] Dymond took 12*l.* to drop a prosecution against one Pilkington, for carrying off men for the Pretender's service. State other misdeeds of Thompson, and what they (the Com[rs]) had done to prevent the running of wool, so that smuggling in their opinion does not continue to nearly the same degree as formerly. Assure their Lordships of the groundlessness of his assertion that he had complained to the Com[rs] of certain vile language used by M[r] Sadler, one of the surveyors general, affecting his Majesty, and that they cannot without indignation hear such a charge. Also assure their Lordships of the falsehood of the memorial and letter signed by Thompson and Elias Barnes. Believe that the most substantial protestant merchants are of the same opinion as the Com[rs], that the running of wool is mischievous, and that dishonest trade has been mostly used by Papists, who may be presumed to be enemies to the Constitution and welfare of both nations. Allude to the practice of running East India goods into Ireland; the same having received the drawbacks in England. One Murphy gave information against thirty persons who assisted in seizing their officers while a French "dogger" was loaded with wool in the co. of Wexford, and the said Murphy

1723. VOL. CCXLIII.

assisting the Sheriff against the offenders, was taken up on the evidence of a person of vile character, who made him drunk, and conveyed two pewter shillings into his pocket, and immediately had him secured as a coiner and hanged on the evidence of the informer only. Custom House, Dublin, Jan. 11, 1722–3.

Minuted:—"17th Janry 1722. To the Lords Commissrs for Trade and Plantations.

Three other papers on the same subject. 13 *pages*.

14 Jan. 4. Copy of "A. Cracherode's Rept concerning the King's title to the mannrs of Westmr and St James's and the Baylywick of St James's." Dat. 14o January 1722." Gives an epitome of the letters patent, &c. relating to the above title. 3½ *pages*.

[? About 15 Jan.] 5. "Memorial to the Right Honble the Lords Commissioners of His Majties Treasury, concerning the expenses of prosecutions for crimes and other suits carried on in behalf of the Crown in Scotland."

"Before the Union his Majties Solicitors Genll paid out what money was necessary for defraying charges of prosecutions for crimes and other suits carried on in behalf of the Crown, and were annually reimbursed of the money so laid out.

"Since the Union no method has been established how such expence should be defrayed, but during the time Sir James Stewart was Solicitor, who continued in that office till the year 1701, money was impress'd by the Treasury into his hand for those purposes.

"Since the year 1717 that Mr Dundas was called to be Solicitor no money hath been impress'd into the Solicitor's hands for those purposes, nor have they been reimbursed of what they have been obliged to lay out in such prosecutions or in defence of the rights of the crown."

It is a very great prejudice to the King's service that no fixed method is established how such expenses should be defrayed.

There remains due to Mr Dundas of what was paid out by him when he was Solicitor, 181*l*. There remains due to Mr Stewart's son 60*l*., "laid out by his father when he was Solicitor anno 1720," and there remains due to Mr Binning and Mr Sinclair, the present Solicitors, laid out before the 22nd of December last, 165*l*. 5*s*. 8*d*., a copy of the accounts whereof is annexed.

The copy of account referred to. Sworn 15 Jan. 1722–3. 5 *pages*.

21 Jan. 6. Copy of report of the Lords Justices of Ireland to the Lord Lieut. of Ireland on the petition of Mr Mason, eldest son and administrator of Sir John Mason, Knt, deceased, who had petitioned on behalf of his brother and sisters for a new lease for 61 years from the expiration of the present lease of the town of Passage, and of the lands in the petition named, set apart by the Act of Settlement for raising 300*l*. per ann. for the maintenance of H.M. Fort of Duncannon. Are of opinion that it is reasonable to comply with the proposal.

1723. Vol. CCXLIII.

The petition and reference thereof to the Com[rs], and copy of a letter on the same subject, signed "H. Lingen." 6 *pages.*

[? About 22 Jan.] 7. Petition of William Underwood, Esq., to the Lords of the Treasury. In 1717 petitioner applied to the Com[rs] of the Treasury by petition setting forth his title to the remainder of a term of years in two old houses in the parish of S[t] James', Westminster, and praying for a renewal. M[r] Cholmley, the Surveyor General, had reported on the petition: prays that the General's "rate" may be read, and that orders for the renewal may be given.

Minuted:—"22[d] Jan[ry] 1722-3. To ꝑsent Surv[r] Gen[l] to reconsider." 1 *page.*

23 Jan. 8. "A. Cracherode's particular of causes now under prosecution with states thereof. 23 Jan. 1722." 8½ *pages.*

[? About 23 Jan.] 9. Memorial of the Corporation of the Royal Exchange Assurance, to the Lords of the Treasury. The Corporation advanced 156,000*l.* for an annuity, on which sum they had tallies and orders struck at 4*l.* per cent. per ann. until the redemption thereof by Parliament: but they were mostly for large sums and not transferable or assignable: pray that on return of the same, others may be struck of 500*l.* value.

Minuted:—"23 Jan[ry] 1722. Orderd." 1 *page.*

24 Jan. 10. A. Cracherode to Horatio Walpole, Esq. M[r] Burkley has engaged him to assist in correcting the press for Layer's trial to be published next Monday. Asks that my Lords may be moved for the moneys mentioned in the enclosed memorial.

Accompanied by a memorial from M[r] Cracherode. The 500*l.* last imprested to him have been expended on Layer's trial, and the adjournment of the special Commission of oyer and terminer in Essex, and bringing several libellers to their trials, &c. Prays 100*l.* more on account, and 250*l.* for his half year's salary and allowance for clerks. 24 Jan. 1722. 2 *pages.*

31 Jan. 11. Report of J. Pulteney, Surveyor General, to the Lords of the Treasury. Has had under his consideration the state of the revenues belonging to the dissolved Hospital of the Savoy now in the Crown. Caused a particular view and inquiry to be made into the present condition and yearly value of the several tenements and other buildings belonging to the site of the Hospital, a plan whereof is now lying in his office. Finds that there are five messuages fronting to the Strand, and two other tenements situate backwards, all inhabited by persons whose names and pretensions for holding the same are mentioned in a copy of return annexed, made on the aforesaid inquiry, by which it appears that all the messuages are very much out of repair and require to be rebuilt, that the present occupants have no leases and are in very mean circumstances and incapable of paying a reasonable rent. Advises the letting of the property at a ground rent, whereon the seven houses stand. The other buildings which stand within the gate or precincts of the Hospital are either in lease or used as barracks

1723. VOL. CCXLIII.

or chapels for Divine Service to accommodate the several Protestant congregations. Asks that the books and muniments relating to the property, which are said to be in some offices in Doctors' Commons, may be delivered up to him. 31 Jan. 1722-23.

The "return" referred to.

Minuted:—"Feby 1722-3. Prepare a warrant for ye delivery of ye books, papers, &c. relating to ye land revenues of ye Hospital of the Savoy, as set forth in ye s^d report, into ye hands of ye Surveyor Gen^ll." 8½ *pages*.

[? About 1 Feb.] 12. Petition of his Majesty's servants belonging to the German Chapel at St. James's Palace, to Robert Walpole, Esq., First Com^r of the Treasury. They (and their families) depend for subsistence on their salaries, and they are reduced to great straits by the arrears remaining unpaid. On Michaelmas day last a whole year was unpaid: pray for payment.

Minuted:—"To be paid what is [due]. 1 Feb. 1722-3." 1 *page*.

2 Feb. 13. John Buchan to —— [Apparently being charged with conniving at smuggling] declares that all he did was to send to Mr Paterson about sixteen loads of peats; but as to unloading or receiving any deals it is most malicious and notoriously false. Believes the Officers of Customs at Aberdeen will attest that as a Justice of the peace in this county, he has always rather been assisting in discovering frauds to the prejudice of the Public revenue, than conniving at, or encouraging, any such practices as Mr Howell seems to insinuate. Old Aberdeen, 2^d Febry. 1722.

Minuted:—"Report read. Agreed to and the informers rejected and dismist." 1 *page*.

2 Feb. 14. Report of Mr W. Lowndes to the Lords of the Treasury on the petition of Dame Anne Tipping [only daughter and executrix of Lady Letitia Russell]. King James the Second granted to Katherine, Countess of Dorchester, a pension of 3,000*l*. per ann. for 5¼ years out of the English Exchequer. This expired at Lady day 1691. By the same patent he granted her several quit rents in Ireland, amounting to 5,000*l*. per ann., for 99 years, "if she should so long live," at a rent of 1,500*l*. per ann. The term expired upon the decease of the Countess about three years ago. By the same patent his late Majesty granted to Lord Preston and other Trustees "all the said quit rents" after the above term for 7 years at 6*d*. per ann. This term is now existent, and would be a security for arrears of the pension of 3,000*l*. per ann., which was granted for 5¼ years, and for the quit rents themselves during the term of 7 years. Their Majesties (by 4 Will. and Mary) in satisfaction for salary, arrears, &c. due to Thomas Cheke, Esq., Lieut. of the Tower of London, and in consideration of a release thereof executed by the Lady Letitia Russel, who was relict and executrix of the said Thomas Cheke (which arrears were computed at 10,000*l*.), granted to Conyers and Colladon an annuity of 600*l*. per ann., to be paid out of the reserved

rent of 1,500*l.* per ann. payable by the Countess for the quit rents, and out of the residue of the quit rents of 5,000*l.* per ann., and out of the residue of the quit rents which during the seven years granted to Preston and others should be payable "in trust for their Majesties," &c. The said annuity to be held for 31 years from Lady day 1692. This term will expire at Lady day 1723. [The report sets out some further particulars of the grant as well as the effect of other documents, and states that if the account last mentioned were admitted, there remained unpaid upon the 600*l.* per ann. 3,161*l.* 17*s.* 2*d.*: besides which the lady Russell's pension ran in arrear about 17 years before she received one penny, and the subsequent payments were made in a very dilatory manner. Reminds their Lordships of the effect of the Act of 11 Will. III. as to quit rents belonging to the Crown of Ireland on 13 Feb. 1688, &c. In case his Majesty shall be inclined to charge the existing terms or either of them with the arrears of the 600*l.* per ann., and with a sum in gross to make good the dilatory payments and the great trouble and charges sustained by the petitioner and her mother, he (Mr Lowndes) has no objection thereto. 2 Feb. 1722–3.

Also two queries written on a separate paper. 3½ *pages.*

[? About 5 Feb.] 15. Petition of George Turbill, "Register to the Commissioners and Trustees for the Forfeited Estates acting in England," to the Lords of the Treasury. By the act passed in the last session the forfeited estates in England which shall remain unsold after 29 Sept. next are devested out of the Comrs and Trustees, and vested in his Majesty for the use of the public. The Comrs have determined all the claims made before them, amounting to 2,000*l.*, and have caused their determination to be entered of record. The forfeited estates have been sold to purchasers for 250,000*l.* and upwards. Frequent disputes will arise, and for the adjusting thereof it will be necessary to have recourse to the records, and it is necessary that the records should be deposited in some public office, and that some person should be appointed to have the custody of them, as was done upon the like occasion in Ireland upon the expiration of that Commission. As petitioner has acted as Register under the Commissioners, and has drawn up all their determinations and decrees, he prays that he may be appointed.

Minuted:—"31st July 1723. Agreed to. My Lds think proper that a salary of 150li p ann. be allowed to him for his own trouble, the rent of an office, clerks, and all incident charges whatsoever. Mr Lowndes will prepare a proper instrumt."

Letter from the Comrs to the Rt Hon. Robert Walpole, Chancellor of the Exchequer and First Lord of the Treasury, recommending the petitioner. Dated 5 Feb. 1722–3. 3 *pages.*

7 Feb. 16. Certificate of the Commrs for building fifty new churches in London and Westminster, of the necessity that 20,000*l.* should be forwith raised by way of loan from natives or foreigners, bodies politic or corporate, willing to lend the same upon the credit of the

1723. Vol. CCXLIII.

fund of 21,000*l.* per ann. charged on certain duties of coal and culm. Palace Yard, Feb. 7, 1722. 1 *page.*

[? About 7 Feb.] 17. Petition of Elizabeth Cameron, widow, to the King. Petitioner is the widow of Major Daniel Cameron, deceased, son of Sir Evan Cameron, of Lochiel, in the north of Scotland. The Major was a person of great loyalty and zeal for his Majesty's interest, and procured leave to come home to Scotland in the beginning of the late Rebellion in hopes to have prevented by his endeavours his elder brother and other relations from embarking in so unnatural a design, and though his endeavours had not the desired effect as to his brother and some others, yet he had the honour of prevailing with many of his numerous and powerful clan to desist from it, and gave encouragement to others whom he knew to be well affected to his Majesty, by furnishing them with arms at his own expense for the suppressing and bringing in of the rebels. His great loyalty and zeal were the cause of his death, for having broken his constitution with the fatigues and hardships of that service and in bad weather, he died on the 26th of March 1718 in the Highlands. All which facts are certified under the hands of the Rt Hon. the Earls of Southerland, Lauderdale, and Hindford, the Lord Terphuhen, Brigadier Preston, Col. Blackader, and other persons of note and distinction.

Petitioner's "insuperable" loss was attended with circumstances very uncommon and inhuman, for while petitioner's husband lay a dying in one room, and petitioner in labour in another, the house was surprised by a party of the rebel brother's friends, who stripped her not only of all her goods, but likewise of the writings and other papers belonging to her, and to complete the scene of cruelty a set of bagpipes and drums were ordered to play upon them day and night for some time. Prays for support for herself and two small children. Referred, 7 Feb. 1722–3.

Minuted:—"22 Feb. 1722–3. Nothing can be done in this." 1 *page.*

8 Feb. 18. Report of the Barons of the Exchequer of Scotland to the Lords of the Treasury. Have examined the warrant prepared for H.M. signature for granting and conveying to John Mercer, writer in Perth, and his heirs, the lands of Craigie Miln and others, all lying in the shire of Perth, "proceeding upon the resignation of Mr John Paterson, of Craigie." The signature contains a *De novo damus* and "taxing of the Waird holding," but they do not find that there are any non-entry duties or casualties and "forfaultures by recognition or escheat" affecting the said lands which will be discharged by the *De novo damus* if his Majesty grant the same. The yearly value of the rents is 40*l.* 16*s.* 8*d.* Edinbr, 8 Feb. 1722–3. 1 *page.*

9 Feb. 19. Memorial of John Pulteney, Esq., Surveyor General of H.M. lands, &c. Has had under his consideration a referred petition of Francis Taylor, gent., for a lease of Colstable Farm and Chesworth Lodge, in the county of Sussex. Finds, by a return made to him by some gentlemen living in that neighbourhood, that there

1723. VOL. CCXLIII.

were growing on the lands in the possession of Jesse Walder (one of Mr Taylor's under tenants) 300 trees, making 150 loads of timber, and that some time before, 25 trees had been cut (in breach of the lessee's covenant), though when this view was taken no more than 21 trees were lying on the ground, computed to make 20 loads and 22 foot of timber, and that upon the premises there are between 30 and 40 acres of underwoods, which they say belong to the tenants. Thinks these 21 trees had better be sold for his Majesty's use, and that strict inquiry should be made after the other four, and that other trees judged fit should be cut and sold for H.M. benefit, reserving sufficient timber for the use of those farms, and excepting such trees as are now growing on that part enclosed within Mr Eversfield's Park, from whom he (the Surveyor) has a memorial desiring their Lordships to grant him a lease of that land (about 44 acres). Mr Eversfield hopes the trees will be left standing as an ornament to his park. All which he (the Surveyor General) intended to have laid before their Lordships in his report upon Mr Taylor's petition (whose name is used in trust for Mr Hoar, of London, goldsmith), but some doubts have arisen as to part of the lands adjoining to Chesworth Lodge, whether the same are thereto belonging, which may retard the report.

Minuted :—" 11 Feby 1722–3. To be done accordingly." 2 *pages*.

14 Feb. 20. Memorial of Sir Thomas Hewett, Knt, Surveyor General of H.M. Works, to the Lords of the Treasury. Is informed by Sir James Thornhill that Mr Walpole had ordered him to put a memorial into the Treasury relating to the painting of the large square room at Kensington. Before Michaelmas last he attended his Majesty at Kensington about finishing the three large rooms in the new building, and showed H.M. several sketches of mosaic work, &c. for painting the ceiling of the great square room. His Majesty chose one of them. He (the Surveyor) ordered a model to be made, and Sir James Thornhill painted it, and his Majesty approved of it, and commanded him (the Surveyor) to tell the Vice-Chamberlain to treat with Sir James Thornhill for the price, and that it should be done out of hand. Scotland Yard, 14 Feb. 1722. 1 *page*.

16 Feb. 21. A. Cracherode (in answer) to Christopher Tilson, Esq., as to what weekly or daily allowances have been paid to prisoners of State for their maintenance. By order of the Lords of the Treasury, "dated in Sept. 1716," he paid Lord Duffus, a prisoner in the Tower, three pounds a week for his subsistence, and by another order from them "in March or April 1717" he paid the Earl of Cornwall and the Lord Nairn (two other prisoners in the Tower) three pounds a week apiece, for their maintenance, which are all the State prisoners he ever had any orders to subsist. Thinks himself obliged to observe that he believes their Lordships, in settling those allowances, had regard not only to the quality of the prisoners, but to their having forfeited their estates by the high treason of which they stand attainted, and to the public

1723. VOL. CCXLIII.

being in possession of their forfeited estates. 16 Feb. 1722. 2 *pages* (*quarto*).

16 Feb. 22. Copy of the petition of Sir William Seton to the Lords of the Treasury, of the reference of the same to the Barons of the Exchequer of Scotland, and of their report on the petition. The last named certifies that her late Majesty by letters, under her privy seal of Scotland, of 1 Oct. 1705, constituted Sir William Seton General Collector of the rents of the several Bishoprics mentioned in his petition, with powers to retain money for remuneration of himself and sub-collectors. Sir William continued the receipt 'till 1714. Upon presentation of his account the Court did not pass the same, but directed processes against the Receivers to oblige them "to produce their rights thereto." Most of the difficulties are now removed, so that the petitioner's accounts will now be carried on and passed. The craving of 108*l*. per ann. for incident charges they conceive may be reasonable to be allowed. Edinburgh, Exchequer Chamber, 16 Feb. 1722–3. 3 *pages*.

16 Feb. 23. Memorial of John Anstis, Esq., Garter King of Arms, to the Lords of the Treasury. The memorial delivered to their Lordships by the Officers of Arms for their largesses consisted of two articles: (1.) Largesses due upon the creations of the nobility, which have been constantly paid to them even to 7 Oct. in the 1st year of H.M. reign, as appears by certificate annexed. (2.) Largesses or rewards due to these officers (13 in number) for waiting on His Majesty to chapel on high festivals, amounting to 41*l*. yearly, which sum has been annually paid from the commencement of the reign of Edward III. [Refers to places where the payments are recorded.] The Heralds in all foreign Kingdoms not only enjoy the like rewards, but which is very remarkable, if foreign heralds attended here on any of the festivals the Crown likewise ordered them payments upon this account. [Again refers to recorded evidence.] Heralds' Office, 16 Feb. 1722–3.

Also two copies of documents in corroboration.

Minuted:—" 11 Sept. 1723. Prepare a state of what is due for the K's time for creation fees. The Largesses to be revived from this time only being 41li p añ."

There is also on the back of the document:—" Due for Creation Fees for 42 Titles of Honour 215*l*." 3 *pages*.

22–28 Feb. 24. Petition of the six poor Gate-keepers in his Majesty's private Road leading to Fulham, to the Lords of the Treasury, for payment for three years' work on the road, the Surveyor of His Majesty's private Roads (William Watkins, Esq.) having promised to obtain for each of them 5*l*. per ann.

Minuted:—" 22d Feb. 1722–3. The allowce of 5li p ann. each to be established in the Office of Works, and to be pd from the time they were employed in this service."

Accompanied by two letters from the Surveyor, one of which is addressed to Mr Tilson; both relate to the above claims. The second states as follows:—" The gates on the Fulham roads are 6,

1723. VOL. CCXLIII.

viz.:—The first at the entrance at the backside of Buckingham house, the 2d over against Chelsea Colleige, the 3d at Chelsea Lane end, for which I pay ten shill. p an., the 4th at the World's End, for which I pay 3 pound p an., there being about half an acre of garden ground belonging to it. The 5th at Sandy End, the sixth and last at Fullham 20 shill. rent; in all 4*l.* 10*s.* ground rent. The Gate-keepers have workt on the road thro 3 years past, wch is ever since the houses were built, in hopes and upon my promise that I would use my endeavours to obtain some small allowance for them." 4 *pages.*

7 March. 25. Report of A. Cracherode to the Lords of the Treasury on the petition of Francis Woodcock, Keeper of H.M. Gaol for the county of Bucks, who sets forth that, at his own charge, he provided for and subsisted the several persons (in the schedule delivered in with the petition), prisoners in H.M. county gaol, from the times of their respective sentences of transportation till they were transported; for which he never received one penny from the Sheriff. By the certificate of Mr Jonathan Forward it appears that he received the sixteen prisoners named in the schedule, on 17 Oct. 1721 (except Robert Walter and Richard Harris, who, the petitioner insists were to transport themselves, and did transport themselves), and that he transported them. Two shillings and sixpence a week was the rate charged for each of them; but the petitioner had not been at the charge of maintaining them, and if he had been, the Sheriff of the county was the proper person to make him satisfaction. Since this is the first application that he (Mr Cracherode) knows to have been made to their Lordships by any gaoler upon this head for maintenance of convicted felons to the time of their transportation, submits whether their Lps will make a precedent in favour of the petitioner. 7 March 1722.

Minuted:—"15th Mar. 1722. Write to the Under Sheriff to know whether these demands are just, and if they are, why they are not paid by him and to be allowed on the Sheriff's accot."

The petition referred to. 2½ *pages.*

19 March. 26. Mr Christopher Cass to the Rt Hon. Robert Walpole, Esq., Chancellor of the Exchequer. Upon the demise of Mr Edward Tufnell, mason to Westminster Abbey, in 1719, applied to the Dean and Chapter, "and offered a proposal of 20s per cwt. less than the then prices," upon which the Rt Rev. the Bp of Rochester desired him to set down the prices proposed against the former ones given, which he did. He was assured that no person should either read or copy the same, or use them to his prejudice. In his absence his Lordship sent for the present mason and read the prices to him, which he accepted, and was given possession of the business. His Lordship ordered the Clerk of the Works to inform him (Mr Cass) that he was under some obligations to employ the present mason, and that he would make him (Mr Cass) some satisfaction. Waited on his Lordship at Bromley, who told him that he was writ to by his brother, the minister of Highgate, in behalf of the present mason, but he would endeavour to procure him (Mr Cass) 100 guineas for

1723. VOL. CCXLIII.

his services. Could not but think himself highly injured. Thinks that his Honour (who, with the L[d] Chief Justice of the King's Bench, are Comm[rs] for repairing the Church) will be of opinion that he has been hardly used, and that he should be put into the possession of the business. March 19, 1722–3. 1 *page.*

21 March. 27. A minute of the Com[rs] for building Churches, ordering that the Treasurer to the Commission (Nathan Blackeby, Esq.), advise with M[r] Lowndes, Secretary to the Lords of the Treasury, to ascertain whether it is proper for the Board to direct the interest to be paid to the workmen employed in building New Churches from the date the tallies bore to the day they were issued to them. Dated, Old Palace Yard, Westminster, 21 March 1722–3.

Minuted:—"8th April 1723. Deliver the tallys and orders to the workmen with the Interest due thereupon."

Also the petition of the workmen to the Commissioners. 2 *pages.*

21 March. 28. Report of the Surveyor General of his Majesty's Woods to the Lords of the Treasury on the memorial of the Earl of Rochester praying their Lordships to supersede so much of the Royal Sign Manual for raising 2,000*l.* by wood sales for his especial service as relates to felling wood in Richmond Park and Whichwood Forest, of which park and forest he is Chief Keeper and Lieutenant. Finds that there are (notwithstanding the late sales) several thousand pollard trees fit for nothing but fuel, and unless now taken for the King's service will be entirely lost to the Crown. The wood in Richmond Park is rather for ornament than profit. Has been very careful in the choice of the trees to be felled. If their Lordships indulge Lord Rochester in his request the sum of 2,000*l.* required by his Majesty to be raised for his especial service cannot be raised this year.

Also the memorial.

Minuted:—"26 Mar. 1723. Send a copy to Lord Rochester and let him know the Surv[r] is to proceed and y[t] their Lordp̃s believe he will meet with this favour and assistance." 2 *pages and* 2 *halves.*

25 March. 29. "An Acco[t] of what was wanting at Lady day 1723 to clear pencõns and annuities payable at the Exchequer." 5 *pages.*

25 March. 30. Order in Council on the petition of the Governor and Company of Copper Miners in the Principality of Wales praying that his Majesty will grant them the like privileges as were allowed to other Companies in having some particular marks impressed on such silver as they shall carry to be coined in the Mint: referring the matter to the Lords of the Treasury. 25 March 1723.

Minuted:—"May 22, 1723. Sign Manuall to be prepared as in y[e] case of ye S.P.C., &c."

The petition referred to, in which they mention that the "elephant" was struck on the gold imported by the Royal African Co., the "Feathers" for the Mine Adventurers, and "Roses and Feathers" on the silver refined by the Governor and Company for

1723. VOL. CCXLIII.

smelting lead with pit coal and sea coal. The petitioners asked to have impressed on their silver "the letters W.C.C. under the head" and on the reverse side "Feathers quartered and [illegible]" 2 *pages*.

25 March. 31. Order in Council on a report of the Lords of the Admiralty made by them on the petition of Edward Vernon, Esq., relating to his expenses for bringing from Jamaica to England, Richard Tookerman, to answer for the felonies, piracies, and other illegal practices committed by him in the West Indies, of which the petitioner, when Commander-in-Chief of H.M. Ships attending on the Island of Jamaica, thought it incumbent on him to take cognizance.

Refers the Report to the Lords of the Treasury to consider how petitioner may be reimbursed.

Minuted:—"Aprill 9, 1723. Orderd out of old stores. 26th Do. Warrt signed." 7 *pages*.

[After 25 March.] 32. Memorial of Charles, Earl of Lauderdale, General of the Mint in Scotland, to the Lords of the Treasury. By an Act of 1 Geo. I. the Lords of the Treasury are empowered to defray the expenses of the Mints of England and Scotland, so that they do not exceed 15,000*l.* By a sign manual petitioner (out of money to be issued to him out of the Exchequer) is charged with paying the salaries of the officers of the Mint in Scotland, and with the charges of the coinage, &c., and the repair of the dwelling-houses of the officers. And he is commanded to cause his Majesty's moneys of gold and silver to be coined of the same forms with those coined in England, and with the same inscriptions, and to set under His Majesty's effigies the letter E., to distinguish the moneys coined at Edinburgh from those coined at London. Since the year 1709 there has been no coinage in the Mint in Scotland, and this has caused a scarcity of coin, &c. The last sum issued for defraying salaries, &c. was 1,400*l.* for one year and a quarter to Lady day 1721. Two years is now due. Prays that a suitable sum may be imprested for defraying the coinage for the salaries and for the fabric. 2 *pages*.

26 and 27 March. 33. Copy or draft of Treasury Minutes for 26 and 27 March 1723. [The importation of Tobacco is the principal subject of the Minutes.] 2½ *pages*.

27 March. 34. "An accompt of the debt due and owing on the pensions payable in the office of Walter Chetwynd, Esq., from Lady day 1722 to Lady day 1723." Dated 27 March 1723. 7 *pages*.

28 March. 35. Lord Carteret to the Lords of the Treasury signifying the King's pleasure that, as a special bounty, 100*l.* should be allowed to Mr Andrew Pfeffer, printer, of the city of Coire, in the country of the Grisons, who had some time since dedicated to the King a translation of the Bible into the "Romansh" tongue, or to Mr Francis Manning, H.M. late Resident in Switzerland, for the use of the said Pfeffer. Whitehall, 28 March 1723.

Accompanied by a letter from Mr Manning (unaddressed) begging that the above letter may be complied with out of hand. 3 *pages*.

VOL. CCXLIII.

1723.
26 and 29 March 36. Two affidavits in proof that Sir Valentine Browne, Bart., deceased, was in the year 1688, and for many years before, in possession of the town and lands of Ross Castle and Islands thereunto belonging: and that he, about the year 1688, built a dwelling-house adjoining to the Castle, with a large Court surrounded with a wall, &c., which was finished in the year 1688, and must have cost at least 2,000*l.*, and since the year 1691 they have been made use of as a garrison, whereby the house has been ruined and the woods have been destroyed by the garrison. Dated 26 and 29 March 1723. 2 *pages.*

6 April. 37. Certificate of Francis Ligo, Deputy Sheriff of Buckinghamshire, to the Lords of the Treasury, that the several prisoners in an enclosed account were convicted and transported at the several times contained in the account; and that they were, from the times of such their several convictions to the times of their transportation, subsisted and provided for by Francis Woodcock, for which he had no allowance, although it had been craved. Conceives that till the year 1720, no persons being particularly appointed by the Judges of Assize to contract for the transportation of felons, it was not known, on the sheriff's last petition for allowances, when the charges of subsisting the convicts would end; the general directions in the Act of Parliament for transportation of felons being found not sufficient for that purpose. Aylesbury, April 6, 1723.

On the other side is the warrant for the payment of the claim. There is also the account referred to, an affidavit and a certificate of the receipt of the prisoners and of the transport of the same. Signed "Jon^{a} Forward."

Minuted:—"18th April 1723. Prepare a warr^{t}." 5 *pages.*

[? About 8 April.] 38. "Memorial and petition" of the Mayor, Aldermen, &c. of the town and port of Bideford, in the county of Devon, to the Lords of the Treasury. Allude to a memorial presented to their L^{ps} by the port of Barnstaple in respect to "a cavil" raised about Dispatches issuing from the Custom house for shipping and unshipping goods at Appledore. Set forth that Bideford is an ancient and very considerable trading port, and that the revenue has amounted to some hundred thousand pounds, and has deserved better of the present Establishment than Barnstaple, as they furnished their late Majesties with several thousand men for the Royal Navy, and with above fifty sail of stout transport ships for the reduction of Ireland, when Barnstaple could not or did not set out five: that their river being within these twenty years so altered and choked with sand that a vessel of 80 tons, without being lightened, cannot even on spring tides come within the prescribed limits of this port (although before, their ships of three or four hundred tons came up to the Key), and the limits of Barnstable being unnaturally extended so far on both sides of their River it is "impossible to bring in or send out their laden ships above them"; and the only place in the whole harbour for ships to ride afloat to complete their lading when outward, or to lighten when inward bound, is the Pool between,

1723. VOL. CCXLIII.

"or made by the rivers of Bideford and Barnstable": that therefore the prohibition of this well-known ancient and agreed method of their Dispatches, and the taking them from Barnstaple must unavoidably be attended with such hardships as well as charge to the Crown and the merchants as must destroy their open fair trade, thereby lessen H.M. revenue, starve the poor, and prove the great impoverishment if not utter ruin of this large populous town: * * * that an attempt was made before the Civil Wars by the people of Barnstaple to subject the merchants of this port to the discharge of their goods and to the payment of the keyidge there (which would now be the consequence of taking out Dispatches thence), but the latter being the right of, and ever paid to, the noble ancestors of the present noble proprietors of this manor, the R^{t} Hon. the Countess Grandville and Lord Gower, and the former appearing impracticable, their designs proved ineffectual. Notice instances of fraudulent dispatches from the other port. Hope they shall not be sacrificed to the false insinuations of their envious neighbours or of unthinking officers, who have, for some years past, fomented the present differences: pray that their ancient privileges may be continued.

Minuted:—"8th Apr. 1723. Read." 1 *large page.*

10 April. 39. Com^{rs} of Customs, Scotland, to the Lords of the Treasury. Acknowledge the receipt of their L^{ps}' order to prosecute, by English bills in the Exchequer, such persons as they suspect of fraudulent practices in the importation of tobacco into Scotland. Will prosecute without loss of time the persons referred to, as they have hitherto upon several occasions attempted to recover the King's duties by bills of this nature without success. Ask for an experienced lawyer from England to carry out the same. Custom House, Edinb^{r}, 10 April 1723.

Minuted:—"Aprill ye 16, 1723. A letter to be drawn in answer that my Lords wonder that they, having so often tryd to recover the King's dutys by English bills, which method (as they acquaint my Lords in this lre) has constantly fail'd, yet have never represented the same to the Treary.

"That their Lordps, who are determin'd to obviate such ineffectual attempts of prosecutions for the future, do direct the Comm^{rs} to transmit to them the several instances wherein they have preferred English bills to recover the King's dutys; together with all the forms and progress of each particular prosecution, that their Lordps may inform themselves of the defects in this method, and give the proper instructions to prevent the like for the future." 1 *page.*

12–23 April. 40. Bill of extraordinary expenses of Charles, Lord Whitworth, H.M. Ambassador Extraordinary and Plenipotentiary at the Congress in Cambray from 10 Dec. 1722 to 9 March 1722–3. Dated Cambray, 12–23 April 1723.

With a notice at the foot that it was allowed by Lord Carteret. 1 *page.*

VOL. CCXLIII.

1723.

[About 16 April.] 41. Report of Mr Christopher Tilson to the Lords of the Treasury on the memorial of Gilbert Pepper, Esq., late undertaker for sick and wounded seamen and prisoners of war for the Kingdom of Ireland. The claim is for 403*l.* 4*s.* 9*d.* interest and charges on bills of Exchange drawn by the memoralist on the Com^{rs} for sick and wounded in the last war, but returned by the merchants (tho' accepted by the Com^{rs}), for non-payment in time. Memorialist must have well understood that there would be delays in time of war, and the Com^{rs} must have submitted to greater rates. A multitude of dormant demands and an immense sum will be revived if their L^{ps} give way to the memorialist.

Minuted:—"Aprill ye 16, 1723. Agree to ye Report." The memorial (the above report being written on the back of it) and a report of the Com^{rs} for sick and wounded on the same subject. 3 *pages*.

[About 17 April.] 42. Memorial of Francis Burton, Esq., Receiver General of the deductions of 6^{d} *per lib.*, to the Lords of the Treasury. Is passing an account of the deductions, and lays the annexed account of the charges which he has been at before their Lordships. Prays that they may be allowed. Also asks to be allowed for an office and a clerk.

Minuted:—"17 Apr. 1723. 100 p ann. for clerk h^{o} rent and all conting."

The account referred to. 2 *pages*.

17 April. 43. Petition of Leonard Woodeson, Clerk to Mr Surveyor and the rest of the Com^{rs} of the Board of Works, to the Lords of the Treasury. Petitioner, in pursuance of their Lordships' warrant, was prevailed upon by the Surveyor, and Board of Works, to lease the House called Essex House in Essex Street, for the use of the Cottonian Library, at a rent of 140*l.*, beside the parish duties and other outgoings reckoned at about 12*l.* per ann. more. A half year's rent is due, and 6*l.* for the parish duty, but the landlord will not submit to the defalcation of the Civil List tax of 6^{d} per £ deducted at the Exchequer; but will force the petitioner by law to pay the full sum. Prays that the money may be paid to the Paymaster of Works, to be by him paid to the landlord; and that he (the petitioner) may be saved harmless.

Minuted:—"17th April 1723. My Lords agree to the petition." 1 *page*.

9 May. 44. Report of Walter Chetwynd, Esq., to the Lords of the Treasury, on the petition of James King, Clerk. In consideration of a debt of 4,000*l.*, and about 1,500*l.* interest due from the Crown to Thomas King, Esq. (petitioner's father), upon account of the Royal fishery of herrings in King Charles the Second's time, a pension of 300*l.* per ann. was granted by King Charles II. to the above Thomas King, who received it during life. By his death it was reduced to 100*l.* per ann., and continued to Alice, his widow, who received it till her death. Petitioner is "the only child" of the above Thomas and Alice, and is advanced in years, and had a considerable loss by the

1723. Vol. CCXLIII.

pulling down of the late Chapel in Spring Gardens (where he was preacher, and from whence he had his chief maintenance), and the principal debt has never been repaid. Thinks the petitioner so far an object for his Majesty's bounty, that his mother's pension of 100*l.* per ann. might be continued to him in satisfaction of all pretensions. 9 May 1723.

Minuted :—"16 Julii 1724. *Vid.* the Minutes."

[The Minutes for this period are not known to exist.]

Also the petition. 2 *pages.*

10 May. 45. Report of the Attorney and Solicitor General on the memorial of the Chief Cashier of the Bank of England in relation to the carrying out the Act passed in the "present session of Parliament," and praying directions whether Trustees may be permitted to receive the principal, notwithstanding the minority of their wards, and whether such infants as have stocks in their own names may receive the same by their guardians. Certify that in respect to the first question they are of opinion that where trustees are appointed by deed or will, in whom the legal interest of the annuity is vested, in such case the Cashier may safely pay the principal money payable for the redemption of any annuity to such Trustees, notwithstanding the minority.

As to the second question, they conceive that the principal money payable for the redemption of any annuity cannot be safely paid to an infant, but in cases where there is a guardian appointed by the deed or will of the father, the principal money may be paid to such guardian, and he may give a discharge; and in other cases where there are no such trustees or guardians, the course of the Court of Chancery is, upon a bill preferred in the name of the infant by some person as his next friend, to direct the money to be brought before a Master of the Court, and to be placed out at interest for the benefit of the infant. 10 May 1723.

The memorial referred to. 3 *pages.*

13 May. 46. Barons of the Exchequer of Scotland (Smith and Scroop) to Horatio Walpole, Esq. Upon consideration of the account of prosecutions in the Court of Exchequer in Scotland for the recovery of duties lately transmitted to the Lords of the Treasury by the Com[rs] of the Customs (Scotland), think that considering the circumstances of juries in Scotland the most effectual method to bring in the Crown duties will be by way of English Bill. As to the particular instances of prosecutions already carried on that way, it appears they are very few. That as to the determination in relation to the Prizage Duty, the Court was divided in opinion, three against two: that wherever any prosecutions are carried on that way, for duties, if the defendants can cover themselves by any claims of exemption by private rights, the determinations in such causes will in all probability go against the Crown. In other instances where proper care is taken rightly to found the demands of the Crown, if the solicitors effectually prosecute the same, there will be a reasonable expectation of success. There ought to be directions to the Commissioners of Customs to imprest into their [the

1723. VOL. CCXLIII.

solicitors] hands, from time to time, so much money as will be necessary for carrying on such causes; the want of which has been alleged as an excuse for not doing it. Some of the persons appointed by the Crown have not seemed to attend upon that business as by their duties they ought, and without diligent and skilful officers it is not to be expected the business of the Crown should be carried on as it ought. Cannot say whether there be any mistake in the return made by the Attorneys of the Court in the cause in which the demurrer is said to be overruled; but it is very plain there might have been a prosecution carried on either by an amended Bill or Enforcing Answers to the Bill upon which the Demurrer is founded. That, and the cause against Williamson, to which they say there was no answer put in, appear by the said account to be the only causes carried on in the said Court since the Union, for the recovery of duties of Customs, where there was no pretence of private rights, though the Court has often intimated to the proper officers that to be the most effectual way of prosecuting for the Crown revenues. Several causes of that nature have been carried on in the Exchequer with effect in respect to Excise Duties, but why no more have been commenced with respect to Custom duties they know not. Serjeants Inn, Fleet Street, May 13, 1723.

At the foot is the "Establishm^t of the Customs" (Scotland).

Report of the Com^rs of Customs, Scotland, sending an account of the instances wherein they have prosecuted by English Bills in the Exchequer, &c., also their solicitor's letter and a copy of a letter written to him by the Com^rs.

Accompanied by the documents referred to. 10 *pages*.

14 May. 47. Thomas Scott to Mr Walpole. By command of the Duke of Roxborough acquaints him that he has laid the papers he received before the King, and has by his Majesty's order sent directions to the Advocate in Scotland to make a strict inquiry into the matters whereunto those papers relate, and to prosecute the offenders when discovered. His Grace has likewise signified his Majesty's pleasure to Brigadier Preston that, in case the troops already quartered at Perth are not sufficient for that service, he should forthwith send such a number thither as shall be necessary to assist the civil Magistrates in the legal execution of their offices, so that the like disorders be prevented for the future. This letter is to be laid before the Com^rs of the Treasury. Whitehall, 14 May 1723.

Minuted:—"Read." 2 *pages*.

14 May. 48. Report of the Com^rs of Customs, Scotland, to the Lords of the Treasury, in reply to a letter of Mr Walpole of the 1st inst., on the discovery they had made of the collusion amongst their officers with respect to the seizure of the mother-of-pearl shells. Dated 14 May 1723.

The following is given as the abstract of it:—

"They sent the Collector of Dumfries to view the shells at 'Kerkenbright,' and by what he writes, and by a letter come to their hands (copy whereof is enclosed), they are confirmed in their

1723. Vol. CCXLIII.

suspicion of the Collector of Kerkenbright being concerned in the collusive seizure. The Com[rs] send inclosed a particular acco[t] of the shells, samples whereof they have sent to the Com[rs] of the Customs here, to show the East India Comp[a] and others that they may be bid for in the Excheq[r] in Scotland the next terme, w[ch] begins the 1st June. And since they find them of such value, the Com[rs] to secure them have ordered them to be brought up under a guard to the warehouse at Leith. They say wrong samples of these shells were at first showed them."

There is also the account above referred to. 6 *pages.*

23 May. 49. The Lord Lieut. of Ireland (Grafton) to the Lords of the Treasury. Has thought himself obliged to recommend to his Majesty the petition (copy enclosed) of the surveyors, tidewaiters, supernumeraries, watermen, and their families at Ringsend belonging to H.M. Customs of the Port of Dublin and other protestant inhabitants there, setting forth that that place is distant from their parish church above a mile and a half, that a river interfering in several places of the Road with it, renders the passage in the winter season and after any sudden rains very dangerous and often impracticable; that a great number of the inhabitants are moreover obliged to so constant an attendance on their duties of their respective charges, that they dare not venture to be so far absent even on Sundays; that an Act of Parliament was some time ago obtained for building a chapel there for their more easy attendance on Divine service, which chapel has been hitherto provided with a Lecturer every Lord's day by the charitable care of the Archbishop of Dublin, as they have no fund for the support of a resident curate to perform the offices of christenings, burials, visitations of the sick, &c., the occasions for which daily occur in a place so full of it's own inhabitants, and which is besides a common resort of many seafaring persons who frequent the harbour of Dublin; wherefore the petitioners pray his Majesty to establish some yearly allowance out of the revenue of the port of Dublin to maintain a constant resident curate amongst them. His Majesty has lately signed a warrant for establishing such minister or curate. Asks for an allowance of 100*l.* per ann. to be placed on the revenue establishment of Ireland for the same, to continue till some other provision should be made for him in the way of a parochial assessment, which design there is a probability of effecting. Bond S[t], 23 May 1723.

The copy of the petition referred to. 6 *pages.*

25 May. The same to the same as to the expense of shipping and provisions procured for the embarkation of the six regiments of foot brought over from Ireland to this Kingdom the last summer. Asking for the money to be reimbursed to the Deputy Vice-Treasurer of Ireland. Bond Street, 25 May 1723. 2 *pages.*

25 May. 50. Copy of letter of the same to the Lords of the Treasury, laying before their Lordships the minutes and resolutions of the Barrack Board in Ireland, by the last of which (of 20 Jan. 1721) he

1723. Vol. CCXLIII.

is desired to represent to his Majesty the necessity there is of supplying the barracks of Ballinrobe and Cork with bedding and utensils, and to endeavour to obtain his Majesty's letter for the payment of 828*l.* 4*s.* 4*d.* to put the barracks in order, that sum having been embezzled by Col. Richard Morris, Quarter-Master. 25 May 1723.

Minuted:—"28th August 1723. Prepare the proper lre."

The minutes and resolutions referred to. 4 *pages.*

27 May. 51. Lord Carteret to the Lords of the Treasury, "signifying the King's pleasure to pay Mr Davenant 1,300li for his service at Rome and other parts of Italy after his allowance as envoy ceased." May 27, 1723. 1 *page.*

27 May. 52. Mr Vice-Chamberlain Coke to ———. Reminds his correspondent that the report from Mr Surveyor, relating to the piece of land adjoining to his Majesty's garden house at Windsor, of which one Hawkings is endeavouring to get a lease, is returned to the Treasury and will pass if his correspondent does not stop it. It would be a great inconvenience to his Majesty's house being so very near. There is an estimate at the Treasury for altering the windows in the presence chamber at Kensington, which he begs may be despatched that the "works" may do it before the Princesses go to Kensington: it being the room through which the company is to come to the Drawing Room. St James's, Monday, 27 May 1723.

The Report of the Surveyor General, which describes the above land as "a peice of wast ground containing about three quarters of an acre lying upon the Castle Hill in Windsor (in the county of Berks), southward from the Castle Wall, and adjoining to the petitioner's house."

Also a rough plan, and the petition.

Minuted:—"6th June 1723. My Lords being informed by Mr Vice-Chamberlain Coke that ye granting what is desired wilbe a great inconvenience to his Mats house, their Lordps do thereupon forbid any further proceeding on this report." 6 *pages.*

28 May. 53. Lord Carteret to the Lords of the Treasury. His Majesty having occasion to employ Salomon Negri, a native of Damascus, in the interpretation of the Oriental languages, desires their Lordships to give the necessary directions for paying him a yearly allowance of four score pounds. Whitehall, 28 May 1723.

Minuted:—"3d Janry 1723-4. Prepare the proper warrant." 1 *page.*

[? About 28 May.] 54. Petition of William Hamilton, H.M. Almoner in Scotland, to the Lords of the Treasury. The allowance on His Majesty's birthday to bedesmen and other poor is only 108*l.* 6*s.* 8*d.*, and falls short of the charges, which increase according to the number of His Majesty's years. The increase this year (1723) is 32*l.* 9*s.* 6*d.* Prays for a dormant warrant to pay the surplus. Undated, but ? about 28 May (the King's birthday).

Also the "account of the charges." 2 *pages.*

1723. VOL. CCXLIII.

29 May. 55. Lord Carteret to the Lords of the Treasury. Henry Davenant, Esq., H.M. late Envoy extraordinary to the Great Duke of Tuscany, the Dukes of Parma and Modena, and the Republic of Genoa, having returned from his employment, his Majesty grants him a pension of 500*l.* a year during pleasure or until again employed: their Lps are to give the necessary directions. 29 May 1723. 1 *page.*

29 May. 56. The same to the same. Thomas Crawfurd, Esq., the King's resident at the Court of France, has represented to His Majesty that his appointments as Secretary of the Embassy at the Court of France were, upon the revocation of the Earl of Stair, determined at Midsummer 1720, and that his appointments as Resident commenced at Midsummer 1722; during which two years he did, by order of the then Secretaries of State, constantly correspond with and transact affairs for his Majesty's service at the Court of France; but has received no allowance for the same. His Majesty is willing that he should receive 40*s.* a day, as if he had been continued Secretary to the time of his being appointed Resident: and their Lordships are to give the necessary directions.

Also a note from Mr Crawfurd, unaddressed, reminding the person to whom sent, of his promise. On the back is:—"200 bounty."

There is a docket on the back which states that the sum due will amount to 1,460*l.*, and adds:—"Memdm 265li was paid him in May 1722 as soe much expended for his Mats service at Paris. Qry if that same is to be deducted." 2 *pages and a few lines.*

31 May. 57. Report of Mr James Moody to the Lords of the Treasury, on the petition of "Rafel Romen Lorenzo Garrido and Iame Juan Leonardo, Undertakers for his Majesty's fortifications of St Phillip's Castle, in the Island of Minorca," as to whether a demand for 862 dollars 6 reals for work done in that castle was not included in Brigadier Petit's accounts certified by the late Commissioners of Army Debts, or whether the same was ever before that Board, and in what manner it was considered by them. Does not find that any application was ever made to the Commissioners for the Army Debts for the payment of the said 862 dollars during any of the commissions for determining those debts.

Also two other papers on the same subject. 7 *pages.*

[? About 1 June.] 58. Petition of Thomas Barlow to the King. Has made "a large road directly from Hanover Square Buildings by Oliver's Mount to the walls of Hide Park for coaches and horses only for the accommodation of the noblemen, gentlemen, and other chief inhabitants in the new buildings adjacent." Asks his Majesty to permit a passage to be made from the road into Hide Park as a very great conveniency to the same inhabitants and no detriment to his Majesty. The Ranger of the Park has no objection thereto, as appears by his letter annexed. 32 signatures.

The letter referred to, signed Henry Portman. Dated Bryanstone, 1 June 1723. 2 *pages.*

1723. Vol. CCXLIII.

1 June. 59. A certified copy from the Council Book "of all the Journals of the General Assembly" of the Province of New Hampshire from the 10th of December 1722 to 1 June 1723. Signed:—"Richard Walden, Cler. Con." 33½ *pages.*

[After 2 June.] 60. Memorial of Margaret, the widow of James, late Earl of Panmure, to the King. Soon after the attainder of the late Earl, His Majesty was, by Act of Parliament, enabled to make such provision for, and settlements upon the memorialist, as she would have been entitled to in case her husband had been naturally dead. The Barons of the Exchequer reported on a petition which she presented, but a doubt arose how far the interest of a bond granted to the memorialist by her husband could legally be granted by his Majesty. It being now decided that the memorialist has a right thereto from Whitsunday 1723, she prays his Majesty to grant her the same.

The copy of the report referred to, and copy of "signature" in her favour, dated 28 Aug. 1718. [This relates to the castle, office, house, and yards of Brechin, and yearly annual rent of 10,000 marks "Scots money" to be taken from the Baronies of Brechin and Navarr and the Barony of Panmure and the teinds of "both the said Baronies," and other properties are also therein specified.] 12 *pages and two halves.*

6–17 June. 61. The draft of the Minutes of the Commissioners of the Treasury between the 6th and 17th of June 1723.

[The *Minute Book* which includes this period is not known to be in existence.]

In the Minute of 12 June their Lordships ordered a warrant for various sums, amounting to 1,730*l.*, in favour of various persons (specified) who were "witnesses or otherwise in the business of the conspiracy." [The conspiracy was that of which the King was said to have received information in the beginning of May 1722.] 12 *pages, quarto.*

[? About 10 June.] 62. Petition of Richard Tonson, Esq., to the Comrs and Chief Governors of H.M. revenue of Ireland. Prays relief for the loss of his boat used as a Customs boat by the officers of the port of Baltimore. The same being lost in quarantine service.

Received June 10, 1723.

Also two affidavits and a certificate thereon. 2 *pages.*

14 June. 63. "A particular of the causes now under prosecution with states thereof." Signed: "A. Cracherode. 14o Junij 1723." 10½ *pages.*

14 June. 64. Resolution passed at a meeting of the Directors of the subscribed Equivalent debt, recommending thirteen persons to be the first directors in the Charter for Incorporating the Proprietors of the Equivalent Debt, and another resolution as to their qualification. Friday, 14 June 1723. 1 *page.*

[About 15 June.] 65. Report of the Barons of the Exchequer in Scotland to the Lords of the Treasury, on the memorial of Simon, Lord Lovat, as to payments out of (1) the lands of Beaufort and others, part of the estate of Alexander McKenzie, late of Frazerdale, and (2) out

1723. VOL. CCXLIII.

of the priory of Bewlie and lands of Kilmaroch, part of the same estate, which stand charged in the Bishop's rental with the payment of a few duty to the Bishop of Ross.

The petition (referred 15 June 1723). Also copy of an unfinished warrant granting the few duties above named to Lovit William Fraser, merchant and Baily of Inverness.

Minuted:—"11th Septr 1723. Respited." 3 *pages*.

17 June. 66. Report of the Surveyor General (J. Pulteney) to the Lords of the Treasury on the memorial of Charles Wither, Esq., Surveyor General of His Majesty's woods, so far as the same relates to his proposal that all the woods of his Majesty's lands be surveyed as the leases come hereafter to be respectively renewed, and that proper certificates be made of the timber growing thereon: gives his method of proceeding, when any application for a lease of crown lands is referred to him, to ascertain what trees are growing on the estate, &c. The returns are seldom as satisfactory as that which was made in the case of Colstable Farm in the memorial mentioned. Believes that great waste is committed by the tenants in cutting down timber trees. Thinks that all such trees should be duly in charge before the proper auditors, in like manner as the lands whereon they grow. If the covenant which is or ought to be in all crown leases of lands, whereon timber trees are growing, were duly complied with, the lessees being obliged to deliver to the auditor every seventh year "terrars" or true accounts of the number of timber trees, and if future leases obliged the tenants to certify the growth of the trees, and how many were fit to be cut, he hopes it may answer Mr Wither's proposal. 17 June 1723.

Extract from Memorial of 30 May 1723 on the same subject. Letter referring Mr Wither's memorial to the Surveyor General for the above report.

The Memorial *minuted* "16th May 1723. Make copies of these warrants mentiond by the Survr that my Lords may give proper directions thereupon." 5 *pages and* 2 *halves*.

[? About 17 June.] 67. The Chairman of "the Committee to enquire into the project commonly called the Harburg Lottery," and of three other Committees, to ——, recommending their clerk, Mr Lucas Kenn, for recompense for his attendance on the Committees.

Minuted:—"June 17, 1723. My Lords cannot encrease the charge of clks. beyond wt it has hitherto been." 1 *page*.

20 June. 68. Memorial of the Duke of Richmond to the Lords of the Treasury. The late Duke, about thirteen years ago, obtained a grant of a lease from Queen Anne, of a piece of ground in the Privy Garden in Whitehall, for 31 years, at the rent of 20*l*. a year, whereon he built a house at a very great charge: prays for a renewal for 31 years, and for the inclusion in the lease of a small piece of ground, containing about 60 ft. in length and 30 ft. in breadth, lying contiguous to the house. June 20, 1723.

Minuted:—"21st June 1723. Refer the first part to the Survr, the latter part being engaged." 1 *page*.

1723. Vol. CCXLIII.

[After 24 June.] 69. Petition of John Rowley, master of the mechanics to his Majesty, to the Lords of the Treasury. Pursuant to His Majesty's orders, "petitioner has lately repaired the great solar systeme & made several new additions to the same, particularly a new pedestal & sphere richly carved, gilt, glazed, &c.," for which he conceives that he deserves 500*l.*; has likewise made for his Majesty's own use a curious silver universal pocket dial, value 30 guineas, and there is due to him upon a late allowance of 100*l.* per ann. 150*l.* by sign manual, dated 24 June 1723: prays payment. 1 *page.*

[After 24 June.] 70. Memoranda of accounts to be stated of what is due (1) to Mr Wych, his Majesty's resident at Hamburgh, and (2) to the widow of Mons. De Robethon for her pension. The state of the debt to them is on the back. There was due to Mr Wych at 3*l.* a day from 14 Feb. 1712–3 (three months being advanced to him) at the Queen's death 231*l.* and for half a year's extraordinaries 150*l.*, and there was due to the widow 125*l.* *Parts of* 2 *pages.*

[? About 25 June.] 71. "Memorial and petition" of James Woodside, late Minister of the Gospel at Brunswick, in New England, to the Lords of the Treasury. He, with about 40 families, consisting of 160 persons, in the year 1718 embarked on a ship at Derry Lough, Ireland, to settle at Casco Bay, in the province of Maine, New England. They made a settlement at a place called by the Indians Pegipscot, but by them Brunswick, within three miles of Fort George. After petitioner had built a large garrison house (at his own expense), which was fortified with palisadoss and two large bastions, and after he had made considerable improvements, the Indians came and drove out the inhabitants upon "pretence they had no right to settle there. Upon this surprise the inhabitants fled (most of them naked out of their beds) into petitioner's house, and those next Fort George fled thither and were supplied with provisions in both garrisons until the Indians withdrew." The Indians being prevented from murdering his Majesty's subjects, in revenge to petitioner, "killed all his cattle with all his provisions & moveables they could come at," and as petitioner had about 40 head of cattle and about 60 swine, petitioner and his family were great sufferers, as appears by the certificate of the Governor.

The copy of the certificate referred to. Dated London, June 25, 1723.

Minuted:—"5£ p Mr Lowther." 1 *page and a few lines.*

[? About 26 June.] 72. Memorial of William Minshull, of Gray's Inn, Esq., to the Lords of the Treasury. "Was ever stedfast to the protestant interest, and so far distinguished himself in the worst of times that he was prosecuted, together with the late Earls of Rivers, Macclesfield, Warrington, Lord Brandon, and other worthy patriots at the assizes held for the county of Chester, by a presentment brought down by the then Chief Justice Jeffreys and form'd to cast an odium and leave defenceless those noble Lords, and other persons of quality, to the number of twenty-six, who vigourously opposed Popery and arbitrary power: which unprecedented presentment was carried on after by Sir Edward Herbert, Chief Justice for ye

1723. Vol. CCXLIII.

said county of Chester, upon the late King James his Accession to the Crown; but was baffled by the noble stand that was made by the presented Lords & Gentlemen & so 'droped,' upon barely taking security for their well abearing to the Government." Memorialist was zealous for the late Revolution, and was one of the first that appeared in arms and is well affected to the present Settlement. For his services King William appointed him attorney for the counties of Chester and Flint, and memorialist put a stop to the frequent riots and treasonable practices of the malcontents, and brought several of the ringleaders to condign punishment. Memorialist also broke the knot of clippers and coiners in the counties of Chester, Flint, and Staffordshire; having prosecuted several hundreds of them and other criminals, with no allowance for the prosecution. Memorialist made the breviates himself, there being no solicitor for the Crown for Chester and Flint. Hoped to have succeeded to be Puisne Judge as was usual, but on the accession of Queen Anne was removed to make room for Mr Winnington, who was made her Majesty's Attorney for Chester and Flint, and some time after Puisne Judge of Chester for life. Memorialist is past 70 years old, and had his whole fortune intr[usted] with his nephew, late member of Parliament for Bramber, in Sussex, who has ruined himself and family, and has absconded, leaving memorialist indebted several hundred pounds, and wholly incapable to pay the same: prays his Majesty's bounty.

Minuted:—"26 June 1723. My Lords cannot do anything in this petition."

Another undated memorial setting forth the same matters at a little later period. 2 *pages*.

27 June. 73. Memorial of Sir Roger Mostyn, Bart., late Paymaster of the Marines, to the Lords of the Treasury. The Auditor of Imprests having finished his account, he (Sir Roger) lays before their Lordships his cravings for the expenses he has been at to the officers employed in his office, and for the incident charges. Begs that the nature of his services may be considered, and the great charges and difficulties he has laboured under since the termination of his patent, viz., by having his account lie open so many years, and his estate subject to extents and other things which he states: prays their Lordships' favour in granting his cravings, and such compensation as shall seem most fit.

Minuted:—"3^d July 1723. See what allowances have been made to former Paym^rs of the Army & Trea~ers of the Navy in passing their Accounts & for their Clerks & Deputy, & to examine the particular articles in the annexed cravings. Mr Tilson to state & examine."

The schedule of cravings. Also a memorial of 11 June 1719 on the same subject, and six other papers connected with his affairs. 13 *pages*.

1723.

VOL. CCXLIV., 1723. July–December.

[? About 1 July.] 1. Petition of John Nevill, Physician to his Excellency Robert Wallpool, Lord Chief Treasurer and Principal Secretary of State, one of the Lords of the Regency, and of his Majesty's Honble "Privi Councel." Has been robbed twice and beaten with his daughter coming "from Ireland hither." Had endeavoured all he could to get practice, or something else to do, but could obtain no manner of business if he would give his life for it'; which obliged him (having 5 children and a very aged father to maintain) to petition the Honble French Committee, who promised as soon as they received the Royal benevolence out of the Treasury (as usual) they would consider him handsomly, to enable him to go hence and follow his business. Had petitioned the Treasury to yield the money to the French Committee. Petitioned also his "Lordship" for relief, until the Committee pay, as he and his family were starving, but was never honoured with an answer. There are thousands of the French poor who are actually perishing as well as the petitioner. Petitioner is well born and educated, and the "15th physician from father to son, has had the happiness to serve 4 crown'd heads by land & by water as Doctor, and is now reduced to expostulate; he and his family being almost naked & bear foot, nay some days without any manner of subsistence in a Christian & plentiful contrey." Asks his excellency if he will generously inform him when he thinks his Majesty's benevolence Royal, will be paid, and to grant him present relief.

The petition has the following postscript to it:—"Was y^r^ L^d^ship & ye whole Goverm^t^ really sensible w^t^ y^r^ pet^rs^ has been his dezasters, & w^t^ he has suffer'd & suffer still, they would draw tears from y^r^ noble eyes, and move y^r^ Lordship to yeild an immediat & comfortable answer in granting both his petitions, wch y^r^ petr beseecheth God to move you all to, &c. He waits below stearving, &c."

On the outside is:—"Vouchsafe to read and grant this petition my Lord for God's sake: for y^r^ pet^r^ & family are stearving, stearving, stearving & naked to, &c."

Minuted:—"1st July 1723. Enquire into the petitioner's case." 1 *page*.

[? About 1 July.] 2. "Memorial of the Honble Mrs Patricia Ballentyne to the Right Honble the Lords of the Treasury, recommended by the Duke of Devonshire." Is the only descendant, alive, of Patrick, Earl of Forth and Brantford, who was General under Gustavus Adolphus in Sweden, and under King Charles the 1st during the Civil Wars, and who performed his duties with universal approbation, and expended of his own money above 10,000*l.* in that King's service; of which memorialist, who is his next heir, has never recovered anything. "Lady Jean Ruthven, his only daughter, when she

1723. VOL. CCXLIV.

belonged to the late Princess Sophia, the King's Royal mother was married in Germany to James, Lord Forrester," memorialist's father, whose estate and honour descended to a collateral branch, being unfortunately murdered, left her very poorly provided. Has avoided as much as possible to beseech relief until now, in her great age, when she is reduced very unwillingly to claim some benefit of the merit of her grandfather, who never was a charge to the crown: prays to be provided for on the civil list.

Minuted:—" 1st July 1723. My Lords cannot advise at this time any new pencon, the King being abroad." 1 *page*.

17 July. 3. Lord Carlisle to "My Lords." His Majesty having appointed an allowance of 40*l*. to be issued out of the Treasury for the Swainmote Courts of Windsor Forest, and the time for holding the courts drawing near, desires an order for the payment of the 40*l*. for this year.

Minuted:—" 40li for holding the Swainmote Court. 24th July 1723. Prepare a warrt." 1 *page*.

22 July. 4. Report of the Postmasters General (Carteret and Walpole) on the petition of Thomas Liddiard, Edward Savage, and Stephen Packer, respecting the appointment and discharge of the duties of the Deputy Postmaster of Hungerford (Thomas Nodes) who, as well as his predecessors, had the inspection and management of the several towns and places following; viz.:—Hungerford, Great Bedwin, Pewsey, Upperhaven, Netherhaven, Amesbury, Stoke, Lavington, Westbury, Trowbridge, Bradford, Warminster, Shipton-Mallet, Bruton, Wells, Froome, and Mere, in the counties of Berks, Wilts, and Somerset. The Postmasters had prosecuted the securities of the Deputy Postmaster who had made default in his accounts, owing the Crown 1,112*l*. 9*s*. 1*d*. The securities had been allowed to issue an extent and had taken his goods into their possession, but had not accounted for them, and had filed a bill in equity against the Postmasters. General Post Office, Lond., 22 July 1723.

The petition on which is this Minute:—" Report of Postmr Genll annexed. 2d 7br. 1723. Read & agreed to." 4 *pages*.

23 July. 5. Charles Delafay (by command of the Lords Justices) to the Lords of the Treasury. Sends petition of the South Sea Company praying for a grant of his Majesty's interest in the reservations made by the King of Spain upon the gain to arise from ships allowed to be sent to the South Sea, which reservations were by his Catholic Majesty assigned to the King: acquainting their Lordships that his Majesty condescended to the petitioner's request, and directed their Lordships to cause a grant to be passed pursuant to the prayer of the petition. Whitehall, 23 July 1723.

The petition referred to. 3 *pages*.

[? About 24 July.] 6. Petition of Daniel Bachelier to the Rt Hon. Robert Walpole, First Lord of the Treasury and Chancellor of the Exchequer. Presents again this memorial, to put his honor in mind of the letter he wrote a few days before his Majesty's departure, in which was enclosed a certificate of the Earl of Stair of petitioner's services

1723. VOL. CCXLIV.

"done in France to his Majesty during the ambassy of that Lord to the French Court," and these were of such a nature that they drew upon him the resentment of the French King, by whose order the estate of the petitioner, exceeding much the pension of 300*l.* given him here, was confiscated. His Honor had told petitioner the next day at Court that he would not forget him (the petitioner), which encouraged him to present a letter last week to ask that the arrears of his pension might be forthwith paid, because he and his numerous family were reduced to great extremities.

Minuted:—"24 July 1723. W^t is his pencõn & w^t due thereupon. 300^li p ann. payable by Mr Chetwynd, one year due at Midsm^r 1723. 25 July 1723. He is paid as far as the rest." 1 *page*.

[? About 26 July.] 7. Memorial of William Wood, Esq., to the Lords of the Treasury, in relation to the securities he has to give in accordance with the indentures between his Majesty and memorialist for coining copper money for Ireland and mixed metal for all his Majesty's dominions in America.

Minuted:—"26th July 1723. To the King's Remem^br or his Dep^ty to exam. the sufficiency & rep^t."

On the next page are proceedings thereon.

With this memorial is a petition of the Provost and the rest of the Company of moneyers of H.M. Mint, in which they state that they have been a Corporation for 400 years, and that they understand Mr Wood has obtained the above grant with liberty to set up a mint at Bristol. Think it their duty to represent that in the reign of the late King James a grant was obtained for coining tin halfpence and farthings, out of the Mint, which gave many evil-disposed persons an insight into the art and mystery of coining, which occasioned the speedy adulteration of the silver coin, and in a few years vast quantities of counterfeit money appeared, to the great prejudice of trade and loss to the nation. Are now willing to contract with the memorialist on the same terms as they did with Sir Jo^s Herne and others for coining copper in the reign of King William and Queen Mary: ask for consideration. Undated. 2 *pages*.

31 July. 8. Barons of the Exchequer of Scotland to the Lords of the Treasury. Transmit draft of signature for granting to Arthur Balfour and his five brothers and sisters, children of John Balfour, late of Fairney, 500*l.* each, out of the surplus of the estate of Burleigh, forfeited by the attainder of John Balfour. Edinb^r, Excheq. Chamb^r, 31 July.

The "draft" referred to.

Minuted:—"2 7ber 1723. Agreed." 4 *pages*.

31 July. 9. Report of the same Barons on the petition of Alexander Murray, of Stanhope, Esq. Are of opinion that by virtue of an Act of Parliament made in Scotland in 1592 "a right is communicated to the subjects" here, to obtain from his Majesty such grant as is asked for by petitioner, for working and carrying on mines in his own lands; and that the "signature" transmitted is valid and

1723. VOL. CCXLIV.

effectual, though there is no concurrence of a master of metals, as required by the Act, that office having been long disused. The duty reserved to his Majesty must be collected by such officer as his Majesty shall see fit to appoint, it being impracticable to carry on the course of refining the ore in the manner as by the Act is directed. Same date.

The mine was in Argyleshire.

The petition and "signature."

Minuted:—"6 Feb. 1723-4. To be transcribed for his Mats signature." 5 *pages*.

31 July. 10. Report of the same on the petition of Alexander Brodie, of Brodie, Esq. Certify that by the certificate of the Treasurer's Remembrancer there became due, of casualties upon the enfeofment of James Brodie, of Brodie, the petitioner's brother, in the year 1715, as heir to his father in the lands of Brodie and others 88*l*. 9*s*. 3*d*., and petitioner upon his enfeofment in the same lands (in 1721), as heir to his brother, is charged with, and liable to pay 110*l*. 16*s*. 9*d*. "as the taxtward" and other duties due to his Majesty. Same date.

Minuted:—"20 Aprill 1724. Agreed." 2 *pages*.

31 July. 11. Report of the same, sending the "draught of a signature for granting to Mrs Margaret Robertson, sister to Alexander Robertson, late of Strowan, for the subsistence of herself and the poor nephews and nieces of the said Alexander Robertson, the estate of Strowan, forfeited to the Crown by a decreet of the Parliament of Scotland."

Also the draft referred to.

Minuted:—"Septb 23d, 1723. Agreed." 4¼ *pages*.

1 Aug. 12. Report of A. Cracherode to the Lords of the Treasury, as to five persons seized in Scotland on board a ship which belonged to Peter Tartone, a French merchant, wherein himself and crew were murdered. One Philip Roche had been committed to Newgate on 11 Aug. 1722, by order of Lord Carteret, on suspicion of the murder, and for piracy in running away with the ship and lading. There was a necessity to bring over two persons from Ireland in order to convict Roche. They and others had applied to be reimbursed. Certifies as to their coming to give evidence. There were four other persons also sent from Dartmouth to give their evidence: all very material witnesses. Upon the evidence given, he was convicted. 1 Aug. 1723.

Minuted:—"1o Augti 1723. 14th Do. Mr Cracherode to pay 260li to Stritch and 100·12·6 to Trevett."

Also six letters and an account (sworn) and another account. 13½ *pages*.

2 Aug. 13. Report to the Lords of the Treasury of Matthew Barton, clerk and controller of the coinage of copper farthings and halfpence, to be coined for the service of Ireland, viz., that the "fillets and moneys according to the assays are in goodness of copper and weight agreable to the contract of Wm Wood, Esq., as prescribed in the grant to him from his Majesty. Aug. 2, 1723.

Minuted:—"5th August 1723. Read. A copie of this to be sent to Ireland. Copy made and letter signed."

1723. VOL. CCXLIV.

W. Wood's petition, in which he asks that the report should be made. 2 *pages*.

[? About 7 Aug.] 14. "The memorial of Mr Jno Coupland, relating to over-payments and fees, &c. in the Treas[urershi]p of the late Lord Viscount Falkland; with a copy of the Lords of the Treasury's warrt for the allowance thereof."

Minuted:—"7th August 1723. The Commrs Navy to certifie if it appears that these sums for short allowance have been paid by ye agent victualler at Portsmo; and likewise by ye Treasurer of the Navy upon ye ship's books, whereby it may appear that double paymt has been made to ye same persons for the same service." 7 *pages*.

8 Aug. 15. The Secretary to the South Sea Company (D. Wescomb) to H. Kelsall, Esq. In answer to a letter requiring more exact information, as to four articles in the South Sea Company's memorial, for allowing extraordinary charges arising by the late subscriptions. Acquaints him, for the information of the Lords of the Treasury, (1) as to the 500*l*. for house rent, the thing required so much haste and expedition that the company was forced to buy the houses wherein the subscriptions were taken, at a cost of 10,600*l*., besides 2,000*l*. more to make them fit. The houses are so old that they must be rebuilt or be unfit for service. *Minuted*:—"Agree." (2) As to the payment of 500*l*. to the Clerks at the Bank; it was *bonâ fide* paid. *Minuted*:—"Agree." (3) As to 500*l*. for contingent charges, called Mr Safford's disbursements, they consist of sundry disbursements charged in his book for subscriptions. *Minuted*:—"Disallowed." (4) As to the solicitor's disbursements, 300*l*. was paid him for advising with counsel, drawing cases relating to subscriptions, &c. *Minuted*:—"Allowed." South Sea House, 8th August 1723.

Report on the same subject. Signed, H. Kelsall.

Minuted:—"11th Augt 1723. Read. The minutes are set against the several articles. The report of the other articles is agreed to." 3½ *pages*.

20 Aug. 16. John Wentworth to "My Lords." Sends copies of the Journal of the General Assembly of the Province of New Hampshire from 10 Dec. 1722 to 1 June 1723. The stores in H.M. Fort William and Mary, at New Castle, are very small and low. Hopes Governor Shute has made proper applications for some recruits, otherwise they will be in a very poor condition. Also sends Mr Collector Armstrong's accounts to the 25th of June 1723, from which time Butts Bacon, Esq, was admitted collector. There being no officer in this place appointed from home to take care of H.M. woods, &c., the writer will take all possible care to prevent spoil. Mr Armstrong, who had a deputation from Mr Burniston, the Surveyor General, has left with the writer his deputation and instructions. Suggests to their Lordships that the commanding officer of this Province, seeing every thing that passes, is likely to serve the King's interest more effectually in the preservation of his

1723. VOL. CCXLIV.

Majesty's woods than any Deputy or Sub-deputy Surveyor, and the people will stand in more fear of him. Has served as Lieut. Governor of H.M. Province of New Hampshire near six years, and has spent and still spends 300*l.* a year more than his income; and this he does cheerfully and willingly to support the honour of his Commission. The Governor in Chief residing in Boston, the whole charge lies on the Lieut. Governor, and the income does not amount to 200*l.* a year, when the Governor of Boston or any Chief Governor is in the country. Prays that his circumstances may be considered, and that he may have such an allowance as to enable him to do the duty of Surveyor of H.M. Woods, which is now more immediately under his care, and cannot be carried on without considerable charge. Resolves not to make a penny perquisite of the place, because he will not be under any obligation to the cutters of timber. It is his great misfortune that he is not known to their Lordships. Is known to Col. Shute, his Governor, and to Governor Phillips, of Nova Scotia, from whom their Lordships may have his character. Province of N. Hampshire, August the 20th, 1723.

23 Aug. 17. Memorial of Anthony Cracherode to the Lords of the Treasury. The 3,150*l.* imprested to memorialist has been all expended, partly in discharge of their Lordships' warrants for considerable rewards to many persons, and partly in his Majesty's other affairs. Has been ordered to pay various further sums. Prays that their Lps would order him 1,680*l.* on account, and the further sum of 500*l.* to carry on H.M. affairs. 23 Aug. 1723.

Minuted:—"23 Aug. 1723. My Lords have this day signd a warrt for 1,000li to be imprested to him, and order another warrt for 1,000li more to him." 1½ *pages.*

26 Aug. 18. Samuel Heckford to the Secretaries of the Lords of the Treasury. In the absence of Mr Jobber (who was brought over from Ireland to give evidence against Roch, executed for piracy) applies to have Mr Jobber's claim laid before their Lordships that Mr Cracherode may be ordered to reimburse him the sum of 86*l.* 16*s.* paid by him on this business. Norfolk Street, 26 Aug. 1723.

Letter of Michael Stretch, enclosing copies of two letters from the Lords Justices of Ireland, also petition of Edward Trevett, of the Kingdom of Ireland, mariner, another witness in the same case praying for satisfaction.

Minuted:—"28th Augt 1723. My Lords do not think fit to do any thing in this." 4 *pages and* 2 *halves.*

27 Aug. 19. Report of A. Cracherode to the Lords of the Treasury on the petition of William Rhett, junior, merchant, asking for an order for payment of 442*l.* 10*s.* 4¾*d.* due to the captors of two pirate vessels whose crews were executed for piracy at South Carolina. The petitioner applies for the above sum as agent for the captors. Certifies that petitioner is the agent and capable of receiving the sum due, and to give a discharge for the same. 27 Aug. 1723.

The petition. 3 *pages.*

1723. VOL. CCXLIV

28 Aug. 20. "A state of the coal duty granted for building churches, &c." 2 *pages*.

30 Aug. 21. Memorial of Serjeant Richard Atherton to ——. Memorialist and two others detected and convicted Thomas Ward of speaking treasonable words, and memorialist attended the Lords of the Treasury [thereon] as often as his duty in the guards would permit him; but the camp in Hyde Park, &c. prevented his receiving H.M. bounty. Memorialist before the conviction wrote the Minutes of the House of Commons "in company with the person convicted as above," but the latter being employed again last sessions of Parliament "memorialist resented it, so far that he thought it very dishonourable to associate himself with persons known to be disaffected to his Most Gracious Majtie King George," and whose company and conversation memorialist utterly detests and abhors: therefore memorialist quitted the writing upon "Ward being employ'd again."

Certificate as to the words used, which were :—" G–d damn your King George, he is no King, and I am as good a man or better than he, for you don't know who is your King, for which words the said Ward was convicted and suffered according to law." At the foot is :—

" Memor that the said Ward was whip'd at the cart by the comōn hangman from the gate in King Street, near the Cock Pitt, Whitehall, round Pallace Yard, Westmr."

On the back is a note from Mr Chr. Tilson to Mr Cracherode, and reply from the latter that the prosecution was not under his management and he knew nothing of it. 2 *pages*.

7 Sept. 22. Ba: Adams to the Lords of the Treasury. Has been in London and other ports and finds there are tidesmen put on all "outerbounds" at a charge at least of 2 or 3,000*l*. per ann. and not 2*d*. advantage: for there is a very great Guinea and Virginia trade, and the Guinea man usually carries a hogshead or 2 of tobacco for the use of the negroes, and they stow it away for fear of the sailors; and neither sailor nor tidesmen ever sees it after stowing, till they come to Guinea, and a tidesman does as much good there as he would do "if a top on Bansted downe." Likewise Virginia men perhaps take a box of pepper for their own use, which they cannot be without, no more than the Guinea men without tobacco, and these have two officers a piece, likewise at 6s per day charge for each ship; and ships bound to other parts take some trusses of tobacco. It cannot be imagined that merchants for trifles would run the risk of having their ships exchequered, and lose their voyages, besides other penalties. At the several ports of this kingdom there are seldom less than 30 "outerbounds," if not 40, at 6s a day each; or at least 4s a day each ship. If their Lordships think this expense may be saved, it is all the satisfaction that is desired. September 7, 1723.

Minuted:—" 8 Septr 1723. Read & disapproved." 1 *page*.

11 Sept. 23. Report of the Postmasters General (Carteret and Walpole) to the Lords of the Treasury on the petition of William Trench, Esq.

1723. VOL. CCXLIV.

The petitioner has produced several certificates, some of them recommending him as deserving protection and encouragement in the maintenance of the Lighthouse at the Skerrets, and all of them alleging the continuance of the lighthouse to be very necessary and useful for such ships as pass these seas. The Irish packet boats have the benefit of the Skerrets' lights, in common with other ships which trade upon that coast; but the packet boats upon their several stations have hitherto in this respect been put upon the footing of the men-of-war and have ever been exempted from paying to any lights, or ony other duties whatsoever. If their Lordships think fit to order it otherwise, in this particular case, it may prove to be a precedent "that may very much prejudice the service which, in the nature of it, requires the utmost freedom from all such matters, which may occasion delay or interrupt the service upon any pretence whatsoever." General Post Office, London, Sept. 11, 1723.

Minuted:—"16 7ber 1723. Allow 200li."

The petition referred to; also a letter from the Lord Lieut. of Ireland docketed:—"Lord Lieut. of Ireland, proposing 50li p ann. to be allowed Mr French out of the Post Office for the benefit the Pacqt boats receive from the lighthouses at Skerries, with a retro-speccōn of 5 years, being about the rate of 1d p ton."

Minuted:—"28th June 1723. Warrt to be pꝑared accordingly."

The petition sets forth that from the frequent loss of ships, seamen, and passengers, on the north-west coast of Wales and the Isle of Man, it was determined to erect a lighthouse on the dangerous rock Skerries, which is a mile long, about three leagues from Holyhead in the entrance to that Bay; by the benefit of which the Packet boats might, in the darkest night, with great safety, sail into and out of Holyhead. Petitioner passed letters patent in 1714 to carry out and support the work, and his only son (just come from his travels) was to superintend the building of the light. The work was begun by his son and six seamen, who, when bringing materials from Dublin, were all lost, and the work remained neglected till 1717, when petitioner at his own expense, amounting to near 3,000*l*., erected the Light House, which is about 150 feet higher than the sea. On the 4th of Nov. 1717 a fire was kindled therein and ever since was supported at petitioner's expense [to] serve the traders to Chester and Liverpool, who are the only part of the navigation that contribute towards supporting the light; so that for want of due support petitioner is yearly near a hundred pounds out of pocket; some pretend that the lighthouse was erected chiefly for the benefit of the Packet Boats, others say they cannot be obliged to pay the 1d per ton, but by an Act of Parliament. Finding his fortune impaired very much, petitioner once determined not to continue the fire until he obtained an Act of Parliament; but fearing the public might suffer if delay or damage happened to the Packet Boats for want of the light in dark nights, he laid his case before the Lords Justices of Ireland. They laid the matter before the Lord Lieut., who thereupon made the proposal above referred to. 7½ *pages.*

1723. Vol. CCXLIV.

[? About 11 Sept.] 24. Petition of Sarah Stuckey, widow, to the Lords of the Treasury. Valentine Stuckey, father to petitioner's late husband, being linen draper to King Charles II., there was due to him 2,500*l.*, and a further sum of 210*l.* 14*s.* 3*d.* for money lent. King James II. gave orders for the payment of the "2,000*l.*," but before any advantage could be had thereby he departed this realm, so that the money remained unpaid. In consequence thereof petitioner's late husband had to sell a freehold estate of 400*l.* per ann., part of which was settled in jointure on petitioner, whose husband died, leaving nothing more than a small leasehold estate held from the crown. Petitioner had applied for a renewal of the lease, and now asks that the fine of 130*l.* set by the Surveyor should be remitted.

Minuted:—"11th Septr 1723. Rejected." 1 *page*.

13 Sept. 25. Report of Sir Isaac Newton to the Lords of the Treasury on the memorials of the "General" and Master of H.M. Mint at Edinburgh. Represents that by the Coinage Act of the last session, H.M. sign manual directed to the General (17 Nov. 1718) is become void, and a new one may be procured to the Master for putting in force the indenture between the late Queen Ann and the Master until a new indenture shall be made, and that 2,100*l.* [should] be imprested upon account to the Master for the service of that mint as desired. Mint Office, 13 Sept. 1723.

Minuted:—"13 7ber 1723. Agreed."

The memorials and a copy of the sign manual referred to. 5½ *pages*.

24 Sept. 26. Barbadoes. Henry Worsley to the Lords of the Treasury. Encloses (1) the reply of William Dalrymple, Esq., Receiver General of his Majesty's casual revenue, and of John Ashley, Deputy Auditor General, to the representation (formerly sent) of the Custom House officers touching the casual revenue; (2) the Custom House officers' rejoinder to the reply. This he left entirely to their Lordships, being a sort of party concerned in the quarrel, having ordered the Custom House officers to sell the seizures themselves, and not have them sold by the Provost-Marshal, which is not only more expensive, but, as he is informed, was never the practice before; and (3) an account of the fines and forfeitures at the last court of Grand Sessions. Barbadoes, 24 Sept. 1723.

Accompanied by the enclosures referred to. Besides which with (No. 1) there is another paper containing copies of various documents on the same subject, and with No. 3 is a letter of an earlier date as to proposals for dividing and selling certain brandies. 32 *pages*.

27 Sept. 27. Report of the Surveyor General (Pulteney) to the Lords of the Treasury, on the petition of the Dowager Lady Clarges for a reversionary lease of the six messuages more particularly described therein. Finds that Thomas, late Lord Jermyn, and others, were legally entitled to the premises in trust for the late Lord Dover for two several terms of 29 and 20 years. These were granted by King Charles II. in trust for the late Earl of St. Albans, and will expire at Mich. 1740. They, the Lord Dover and his Trustees, demised the

1723. Vol. CCXLIV.

tenements to Sir William Clarges, Bart., late husband to petitioner, his executors, &c. for 28¼ years, from 25 June 1711, which will expire at Mich. 1739. Sir Walter Clarges devised the same messuages, which are situated together on the south side of Piccadilly, to petitioner (being part of the Bailiwick of St James's). Four of the six messuages have a frontage of 72 feet to Piccadilly and in depth 77 feet. They are worth at a rack rent 115*l.* per. ann. Two others have 32 feet frontage on Piccadilly, and are 77 feet in depth, and are worth 100*l.* per ann. Has made a report on the petition of Thomas Lobb, Esq., for a reversionary lease of the two last messuages. It appears that the tenant right of these two is in the Lord Dover's trustees, &c. Petitioner is the next and immediate crown tenant, and a lease may be granted to her for 33 years from Mich. 1740, for a fine of 282*l.* 8*s.* 7*d.*, reserving a rent of 2*s.* 6*d.* in the pound amounting to 26*l.* 17*s.* 6*d.* per ann. But if a lease be granted of the four first only, then a fine of 130*l.* will be a valuable consideration, reserving a like rent of 2*s.* 6*d.* in the pound amounting to 14*l.* 7*s.* 6*d.* per ann. 27 Sept. 1723.

Also the petition.

Minuted:—"Wt signed for 2 of these Houses in ye name of Thomas Lobbe." *Again*:—"29 April 1725. Caveat entred by Mr Folkes on ye behalfe of the coheires of the late Lord Dover." 5 *pages.*

30 Sept. 28. An accompt of the debt due and owing on the pensions payable in the office of Walter Chetwynd, Esq., from Lady Day 1723 to Michaelmas 1724. Dated 30 Sept. 1724. 11 *pages.*

1 Oct. 29. Address of the House of Commons of 1 Oct. 1723, recommending Lieut. Col. Samuel Freeman to the Lord Lieut. of Ireland for a suitable provision to be made for him. Also his petition to the House of Commons which states that he had served in all the wars of Ireland, Flanders, and Spain.

Minuted:—"Warrt signd 5 Aug. 1724." 2 *pages.*

9 Oct. 30. Address of the House of Commons recommending to the Lord Lieutenant of Ireland George Macartney, William Maynard, Edward May, Thomas Pearson, Talbot Ivory, and Enoch Sterne, Esquires, and others concerned in the Quarentine duties. 9 Oct. 1723.

Also their petition.

Minuted:—"Warrt signd 7th Augt 1724. 2 *pages.*

11 Oct. 31. Address of the House of Commons on the petition of Quarter Master Charles McFaden, setting forth his services in the Army, and that he is the only officer living of the late Brigadier Wolseley's regiment of horse now unprovided for, and praying that he may enjoy the same benefit with the rest of his fellow soldiers in relation to half pay, recommending him to the Lord Lieutenant for the same. 11 Oct. 1723.

Also his petition in which he says he was one of fourteen who turned King James's guns upon his army at Newtown which occasioned an entire victory, and he engaged so closely at the

1723. VOL. CCXLIV.

Boyne that his troop were all cut off to nine men, and he received so many wounds that day that he has been incapable of providing for himself ever since.

Minuted:—" Warr[t] signd 7th Aug[t] 1724." 2 *pages*.

12 Oct. 32. Address of the House of Commons, Ireland, to the Lord Lieut. on the petition of the Hon. Richard Stewart, Esq., for himself and others concerned in the Colliery of Ballycastle, Antrim. The address recommends that 2,000*l*. be paid to them to enable them the better to carry on the Colliery. 3½ *pages*.

14 Oct. 33. P. Laurans to the Hon[ble] M[r] Lownds, Secretary at the Treasury. Asks him to read the enclosed petition to the Lords of the Treasury.

The petition referred to. It relates to a machine "infallibly proper for the discovery of the longitude upon sea" which the petitioner Peter Laurans had attained to the knowledge of making. He is destitute and asks that a sum of money which he understands has been collected and lodged with their Lordships may be handed over to him. *Minuted*:—" Read 16 Oct. 1723. My Lords cannot order any money upon this petition." 3 *pages*.

15 Oct. 34. J. Fauquier to Christopher Tilson, Esq.—Desires that the Treasury order to be executed by him may be put upon the back of the proposal itself as was done in other cases. 15 Oct. 1723.

Accompanied by an "abstract of M[r] Grotes Contract for sale of Tyn, &c., dated the 24th day of June 1723, with Mr. Fauquiers proposition with relation to the said tyn."

Minuted:—" Proposall agreed to." 3 *pages*.

[? About 16 Oct. 1723.] 35. Petition of Sir Polycarpus Wharton, Bart., to the Lords of the Treasury asking for payment of a balance due to him on his father's (Sir George Wharton's) account who was Treasurer and Paymaster of the Ordnance and died on 12 Aug. 1681. Petitioner has been a great sufferer by the Office of Ordnance occasioned by their breach of contract with him for eleven years ending 1698. To prevent his ruin, employed his thought upon "his shell" of which he annexes a description, and asks to be allowed a speedy trial of it.

On the annexed leaf is:—" A description of the service of Sir Polycarpus Wharton's shell to be shott out of three severall natures of cannon used now only in the lower and midle tere of the first and lower teres of the second and third rate ships of the English fleet, but (with submission) may hereafter be also used in smaler ships to carry a much lesse number of cannon, but of the highest nature of the three belowe specifyed."

[The principal merit of the shell appeared to be that it could be fired like common ball, and when it pierced the enemies ships it would burst into thirty or more pieces.]

Minuted:—" 16 Oct. 1723. Read, and my Lords can do nothing herein."

There is also another paper docketed:—" S[r] Polycarpus Whartons case on his fathers account, No. 20."

1723. VOL. CCXLIV.

It contains much of the information found in the petition. 3 *pages.*

28 Oct. 36. "Abbreviat by Sir Robert Sinclair, Barr[t], receiver General in Scotland of receipts, payments, & remains of the rents and profits and sale of the forfeited estates in Scotland the twenty eight of Octo[r] 1723, exclusive." 1 *large page.*

31 Oct. 37. "Resolution of y[e] House of Lords in favour of Luke Netterville, Esq.," who was reduced to the utmost extremity, and had been received into the Church of Ireland by the Bishop of Dublin 16 years since. He had "educated his children in that faith," and asked to be recommended to the Lord Lieutenant for civil employment. The Resolution recommends him to the Lord Lieutenant for civil employment, he being the first of his family who has been received into the Church of Ireland, and orders Lord Charlemont and the Lord Baron Ferrard to attend the Lord Lieutenant with the resolution. 31 Oct. 1723. 1 *page.*

6 Nov. 38. Report (signed) of the Mayor and Jurats of Queenborough to the Lords of the Treasury. Had received a complaint in a letter from the Treasury of 15 Oct., made against them by persons employed by the Navy Board, viz., "that they were obstructed in the experiment of raising water on a piece of ground belonging to his Majesty near Queenborough," and their "Lordship's intentions that they should be permitted to proceed in the manner they thought fit." When these gentlemen came at the end of September they began directly to bore the well in the castle ground, and could not think it became them to take any notice of the Corporation, who had been in possession above three score years, and who claim a jurisdiction over it by charter; but they were in no ways interrupted; the Corporation resolved to represent the matter to their Lordships. The gentlemen succeeded in finding water, but obstructed the people (who were in great want) from having any. Give an account of the nature of the obstructions. The Mayor submitted to this ill treatment. After treating the Corporation in this manner, these gentlemen intermixed some aspersions in the account of their proceedings, in hopes of preventing their Lordships future favour to the Corporation, and were guilty of other incivilities and rudeness. Apprehend all this is occasioned from opposing the Commissioner in leasing the castle land for his own use; for Mr. James Young Master "Attendance" of Chatham Dock and Mr. John Ward, Master Shipwright of Sheerness Dock (two of the persons employed) publicly declared in the town that the Corporation might thank themselves and see what they had got by petitioning. The Corporation have the utmost zeal for his Majesty's service and are ready to submit to their L[ps] consideration their pretensions to this piece of ground. Pray that no proposal for conducting the water through the land belonging to the Corporation or for debaring them the free use of it (hitherto enjoyed) will be approved by their Lordships without admitting the Corporation to be heard. Queenborough, 6 Nov 1723.

1723. VOL. CCXLIV.

[The letter of 15 Oct. above referred to is entered in the Treasury Letter Book, Vol. 17, p. 393.]

With the report is a letter from the Navy Board of 10 Oct. 1723, enclosing copy of another letter on the same subject. The letter of the 10th of Oct. has this minute on it:—

"12th 8br 1723. To the Mayor & Jurats of Queenbro desiring them not to proceed in stopping the offrs of the Navy & that my Lords will consider what is proper to advise his Maty relating to the grant of the Castle & other the lands there." 8 *pages*.

11 Nov. 39. Report of Mr George Treby to the Lords of the Treasury on the memorial of Major James Cunningham, Deputy Governor of the Garrison of Fort William in North Britain who claimed 91*l*. 12*s*. 6*d*. for intelligence, extraordinary expenses and maintaining prisoners during "the Rebellion in the year 1719." Finds that 150*l*. was annually allowed for contingencies &c. on the establishment of that garrison; that in 1719, 50*l*. was allowed to Sir Robert Pollock, the Governor, for intelligence &c., besides other sums for expresses &c., amounting to 460*l*. 19*s*. 9*d*. As for his demands in attending the General, conceives that it is every officers duty to bear such expenses out of his pay and that any additional allowance would be a dangerous precedent. Whitehall, 11 Nov. 1723. 1 *page*.

11 Nov. 40. Mr William Cowper Clerk of the Parliament to William Lowndes, Esq. as to a payment of a fine by him into the Receipt of the Exchequer; and as to his discharge therefrom. Thinks he might have doubted how the Lords Comrs or any Court of Revenue could take regular notice of fines set upon record, or in the High Court of Parliament, without some previous estreat made of the record in form: asks him to ascertain how the matter stands. Essex Street in the Strand. 11 Nov. 1723.

Also copy of a standing order of the House of Lords of 3 April 1624, in respect to mitigation of fines. 3 *pages*.

21 Nov. 41. Report of the Barons of the Exchequer of Scotland to the Lords of the Treasury on the draft of a "signature" for continuing and "prorogating" to John, Earl of Bute his heirs and assigns, a lease of certain tithes within the Isle of Bute, granted by her late Majesty to the deceased James, Earl of Bute, for 19 years from Whitsuntide 1705, "and that for the further term of nineteen years"; as also for granting to the Earl for 19 years certain other tithes and few duties, in that Island, belonging to his Majesty "as come in place of the Bishop of the Isles"; paying for the same 11*s*. 1*d*. $\frac{1}{3}$ sterling. Edinburgh, Exchequer Chamber, 21 Nov. 1723.

The draft referred to. 5½ *pages*.

22 Nov. 42. Barbara Crow to his "Excellency." Has enclosed certificates of her not having received any consideration for her service as body laundress to H.R.H. the Princess of Wales from Mich. 1714 to Mich. 1715. Asks for a warrant for the same. "Novr ye 22d 1723."

On the dorse is the following report by Christopher Tilson. "The princes's Body Laundress has 200*l*. p ann. whereof Barbara

VOL. CCXLIV.

1723.

Crow has 100*l.* and a German who dos the work has the other 100*li.* p ann.

The prince, princess, and their family were kept at the King's charge the 1st year of his reign, and notwithstanding Mrs Crow came over body laundress yet (as Mr. Lowman certifies) she had no allowance whatsoever for that year. The Countess of Buckenburg certifies to the same effect and that she has often (tho' in vain) sollicited her payment. The Prince before his revenue was setled received 70,000*li.* without account to be disposed as he should direct, besides which I find there was 5,000*l.* issued to Mr Molyneux for the Prince's use, but intended as the warrant expresses, to be repaid to the King out of such annual revenue as should be setled upon him.

It dos not appear that this 5,000*li.* was ever repaid. Mrs Crow cannot assure me but that there may be others in like circumstances as to that year's arrear with herself, if so, the paying her alarms all the rest, and your Lordships will easily judge the consequences thereof.

If Mr Lowman's certificate is obtained that she is the only instance, then she is in a proper way for your Lordships favour, otherwise it will be adviseable to obtain the repayment of the above 5,000*l.* before any demands of this kind be yielded unto.

Minuted:—"6 Xber 1723 read." 2 *pages*.

[? About 24 Nov.] 43. Petition of George Roe and Simon Sherlock in behalf of themselves and about sixty more creditors of James Leathly, Benjamin Taylor, and James Dugg[an] who where partners in clothing several regiments in Ireland, addressed to the Knights, Citizens, and Burgesses in Parliament assembled, praying them to recommend their case to his Majesty that they might have such reparation out of the estate of Sir William Robinson, Deputy Vice Treasurer General of Ireland (who, they complain, had illegally extorted several sums from them) as the justice of their case required.

Also copy of a letter from the Lord Lieut. and Privy Council in Ireland sending and recommending a bill for the relief of the above creditors. Dated 24 Nov. 1723. 3 *pages*.

26 Nov. 44. Report of the Lord Lieut. of Ireland to the Lords of the Treasury on the memorial of Captain John Southby, praying to be restored to half pay. The Lord Lieut. says:—"this gentleman having already resign'd his employment in the revenue to render himself capable of being restored to half pay, which by his former service in the army he had acquired a title to, I think I may reasonably recommend his application to your Lordships." Dublin Castle, 26 Nov. 1723.

The memorial and two other documents, on the same subject and copies of the same with one short extract from a letter in addition. 6 *pages and* 2 *halves*.

29 Nov. 45. Report of the Comrs for Hawkers and Pedlars to the Lords of the Treasury on the petition of Richard Goodman. Were informed by Mr. John Brown, their officer for the North Parts of England,

1723. VOL. CCXLIV.

that the petitioner had been serviceable in discovering persons who traded without licences. He had "convened" a Scotch pedlar before a justice of the peace who would not convict him. The pedlar thereupon brought an action for false imprisonment against petitioner, who, however, obtained a verdict and had a certificate for treble costs. Petitioner, however, had not produced the record of the trial with a bill of his charges in defending the suit as he had undertaken to do. Hawkers Office, 29 Nov. 1723.

The petition referred to. 2 *pages*.

[? About 29 Nov.] 46. Petition of James Leppan "to the R^t^ Honble Mr Robt Walpole Esq." Was the only evidence for his Majesty at Carlisle against the rebels, and afterwards was commanded by the Duke of Roxborough to go into Scotland with Mr. Paxton "upon Ire and Termire"; where he was desperately wounded by some of the Government's enemies, and expected nothing but death till the Duke of Roxborough sent money and orders for him to come to London, where he lies in miserable condition confined in the Marshalsea Prison, Southwark, for debt, and where he must perish unless he has Mr. Walpole's assistance. Has petitioned the Treasury for a sum of money to discharge him from this place of torment and keep back his pension of 30*l.* a year until the sum is repaid.

Minuted:—"Rejected 29th 9br 1723." 1 *page*.

5 Dec. 47. "State of the prosecutions carrying on [in the] Court of Exchequer in Scotland by English bills against the merchants in Glasgow; in obedience to ane order from the Right Honourable the . : . . . Commissioners of His Majesty's Treasury, dated the 27th of March 1723." Custom Ho: Edinbr 5th December 1723. 3 *pages* (brief size). 3 *pages*.

7 Dec. 48. Memorial of Mrs Ruperta Howe, Chief Rangeress of Alice Holt and Woolmer Forests in the county of Southampton, to the Lords of the Treasury. The repair of the several lodges of these forests would amount to 373*l.* and upwards, which she hopes their Lordships would order as well as the four years salaries of the keepers, at 130*l.* per ann. She also asks that the lodgings in Somerset House, in which she lives, may be repaired. 7 December 1723.

Three other documents connected therewith. 5 *pages*.

[? About 13 Dec.] 49. Memorial of William Wood to the Lords of the Treasury. In the patent granted to memorialist for the American coin, there is mention of three several assays, viz., in the lump or ingot, in the fillet and in the coin, whereas two of them are needless; because the only end is to secure the goodness of the coin, and if that be according to the standard and will bear the assay, it is impossible that the ingot or fillet, from whence it was taken, should be bad: prays that the two fillets which he has seen may be accepted, the one to be kept in the Treasury and the other delivered to the Controller as standard for the coinage.

Minuted:—"13th Decr 1723. To the Comptr to certify if he agrees to this proposition."

1723. VOL. CCXLIV.

Certificate at the foot that the Controller of the American coinage agrees to the memorial, provided he may have an order from the Treasury to pass the coin on proof of its malleability only: the patentee being always answerable for the compound. 1 *page*.

[? About 4 Dec.] 50. Memorial of the Managers (being 15 in number) appointed by the Lords of the Treasury to finish the work left unfinished by the first managers of the subscriptions to the South Sea Company on the Act 6 Geo. I. They describe the nature of the work they had performed, which consisted, amongst other things, in reducing seventy-seven volumes, of which the original subscriptions and lists consisted, into twenty-two volumes. To each of the twenty-two volumes there was a preface affixed, in which many errors and mistakes that appeared in the original subscription books, are certified into the Exchequer: praying consideration for their services.

Minuted:—"4 Xber 1723. Agreed at the rate of 150li p ann. and incidts to be paid all in discha of ye Commrs." 1 *page*.

[? About 17 Dec.] 51. Memorial of Mrs Elizabeth Bridges to the Lords of the Treasury. There is due to petitioner from the late Queen Anne 102*l*. 10*s*. 3*d*. for rent of her house hired by the Comrs appointed to settle the Treaty of Commerce between Great Britain and France from 8 Feb. 1713 to 1 Aug. 1714: prays that the money may be ordered.

A certificate in corroboration of the memorial dated 17 Dec. 1723. 2 *pages*.

19 Dec. 52. Report of the Commrs for licencing Hawkers and Pedlars to the Lords of the Treasury. In obedience to their Lps commands they were directed to open the door of the Office of Thomas Tomkins their cashier, in the presence of his sureties, and to inspect his books, chests and papers, and to give their Lps an account of the state of his cash, and likewise to seal up again the chests and office in the presence of the sureties. They opened the office and examined the papers and accounts which were in the utmost confusion. "There was not any bank or goldsmith note," and only a few bills amounting to 20*l*. 13*s*. As for specie, there was none. Upon this the sureties declared themselves satisfied and declined any further inspection. The sureties of their free will delivered up the key to the Comrs. The annexed estimate will show the amount which Tomkins stood indebted to the Crown. Hawkers and Pedlars Office, 19 Dec. 1723.

The estimate of the debt referred to amounting to 41,321*l*. 6*s*.

Also three other papers connected with these affairs, two of them being of a little later date, of which one relates to the appointment of a succeeding cashier. 8 *pages*.

12 Nov. to 30 Dec. 53. Various letters and proposals of Mr Arch. Hutcheson addressed to [? the Secretary of the Treasury] in respect to the pension of 5,000*l*. per ann. granted to the late Duke of Ormonde by the late Queen, to enable him to discharge his debts, which pension was assigned to Mr Cotton, Mr Clayton, and Mr Hucheson in trust to pay his debts amounting to upwards of 45,000*l*.

1723. VOL. CCXLIV.

In one of the letters (25 Nov. 1723) he says it would be a great satisfaction to the Earl of Arran to have these debts discharged, and likewise that due from himself to the public. He further says, if his proposal were accepted by the warrant that would be granted there would be paid out of the revenue of Ireland to the Public of Great Britain at Christmas next (1723) 10,000*l.*, and at Christmas 1724, 10,000*l.* more, which are the sums due from the Earl of Arran, who by act of parliament was enabled to purchase his brothers forfeited estate.

The letter of 30 December 1723 states that 30,000*l.* of the 50,000*l.* payable to the Public of Great Britain by the Earl of Arran, pursuant to the Act, had been paid. 14 *pages and* 4 *halves.*

54. Memoranda as to petitions, enquiries thereon, copies of orders and minutes relating to the "droits" of the King's Heralds and Pursuivants at Arms being 13 in number. The paper seems to have been prepared for the information of the Lords of the Treasury. It states that there were seventy creations of peerages since Sept. 1715. The date is probably 1723 or 1724. 1 *page.*

55. Petition of Margaret Baliol to the Lords of the Treasury. Asks for delivery to her of her Letters patent, warrant accounts &c mentioned in the printed case annexed, to prevent her (who has exhausted all her substance) and sixty of her family, from perishing. She adds, "Your Lordships know it is your oppress'd petitioner's birthright and patrimony and inheritance for them and their heirs and that it is his sacred Majesty's gracious comãnds that we should be invested in our property." Prays to be admitted to his Majesty's bounty at Christmas. Undated, but ? 1723.

Also the printed copy of her petition to the House of Commons, $17\frac{22}{23}$. 3 *pages.*

56. Petition of Edmund Britiffe, Thomas Newman, and Thomas Guenault, Paymasters, and Peter Leheup, Comptroller of Exchequer Bills, to the Lords of the Treasury. The million of Exchequer Bills (9 Geo. [I.]) are discharged and cancelled within a small sum. There remain outstanding 919,912*l.* 10*s.* in Old Exchequer Bills. Pray to be continued to receive, discharge, and cancel the same. [? About 1723.]

Also memoranda as to enactments in 8 Geo. [I.] 2 *pages.*

57. Draft of a warrant of the Lords Justices, on behalf of the King, addressed to the Attorney and Solicitor General, requiring them to prepare a bill to pass the great seal for a grant and assignment from his Majesty to the Governor and Company of Merchants of Great Britain, of the shares or proportions of 10 per cent. of all profits and gains on goods, merchandise, and ladings of two ships called the Bedford and Elizabeth, which were allowed by the assiento contract to trade for one voyage only, and of 5 per cent. of the net gain of all the three parts belonging to England of the ship allowed to trade yearly to the Indies during the term of that contract, which shares were reserved to the King of Spain and

VOL. CCXLIV.

1723. by him left to be disposed of by the late Queen Anne, and since her decease have devolved on the present King. Dated — 1723. 6 *pages.*

58. Draft of a warrant by the Lords Justices to [the Attorney and Solicitor General] to prepare a bill containing an Indenture as therein set forth.

Docketed:—"Indenture for settlem[t] of part of the Island of St. Christophers, w[ch] was rendered by France, pursuant to the Treaty of Utrecht." Dated — 1723. 11 *pages* (*brief size*).

59. "Copy of an Act passed in North Carolina in the year 1723 intituled An Act for Settling the Titles and bounds of lands." [The copy perhaps was made some years later.] 11 *pages.*

[1723 or 1724.] 60. Memorial of Lieut. Col. Laurence Armstrong to the Lords of the Treasury. Their L[ps] directed by warrant of 31 Jan. 1722 the secretary-at-war to prepare a warrant to pay memorialist 800*l.* for his services and losses in North America. The secretary alleges there is no fund for payment thereof. Will be obliged to dispose of his commission to prevent being cast into prison, which, after 29 years faithful service, memorialist hopes their L[ps] will not permit. Prays directions may be given for payment.

Minuted:—"My Lords can give no other directions."

[This matter is referred to in the *Register of Papers*, p. 185, under 8 April 1724, and again at p. 195, under 19 May 1724. The entry in the last is "Col. L. Armstrong rel. to 800[li] ordered him for services at Canso. Recall the letter to y[e] late Secr̃y at War and direct it to Mr. Pelham the present Secr̃y."] 1 *page.*

[? 1723 or 1724.] 61. A draft or copy of a report of the Commissioners for forfeitures, Scotland, entitled:—"A further report humbly offer'd by the Commissioners and Trustees for the forfeited estates who acted in Scotland, &c." They remark amongst other matters that in the year 1719 they determined 350 claims, and in 1721 and 1722, 205 claims, and there remain 998 claims; and a great number of these have been under their consideration. Appeals have been entered in 53 cases, &c. 22,737*l.* have been ordered to be paid into the Exchequer of Scotland. Give reasons why the sum is not greater and though they have used all the powers vested in them which they could give to stewards or factors for recovering the rents, &c. of the forfeited estates in the northern parts of the Highlands and Isles of Scotland, they have proved too weak for the opposition made by the tenants of those estates. Mention as a proof that in October 1721, William Ross and Robert Ross, their factors, on the estate of Seaforth, Glenmoriston, Strathglass, &c. going upon the estates, to perfect the rentals and collect the rents, were opposed by armed force. In this service William Ross was wounded and his son killed, and others were wounded. The charge of the Commission had been between 24 June 1716 and 24 June 1722, 58,641*l* 5*s.* 6¾*d.*; the income and expectations 61,231*l.* 13*s.* 8¼*d.* The Com[rs] and Trustees in Oct. 1719 sold the several estates follow-

1723. VOL. CCXLIV.

ing to Robert Hacket and John Wicker, Esqres (which were afterwards transferred to the Governor and Company of Undertakers for raising the Thames water in York Buildings), viz., the estate of Winton for 49,942*l.* 18*s.* 4½*d.*, the estate of Panmure for 53,027*l.* 8*s.*, the estate of Kilsyth for 15,949*l.* 3*s.* 4*d.*, the estate of East Reston for 1,698*l.* 0*s.* 5¼*d.* In Oct. 1720 they sold to Robert Hacket for the use of the above Governor and Company the estate of Southeske for 42,299*l.* 7*s.* 4$\frac{5}{12}$*d.*, the estate of Linlithgow for 18,511*l.* 10*s.* 10*d.*, the estate of Marishall, including part sold to Mungo Graeme of Gorthie, Esq., for 45,333*l.* 9*s.* 4⅔*d.*, the estate of Fingask for 9,384*l.* 1*s.* 11⅓*d.*, the estate of Pitcairn for 567*l.* 5*s.* 3⅓*d.*, and sold to the Lord Blantyre, Sir James Hamilton, Mr. James Graham, and others. The estate of Keir for 10,412*l.* 15*s.* 9$\frac{7}{12}$*d.* to John Nairn of Greenyards, Esq., the estate of Bannockburn for 7,341*l.* 1*s.* 3*d.*, and to Mungo Graeme of Gorthie, Esq., the estate of Innersnait for 820*l.* The Commissioners also settled eighteen estates for sale in October last, but it appeared to be the interest of the public to defer the same for some time; so that there remain thirty estates, amounting to the yearly value of 11,404*l.* 9*s.* 3⅓*d.*

There is also a balance sheet of the Receiver General for Scotland upon account of the forfeited estates (undated) which relates to some of these estates. 9 *pages.*

[? 1723.] 62. Petition of John Hamilton late Head Distributor and Collector of H.M. Stamp Duties of North Britain to the Lords of the Treasury. The Scotch Parliament recommended him to Queen Anne as having been instrumental in preventing the repeal of the penal statutes against Papists in the reign of King James. To satisfy him for his losses on that occasion (amounting to 1,000*l.* at least) he was appointed head distributor and collector of H.M. Stamp duties in North Britain in the year 1711, &c. When first appointed, met with such fierce opposition and great difficulties, that his life was frequently in danger, but surmounted all difficulties and put the collection of the duties in the clear and easy method it now is. Came to London in 1722 to get his account and losses allowed him, and was here for sixteen months. Has been removed for non-payment of his balance. Offered to receive only one third of his salary and had commenced the first payment that way for one quarter. Refused 800*l.* offered to him for his post about 12 months before he was turned out. His dismission not only deprived him of the offer of the 800*l.*, but precluded him from such advantage as Mr. Pitcairn, late Under-distributor for Edinburgh and Leith, had, (when he was turned out for non-payment of his balance of 232*l.*) of getting his arrears paid for him by Mr. Borthwick, his successor in that office, and as Mr. Columbine, late Collector, who had 500*l.* from Mr. Johns, his successor, who "besides sould office as a Lieutenant in the Army in Exchange of Columbine's Office as Collector." On his admission to his office was required to lay aside all other business. Prays that he and his sureties may be discharged of the balance, and in consideration of his claim of the 1,000*l.* and the above three great advantages, of which he has been deprived, by his dis-

1723. VOL. CCXLIV.

mission, he may be allowed some moderate support for himself and family.

Also a copy of the same with a few trifling alterations. 2 *pages.*

[? End of 1723.] 63. "An acco^{t} of disbursm^{ts} and expences made by Bap^{t} Nunn in apprehending the Blacks from ye 20th day of May 1722, at wch time the said Nunn took up a greyhound wch the night before Shorter and gang had used in killing his Ma^{ts} deer in the Forest of Windsor as appears by the oaths of several persons since apprehended." The expenses are continued until 29 Sept. [1723]. The total disbursements were upwards of 470*l.*, and there is some curious information as to the hazards, &c. of apprehending the "Blacks" who appear to have been poachers.

Minuted:—"600^{li} to Crachrode." 14 *pages.*

[Perhaps about 1723.] 64. An abstract or notes of certain Acts of Parliament touching annuities, when payable, &c. *Docketed:*—"How the several Fonds are redeemable." Undated. 5½ *pages.*

VOL. CCXLV. 1723. CLASSIFIED.

1. Reports of the Controllers of the Accounts of the Army (Medows and Bruce, and in one instance, H. R. Westfaling added) to the Lords of the Treasury. (1.) On the state of the accounts of the Regiments of Foot commanded by the late Major General Wightman, the late Brigadier Bowles, and Col. Thomas Harrison. (2.) On the memorial of Captain Verman on behalf of the Captains of Col. Franke's late Regiment. *Minuted:*—14th Augt 1723. My Lords do not think fit to give any directions in this matter." (3–8.) On memorials of Mr. Missing, Contractor for Victualling the Garrisons of Placentia, Annapolis Royal and Gibraltar. 36½ *pages.*

2. "An Accompt of the debt which at Michaelmas day 1723 was due and owing to his Majesty's servants and others payable in the Treasurer of the Chamber's Office, distinguished under General heads of expence, and by the several quarters in which the same became due and payable." *Signed:*—"C. Stanhope, Treařer of the Chamber's Office, October 1st, 1723."

Another Account for the quarter ended at Midsummer day 1723. Dated 12 Dec. 1723.

Also certificate of arrears due to Mr Daniel Malthus, Apothecary to her late Majesty's person. *Minuted:*—"27th Feb. 1722. A moiety ordered out of the first money that shall come into the Excheq^{r} of the Queen's arrears." 11½ *pages.*

1723. VOL. CCXLV.

3. Four warrants signed "Holles Newcastle" to the Master of the Great Wardrobe to provide a large folio bible for the use of the Warders at the Tower, and various articles of furniture at other places. 5 *pages.*

4. Four papers connected with the Civil List. The first is:—"A Declaracōn of the expence on acco^{t} of the Civil List for the year commencing Mic̄has 1722 and ending Mic̄has 1723," &c. Two others are "Gross and Nett Income of the Civil List Fonds stated from the Weekly Certificates transmitted to the Treasury." 19½ *pages.*

5. Reports of the Com^{rs} of Customs to the Lords of the Treasury and one or two other papers connected with Customs affairs. The reports are chiefly on smuggling cases, one of which relates to the division of the shares, arising out of the seizure of 10 smuggling vessels, between the Commander of the "Solebay" man-of-war and the Custom House Officers. There is also a letter relating to the expected arrival on the coast of St. Malo of a French ship infected with the plague, and a report as to ships coming from Egypt, from which there was a fear of plague.

Another letter relates to a complaint of rudeness on the part of Officers of Customs in examining the baggage of the Morocco Ambassador. 46 *pages and* 6 *halves.*

6. Two Memorials and a Report of the Com^{rs} of Excise to the Lords of the Treasury (1) as to auditing the accounts of the duties on hides; (2) as to a petition of Robert Payne and a bond for 5,000*l.* given by Thomas Crabb Junr to one of the Collectors of Excise; and (3) as to the resignation of Mr Isaac Hide one of the General Accountants in the office, and the recommendation of successors. 9 *pages.*

7. Various financial papers, including:—"A state of the Public Debt at the Receipt of his Maj^{tys} Exchequer;" an "Abstract of the gross and nett produce of the several revenues under the management of the Commissioners of Excise, in that part of Great Britain called Scotland;" a "State of the supplies for the year 1723." &c. 23 *pages* (*some double*).

8. Memorials &c. connected with Lottery affairs; the first relates to exchange of tickets for certificates and is minuted:—"17 July 1723. Renew ye com^{n} with Musgrave and Newnham instead of Arnold and Duncomb." 4 *pages.*

9. Memorials chiefly signed "S. Compton" or "Robt Jacomb Dep^{y}" addressed to the Lords of the Treasury representing the necessity of remittances to Port Mahon and Gibraltar, and enclosing proposals from Henry Furnesse to give his bills at the rates he specifies. Also other demands for pay of guards and garrisons in Great Britain and elsewhere. Dated Horse Guards. 18½ *pages.*

10. Four papers addressed to the Lords of the Treasury entitled:—"Abbreviate by Sir Robert Sinclair, Barr^{t}, Receiver Genl in Scotland; of receipts, payments and remains of the rents and profits and sale of the forfeited estates in Scotland." 1 July, 1 Sept., 1 Oct., and 1 Dec. 1723.

1723. VOL. CCXLV.

Also "an account of what money has been paid into the Excheq of Scotland from the rents, profits and sale of the forfeted estates, from the commencement of the commission for forfeitures there; what has been paid thereout to creditors or otherwise and what now remains therein (vizt) on the 8th July 1723." 5 *large pages.*

11. Certificates or memorials signed:—"Jno Monteage Acco^{ta} Gen^{ll}" and one signed:—"Gilbert Heathcote, Govr" [of the Bank of England] addressed to the Lords of the Treasury as to the state of the capital, or joint stock, erected by Act of Parliament 1 Geo. cap. 19. and transferable at the Bank of England: also as to the deficiency to be made good to the Treasurer of the Navy appointed by act of the 5th year to be supplied out of the general yearly fund of 724,849*l.* 6*s.* 10$\frac{1}{5}$*d.* established by another act 3 Geo. [I.] &c.

In that of 28 Jany it is mentioned that the Bank was to receive 3*l.* per cent. for paying the interest at their own cost as also in reward for their service upon all bills to be circulated by them, so long as they shall exceed one million in principal, and an allowance after the rate of 20*s.* per cent. per ann. for the like when under a million. And further that the Court of Directors of the Bank of England memorialise for six months allowance.

The memorial of 3 May is docketed:—"Relating to Exchequer Bills, The Loan to ye Trea͞rer of ye Navy and the charges for the annuity offices." 8 *pages.*

12. Three reports of the Com^{rs} for Taxes to the Lords of the Treasury (1) recommending the augmentation of the salary of the General Surveyor of the Duties on Houses in London the same being at present 70*l.* per ann. and further recommending that Mr Thomas Sanderson, a surveyor in the country, be appointed for London, Middlesex, and Westminster, and that Mr James Underwood, a surveyor in Staffordshire be appointed in the room of Mr Sanderson and that Mr Robert Winniatt the present General Surveyor of London, &c. be removed to Staffordshire.

Minuted:—"4th Feb. 1722–3 My Lords agree to this representation."

(2) On the backwardness of the payments of Sir Robert Sinclair, Bart., Receiver General of the land taxes in Scotland. Also as to the difficulty of prevailing with the regiments quartered in Scotland to take their subsistence of the Receiver: asking that orders may be given to the troops to take their subsistence from the Receiver General. Memorial enclosed.

Minuted:—"12 June 1723. A l͞re to ye D. Payma^{r}, Mr Jacomb to attend on Fryday & Mr Douglas to the Barons ab^{t} the arrears."

(3) On the backwardness of the Receivers Payments on the Land tax, 1722. Several counties and several Receivers are more remiss than they have been in former years notwithstanding the threatening letters sent to them. Have very little power to compel the Receivers to clear and pass their accounts till Michaelmas term after the expiration of the year, and then only

1723. VOL. CCXLV.

by mean-process, to which they are not obliged to plead till the term following. 5 *pages.*

13. Papers of the Surveyor General and the officers of the Board of Works, viz., (1) Report on the Memorial of Charles Earl of Carlisle, late Constable of the Tower of London as to the state of repair of certain houses of the officers and warders which are also places of reception for prisoners. The estimated cost for repair is 4,922*l.* 0*s.* 2*d.* A new building would be of more service if a convenient place within the Tower could be found. There is a strong large Tower commonly called the White Tower which may be very proper and secure for prisoners and large enough for such a purpose without taking away the Record Office. This may answer all ends and at a reasonable charge and much less than a new building, &c., which may be thought to crowd up the spaces and obstruct the air.

Minuted:—"Agreed to. The repairs to be done gradually." (Also the memorial) (2, 3, and 4) States of the Debt in the Office of Works. 6½ *pages.*

VOL. CCXLVI. 1723.

DOCUMENTS for which a brief description suffices.

Date.	Description of Document.	From	To	Purport.
4 Jan.	1. Petition -	Samuel Burridge, of Tiverton, in the co. of Devon.	Lords of the Treasury.	Asks to succeed the late Mr. George Thorne as Receiver General of land tax for part of the county of Devon.
[? about 11 Jan.]	2. Do. - -	John Smith and George Leslie, Deputy Chamberlains for joining Tallies in the Court of Exchequer.	Do. - -	For payment of their fees (151*l.* 18*s.* 6*d.*) on payment into the Exchequer, by the Recr. General, of 1,500,206*l.* 3*s.* 9*d.* on account of customs. 1¼ *pages.*
15 Jan.	3. Representation	Comrs. of Customs, Scotland.	Do. - -	As to shells of mother of pearl imported at Kirkcudbright (supposed from Ostend) with design to have them condemned in the Court of Exchequer and afterwards sent to England prejudicially to the East India Company. *Minuted* :—"23rd Janry. 1722. The E. I. Company to have a copie of this representation." 1 *page.*

Date.	Description of Document.	From	To	Purport.
16 Jan.	4. Letter - -	Bernard Cook - -	Right Hon. — -	Begs that he may be dispatched being mightily wanted by his distressed family at Barbadoes. *Minuted*:—"To have 100*li*. notwithstanding ye report." 1 *page*.
17 Jan.	5. Estimate -	—	—	Navy debt as it stood 31 Dec. 1722. 2 *large pages*.
17 Jan.	6. Memorial -	Comrs. for Forfeitures in England.	Lords of the Treasury.	For an order to the Exchequer to pay their salaries and those of their subordinates. Also the account of their salaries. 3 *pages*.
19 Jan.	7. Letter - -	Robert Blount - -	The Hon. Horatio Walpole.	As to a warrant for commencement of the payment of his pension. Also a certificate on the same subject. 2 *pages*.
22 Jan.	8. Do. - -	Thomas Jekyll -	—	Encloses a letter for the Lords of the Treasury as to the suppressing of smuggling at Southampton. *Minuted*:—"26th Janry. 1722 to Comrs. Customes to report their opinion." Also the letter named. 2 *pages*.
23 Jan.	9. Do. - -	W. Lowndes - -	Lord — - -	For the issue to Walter Chetwynd, Esq., of 200*l*. by way of imprest, the same to be paid to Sir Rowland Gwyn. 1 *page*.
28 Jan.	10. Petition -	Daniel Brattell -	Lords of the Treasury.	Petitioner's grandfather, father, and uncle have been successively assaymasters for upwards of fifty years; prays to succeed his uncle. Also certificate of the truth of the petition. Signed Wm. Thompson and Isaac Newton. *Minuted*:—"Mr. Hopton Haynes to have this office. Warrt. signd 7th Feb. 1722–3." 1 *page*.
1 Feb.	11. Do. - -	Jane Stuart - -	The Rt. Hon. Robt. Walpole, Esq., and other Lords of the Treasury.	Petitioner was widow of Jonathan Stuart, a drum major (whose services she states). Prays bounty. Three certificates and a recommendation of her case. 1 *page and* 3 *parts of pages*.
3 Feb.	12. Letter - -	Victualling Comrs. -	Mr. Scrope -	Sends an account of the money payable upon the course of the victualling. 1 *page*.

Date.	Description of Document.	From	To	Purport.
6 Feb.	13. Copy of Order in Council, Minute of the Lords of the Treasury, &c.	—	—	Respecting the ship "Hannah" and her lading under quarantine in Standgate Creek. $3\frac{1}{2}$ *pages.*
9 Feb.	14. Estimate -	—	—	Debt of his Majesty's [Dock-] Yards. $\frac{1}{2}$ *page.*
9 Feb.	15. Letter - -	F. Osborne - -	Wm. Lowndes, Esq., at his house in Duke St., Westminster.	As to arrears due in the Queen's time. His son was taken away suddenly, leaving seven daughters and heavy debts. Mr. Wallpole was very cruel in taking Mr. Osborne's pension at his age. 1 *page.*
11 Feb.	16. Draft of Minutes.	—	—	Minutes of the Treasury Board of 11 Feb. 1722-3 relating to buildings in the Savoy, and to papers concerning the revenue of the Hospital. 1 *page.*
14 Feb.	17. Memorial -	Henry, Earl of Lincoln, constable of the Tower of London.	Lords of the Treasury.	Recommending 50*l.* a year to be added to the salary of "Gentleman gaoler," which was but 20*l.* per ann. *Minuted:* — "18th Feb. 1723. My Lords have taken his Mats. pleasure upon this meml1., and direct a lrõ to the Secretary-at-War to place this additional salary upon the Establishment." 1 *page.*
22 Feb.	18. Letter - -	Lord Townshend -	Do. - -	For directions to be given for the payment of the reward to James Peck and two others who apprehended the murderers of Anne Bristow on Smalbury Green. 1 *page.*
1 Mar.	19. Memorial -	Charles Edwin, executor of Samuel Edwin, Esq., late Usher of the Receipt of the Exchequer.	Do. - -	Por payment of 998*l.* 5*s.* $10\frac{1}{4}$*d.* due for discharging wages of watchmen, &c. at the Exchequer. Also a duplicate with slight verbal alterations. 2 *pages.*
14 Mar.	20. Do. - -	Comrs. of Customs (Scotland).	Do. - -	Queries relative to the deduction of 6*d.* in the pound on salaries of officers. Enclosing another paper on the same subject. 3 *pages.*
[? About 15 Mar.]	21. Petition -	Samuel Taylor, one of the messengers of the Great Chamber to the late Queen Anne.	Do. - -	For payment of 210*l.* 13*s.* $7\frac{1}{2}$*d.* due to him. Also certificate thereof. 2 *pages.*

Date.	Description of Document.	From	To	Purport.
21 Mar.	22. Draft of Minutes.	—	—	Of Minutes of the Treasury Board for 21 March 1722-3. Also a letter from "Everslame Bestose" asking their Lordships to order him money. 2 *pages*.
[After 25 Mar.]	23. Petition -	Henry Tatlock, laceman, and others.	Lords of the Treasury.	For money due to them for supplying the stable liveries of her late Majesty. Also a previous petition which is *minuted* thus:— "19th Decr. 1722. To be consider'd when any money comes into the Exchr. upon this account." 2 *large pages*.
[? About 27 Mar.]	24. Representation	Comrs. of Excise (Scotland).	Do. - -	As to exceptions to the deduction of 6*d*. in the pound out of salaries, &c. Also "Genll. list of the usuall payments made out of His Majesty's revenues of Excise, &c. in Scotland." *Minuted*:—"27th March 1723. Prepare a S. M. according to the precedent." 2½ *pages*.
[After 8 Apr.]	25. Memorial -	William Watkins, Esq.	Do. - -	Asking for payment into the Paymaster of the Works' hands, of the allowance to the six gate keepers, that the memorialist might receive his pay as Surveyor of H.M. Private Roads, 1 *page*.
[? About 11 Apr.]	26. Petition	Frances Wyndham -	Do. - -	King Charles II. granted her father, Sir Francis Wyndham, Bart., an annuity of 600*l*. per ann., and to Ann Wyndham his wife, a like annuity of 400*l*.; for services rendered to the King after the battle of Worcester. The grant was afterwards changed to petitioner and her sister (200*l*. each for life). These annuities were in arrear in 1714, 2,550*l*.; and 675*l*. was also due to Rachel her sister (deceased) as bedchamber woman to Queen Mary. 100*l*. is due to petitioner to Midsummer 1714: prays for the latter, and for further directions as to the arrears. Also a certificate. 2 *pages*.

Date.	Description of Document.	From	To	Purport.
18 April	27. Letter -	J. Veel, for the Secretary to the Trustees of South Sea Co.	—	*Docketed:* — "18 April 1723. A letter from the Trustees of the South Sea House relating to Mr. Hawes stock." 1 *page.*
21 April	28. Do. -	Leonard Wooldeson	Charles Dartiquenave, Esq., Paymaster Genl. of H.M. Works, Surrey St., St. Jameses.	Represents the particulars of the large debt due to him from the late Queen. The Chancellor is to be at the Treasury to-morrow morning, when it is expected that the remainder of the Queen's money will be distributed. 2 *pages.*
23 April	29. Do. -	George Turbill -	William Lowndes, Esq.	For a quarter's salary due at Christmas to the Comrs. for forfeited estates in England. *Minuted:* — "23rd April 1723. Order'd." 1 *page.*
[? About 29 April.]	30. Do. -	J. Laborde -	"My Lord"	Is sent by "Mademoyselle de Malause" to wait upon his Lordship to receive his commands. *Minuted:* — "26th April 1723. Prepare a warrt. for 500*li.* bounty." 1 *page, quarto.*
30 April	31. Memorial -	Nehemiah Arnold and John Duncombe.	Lords of the Treasury.	State what their services have been in forwarding the present Lottery, and ask to be continued in their Commission. 1 *page.*
1 May	32. Do. -	Philip Cavendish, Treasurer of Greenwich Hospital.	Do. -	For money to be issued, 18,000*l.* being due for works at Greenwich Hospital. 1 *page.*
3 May	33. Certificate -	—	—	"Of the dividends recd. by Mr. Henning upon the King's stock in the S. S. Company." ½ *page.*
15 May	34. Letter -	T. Marten, Secretary to the Trustees for sale of estates of Directors of the South Sea Co.	William Lowndes, Esq.	The Trustees do not recommend intermeddling with the estate (which is extended) of Sir Harcourt Master, one of the directors. *Minuted:* — "Read." 1 *page.*
[? About 16 May.]	35. Estimate -	—	—	Of the "Seaman's Monitor" to be distributed among the officers and seamen on board H.M. men-of-war. *Minuted:* — "16th May 1723. Prepare a warrt. in the name of the Bookseller." 1 *page.*

Date.	Description of Document.	From	To	Purport.
[After 17 May.]	36. Certificate -	Col. Manning and Captain Legg.	First Lord of H.M. Treasury.	Had Mr. Layer under their care, in the Tower, from 20 Sept. 1722 to 17 May 1723. ½ *page.*
[About 20 May.]	37. Petition -	Jonathan White -	Lords of the Treasury.	To be admitted as a settled man to the Tide Office. Encloses similar petition to the Comrs. of Customs, dated 20 May 1723, and a testimonial. 3 *pages.*
21 May	38. Letter -	Lord Townshend -	Do. - -	The King's pleasure is that they should issue to George Tilson, Esq., Under Secretary, 300*l.*; to Mr. John Wace, First Clerk, 200*l.*; and to Mr. John Courand 100*l.*, for extraordinary expenses, as they were attending his Majesty during his absence out of the Kingdom for the affairs of the Secretary's office; besides which 3*l.* per day, 20*s.* per day, and 10*s.* per day is to be allowed to them respectively as board wages. 1 *page.*
21 May	39. Copy of similar letter.	Lord Carteret -	Do. - -	Similar order in favour of John Anthony Balaguier, Esq., Under Secretary (300*l.*), Mr. Daniel Prevereau, First Clerk (200*l.*), Mr. Edmund Tigh, Clerk (100*l.*), Joseph Noble, Chamber Keeper (20*l.*), for extraordinary expenses as above; besides which they are to be allowed 3*l.*, 1*l.*, 10*s.*, and 5*s.* per diem respectively as board wages. 1 *page.*
21 May	40. Petition -	Elizabeth Wightman	The King - -	Is daughter to the late Major-General Joseph Wightmau, and is left without bread. Asks to be provided for. (French.) *Minuted:*—"May 21, 1723. 100 bounty." 1 *page.*
23 May	41. Do. - -	Colonel Charles Cadogan.	Lords of the Treasury.	His regiment of foot (being the King's own) used to be allowed about 100*l.* each clothing, as trophy money. For the last four years has had to provide colours, clothes, &c. Prays payment of 400*l.* for the same. *Minuted:*—"June the 6th, 1723. Refer to the Secretary at War to report what has been the practice, and out of what mony it has been usually paid." 1 *page.*

1723. Vol. CCXLVI.

Date.	Description of Document.	From	To	Purport.
24 May	42. Letter - -	P. Whichcote -	Mr. Walpole -	The Lord Lieut. of Ireland is very desirous to have the warrant signed before the King's departure. The purport of the warrant is not given, but it related to a favourite scheme of the Archbishop of Dublin. 1 *page, quarto.*
29 May	43. Do. - -	Lord Townshend -	Do. - -	As to the claims of the wife of James Gartside [on account of her husband's services]. Three other papers in connexion with her husband's affairs. 4 *pages.*
30 May	44. Memorial -	Comrs. for Taxes -	Lords of the Treasury.	Proposing the discharge of Mr. Thomas Gwyllim, a surveyer of the duties on houses in co. Merioneth, and recommending a successor. Two other papers on the same subject. *Minuted:*—"12 June 1723. Agreed." 5 *pages.*
30 May	45. Account -	—	—	"Produce of small branches of Civill List, &c., from Mich'as 1722 to Lady day 1723. Exchequer. Auditor's Office." 1 *page.*
30 May	46. Account or return.	Comrs. of Alienations	Lords of the Treasury.	Computation of the produce of their office. 1 *page.*
3 June	47. Copy of Warrant.	—	—	Consolidating English and Scotch Boards of Customs. 9 *pages.*
[? About 5 June.]	48. Two Petitions and two ac-accounts.	Bernard Lintot, William Taylor, and Jacob Tonson.	Lords of the Treasury.	Respecting payment for printing copies of report, &c. of Committee appointed by the House of Commons to examine Christopher Layer and others in connexion with "the conspiracy." Each *minuted:*—"5th June 1723. Prepare a warrt." 4 *pages.*
[About 5 June.]	49. Memorial -	Loftus Cliffe -	Lord Townshend, H.M. Principal Secretary of State.	Was 27 years collector of the port of Ross, Ireland, and was dismissed without any reason in 1716. His father was a sufferer for King William. Prays a letter recommending his case to the Lords of the Treasury. *Minuted:*—"June the 5, 1723. A letter to be wrote accordingly." 1 *page.*

Date.	Description of Document.	From	To	Purport.
10 June	50. Petition	Samuel Mayo and Thomas Carter.	—	Praying for consideration for their services in giving evidence in all matters relating to "the ship Phenice, Captain Halstead, &c." also upon the trials of Plunkett, Kelly, and the Bishop of Rochester. Petitioners could not get their bread at sea without hazard. *Minuted* :—"To subsist to this day & a months advance to carry 'em home. 1 *page*. [*See also* 16 Sept.]
11 June	51. Letter and Memorial.	J. Burchett (Admiralty).	Secretaries to the Treasury.	As to the deductions of 6*d*. per month for Greenwich Hospital from Marine soldiers amounting to 5,525*l*. 19*s*. $5\frac{3}{4}$*d*. 5 *pages*.
11 June	52. Letter - -	E. Mason - -	—	His Majesty has granted him an annuity of 100*l*. per ann. and 100*l*. for his present exigencies. Hopes he will complete the Royal goodness. 1 *page*.
18–29 June	53. Do. - -	Lord Townshend -	Lords of the Treasury.	His Majesty's pleasure is that their Lordships should forthwith order 1,000*l*. to be issued without account and paid into the hands of Charles Delafaye, Esq., secretary to the Lords Justices to answer bills drawn on them for postage, staffetes, expresses, &c. being the charges of the two principal Secretaries of States staying at Hanover. 1 *page*.
19 June	54. Letter and Memorial.	J. Burchett (Admiralty).	Secretaries of the Lords of the Treasury.	As to the deductions of 6*d*. per month from the late six Marine Regiments for the use of the Chest, which had not been paid over to the Governors of the Chest. $4\frac{1}{2}$ *pages*.
24 June	55. Account -	—	—	Of money advanced on tin at Hamburgh and of tin sold at Hamburgh by John Gore. 1 *double page*.
[? About 26 June.]	56. Memorial -	Royal Academy of Music.	Lords of the Treasury.	For a warrant to pay 1,000*l*. out of the Bounty Office and for 200*l*. to defray the taxes and other expenses attending the receipt of the 1,000*l*. which his Majesty allowed. *Minuted* : — "26th June 1723 1,000*li*. order'd." 1 *page*

Date.	Description of Document.	From	To	Purport.
[? About 1 July.]	57. Petitions, &c.	Colin Campbell -	Lords of the Treasury.	For consideration having lost his employment by the Union, before which he was possessed of the office of Clerk of the Coquets and Searcher at the Port of Preston-Pans, Dundee, Montrose, Inverness, and all the ports by North Tay. One of the papers is *minuted*:—"1st July 1723. There is no vacancy. My Lords will give him an office when vacant in Scotland of the value of that which he lost." *7 pages.*
[? About 4 July.]	58. Petition -	James Woodburn, Pratique Master in the Port of Belfast.	Chief Comrs. and Governors of H.M. Revenue of Ireland.	For payment for his services for 29 kalendar months connected with the performance of quarantine. At the foot is a testimonial to his services. 1 *page.*
8 July	59. Letter - -	Edward Parsons -	Horatio Walpole, Esq.	Sends account of taxes for the year 1722. Has received no more than 6,600*l.* which he paid into the Receipt of the Exchequer. Also the account referred to. On the back is a *minute* concluding "that the Lords are well satisfied, Mr. Parsons has paid all he has recd." $2\frac{1}{4}$ *pages.*
9 July	60. Petition -	Nathaniel Hunter, of Dublin, pilot.	Comrs. and Chief Governors of the Revenue in Ireland.	For relief having been exposed to injury by bringing a ship under quarantine. 1 *page.*
11 July	61. Certificate -	J. Burchett (Admiralty).	Lords of the Treasury.	Of clerks who had paid the land tax for 1722. 1 *page.*
16 July	62. Account -	—	—	Of taxes paid by the Secretary of the Admiralty and his clerks in the years 1719 to 1722 which have not been reimbursed. *Minuted*:—"26th July 1723. My Lords give orders for the payment of the taxes of the clerks as usual." 1 *page.*

Date.	Description of Document.	From	To	Purport.
18 July	63. Memorial -	Comrs. of Forfeitures for England.	Lords of the Treasury.	For their salaries and those of their inferior officers; together with incident charges; also letter to Mr. Lowndes on the same subject. *Minuted*:—"Order'd." 2 *pages*.
[? About 24 July.]	64. Petition -	Richard Burren, Surveyor of Searchers in the Port of London.	Do. - -	For an addition of 50*l.* per ann. to his income. *Minuted*: — "24th July 1723. My Lords will not increase his salary. 1 *page*.
26 July	65. Letter - -	Comrs. of the Navy -	Secretaries of the Treasury.	As to the state of Mr. Hampden's accounts as late Treasurer of the Navy. 2 *pages*.
30 July	66. Do. - -	Comrs. of Customs, Scotland.	Horatio Walpole, Esq.	For the appointment of a successor to Mr. Jessop Boughton, Secretary to the Board since the Union, who is "confused in his understanding." Recommending also an allowance of 20*l.* per ann. by way of superannuation to Mr. Boughton. 2 *pages*.
31 July	67. Certificate -	Barons of the Exchequer, Scotland.	Lords of the Treasury.	There is only 254*l.* 15*s.* 11¼*d.* in the Receiver General's hands of the Bishops' rents at his Majesty's disposal. Encloses memorial "for the Chancellor of the Exchequer." 2 *pages*.
[After July.]	68. Memorial -	Thomas Moore, Esq., late Paymaster General of the Forces.	Do. - -	As to the balance of his account, &c.; asked to be allowed 300*l.* a year for three years and two months. Sir Roger Mostyn was allowed 300*l.* a year for eight years and three months for his trouble. 1 *page*.
1 August	69. Representation	Barons of the Exchequer, Scotland.	Do. - -	Recommending their agent at London, Mr. Joseph Tudor, to be put on the establishment of Scotland, as he had only a small allowance by way of incidents. Exchequer Chamber, Edinburgh. 1 *page*.

Date.	Description of Document.	From	To	Purport.
2 August	70. Letter - -	Thomas Woolley -	Horatio Walpole, Esq.	For the Directors of the East India Co. Acquaints the Lords of the Treasury that it is but lately the arrears for the duties on the Company's unrated goods were stated according to the new method of computation, which the Company always apprehend to be very severe. The Directors are providing to discharge the dues. 1 *page.*
8 August	71. Memorial -	Philip Cavendish, Esq., Treasurer of Greenwich Hospital.	Lords of the Treasury.	The creditors for the building are very impatient and continually soliciting for relief; pray for an order for the payment of the remainder of the debt, being upwards of 18,000*l.* 1 *page.*
[? About 9 August.]	72. Petition -	Thomas Bishop of Sodor and Man.	Do. -	Prays payment of the 100*l.* in arrear, due to the poor clergy of his diocese for the year 1713. *Minuted:* — "9th Augt. 1723. To be inserted in the List of the Queen's Creditors." 1 *page.*
[About 14 Aug.]	73. Memorial -	Captain John Verman and others.	Do. -	On behalf of himself and the Captains of Col. Franks's late regiment of foot, prays that Mr. Thomas Moor of the Paymaster's office and Mr. Gough may be compelled to account with them. *Minuted:* — "14 Augst. 1723. The Lords do not think fitt to give any directions in this matter." 2 *pages.*
26 Aug.	74. Letter - -	Andrew Shields -	—	Is] afflicted with a tedious indisposition. Has nothing but his salary as an extraordinary page of the bedchamber, which is a year in arrear at Michaelmas next. Bath. *Minuted:*—"11th 7br. 1723. To be paid as far as the rest of the pages are." 2 *pages.*
27 Aug.	75. Do. -	Board of Trade -	Rt. Hon. Robert Walpole, Esq.	For an order to have the House quitted by the Earl of Clarendon allotted to the Board for an office. *Minuted:* — "The Board of Workes to put the Lords of Trade in possession of that part of the Lord Clarendon's house which stands in Privy Garden. 29 Augt. 1723. Letter signed." 1 *page.*

1723. VOL. CCXLVI.

Date.	Description of Document.	From	To	Purport.
28 Aug.	76. Report -	A. Cracherode -	Lords of the Treasury.	On the petition of Stephen Smith and others praying the reward of 100*li.* for taking and convicting a highwayman. *Minuted:*—"My Lords do not conceive this case to be within the meaning and intent of the proclamation." Also the petition. 2¼ *pages.*
[? About 31 Aug.]	77. Memorial -	Charles Christian, engraver.	Do. - -	For consideration for his services in having given evidence in the Houses of Lords and Commons as to two seals. *Minuted:* — "31 Augt. 1723. 50*li.* per the hands of Mr. Cracherode." 1 *page.*
[? About 4 Sept.]	78. Do. - -	The widow and administratrix of Thomas Russel, of St. James's Market, butcher.	[Do.] - -	For payment of 621*l.* 19*s.* 4¾*d.* due on a contract made in 1713, with the Board of Green Cloth, to supply her late Majesty with meat. *Minuted:*—"4th 7br. 1723, My Lords order a moiety to be paid." 1 *page.*
6–17 Sept.	79. Letter - -	Lord Townshend -	Mr. S. Walpole -	The money for extraordinary expenses at Hanover is nearly expended; another 500*l.* will be wanted. The under secretaries and clerks have three months due to them. Desires the allowances to be made as the King signified before his departure. 2 *pages.*
6–17 Sept.	80. Do. - -	Ste. Poyntz - -	Mr. Lowther -	Asks him to receive Mr. Chancellor of the Exchequer's commands upon two bills payable to the order of Mr. Michael David. *Minuted:*—"16 7br. 1723. Mr. Lowther to accept these bills as also bills for 500 more which will come. 1 *page, quarto.*
10 Sept.	81. Presentment -	Comrs. of Stamp Duties.	—	For Charles Symister to be a stamper in the room of Edward Cooper, deceased. ½ *page.*
[? About 11 Sept.]	82. Letter - -	—	—	As to payment of [reward] of 100*l.* for a robbery "committed upon William Fitser." *Minuted:* — "11th 7br. 1723. My Lords order the proper letter to be signd in this behalf." 4 *lines.*

Date.	Description of Document.	From	To	Purport.
16 Sept.	83. Petition -	Samuel Mayo and Thomas Carter.	The Chancellor of the Exchequer.	Was evidence aginst Capt. Halfhead, &c., and attended both Houses of Parliament and received subsistence money to 12 Aug. last. Pray to be rewarded for lost time and to be provided for in the Customs as they cannot get their bread at sea for fear of the Jacobites. There are two letters on the back respecting the petitioners' case. They received 2*s.* 6*d.* a day each to 14 June when they were discharged. 16 Sept. 1723. 2 *pages.*
16 Sept.	84. Letter - -	F. Osborne - -	William Lownds, Esq.	Does not doubt his "friendly assistance if there be rome for it" for some family (not named) who have been long sufferers. 1 *page, quarto.*
19 Sept.	85. Warrant (copy). -	Lords of the Treasury.	Edward Carteret and Geoffrey Walpole, Esquires, H.M. Postmasters General.	For 200*l.* to be paid to William French, Esq., in aid of keeping up the Light House on the Rock called the Skerries lying about three leagues from Hollyhead, in the entrance to the bay. 1 *page.*
[? After 27 Sept.]	86. Petition -	Martin Lewin, gent., late head Marshal of the city of London, John Dyer, and Edward Herring.	Lords of the Treasury.	Petitioners together with the late Jonathan Wild apprehended Humphrey Anger for highway robbery at Hornsey, Middlesex. Pray for the reward of 100*l.* Also a certificate. 2 *pages.*
[? About 28 Sept.]	87. Memorial -	Comrs. and Receiver of Alienations.	Do. - -	As to deduction of sixpence in the pound from pensions, viz., from 500*l.*, part of 2,000*l.* per ann. to the Duke and Duchess of St. Albans, and from 1,546*l.* 12*s.* per ann. payable to the Hanaper. *Minuted*:—"28 7br. 1722–3. The pencõn exempted.—Hanaper to pay. Wt. signed." 3 *pages.*
[? About 30 Sept.]	88. Petition -	Jane Gunthorpe -	Rt. Hon. Robert Walpole, Esq., First Lord Commissioner of the Treasury.	For arrears due from King William and Queen Anne to her late husband George Gunthorpe, confectioner, and to herself as table laundress to her late Majesty. *Minuted*:—" 30 7br. 1723. List of arrears." Also a certificate. 2 *pages.*

1723. VOL. CCXLVI.

Date.	Description of Document.	From	To	Purport.
5 Oct.	89. Account -	—	—	Of the debt due on the pensions payable in the office of Walter Chetwynd, Esq. Mich. 1722 to Mich. 1723. 12 *pages*.
8 Oct.	90. Memorial -	"George Lord Parker," one of the Four Tellers of the Exchequer.	Lords of the Treasury.	For directions to be given as to a loss by reduction of guineas from 21*s*. 6*d*. to 21*s*. Exchequer, 8 Oct. 1723. 1 *page*.
9 Oct.	91. Certificate	Comrs. of Alienations.	Do. - -	Produce of the office for six months, viz., to Mich. 1723. 1 *page*.
11 Oct.	92. Memorandum	—	—	As to the subsistence of Capt. Gustavus Bahr who was sent for from Hanover to give evidence in the prosecution for condemning the ship "Revolution formerly in the Pretender's service." Oct. 11, 1723. *Minuted*: — "12th 8br. 1723. Mr. Lowther to subsist Capt. Bahr untill the process against the ship 'Revolution' is ended, the money to be afterwards replaced to Mr. Lowther out of the produce of the ship upon condemnation." Again: —5*sh*. per diem from 2d Augt. till the tryall. 30*s*. to carry him home." 1 *page*.
7 Nov.	93. Proclamation (copy).	The Hon. John Wentworth, Esq., Lieut. Governor of the Province of New Hampshire.	—	Giving public notice that Robert Armstrong, Esq., late Deputy Surveyor of Woods in the province, has embarked for Great Britain, and no successor being appointed, he (the Lieut. Governor) has constituted Mr. Edw. Hall, of Exeter, to be Deputy Surveyor. Also the form of oath to be taken. 2 *pages*.
8 Nov.	94. Letter - -	Ch. Delafaye - -	Lords of the Treasury.	Transmits a petition of William Prust, a material evidence in a suit in the Court of Admiralty, for the condemnation of the ship "Revolution" for directions thereon. The petition and a schedule entitled: "An account of what I have lost by upposing the Pertenders sarves." 3 *pages*.

Date.	Description of Document.	From	To	Purport.
20 Nov.	95. Letter - -	Sir Gilbert Heathcote.	—	For process in the Exchequer to be stayed against Mr. Madockes for not accounting as Paymaster. Bank. 1 *page, quarto.*
[? About 22 Nov.]	96. Memorial -	Officers of the Four Troops of Horse Guards.	Rt. Hon. George Lord Newburgh, Lieut. Genl. of H.M. forces, and Captain and Colonel of the third troop of Horse Guards.	Several repairs are wanted for the accommodation of the troops. *Minuted:* — "20th 9br. 17... The Survr. of the Horse Guards to report what is wanting and an estimate of what the repairs will come to." 1 *page.*
[About 26 Nov.]	97. Representation	John Dive for Thomas Smith, Esq., Exec. of the Rt. Hon. John Smith, Esq., deceased, one of the four Tellers of the Exchequer.	Lords of the Treasury.	For delivery up of the bonds of the sureties of the late Teller of the Exchequer. Also certificate of the Auditor of the Receipt of the Exchequer respecting moneys handed over to another Teller. 2 *pages.*
November	98. Estimate -	Hugh Warren, Surveyor of the Guards.	Lords of the Treasury.	For necessaries and repairs to the Horse Guards, Tilt Yard, and offices thereunto belonging. 1 *page.*
November	99. Petition -	Edward Wynn, steward to Richard Norton, of Southwick House, Southampton, Esq.	Do. -	For charges, fees, &c. attending the apprehension, &c. of four blacks lately executed. Bill of the expenses. 3 *pages.*
4 Dec.	100. Memorial -	Anthony Cracherode.	Do. -	Has several criminals to prosecute at the Old Bailey. Prays for half a year's salary (250*l.*) and for 500*l.* on account. 1 *page, quarto.*
6 Dec.	101. Letter - -	Ch. Delafaye -	Do. -	For 200*l.* to be ordered him for the clerks and servants of the Secretary's office for attendance on their Excellencies during the King's absence, and for 500*l.* to himself. *Minuted:* — "500*li.* to himself for his attendance on the Lords Justices as their Secry and 200*li.* to be distributed among the clerks. 1 *page.*

Date.	Description of Document.	From	To	Purport.
6 Dec.	102. Letter - -	John Eyles - -	Mr. Carkesse	*Minuted:* — "To Mr. Carkesse that the Chevalier Eon have the allowance of 2 tons of wine as a minister of the K. of Spain, and that the 75*l.* wt. chocolate seized by the Cust. Ho. Officers be delivered to him upon Mr. Lowthers paying the duty." 1 *page* (*quarto*).
10 Dec.	103. Presentment -	Comrs. of Stamp Duties.	Lords of the Treasury.	For Richard Dovey to be Inspector of Gaming Houses, &c. in the room of Geo. Portsmouth, deceased. ½ *page*.
10 Dec.	104. Memorial -	Comrs. of Excise	Do. -	"Desiring that the officer who commands the detachm. at Blandford to prevent the running of goods may assist in executing warrts. to seize the murderers of one Purchase." *Minuted:* — "13th Jan. 1723–4. To Mr. Treby Secry-at-War to take the King's orders upon this memorial." Also a letter signed "James Furnell on the same subject." 2 *pages*.
13 Dec.	105. Letter - -	Comrs. of the Navy -	Mr. Lowndes -	As to the Estimate of the debt of the Navy. Also an abstract and another letter. 3 *pages*.
17 Dec.	106. Do. - -	Do. - -	Do. -	On the debt of the Navy and as to what money has been paid into the Exchequer to discharge Mr. Hampden's balance as Treasurer of the Navy. Certificate of Imprest Money repaid to Richard Hampden, Esq. 2 *pages*.
20 Dec.	107. Letter - -	Sir George Oxenden	Lords of the Treasury.	Declines to accept the stewardship of the manor of Wingham, to which their Lordships had appointed him. *Minuted:* — "21 Decr. 1723. Prepare a warrt. appointing Mr. Thos. Winter, steward of this mannor with a clause of revocation of the grant to Sir Geo. Oxenden." 1 *page*.
[? About 24 Dec.]	108. Account -	—	—	"Revenue Acct. Isle [of] Providence." 2 *pages*.

Date.	Description of Document.	From	To	Purport.
24 Dec.	109. Report - -	Comrs. of Customs (Scotland).	[Lords of the Treasury.]	"Concerning the sureties for John Haldane Collector of the Customs and Salt duties at Preston-Pans. Edinborough. 24 Decr. 1723. *Minuted* :— "13th May 1724. Read." [Haldane was indebted to the Crown, 3,500*l.*] Also the memorial of the sureties. 3 *pages.*
[After 24 Dec.]	110. Copies of Receipts, &c.	—	—	For salaries paid to Gentlemen and grooms of the bedchamber and to the Comrs. of Trade, by Mr. Richard Powys, &c. The last dated 24 Dec. 1723. 2½ *pages.*
25 Dec.	111. Abstract -	Matthew Pennyfather, Comptroller and Accountant General.	—	Of the produce of His Majesty's Revenue in Ireland, for one year ended at Christmas, 1723. 1 *page.*
[? Dec.]	112. Memorial -	Piercy Kirk, Esq., House Keeper of Whitehall.	Lords of the Treasury.	For payment of a debt of 390*l.* 8*s.* 11¼*d.* due from the late Queen Anne. Also a certificate. 2 *pages, quarto.*
[? Dec.]	113. Petition -	Alexander Carleton	Do. -	Has been applying for his debt for brass and iron goods for 24 years. Is a younger brother, of good family. The Treasury has usually given him annually 50*l.* bounty money: prays to be ordered 50*l.* this Christmas. 1 *page.*
1723.	114. Petition -	John Wilson, one of the Land carriage men for the Port of London.	Hon. — Edgecomb, Esq., one of the Lords of the Treasury.	Prays for restoration to his employment, being dismissed through the representations of two other custom house officers, in connexion with a seizure of uncustomed goods below Gravesend. 2 *pages.*
1 Jan.–31 Dec.	115. State of Account.	—	—	Of Joseph Gascoigne, Esq., late Receiver General of H.M. patrimony in the Island of Minorca, between 1 Jan. 1712 and 31 Dec. 1723. 2½ *pages.*
[End of 1723.]	116. Account -	William Johnson, Solicitor.	—	Of persons indebted to the revenue on salt in Mich. term, 1723, and of the proceedings against them and of what has been recovered. 7 *pages.*

1723. VOL. CCXLVI.

Date.	Description of Document.	From	To	Purport.
[? 1723.]	117. Petition -	Master of the Barges and 48 watermen to His Majesty.	Lords of the Treasury.	For an order to pay them for a small bill of services rendered, and for their salaries to Christmas 1722. 1 *page.*
[? 1723.]	118. Memorial -	Robert Monro and Henry Cuningham, Esquires.	Do. -	Praying for reappointment of Thomas Dishington, formerly salt officer at Innerkiethen, in the collection of Barrowstowness. 1 *page.*
[? About 1723.]	119. Petition -	Maurice Hayes, of the Kingdom of Ireland.	Robt. Walpoole, Esq., First Comr., &c.	Discovered the conspiracy against King George and Government. His Majesty ordered petitioner the bounty of 40*l.* per ann. in Oct. 1722. Prays that it may be paid. 1 *page.*
[Perhaps 1722 or 1723.]	120. Petition -	Elizabeth Murray, widow and relict of Anthony Murray, Esq., deceased.	Do. -	For continuation to herself of her husband's pension [Her husband had the honour to be known to the King in Hanover.] 1 *page.*

VOL. CCXLVII., 1724.

[Beginning of 1724.] 1. New years gifts to the Secretaries, "the Lords" and the clerks at the Treasury. 4 *pages, quarto.*

[? Beginning of 1724.] 2. Petition of William Hawkins, Esq., Ulster King of Arms, of all Ireland, in behalf of himself and others of the State Officers. It has been the custom for the petitioners to have new robes every third year. The last were delivered to them on His Majesty's birthday, 1721. 820*l.* is the sum constantly allowed. All the materials must be had from London, and the work takes a considerable time. Prays the issue of the money so that the clothing may be timely finished for the birthday [28 May]. 1 *page.*

[? After 1723.] 3. "Mr Brownes case." A case submitted for Counsel's or the Attorney General's opinion, on the claim of Robert Browne, executor of Elizabeth, wife of Thomas Browne of London, scrivener (to whom the Duke of Buckingham had assigned his pension of 2,500*l.* a year for advances thereon), the point being whether, under the patent 26 Car. II., the arrears could be paid out of the hereditary excise. The opinion is in favour of Mr Browne's demand. It has no signature. 2 *pages.*

1724. VOL. CCXLVII.

On the back is:—"1° W. & M. 600,000li for payment of the wages due to ye servts of ye late King Charles ye 2d, wch were his servts at the time of his decease, to be paid in such manner and proportion, and to such of them, as his Maty shall direct." 2 *pages.*

[? 1724.] 4. "Equivalent Charter. The amended draught."
The King's will is that the Attorney and Solicitor General prepare a bill for the Royal signature in the words of the draft. 29 *pages.*

9 Jan. 5. Two memorials of the several established and supernumerary Tidewaiters who served in the last quarantine in the Port of Dublin, to the Comrs and Chief Governors of the Revenue of Ireland for their case to be considered.
Received Janry 9, 1723–4. 2 *pages.*

13 Jan. 6. Petition of Ruperta Howe, widow, to the Lords of the Treasury. As relict and executrix of Emanuel Scroop Howe, Esq., is possessed of the office of Lieut. Chief Ranger or keeper of the forest and chace of Alice Holt and Woolmer (Southampton) with power of substitution of underkeepers or foresters for the remainder of the term of 45 years. Petitioner granted the office of Deputy or underkeeper of the Lodge or Walk, called Goose-Green Lodge, in Alice Holt Forest, to Col. Pendlebury for 29 years, he covenanting to do repairs and not to grant away the office, unless to a person qualified and approved by the petitioner. He has, however, in consideration of 800*l.* granted the same to Col. Charles Frampton, who has committed spoil in cutting down trees and taking deer and game, and he perseveres in the same. The Attorney General has reported on the case and petitioner asks that he (the Attorney General) may review his report and that their Lps would give directions for the future preservation of his Majesty's interests. Jan. 13, 1723–4. 2 *pages.*

[? About 16 Jan.] 7. Petition of Jezreel Jones to the Lords of the Treasury for allowance of 30*s.* a day for interpreting, coach hire, &c. whilst attending audiences of his Majesty, the Prince and Princes[s], &c. and for his journey to Portsmouth, and for seeking for a house for the Morocco Ambassador. The amount claimed was 102*l.*, viz., from 6 Nov. 1723 to 13 Jan. 1723–4.
Minuted:—"16th Jan. 1723-4 order'd." 1 *page.*

22 Jan. 8. The Lord Lieut. of Ireland (Grafton) to the Lords of the Treasury. Transmits the petition of John Rathborne of Dublin, merchant, together with copies of the reports of the Attorney General and Surveyor General thereupon, to whom he had referred the petition. The petition sets forth that the passage from the Blind Quay to the Castle of Dublin, was very narrow and incommodious, and the Lord Lieut., upon the complaint of the House of Commons in 1710, ordered a new way or passage to be opened to the Castle. Petitioner was seised of two houses on Corke Hill standing on the ground required, and an agreement was made with him to give him all the ground over which the present passage to the Castle leads,

1724. VOL. CCXLVII.

also that piece adjoining whereon Toms Coffee House stood, in place of 30 feet of his ground for a way into the Castle: The plan at first projected for rebuilding the Castle was changed, whereby that side of the Castle, which lies next to Castle Street, was to be brought about 25 feet nearer to the street. This could not be done without encroaching on the ground intended to be conveyed to the petitioner to the extent of 25 feet in depth and 50 feet in length. The Government in 1712 came to a new agreement with him, to give him 600*l.* in consideration of this last piece of ground, &c. The petitioner further sets forth that he had pulled down his houses, &c. to carry out the arrangement and that there was due to him 1,198*l.* 17*s.* 6*d.* by the non-conveyance of the ground to him, &c. The Lord Lieut. asks for a warrant to pay him that sum and for the King's authority to convey the land.

The petition, &c. referred to and abstract of the papers. 10½ *pages.*

23 Jan. 9. Order in Council on the memorial of the Com^rs of Admiralty proposing that his Majesty should give the produce of the pirate sloop "Ranger" condemned at Rhode Island, to the Commander and crew of H.M. Greyhound referring the matter to the Lords of the Treasury. Dated 23 Jan. 1723.

Minuted:—"19th October 1725. Capt. Peter Solgard Commander of the Greyhound with his officers and ships Company is to have the sum of 314^li or thereabouts divided amongst them; being the produce of the pyrate sloop called the Ranger taken by them and condemned in the Admiralty Court of Rhode Island: provided no legall claime has been made to the said sloop on anything found on board her when taken within a year and a day since condemnation. This on reading an Order of Council relating hereto. Dated the 23 January 1723."

Also copy of the memorial. 2 *pages and* 2 *halves.*

29 Jan. 10. Report and supplemental report of Mr Christopher Tilson to the Lords of the Treasury upon the proportions to be allowed to the South Sea Company for additional charges of management in respect to the increase of their capital by virtue of the Act 6 George I. Dated 15 April 1722 and 29 Jan. 1723–4.

Minuted:—"17 July 1722. Let ye South Sea Directors have a copy hereof." [This must apply to the report of 15 Apr. 1722.]

There is also another paper on the same subject. 8 *pages.*

[? About 29 Jan.] 11. "Memorial and humble petition" of Sir Lawrence Anderton, Bart., to the Lords of the Treasury. Memorialist in August last, presented a memorial to their Lordships setting forth:—that Francis Anderton, Esq., his younger brother, had wrongfully possessed himself of petitioner's estate, during his residence in foreign parts; and in 1716 had been convicted of high treason for being concerned in the Rebellion:—that the Trustees of the forfeited estates had seized petitioner's estate and dismissed his claim made thereto. On appeal, the Court of Delegates reversed the Com^rs decree, whereby the

1724. VOL. CCXLVII.

estate was declared forfeited by the said Francis to the public; but, in regard that petitioner had been educated in a Popish Seminary beyond the seas, contrary to the Statute 1 Jac. I., the Delegates decreed petitioner incapable of taking the Estate, otherwise than upon the terms of the Statute. The petitioner since his return to England, having been instructed in the doctrines of the Church of England, renounced his errors and conformed himself to the latter Church, and took the oaths, and hoped the Com^rs would have delivered to him his deeds and left him to get in the arrears of rent. Upon his petition the deeds were delivered over to him. The Com^rs received 3,591*l.* 6*s.* 10*d.* for rent of petitioner's estate, and paid it into the Exchequer, and part still remains in the hands of the tenants or of their Agents, and the tenants being terrified by the threats of the Agents refuse to pay petitioner the rents. Petitioner is advised by Counsel (opinions annexed) that he is entitled by his conformity as well to the money in the Exchequer, as to the money in the Receivers and tenants hands. When any estates were claimed in Scotland and the claim was allowed, the rents received by Com^rs Agents were refunded to the claimants: prays for issue of warrants to repay the money to petitioner which was paid into the Exchequer, and an order to the Agents and tenants to pay him the rents.

Minuted:—"1 May 1724 Sr Lau. releases the m^o already paid for ye pub. use. Prepare an authority for ye Rem^r as desired."

The former petition and the opinions referred to: also some memoranda upon the case. The last dated opinion is on 29 Jan. 1723. 9 *pages.*

4 Feb. 12. Two letters of Jezreel Jones (1) to the R^t Hon. Robert Walpole, Esq., and (2) to the Lords of the Treasury explaining his accounts as well as errors in them in connexion with the Morocco Ambassador's affairs. In the first letter he says:—"I have known the Morocco Amb^r many years, I have been conversant with him and many others of his countrey and especially of the great ones." In the second he complains that some persons had "lessen'd" him to the Ambassador, saying he was only sent to conduct him up, and was refused "to goe with his Ex^cy in the coach at his audience of his Maj^ty, the Prince, and the Princess;" as he used to do in her late Majesty's reign, with his Excellency's predecessors. His Excellency told him that he had desired Mr Mohamet to acquaint His Majesty, that he (Jones) had wronged him by receiving an imprest and had never paid him any part of it. The Ambassador complained also that he had charged a bill for money lent by his Excellency's landlady. He says, "I answered, I had paid her that bill, and other demands out of the imprest I had of the Governm^t for his ease and use; also in discharge of 300^li I had received, I discharged what I paid her for the time of his Ex^cy's being at her house with his retinue, Lyon, Ostrichs, and all other the expences which the Government had entrusted me with, on his account," &c. Dated 4 Feb. 1723–4.

The account referred to. 7 *pages.*

Vol. CCXLVII.

1724.

7 Feb. 13. Resolution of the House of Commons in Ireland for an address to the Lord Lieut. to lay before his Majesty the petition of George Roe and Simon Sherlock for themselves and sixty creditors of James Leathley and others, army clothiers, in relation to money illegally extorted from them. 1 *page*.

7 Feb. 14. "Address of the House of Peers in Ireland in favour of their officers." There is a list of the officers whom the House proposed should be rewarded for their extraordinary services together with the sums. 1 *page*.

8 Feb. 15. Petition of Monsieur de l'Hermitage to Mr Walpole praying him to facilitate the payment of part of the pension of the Count de Heun, a German gentleman, who had changed his religion four or five years since and was in needy circumstances.

Minuted:—"150 p ann. p Mr Chetwynd paid to Michas 1722." On the back is:—"Ordered."

At the foot is a letter from the brother of [Sir Robert Walpole] unaddressed; asking him to move his brother that part of the poor gentleman's pension might be paid as a great act of charity which would much oblige the Dutch Ambassador here. Dated Paris, February 8–19, 1723–4. 1 *page*.

8 Feb. 16. Report of the Barons of the Exchequer of Scotland to the Lords of the Treasury on the petition of Alexander Murray, Esq. For twenty years past petitioner has yearly paid the Crown "as come in place of the Bishop of Galloway" 5*l*. 11*s*. 1*d*. ⅓ in name of tack duty for the tithes of the lands of Broughton; and likewise yearly certain small feu duties for the lands of Outten Gallows and others held of the late Bishop of Galloway amounting to 3*l*. 15*s*. If the lease of the tithes of Broughton be renewed with the same reserved rent or tack duty, a composition will be due, of about 82*l*. It appears by the certificate of two of the Justices of the peace of the County of Galloway, and from information of others, that the want of a bridge over the river of Fleet (mentioned in the petition) which was lately carried off by a violent flood, is not only a great loss, but in the winter (for the most part) prevents all communication and travelling between Port Patrick and the Western Parts of Scotland, and Carlisle, and the Western Parts of England. The estimate for a bridge is 300*l*. The building of bridges is a public work, and by law ought to be done by the county; but from the circumstances of that country, it is not practicable to have the bridge built: propose that petitioner should have a new lease for 19 years on the same terms and rebuild the bridge, laying out at least 260*l*.

Also the petition, the lower portion of which is lost. 3½ *pages*.

8 Feb. 17. Report of the same to the same on the memorial of Mr James Houston, minister at Kirkliston. Her late Majesty granted to the deceased Mr Thomas Miller, minister of the same church, for life, the feu duty payable to the Crown for the lands and tithes of Hallyeards, containing the lands and tithes of Halburys [Hallbarns

1724. VOL. CCXLVII.

in the memorial] and others extending to 66*l.* 19*s.* 8*d.* Scots, or 5*l.* 11*s.* 7*d.* $\frac{2}{3}$ sterling. The memorialist was admitted minister 26 Sept. 1716, and has a numerous family, and it will be a proper act of his Majesty's bounty, if he will grant him the feu duties named, from the death of his predecessor during his ministry.

Minuted:—"Warr^{t} signd 5th Augt 1724.

Also the memorial referred to. 3 *pages.*

8 Feb. 18. Report of the same to the same on the petition of Margaret Macdonald, widow of Sir Donald Macdonald of Slate, on behalf of herself and the four daughters of Sir Donald. The Report sets out some particulars of the marriage articles of Sir Donald also of certain bonds providing for his wife and daughters. The Barons are of opinion that the widow and daughters would have been entitled to their jointure and several provisions but for the attainder and forfeiture of Sir Donald. Under the Act passed in the fourth (? sixth) year of his reign entitled:—"An Act for explaining the nature of conveyances to be made to the purchasers of the forfeited estates by the Commissioners and Trustees acting in Scotland, &c." his Majesty may grant the same in the same manner out of his real and personal estate as if Sir Donald had not been attainted and his estate not forfeited. The Barons have caused the accompanying two drafts of signatures for grants to be made to the widow and daughters. Edinburgh, Exchequer Chamber, 8 Feb. 1723–4.

Also the two "signatures."

On the back is:—"June ye 5th read and agreed." 9½ *pages.*

10 Feb. 19. Copy of Order of the Court of Exchequer Chamber, confirming the appointment of Mr James Abercrombie as his Majesty's limner and painter in Scotland for life (Andrew M^{c}ilraith having been nominated thereto). "Die Lunæ 10mo Feb^{rii} anno 10mo R.R^{s}."

Also copy of the appointment of the said James Abercrombie, jun^{r}, "of Glassaugh," who is described as having a genius for the art.

On the outside these are addressed to Captain Alexander Abercrombie of Glassaugh, Member of Parliament, at Oldmans Coffee House, near Charing Cross, who was father of the artist. 2 *pages.*

11 Feb. 20. Report of the Barons of the Exchequer of Scotland to the Lords of the Treasury. His Majesty had signified that John Earl of Rothes should be discharged from the balance due upon his account, as Chamberlain of Fife and Strathern, for the year 1720 and preceding years; and also from the sums chargeable on him as principal sheriff of the shires of Fife and Aberdeen, for the year 1721 and preceding. As Receiver and Chamberlain of H.M. rents of Fife and Strathern, the sum of 1,308*l.* 8*s.* 5*d.* was due to him on his salary of 320*l.* per ann., and he was chargeable for 607*l.* 17*s.* 8*d.* $\frac{2}{12}$ as sheriff of the shire of Fife for 1721 and preceding, and with 328*l.* 12*s.* as sheriff of the shire of Aberdeen. Caused the annexed draft of a warrant to be prepared to discharge the Earl of the balance on passing his account. 607*l.* 17*s.* 8*d.* $\frac{2}{12}$ are payable

1724. VOL. CCXLVII.

by the Earl of Leven, who petitioned his Majesty for that amount. 11 Feb. 1723–4.

The draft referred to. 4 *pages.*

13 Feb. 21. Memorial of Jacob Tonson, junior, of London, bookseller to the Lords of the Treasury. Intends (as authorised) to proceed in the reprinting and publishing a new edition of Rymer's Fœdera in 17 vols., folio. The Treasury was at the sole expense of publishing the book now extant and the number fell short of supplying the Ministry and other Chief Officers of State, Foreign Ministers, and Societies of Learning, and the price of the book has risen to upwards of 100 guineas. Proposes to supply fifty complete sets or more in 17 vols., folio, at 30 guineas each, in quires; to be paid in three instalments. 13 Feb. 1723.

Another paper containing some other particulars touching the same subject. 2 *pages.*

17 Feb. 22. Report of the Barons of the Exchequer of Scotland to the Lords of the Treasury as to (1) the passing of the accounts of money imprested to Charles Earl of Lauderdale, General, and John Montgomery, Esq., Master of the Mint at Edinburgh; (2) the putting a stop to the passing of the grant of 500*l*. a piece to the six children of John Balfour out of the estate of Burleigh until a representation thereof made by the Com^rs^ and Trustees for forfeited estates in Scotland had been examined; and (3) the allowances to the clerks of the Court of Delegates which they see no reason to stop. 2 *pages.*

[? About 19 Feb.] 23. Mons. Fabrice to M^r^ "Tillotson" introducing the bearer Capt. Gustavus Behre, whom he had sent for from Sweden, as a witness against the last conspirators, and whom Lord Townsend has sent here from Hanover as a witness for the confiscation of the vessel of the Pretender, named "the Revolution." He was promised his subsistence, and Lord Townsend, Mr Walpole, the Duke of Newcastle and his brother had assured the writer twenty times it was a settled thing, but notwithstanding, they have put him off at the Treasury two months from day to day. Lord Townsend has promised that Mr Tillotson will give him (the Captain) a letter of recommendation to his brother at the Treasury. (French.)

Similar letter from the same to the Hon. Mr Pelham, one of the Lords of the Treasury, giving the same particulars, except that he had then been seven months without receiving the pay promised him.

Minuted:—"19th Feb. 1723–4. See what has been paid to him and whether he has any settled allowance."

Also the following note:—"By minute dated 18 Oct. 1723, Mr Lowther was directed to subsist Capt. Bahr. at 5^s^ p diem from 2 Augt 1723 and has paid him thereupon to the 22^d^ of Jan^ry^ last 43^li^ 5^s^.

Also petition (undated) of the same captain asking for a larger allowance. 5 *pages.*

22 Feb. 1723–24. 24. Report of Charles Wither to the Lords of the Treasury on the petition of James Sammells and others, fullers; praying their

1724. VOL. CCXLVII.

Lordships to grant them a licence to dig fuller's earth, in a place called Clay-pitt bottom, in the New Forest, it being very scarce near the City of New Sarum, where petitioners dwell, and where there is great occasion for it to carry on the woollen manufacture in which they are concerned. Does not find that the licence they ask can be any detriment to the forest, provided they are confined to the spot of ground in their petition mentioned, which is an old clay pit in Ashby Walk, near the parish of Hale; nor does he apprehend that the petitioners have any design to export the clay they intend to dig to foreign parts, the pit being above 12 miles from any sea port. Advises that they should give security not to abuse the liberty granted them, and should give notice to the Keeper of the Walk when they design to remove any clay. Suggests also that they should pay some small acknowledgment for this liberty. February 22, 1723.

The petition is annexed which has a minute on it from which the above report resulted. It has the following further minute: "My Lords agree to the report, and direct the Surv[r] to advise what acknowledgment would be reasonable for them to pay to the Crown." 2½ *pages.*

29 Feb. 25. Lord Lieut. of Ireland (Grafton) to the Lords of the Treasury. On an application of Lord Harry Powlet, Colonel of the Battle Axe Guards, and of William Hawkins, Esq., Ulster King-of-Arms, for the usual allowance of clothing against the King's birthday. Finds that it has been the constant custom to grant these allowances every third year. 29 Feb. 1723. 1½ *pages.*

29 Feb. 26. Report of A. Cracherode to the Lords of the Treasury. Laid the annexed petition of Daniel Cox, Gent., late Under-Sheriff for the co. of Warwick, before the three judges who went the Midland Circuit, praying for payment of 277*l.* 15*s.* for his disbursements in executing the Office of High Sheriff for the county upon the death of Randal Croxhall, Esq., in obedience to the late act. Encloses the judges' opinion on the case.

Also the covering letter from the Treasury, the petition which gives the items of the disbursements and the opinion of the judges, which is that the Crown ought to bear the expenses of the Under-Sheriff, but that they are not proper judges of the particulars although there is nothing that appears extravagant. 4½ *pages.*

2 March. 27. Sir R. Raymond [Justice of the King's Bench] to ———. His patent bears date 31 Jan. last, and upon the General warrant for payment of the judges salaries, payment of any salary, more than from the date of the patent, is refused, without there are directions from the Lords of the Treasury. Is informed that such directions have been generally given for payment of the succeeding judge, up to the time his predecessor was last paid; which in his case would be from 28 Nov., the last day of Mich. term, to which day the Lord Chief Baron Eyre was paid. This has been done in the cases of all the judges lately and was so, so long ago as when his father was made a Judge, now nearly 45 years previously. Asks

that this may be mentioned to Mr Walpole and that an order may be procured for him. Mar. 2, 1723.

The following memoranda are on the back of the document:—
"Sr Jams Montague paid to the day of his death and Sr Robt Eyre who succeeded him, paid, not only the whole term, as one of the Justices of the King's Bench, but also so much more as, together wth what paid to Montague, made up the whole term as Ld Chief Baron.

"Chief Baron Bury paid to the day of his death, and Gilbert, who came in a Baron thereupon, was paid the whole Trinity Term, tho' his patent bore date but 6 days before the end thereof.

"Many other instances may be found to make it appear that the King is to save nothing by the death or removal of any the judges; for the judge who comes in, always prevails to get so much as, with what paid his predecessor, shall make the salary compleat and more, I believe, sometimes." 3 *pages, quarto.*

[? About 3 March.] 28. Petition of Robert Peter, late Receiver General of the taxes for the county of Hertford, to the Lords of the Treasury for allowance or remittance of 7,305*l.* 7*s.* 4*d.* interest at 10*l.* per cent. and allowance of 580*l.* 10*s.* for extra charges [arising out of the settlement of an old debt to the Crown].

Minuted:—"3d March 1723. My Lords adhere to their resolution not to make any allowances of this kind for the future."

A report and certificate (which should accompany the petition) are not now with it. 1½ *pages.*

12 Mar. 29. "Address of the Commissrs of the late Genl Assembly of the Church of Scotland & reference."

The address is to the King and is as follows:—

"The state of the Highlands and Islands of Scotland with regard to the multitude of Papists is very lamentable, for some of the remote Islands are wholly inhabited by Papists, and in diverse parishes on the continent the greatest part of the people are popish, and many of these are perverted of late years by the cunning and industry of popish priests and jesuits who traffick amongst them in great numbers.

"These parishes are of so great extent, being from thirty to fourty miles and upwards of length, and so embarrassed with lakes, rivers, and impassable mountains and marishes, that one minister in each of them, and one school for which only our law makes provision, cannot suffice for instructing the inhabitants, so as either to recover the seduced, or preserve the rest from infection; especially when in some parishes for every protestant teacher, there are six popish traffickers practising incessantly amongst them.

"It will be evident to your Majestie in what eminent danger this increase of popery puts our holy religion, and the protestant succession in your Royal Family, upon which, under God, the security of our religion and of all our other valuable interests does depend, and that it is of the greatest importance to find out effectual remedies to this growing evil.

1724. VOL. CCXLVII.

"The instructing of these poor, ignorant, misled people in the knowledge of the principles of the true Protestant Religion and of virtue, seems to be the only effectual way to make them both good christians and loyal subjects; to this end, the ministers in these parts labour with indefatigable industry, and the Assemblies of this Church, for the assistance of these ministers, have made provision out of the yearly allowance given by your Majestie to the Church, for as many preachers and catechists as they can maintain, and the Society in Scotland for propagating Christian Knowledge have settled as many charity schools in these parishes, as the interest of their stock will support. Yet all these helps come far short of what is necessary for preserving and recovering that people from the contagion of Popery and Jacobitism, with which they are infected.

"The late General Assembly having had this matter under their most serious consideration, did appoint us, in the most dutiful manner, to lay the same before your Majestie, and most humbly and earnestly to plead, as we now in their name beg leave to do, that your Majestie will be graciously pleased, out of your Royal bounty, to allow a suitable fund yearly during your Majestie's pleasure, toward the assisting the ministers of this Church in instructing the people in the knowledge of the protestant religion, preventing the growth of popery, and recovering such as have been misled by popish emissaries, and for maintaining more preachers and catechists to travel through the foresaid counties, where Popery so much prevails, and for defraying the expences of processes that may bee needful toward the suppression of popery and preventing the 'furder' growth thereof. Edinburgh, 12th March 1724."

Referred to the Lords of the Treasury, 30 March 1724. 2 *pages.*

13 March. 30. Report of the Comrs for forfeited Estates, to the Lords of the Treasury, in explanation of their account, which differed with an account of sums paid into the Exchequer on account of Forfeitures. Also offering facilities for further explanations, if necessary. Fig Tree Court, Inner Temple, 13 March 1723.

Also a statement of the account. 5 *pages, injured.*

[? About 13 March.] 31. Petition of the Merchants of London to the Lords of the Treasury. In the annexed petition the merchants of London complained of the many holidays kept at the Custom House (contrary to law), and that the officers do not duly attend at other times, and that the Searchers take exorbitant fees. This petition was referred to the Comrs of Customs [on 13 March 1723–4]. The present petition represents that the Comrs are the chief cause of so many holidays. By their want of attendance they have no power over the Searchers (being patent officers). Petitioners cannot expect any redress from them. Pray that they may be heard at the board, and that their Lps would order that no holidays be kept but such as are appointed by law, and that one Commissioner attend every morning at 9 o'clock in the Long Room to dispatch merchants' business, and that if, for the future, the searchers presume to take

1724. VOL. CCXLVII.

more fees than warrantable by law, the Com[rs] will proceed against them with the utmost severity.

Also the petition referred to, in which the merchants complain that ships are often disappointed of their voyages by not being ready to embrace a fair wind, and that sometimes goods cannot be taken ashore to reap the benefit of a market before other ships come in.

Both petitions have numerous signatures. 2 *large pages.*

23 Mar. 32. "Observations on the Treãry warr[t] to the Surveyor Gen[l] of woods. Dated 2[d] October 1723." The observations relate to various matters in connexion with Woolmer Forest and Alice Holt Forest, of which Mrs Ruperta Howe was Chief Ranger. It was proposed that the latter, joined with the verderers, should prepare proper instructions for the under-keepers to observe. Dated "March the 23, 1723-4." 2½ *pages.*

[About 24 Mar.] 33. Report of Walter Chetwynd, Esq., to the Lords of the Treasury on the "pretensions" of M[rs] Margaret Swintoun to a pension of 50*l.* per ann. payable out of the Civil List. It appears that the said Margaret Swinton (formerly Margaret Douglas) was the true and lawful wife of Col. Charles Swintoun, and that the petitioner and complainant, Alice Swintoun, was not his wife, but is one Alice Newman (who takes upon her the name of Swintoun) by whom the Colonel owned he had had children, but always denied he was ever married to her.

Also the petitions of Margaret, widow of Col. Charles Swintoun, and of "Ailce" Swinton, widow and relict of the late Col. Swintoun, a letter, a marriage certificate, and two affidavits. 8½ *pages.*

[? About 25 Mar.] 34. "An acco[t] of what was wanting at Lady Day 1724 to clear all fees and salaries payable at the Exchequer to that time."

It gives a list of all the persons and the amounts due to them. 4 *large pages.*

26 March. 35. A schedule of deeds, writings, and papers relating to the late dissolved Hospital, commonly called the Savoy made pursuant to a warrant of the right Hon[ble] the Lords Commissioners of His Majesty's Treasury and delivered to John Poulteney, Esq., Surveyor General of His Majesty's lands, &c. by John Huggins, Esq., this six and twentieth day of March 1724. *A book of* 12 *pages.*

28 Mar. 36. "An account of the copper coynage of half pence and farthings for the service of Ireland as it appears by the several abstracts transmitted from Bristoll to the 28th of March 1724." 1 *large page.*

31 March. 37. Report of the Com[rs] for Taxes to the Lords of the Treasury on the petition of the Lady Biddulph, widow and relict of Sir Michael Biddulph, Bart., deceased, one of the sureties of Morgan Whitley, formerly receiver general of Cheshire and North Wales. Sir Michael (having obtained an Act of Parliament) compounded for his part of Whitley's debt and paid the composition (5,859*l.* 1*s.* 10*d.*)

1724. VOL. CCXLVII.

into the Exchequer Morgan's debt after Sir Michael's payment, amounts to 32,221*l.* 13*s.* 1*d.* Are of opinion that where estates and effects of Receivers are concealed, it would be for the benefit of the public, if an Act of Parliament were obtained, to empower their Lps to gratify discoverers of any estates out of the produce of the same. By this means their Lps might show indulgence to the petitioner. 31 March 1724.

Minuted:—"15th April 1724. My Lords think they have no power to dispose of moneys recovered on accot of taxes, the same being appropriated."

The petition referred to. 3 *pages.*

31 March. 38. "Copy of the Auditors of Imprests' Report on Capt. Martin's and Col. Arnott's accots as Paymasters of the Almanza Prisoners."

Also the memorial of Col. John Arnott.

Minuted:—"Read & the necry wts to be prepared for his discha." 19 *pages.*

13 April. 39. Representation of Sir Isaac Newton to the Lords of the Treasury concerning the proposed trial of the Pix, of copper moneys coined by Mr Wood at Bristol, viz., that the moneys there reserved for a trial are kept locked up in a box or pix, under the keys of Mr Wood and the Controller of that coinage, or of their deputies. The trial thereof may be most authentic and satisfactory, and something cheaper if the box, before being opened, be brought up to London and the moneys be tried in his Majesty's Mint in the Tower, by his Majesty's Assay Master, before such person, or persons, as their Lps or his Majesty in Council shall appoint to see the trial performed, and to report the event to their Lps and before the officers of the Mint and the parties concerned, viz., Mr Wood and the Controller of that coinage (who are both in town) and before their deputies and one or two gentlemen of Ireland. And at the same time any other copper moneys, old or new, may be tried there, before the persons above named, and the weight and value ascertained and compared with the value of the copper moneys now coined at Bristol, and the trial may be reported to their Lordships.

But if their Lps had rather that the copper pix be tried at Bristol, he will look out for a man to do it and treat with him and see him instructed. 1 *page.*

21 April. 40. Petition of John Mackpheadris, merchant, to the Lords of the Treasury, asking that his proposal for the payment of his debt to the Crown and for his release from confinement may be accepted. Petitioner traded and employed several hundred men and paid yearly about 10,000*l.* to the Customs and Excise, and at one time acquired 100,000*l.*, but by misfortunes of the seas, &c. lost the greatest part of it. 1 *large page.*

30 April. 41. The Lords of Trade to the Lords of the Treasury, on the petition of Sir Charles Cox, praying for an arrear of salary due to his brother Samuel Cox, Esq., as President of the Council and Commander-in-Chief of Barbadoes. By his Majesty's instructions to the

1724. VOL. CCXLVII.

Governors of Barbadoes, the Presidents of the Council there, acting as Commanders-in-Chief of the Island, during the absence of the Governor, are entitled to the moiety of his salary; but they do not see how Mr Cox can justly claim any pay whilst another person actually discharged the duties of the office. April 30, 1724.

A copy of the above and a copy of H.M. Instructions. (19th and 111th clauses.) 6 *pages.*

[? About 1 May.] 42. Petition of Andrew Trebeck to the Lords of the Treasury. Officiated in the Royal Chapel during the absence of the Court for several years in the reign of the late Queen and that of his present Majesty, for which the usual allowance is 15*l.* for reading prayers and a guinea for each sermon. From Aug. 1713 to Aug. 1714 the Queen continuing at Windsor till the middle of February, he read daily prayers and preached 32 sermons in the said chapel, for which there is an arrear of 48*l.* 12*s.* Prays payment.

Certificate in corroboration. Dated 1 May 1724. 2 *pages.*

[? About 1 May.] 43. Memorial of Peter Capon to the Lords of the Treasury. There was an order of the Treasury to pay 50*l.* for memorialist's charges in going to New England to purchase provisions for the garrison of Annapolis Royal and Placentia. By his detention at the Treasury for the above order, the vessel sailed, in which memorialist had embarked his baggage, and he could not overtake it in the Downs, or at Plymouth. These journeys and the charges of provisions bought at Boston in New England, far exceeded that sum, and almost ruined petitioner, and necessitated his selling his commission, and the 50*l.* has become a charge on the regiment where he has no effects: prays that the Paymaster General may remove the charge from him and place it to the account of provisions for those garrisons.

Minuted:—"1 May 1724. My Lords can give no directions herein." 1 *page.*

2 May. 44. Petition of Edward Shaftoe, gent., to the Lords of the Treasury. Petitioner was father to the late Captain John Shaftoe, one of the four officers shot at Preston, and was drawn into the Rebellion by the latter; but soon after the town was taken offered himself as a witness against the rebels to prove the Rebellion and the proclaiming of the Pretender in all the market towns through which they marched. Petitioner, with Mr Calderwood, proved this upon every trial at Liverpool, and at most of the trials elsewhere. Mr Calderwood was rewarded with a sum of money and a pension of 40*l.* per ann., but petitioner received no more than subsistence of meat and drink, and was discharged with only 40*s*, and after six years was ordered 40*l.* Is 78 years of age, and now reduced to extreme necessity. Prays speedy relief.

Also two certificates in his favour, one being dated 2 May 1724. 3 *pages.*

2 May. 45. Lord Lieut. of Ireland (Grafton) to the Lords of the Treasury. Sends several parliamentary recommendations presented to him

1724. VOL. CCXLVII.

during the last session, viz., addresses (1) in favour of Luke Netterville, Esq., for some provision to educate his children. He is the first of his family received into the Communion of the Church of Ireland. (2.) On the petition of Nicholas Grueber, merchant, for 1,000*l.* to be granted to him to encourage him in making gunpowder to supply the Government. (3.) Recommending a grant of 2,000*l.* to Richard Stewart, Esq., and partners to enable them to carry on the colliery of Ballycastle, Antrim. (4.) On the petition of Brigadier General David Crichton, recommending him to be replaced on half pay. (5.) In favour of Lieut. Col. Freeman for his long services and misfortunes. (6.) In behalf of Major Philip Dunbar for services in the War of Ireland, Spain, and the West Indies (for half pay). (7.) On the petition of Quarter-Master Charles MacFaden, of late Brigadier Wolseley's regiment of Horse (for half pay). (8.) On the petition of George Roe and Simon Sherlock, in behalf of themselves and other creditors of James Leathley and others, partners in clothing several regiments. This concerns sums illegally extorted from them by Sir William Robinson, deceased, when Deputy Vice Treasurer. (9.) On the petition of William Molesworth, Esq., H.M. Surveyor General of Lands, for increase of salary. (10.) In behalf of Gustavus Hamilton and others of the late Lord Wharton's regiment for an arrear of half pay.

Minuted:—"Prepare w^ts^ accord^g^ to ye addresses." *5 pages.*

4 May. 46. The same to the same. It being customary for the Crown to grant to several officers both in England and Ireland, through whose hands the bills of every session of Parliament pass, certain allowances, for their trouble; he (the Lord Lieut.) sends a list of allowances due, and prays their L^ps^ to obtain H.M. warrant for payment (the sum being 1,266*l.* Irish, and 843*l.* English).

The only account with the letter is for 145*l.* for 21 Public Bills put into form by the Clerk of the Council—the titles of the Bills are given. There is also a memorandum of the fees due to the Usher and Keeper of the Council Chamber in Ireland for the same bills. *3 pages and 3 parts of pages.*

[After 4 May.] 47. Sums issued to Sir Luke Schaub upon account of his journey to, and residence at, Paris, between the 4 of March 1720–1, and the 4th of May 1724, being 3 years and 61 days. At the foot is a memorandum which shows that his claim was for 12,120*l.* 1*s.* 11*d.*, and that he "stood his Ma^ty^ for the above mencōned time in about 4,030^li^ p ann." *1 page.*

4 May. 48. Report of the Surveyor General (John Pulteney, Esq.) to the Lords of the Treasury. Has viewed the buildings adjoining H.M. Palace of Somerset House, to see whether there are any encroachments and nuisances that may endanger or annoy the same. Finds that in 1694 King William and Queen Mary, by letters patent, granted to the late Earl of Dorset, the inheritance of thirty-two tenements standing on several pieces of ground, heretofore part of

the lands belonging to Somerset House and adjoining the palace; the greatest part of which front the Strand, and are situate between Strand Lane, East, and the Duchy Lane, West. The closets, or back parts of those situate East of Somerset House Gateway, are set upon the Palace wall, about four inches; and the inhabitants of several of the houses have taken down some parts of the wall, to gain light to them; which may be of ill consequence in case of fire. The vaults belonging to those houses are close to the palace wall, and the "currents of them" are laid into the drains belonging to Somerset House. There is standing in that part of the palace called the cistern yard a building near adjoining to the wall, and a closet or small building between the yard and the long court adjoining to one of the front houses; both of which might be taken down to prevent fire. In the Strand Lane there is a tenement inhabited by one of the beadles of the parish of St. Clements Danes, which is built across the lane, with a passage underneath. The timbers are fastened into the wall of Somerset House, part of which has been pulled down, and a chimney belonging to the Beadles house is built up with the wall, and stands thereon. Adjoining to which last-mentioned house is a building called the Old Waterhouse, belonging to the palace, which is also built across the lane and joined to the palace wall. It is a decayed building of no use. If both are pulled down, the garden wall on that side will be clear of any building for the full breadth of the lane. In the same Lane, and adjoining the East side of the Palace, there is a house called the Fish, Ale House, which stands close to the Palace wall, through which two window lights are made. And the vault belonging to the ale house (which lies to that part of the Palace where the Countess of Dalhousie now lives) having sometime since soaked through the wall, it annoyed the said lodgings, but the clerk of the works says this has been amended.

On the West side of the Palace, Mr. Brysan (the tenant or assignee of Sr Robert Davers who is lessee of several houses in Duchy Lane) has erected a building close to H.M. stables—inclosed with a pale of about six feet, the backyard, &c. This is an encroachment. Gives some other particulars of the vaults of the tenants.

The letter which led to the above report. 4½ *pages.*

[? About 9 May.] 49. Petition of John Lawton, one of the Deputy Chamberlains of the Exchequer, to the Lords of the Treasury. Petitioner and a brother officer (in 1718 and 1719) laid the condition of the Records under their care before their L^ps^, and the House of Lords delivered an address thereon to his Majesty. Was in hopes of receiving some commands thereon, but as he has not, informs their Lordships that many very valuable records in the Chamberlain's office are in a very perishing condition, and a great number of others are in much confusion for want of a person to methodize them, &c. asks to be employed thereon. [The records referred to are those in the "Court of the Receipt of the Exchequer."]

1724. VOL. CCXLVII.

Minuted:—"Prepare proper warr[ts] appointing John Lawton, gent., to methodize & abstract these records at a salary of 200[li] p. ann. for himself, 100[li] p. ann. for his first clerk, 70[li] for a second & 50[li] for the 3[d]."

Also a certificate of the necessity of the work and of Lawton's fitness for the same. Dated 9 May 1724. 1½ *pages.*

9 May. 50. Certificate of the Auditors (signed) addressed to the Lords of the Treasury as to the condition in which the Earl of Cadogan's accounts, as Master of the Robes, remain. If the Earl deliver in his accounts for two of the three years for which he is in arrear, to wit from Lady day 1721 to Lady day 1723, and proceeds to exhibit his accompt for the next year within the time prescribed, there will be no objection to their L[ps] granting a warrant for stopping the process which is issuing againt him. 9 May 1724.

Minuted:—"8 June 1724. Agreed to." 1 *page.*

13 May. 51. Memorial of John Pulteney, Esq., Surveyor General of H.M. lands, &c., to the Lords of the Treasury. Since his memorial of 31 Jan. 1722–3 relating to the tenements and other buildings within the precincts of the dissolved Hospital of the Savoy, has had under his further consideration the state of the land revenues formerly belonging thereto, but now vested in the crown. Finds that the revenues consist for the most part of small parcels of land scattered in several counties, some whereof where granted under the common seal of the Hospital, for twenty-one years, and others for three lives. Shall only trouble their Lordships with an account of (1) such of them whereof the leases for years are expired, and (2) of others granted above thirty years ago for three lives, which may probably be determined. None of these estates appear to have been renewed since they came to the Crown.

Under head No. 1 are:—Lands called Greenthwait in the county of York; lands forming part of Sutton Grange in the parish of Galtres in the county of York; Abingdon Mills in the county of Northampton; lands in East Haddon in the same county; and Harpool Mills in the same county.

Under head No. 2 are:—Houses and lands at Mile End in the county of Middlesex; two messuages and lands in Cudworth in the county of York; houses and lands in Sharleston in the same county; the site of St. Dewes Hospital in the county of Northampton; lands in West Haddon in the same county; and lands in Garstang and Agberth in the county of Lancaster.

Advises that the receiver be directed at his next receipt of rents to demand of the lessees whether any, and how many, of the persons for whose lives his premises were granted, be then living, and what proof he has, &c. The great charge of passing an Exchequer lease may discourage the tenants of small holdings from renewing their leases, and from paying fines; so that the fines must be greatly lessened or the passing of Exchequer leases of small estates will be impracticable. Draws attention to his memorial of 30 May 1723, in which he proposed that such persons as their Lordships should think fit

1724. VOL. CCXLVII.

should advise in what manner small estates not exceeding 20*l.* "on the rack" may be leased. 13 May 1724.

Minuted:—"Read."—Again:—"Mr Surveyor & Mr Scroop to consult abt easing ye exp. of Exr leases." 6½ *pages.*

15 May. 52. Report of S. Godolphin, Auditor, to the Lords of the Treasury on the petition of Nathaniel Boothe, Esq., for a reversionary lease of the *Pre* and *Post* fines in Cheshire, Chester, and Flint, upon more easy terms than his former grant, as some years came short of the reserved rent to the Crown; and to make up the term in being, to 31 years. He (the Auditor) has annexed an account of the profits of those fines from 1714 to 1720 whereby their "Lordships will be best able to value the premises." 15 May 1724.

The petition and account referred to. 3 *pages.*

18 May. 53. Report of Sir Isaac Newton to the Lords of the Treasury on the petition of Mr John Walker in respect to claims of Dr Justus Brandshagen who (with Thomas Hamilton) went down to Scotland to survey Sir John Erskin's mine. Objects to his claims, he having been paid and having given receipt in full. He (Sir Isaac) knows of nothing more due to either of them from the Crown than what they have already received. Mint Office, 18 May 1724.

Minuted:—"Read. "My Lords agree to the rept."

Docketed:—"Report on the petition of John Walker creditor of Justus Brandshagen for 10li 10s 0d." 1 *page.*

18 May. 54. Extract of report of 18 May 1724 on Jamaica laws made by the Attorney and Solicitor General to the Commissioners for Trade and Plantations. No revenue, except the rents reserved, will subsist after the determination of the present Revenue Act. The laying on new taxes on the people will depend upon the question whether Jamaica is to be considered merely as a colony of English subjects, or as a conquered country. If a colony of English subjects, they cannot be taxed but by the Parliament of Great Britain, or by the consent of some representative body of the people of the island; but, if a conquered country, they may be taxed by the authority of the Crown.

Also another and more brief extract from the same opinion.

[The extract was probably made at a later date.] 3 *pages.*

20 May. 55. Memorial of Jacob Tonson, junior, of London, bookseller, being a repetition of his memorial of 13 Feb. 172¾. May 20, 1724.

Minuted thus:—"W. H. at Hampton Court to ge [? give] Mr Tench ballce Equivalent."

There is also a copy of the subordinate paper noticed at p. 263, under 13 Feb. 2 *pages.*

[After May.] 56. Memorial of Thomas Lewis, Clerk to the Comptroller of H.M. Stamp Duties in North Britain, to the Honble Baron Scrope, Secretary to the Rt Hon. the Comrs of the Treasury. Gives an account of his having left his employment in England, to go to Scotland, and of his employment in the Stamp Office, Edinburgh

1724. VOL. CCXLVII.

until the Comptroller desired his dismissal. The latter would have had him deliver up his keys, but he refused. This brought down his creditors on him and forced the memorialist to take a journey to London on foot, and since his arrival he understands Mr Anderson is put in his room. Altho' he has not the honour to be personally acquainted with Baron Scrope, yet he believes the latter has several times seen his writing when employed by Mr Bowles in the Exchequer; prays the Baron to use his interest that he may be replaced, or for other employment. Undated, but? after May 1724, because Scrope was Baron of the Exchequer of Scotland in that year (*see* North Britain Book, Vol. VII., p. 161), and by the last clause of the memorial he had ceased to fill that office. 2 *pages.*

[? About 5 June.] 57. Petition of Richard Dowdeswell and Pakington Tomkyns to the Lords of the Treasury. Are security, in 6,000*l.*, for the late Secretary for licensing Hawkers and Pedlars, who, not being proof against the temptations of Change Alley, was deeply involved in the general calamity of the South Sea and other bubbles. Petitioners have not such a sum of ready money at command as they stand engaged for, and hope for time to raise the same. Petitioner Tomkyns labours under the further difficulty that what small estate he has, is all settled, excepting a third share of the ground rents of Spittle Fields Square and the Market; and the Rev. Wm Lucy, lately suddenly deceased, was the proprietor of another third, and was empowered to sell the whole; which his death prevented. He has now left the same by will to be disposed of; and the will is likely to be controverted; pray that no process may be ordered out against them.

Minuted:—" 5th June 1724. To be considered when the Attor. Gen^ll^ makes a return to the reference touching this matter." 1 *page.*

8 June. 58. Certificate of arrears due from her late Majesty Queen Anne, unto Sir John Shadwell, third Physician to her late Majesty. The amount was 295*l.* 2*s.* 9*d.* His salary was 200*l.* per ann. Treasurer of the Chambers Office, June 8, 1724.

Minuted:—" 19 June 1724, a w^t^ for 800^li^. Warr^t^ sign'd." 1 *page.*

[? About 8 June.] 59. Memorial of John Preston, Esq., Remembrancer of the City of London, to the Lords of the Treasury. There have been, time out of mind, paid and allowed yearly to the Lord Mayor, Aldermen, Sheriffs and Principal Officers of the City of London, certain sums in lieu of wine impost, which money was formerly paid at the Custom House without any fees. Upon appropriating the several duties on wines the money has been, for some years, paid at the Exchequer by order from the Treasury and the fees attending the receipt have been directed by their Lordships to be repaid to Christmas, since which they are in arrear, viz., 62*l.* 12*s.* 6*d.*

Minuted:—" 8th June 1724. Rejected."

Also the Account.

Also a letter? of a previous date from the same to the Lords of the Treasury to the same effect. 2 *pages and* 2 *halves.*

1724. Vol. CCXLVII.

[? About 19 June.] 60. Memorial of Captain Thomas Scott to the King. Had under him the command of some of H.M. Ships in the Mediterranean and repaired to Algiers in 1721, and again in 1723, with instructions from His Majesty on several heads to be negotiated with that Government. Had the good fortune to accomplish the business agreeably to His Majesty's intentions, and for the advantage of the Trade of his subjects. It has been customary on affairs with the States of Barbary to make presents, and the Dey of Algiers intimating his expectations of that kind, memorialist, in his own name, made considerable presents to the Dey and his principal ministers, which facilitated the bringing matters to a prosperous issue. These negotiations led memorialist into extraordinary expense, besides the presents, and as he acted in a ministerial way, and foreign to his ordinary employment as Commander of H.M. Ships, he submits his case for Royal consideration.

Minuted:—" 19 June 1724. A w^t^ for 800^li^. Warr^t^ signd." 1 *page*.

[? About 22 June.] 61. Petition of Samuel Grey to the King. King Charles II. by lease in the 20th year of his reign granted to Henry, Lord Arlington, the manor of Mariebone (Middx.), and the park or late park, or enclosed grounds disparked, called Mariebone Park, for 60 years, at a rent of 36*l*. 14*s*. 6*d*., which will expire at Lady Day 1728. His late Majesty King William III. in the year 1696 granted the manor, park, and premises, to Charles Bertie, Esq., and others, as trustees for the then Duke of Leeds, from the death of the then Queen Dowager, for 31 years at a rent of 3*l*. 18*s*. 4¼*d*., which term commenced 2 Dec. 1705, the day of the death of the Queen Dowager, and will expire about 3 Dec. 1736. It is in his Majesty's power to grant such further term in the estate as, together with the remainder of the term granted to Charles Bertie, Esq., and others, will make up 31 years at the rent of 36*l*. 14*s*. 6*d*. Prays for a grant of the same.

Minuted:—" 19th May 1724. The Surv^r^ Gen^ll^ to make a particular in order for a lease."

Referred to the Surveyor General 22 June 1724. 2 *pages*.

25 June. 62. Report of the Com^rs^ for Salt (Scotland) to the Lords of the Treasury. It is referred to them to report on the petition of Robert Dalrymple, Esq., in behalf of the Earl of Wemyss, and on the state, nature, and forwardness of the proceedings against the Earl in the Court of Exchequer; and in case there be no objection, the reference directs process to be staid upon so much of the petition as relates to 6,962 bushels of native salt shipped at the harbour of Methel. Have previously reported thereon on 18 March 1717–8; and the Barons of the Exchequer also reported thereon on 31 Dec. 1719. For the reasons given, and as his Lordship now regularly accounts with their officers for the duties of all the salt he makes, they have no objection to the staying of process. Salt Office, Edinburgh, 25 June 1724.

Also the two reports referred to. 8 *pages*.

30 June. 63. Report of the Barons of the Exchequer of Scotland to the Lords of the Treasury on the memorial of Robina, Countess Dowager

1724. VOL. CCXLVII.

of Forfar on the behalf of John Lockhart of Lee. It appears that there is due to the Crown by the enfeofment of John Lockhart in January then last, "in the barony of Lee and others," as heir to James Lockhart, deceased, his late father, 75*l.* 0*s.* 9¼*d.*, which sum his Majesty may remit as desired.

Also the memorial.

Minuted:—"Warr[t] signd 30 July 1724." 3 *pages.*

VOL. CCXLVIII. JULY—DECEMBER.

---

3 July. 1. Papers connected with the accounts of Sir Alexander Brand of Brandsfield, for rents of Orkney and Shetland. The first is a letter from him, dated 3 July 1724, asking his correspondent to consider the enclosed papers and hear thereon Mr. Johnston, who was Secretary to King William at the time when he (Sir Alexander) served the government with his fortune, or that Mr. Scroop should talk to Mr. Johnston thereon. The second is an account of the charge and discharge of Sir Alexander Brand for the rents. The third is a copy of the reasons for the articles in Sir Alexander's account. The fourth is entitled: "An exact & faithfull abstract of a decree of the Court of Exchequer of the Kingdom of Scotland, pronounced against Sir Alexander Brand, for the arrears of the Crown and Bishop's revenues due & owing by him to her Majesty, conform to an obligation of farm, or a lease made & entered into by him for the Islands of Orkney and Zetland, &c." On the outside it states that it is for the years 1693, 1694, 1695.

There is also a printed paper relating to the affairs of "Bailly Brand" who in 1693 was recommended "to be Stewart and Justiciar of Orkney and Zetland in Robert Alphingston of Lapney's room."

Besides these are five other papers touching Sir Alexander Brand's affairs, one being a duplicate. 22 *pages.*

3 July. 2. A closely written paper (half being left for margin) entitled: "Memor. concerning the Equivalent Charter."

The first memorandum is: "The powers in this Charter being to chose Directors for management [are], to divide the Annuity which by Act of Parliament is payable quarterly, and to transfer the stock to natives, or foreigners, and to bodies politick, as well as to individuals."

The other memoranda relate to the stock, and to purchase and sale of it.

One of the observations made is: "That the operations here mencõned may effectually prevent the Stocks either becoming a bubble, or being blown upon, and settle the property in the hands of such as like to have their money estate sure, equal and marketable."

1724. VOL. CCXLVIII.

With the paper is a copy of a Resolution, dated 3 July 1724, at the meeting of the Directors of the subscribed Equivalent Debt recommending the appointment of the thirteen persons named to be the first directors in the "Charter for Incorporating the Proprietors of the Equivalent Debt." 3 *pages.*

6 July. 3. "Mr. Manning's memorial to the Lords of the Treasury about his bill of Extraord[ys], 16th July 1724."

The warrant for paying him 1200[li] in full, was ordered by the late Earl of Oxford, in the late Queen's time, and the annexed Bill of Extraordinaries was not signed and allowed till after his present Majesty's Accession, so that the Treasury could have no cognizance of it, and the words "in full" could only extend to what lay before the Treasury. The bill of extraordinaries has only lately been presented. Prays that the bill may be allowed. The bill was lost or mislaid by the late Mr. Powys and is for money laid out of a minister's own pocket for the public service. Believes this was never refused when transmitted to the Treasury by the Secretary of State's order. 6 July 1724.

Accompanied by another paper commencing "M[r] Manning her late Majesty's Secretary to the Republick of the Grisons, humbly craves allowance of the following summes by him expended from July 18th 1712 to July 18th 1713.

On the back of this is:—"18 Dec[r] 1713. M[r] Manning was paid 442[li] on his allowances as her late Ma[ts] Secretary to the Republique of Grisons to the 3[d] of August 1711, when he had direc̃ons signified to him to return home. And on the 17th Dec[r] 1714 he was also paid 1200[li] out of the late Queen's arrears in full satisfaction of all demands or pretenc̃ons which he had or might claim for any allowances or services by him performed there, after the time of his being recalled." 6½ *pages.*

[After 16 July.] 4. Memorial of Alexander Stevensone to the Lords of the Treasury on behalf of the Duke of Portland, Governor of Jamaica, in answer to objections raised against the revenue bill of Jamaica transmitted for his Majesty's approbation, as far as relates to the Public Revenue of the Island.

The objections answered are:—(1) The apprehended deficiency of the revenue; (2) the discharge of the debt. The opinion is expressed that the funds granted by the Assembly are amply sufficient. By the Duke's management the debt which, at his arrival, was 26,000*l.* is reduced to 9,800*l.*, and it is computed there will be an overplus of 6,000*l.*; (3) The lowering of the duties on indigo and sugar; (4) the contingency of an overplus; (5) the accounting by the Receiver General of Revenue to the Governor, Council and Assembly only, or "to a Committee thereof."

Accompanied by the copy of a letter from M[r] Scrope of the Treasury to the Com[rs] for Trade raising all the above questions. 3 *pages.*

17 July. 5. Report of M[r] William Tompson of H.M. Mint to the Lords of the Treasury on the petition of M[r] W French who prays to be

1724. VOL. CCXLVIII.

reimbursed, what he expended in taking up two coiners (Hicks and Miller) at Timsbury near Bristol, and for prosecuting them, and to be allowed the accruing charge in carrying on the prosecution. In favour of allowing him his charges about the prosecution. Mint Office, July 17, 1724.

Also the petition. 3 *pages.*

22 July. 6. J. Holbech to——. The laying the great annoyance of dust by watering the broadway before the Horse Guards and Whitehall is done at the instances of the several public offices, near adjoining, by a voluntary contribution; but this comes short of the real annual expense at least 30*l.* The Treasury ordered 20*l.* last summer towards the deficiency, but as the way is now opened to King St., Westminster, as wide as the old broadway, this has doubled the charge, "and there is only the Plantation Office (now removed) to give assistance to the encreased charge"; therefore he begs that their Lordships may be moved for payment of the 20*l.* for this summer's watering the old way, and that the additional charge may be represented to their Lordships occasioned by the width of the parade before the cockpit, which is not done for less than 50*l.* a year more. The whole expense comes to above 110*l.* per ann., but the contributions to the old work do not exceed 52*l.*; prays for some allowance to help this great deficiency for the future. 22 July 1724. 2 *pages.*

28 July. 7. Report of the Barons of the Exchequer of Scotland to the Lords of the Treasury on the petition of Sir Arthur Forbes of Craigyvar, Baronet. The part of petitioner's estate which holds ward of the Crown, is of about the yearly value of 88*l.* 7*s.* 6*d.* sterl.; and the other part of his estate is about 639*l.* 16*s.* 8*d.* sterl. The petitioner, being a minor of the age of twelve years at the death of his father (May 1722) his Majesty, by the law of Scotland, is entitled to the rents and duties during the minority; subject, however, to the entertainment of the vassal, in case he has no other estate. And on account of the ward lands, his Majesty is entitled likewise to two years value of the petitioner's whole estate, which is called the Casualty of Marriage. The debts affecting the estate are about 6,184*l.* sterl., together with annuities, &c. extending to 195*l.* 13*s.* 10*d.* so that "the avail, of the marriage" may be estimated at about 455*l.* 8*s.* 4*d.* sterl. The Crown has granted in some cases such casualties in favour of its vassals. 28 July 1724.

Minuted:—"17th March 1725. Agreed to."

Also the petition. 5 *pages.*

29 July. 8. Report of the Barons of the Exchequer of Scotland to the Lords of the Treasury upon the deduction of sixpence in the pound to be made out of certain payments mentioned in their Lordships warrant of 14 July 1724 which instructed them to examine into the execution of H.M. warrants to the Comrs, Receivers and other officers of H.M. revenues in Scotland, and to cause this deduction to be made. They would at their first meeting next term take this matter again into consideration. 29 July 1724.

1724. Vol. CCXLVIII.

Also a memorial of the Com[rs] of Customs, Edinburgh, referred to in the report. 5 *pages.*

[? About 31 July.] 9. Petition of Edward Norris of Speake in the county of Lancaster, Esq., to the Lords of the Treasury. Doctor Killegrew, late master of the Hospital of the Savoy demised to Thomas Norris, late of Speake, Esq., deceased, several lands in Garstange alias Garston in the co. of Lancaster (by estimation 20a. 2r. 20p.) at the rent of 4*l.* 1*s.* for three lives "which lives are now dead." Prays to be admitted tenant.

Minuted:—"31st July 1724. My Lords will not advise the granting of any Savoy leases." 1 *page.*

[? About 31 July.] 10. Petition of Richard Page, Esq., to the Lords of the Treasury. Petitioner's late father was surety for Thomas Perrin and Richard Gottley, merchants, on account of tobaccos imported, and upon their failure an extent was issued in 1712, and several estates of petitioner's father were seized; amongst others, the manor of Uxenden and other farms in the parish of Harrow-on-the-Hill, in the co. of Middlesex. Application was made to purchase the estates in Harrow for petitioner whilst he was a minor, which was refused. Mr. Huggins, warden of the Fleet Prison (from whence Mr. Perrin had escaped), being liable to answer to the Crown for the same, applied to purchase the crown title, to indemnify himself and bid 1,500*l.* for the same. The petitioner's guardians supposing the estates to be freehold (they being found to be so by inquisition in 1721) bid 1,200*l.* for the crown title. Since that, by an expensive trial, it has been found that the lands are copyhold and not liable to the debt; prays that the sale may be put a stop to, and that petitioner may purchase at a reasonable price.

Minuted:—"31 July 1724. My Lords, upon a report of this case, made by the Comm[rs] Customes, did, on the 10th June last, sign a warr[t] directing the Comm[rs] to cause the estates to be sold to the best bidder, towards discharge of the crown debt pursuant to the advice of the said Com[rs]; & do not see any reason to alter or revoke their said warrant." 2 *pages.*

[? About 31 July.] 11. An application to the Lords of the Treasury from John Sydenham, agent for his Majesty in connexion with:—

"An accompt of money due to his Majesty being the proceed of wreck goods taken up by virtue of a grant to Jacob Rowe, Esq."

Prays that his expenses (450*l.*) may be allowed.

Minuted:—"31st July 1724. The proprietors to lay an account of the King's $\frac{1}{10}$ before my Lords." 2 *pages.*

6 Aug. 12. Trustees of Forfeited Estates, Scotland, to the Lords of the Treasury. Have received a copy of a report made by the Barons of the Exchequer of Scotland in favour of a grant to be made to the children of the late Col. "Bellfour" out of the estate of Burleigh pursuant to a power given to his Majesty to make a provision for them out of that estate. 6 Aug. 1724.

1724. VOL. CCXLVIII.

The report of the Trustees referred to. 28 July 1724. Memorial of Margaret Balfour, eldest daughter of Robert, Lord Burleigh, deceased, and four other documents. 16 *pages and* 2 *halves.*

6 Aug. 13. Order in Council on the annexed report from the Lords of the Committee of Privy Council relating to the patent granted to William Wood, Esq., for coining half pence and farthings for Ireland; approving thereof, and ordering that the Lords of the Treasury give the proper directions, that he shall not coin or import into Ireland more half pence and farthings than 40,000*l.* Dated 6 Aug. 1724.

The report mentioned, and copies of three other documents on the same subject.

In one of these it is mentioned that a pound of copper is coined into 23 pence, and the intrinsic value of the copper per pound is 13 pence, in another that there was coined from Lady day 1723 to March 28, 1724, in half-pence 55 tons 5 cwt. ¾ qrs. and 12 ounces, and in farthings 3 tons 17 cwt. 2 qrs. 10 lb. 8 oz. avoirdupois. 60 half pence weighed 14 oz. troy, and eighteen pennyweights, and 30 farthings weighed 3 oz. 3 qrs. and 46 grains. The weight of old half pence in some previous reigns is given, and the inscriptions on the coin are given. 31 *pages and* 2 *halves.*

7 Aug. 14. Com[rs] for Salt Duties to J. Scrope, Esq. [Treasury]. Are surprised to find themselves censured for remissness in calling for their papers from the Treasury, it being their constant practice, when they send any representations or memorials to the Treasury, to order their messenger that delivers them, to inquire frequently for them, as they are assured he does. The memorials of 14 June and 21 Nov. 1723 were delivered into the Treasury Chambers at the times they were dated; and upon inquiry after them, some time afterwards, the messenger was told they could not find any such papers, and they (the Com[rs]) repeated the contents in a new memorial. As to the warrant on their memorial of 14 Jan. 1720, they could hear nothing of it, though frequent inquiry was made; but being at last informed that it was lost, they transcribed it into their memorial of 17 May 1722. Salt Office, 7 Aug. 1724. 1 *page.*

8 Aug. 15. Report of the Surveyor General (Pulteney) to the Lords of the Treasury, on the petition of Samuel Clark, Esq., praying for the grant of the lease of a parcel of concealed Low Marsh land, lying in the parishes of Hueish and Ham, or one of them, in the co. of Somerset, called Wagg Moor. The petitioner alleges that these lands are used without any claim of right by the inhabitants of the towns near thereto adjoining, as waste ground, in common to all of them. M[r] Auditor Jebb has certified that these lands have never been granted or leased, or in any charge before him. Thinks it his duty to encourage any discovery of this kind. Neither the Crown's title, quantity, condition, nor value appear in any inquisition, survey, &c. Cannot advise the grant of a lease thereof, until

1724. VOL. CCXLVIII.

enquiry has been made. A commission of enquiry is what has been usual in such cases; nevertheless in 1662 (in a case of concealed lands) finds a letter of enquiry in the nature of a commission was signed by the Lord Treasurer, Southampton, and directed to some of the principal gentlemen of that country, whereby they were in his Majesty's name authorized to inform his Lordship of the crown's title, &c. As the commission of enquiry would be expensive, recommends a similar letter to that last suggested to be sent. Upon the return to such a letter of enquiry a lease might be granted.

On the 6th of April last, on the petition of John Denew, merchant, and others, for a lease of other concealed lands in Somersetshire, he made the like report. 8 August 1724.

The petition referred to. 4 *pages*.

19 Aug. 16. Report of the Treasurer of the Chamber (Charles Stanhope, Esq.) to the Lords of the Treasury, on the petition of the Executors of Theodore Randue, Esq., late housekeeper of H.M. Palace of Windsor Castle. Cannot find from the office books that any allowance was ever paid to any person keeping the Garden House. Her late Majesty purchased the house and gave it to the Prince of Denmark, who placed Mrs Browne there as housekeeper at an allowance of 40*l.* a year. After his decease Her Majesty continued the salaries of his servants not otherwise provided for, and gave orders for placing this allowance upon the pension office, and she was paid until her decease. Before her Majesty's decease (Mr Browne being dead) she ordered Mr. Randue to take care of the house, and if an allowance shall be thought proper to be made to his executors, his Majesty's sign manual will be necessary. 19 August 1724.

Also the petition of the Executors.

Minuted:—"15th 8br 1724. There being no established allowance to the late Mr Randue, the Executors can have no claim upon the Crown." 3 *pages*.

29 Aug. 17. Comrs of Revenue (Ireland) to the Lords of the Treasury in reply to their Lordships letter of the 18th, together with the copy of the bond entered into by Mr Wood, patentee for the copper coinage for Ireland. Assure their Lps they never gave any orders to prevent the circulation of the half pence. As to their Lps commands to the Officers of Customs not to receive, in any one payment, above five pence half penny in copper coin, represent that, from the disorder this nation is in at present, about these half pence, and the declarations that have been signed by all sorts of people and published, they will not receive or utter them. They (the Comrs) are under the utmost difficulties how to execute the commands. The letter or order will be understood by their collectors and other officers as a strong intimation "that they are [only] to receive five pence half penny, or any less summ of ye said half pence in any one payment." Repeated pamphlets and papers, dispersed over the kingdom, have "inculcated into the minds of the people" that all the King's duties are to be paid in sterling money or current money of England. And though they apprehend that Mr Wood's half pence are

1724. VOL. CCXLVIII.

not intended by their Lordships to be paid otherwise than by way of change, yet the prejudice against them is such, that this argument will have but little force. They (the Com^{rs}) apprehend that if, by their orders, the collectors and other officers were obliged to take these half-pence, such orders would be thought arbitrary, and would bring a difficulty on the revenue, the whole nation thinking they may safely refuse them, the King having declared in his patent that none shall receive them but such as are willing. It is with extreme regret that they return any other answer than a ready compliance, and nothing but the public quiet of the kingdom and their apprehension of ill consequence to the revenue should hinder them from obeying; the uneasiness that people of all ranks are in, being greater than can be imagined by any that are not on the spot. Are not able to judge if the officers of the ports in England can be made to cheque Mr Wood, that he may not export above the 40,000*l*. mentioned; for they apprehend that, as the far greatest part of the current money in this kingdom is clandestinely exported from other countries, so it is to be feared that great quantities of this copper coin may be exported from England without the privity of any officer, as well as counterfeits of equal value with Mr Wood's coin exported from Holland and other places.

Custom House, Dublin, 29 Aug. 1724. 2 *pages*.

21 Sept. 18. Report of the Surveyor General (Wither) of H.M. Woods to the Lords of the Treasury, on the memorial of his Grace the Duke of Bolton, Lord Warden of the New Forest in the county of Southampton. His Grace thinks it for the advantage as well as for the beauty of the forest to make a riding between Burleigh and Lyndhurst, the change will amount to about 60*l*. The dotard and other trees will defray the charge. Is of opinion that the riding proposed will greatly contribute to the advantage and beauty of the forest, and that it will be of so great use that their L^{ps} will be importuned to cause other ridings to be made through the great thickets of the New Forest. Sept. 21, 1724.

Minuted:—"12th 8^{br} 1724. Agreed to."

The memorial referred to. 2½ *pages*.

21 Sept. 19. "Copy of a Resolution of the York Buildings Company in relation to the Annuitants. Sept. 21, 1724."

It is to the effect that Annuity Bonds which had been issued by "the Governor & Company of Undertakers for raising the Thames Water in York Buildings" for payment of annuities on Lottery prizes, should be charged on all the manors, lands, &c., belonging to the Company. 1 *page*.

22 Sept. 20. Memorial of John Pulteney, Esq., Surveyor General of His Majesty's Lands, &c., to the Lords of the Treasury, in relation to certain Exchequer leases of lands and tenements in Dringhouses, Middlethorp, and Beverley, in the co. of York, long since expired; the profits of which lands have been withheld from the Crown for about twenty two years. Suggests that steps should be taken for the immediate recovery of possession. Memorialist observes "As

1724. Vol. CCXLVIII.

the profits of these premises have long been withheld from the Crown for want of your Lordships being duly apprized of the expiration of the term for which they were granted, so may it reasonably be presumed that other Crown lands are wrongfully held over, by the tenants, after the determination of their respective leases; to the lessening of his Majesty's land revenue and to the endangering the loss of the lands, by their being long concealed; which I find to have been the case of some Crown Lands. For remedy whereof, if I had a due cognizance (in virtue of my office) of what Crown leases pass under seal, I should think it my duty to lay before your Lordships, from time to time, an account of all such leases as were expired or near expiring; but as nothing further appears in my books than the rating of the particulars; after which leases are sometimes dropped; and as other leases which pass under seal are many times made to commence from their several and respective dates, of which dates I have no cognizance whereby to know the certain times when these leases expire, therefore in my memorial of the 30th of May 1723 I humbly offered that the proper officers (with whom all Crown leases are, or ought to be inroled,) might be directed to lay before your Lordships a list of such leases for years, as were then expired, or were expiring," &c., "whereupon your lordships were pleased to give such directions accordingly," &c. 22 Sept. 1724.

Minuted:—"23 7^{br} 1724. Read & agreed." 2½ *pages.*

26 Sept. 21. Memorial of Hugh, Archbishop of Armagh, to the Lords of the Treasury, praying for an order to the Treasury in Ireland, to pay him the rents received by them from the time of his predecessor's death, and that he may receive the arrears. 26 Sept. 1724.

Minuted:—"30 7^{br}. Prepare the usual Warr^{t} if there is any preced^{t}." 1 *page.*

29 Sept. 22. [Ireland.] "Payments by warrants of concordatum from Christmas 1721 to Michaelmas 1724.

"Exam^{d} ꝑ John Pratt, Dep. Rec^{r} Genl."

At the end is: "His Majesties letters dated 8th August 1722 for allowing paym^{ts} made by warrants of concordatum over & above ye allow^{ce} on the Establishment of 5,000^{li} ꝑ annum clear'd that fund to Christmas 1721 & no further." 13 *pages.*

29 Sept. 23. A similar paper containing payments for military contingencies for the same time. 8½ *pages.*

[? 29 Sept.] 24. "Acco of the sums granted in Parliam^{t} to make good the deficiency of the general fond and of the supplys for the years 1722, 1723, & 1724." 2 *pages.*

29 Sept. 25. "An accompt of what has been received and paid for repairing the collegiate church of St. Peter Westm^{r} & chappels of the same between Michmas. 1716 & Michmas. 1724 out of the duties on coals." 1 *page.*

1724. Vol. CCXLVIII.

30 Sept. 26. "Certificate and memoriall of Jno Lawton relateing to the Records in the Exchequer 30 September 1724."

Certifies that since the 27th of July "three clerks, viz., Mr Stewart, Mr Smart, and Mr Longbridge have been employed in the Chapter House in brushing, making clean, and putting the rolls of the Court of Common Pleas of the reigns of Henry the 4th, 5th, 6th, Edward the 4th, and Henry the 7th upon dusted dry matts, about 40 of which rolls by reason of their having lain long upon matts on a damp stone floor, and seldom mov'd or dusted, are perishing, which have been separated from the rest and open'd for the benefit of the air.

"The above-named clerks are also emptying the chests wherein the aforesaid Common Pleas Rolls ought properly to lie, that therein the said rolls may be put, those chests having been fill'd with Star Chamber Records, which records, with a great heap of the same sort lying upon the chests, the clerks are now cleaning and putting into other places more convenient; that huge heap having been so exposed to dust and to the damps, occasioned by the broken windows, that many thereof are likewise rotting."

Asks that presses, &c. may be made for them and the windows mended and the roof repaired, and that some small necessaries may be supplied by the Ushers of the Exchequer, and for the payment of "the salary quarterly."

The office of the Custos Brevium being overstocked with writs of divers kinds, that office has given notice that the writs of the reigns of King Charles the 2d and King James the 2d are to be transmitted into the Court of the Receipts of the Exchequer, where there is not room fit to receive them. If their Lordships should think convenient to appropriate the two rooms where the old port books lie (which rooms were reported necessary to augment the conveniences for records in the Exchequer, by the Lords Committees, appointed to inspect the offices of records, who viewed them), and if their Lordships would direct shelves to be made in the rooms, the writs might be received.

Minuted:—"My Lords agree to this meml l as to his salary, but the other part relating to repairs to be consider'd." 1 *page.*

[After 29 Sept.] 27. "An accot of what was wanting at Michmas. 1724 to clear all fees and salaries payable at the Exchequer to that time." 2½ *large pages.*

[After 29 Sept.] 28. A similar account of what was wanting to clear pensions and annuities at the same time. 2 *pages.*

[After 29 Sept.] 29. "The debt to his Mats Foreign Ministers for one year and three quarters from Xmas 1722 to Michas 1724 being seven quarters."

Also "the names and characters of his Majesty's several Foreign Ministers, where residing, and the amount of their annual expence."

1724. Vol. CCXLVIII.

The following is the list of them :—

Charles Lord Whitworth at Cambray Alexander Lord Polwarth ibm Wm Stanhope, Esq. in Spain Horatio Walpole, Esq. at Paris	Ambassadors
John Molesworth, Esq. at Sardinia Wm Finch, Esq. in Holland	" Envoy & Plenipos."
Thos Lumley now Sanderson, Esq. Lord Glenorchy, Denmark Thomas Scot, Esq. —— Dubourgay, Esq., Prussia	Envoys extrary.
Thomas Dayrolle, Esq., States General Cyril Wych, Esq. with the Hans Towns Wm Leathes, Esq. wth the United Netherlands Robert Jackson, Esq. at Sweden Thomas Crawford, Esq. at Paris	Residents.
Charles Hudson, Esq. at Algier Benj. Lodington, Esq. at Tripoli	Consuls.
Robert Sutton, Esq. at Cambray Charles Holzendorff, Esq. at Madrid	Secretaries
Thomas Lascells at Dunkirk Mons. St Saphorin at Vienna Benj. Keen at Madrid	Agents at

Thomas Coleman, Esq. Resident to the Great Duke of Tuscany. 2 *pages.*

[About 30 Sept.] 30. " Representation and request of Thomas Acherley Gent." to the Lords of the Treasury. Has observed that in the dry summer of the year 1717 the demands for water increased so much that the owners of Hampstead water works increased and enlarged their ponds, declaring they should not want " tenants " if they could supply water. Conceived that all attempts to furnish water, except by another river, would be fruitless. Was acquainted with the River Colne at St Albans, and observed its great fall and the great length from St Albans to Staines, where it issues into the Thames. Guessed that the water lay high enough and in the winter of 1717, levelled the ground along the high road between St Albans and Hampstead ponds, and found that St Albans River lay as high as the highest steeple in London (except Paul's). Attempted to obtain an act of parliament in 1718, 1719, and 1720. A committee reported that the scheme was practicable and useful. A bill was brought in and read a first time and ordered to be read a second time: but the millers of Hertfordshire and others raised such an opposition that the bill was laid aside. To avoid the Hertfordshire millers, petitioner examined the river and found that all the brooks in Hertfordshire, viz., the Gade, Bulborne, Chesham Waters, and other Great Springs, all join the River Colne above Rickmansworth, and there make a vast river. And the Gultchwell springs in Middlesex run into the same River Colne, near two miles below Rickmansworth. Petitioner contracted with the owner of Gultchwell

1724. VOL. CCXLVIII.

springs, the level whereof he found high enough. Found that they yielded a quantity of water sufficient to serve plentifully all the western parts of Westminster and London. But one Mr Blackmore and others, grafting upon petitioner's invention, endeavoured to supplant him and pretended that waters might be brought from a branch of the River Colne, called Cowley Stream, which drives the powder mills at Hounslow Heath. They printed a plan for that purpose, and found friends in the session of parliament, 1720–21, sufficient to discourage petitioner's design and to embrace theirs.

Upon examination, their project was found impracticable, as the level was much too low, and their attempt was unsuccessful. Petitioner made a further attempt in 1722–23, but was still unsuccessful. Renewed his attempt in the sessions of 1723, and a committee reported it to be practicable and useful, as appears by a copy of their report annexed; but petitioner was again unsuccessful, because Mr Blackmore set up another plan, in imitation of the Gultchwell plan. Petitioner is advised that, although his design is the best and most practicable, and will accommodate a vast number of his Majesty's subjects, and will add not only great ornaments, but great conveniences to his Majesty's palaces of St James, Whitehall and Kensington; yet it is too difficult to be undertaken, without the encouragement and assistance of the Government, in relation to the passing of an Act, as was proved by the example of the New River; forasmuch as Sir Hugh Middleton and his partners could never make any considerable progress against the opposition they met with, until King James the First afforded them his countenance and assistance. That example is worthy of imitation in regard his present Majesty's subjects, who now want water, are as numerous as were those that wanted it above 100 years ago, and were supplied by the New River undertaking. Prays their Lordships to recommend the "invention" to his Majesty, to the end that an Act of Parliament may be obtained, and that he may be recompensed for his pains.

Accompanied by the report referred to, which gives some engineering and other evidence of witnesses as to the practicability of the scheme.

Also a nicely executed plan or map which appears to have been prepared by the petitioner.

Minuted:—" 30th 7br 1724. Read." 5 *pages.*

[? About 8 Oct.] 31. Petition of Sir John Vere Kennedy, Bart., to the Lords of the Treasury. His Majesty appointed petitioner's younger brother Andrew Kennedy, Esq., conservator of the privileges of the Royal Boroughs of Scotland in the Netherlands, upon the decease of petitioner's father (the late conservator), with whom petitioner was joined for twenty years. The grant of the office was given to petitioner's brother in express words for the subsistence of his and petitioner's mother and family; but, though his mother was dead and most of the family provided for, his brother had not afforded petitioner any relief. Has, however, received private and public relief from their Lordships; asks their Lordships to order a small sum to be paid to him for the support of his numerous family.

Minuted:—"8 Oct. 1724. Read."

Also a memorial from the same to the Rt Hon. Robert Walpole, Esq., one of the Lords of the Treasury, on the same subject. Undated. 2 *pages*.

10 Oct. 32. Report of the Surveyor General (J. Pulteney) to the Lords of the Treasury on the memorial of Edward Southwell, Esq., tenant to the Crown, for the greatest part, of Old Spring Garden, representing that many encroachments had been made on H.M. ground there by owners of property situate on the north side of the said garden; by reason whereof, there is not room for the turning of coaches that frequently attend on foreign ministers and other persons of distinction, who pass that way, to and from St James's Park; and memorialist is very much obstructed in going to and from his now dwelling house; therefore prays that these encroachments may be viewed and removed. Finds that the garden was formerly enclosed by a brick wall belonging to his Majesty; whereon the owners of the houses on the north side thereof have brought forward their fronts and struck out window lights to their ground rooms and also made doorways through the wall into their houses; as appears by several pieces of the old wall now standing with the copings thereon: they have likewise made areas to their houses, which are enclosed with rails; and have set posts upon his Majesty's ground. These encroachments ought not to have been made. The grievance may be redressed by obliging the encroachers to take away their posts and set their rails within two feet six from their houses; so as to leave room for coaches to turn in that part of the garden which lies nearest to the entrance into St. James's Park. Their areas, window lights, and doorways may continue as they are during his Majesty's pleasure only; and under such acknowledgment of his Majesty's right to the old wall, and the ground within it, as may be proper to preserve that right. In the like case in 1703 of encroachments on St. James's Park wall, the then Surveyor General proposed that every encroacher might have a lease of his encroachment, at a small rent by way of acknowledgment, but it does not appear that anything further was done; it being reasonable to believe that the great charge of passing an Exchequer lease, made such a proposal then impracticable; nor can he think it will be less so in the present case. Proposes that the owners should acknowledge their encroachment by an instrument in writing. Some vaults have been dug under this garden extending to the kennel or watercourse, which vaults belong to the houses inhabited by John Emery, vintner, and others. Suggests that leases should be made of these vaults. Specifies some other encroachments of a like nature there which ought to be forthwith removed. Upon notice to the persons concerned none, who attended the Surveyor, pretended to have had any licence or proper authority for the making of the encroachments. 10 Oct. 1724.

1724. Vol. CCXLVIII.

Minuted:—"6th 9br 1724. Agree to the Report. That part which he proposes to be held by a lease, vizt the wine vaults is agreed to." 5 *pages*.

14 Oct. 33. Address of the Presbitry of Abertarf to the King on the reformation of the Highlands of Scotland and the evangelization of the inhabitants thereof; laying before his Majesty the state of the bounds under their inspection, and what they judge most for the advancement of the glory of God, the peace of his Majesty's government, &c. The same (*i.e.*, the bounds) consist of five ministerial charges or parishes, some of which are twenty four miles in length, and twenty in breadth; the whole being about 150 miles in circumference, in which there are many papists and no legal schools, save what are settled by the Society for Propagating Christian Knowledge; so that these people cannot but be brought up in ignorance, and thereby become an easy pray to popish priests, jesuits, emissaries from Rome, and other disaffected persons. The General Assembly of this national church judged it one good expedient, for advancing true religion and his Majesty's interest, to erect four new presbyteries and a synod whereof their bounds are a part, &c. It is an absolute necessity that new parishes be erected, and more schools planted; and till this is obtained preachers of the gospel and catechists should be employed to instruct the people. And as their stipends are small, and no assistance to be expected in this poor country, they ask for some allowance from the royal bounty. King William and Queen Mary bestowed 30*l*. yearly as a salary for a schoolmaster at Fortwilliam; but the Bishop's rents out of which the same came, having been otherwise disposed of, that school sunk; to the great loss of the country. If it were re-established, it might prove of great use, not only for teaching literature, but also loyal principles. Have prevailed with Mr John Mc Bean, a person of piety, good literature, and loyalty, to take up that school; but if the salary be not punctually paid to him, he must soon give over. Pray for an allowance for maintaining preachers and catechists until some new parishes are erected: as likewise for the re-establishment of the salary of 30*l*. per ann. for the school at Maryburgh, payable to Mr John McBean. Abertarf, 14 Oct. 1724.

Referred to the Lords of the Treasury. 3 *pages*.

[? About 15 Oct.] 34. Petition of William Elphinston, gent., to the Lords of the Treasury, in relation to a crown debt of 200li besides interest for above 20 years, and the reversion of an estate of 250*l*. per ann. Petitioner in his own name took out administration, and prosecuted the suit for the Crown and others at his own expense; but finds that administration for the Crown will be of greater use in the prosecution of the suit. Is ready to renounce his administration to the Crown. Prays that he may procure administration for his Majesty's use and may have one half of what shall be recovered.

Minuted:—"15 Oct. 1724. Petn rejected and the King to be put to no charges about the same."

Also a previous memorial and report on the same subject. 3½ *pages*.

VOL. CCXLVIII.

1724. [? About 15 Oct.] 35. Memorial of Colonel George Douglass, Sir William Hope, Col. Geo. Somerville, William Steuart, physician general, and George Preston, surgeon, to the Lords of the Treasury. Were paid out of the Treasury of Scotland before the Union; but upon the Union, were, by royal warrant, placed upon the contingencies of the forces allowed upon the establishment of Great Britain, and continued to be so paid till 25 Dec. 1717. They were then postponed until 25 June 1720, when his Majesty, by warrant, continued their pay, which they still enjoy. By the deficiency of the fund, they are now in arrear two years and a half. Hope, as Capt. Walter Lockhart has lately obtained his allowance, that their Lordships will give directions to satisfy them.

Minuted:—"15 Oct. 1724. My Lords have no fund in their power to satisfye these arreares." 1 *page.*

24 Oct. 36. Report of the Surveyor General (Pulteney) to the Lords of the Treasury. As directed, had treated with Mr Chichley, secretary to the Archbishop of Canterbury, for the renewal of the lease of his Majesty's two barge houses, and the barge-master's house at Lambeth. On surrender of the existing lease of 13½ years, a new lease of 21 years was agreed to on payment of a fine of 25*l.* at the present rent of 40*s.* per ann.

Also letter from the Lord Chamberlain to the Lords of the Treasury for orders to be given for renewing the lease, and a letter referring the matter to the surveyor.

Minuted:—"6th 9br 1724. Agreed to. Prepare a warrant to the Recr of the Land Revenue of Surry for this sum."

There is also an earlier letter from the Vice-Chamberlain on the same subject. 4 *pages.*

Oct. 37. Report of Sir Isaac Newton to the Lords of the Treasury on a new double silver seal made by Mr James Gerard for his Majesty's Bahama Islands in America. It is made according to his Majesty's warrant. By an impression taken from it and kept in the Mint, finds the work to be very good, and the price of the silver and work is reasonable. "Mint Office, Octob."

Also a description of the seal delivered by the engraver to his Majesty in Council, with a note of its reference to the principal officers of the Mint for a report to be made.

Minuted:—"6th 9br 1724. Agreed to." 2½ *pages.*

17 Nov. 38. Representation of the justices of the peace of the shire of Clackmannan in Quarter Session, Nov. 17, 1724, to the Lords of the Treasury, commencing:—"Victual of the growth of Scotland being more than sufficient for the consumption of all the inhabitants thereof, several acts were past in the Parliament of Scotland for restraining the importation of victual of any sort, except in case of scarcity and dearth; and especially from Ireland where victual abounds, and which lyes near the western coasts, and the execution of these laws was committed to the justices of the peace, sheriffs, and other judges. And several particular commissions were granted

1724. VOL. CCXLVIII.

from time to time for guarding the said western coast, which had not the wished effect, till at last the Privy Council of Scotland did enter into a contract with certain persons of honour and interest, who became obliged to be answerable for every quantity of meal, less or more, that should happen to be imported to Scotland upon the western coast, under the penalty of the value of the victual so imported, and that should not be seized, or the importers duly prosecute. This contract was to endure for three years, and was execute with such fidelity and diligence, that very soon after the commencement thereof all importation from Ireland was effectually stopped, to the great satisfaction and advantage of all the heritors of Scotland, whose rents for the most part depend upon the sale of victual." The gentlemen who contracted with the Privy Council were at great expense beyond the Government allowance, and the extra expense was by Act of Parliament of Scotland of 3 March 1707 declared to be a public debt, and was paid accordingly, &c.

The contract not being renewed after the Union, the importation of victual from Ireland was not only begun as soon as the contract ceased, but whereas nothing but meal was formerly imported, for several years corns of all kinds have been imported in great quantities, and Ireland being a country that abounds with everything that is proper for the consumption of Scotland, black cattle and everything is brought plentifully. The country people on the coast find their advantage, and so encourage the importers that they are too hard for the judges or the Commissioners of Customs. The people have also enlarged their smuggling trade, and run immense quantities of brandy from Ireland and the Isle of Man. This smuggling being a great prejudice to the revenue, as well as grievous to all the heritors in Scotland, they (the magistrates) recommend a similar contract to be entered into, to that above referred to. Sir John Schaw, whose estate and interest lie upon the western coast, by whose activity and diligence the former contract was rendered effectual, would undertake again to serve. 1½ *pages.*

17 Nov. 39. Report of the Speaker of the House of Commons to the Lords of the Treasury on the petition of Paul Joddrell, Esq., Clerk of the House of Commons, praying to be paid 1,807*l.* 19*s.* 8*d.* for ingrossing public bills, making copies of bills, &c. for the service of the Treasury. Finds that the allegations are truly set forth. Submits that petitioner should be allowed 1,500*l.* for the services mentioned, and for keeping the journals of the House in a better manner than ever had been done by any of his predecessors, and for his faithful and diligent discharge of his duty as Clerk of the House of Commons since his Majesty's accession.

The petition and three other papers. 6 *pages.*

[? About 20 Nov.] 40. Petition of Lieut. Ralph Bethel to the R[t] Hon. Robert Walpole, Esq. Was the first that discovered, and gave information, of the intended insurrection and subversion of Government, at Oxford, in the beginning of the late Rebellion; and gave evidence against Gordon, Doril, and Kerr, who were convicted and executed

1724. Vol. CCXLVIII.

for receiving money from Adams, the cook, in Shoe Lane, for the Pretender's service. Was promised to be provided for, &c. Prays that some provision may be made for him.

Also a certificate touching petitioner's case.

Minuted:—"20th 9br 1724. See what has been paid to him by Mr Cracherode or any other person."

On the back of the paper are divers notes of reports by Mr Cracherode as to payments made to the petitioner. 3 *pages.*

25 Nov. 41. Report of the Surveyor General (Pulteney) to the Lords of the Treasury on the petition and case of Simon Mayne, Esq., so far as the same may relate to his having a lease of certain tithes [in Dinton, in the co. of Bucks] therein mentioned. Finds that soon after the Restoration these tithes were, by Act of Parliament, vested in the Crown, upon the attainder of petitioner's father, and that in 1662, a lease of them was granted to Sir William Smith for 31 years at the rent of 5*l.*, &c. States other circumstances in connexion with the above tithes which are issuing out of his own lands. Recommends a lease to be granted to the petitioner for 10½ years, to commence from Lady-day 1745, when the present lease will expire. 25 Nov. 1724.

Also the "case" and the petition. The former is *minuted:*— "Prepare a warrt for 200li." 4½ *pages.*

25 Nov. 42. Report of A. Cracherode to the Lords of the Treasury on the memorial of Mary, the wife of William Prust, praying for the remaining part of 149*l.*, being her husband's charges during the suit, depending in the Court of Admiralty, for the condemning of the ship "Revolution." Their Lps had ordered him 100*l.* and promised the remainder when the ship was sold. Prust and his wife came over from Genoa to give evidence. Recommends that the balance be paid. 25 Nov. 1724.

Minuted:—"25 Novr 1724. Out [of] money arising by old stores."

The petition and four other documents on the same subject. 7 *pages.*

1 Dec. 43. William Mowbray to ——. The Comrs for Stamp Duties have agreed to purchase the chambers and apartments in New Square, Lincoln's Inn, for the use of the Crown. It will be necessary to have the premises conveyed to trustees for the use of the Crown, and to have the trust declared, and also to have other trustees named for vesting certain long terms for years that are to be assigned for protecting the inheritance. Is directed by the Comrs to desire his correspondent to mention the affair to the Lords of the Treasury, in order to know who their Lordships would have named as trustees on behalf of the Crown, &c. Essex Street, 1st Dec. 1724. 1 *page.*

10 Dec. 44. Report of the Comrs for Hackney Coaches to the Lords of the Treasury on the petition of James Cooke. The allegations are true, viz., that it is petitioner's business to take care of the house

1724. Vol. CCXLVIII.

where the office is kept, to attend the Com^rs^ on board days, to take in the complaints brought against hackney coachmen and chairmen, and to give out orders for coachmen to have new numbered plates in case they are worn out or lost, and to measure such distances as may be disputed. His salary is 40*l.* per annum, and the allowance for measuring is hardly above 5*l.* per annum. Recommend an additional 20*l.* per annum. 10 Dec. 1724.

Also the petition. 2 *pages.*

10 Dec. 45. Petition from the same Com^rs^ to the same. Their salary was formerly 200*l.* per ann. The revenue from the 700 hackney coaches was then but 2,800*l.* per annum, and the Com^rs^ salaries were reduced to 100*l.* per ann. There are now 800 coaches each paying 13*l.* per ann., and 300 chairs each paying 10*s.* per ann. The revenue is 10,550*l.* per ann., besides fines for offences, usually amounting to 100*l.* per ann. The salaries and incident charges seldom amount to 1,500*l.* per ann. The revenue and trouble are both increased. The receiver and others have applied for increase of salary, which the Com^rs^ recommend. The Com^rs^ thankfully acknowledge his Majesty's bounty and their Lordships favour for their present salaries (150*l.* per ann.), but ask for an advance. Same date.

Minuted:—"Read. 19 8^br^ 1725." 1 *page.*

10 Dec. 46. Report of the same Com^rs^ to the Lords of the Treasury on the petition of Mr. Edward Wharton, as to an addition to his salary. Same date.

The petition referred to. 2 *pages.*

14 Dec. 47. Report of the Surveyor General (Pulteney) to the Lords of the Treasury on the proposed purchase of the estate of Mr Serjeant Darnell, consisting of a piece of ground in Windsor, whereon several coach-houses are built. Finds that the piece of ground agrees with Mr Negus's plan annexed. The buildings are slight and will cost about 600*l.* to fit them for his Majesty's service; and they may require to be rebuilt at the end of 20 years. In 1706 they were surveyed by the Surveyor General (Travers) and the Surveyor of Works (Sir Christopher Wren), and were valued at 2,200*l.*, exclusive of the ground, which Mr Serjeant says is worth about 700*l.* Mr Serjeant informs him (the Surveyor General) that he holds the same with other premises by lease from the Dean and Canons of Windsor for 40 years, renewable every 10 years, &c. Gives other particulars of the way the property is subleased, &c.

Finds by the entries in his office and by the annexed certificate of Mr Auditor Jett's deputy, that in the lease granted by King William, in 1695, of several parcels of land at Frogmore, in Windsor, and of a farm called Shaw Farm, there is a proviso whereby his Majesty may resume four acres, part of a close of eight acres, adjoining to Frogmore House, for the building of a mews there, whenever his Majesty shall think fit, &c. The timber necessary may be furnished out of Windsor Forest. Mr Negus says it will be necessary either to build a mews on his Majesty's ground, or to take a lease of Mr Serjeant's mews, there not being a sufficient number of stables and coach-houses to be hired at Windsor, for his Majesty's accommodation when the Court is there. 14 Dec. 1724.

Six papers, including a plan and a report by Mr Negus, connected with the subject of the above report.

Minuted:—"17th Decr 1724. Read vid. min." 12 *pages*.

15 Dec. 48. The vicar, churchwardens, and other gentlemen of the vestry of St Martin's in the Fields to John Scrope, Esq., one of the Secretaries to the Lords of the Treasury. Acknowledge the receipt of his letter announcing his Majesty's goodness in declaring that he will provide their new church with an organ at his own charge, for which extraordinary instance of his favour they are truly sensible, and it will be their constant endeavour to support the honour and interest of his Majesty and the Royal Family, as they have declared more at large in a minute entered in their vestry book. Have concluded an agreement with Mr Shrider, who is reputed a skilful and experienced organ builder, and serves his Majesty in that capacity; and whose draft of an organ for their new Church, and estimate of the charges of it, have been examined and approved of by the ablest and fairest judges. Fifteen hundred pounds will be necessary to comply with the agreement, and they beg that that sum may be paid to the Rev. Dr Pearce, their vicar. St Martin's in the Fields, 15 Dec. 1724. 2 *pages*.

19 Dec. 49. J. Burchett to the same. Has communicated to the Lords of the Admiralty the letter and papers touching the demands of Col. Philips, for building, manning, and maintaining a sloop for the service of the government of Nova Scotia. The Lords of Trade have given their opinion to the Lords of the Treasury that either a small ship of war should be appointed to attend the Colony, for the safety of the coast and prevention of illegal trade, or that the governor should be allowed the hire of a sloop for that purpose. The Lords of the Treasury being of opinion that the Governor Col. Philips's charges should be reimbursed by the Navy, he (Mr. Burchett) is commanded by the Lords of the Admiralty to say that they conceive the expense of the sloop ought not to be defrayed out of moneys granted for the Navy, and that when vessels have been fitted out by the Governors of his Majesty's Islands or Plantations abroad, the inhabitants have borne the charge thereof. Is further directed to say that when ships shall be sent to guard the Newfoundland Fishery, one of them will, as in the last year, be appointed to attend on Placentia and Nova Scotia, so long as the fishery doth last, for in the winter season no ship can be of any service in those parts by reason of the ice. Returns the papers and accounts.

Also the letter of the Board of Trade and "Journal of His Majesty's vessel the "William Augustus" in the service of the Government of Nova Scotia, for the perusal of the Rt Honble the Lords Commissioners for Trade, &c." 14 *pages*.

22 Dec. 50. Lord Lieut. of Ireland (Carteret) to the Lords of the Treasury. Transmits a memorial from Thomas, Lord Southwell, praying

1724. Vol. CCXLVIII.

for a pension of 400*l.* per ann. Recommends his Lordship as a person very deserving of his Majesty's favour. Dublin Castle, 22 Dec. 1724.

The petition referred to. States that petitioner's father, who was a zealous promoter of the establishment of the Palatines in Ireland, granted leases for three lives to them upon his estate in the county of Limerick, by means whereof they have become a flourishing Protestant Colony. Petitioner's father was mistaken in his notion of the power given him by his marriage settlement, he being thereby enabled to grant leases for no longer term than 21 years. Memorialist, for the strengthening of the Protestant interest, and in compassion to the distressed strangers, was willing (although to his great loss) to confirm their leases, although he might lawfully have avoided the same.

Five other papers relating to the same matter.

There is a long docket on the back ending :—"it does not appear that Lord Southwell put other tenants out, to let the Palatines in; but if so, all loss seems to be repaired by the 1451li. paid as above [*i.e.*, out of the revenues of Ireland]. Planting people on an estate savours much more of improvement than loss. The loss here is said to be 192li. 7*s.* ꝑ ann. Yet 400li. ꝑ ann. pension proposed; tho' the real yearly value of the whole estate, supposing it had been set without loss, is but 463li. 17 ꝑ ann." 12½ *pages.*

31 Dec. 51. Comrs of Forfeitures to John Scrope, Esq. Send, in answer to his letter, an abstract of the accounts transmitted to the Lords of the Treasury from Scotland "between the York Buildings Company and the public." Touching claims on the estates bought by the Company. 31 Dec. 1724.

Also the abstract referred to. 7½ *pages.*

[? 1724.] 52. Memorial of the managers appointed to take in and enter the tickets of the Lottery 1723, and deliver out certificates in lieu thereof, to the Lords of the Treasury. The office has a complicated work to perform, and the managers have not only expended the 600*l.* ordered on 6 Dec. 1723, but the further sum of 21*l.* 2*s.* 0½*d.* Ask for a further sum of 600*l.* for incidents.

Minuted :—"Wt signed." 1 *page.*

[? 1724.] 53. Memorial of the late Comrs of the Forfeited Estates in England to the Lords of the Treasury. The Governor and Company for raising Thames water in York Buildings, contracted with memorialists for the purchase of part of the Lord Widrington's estate in the county of Northumberland for 57,000*l.* The Company have not completed their contract, but have paid money on account. There was due to the public on 25 Dec. 1723, 8,930*l.*, and for interest unpaid 4,948*l.* 6*s.* 10¾*d.*, besides interest for the 8,930*l.* from 25 Dec. 1723.

Also the copy of contract and account. 4 *pages.*

[Perhaps 1724 or 1725.] 54. Memorial of John Sydenham to the Lords of the Treasury. Has ever since Sep. 1, 1723, attended their Lordships, and prays to be reimbursed for his expenses in attending expeditions on

1724. Vol. CCXLVIII.

wrecks to the amount of 459*l.* 10*s.* Is out of pocket 249*l.* 19*s.* 7*d.* It was their Lordship's intention that he should have 5*l.* per cent. on the whole, but by a mistake of the clerk, he has received no more than 10*s.* per cent., by which he will lose above 830*l.* Prays payment.

Also the account. 4 *pages.*

[1724.] 55. Schedule of sums payable, or paid, to persons engaged at the Congress of Cambray about the "Treaty of Cambray." [? During the year 1724 after April.] 1¼ *pages.*

1724. 56. Memorial of the late Com^rs and Trustees for the sale of Forfeited Estates in England to the Lords of the Treasury, praying payment of half a year's salary. The power of selling the estates determined at Michaelmas 1723; but other powers continued and they had to attend above six months later. (Signed.) 1 *page.*

1724. 57. Another petition from them for a quarter's salary. 1 *page.*

[1724.] 58. Petition of Joseph Cagnoni, James Antonio Migliorucci, and Anthony Francis Bartolini, merchants. Are natives of Florence, and reside in London for trade purposes. By the late Act, intitled "An Act for granting an aid to your Majesty as well by a land tax, as by several subsidies and other duties payable for one year," petitioners are not exempted from taking the oaths of allegiance and supremacy, or paying double taxes. Pray that the Com^rs or assessors of the duties in London may exempt them from paying the double taxes. English merchants living in Leghorn and Florence are never required to take any oaths, nor are subject to forfeiture or double taxes. [1724. The Act passed in that year. See *Historical account of Taxes under all denominations, page* 370.] 1 *page.*

1724. 59. "A plann of Port Royall in South Carolina 1724." 1 *double page.*

[1724.] 60. Memorial of the R^t Hon. Charles, Earl of Arran, to the Lords of the Treasury. A pension of 5,000*l.* per ann. was granted to James, Duke of Ormond, for 15 years from Midsummer 1713, to pay his debts, &c., which pension was assigned to Archibald Hutcheson, Esq., John Cotton, Esq., and Alexius Clayton, Gent., for securing several of the Duke's debts. The Duke was attainted of high treason, and his estates vested in Com^rs. Memorialist is declared purchaser of all the estates for 50,000*l.*, subject only to such debts as are charged thereon. At Mich. 1721 the arrears of the pension were sufficient to pay the debt of 30,244*l.* 10*s.* 2½*d.* Prays that the 21,136*l.* 8*s.* 4*d.* still due to Hutcheson and the others may be paid. Memorialist is willing to discharge the remainder of the 50,000*l.* purchase money. 1 *page.*

1724. 61. "Memorial of the three Macers of the Court of Justiciary in Scotland 1724" to the Lords of the Treasury. Pray for payment of their salaries at 5*l.* a year reported on in 1720 and since unpaid,

1724. VOL. CCXLVIII.

and also for 99*l.* 7*s.* 9*d.* for serving criminals with indictments, summoning juries, &c.

Also copy of a report of the Barons of the Exchequer of Scotland on the same subject. 2 *pages.*

[? 1724.] 62. Memorial of Sir James Mackenzie, of Roystoun, Sir William Calderwood, of Poltoun, and David Erskine, of Dun, three of the Judges of Justiciary, to the Lords of the Treasury. "By the eldest laws in Scotland, the Justices General and his Deputies are bound to hold the Justice Airs, or Circuit Courts, twice in the year, viz., spring and harvest. By Act 3 Sess. 3 Parl. Ch. 2, entitled Act for regulation of Judicatories, the Court of Justiciary is to consist of the Justice General, Justice Clerk, and five Lords of Session, and all of them invested with the same and equal jurisdiction and power in all criminal causes. By the same Act circuit courts are to be kept once a year," &c. "Until the Union these Courts were not regularly kept," but upon the Union, the old laws were revived, and each of the judges had an allowance of 200*l.* sterling, for charges of each circuit. By Act 10 Anne the circuit courts were to be kept once a year, and by subsequent establishments each judge was only allowed 100*l.* Upon the death of Sir Gilbert Elliot, of Minto, who died in the beginning of May, 1718, Sir James Mackenzie kept the western circuit alone. Relate other instances of the circuits being kept alone. The judges are at great charges, and when one judge goes and keeps the courts the charge is equal to when both go.

The pension of the five judges is no more than the old salary of 100*l.* per ann. to each. Pray that his Majesty will order each of them the other 100*l.* Also pray that when they go the circuits alone, they may have their colleagues' allowance. [? 1724. His Majesty's letter of 16 March 1723 is mentioned.] 3 *pages.*

[? 1724.] 63. Memorial of Walter Chetwynd, Esq., Paymaster of H.M. annual pensions and bounties, to the Lords of the Treasury. Is accountable at the Exchequer for sums under 30*l.* per ann., and for charities, and the annual sum of 15,000*l.* payable to the French Protestants. Prays payment of the poundage paid by him at the Exchequer at 6*d.* in the pound, amounting to 2,505*l.* 9*s.* 1*d.* [After Christmas 1723.] 1 *page.*

[? After 1724.] 64. "Sir Alexander Anstruther's case."

Upon the "information given against him in October 1724 for washing and diminishing the coin of the Kingdom, he was removed from the Fleet (where he lay for a debt due to Mr Christie) to Newgate, where he has remained ever since, in a deplorable condition, having been put among the common malefactors," he was exposed to hardships which at his advanced age have brought so many infirmities upon him, that his life is in great danger. His Majesty having pardoned him his crime, a warrant was signed by the late lords justices, but the signing of the bill was stopped on account of a dispute between the warden of the Fleet and Mr Christie, as to whether Sir Alexander would not be freed from

1724. VOL. CCXLVIII.

the debt by the pardon. Prays that he may enjoy the benefit of the pardon, and that he may be "relieved" out of Newgate, where he now is in irons. 1 *page.*

[Between 1721 and 1725.] 65. Copy of a letter of the Lord Chancellor (Macclesfield) to the Lord [Chief Justice?]. His Majesty has declared his desire that advantage should be taken of the yearly meetings of Parliament, to frame useful laws for the benefit of his subjects in their private property and commerce, and for the encouragement of industry and the easy redress of fraud and oppression, and that the annual provisions for securing the public peace may be constantly accompanied with one or more of such laws. As the exercise of the royal authority in the administration of justice is in so great a degree deposited with his Lordship, and the rest of the Lords, the Judges, and as his Lordship's wisdom and experience must discover what are the defects, and what may be the improvements of the laws in being, and as his Lordship is considered to be his Majesty's counsel in affairs of that nature, his Majesty signifies his pleasure that his Lordship shall consult with the rest of the judges, and consider what alterations in the old laws or additions of new ones (relating to property, contract, frauds or the administration of justice, or other heads, which may occur to him) may be of public service, and prepare the same for the consideration of Parliament. This may prove a long and difficult work, and his Majesty is far from expecting it to be done at once; but his pleasure is that it be immediately set about, so that something may be offered to the approaching session, and so successively in every session till the whole shall be accomplished. Leaves it to his Lordship's discretion, but there is one particular which he (the Lord Chancellor) has often reflected upon as requiring especial attention, and that is the Law of Executors, which now stands so that it is difficult for an honest executor to be safe, or for a dishonest one to be brought to justice. Wishes it should be taken into consideration as soon as convenient, but does not expect it this session. Their Lordships will probably begin with something which may be sooner perfected. Undated, but between the creation of Lord Macclesfield 1721 and the end of his Chancellorship, Jan. 4, 1725. 2 *pages.*

[? About 1724.] 66. Petition of Martha, widow and administratrix of Robert Inwood, deceased, to the Lords of the Treasury. Petitioner and her husband were at the Court of St Germains in the service of King James after his abdication, and before the plot to assassinate King Will. III. Her husband had very great advantages of being let into the secrets or mystery of the affairs then and there contriving against King William. On his return to England, caused a full discovery of these plots, and in pursuance thereof Thomas Pyke and others were convicted of high treason and executed, and sundry noblemen's estates "were confisticated" through petitioner's husband's information. For his services he received a pension of 50*l.* per ann. Her husband died in Feb. 1722, leaving four children. Asks for their Lordships' bounty. 1 *page.*

1724. VOL. CCXLVIII.

[Undated, but ? 1724.] 67. Petition of the Hon. Janet Ker, *alias* Murray, widow and sole executrix of Lord Charles Ker, late director of his Majesty's "Chancellary" in Scotland, in behalf of herself and her eleven fatherless children, to the Lords of the Treasury: praying to be paid the losses sustained by her husband since the Union: viz., at 143*l*. 7*s*. 9½*d* a year from 1 May 1707 to 10 March last (the time of her husband's death), amounting to 2,417*l*. 12*s*. 7*d*. Undated but the amount would show it to be seventeen years after 1707.

Enclosing copy of an earlier petition and report. 4 *pages*.

[? 1724.] 68. "A state of the case as to Mr Townley, the late cashire of the Wine Licences," apparently submitted for counsel's opinion to ascertain if the Comrs could proceed against him and the heirs of Moor, his surety, so as to get judgment. Undated, but after July 1724. 3 *pages*.

[Perhaps 1724.] 69. [Anonymous] to Rt Hon. Robert Walpole, Esq. Encloses for consideration the case of Francis Sirr, a silk merchant in St Clement Danes, who was defendant in an action against John Snow, an informer. The offence charged on the defendant was receiving run goods. Undated, but apparently before Walpole was made a Knight, and after 1722–3. 6 *pages*.

VOL. CCXLIX. 1724. CLASSIFIED. PART 1.

1. Particulars of the causes under prosecution with the states thereof. Prepared by A. Cracherode, showing the name of the plaintiff and defendant in each cause and an epitome thereof. 31¼ *pages*.

2. Two accounts connected with the Treasurer of the Chamber's department and a letter relating to the defraying "the expense of the ensuing Maundy." 11 *pages*.

3. Letters from the Lord Chamberlain and Vice-Chamberlain of the household to the Lords of the Treasury, viz.: (1) for payment of 5*l*. a week to his Excellency Hag Abdeleader Perez, Ambassador from the Emperor of Morocco for his diet; (2) for 300*l*. for Mr Kent, who had finished the Presence and Council Chambers ceilings, in grotesque painting, according to the designs shown to his Majesty; (3) for 500*l*. to Sir Clement Cotterell, Master of the Ceremonies, as a present from his Majesty to Mons. Chavigny, Envoy Extraordinary from France; and (4) for 500*l*. to the Ambassador from the Emperor of Morocco, and 100*l*. each to his companion and secretary, and 50*l*. for clothing for the Ambassador's slaves. 5 *pages*.

1724. Vol. CCXLIX.

4. Various papers connected with the Civil List; principally accounts of the debt. 11 *pages.*

5. Reports of the Com[rs] of Customs to the Lords of the Treasury, including letters from their Secretary: (1.) On the memorial of the Earl of Cadogan for exemption from customs, of four small pieces of hangings after the manner of Tenniers, and two pieces of the History of Jupiter, from Holland; which served as furniture in his house at the Hague, when he was ambassador there. [The Com[rs] have no objection thereto.] (2.) On the petition of Richard Page, whose father was seised of certain lands in the parish of Harrow, Middlesex; petitioner was seised of lands for life and copyhold there, &c. His father was security for certain tobacco merchants who failed, and an extent was issued against his father, and a second extent against petitioner's copyhold lands: prays for stop of prosecution. A trial of the case was recommended to ascertain if any of the lands are copyhold. [*Minuted*:—"Process to be stayed till the next issuable term. Lre writ. 15th Febr[y] 1723."] (3.) On the petition of Bridget, wife of W[m] Botting, of Nuthurst (Sussex), for a reward for discovery of certain persons who assaulted the Officers of Customs of the port of Lydd. (4.) Letter and memoranda as to Treasury fees for London and out-ports and Plantation Establishment. (5.) Enclosing "list of superannuated officers at pension." (6.) On the baggage of Count Staremburgh, the Emperor's Ambassador, and Mons. Chavigny, Envoy from the Court of France. (7.) On the memorial of the Com[rs] of Customs in Scotland relating to the impresting money by the Receiver General, at Edinburgh, to the Collector of port Glasgow. *Minuted:*—"Agreed to. Warr[t] signed 21st May 1724." (8.) On the petition from William Broderick, Esq., late Attorney General of the Island of Jamaica, for a reward for his services. (9.) On M[r] Rogers' bills for expenses in suppressing smugglers and owlers. [*Minuted*:—"War[t] signed in full of all his demands."] (10.) Memorial (without report) relating to a warrant issued for John Brown to be collector of Pocomock in Maryland. [*Minuted*:—The Com[rs] to grant y[e] deputation to Brown. Letter signed 14 July 1724.] (11.) Laying before their Lordships an account of the produce of the revenue, viz., the further subsidy of tonnage and poundage and other duties, &c. 64 *pages or parts of pages.*

6. Memorials of the Com[rs] of Customs for Scotland to the Lords of the Treasury:—(1.) About the establishing of officers at Glasgow Town, &c. [*Minuted*:—"13th May 1724. To Comm[rs] Cust. in Scotl. to use their endeavours with the magistrates & merch[ts] of Edinburgh & Glasgow to make them agree to the continuance of the execution of this method for another year & that the officers presented in this mem[ll] are to continue to act in the same manner & to be paid in the same way they now are for the time this method shall be continued."] (2.) On the neglects of M[r] Charles Eyre, solicitor to the Board. He has been one great occasion that the provisions of law against clandestine trade have

been eluded, and advantages given to the unfair traders openly to insult the officers of the revenue and carry on their illegal designs with impunity. Recommending his dismissal and the appointment of Mr Peter Wetherburne, advocate, practising in the Exchequer Court. (3.) For a clause in an Act to be obtained to restrain the extravagant number of landing places in use in Scotland. (4.) On taking illegal fees from the merchants. Have discovered "that a great scene of fraud and corruption has been carried on by several of the officers at Leith. The salaries are so low that there is a temptation to accept bribes. Advise that the officers should have better encouragement, and that instead of the five land-waiters on the present establishment at 35*l.* per ann., and two coast-waiters at 25*l.* each, the office of coast-waiter, as distinct from land-waiter, should be sunk, and instead thereof, four land-waiters and two coast-waiters be appointed land-waiters and coast-waiters at 45*l.* per ann. each, and some other minor changes. Propose also to fill up vacancies from the outports, to make the officers more vigilant, and less liable to corruption, from the expectation of preferment to a better salary. (5.) For sinking the officers on the establishment of Lewis and Campbeltown. (6.) On the repeated complaints from the officers of Glasgow Town that they are not only insulted by the common people in the execution of their duty, but that the provost there, with some of the justices of the peace, instead of supporting them, have in several instances made use of their authority to obstruct them. "As such proceedings are contrary to law, and as these magistrates assume a power of determining seizures which the law vests in the Court of Exchequer only", they are advising with the Lord Advocate as to the method they can be most effectually prosecuted, and accordingly shall proceed against them as far as the law will permit. (7.) Concerning the Receiver General's office. (8.) On the Order of Council of 21 June 1714, "that no person is to be admitted into any employment in the customs in any of the out ports of Great Britain who are inhabitants in such out ports," proposing for the better service of the revenue, to revive that practice in future presentments to their Lordships for supplying vacancies. [*Minuted:*—"24th 9br 1724. My Lords concur with their presenting."] (9.) Encloses copy of the opinion of the King's Advocate upon the obstruction of the Justices of the Peace, offered to the officers at Glasgow Town in the execution of their duty. His opinion is "that there is no law obliging merchants to take permits, by reason whereof the justices cannot be prosecuted." Also two other papers on the same subject. One being a representation of the justices of the peace for the shire of Edinburgh [which is in the same terms as that of the justices for the shire of Clackmannan noticed in this Calendar under 17 Nov. 1724]. 42 *pages.*

7. Estimates of extraordinary and other expenses connected with the land forces; also an estimate of the charge of the office of ordnance. (The last document is in duplicate, but one copy has an additional signature.) 8 *pages,* 13 *lines.*

1724. VOL. CCXLIX.

8. Reports of the Com[rs] of Excise to the Lords of the Treasury relating to :—(1) receipts from the "duty on malt for the Lottery 1722"; (2) the smugglers concerned in "the murder of Purchase," who were skulking about Shaftsbury and whose number was so great that the civil magistrates dared not, without a military force, execute the warrants granted for apprehending them. Also relating to the dragoons lately ordered to Blandford, who are now planted one half at Pool and the other half at Christ Church, where they are not serviceable; (3) the troops last mentioned as at Pool and Christ Church: advising that they should remain there; and that other forces should be placed at Shaftesbury. [*Minuted*:—"Lre writ to Secry at Warr"]; (4) the time the several revenues under their care, which are applicable to the payment of the Civil List, take to adjust. The computation of the half-yearly produce of the revenues applicable to the Civil List should be made from the half-yearly payments into the Exchequer, and not from the half-yearly estimates; (5) the several accounts of the produce of the hereditary and temporary duties of excise; (6) warrants of distress issued against several persons at Yeovill, against whom judgments had been obtained for resistance to the officers. The constables will not assist in the execution of the justices' warrants. The method taken for avoiding payment of the duties on cider has been for private persons to retail their cider, and receive money for it under colour of selling apples and other things for ten times their value, and pretending that the cider is given them for nothing. 27 *pages*.

9. Papers relating to fees received at the Treasury for three disjointed months. 10 *pages*.

VOL. CCL. 1724. CLASSIFIED. PART II.

1. Various financial papers, including "an abstract of the produce of his Majesty's revenue in Ireland," income of the Aggregate Fund, payments to the South Sea Company on their increased capital, produce of the hereditary and temporary excise, &c. 21 *pages*.

2. A series of abbreviates of accounts by Sir Robert Sinclair, Bart., Receiver-General in Scotland, of receipts, payments, and remains of the rents and profits and sale of the forfeited estates in Scotland. 1 Jan. to 28 Nov. 1724. [There are some, perhaps, missing.] 14 *pages*.

1724. VOL. CCL.

3. Forfeited estates, Scotland.

Two accounts relating to the purchase money of the estates of (1) Fingask, and (2) Southesque and Linlithgow. 2 *double pages.*

4. Five letters from the Com^{rs} of the Navy to the Secretary of the Treasury, and one from them to Mr. Burchett, Secretary to the Admiralty: viz. :—

(1 and 2.) On the debt of the Navy. (3.) To Mr Burchett. Observe that by the votes of the house of Commons, Sir John Evelyn is about to purchase of the King the inheritance of certain lands and tenements in or near Deptford, Kent. Have ordered the officers of Deptford to give their opinion what ground is absolutely necessary to be added to the yard. This they have done. Agree with their sentiments, that if nine acres of meadow land were joined to the yard, and the way to Sir John Evelyn's house removed, it would render the yard much more commodious and safe. Sir Dennis Gawden, in 1681, granted a lease to his Majesty of about 2½ acres of land adjoining the dock by the water-side for 36 years, at 5*l.* per ann., and 100*l.* fine, the same being held of Mr Evelyn, and as that lease began to wear out, the Navy Board began to treat for the purchase thereof. Large and unreasonable sums were demanded, particularly 5,000*l.* for a lease of 51 years. No agreement was concluded till 1712, when 2,050*l.* was agreed to be given for the fee-simple. Nevertheless, they are in doubt whether this may not, as well as the other nine acres (necessary to be joined to the yard), be part of the lands Sir John Evelyn is suing for the inheritance of; and if so, they propose that both may be reserved for his Majesty's service: or if these are parcels of his own land, that some consideration may be made to him for the nine acres of meadow, in case the Act passes. (Copy dated 13 March 1723/4.) Also the copy of the letter from the officers of H.M. yard at Deptford on the same subject. (4.) On the memorial of Sir Barnham Ryder. Find that there is about 3½ years to come of the lease held from him on behalf of his Majesty for the house in which one Naval Treasury Office is kept. The rent is 160*l.* The last fine upon a lease of 21 years was 1,333*l.* 6*s.* 8*d.*, &c. Ask that the memorial may be laid before the Com^{rs} of the Treasury, as Sir Barnham's inclination is rather to dispose of it to his Majesty than to any other purchaser. The Com^{rs} think his demand is great. If this cannot be had on reasonable terms, some other place might be timely secured. The letter encloses Sir Barnham's memorial. [*Minuted*:—"3 Nov. 1724. Lre. to Navy hereupon." (5.) On the debt of the Navy, also two States of the debt of the Navy. (6.) Enclose copy of the opinion of persons ordered by them to take a survey of the house in Broad Street used for the office of the Treasurer of the Navy. Mr Ryder, Sir Barnham's brother, was entitled to treat for the sale, and offered it at 8,250*l.*; estimating the house at 330*l.* per ann. and at 25 years' purchase. The Com^{rs} thought this very extravagant, and Mr Ryder reduced it to 23 years' purchase (7,590*l.*). The Com^{rs}' surveyors

1724. Vol. CCL.

valued it at 3,236*l.* Mr Ryder would not further reduce the 7,590*l.*, but offered to treat for a renewal of the lease. The copy of the survey of the house. 17 *pages.*

5. Three memorials from the Paymaster-General's Department to the Lords of the Treasury for payments for victualling Gibraltar, for guards and garrisons, and for remittances for Minorca and Gibraltar. 4 *pages.*

6. Three applications from Mr Francis Negus to the Rt Hon. the Chancellor of the Exchequer for the issue of money for the extraordinary expenses of H.M. stables. Also an account of the debt of the same. 6 *pages.*

7. A broken series of warrants to the Master of the Great Wardrobe and his deputy, for delivery of articles out of the Wardrobe. Numbered between 3 and 39, with many breaks. Also two other papers relating to the debt of the Great Wardrobe. 21 *pages or parts of pages.*

8. Various papers relating to the business carried on by the Office of Works. They include charges "for his Majesty's busts and pedestals sent to Hanover," for works at Royal palaces, public offices, and buildings, for works at St James' Park, for watering the roads in Hyde Park, for expenses of Mr Nicholas Du Bois, H.M., master mason employed abroad in H.M. service, for repairs in Bushey Park (damaged by the late high winds), for repairs at the mews at St James's, for alterations at Windsor, and for expenses of Mr John Stourbridge, "chief clerk of H.M. works." 20 *pages.*

9. Eight carefully drawn reports to the Lords of the Treasury made by Robert Paul, Richard Sankey, and Samuel Kettilby, appointed to make a general survey of the Ports in Scotland. There is the following table of contents at the beginning :—

"Report No 1. The course of our Survey and the method of our proceedings at the several Ports. Copys of directions suited to reform & instruct the officers in their ordinary business, prepared & left with the commissioners at Edinburgh, to be observed by the officers for the future.

"Report No 2. A list of officers whom we found unfit for the service, by age, infirmity or otherwise, with our reason for the same.

"A List of officers proposed to be removed to other ports and of officers proper to be removed from other ports to supply their places.

"Observations on the conduct of some officers whom we think very censurable.

"Report No 3. A list of officers who have neither taken the oath of office or oaths to the Government.

"A list of officers who have taken the oath of office, but have not taken the oaths to the Government.

1724. Vol. CCL.

"A list of officers who have taken the oaths to the Government, but have not taken the oath of office.

"The occasions from whence the said neglect of taking the oaths proceeded.

"Report N° 4. The method which had been practiced in discharging tobacco at Port Glasgow, Greenock, and other ports.

"The care taken in the discharge of the tobacco imported into Scotland in the year 1723.

"The method practiced in exporting tobacco to foreign ports.

"The practice of sending tobacco coastwise and by land carriage into England and the method of granting permits.

"Report N° 5. Frauds practiced in importation & exportation of wines.

"Frauds practiced in importation & exportation of all other goods besides wines and tobacco.

"Frauds in goods brought & sent coastwise from Scotland to England & from England to Scotland & from port to port in Scotland.

"Merchants who have endeavoured to corrupt the officers.

"Officers who have been deforced & abused in the execution of their duty.

"Sources & springs of the said frauds, corruptions & abuses.

"Report N° 6. Alterations humbly proposed of ports, members, creeks & keys.

"Alterations in the stations & boats & officers on the coast and what additional boats & officers are necessary.

"The usefulness of sloops & where proper to be stationed.

"Further regulations or remedies humbly proposed for the service of the revenue.

"Report N° 7. Observations on examining the officers belonging to Newcastle, Berwick & Carlisle with respect to goods passing into England over the borders.

"Additions & alterations humbly proposed of officers on the borders.

"Final Report N° 8. Observations concerning fees taken by the officers in Scotland.

"A Table of fees humbly proposed to be establish'd.

"The close of the whole." 121 *pages.*

VOL. CCLI. 1724.

DOCUMENTS for which a brief description suffices.

Date.	Description of Document.	From	To	Purport.
6 Jan.	1. Estimate -	—	—	Of debt for transport service with covering letter. 2 *pages*.
7 Jan.	2. Letter -	Lords of the Privy Council.	Lords of the Treasury.	For 200*l*. to be paid to William Sharpe to be distributed to the under clerks of the Council. Council Chamber. 1 *page*.
8 Jan.	3. Estimate -	—	—	Of the debt of the Navy. 2 *large pages*.
10 Jan.	4. Attested copies of Commission.	—	—	Appointing George Townshend, jun., and others, Commissioners for duties on Hawkers and Pedlars. 7 *pages*.
20 Jan.	5. Memorial -	J. Hancock, yeoman of the Robes.	Lords of the Treasury.	For the issue by way of imprest of such part of the nine months' salary due to the Officers of the Robes, as their Lordships thought proper. *Minuted:* — "12th Feb. Orderd. No further than Michas." 1 *page*.
21 Jan.	6. Letter -	Lord Townshend -	Do. - -	For payment of board wages to Mr. George Tilson, Mr. John Wace and Mr. John Couraud; the King having returned from his German dominions to St. James's Palace. *Minuted:*—"Agreed." 1 *page*.
21 Jan.	7. Account -	—	—	Of moneys paid into the Exchequer since Lady Day 1723, from rents, sales, &c., of the Forfeited Estates. 1½ *pages*.
22 Jan.	8. Letter (copy)	Lord Lieut. of Ireland (Grafton).	Lords of the Treasury.	For allowance of the pay of Viscount Shannon whilst attending Parliament in Great Britain, by which he incurred the tax of 4*s*. in the pound on absentees. The tax was laid on his salary as Commander-in-Chief of H.M. Forces and colonel of a regiment of horse. 1½ *pages*.

1724. VOL. CCLI.

Date.	Description of Document.	From	To	Purport.
23 Jan.	9. Letter -	Lord Townshend -	Lords of the Treasury.	For the same present as was given to Mons. Van Borsseles, to be given to Mons. Ernest Pesters on his taking leave of His Majesty when sent by the States-General as their Deputy to the King of Hanover upon extraordinary affairs. *Minuted:* — "The usual present." 1 *page*.
31 Jan.	10. Bill -	Officers for Licensing Hawkers and Pedlars.	Do. - -	Salary bill. 1 *page*.
3 Feb.	11. Estimate -	—	—	Debt on the Navy and Victualling course. 2 *pages*.
[? About 4 Feb.]	12. Petition -	Henry Tyson -	Lords of the Treasury.	For a year and three-quarters' pay as Messenger of the Robes. *Minuted:* — "4th Febry. 1723–4. To be added to ye establ." 1 *page*.
[After 10 Feb.]	13. Copy of Minute	—	—	Copy of Minute of Council held at Fort George in New York, Dec. 2, 1721, for an addition to the salary of the Clerk of the Council. 1 *page*. Also a memorandum. 2 *pages*.
17 Feb.	14. Report -	Barons of the Exchequer, Scotland.	Lords of the Treasury.	On the petition of Mr. Alexander McBean, minister of Inverness, who had served as schoolmaster for eight years and received no more than two years' salary. Have no objection to his being satisfied the 180*l*. as prayed. Also the petition. *Minuted:* — "28th Apr. 1724. Agreed to." 3½ *pages*.
[? About 18 Feb.]	15. Memorial -	Joseph Hancock, agent to the Garrison of the Isle of Wight.	Do. - -	Praying on behalf of the Earl of Cadogan, Governor of the Isle of Wight, that 800*l*. might be laid out in repairs of the Castle of Carisbrook. *Minuted* on 28th Janry. 1722. It has the following inclosed:—"Memorandm. for the Rt. Hon. Mr. Walpole. Lord Cadogan desires he will be pleased to direct the 800*li*. for repairs in the Isle of Wight without account.—18th Feb. 1723. Agreed to." 1 *page*.

1724. VOL. CCLI.

Date.	Description of Document.	From	To	Purport.
24 Feb.	16. Letter - -	Comrs. for Forfeitures.	Lords of the Treasury.	In answer to one from Mr. Scrope in respect to the affairs of their Commission. 300,711*l.* 14*s.* 9*d.* have been paid into the Exchequer. There has to be issued to claimants 45,089*l.* 2*s.* 3*d.*, and to the Commissioners and other officers, 79,857*l.* 14*s.* 11½*d.* Also abstract of the produce of the forfeited estates in England and Ireland. 5 *pages.*
26 Feb.	17. Account -	—	—	Gross and net produce of the duty of silver plate and hops, North Britain. Excise Office, Edinburgh, 26 Feb. 1723–4. 1 *large page.*
26 Feb.	18. Memorial -	George, Earl of Halifax, Ranger of Bushey and Middle Parks.	Lords of the Treasury.	For repairs or new walls, palings, and drains to be made in those parks. 1 *page.*
27 Feb.	19. Account -	--	—	Of the produce of the duty on home made salt under the management of the Comrs. of Customs, Scotland. From Mich. 1715 to 29 Sept. 1722. 1 *large double page.*
[About 2 March.]	20. Petition -	John Saftin, late collector of Customs at Montrose.	Lords of the Treasury.	Was removed to be better provided for in England, having been a sufferer in the execution of his office in the rebellion in Scotland. Was allowed 100*l.* per annum for subsistence. Prays to be put on the establishment of pensions until provided for. On the back are memoranda of the sums paid to him. *Minuted*:—"2 Mar. 1723–4. Wt. for 100." 1 *page.*
7 March	21. Letter -	Comrs. of Alienations	Do. - -	Send account of their receipts and propose to send accounts of receipts and disbursements four times in the year. 1½ *pages.*
20 March	22. Bond -	—	—	"The Bank's bond for the Receivers of the Lottery on Malt, 1724." "David Le Gros, Secretary." 1 *page.*

1724. Vol. CCLI.

Date.	Description of Document.	From	To	Purport.
20 March	23. Bond	—	—	"The Receivers Bond for the Lottery on Malt, 1724." 1 *page.*
26 March	24. Petition	John Bird of the city of Coventry.	Lords of the Treasury.	Asking to be appointed Receiver-General of the Land Tax for the county of Warwick and city of Coventry. 1 *page.*
31 March	25. Certificate	Comrs. for Alienations	Do.	Of the receipts and expenses of their office. 1 *page.*
2 April	26. Report	Comrs. for Salt.	Do.	Send list of all superannuated officers who are pensioners, with the amounts received. Also the list. 2 *pages.*
10 April	27. Letter	Lord Chamberlain (Holles Newcastle).	Do.	As to having the wine imported by him on his arrival, custom free. Desires that all the favour and civility may be shown to him consistent with the law. 1 *page.*
11 April	28. Do.	F. Osborne	William Lowndes, Esq.	Is sorry to see that Mr. Lowndes' father is dead. Hoped he would have got the arrears due to Mr. Osborne. Their misfortunes are so pressing that he (Osborne) ought to try all he can. 1 *page.*
13 April	29. Do.	Sir Isaac Newton	Lords of the Treasury.	The Clerks and Under Officers of the Mint who have less than 40*l.* per annum have had their salaries increased by one fourth, except the porter: prays that the salary of the latter may, in like manner, be increased. ½ *page.*
14 April	30. Memorial	Constable of the Tower of London (the Earl of Lincoln).	Do.	Recommending William Butt, one of the yeomen warders, for the allowance of 5*s.* a day, the same as was allowed to George Kelly and John Plunkett, prisoners. Dennis Kelly, Esq., a prisoner had refused to pay anything to Butt, who had provided everthing necessary whilst he was lodged in his (Butt's) house, St. James's Square. 1 *page.*

Date.	Description of Document.	From	To	Purport.
14 April	31. Memorial -	J. Gilbert, Sub-Almoner.	Lords of the Treasury.	For money for alms for the poor at the gate, for private pensions, for two Arabic professors at Oxford and Cambridge, and for Lady Frances Keightley. *Minuted* :— "21st Apr. 1724. Order'd." 1 *page*.
[? About 16 April.]	32. Petition -	Isaac Carea, merchant.	Do. - -	To be acquitted from a verdict of 200*l*. obtained against him for "running" snuff, on payment of such satisfaction as he can make. Also affidavit and certificate connected therewith. *Minuted* :—" Warrt. signd. 7th Augt. 1724." 2 *pages*.
23 April	33. Letter -	Board of Trade -	[Do.]	Their Lordships clerks have detained a portion of the salaries of the members of the Board of Trade, which is treatment they ought not to submit to. 2 *pages*.
[? About 28 April.]	34. Petition -	Walter Turner and Edmund Aubery.	Do. - -	For consideration of their case. 2,481*l*. 19*s*. were owing to them for coaches and livery, on contract, during the late Queen's reign. *Minuted* :—" 28Apr. 1724. They have been favoured already." 1 *page*.
30 April	35. Letter -	Lord Townshend -	Do. - -	Mons. van Heck, of Leyden, has disbursed for His Majesty's service 150*l*. beyond his usual allowance of 200*l*. His Majesty desired that their Lordships should be certified thereof. *Minuted* :—" Orderd. 8th May 1724." 1 *page*.
4 May	36. Do. - -	Lord Lieutenant of Ireland (Grafton).	Do. - -	Asking their Lordships to lay before the King the recommendation of the House of Lords (Ireland) in favour of the officers and servants of the house, that a grant of the allowances set opposite their names may be made. Also a list of the officers and sums. 2 *pages*.
4 May	37. Do. - -	"Late" Lord Lieut. of Ireland (Grafton).	Do. - -	For a recompense to those who attended the late quarentine. 2 *pages*.

1724. Vol. CCLI.

Date.	Description of Document.	From	To	Purport.
4 May	38. Letter -	W. Jessop, Receiver (Alienation Office).	Lords of the Treasury.	Certifying the amount received in the Alienation Office for the month of April. 1 *page*.
7 May	39. Do. - -	Lords of the Admiralty.	Do. - -	The salaries of the officers on the "ordinary" and other establishment of the Navy to cease from 25 March last. 1 *page*.
20 May	40. Release -	Sir Lawrence Anderton of Lostock, Lancashire, Bart.	Trustees for Forfeited Estates in Great Britain and Ireland.	For 3,494*l*. 9*s*. 8½*d*. paid into the receipt of the Exchequer by the trustees. There is a note that it is enrolled on the Close Roll. 1 *page*.
21 May	41. Memorial -	Managers and Directors of the Lottery for 750,000*l*.	Lords of the Treasury.	For 1,200*l*. to be paid to Christopher Rhodes, one of the managers, for salaries and expenses of the office. 1 *page*.
22 May	42. Report -	Deputy Auditor of Imprests (Jeremiah Oakeley).	Do. - -	On the "occasions" which delay the passing the late Mr. Fernes account as Receiver-General and Cashier of Customs. 1½ *pages*.
23 May	43. Letter -	Ann Stanley -	—	Asks for an order for the payment of the arrears due to Sir John Stanley. *Docketed*:—"Due to Sir John Stanley on his pension of 400*li*. p ann. payable by Mr. Chetwynd one year and a half at Lady day 1724, 600*li*." *Minuted*:—"To be paid a year." 2 *pages*.
27 May	44. Statement -	—	—	State of the prosecutions carrying on in the Court of Exchequer, in Scotland, by English Bill, against the merchants in Glasgow. 2 *large pages*.
[? May]	45. Petition -	Robert Peters, Esq., late Receiver-General of Taxes, co. Hertford.	Lords of the Treasury.	For 236*l*. 10*s*. expended by him in bringing to London the moneys by him received between 1707 and 1712. Also an affidavit. *Minuted*: —"May 1724. Wt. to Audr. to give allowce. in his accot. of 580*l*. 10*s*." 2 *pages*.
[After May.]	46. Do. - -	John Baskett [King's Printer].	Do. - -	For his charges of printing reports and laws for the government service. 5 *pages*

1724. Vol. CCLI.

Date.	Description of Document.	From	To	Purport.
[? About 9 June.]	47. Statement -	—	—	*Docketed:* — "Mr. Auditor Harley's case recd. ye 9th of June 1724. As to auditor's fees and allowances." 1½ *pages.*
16 June	48. Account -	Excise Office -	—	"A compare account of the net produce of the hereditary and temporary rates and dutys of Excise, with the payments into the Exchequer, and the pensions, &c. paid at this office out of the said net produce, from Michaelmas 1715 to Lady day 1724." Excise Office. 1 *page.*
[? About 18 June.]	49. Memorial -	Henry Lowman on behalf of John Fox, Esq., once an Officer of the Board of Green Cloth.	The Chancellor of the Exchequer.	His pension was reduced in King William's time to 200*l.* per ann. This he received during Queen Ann's reign, after which he was struck off the list; 15*l.* per quarter is prayed for him; he being 85 years old, and almost childish. *Minuted:* — "18th June 1724. 10*li.* p Mr. Lowther." 1 *page.*
[? About 24 June.]	50. Account -	—	—	Of the gross and net produce on the importation of tea for seven years ending Midsummer 1724. 1 *page.*
2 July, &c.	51. Certified copies	—	—	Of documents connected with Barbadoes, viz., touching fines at the grand sessions connected with bonds entered into by Philip Kirton, of Christ Church, Barbadoes, gent., and John Goodwyn, of St. Michaels, in the same island, gent., as sureties of Richard Rycroft, of Christ Church, gent., and concerning two courts held at Barbadoes, at the second of which the recognizances of the above sureties were estreated. 12 *pages.*
6 July	52. Letter - -	Fr. Negus - -	The Rt. Hon. R.	Prays him to direct 250*l.* for the King's huntsmen. 1 *page, quarto.*

1724. VOL. CCLI.

Date.	Description of Document.	From	To	Purport.
[? About 17 July.]	53. Memorial -	Charles Mason, late Treasurer of the Transports.	Lords of the Treasury.	For a further warrant to Christopher Whittingham, to continue to receive and pay into the Exchequer the rents of his (Masons) estate two years longer; and that any process may be countermanded. Also a certificate of the Deputy Auditor thereon. $2\frac{1}{2}$ *pages.*
17 July	54. Letter -	W. Powlett - -	—	The Bishop of London desires directions to be given for payment of the salary due to the Whitehall preachers. 1 *page, quarto.*
3 Aug.	55. Do. -	Roger Hudson -	—	For an order for 450*l.* for a year and a half's rent for "Moat Park," to Mr. Arthur Van Sittart. 1 *small page.*
[? About 7 Aug.]	56. Petition -	Gustavus Hamilton, Esq.	Lord Lieut. of Ireland (Grafton).	For his half-pay as cornet of dragoons in the late Lord Wharton's regiment from 1710 to 1715. Also resolutions thereon of the House of Commons. *Minuted*:—"Warrt. signd. 7th Augt. 1724." $3\frac{1}{2}$ *pages.*
12 Aug.	57. Memorial -	Richard Hampden, Esq., late Treasurer of the Navy.	Lords of the Treasury.	For a warrant to the Barons of the Exchequer to stay proceedings on certain distringases, and to stay the levying of an estreat for 500*l.* 1 *page.*
[? About 13 Aug.]	58. Petition -	John Martin, "Keeper of the lyons."	The King -	For the grant of that office which (he says) had been unwarrantably possessed, and after several solemn hearings in the Court of Chancery, &c. the fraud was detected. *Minuted* · — "13 Aug. 1724. Rejected." 1 *page.*
[? About 18 Aug.]	59. Do. -	Elizabeth Ferne, Executrix of Henry Ferne, Esq., late Receiver General of Customs.	Lords of the Treasury.	For directions to be given to the Comrs. of Customs to make their report, or order the bonds standing out for interest to be prosecuted, that she may pass her husband's final account. Referred to the Comrs. on 18 Aug. 1724 to report. Also a previous petition from her, which was ordered to be reported on 23 July 1724. 2 *pages.*

Date.	Description of Document.	From	To	Purport.
17 Sept.	60. Memorial -	Christopher Tilson and six others.	Lords of the Treasury.	Ask to be re-appointed as managers for exchanging the tickets of the present lottery (1724) which is above two-thirds drawn. *Minuted:*—"17 7br. 1724. Agreed, and Geo. Morley to be added to the No." 1 *page.*
18 Sept.	61. Do. -	Anthony Cracherode	Do. - -	Praying for 1,500*l.* upon account to pay his Majtie's. clerks in court, and Mr. West, counsel to the Board of Trade. *Minuted:*—"23 7ber.1724. To be consd. with ye cash after Michas." 1 *page.*
19 Sept.	62. Letter -	Comrs. of Customs, Dublin.	Do. - -	Encloses copy of a letter received from Mr. Hopkins, Deputy Controller of the copper coinage for Ireland, giving an account of half pence and farthings coined by Mr. Wood, the patentee. The copy referred to. 2 *pages.*
21 Sept.	63. Memorial -	Edmund Britiffe, Thomas Newman, and Thomas Guenault, Paymasters of Exchequer Bills.	Do. - -	Crave allowance of 87*l.* 11*s.* 11*d.* disbursed by them. *Minuted:* — "8 October 1724. Agreed and ordered." 1 *page.*
[? About 29 Sept.]	64. Letters and account, &c. (Copies.)	Samuel Reed -	John Somforth, Esq., Douglas, Isle of Man.	Concerning tobacco shipped to the Isle of Man. The account is from 25 March to 29 Sept. 1724. 5 *pages.*
29 Sept.	65. Account -	? Comrs. for Wine Licences.	Lords of the Treasury.	Of the gross and net produce of that part of H.M. Civil List which arose by wine licences for a half year. 1 *page.*
[After 29 Sept.]	66. Memorial -	John Montgomery, Esq., Master of the Mint in Scotland.	Do. - -	For so much salary for the Mint as their Lordships shall see fit (two years and a half being in arrears). Also certificate from the "General" of H.M. Mint at Edinburgh as to the balance on his account. Dated 29 Sept. 1724. 2 *pages.*
6 Oct.	67. Presentment -	Comrs. for Stamp Duties.	Do. - -	For Mr. George Maccubine to be a stamper in the room of John Cleghorne, deceased. *Minuted:* — "Warrt. for John Spicer to succeed Cleghorne. Sign'd 7th Oct. 1724." ½ *page.*

Date.	Description of Document.	From	To	Purport.
8 Oct.	68. Certificate -	W. Ashburnham and Cor. Cayley (Alienation Office.)	Lords of the Treasury.	Of the produce of the office. 1 *page.*
1 Nov.	69. Letter -	Lord Stair - -	The Rt. Hon. Mr. Walpole.	Reminding him that he (Mr. Walpole) thought Col. Kennedy and Dr. Lidderdale should be paid the respective sums of 200*l.* and 100*l.* *Minuted* :—" 1st 9br. 1722. 100*li.* bounty to Lidderdale." 1 *page.*
6 Nov.	70. Do. -	Lord Townshend -	Lords of the Treasury.	For allowance to his secretaries and clerks attending at Windsor. *Minuted* : — " 11th 9br. 1724. Agreed to." 1½ *pages.*
6 Nov.	71. Do. -	Duke of Newcastle -	Do. - -	Do. *Minuted* as above.
[? About 12 Nov.]	72. Petition -	Henrietta Ramondon, daughter and executrix of Dr. Thomas Lawrance, 1st Physician to her late Majesty Queen Anne.	Do. - -	For payment of 240*l.* 5*s.* 6*d.* due to her father or a part thereof. Also a certificate from the Treasurer of the Chamber's Office corroborating the claim. Dated " 12th Novr. 1724." 2 *pages.*
18 Nov.	73. Letter -	Lord Chamberlain of the Household (Grafton).	Do. - -	For 110*l.* to be paid to John Engliss, Esq., Marshal of the Ceremonies, as a present from his Majesty to Chevalier Espaleta, Secretary to the Embassy from the King of Spain. 1 *page.*
21 Nov.	74. Receipts -	J. Bayley - -	Henry Kelsall, Esq.	*Docqueted* : — " Rect. of quit rents to Lord Tankerville." (Norfolk, Hempton Priory.) 2 *pages.*
21 Nov.	75. Warrant -	Lord Chamberlain of the Household.	Master of the Jewel Office (the Hon. James Brudnall, Esq.).	For a new silver trumpet. At the foot is :—" Let this warrant be executed and a new trumpet delivered according to the tenor thereof, provided the old trumpet mentioned therein to be broken and worn out, be at the same time delivered up to the Master of the Jewel Office for his Mat's. use." 1 *page.*
[After 21 Nov.]	76. Account -	—	—	Balances due from the York Buildings Company to the public according to the account stated by the Commrs. for forfeitures in Scotland. 1 *page.*

1724. VOL. CCLI.

Date.	Description of Document.	From	To	Purport.
1 Dec.	77. Report -	Sir Charles Farnaby	Lords of the Treasury.	Balances due from George Murray and Robert Murray, late paymasters of the lottery. *Minuted:* —" A lrẽ writ to Robt. Murray." 1 *page*.
3 Dec.	78. Letter -	Duke of Newcastle -	Do. - -	For directions to be given to defray the charge of the prosecution of Robert Elstone, late master of a merchant ship, for murder of two of his men. Also copy of a letter from the Comrs. of the Admiralty on the same subject. 2 *pages*.
4 Dec.	79. Do. -	Lord Lieut. of Ireland (Carteret).	Do. - -	Recommending Lord Blayney for the continuance of his additional pension of 300*l*. per annum five years longer. *Minuted:* — " 14th Decr. 1724. The King's pleasure to be taken hereupon." Also the petition to the King of "Cadwallader, Baron Blaney of Monaghan," Ireland. 3 *pages*.
8 Dec.	80. Do. -	Do. - -	Do. - -	" Transmitting accounts of the overdrawings on the Concordatum [and] military contingencies, between Xmas. 1723 and Michas. 1724, in order to the placing thereof on the revenue at large." 2 *pages*.
8 Dec.	81. Do. -	Do. - -	Do. - -	Recommending Major General Thomas Pearce for an addition of 6*s*. 8⅔*d*. per diem to his pay as Major General, as he has distinguished himself by his vigilence and care. Also the Major General's petition. 2 *pages*.
[? About 17 Dec.]	82. Petition -	Roger Garth -	Do. - -	For a reward for attending their Lordships with evidence against the late Bishop of Rochester. *Minuted:* — "17th Decr. 1724. 350*li*. in full of all his services and expences. Prepare a warrt. to Mr. Cracherode." 1 *page*.

1724. VOL. CCLI.

Date.	Description of Document.	From	To	Purport.
19 Dec.	83. Letter -	J. Burchett (Admiralty).	John Scrope, Esq.	As to the charge for prosecution of Robert Elston, late master of a merchant ship, for killing two of his men; the Attorney and Solicitor General having given their opinion that "the fact was not committed within the jurisdiction of the Admiralty," they (the Lords of the Admiralty) have nothing to do with the prosecution of the prisoner. 1 *page.*
21 Dec.	84. Do. -	Lord Chamberlain of the Household.	Lords of the Treasury.	His Majesty's pleasure is that they give orders for the payment of 500*l.* to the Right Hon. the Earl of Essex, as a present to buy a jewel. 1 *page.*
23 Dec.	85. Do. -	Lord Lieut. of Ireland (Lord Carteret).	Do. - -	Sends petition of Lieut. Anthony D'Orval de Preugnie with copy of another formerly presented to his Majesty, and of the proceedings thereon. Petitioner served in the reduction of Ireland, and left the service for his wounds; recommends him for half pay. Also the papers referred to. 5 *pages.*
25 Dec.	86. Account -	—	—	The reasons for the increase on salary bills (? Excise) to 25 Dec. 1724. 1 *page.*
[Undated but ? 1724.]	87. Report -	Christopher Tilson -	Lords of the Treasury.	On a claim of Herbert Rudhale Westfaling, Esq., for a years salary for himself, secretary, and clerks and for contingencies of the office for stating army debts. The demand cannot be paid unless a new provision be made by Parliament. Also some further notes on the same subject. 3 *pages.*

VOL. CCLII. 1725. JANUARY—MAY.

[Beginning of 1725.] 1. "New Years Gifts or other annual dues for the Lords."
"New years guifts paid & distributed by Mr Scroop."
"New years gifts or other annual gratuities for the Secretarys" [of different departments].
"New years gifts or other annual gratuities for the Clerks" [in different departments]. 3 *pages.*

1725. 2. Estimate of the charge of the Office of Ordnance for 1725. Signed. 1 *page.*

2 Jan. 3. "Attorney General's (Yorke's) opinion as to the pretensions of Greenwich Hospital upon the Coal Duties." The opinion is that by the Act 5 Geo. I. the sum of 6,000*l.* per ann. appropriated to the Hospital is not continued to Lady day 1751. 1½ *pages.*

7 Jan. 4. "State of Lady Lætitia Russell's annuity to Easter 1723," signed by "Matt. Pennefather, Compr & Acct Genl."
Also "copy of the King's letter to Lord Lieutt for paying the arrears of Lady Lætitia Russell's pencōn." 4 *pages.*

7 Jan. 5. James Graham to ——. Hopes he will not decline to give his countenance and assistance in forwarding his (Graham's) claim to a salary, now that he has a nearer opportunity to do him (Graham) good offices. Asks him to put an enclosure into Mr Walpole's hands. Sends also copy of his letter to Mr Walpole. Has written to Alexander Hamilton, "Will's brother," to wait on his correspondent, and receive his commands. Hints that if he thinks it worth while, he may offer Mr Walpole a present. Edinburgh, 7 Jan. 1724/5. 1 *page.*

14 Jan. 6. Comrs of Revenue, Ireland, to the Lords of the Treasury. Sir Michael Creagh, attainted of treason for the Rebellion of 1688, has set forth in his memorial to them (the Comrs of Revenue) that he lent considerable sums to several persons, which sums continued undiscovered; and according to a list these amounted to 22,650*l.*, and in regard the same was vested in the Crown by his attainder, he submitted himself to be considered as a discoverer. By their solicitors report the amount would be near that sum, but most of the debts were granted away and the grants confirmed by Parliament, and others sold for the use of the public by the late Trustees for the sale of Irish forfeitures of 1688; so that 3,000*l.* or 4,000*l.* only appears at present not to have been granted. For recovery of these sums the usual process has been issued. Sir Michael has undergone great difficulties by arrest and otherwise, and the Comrs could not refuse to help him so as to expedite the suits. Sir Michael has lately embraced the Protestant Religion. Have supplied him in small sums amounting to 100*l.*, which they presume their Lordships will approve. Ask for their Lordships commands if he seeks further assistance, of which he will speedily stand in need. Custom house, Dublin. 2 *pages.*

1725. VOL. CCLII.

16 Jan. 7. "Serj[t] Pengelly's opinion how far the Act 5 Geo., for applying the coal duties &c. is affected by the S[o] Sea Act 6 Georgij." 16 Jan. 1724.

With it is also copy of another opinion of the same Serjeant as to whether the 6,000*l.* per ann. granted to Greenwich Hospital by Act 9 Anne is not continued by Act 5 Geo. [I.] until Lady day 1751. 24 Dec. 1724. 2 *pages* (4[to]).

16 Jan. 8. Richard Salter to the R[t] Hon. Robert 'Walpoole,' Esq. Sends a paper which hints "at some persons w[ch] defraud his Majesty 'bassly.'" Also informs Mr. Walpole that there are several of their ingenious hands shipping away contrary to an Act of Parliament to another country, which will be a great damage to our trade.

The paper referred to is entitled "Considerations respecting frauds in drawbacks for duties on tobacco exported from England to Ireland." One of the frauds is thus described: "The Masters of vessels that come into the Irish Ports, with tobacco from England, wait opportunities of 'runing' 28 days, which is the time allowed them by Act of Parliament, before they make entry, and then they make a shew of burning part of the tobacco, as damaged, to the amount of what they had run; then collude with the Collector, Surveyor, or Landwaiter (who call the English Acts of Parliament oppressive Acts) to certify the whole deficiency as damaged, and burn'd; to the defrauding of the crown of all the duty of the tobacco so run; of which there is an instance beyond all dispute, by which it can be made appear that the quantity of tobacco entered and shipp'd off from England, and the quantity certified to be landed in Ireland, differed about 800 pounds in about 3,000 pounds weight." 4½ *pages.*

22 Jan. 9. Memorial of the Surveyor of Woods [Wither] to the Lords of the Treasury. Has received their Lordships directions to pay various sums specified, but represents that no money has ever been raised by him but what has been by warrant appropriated to particular services, and that he cannot pay the sums amounting to 1,285*l.* until authorised by their Lordships to raise money for that purpose. Proposes that money should be raised by felling wood in the forests of Dean, Whichwood, and Cliff. Jan. 22 1724.

Minuted:—"23rd March 1725. Prepare the proper War[t]." 1¼ *pages.*

21 and 29 Jan. 10. "The complaint of Matt. Barton, King's Clerk and Comptroller of the coinage for the service of his Majesty's dominions, &c. in America against W[m] Wood, patentee of the said coinage." Jan. 21, 1724. [The patentee is charged with not complying with the terms of his grant, and treating with contempt every effort of the Controller to make him comply.]

"The answer of W. Wood, Patentee of ye American coinage, to the complaint," &c. He says that the whole complaint is frivolous, and seems only designed to give trouble and vexation to the patentee. Jan. 29, 1724. 2 *pages.*

VOL. CCLII.

1725.
1 Feb. 11. Commissioners of Revenue in Ireland to the Lords of the Treasury, enclosing their report on the petition of Mr Edward Fitz Gerrald, recommending in a particular manner that part of it which relates to the encouragement of the discoverer, whose zeal and hazard as well as expense has been very great. The fourth part of what has been discovered has usually been granted to discoverers. 1 Feb. 1724.

The Report referred to. The Commissioners find that Henry Fitz Gerald the petitioner's father was, in 1690, indicted and outlawed for high treason on account of the Rebellion of 1688, and that he took King William's protection. After this until his death, in 1715, he behaved himself as a peaceable subject. In 1714 Sir Arthur Shaen, Bart., made a lease to petitioner's father for 31 years, at a rent of 133*l.* 6*s.* 8*d.*, and by the same deed Sir Arthur demised the same lands to the petitioner at the above rent, to commence on the expiration of the first term, and for a further term of 31 years after the expiration of the first two terms, to Henry Fitz Gerald of Dublin, which two reversionary terms appear to have been in trust for petitioner's father. Petitioner's father, by will in 1715, devised the premises to petitioner and his heirs male, subject to a portion of 300*l.* payable to his daughter Mary (petitioner's sister). Petitioner and his brother Gerald as administrators became possessed of the premises, and petitioner renounced the errors of the Church of Rome and became a protestant of the Church of Ireland, as appears by certificate enrolled of the Archbishop of Dublin. Dupleacks the discoverer objects, that notwithstanding this, he cannot be taken to be a protestant, as by Act of 8 Anne the petitioner is obliged, besides filing the certificate, to receive the holy sacrament according to the usage of the Church of Ireland, and to make and subscribe the Declaration to prevent the further growth of Popery, and to take and file the oath of abjuration. A certificate thereof is also to be filed. As he has not made it appear that he has complied with these requirements, they (the Comrs) are of opinion that he cannot be deemed to be a protestant within the meaning of the Act. Further set out what were the arrangements on petitioner's marriage, but the petitioner had no power to charge the premises, the same being vested in his Majesty by reason of the attainder of petitioner's father. Thomas Dupleacks petitioned the Comrs in 1722 to be admitted as a protestant discoverer to make out his Majesty's title to the assets, and for a prosecution, and he was accordingly admitted. An information in the Court of Exchequer was exhibited against the petitioner and his brother, and the latter put in his answer, but the petitioner had not answered. Process of contempt issued against him, and the execution of the sequestration was opposed by several persons in arms, who came from the petitioner's house and fired upon and wounded some of the sequestrator's assistants. But it appears by a certificate of several protestants of good estate and reputation in the county where the petitioner resides, &c. that he has at all times behaved himself as a good subject to the Crown. Eleven ejectments were brought in the Court of Common Pleas by

1725. VOL. CCLII.

Sir Arthur Shaen to recover the possession of the lands for arrears of rent, but (for reasons given) those proceedings ceased. Thomas Dupleacks exhibited a bill in the same court against the petitioner and his brother, setting forth that the two reversionary leases were made in trust for petitioner's father, and praying to have the benefit of them and of the lease in possession as protestant discoverer, and suggesting that petitioner's father and himself were both papists. Soon after Sir Arthur Shaen outlawed the petitioner and his brother in an action of debt for rent, and the lands in lease were returned by inquisition as of the yearly value of 40*l.*, *ultra reprisas.* Sir Arthur was put in possession, but the outlawry was reversed and a *custodiam* granted to Mr Richard Nuttall, the Comrs Solicitor, for the King's use, and the lands were lately set to a solvent tenant at 208*l.* per ann. beyond the reserved rent payable to Sir Arthur, a fourth part of which rent of 208*l.* per ann. the discoverer insists to have secured to him.

The petition in which the lands leased to petitioner's father are described as "the severall lands of Knockmt, Banacher, Bracklan, Sarsfieldstown, Scurlocksland, Corbittstown, Balintlevy, Ballinturnan, and Ballinderry in the county of Westmeath."

There is also a petition from him to Sir Robert Walpole, asking that the leasehold lands may be subject to the jointure of 1,400*l.* to his wife.

Further there is a copy of an opinion that Dupleacks, the informer, was not entitled to any share in the discovery.

In the Minute Book, Vol. 25, p. 92 h. (11 Aug. 1725) after stating that the above report had been read, "My Lords adhere to the Report, which is against the petitioner, and leave it to the Commrs of the Revenue to act therein as they have used to do in cases of the like nature." 8 *pages.*

18 Jan. and 3 Feb. 12. Report of the Surveyor General (J. Pulteney) to the Lords of the Treasury on the petition of Edmond, Duke of Buckinghamshire and Normanby, an infant, Katherine, Duchess of Buckinghamshire and Normanby, (his Grace's mother and guardian,) Charles, Earl of Orrery, and other the said Duke's trustees. By patent of 9 Charles I. the King granted to Edmond, Earl of Mulgrave, and his heirs male the Manor and Castle of Mulgrave, and several lands, &c. in Yorkshire, under the yearly fee-farm rent of 62*l.* and 3 pence. His grace is lineally descended from the Earl of Mulgrave, and is seised of the manor, &c., with remainder to the Honble Robert Sheffield, Esq., and his heirs male; reversion in fee to his Majesty. The said Robert Sheffield is far advanced in years and has no issue male. The petition further sets forth that the alum works on the premises may produce great profit, if managed to the best advantage, and that the lands and houses may, with expense, be considerably improved, but no person will engage therein unless he can have an estate or interest in the premises for a competent number of years certain; which by reason of the Duke's infancy, and the contingencies whereto this estate (in taile male) is liable, cannot be granted, so as to bind the Crown, without the aid of Parlia-

1725. Vol. CCLII.

ment. Petitioners pray to be allowed to bring in a Bill into the House of Commons to enable his Grace to grant leases. Is of opinion their Lordships should advise his Majesty to give the leave asked. 18 Jan. 1724.

Also supplementary report on a supplement to the petition, wherein the petitioners set forth that the manor of Seaton with appurtenances was granted to Edmund, Lord Sheffield (afterwards Earl of Mulgrave), by Queen Elizabeth in the thirty fourth year of her reign. This they intended to have inserted in their petition, but it was omitted. He (the Surveyor General) has no objection to the like power as regards this manor as is proposed to be granted in relation to the manor of Mulgrave.

Also the petition and supplement. *5 pages.*

5 Feb. 13. Lord Lieut. of Ireland (Carteret) to the Duke of Newcastle on the petition of Francis Maynard, of the county of Kerry, Esq. Praying for an annual pension on the Establishment of Ireland, or some other provision. Referred the same to the Deputy Auditor General, whose report he transmits, and thinks the petitioner a proper object of the Royal compassion.

There is the following minute in the *Minute Book*, Vol. 25, p. 39*b*, on the reading these documents:—"My Lords thereupon order a warrant to be prepared for placing him on the Establishment of Ireland at 100*l*. p ann. pencõn from Lady day last."

The Report referred to. Petitioner was an officer in the regiment of Sir George St George, which was "broke" in the reign of King William, after the peace of Ryswick; had been sheriff of the county of Kerry; was a Justice of the Peace, a captain of a militia company, &c., and whilst sheriff was at a considerable expense on account of the designed Invasion.

The petition referred to and a certificate with covering letter. *5 pages and 2 halves.*

9 Feb. 14. Representation from the Com[rs] of Taxes to the Lords of the Treasury with an account of the deficiencies in respect to the tax upon Papists. Office for Taxes 9 Feb. 1724. 2 *pages.*

11 Feb. 15. Copy of affidavit of John Russell, writer to the Signet, as to a "Back bond granted by Col. Balfour of Fanney, relating to the Disposition granted by the deceast Robert, Lord Burleigh, to him, and as to the way & manner that the said backbond came to his possession."

"Edinb[r]," 11 Feb. 1724. 1 *page.*

12 Feb. 16. "Draft of the Att[o] General's opinion ab[t] prohibiting the importation of tea from Holland &c. as also a lrẽ from M[r] Woolley Secr[y] to the East India Comp[a] thereupon."

Also the case submitted to the Attorney General. 6 *pages.*

15 Feb. 17. Com[rs] of Forfeited Estates (Scotland) to John Scrope, Esq., asking that the enclosed account may be laid before the Lords of the Treasury.

1725. VOL. CCLII.

The account referred to entitled:—"An accompt of the moneys due by the Governour & Company of Undertakers for raising the Thames Water in York Buildings to the Publick for Principal & Interest conform to the several dates." 2 *pages.*

16 Feb. 18. Representation of the Earl of Halifax, Auditor of the Receipt of the Exchequer, to the Lords of the Treasury. The cash room belonging to the office was broken open by having the lead upon the roof turned up, and by sawing a joist and breaking some plastering. The lock at the end of the chest was forced off, and out of the hole that the lock covered, four entire bags were carried off, a fifth was taken out, opened, and about 200*l.* taken; the remainder in the bag lay on the floor, where was found an old blade of a knife with a piece of cork for a handle "supposed to be brought to strike fire withal, because near it was an old tinn pot with some pieces of touch wood and a gimblet." Gives other particulars. Sent for the officers of works to consult as to what was necessary to be done, and to arrange for a survey of the building to prevent the like misfortune for the future. Relates what steps he took to discover the robbers, as well as the precautions taken to prevent further attempts. Exchequer, 16 Feb. 1724.

The report of the Officers of Works, who suggest that arches should be turned under and over the offices, and the floor paved with stone.

Also two plans.

Minuted:—"Read 4° Mar. & agreed to 500^{li} to be issued to the Usher of the Excheq^{r} for Iron Chests, watch coats, an engine & buckets."

A fuller minute to the same effect is entered in the Minute Book, vol. 25, p. 25. 6½ *pages.*

[After 17 Feb.] 18*a*. Memorial of Captain John Kelly to the R^{t} Hon. Sir Robert Walpole. In 1721, being Captain of an Independent Company at Tinmouth Castle, he caused a seizure of 10 Dutch trading ships, which were condemned and sold for 5,700*l.* By his great fatigue he had a violent fever, and was thought incurable; and his "company," which cost him 1,000 guineas, was given to a Captain on half pay. The Board of General Officers reported that he had sustained a very great hardship. All he had got by the seizure was 150*l.* by warrant from the Lords of the Treasury, which was far short of the expense he was at, whilst the Government was benefitted at least 20,000*l.* Has been a close prisoner in Newgate and the King's Bench upwards of 10 months. His Majesty has granted him 160*l.* per ann. till better provided for, and as he was desirous to end his days in his Majesty's service this would be saved if his Majesty would grant him the first Troop of Horse or dragoons that shall become vacant, or a pension equivalent.

The copy of the warrant for the 150*l.* dated 17 Feb. 1724.

In the *Minute Book*, Vol. 25, p. 44*i*, 3 May 1725, is:—"Capt. John Kelly's peticon for a further reward for his service in dis-

1725. Vol. CCLII.

covering the Dutch smuggling ships a° 1721, hovering about Tinmouth, is read and rejected." 2 *pages.*

17 Feb. 19. Report of the Barons of the Exchequer of Scotland to the Lords of the Treasury on the warrant prepared for the Royal signature granting to John, Duke of Argyle and Greenwich, "the miln and miln lands of Muckart lying within the regality of St Andrews, and the lands of Blackfoord alias Blackshaugh, within the Stewartry of Strathern and Sherriffdom of Perth, holding few of his Majesty as come in place of the Archbishop of St Andrews, and the four oxgate and half of land in Wester Duddingston within the Sheriffdom of Edinburgh holding taxtward of his Majesty, proceeding upon the resignations of Mr John Campbell of Mamore, and George Logan of Burn castle respectively." Find that the signature contains a *de novo damus*, but it does not appear that any of the bygone few duties, &c. will be discharged by the *de novo damus.* The signature contains a disjoining clause and a discharge and dispensation to the Duke of Argyle; but his Majesty may disjoin the lands from the former jurisdiction as they are in his Majesty's gift, and he may reunite them to another. "Edin.," 17 Feb. 1724–5. 2 *pages.*

18 Feb. 20. Representation of the Court of Directors of the "Equivalent Company" to the Lords of the Treasury. The proprietors of the Equivalent debt amounting to 248,550*l.* 0*s.* 9½*d.*, being lately incorporated, acquaint their Lordships that the yearly fund of 10,000*l.*, which to Michaelmas last has been or will be paid in Scotland, is from and after that time, by virtue of the Charter and the Act, to be paid to the Corporation, or to their Cashier. And their Lordships are thereby enjoined to issue their warrants to the proper officers in Scotland to pay the same. In pursuance of the same Charter and Act there becomes also payable to the Corporation the annual sum of 600*l.* for charges of management. Pray their Lordships to issue their warrant for payment of the 10,000*l.* and the 600*l.* They also pray that the latter sum may be made payable from Midsummer 1719, to include unavoidable expenses to which they have been put.

"Res. 18 Febry 1724–5." 1 *page.*

19 Feb. 21. Petition of Nicholas Paxton to the Lords of the Treasury. By order of Viscount Townshend has acted as Solicitor on behalf of the suitors of the Court of Chancery towards obtaining satisfaction from the deficient Masters of that court, for which purpose a great many orders have been made by the Comrs of the Great Seal. Petitioner has likewise taken administration to Mr Dormer, late one of the masters, and has preferred a bill in Chancery to call some persons to account who were indebted to him. Petitioner is suing for administration to Mr Borrett, another master: prays that 300*l.* may be ordered towards reimbursing him for the expenses. 19 Feb. 1724.

1725. VOL. CCLII.

In the *Minute Book*, vol. 25, p. 21*d* (23 Feb. 1724-5), is:—"My Lords order 400li to be issued to Mr Cracherode for law charges, and that out of the same the said 300li be paid to Paxton as an imprest for the purposes aforesaid." 1 *page*.

23 Feb. 22. Application from the Secretary to the United East India Company, to the Lords of the Treasury, renewing the address on behalf of George Benyon, a land-waiter in the port of Bristol, who had discovered a clandestine trade carried on at Bristol and other parts of England with the pirates at Madagascar, viz., for him to be made a land surveyor. It "will be an encouragement to other persons to discover any ill practices they shall know to be carrying on to the disadvantage of the public, and by distinguishing Mr Benyon will protect him from the resentment of the persons who may think themselves hurt by his above mentioned service. East India House, 23 Feb. 1724."

Accompanied by a previous memorial (of 12 July 1721) referred to in the above, on the same subject. 2 *pages*.

24 Feb. 23. Report of the Barons of the Exchequer in Scotland to the Lords of the Treasury on the petition of Alexander McMillan, writer in Edinburgh. Petitioner "is possessed of five receipts for arms valued, apprized and delivered up to the Deputy Lieutenant of the County of Sutherland," in pursuance of an Act of the 1st year of H. M. reign entitled "an Act for the more effectual securing the peace of the Highlands, in Scotland," amounting to 701*l.* 8*s.* sterling. By the Act these sums are to be paid by the Collectors of the Land Tax or Excise. The arms were delivered up to the Deputy Lieutenant, and the parties have not received satisfaction. There has been already paid for arms delivered up 11,483*l.* 7*s.* 11$\frac{1}{6}$*d.*

Also the petition referred to. 4½ *pages*.

24 Feb. 24. Report of the Barons of the Exchequer in Scotland to the Lords of the Treasury, on the petition of Mr Alexander Swinton, of Strathore, in the county of Fife, Scotland. Conceive it reasonable that payment should be ordered him of 90*l.* as the value of the coals made use of by the King's forces during the time of the late unnatural Rebellion in Scotland.

The petition states that the petitioner had a lease of the coal works of Lochgellie, within about five miles of the town of Bruntisland. He had a coal yard on the shore of the town of Bruntisland, in which were deposited for exportation 1,000 loads of great coal and 400 loads of small coal. The rebels, among other places, seized upon the Castle of Bruntisland and upon the coal yard near to it; but soon after, being forced to abandon both, Sir Robert Montgomerie of Skelmerlie, by order of the Government, took possession of the castle and the custody of the coal-yard, where the coals were untouched by the rebels. Sir Robert supplied the garrison in the castle with coals from the coal yard, from November to March or April, and the remainder were used for baking bread for the use of the army who were pursuing the rebels. Endeavoured to make

1725. VOL. CCLII.

the proprietor of the castle, who first seized the same for the use of the rebels, liable for payment; but the Lords of Sessions absolved him. Petitioner's affection and zeal to the present Government is very well known, and about the time of the breaking out of the Rebellion he made a discovery to the Government of a considerable number of arms coming from Holland, which were seized, and for which he was rewarded.

Also a certified copy of the same. 6 *pages.*

24 Feb. 25. Report of the same to the same. On the petition of John Baillie, late Deputy Sheriff of Inverness. It appears that the petitioner did meet with a considerable loss, by the Rebel army, in 1715, entering upon lands belonging to him, near Inverness, and driving off part of the stock. He appeared very zealous for his Majesty's service, and is well affected to the Government; so that he deserves some countenance and favour. As to his proposal to be made collector of Few Duties, payable to the Crown out of the Isles of Lewis, Skye, &c., the lands are forfeited to the Crown, by the attainder of the proprietors, and have been sold by the Trustees for the forfeited estates in Scotland; except the estate of the late Earl of Seaforth, and that is freed and discharged of the aucient few duties, payable to the Crown, so that there is nothing leviable thereout. As to the estate of the late Earl, now in possession of the Crown, not being sold by the Trustees, there is a yearly few duty of 166*l.* 13*s.* 4*d.* sterling payable thereout, which is in arrear for a considerable number of years, by reason the ordinary process of this Court for levying the duty, could not be executed in those remote parts where the estate lies: so that it may not be improper to put the collecting these Few Duties into some such way as is proposed. 3½ *pages.*

[About 25 Feb.] 26. Petition of Elizabeth Collett, widow, to the Lords of the Treasury, for a lease of a wine vault dug under His Majesty's ground, which encroaches upon H.M. Spring Garden.

Referred to the Surveyor-General, 25 Feb. 1724–5. 1¼ *pages.*

26 Feb. 27. Memorial of A. Cracherode to the Lords of the Treasury, asking directions from their Lordships on a letter annexed from the Principal Secretary of State commanding the prosecution of (1) — Brotherton, of the city of Gloucester, for a pretended assault, and (2) of — Creary, a material witness for his Majesty against Wilson and others, for a riot at the camp near the city of Gloucester, also for a pretended assault.

The letter referred to. 2 *pages.*

26 Feb. 28. Letter signed "Fabrice," without address. The bearer has dedicated to the King his travels, which he has published by subscription, and his Majesty has ordered him 200*l.* sterling, as M[r] Walpole told him (the bearer) yesterday, and as he does not know whom to address, and as the writer has known him formerly in Turkey, he has asked a letter of recommendation to one of the Lords of the Treasury to know if orders have been given to the Treasury, and if he can quickly receive the money since it is

1725. VOL. CCLII.

necessary for him to go immediately to Holland to print a French copy of his life. "À Londres le 26 de Fevr. 1724" (French).

Minuted:—"A wt for 200li." 2 *pages*.

[About 29. "The case of Richard Marshall Esq. Studd Master in regard to his allowance forkeeping the studd."

Showing the terms on which he kept the stud during the time of King William, the Prince of Denmark, Queen Anne, and his present Majesty. Since the Duke of Somerset had a grant of the Park and the meadows at Hampton Court, has kept studd for six years to his great loss, by reason of the great quantity of hay which he has been forced to buy, instead of that which he used to have from the meadows. Upon representing his case to his Majesty on 8 July 1724, it was directed to be laid before the Lords of the Treasury for a reasonable allowance to be made above the annual allowance of 18*l*. 4*s*. 1*d*. for each stallion, mare, colt, and servant's horse in consequence of his loss of the hay and after-grass.

Minuted:—"Referd to Mr Negus March 3 1724–5."

Three other copies connected therewith.

In the Minute Book, vol. 25, p. 59*q* (14 June 1725), is a notice that Mr. Marshall "is to be paid at the rate of 171li p ann. for 7 years amounting to 1197li." 5 *pages*.

3 March. 30. Order in Council on the petition of Mark Legaur, mariner, referring his petition to the Lords of the Treasury to consider as to what was proper for the petitioner. 3 Mar. 1724.

The petition states that the petitioner was a mariner on board the "Prudent Hannah," a brigantine of Boston, New England, which on her passage from thence to Virginia was taken by pirates, who took out of her the master and one man, leaving petitioner with two others on board, and putting five of their crew into her, giving orders to follow their ship; but petitioner in the night time ventured to steer her another course, by which means she lost sight of the pirate ship, and two days after he took an opportunity when the principal of the pirates, who commanded the rest, lay dozing with a pair of pistols under his head (petitioner making an excuse to go in for some provisions), seized the pistols from him, and after some scuffle petitioner shot him "into the jaws," and overcame him, and afterwards engaging the rest, three of them surrendered to him. These he secured; the fifth was a Frenchman, who stood neutral. Petitioner sailed to New York with the pirates, where they were tried, convicted, and three of them executed. Petitioner's jawbone was broken, and he was otherwise dangerously wounded, and being an entire stranger here, and very poor, prays that he may receive the rewards for the three who surrendered, as promised by his Majesty's proclamation in 1718.

Copies of two documents in support of his case. 3 *pages*.

6 March. 31. "An account of the monies arisen by the tax upon Papists the sums discharged by certificates transmitted into the Remembrancers Office, and the arrears standing out thereupon."

Addressed "to the honble the Knights Citizens and Burgesses assembled in Parliament."

1725. VOL. CCLII.

Another paper is put with this, but whether it originally belonged to it is a little uncertain. It is docketed :—" Abstract concerning Papists Estates," containing much of what had been enacted in relation to papists and their estates since 1 Geo. I. and making suggestions to render the Act of 3 Geo. I. effectual. Signed " Denis Bond." 4½ *pages.*

11 March. 32. Deposition, taken at Kirkwall, in the county of Orkney, 11 Mar. 1725, of James Laing, merchant in Calfsound, in the Island of Eday, as to the capture of the crew of a pirate ship, which was stranded in endeavouring to come to surprise James Fea, the younger, of Clestrain, giving an account of the plots and counterplots of Mr. Fea and the pirate during several days. Mr. Fea at last succeeded in taking the whole of the pirates, twenty in number, prisoners. 5 *pages.*

[There are three Minutes connected with Fea's affairs entered in the *Minute Book,* Vol. 25, pp. 54*a*, 67*f*, and 83*f*. He petitioned to be rewarded for seizing the pirate Gow and his crew. The bounty to him of 500*l.* allowed by proclamation was enlarged to 800*l.*]

11 March. 33. Lord Lieut. of Ireland to the Lords of the Treasury. Sends petition of Mr James Clarke, late Collector of Kilkenny in Ireland, setting forth his services and sufferings for the Protestant cause in that kingdom, and that through unavoidable misfortunes he became indebted to the King for 2,303*l.*, of which 1,000*l.* has been paid, and that he prays for the remainder to be remitted. The Lord-Lieut. asks their Lordships to consider how far he may be a proper object of his Majesty's compassion.

The petition and a certificate: also a report of the Com^rs^ of revenue, Ireland, all on the same subject.

The petition is *minuted* :—" 13th 8^br^ 1725. To be discharged from the 303^li^ 2·1 upon paying the 1000^li^ said by the Comm^rs^ to be in a prompt way of paym^t^."

Petitioner was in considerable business in the Court of King's Bench, Ireland; and at the instigation of John Forster, Esq., Recorder of Dublin, afterwards Lord Chief Justice, was concerned as agent or manager for the Lord Mayor, Aldermen, Sheriffs, and Citizens in all disputes at that time carried on against them, though he knew he should thereby incur the displeasure of the judges of that Court and hazard the loss of his business, which happened. 5 *pages.*

16 March. 34. The same to the same. Cleonard de Lima and Manuel Demetre, of the Island of Minorca, have made application to his Majesty for 420*l.* in consideration of a robbery committed by some of the garrison at Port Mahon upon George de Lima, since deceased. His Majesty grants the same to them of his special bounty in consideration of the expense of their voyage. Asks for directions to be given for the payment. Whitehall. 1 *page.*

17 March. 35. Joseph Fawcett to the R^t^ Hon. Robert Walpole. Commences :—" Mr Halsey, who I believe respects me, told me that your hono^r^ ordered me to make a bill for the charge, persecution and great expense I have had, or been at, in the Mint affaire (being

1725. VOL. CCLII.

sure I have been instrumental to convert many rebel insolvents, papists and tories) and that without any confused noise or garments rowl'd in blood or halters." Sets forth his zeal for the Government, that he was put to great charges in printing the address to his Majesty, the petition to the House of Commons, the Mint case, "a representation to the House, of Thomas Eaton ye constable's taking money of the miserables," and "the mistakes the select vestry of the parish made in't": to do which, he had to put his valuables "into limbo." He (Fawcett) was prosecuted at Guildford; but Mr Arthur Onslow, the Chairman, brought him off. Had to prosecute Eaton for scandalous words against the King and Government. His poor wife broke her heart under these new catastrophes and left this vale and him with six children. He says, "Great S^r^ I have depended upon you for a resurrection, if you'l say let it be done (twill)."

The following is the postscript:—"S^r^. If the inclosed's thought to be of any service to the Governm^t^ be so kind as to let me know it, and he and I will wait on y^r^ hon^r^. He's ab^t^ 60 years of age, a good schollar and great naturalist, and has made a large collection of rarities, sea plants and other curiosites or rarities of those countreys."

The enclosed rhapsodical papers referred to are entitled:—

(1.) "Melchisedeck illustrated in a true light by Doctor George Hamilton Grierson and also ye plean meaning of the holy sacrament of the Lords Supper."

(2.) "This is to ye publick that Geo: Hamilton Grierson the apostolical Doct^r^ & divine who clears all dark parables and antient prophesies," &c. 4 *pages.*

20 March. 36. Lord Lieut. of Ireland (Carteret) to the Lords of the Treasury. Is of opinion that Captain William Moore's is a compassionate case, and that his Majesty's bounty would be properly bestowed on him.

There may be some doubt whether Lord Tyrawley was properly entitled to half-pay from 13 June 1717, when his regiment was broke, to the 24th Dec. 1720, when his pay determined as General, but from "20" Dec. to 8 June last, the day of his death, during which time he was not otherwise provided for, he was entitled to half-pay as Colonel of a regiment of foot upon the Establishment. 2 *pages.*

[? About 22 Mar.] 37. Petition of Mary Masson, widow, heir, and representative of James Bayne, deceased, to the Lords of the Treasury. As master wright to the Crown James Bayne was employed by the Government in the building of the Palace of Holyrood House, and in repairing the Castles of Edinburgh, Sterling, and Bass, for which he furnished timber and other materials; and by a Committee of the Parliament of Scotland, 81,769*l.* (Scotch money) or 6,814*l.* 1*s.* 8*d.* sterling was admitted to be due to him; for the payment whereof he was recommended by an Act of Parliament to King William, but never received any part thereof, except a pension of 50*l.* per ann.

VOL. CCLII.

1725.

James Bayne and his family's ruin was entirely owing to the non-payment of this debt. Prays for relief or compensation for the debt.

With a recommendation of her case at the end signed by four persons.

On the back is:—"Delivered the 22[d] March 1724. S. Walter." 1¼ *pages.*

[Before 25 Mar.] 38. Memorial of the Earl of Weemys to the Com[rs] of Customs. Lays before the Com[rs] the state of the right of the family of Crawford, under which he claims exemption from duty for his coal exported from the harbour of Methill, also the condition and circumstances of his coallery as well as the port. Will point out the state of the harbour and coallery as they appear from the affidavits annexed. The Regality of the City and Bishopric of St. Andrews had many and great privileges and immunities granted to them; and amongst these, that of a right to the customs of all the ports within the regality; with a power of appointing proper officers for receiving such customs, searching ships and granting "coquets," as may appear by a charter granted by John, Archbishop of S[t] Andrews, to Patrick Larmonth of Darsie, ratified by King James the Sixth, A.D. 1583. From Larmonth of Darsie this right was "apprysed" by Robert Lord Lindsay, who received from George, Archbishop of S[t] Andrews, "a charter of apprysing," A.D. 1610. The family of Crawford Lindsay having proceeded upon this right to exact customs, &c., divers merchants became refractory. This moved the Earl of Crawford to bring an action before the Lords of Council against them and the King's Controller in A.D. 1615, and he obtained a decree. The merchants obtained letters of suspension, but the decree was affirmed. The Earl of Crawford obtained a charter in A.D. 1648, of all and singular the office of great customary or custom of the City of S[t] Andrew and port of the Regality. William, Earl of Crawford, having made over his estate to Sir Thomas Moncrief, for the behoof of his creditors, a charter was (A.D. 1695) granted to Sir Thomas, confirming the right. Memorialist's ancestors having found coal within their estate close by the Creek of Methill, (which lay so deep and must be wrought at so great a charge, that it could not possibly turn to any account by inland sale), built a harbour to export their coals, relying upon their right of exemption from duty. This cost them 9,000*l.* sterling. Petitioner's ancestors "set down" pits at a very great expense, and erected machines for drawing up the water at a cost of not less than 8,000*l.* sterling. The growth of water is no less than 100 tons an hour, and the pits 40 fathoms deep. The neighbourhood is stored with coal pits, which are wrought without any charge at all for raising water, and it is manifest that memorialist can have no sale for his coal within the country, and cannot export without loss, unless the exemption is continued.

At the foot is a copy of a warrant to the Com[rs] of Customs to stay all proceedings until the end of next Whitsuntide term.—Imperfectly dated on the docket, 1724–5, and so must be before

1725. VOL. CCLII.

25 March. There is a further stay of process till Michaelmas term. See *Entries for North Britain*, vol. 8, p. 120. 7 *pages*.

25 March. 39. "Report of the Surveyor of the Woods [Ch. Wither] relating to Highways and Lodges in Dean Forest," addressed to the Lords of the Treasury. Finds that the whole forest, being extra-parochial, the roads in it are not under the care of the officers of any particular parish; but have, from time to time, been repaired at the expense of the Crown. Has caused the highways to be viewed by the forest officers with the assistance of some gentlemen of the county, who have jointly made a return to him that it will cost at least 854*l.* 10*s.* to repair them. Gives the particulars. Has caused Ruardean Lodge to be surveyed, and finds it much out of repair; and its situation so much exposed, that he thinks it would be for his Majesty's service to remove it to a more "sheltry" place. Five other lodges also require repair at a cost of 207*l.* 10*s.* Most of the roads are very narrow and overhung with trees. Proposes to widen them to 30 feet in the clear. The wood and trees might be sold to defray the expense.

Minuted:—"Wt signed." 3 *pages*.

25 March. 40. "A list of the persons pay'd by Jacob Blagny now living," arranged alphabetically under the first letter. They are chiefly French. There is a column for the amount of their pensions per annum paid at Lady day, 1725. Signed "Jacob de la motte Blagny." 6½ *pages*.

27 March. 41. Copy of a letter from the Lord Lieut. of Ireland (Carteret) to the Duke of Newcastle on the state of the debt due from the nation. Thinks it his duty to offer whatever occurs to him for the improvement of the King's revenue which in some respects requires alteration. By an act of 14 & 15 Charles II. for settling the Excise or New imposts upon his Majesty, &c. a Commission of Appeals was erected for the benefit of the merchant, and 'till the year 1702 the Chief Baron, or one of the Barons of the Exchequer, was always in the Commission; but since that time it has generally been composed of persons of less rank, and these employments (as he is credibly informed) have been purchased. It seems to have been the design of the act that this Commission should be a check upon the Officers of the Excise if they should determine too favourably for the merchant against the Crown, &c., but it would be more effectual if the gentlemen in the Commission were of more weight or authority, and absolutely independent of the Commissioners of the Revenue. Is likewise informed that appeals have sometimes remained so long undetermined that the goods have been spoiled before any judgment was passed. Proposes that the two Chief Justices and the Chief Baron in Ireland be made Comrs of Appeals, with a salary of 200*l.* per annum in the room of the three gentlemen who are now in the Commission, whom he proposes to compensate, as he has nothing to object to them personally; and in order that they may have no colour to complain, which otherwise they might have. Some of them, if not all, having purchased their employment. 3½ *pages*.

VOL. CCLII.

1725.

31 March. 42. Report of A. Cracherode to the Lords of the Treasury on the memorial of William Young, in behalf of the captors of the pirate sloop called the "Ranger," whereby he sets forth that on 10 Jan. 1723 Captain Peter Solyard, commander of H. M. Ship the "Greyhound" took the above pirate ship and carried her, together with the crew, into "Road Island"; and on the 12th of July following the pirates (37 in number) were tried and twenty-eight of them convicted of piracy. Therefore the memorialists (on behalf of the captors) prays their Lordships to direct payment of the reward offered by his Majesty's proclamation. Certifies that his Majesty by his proclamation of 21 Dec. 1718 declared that any person seizing pirates and bringing them to conviction should receive a reward for the same, viz., for every commander of a pirate ship, 100*l.*; for every lieutenant, boatswain, carpenter, and gunner, 40*l.*; for every inferior officer, 30*l.*; and for every private, 20*l.*; to be paid by the Treasury. It appears by certificate, annexed, that thirty-seven persons named in the list were taken in the "Ranger," by the "Greyhound," and brought into the said colony to the town of Newport and committed to gaol. Gives the names and rank of twenty-eight of them who were convicted, and states what was due to the captors, amounting to 680*l.* Gives also the names of the persons on board the "Greyhound," the sums due to them, &c.

Also the petition and four other documents connected therewith. One of them is under the seal of the Governor of Rhode Island and that of the Collector of Customs there. 19½ *pages.*

[See also *Kings Warrant Book*, vol. 26, p. 432, where there is a warrant to pay the memorialist 577*l.* 12*s.* 6¼*d.*, for which there was a power of attorney from a large part of the captors.]

2 April. 43. Copy of the Attorney and Solicitor General's report to the Lords of the Treasury on the case of the Comrs and Trustees of the Forfeited Estates in Scotland; the question being whether they were entitled to their salaries during the continuance in the actual execution and performance of their trust. The opinion was that they were entitled. 2½ *pages.*

6 April. 44. Alured Popple to John Scrope, Esq., transmitting the form of a bond to be taken in 1,000*li.* penalty for the execution of the office of Deputy Governor of North Carolina by Sir Richard Everard, Bart. 2 *pages.*

8 April. 45. Lord Lieut. of Ireland (Carteret) to the Lords of the Treasury in favour of continuing the pension of 250*l.* per ann. (which Lord Strangford enjoyed until his death) to Lady Strangford and her son the present Viscount, a youth of 10 years old. They were left in a deplorable condition [without] any thing to subsist them, or to educate the young Lord. Lady Strangford had petitioned for the pension for their support and to educate her son in the Protestant religion, to which his father had become a convert.

There is a Minute of a previous date to this, viz., 17 Feb. 1724, on this subject (see *Minute Book*, Vol. 25, p. 20) as follows:— "See what pencōn the Dowager Viscot 'Strongforth' hath in

1725. VOL. CCLII.

Ireland, for her self or for educating her children in the Protestant religion: and if there be any mr̃e wants for continuing the same, the necessary measures are to be taken for that purpose." 1½ *pages.*

14 April. 46. "A particular of causes now under prosecution with the states thereof." Signed "A. Cracherode." 10 *pages.*

15 April. 47. The Earl of Loudoun to ———. Puts him in mind to give orders for making out a gift of 1,000*l.* yearly to the Church of Scotland to be applied for providing itinerant ministers and catechists in those parts of the Highlands and islands where Popery and ignorance most prevail; this gift being mentioned both in the King's letter to the General Assembly and in his (the Earl's) instructions it appears proper to have it forthwith despatched. It is all the more necessary because the Assembly which is now to meet is to have the applying of the money for the end contained in the gift for this year. Must likewise beg that the person addressed would give orders for a warrant for 1,000*l.* to be paid to him in Scotland, he having the honour to be his Majesty's Commissioner. Sends enclosed, for consideration, a memorial concerning his house rent.

The memorial referred to, which states that the house in Privy Garden in which he lives, wanting repair in her Majesty's time, she promised that if the Earl would advance the money he should have a building lease, and the quit rent should be the third of the value, as it then was; and that the money he should lay out in repairs should be repaid in case Whitehall should be rebuilt, or at his removal from the house. Upon faith of these promises the Earl laid out in repairs 2,400*l.*, but was never able, in the Queen's time, to obtain a lease. After his Majesty's accession he obtained a lease, but without any condition of repayment of his money. By the lease his quit rent is 60*l.* a year, which is the third of the value of the house as improved. The common method in repairing houses which did not formerly pay quit rent is to have the house valued and to get a building lease for the third of the value of the house before the repairs. The Memorialist now pays more than the yearly value of the house. Proposes, in order to make him some reparation for his losses by the above lease, that Mr Walpole should pay the quit rent for five years at Lady Day last, amounting to 300*l.*

In the *Minute Book*, Vol. 25, p. 40, 15 April 1725, is:—"The Earl of Loudoun is to have the usual Bounty of 1,000*l.* now he is going the King's Commr to the Kirk in Scotland." 4 *pages.*

13 Jan.– 15 April. 48. Memorial of Francis Burton, Receiver General of the deductions of 6*d.* per pound, to the Lords of the Treasury, as to there being no deduction upon the rent of the house wherein the Admiralty Office is kept. Further, the Treasurer of Greenwich Hospital pays salaries exceeding 50*l.* per ann. to officers therein who were in like stations to several in Chelsey Hospital from whom deductions were made.

1725. VOL. CCLII.

Besides the memorial are several memoranda and accounts of the same receiver connected with the 6*d.* deductions. Dated between 13 Jan. and 15 April 1725. 8 *pages.*

16 April. 49. Com[rs] for Salt (Scotland) to the Lords of the Treasury. Upon receipt of M[r] Scroope's letter, acquainting them with the discovery of great frauds at the Port of Anstruther in 1719, in the weighing and delivering up of salt to the Custom House officers, they (the Com[rs]) instructed M[r] Alex[r] le Grand, one of the Inspectors of the Out Ports, to repair to Anstruther to examine the books, files, and warrants there, and to copy the documents which their Lordships called for. This he has done, Send copies of the notes or writings. Upon weighing over the salt at Anstruther in 1719, it appeared that great frauds had been committed there, and a stop was put to making out debentures for salt delivered up, &c. Several of those whose debentures continue under stop have prosecuted the collector by bill in the Exchequer, and they expect the case will come on in next term. Salt Office, Edinburgh, 16 April 1725.

Also three papers touching the quantities of foreign salt weighed and delivered up, &c. 7 *pages.*

17 April. 50. "The final report of the Commissioners and Trustees of the Forfeited Estates in Scotland. Presented to the Honourable House of Commons; Saturday the 17th day of April, 1725."

A printed paper with five appendices. 11 *pages.*

17 April. 51. Report of the Attorney General (York) to the Lords of the Treasury, on the petition and memorial of Moyle Breton, Esq., and of Thomas Breton and Anne Breton, in her own right, and of the said Anne (as executrix of Robert Breton and Mary Breton) and of Richard Bate, clerk, and Elizabeth his wife; they the said Robert, Thomas, Anne, Elizabeth and Mary being the five younger brothers and sisters of the said Moyle Breton. The prayer of the petition is that a marriage settlement may be examined, and if found true that directions may be given that the defence of the settlement against the pretences of John Sansome, a collector of Customs in the port of Bristol (who is charged with having fraudulently obtained a bond from Mary Breton) may be acknowledged and allowed, and that the petitioner Moyle Breton's estate and the trust estate, charged with petitioner's younger children's portions, may be discharged thereof. The Attorney General sums up his report by saying that upon the merits of the case, as it stood originally, there was not sufficient foundation for the proceedings upon the extent [issued against Sansome, by virtue whereof all the lands which had been the estate of Mary Breton were extended and seized into the Queen's hands], but the settlement of May 1698 must have prevailed against the title of Sansome or of the Crown under him; and this, he thinks, was Sir Edward Northy's opinion. It is also plain to him that the Court of Exchequer thought there was not sufficient reason for a court of equity to set the settlement

1725. Vol. CCLII.

aside. Is of opinion that it may be proper and advisable for their Lordships by their warrant to authorise the Attorney General to confess the plea of the petitioner, Moyle Breton, to the said extent, and to consent in the Court of Exchequer that the English information be dismissed.

The lands mentioned are—a farm in Boughton Aluph in Kent, "Certain woodlands in Kent containing about 236 acres," and the reversion of Socum Farm, the parsonage farm, and Oliver Girton's farm.

The petition and three other documents. 23 *pages.*

[After 17 April.] 52. A paper docketed:—"Difference between the Commiss[rs] & York Buildings Company's Accounts." The "Commissioners" are the Commissioners of Inquiry for the Scotch Estates. Undated, but after 17 April 1725.

With this is an affidavit (referred to in the above paper) of Robert Packett, formerly one of the Directors of the York Buildings Company, respecting the bidding at the sale of the estates of the late Lords Wintoun, Kelsyth, and Panmure, and other matters connected therewith. 5½ *pages.*

20 April. 53. Lord Lieut. of Ireland to the Lords of the Treasury. The Lords Justices (Ireland) ordered the Deputy Vice-Treasurer to pay 20,000*l.* as required in H.M. warrant. The Lord Lieut. repeated the orders since he arrived. The Deputy Vice-Treasurer informs him that he has not been able to pay more than 4,000*l.* upon that account, as he had to pay current expenses of the establishment, and to remit 20,000*l.* to pay the Paymaster of the Forces in Great Britain, on account of six regiments of foot, lately replaced upon the Irish Establishment. Has ordered him to remit the remainder of the sum mentioned in his Lordship's letter with all possible expedition.

Docketed:—"L[d] Liev[t] ab[t] the residue of y[e] m[o] due from y[e] purchasers of y[e] late D. Ormonds estate." 1½ *pages.*

20 April. 54. Memorial of the Principal Officers of the Ordnance to the Lord Lieut. of Ireland (Carteret). The Board of Ordnance contracted with M. Nicholas Gruebere, merchant, to make 1,000 barrels of gunpowder for H.M. service, at 3*l.* 14*s.* per barrel, amounting with fees to 3,918*l.* 16*s.* 2*d.*: a moiety to be paid him in hand to go on with the work, and the remainder when the last parcel was delivered. The late Lords Justices directed that the Board of Ordnance should receive from the Vice-Treasurer the moiety of the above sum to enable them to pay Gruebere 1,850*l.* (the sum he was entitled to receive in advance). He has since completed the contract and desires to be paid. Move his Excellency to grant his order on the Treasury for the balance.

Minuted:—"A letter to Lord Lieutenant for payment of the sum desired is already drawn upon Letter from Lord Lieut[t] of which this is a duplicate." 2 *pages.*

VOL. CCLII.

1725.

22 April. 55. Lord Lieut. of Ireland to the Lords of the Treasury. By the accounts before "the Commissioners," the balance with which the Deputy Vice-Treasurer charges himself amounts to about 75,000*l.*, being twice as much as the last, which exceeded any of the former. Gives explanations. Transmits an account of the debt and credit of the Kingdom from Lady Day 1723 to Christmas 1724. The accounts will be laid before the Irish Parliament, but it will be so near the beginning of the session, that he will hardly have time to receive the King's commands for supplying so great a deficiency. Is informed that the state of the debt will not differ from what it is computed at in the enclosed papers. Several particular sums are brought in that are due to his Majesty, but not immediately receivable, amounting to 156,852*l.* 16*s.* 2⅝*d.*, which leaves a debt to the Establishment of 134,061*l.* 0*s.* 10¼*d.*, including the 50,000*l.* loan borrowed on Parliamentary credit. But in most of the articles brought to lessen the National Debt there are either anticipations or insolvencies. Believes that the [deficiency] is in some measure to be attributed to the deadness of trade, but is glad to find by the weekly abstracts that trade begins now to recover.

He further observes: "The enclosed papers of accounts are made up pursuant to a method the House of Commons has long gone into; wherein for the sums actually due to the Establishment for any half year, and which one would hope should be ready in the Exchequer, they have always applied the expected produce of the revenue which can never be received till near six months after it is due to his Majesty, and consequently before it can be got in to answer the proper payments another debt of the same amount is accrued. Thus it stands in relation to the quit rents which are payable half yearly, but one half year can never be collected before another becomes due. In the Hearth money it is much worse: for the duty is payable only once a year (vizt the 10th of January) in one entire payment, but is never got in till nine months after; by which means the Establishment must be always very much in arrear, even though the Hereditary Revenue and the additional duties should at last yield all they are computed at."

The total of the Hereditary Revenue and additional duties for the year ending Lady Day 1724 amounts to 486,720*l.* 8*s.* 10½*d.* These, in his opinion, could never support the Establishment. Thinks he has made those who have the most considerable weight in Parliament sensible of the great deficiency, and the necessity of supplying it. Has very good reason to hope that at the meeting of Parliament the generality of the people will be very well disposed to enter into such measures as his Majesty shall judge most proper for the keeping up the honour and dignity of the Establishment. Forbears to talk of any particular methods for raising the money till he shall receive his Majesty's directions.

Minuted:—"Ap[ril] ye 29th read & to be consid^rd."

There is one enclosure only, viz.: the "Account of the Vice-Treasurer's ballance at Christmas 1723." 8 *pages.*

1725. VOL. CCLII.

23 April. 56. Report of the Com^{rs} of Works to the Lords of the Treasury on the memorial of the Duke of Ancaster, Lord Great Chamberlain, accompanied by a plan of the vaults under the Court of Requests at Westminster. Have carefully considered the same, and made plans both as they were before the rebuilding the Court of Requests, and as the vaults now are.

The memorialist states that the Board of Works complain of his putting a padlock on the door of the vaults under the Court of Requests, so that he cannot come at the King's stores lodged there. Was greatly surprised to be refused the key of the vaults, for he has a right to search any rooms belonging to the House when he thinks proper, and therefore put a lock upon it till he was further satisfied. Hopes their L^{ps} will order the removal of the stores, for it is his undoubted right to dispose of all the offices and rooms belonging to either House of Parliament that are not granted by his Majesty's warrant, or desired by either House of Parliament for their service. The usual method is for their Speaker to write to the Great Chamberlain to desire that they may have it. Is satisfied that it is an encroachment upon his rights. They have not had this pretended possession many years. One Margery Duzell remembers above 60 years before the rebuilding the Court of Request, the records of the Court of King's Bench were kept in the passage under the Court of Requests, and never saw nor heard that any of the King's stores were kept there. Edmund Fitz-Gerald also remembers the same. Hopes their L^{ps} will order the delivery of the key to him.

The plan is also with the report and memorial. 5 *pages.*

[In the *Minute Book,* Vol. 25, p. 74*d* (14 July 1725), is:—" Board of Works attending are called in and my Lords order them to make a plan of the vaults under the Court of Requests, and to mark in the said plan what may be for the King's accomodation, what for the service of the House of Lords and Commons, and what for any other necessary occasions, which plan my Lords mean to transmit to the Lord Great Chamberlain for him to take care that the vaults be disposed accordingly."]

25 April. 57. Surveyor of Woods (Ch. Wither) to ———. Asks him to forward the King's Sign Manual for making the several wood sales for the services therein mentioned. The season for felling timber is now at its height, and if deferred a week the bark of all the wood cut would be lost to the Crown; which piece of ill husbandry he would be glad to prevent. 1 *page, quarto.*

26 April. 58. " Surveyor of the Gardens' report upon Mr Wise's and Mr Carpenter's charge of planting in the Lower Wilderness at Hampton Court."

Represents that at the very time this estimate was offered to the Lords of the Treasury the work was actually done without his knowledge, much less without his giving any direction for it. " But as

1725. VOL. CCLII.

the charge of making this new Plantation, the destruction of the old one being occasioned by the overflowing of the Thames, and not any neglect of the Contractors." Their L^ps will please to determine whether it ought to fall upon them or no.

The bill of the work and the following extract from the *Treasury Minute Book* of 4 June 1725:—

"Sr John Vanbrugh's report for a sum demanded by Wise and Carpenter for work done in the Plantacons at Hampton Court without the previous direction or agreement of my Lords is read, and Sr John is to be writ to again thereupon inasmuch as he has not by this Report, given his opinion to my Lords, as, by their letter, he was desired to do." 3½ *pages*.

59. Lord Lieut. of Ireland (Lord Carteret) to the Lords of the Treasury. The Com^rs for passing the accounts of the Kingdom met on the previous Saturday to sign the accounts of the year ending at Christmas 1723, but found that their commission had not been enrolled. By a clause therein it ought to have been enrolled within six months of its date. The Com^rs have represented to him (the Lord Lieut.) that they do not think themselves sufficiently authorised to proceed any further; they doubt whether the persons accounting before them, since the first six months after the date of the commission have been duly discharged. The doubt is founded on an Irish Act of Parliament of 17 & 18 Car. II. Was surprised that the omission should remain so long undiscovered, and that any further scruple should remain with the Com^rs. Directed them to agree with the Solicitor General on a draft of a King's letter for passing a new commission of accounts to remove the difficulties. Forwards a copy. If his Majesty approve of the draft, desires their Lordships will transmit his Majesty's warrant that he may order a commission to be passed.

In the Minute Book, Vol. 25, p. 44, is:—

"Lord Lieut^s letter of the 27 day of Aprill 1725, with a draft of a letter for renewing the Commission of Acco^ts, by reason of a doubt as to the validity thereof, for want of Inrolling the same within 6 months pursuant to a clause therein contained, and the import of an Act of Parliament in that behalf, are read; and my Lords approve the draft, and order the same to be transcribed for the King's hand accordingly." 4½ *pages*.

27 April. 60. L. M. to the Lords of the Treasury. Offers to make discoveries. Hopes to receive a free pardon for all offences committed by him against the Government relating to the revenue of customs and excise on salt. Prays that his discoveries may not come to the Board of Customs. Prays that Mr John Cock, Collector of Customs in Padstowe, and none other may be ordered to go with memorialist to a neighbouring port, where memorialist will show him many private places where many thousand pounds worth of concealed smuggled goods have been hidden. Asks their Lordships to direct to Mr L. M. Post Office, Bodmin.

1725. VOL. CCLII.

On the back is the following minute:—"May 1st eod. ann. Lr̃es writ to s[d] L. M. & to M[r] Cocke Coll[r], Padstowe vide Lr̃e Book [vol. 18] p. 78."

The letters referred to are entered there. The memorialist is assured of their L[ps] protection in any discoveries he may make, and the collector is to assist in the same. 1 *page.*

27 April. 61. Report of the Surveyor of Woods (Ch. Wither) to the Lords of the Treasury. On the memorial of the Earl of Halifax, Chief Ranger of Salsey forest, Northampton. Finds the lawn rails and ring mounds in the forest are much run to ruin, though Lord Halifax has been at considerable charge in repairing them. The cost of repairs would be 202*l.* 15*s.* 11*d.*

Minuted:—"W[t] signed." 2 *pages.*

April. 62. Petition of Josias Thompson, late Coast Surveyor in Ireland, to the King. Has done as much and more in his station to serve his Majesty than any person so employed in that kingdom, and is ruined on that account only by the artifice of a reputed Jacobite surveyor general; and there are those continued in his Majesty's revenue who are known friends to the Pretender, favourers of the wool smuggling trade and defrauders of his Majesty's Customs, &c. On a former petition to his Majesty the King ordered petitioner to be examined, but he has not obtained the benefit thereof, although it is two years past; neither has he received any subsistence since he came into this kingdom by the encouragement of the Lords of Trade, save only 20*l.* at two payments; though a reward of 100*l.* was paid to Elias Barns for services in conjunction with petitioner, and a moiety was intended for him by his Majesty, as Mr. Walpole declared. By a false, malicious, and inconsistent charge exhibited against him by the Surveyor General is deprived of the favour promised him. Prays his Majesty to enable him to return to his wife and five small children in Ireland, who are reduced to extreme want by his endeavours to serve his Majesty.

Docketed:—"Mem. This is the original petition which I deliver his Majesty in April 1725 and which by his orders was sent to the Treasury."

Minuted:—"20th Jan. 1725/6. Upon further consideration of this petition my Lords do not think fit to do any thing in it." 1 *page.*

1 May. 63. John Stainforth to the Lords of the Treasury. Pursuant to their L[ps] commands and warrant has been at Beverley, Collingham, Dringhouses, and Middlethorp, and has viewed and demanded possession of all the lands and tenements in the annexed schedule, and which are included in the lease granted to M[r] Bland. Cannot find that the present possessors of the premises, except the heirs of W[m] Hood, for the estate at Dringhouses and Middlethorp, ever held the same by any lease from M[r] Bland. They have always paid reserved rents to the Crown, or others who claim under that title, and believe their estates to be held in fee. In the paper annexed has given what observations he made upon the premises.

1725. VOL. CCLII.

The paper referred to is in tabular form containing—(1) Names of the present possessors, (2) Lands and tenements granted to lease to Mr Bland [in the places above-named], (3) Reserved rents, and (4) [Observations]. 2 *pages.*

4 May. 64. Report of Sir John Vanbrugh to the Lords of the Treasury relating to a further supply of water at the Cockpit, in case it may be done at little charge, by laying a new pipe from the main near the gun houses. There has, for some time past, been a great scarcity of water about Whitehall, occasioned partly by the great failure of the springs in Hyde Park for want of rain, and partly by the proprietors of the New River water cutting off a branch which served Whitehall for many years past, but which they now pretend to have been only upon courtesy. Has endeavoured to recover some of the springs about the mews and St Martin's Lane, which have been either diverted or choked up many years ago; and has so far succeeded in this search that he believes the additional quantity of water which will now be gathered from them will prove sufficient to supply both the Cockpit and Whitehall without any further aid. 1 *page.*

7 May. 65. Report of the Controllers of the Accounts of the Army (Medows and Bruce) to the Lords of the Treasury on the memorials of Mr Missing, Contractor for Victualling Gibraltar Garrison, as to the quantities and qualities supplied, and what is proper to be done for the better conduct of the victualling affair for the future. They observe that "neither the letter nor meaning of the contract can be understood to enable the contractor to receive from the Government half the price of 19 or 21 months provisions, beforehand, (as it has sometimes happened), and at the same time leave him at liberty to sell 15 or 17 months, and receive the whole amount of that quantity over and above the moiety he had before; nor does it seem necessary, or adviseable, ever to have more than 6 months provisions in store for the garrison, in so hot a country; where the wast and risque is so great."

In their opinion the utmost that can be demanded or expected from the Government in reason or by the contract is, that the contractor be paid always beforehand, one moiety for six months provisions, provided he produce certificates from the commanding officer that there is such a quantity in store, and the other moiety upon the arrival of the monthly lists of the persons victualled. He is overpaid by the account annexed, 2,747*l.* 15*s.* 7½*d.* 5 *pages.*

15 May. 66. Report of the Auditor of Land Revenue (Tho. Jett) to the Lords of the Treasury, transmitting an account or certificate of the names of the Receivers of the Land Revenue of the Crown within his audit, the time to which they have brought in their accounts to be passed, and the remains or otherwise, which appear on the foot of those accounts to be in their hands or owing to them; with a schedule of all the new rents that have been put in charge and given to the receivers to collect since his Majesty's accession; and

1725. VOL. CCLII.

also a distinct rental of all the new rents reserved upon the several leases within the Manor or Bailywick of St James.

The certificate and schedule follow on the report, and the following is a description of the rental:—

67. "The Manor or Baylywick of St James in the county of Middlesex.	A true and perfect Rentall of all and every the rents and revenues, within the said Manor or Baylywick, reserv'd and made payable to the Crown, by virtue of the several and respective Leases thereof made, to divers persons."

It is divided into five columns, viz.:—(1) The names of the Lessees, (2) The dates of the several leases, (3) The premises, (4) The terms of years granted, and (5) The present rents p annum.

At the foot is the following memorandum:—"There was antiently a bayliffe appointed by patent, to collect the rents & proffits of the said mannor or baylywick of St James: But when the same was made parcell of the joynture to [the] Queen Mother and afterwards to Queen Catherine, and the greatest part of the demesnes was in lease to the Lord Dover and the Earl of St Albans, for several long terms of years, under small rents, it was not worth the while of a Bayliffe to collect the same. And were put in charge to the Receiver of the County and have continu'd so to this time.

Since his Maties succession to the Crown, there being many leases made, to divers persons, of several houses, for long terms of years, under the rents of 12*d.* and 6*d.* p annū, payable for each house, and there being likewise other leases made of several pieces or parcells of ground, reserving the like rents of 12*d.* and 6*d.* p annū, payable to the bayliffe or receiver of the premisses for each house standing thereon. And those leases not distinguishing or particularizeing the number of such houses, the Auditor is at a loss to tell what or how many rents to put in charge for the same; therefore I humbly submit it as my opinion, that it would be for his Maties service to have a bayliff appointed for the manor," &c. Signed "Tho. Jett, Audr." 35½ *large pages.*

19 May. 68. Francis Negus to the Lords of the Treasury. Upon the application of the widows of William Lowine, late chief huntsman, and of Edward Ives, late yeoman pricker, and of Roger Webb, late Harbourer to the Buckhounds. His Majesty, in consideration that the huntsmen are his livery servants, has bestowed upon their widows his Royal bounty, in such manner as has been done to the widows of his livery servants of his stables and stud, in lieu of all demands of charity or pensions whatsoever. Prays their Lordships directions as to how the bounty is to be paid.

Minuted:—"To be placed on the extrarys of the stables." 1 *page.*

21 May. 69. Report of the Controllers of the Accounts of the Army (Medows and Bruce) on two memorials of Thomas Missing Esq., contractor for victualling the garrisons of Placentia and Annapolis

1725. VOL. CCLII.

Royal, consisting of 434 men. Have caused a "State" to be annexed denoting the quantities of each species of provisions due to the garrisons according to contract. There is due to the Contractor 1,996*l.* 8*s.* after the rate of 6*d.* per man, per day.

Also the paper referred to. 3½ *pages.*

21 May. 70. Memorial from the Com^rs of Customs, Edinburgh, to the Lords of the Treasury. Had in a previous memorial proposed the building of seven sloops to guard the Eastern and Western coasts and that the King's moiety of the seizures effected by them should be applied to the charge of the sloops. Two of them had arrived and the others are daily expected, but they have received no directions regarding them. Pray their L^ps warrant for paying the salaries of the commanders and crews and for repayment of the cost of the sloops. Conceive that they should have a warrant also from their L^ps to lay aside the two sloops already in use, there being nine sloops in pay instead of seven.

In the *Minute Book*, vol. 25, p. 60*f* (14 June 1725), it states that the above memorial was read "and ordered to be transmitted to the Comm^rs of the Customes here, so as they may report an acco^t of the first cost, with their opinion also as to the proposed Establishm^t and other the matters contained therein." 2 *pages.*

22 May. 71. Report of the Surveyor General (Pulteney) to the Lords of the Treasury. Pursuant to warrant, has caused to be prepared a lease from Sir John Darnall of his mews or stable yard in Windsor unto Francis Negus, Esq., for his Majesty's use, for seven years, from Lady day 1725, at 250*l.* per ann. with the usual covenants. Sends an authentic copy. Was further directed by the warrant to give notice to the Lessee of his Majesty's lands at Frogmore in Windsor, and of the Farm called Shaw Farm, as to a proviso in the lease of those premises, whereby the crown may resume four acres of the close of eight acres, adjoining Frogmore House, to build a mews, to dig earth, &c. Has caused a notification thereof to be delivered to Mrs Elizabeth Aldworth and her sister Mrs Susanna Aldworth, in whom the premises are vested.

With this report are two others of the respective dates of 26 Jan. 1724 and 5 Feb. 1724–5, copy of a Treasury minute and a warrant from the Lords of the Treasury of 13 Feb. 1724–5 to the surveyor to prepare the lease above referred to. Copy of Sir John Darnall's letter to the Surveyor General on the same subject, copy of the "notification" and certified copy of the lease. 11½ *pages.*

25 May. 72. Lord Townshend to the Lords of the Treasury. His Majesty has thought fit that George Tilson and Thomas Townshend, Esq^res, Under-Secretaries, Mr John Wace, First Clerk, Mr Joseph Richardson, Mr George Woodward, and Mr Adam Lawrey, Clerks, and Mr Isaac Burrows, office-keeper, should attend him during his absence [in his dominions in Germany]. His Majesty's pleasure is that their Lordships give orders to pay forthwith to the above persons the sums therein specified.

1725. VOL. CCLII.

In the *Minute Book*, vol. 25, p. 195, 24 June 1726, is: "Mr George Tilson being in disburse the sum of 146. 10. 6 over and above 1,500li issued to Cha. Delafaye for incidents and Extrary charges in my Lord Townshend's office in his Mats last journey to Hanover is to be repaid the same out of the King's money in the hands of Mr Lowther." 2 *pages*.

27 May. 73. Memorial of Richard Carter, late Deputy Commissary of the Marine Forces, to the Chancellor of the Exchequer (Walpole). Has served the Government upwards of thirty years, and was reduced as Deputy Commissary of the Marine Regiments, and put on half-pay as his predecessors were, upon the late King William's establishment, after the Peace of Ryswick. At the request of the Secretary of the Treasury he resigned his warrant as Purser of the Torbay, that he might compile the General Muster Rolls of the Marine Regiments. Was struck off the list of half-pay officers with the late Commissary General of the Marines from 25 Dec. 1717; and, on a memorial to the Treasury, was recommended to the Admiralty (as having been a naval officer) for preferment. Although the Lords of the Admiralty promised to have regard to the recommendation, they had not provided for him. Prays to be reinstated on the half-pay list as Deputy Commissary of Marines (the pay is 53*l*. per ann., but his predecessors had 10*s*. a day), or to be appointed one of the Deputy Commissaries of the Land Forces.

Also copy of a letter and certificate in support of his case. 2 *pages*.

VOL. CCLIII. 1725. JUNE—DECEMBER.

1 June. 1. Order in Council on the petition of Martha, the widow of Sir Robert Johnson. Her husband was commander of several ships of war, and on his return from a squadron of ships sent to the East Indies to destroy the pirates he, with two of his sons, and all his effects, was lost in the great storm at the Cape of Good Hope, and the petitioner is left with four young children in the greatest distress. Prays for a pension. His Majesty in Council, looking upon petitioner as an object of compassion, refers the petition to the Lords of the Treasury.

Also the copy of her petition.

In the *Minute Book*, vol. 25, p. 70, 9 July 1725, is:—"An Order of Councill of the 1st June 1725, referring a peticon of Martha, the widow of the late Sr Robert Johnson, who was heretofore Commander of several ships of warr in the Royal Navy, was read, and as the same concerns a pencõn to be out of the Civil List for her

1725. VOL. CCLIII.

relief, my Lords are of opinion the Rules of the Navy with respect to pencons may better be dispensed with in the petitioner's favour than the Kings Civil List be burthened therewith and order a Report (if called for) to be made to the Council accordingly." 3¼ *pages.*

2 June. 2. Report of the Lords Com[rs] of Trade to the King on the petition of William Toshach, merchant and inhabitant of Placentia in Newfoundland, who states that he was possessed of a large dwelling house near the point of the great Beach, at Placentia, and the same (in A.D. 1720) was taken up by Col. Gledhill, the Lieut. Governor, for H. M. use and comprehended within the new fortifications there; whereby petitioner has lost 80*l.* sterling, for which he asks to be reimbursed. The Lords of Trade admit that the house has been demolished, and that the grounds are included within the limits of the new fortifications, and that satisfaction should be made to the petitioner.

There are also two nicely executed plans:—(1.) "A plan of the Settlement of Placentia with the names of each inhabitant in the French time and the number of Chaloupes of Grave each planter possessed mark'd to their possessions."

(2.) "A particular Plan of the Fort and Settlement of Placentia." 2 *pages beside the plans.*

3 June. 3. "The conditions on which Sir John Evelyn is willing to dispose of six acres, three roods, and thirty poles of his land; being part of the Little Crane Mead, and other lands adjoining to his Matys Dock Yard at Deptford and part with his way to the Thames for the enlarging and accommodating the said yard."

On the opposite page are:—"Navy Office, 3 June 1725. The Navy Board's observations on S[r] John Evelyns proposals."

In the *Minute Book*, vol. 25, p. 85*f*, 28 July 1725, is:—"M[r] Surveyor General and S[r] John Evelyn attending, are called in, and M[r] Surveyor's Report of the 9th of June last on S[r] John Evelyn's peticon for the fee simple of certain lands at Deptford, as also S[r] John Evelyns observacons thereupon, whereby he would lessen the value rated by the Surveyor for converting his term of years in that estate, into an inheritance, pursuant to an Act of Parliament in that behalf are read, and my Lords upon consideracon thereof do agree to the Surveyor's Report *in omnibus*, except the 160[li] rated by the said Surveyor for the value of about 200 young elms growing on the premises which is to be remitted to Sir John and that because they are esteemed as ornamental to the House at Says Court." 2 *large pages.*

3 June. 4. Certified copy of the memorial of James Carstairs to the King, and of the reference thereupon to the Lords of the Treasury. His Majesty, pursuant to a clause in an Act of Parliament investing the forfeited estates, &c., granted the estate of Kilconquhar to James Carstairs, subject to the payment of the debts affecting it, and reserving power to revoke the same grant. Found that

1725. VOL. CCLIII.

nothing less than a sale of the estate would enable him to answer the chief end of the grant, namely, the payment of the debts; and a sale could not be accomplished while the grant continued. His Majesty referred the matter to the Advocate; who reported that the power of revocation, by hindering a sale, would disappoint the intention of the grant. There were other difficulties which could only be remedied by a clause in an Act. Memorialist has found a purchaser who is satisfied with the title. Prays that the King will discharge the grant of the power of revocation.

The *Minute Book*, vol. 25, p. 107, 21 Sept. 1725, states that the petition was read, "And my Lords say it will be a 'president' and of ill consequence, and they cannot advise the doing thereof." 3 *pages*.

11 June. 5. Surveyor of the Woods (Ch. Wither) to the Lords of the Treasury. Has caused Swinly Walk and Lodge in Windsor Forest to be carefully surveyed, and has informed himself of the works and plantations which his Majesty has ordered to be made there for the increase and preservation of the game. Finds that many acres of land are to be ploughed and sown with different sorts of grain, hurdles and gates to be made, &c., which cannot be reduced to a certain estimate. Proposes that he may be authorised to defray the expenses up to Michaelmas out of wood sales, and then to lay a bill of expenses before their Lordships, with an estimate of the annual allowance for the future. 1 *page*.

11 June. 6. Report of A. Cracherode to the Lords of the Treasury on the petition of Oliver Spurrell, shipwright, who had sued Elizabeth Bolton, late of Chatham, Kent, widow, on a bond, and obtained an outlawry against her. A leasehold belonging to her by inquisition was found to be worth 116*l*. 9*s*. On its sale by the sheriff it realised 105*l*. This latter sum the petitioner prayed might be paid over to him toward satisfaction of the debt of 165*l*. Advises that an order of court should be obtained to pay over the 105*l*. (certain deductions being made).

The petition and an affidavit. 4¼ *pages*.

[? About 14 June.] 7. Petition of Thomas Bryan, Keeper of his Majesty's Gaol at Horsham, Sussex. Asking to be paid his great expenses in carrying to London and bringing back Edward Jarvis, alias Thompkin, and Thomas Stoker, two notorious smugglers, who removed themselves by *habeas corpus* to evade the punishment of the law, and were by the Court of King's Bench remanded to Horsham Gaol and remained there until transported.

Minuted:—"14th June 1725. To be paid by Mr Cracherode." 1 *page*.

[? About 14 June.] 8. Petition of Joseph Wight and John Merest, under clerks attending the service of the House of Lords, to the Lords of the Treasury. By their service in the House they are incapable of other employment. They have no fees, and their perquisites so in-

1725. VOL. CCLIII.

considerable as not to be a competent maintenance, and, since the late repairs done to the Parliament office, their assistance to digest and sort the Records and papers therein has been required, for which no reward is given, nor have they any allowance whatsoever for public business.

Also a paper in relation thereto entitled " Extract of a report in relation to the Parliament office &c."

On the back of the petition is :—" There are no less than four under clerks of the House of Commons, who have 50^{li} a year salary a piece."

Minuted:—" June ye 14 : 1725. Read. Nothing can be done." 3 *pages*.

[? About 14 June.] 9. Petition of William Wynne to the Lords of the Treasury.

Petitioners father, Dr Owen Wynne, for his services abroad and at home, obtained a lease for 31 years at 9*l.* a year rent of the " original seal of Anglesey, Carnarvon, and Merioneth, and of the prefines on fines and recoveries acknowledged and suffered at the Grand Sessions, held for the three counties. Petitioner's mother surrendered the lease and obtained a new lease for 31 years. Prays for a concurrent lease for 21 years.

Minuted:—" June ye 14th 1725, read, & nothing done therein." 1 *page*.

19 June. 10. Report of the Attorney General (Sir Philip Yorke) to the Lords of the Treasury on the petition of the Wardens and Commonalty of the mystery of Goldsmiths of the city of London. The petition sets forth that the petitioners, being empowered by several acts of parliament to assay and mark at Goldsmith's Hall all sorts of manufactured plate, to prevent the fraud of the works thereof, have, for several reigns past, kept an Assay Office at their Hall, with an Assay Master, an Assistant, a Weigher, and Drawer, and provided furnaces, coals, coppells, and all other tools and materials necessary for the same. Towards defraying the great charge thereof they have usually taken four grains upon every pound weight Troy, being about one half penny in value ; and for about seven years last have, by agreement made with the most considerable small workers, taken for every sword hilt so assayed and marked, being five pieces, sixpence; for every snuff box, three pence; for spurs, two pence; for buckles, one half penny; and proportionally for other small wares. Notwithstanding all which allowances there hath been a constant deficiency of about 200^{li} per ann. The petitioners present circumstances render them incapable to support the charge any longer, more especially as they are prosecuted by way of information for taking the said allowances, which will occasion the shutting up of the Assay Office, to the lessening of H. M. revenue, and the great detriment of his subjects in general. The petitioners pray their Lordships to grant their warrant of *noli prosequi* to the Attorney General on the information and for further relief.

Upon a hearing of the matter on both sides, the case seems to be that the Company had been a Guild or Corporation by prescription, with certain privileges confirmed and enlarged from time to time

1725. Vol. CCLIII.

by charters; that the "Franchise" of touching and assaying wrought plate or manufactures of gold and silver is vested in the Corporation by Act of Parliament and by Charter; for by the Statute 28 Ed. I. ca. 20 it is ordained that no Goldsmith of England nor elsewhere within the King's dominions shall from thenceforth make any manner of vessel or other thing of gold or silver, except it be of good and true "Allay," that is to say, gold of certain "Touch," and silver of the sterling allay or better, at the pleasure of him to whom the work belongeth, and that none work worse silver than money, and that no manner of silver depart out of the hands of the workers until it be assayed by the wardens of the craft. And further that it be marked with the Leopard's head, and that they work no worse gold than of the "Touch" of Paris, and that the wardens of the craft shall go from shop to shop among the goldsmiths to assay if their gold be of the Touch before mentioned.

And by letters patent of 3 Feb. 20 Hen. VII. the King grants to the wardens and commonalty the right to search, survey, assay, and and govern the gold and silver worked, or to be worked, in London and elsewhere. From which it appears that it is not only a privilege, but a duty laid upon them.

It does not appear by an Act of Parliament or charter that the Company has been expressly empowered to take any particular fee for assaying; but it was admitted on all sides, and is proved by affidavits annexed, that from time immemorial, until about 1716, the fee constantly taken and not disputed for assaying and marking all silver work has been four grains in the pound troy. Though the Company was satisfied with this as a compensation for large plate, they complained that it was not adequate for assaying and marking toys and other small wares, a great number whereof go to a pound troy. This caused some backwardness and neglect in the officers of the Company in receiving such small wares, and the artificers did not bring their work to the office to be assayed and marked, and they made it of baser alloy than by law they ought. Hereupon a petition was presented (copy annexed) to the Committee of the Company in A.D. 1716, signed by fifteen artificers in small wares, being members of the Company, complaining of this abuse, and asking that they should cause the same to be marked. The Company gave public notice that all artificers and foreigners in or near London should enter their marks and bring their works to the Hall to be assayed.

After this notice another paper (copy annexed) was presented to the wardens and assistants of the Company, signed by 25 persons. They complained that many inconveniences would attend the allowance of the assay and touch to foreigners; that it was contrary to the byelaws of the Company, and an invasion of the privileges of the freemen, and they were advised that it might lawfully be refused to foreigners. They prayed that it might not be allowed. They have a proposal to offer to keep out all foreigners from the assay and touch, and to punish all freemen who bring

VOL. CCLIII.

1725.

foreigners' works to the Hall to be touched. It appears to him (Sir Ph. Yorke) that a considerable number of artificers, being freemen, after a meeting, proposed to the Committee the following rates, viz., threepence for assaying and marking each snuff box, one halfpenny a pair for buckles, and sixpence for every sword hilt, and from this time the Company's officers have taken these rates, and twopence for each pair of silver spurs. Notwithstanding the representation and proposal, does not find that the company made any progress in "excluding persons not free from the assay and touch" nor does he conceive "that it could be done by law." The Company's officers continuing to insist on the new rates an information was filed against the assay-master for extortion. It was argued that the offence, if criminal, was the offence of the Corporation, and that the taking the new rates was upon the proposal of the artificers themselves. It was argued that these were only reasonable reward for the labour involved. For the prosecutors it was contended that the rates were extortionate, and that the former allowance was sufficient. However this may be, the rate of four grains per pound troy is a fee established by prescription or usage, and though the circumstances of times and the value of money may alter, that will not authorise the increasing the fee; but such increase will be extortion. In this case the increase is exorbitant, amounting in some instances to above twenty times as much as was taken before. The profits of the assay office do amount to more than is represented by the Company, for the produce of private assays is omitted out of the computation, and that alone amounts to 150*l.* per ann. It would be dangerous to suffer fees to be increased upon such computations. The public is concerned in the redress of this grievance, for the increase falls on the buyer and lessens the export. The information was granted upon motion and on hearing counsel for the petitioners, and in such cases the staying proceedings by *noli prosequi* is very unusual. Is of opinion that his Majesty or the Lords Justices, by warrant, should order a *noli prosequi* to be entered to the information, provided the Company give assurances that for the future they will take no more than the ancient fees, &c.

Accompanied by the petition and twenty one other documents, chiefly affidavits, relating to the case. 56 *pages.*

19 June. 11. Report of the Surveyor General to the Lords of the Treasury on the petition of the Governor and Company of Chelsea Waterworks, who, petitioners say, having been encouraged by Royal Charter, have undertaken to supply the city of Westminster and parts adjacent with water, which (by reason of the great increase of new buildings) is now much needed. Petitioners say that they have so far succeeded as that they intend forthwith to make reservoirs of water to supply the buildings; but they cannot have a proper place to make a reservoir to supply his Majesty's palace at St James and the middle and lower parts of Westminster unless his Majesty will permit them to use the canal or bason lately made in St James's Park, over against Devonshire House, and the old

pond adjoining to the Deer Pen Grove; therefore they pray to have the use of the canal and pond, and that they may be permitted to lay a main or mains from their machines through the park to the pond and canal, and from thence to the proper places, to serve his Majesty's palace and the streets adjoining. Has been upon the place with Mr Negus (the present Governor of this Company), and finds that the petitioners propose to lay their mains from the Park gate next to Buckingham House, and to carry them (with a little sweep) within thirty six feet of the iron rails of the house, in a straight line, of about 1,575 feet, to the head (or south east corner) of the said old pond, and from thence in another straight line of about 840 feet to the head (or south west corner) of the said canal, and from thence to carry a main through the north east corner of the park wall into Piccadilly Road, as is shown by their annexed plan: for the performing of all which works the ground to be broken up is not to exceed six feet in breadth in any part thereof, and the mains are proposed to be of the thickness of four inches from the bore. Which (considering that (as they say) the head of the old pond is not above ten feet higher than their works, and that the canal is not above seventeen feet higher than the pond, and that the distance from the pond to the canal is not great) if due care be taken in the choice of the timber wherewith those mains shall be made, they may so resist the force or weight of the water (which won't be great) as not to want mending in many years.

Their mains being laid in the manner before mentioned, all that upper and most open part of the park which lies south of Hyde Park Road will be preserved from being broken up.

This undertaking may be of great convenience to many of his Majesty's subjects in and about Westminster; and if the petitioners are allowed the use of the canal and old pond for reservoirs his Majesty's palace of St James's may be constantly supplied with a sufficient quantity of water, not only for common use, but for a fountain or other waterwork in the garden of the palace: besides that the canal (which is now dry) and the old pond being kept in good repair and full of water, will be an ornament to the park, and of service in case of fire. If their Lps advise his Majesty to gratify the petitioners, a licence may be granted to them to lay their mains and to make use of the pond and canal for reservoirs of water and to carry it into Piccadilly Road. The same to be held during the King's pleasure.

In the *Minute Book*, vol. 25, p. 69*d*, is:—"Mr Pulteney the Surveyor General's Report of the 19th June last, on the peticon of the Chelsea Waterworks Company for permission to dig and lay mains from the machines to the pond in St James's Park near Devonshire House as well for the benefit of the King's Palace as of the Streets adjoyning is read and agreed to."

Also the petition and a draft of the plan. 4½ *pages*.

30 June. 12. Report of the Attorney General (Yorke) to the Lords of the Treasury on the petition of the Rector and the rest of the gentlemen of the vestry of the parish of St James, Westminster, which sets

1725. VOL. CCLIII.

forth that by conveyance made under letters patent of 4 April, 6 Will. & Mar., the parish of S[t] James is seised in fee of a small piece of ground inclosed with a brickwall, and formerly part of a piece of ground called Pauletts Garden, near the Pest House Ground, in that parish; the same to be used for a burying place only. The petitioners find it necessary to erect a workhouse for such of the poor as can work, and to erect a convenient building for those of great age or suffering from infirmity; and they are desirous to erect such building on a small part of the burying ground, and pray for the Royal licence to enable them. Confirms the petitioners representation of the case. States in addition that the piece of ground has not hitherto been consecrated. Has no objection to what is prayed, and advises how it may be done.

In the *Minute Book*, vol. 25, p. 70*d*, 9 July 1725, is mentioned that the Attorney General's report is "read and agreed to."

The petition referred to. 6 *pages*.

1 July. 13. "Equivalent Comp[ys] Mem[ll] for y[e] ball[a] y[t] shalbe struck on the Rec[rs] Acc[ts] to be paid over to the Company." The memorial is signed by John Mounsey, Sec[ry]. The moneys are payable out of the revenues in Scotland, and his Majesty's warrant is prayed that the balances may be paid over to the Company.

In the *Minute Book*, vol. 25, p. 65, mention is made that the memorial "is read and is to be considered at another time." 1 *page*.

7 July. 14. Memorial of Diana Spencer on behalf of the Duchess of Malborough to [the Lords of the Treasury] as follows:—"Some years ago M[r] Lowndes measured the buildings in the Pall Mall to the passage, that turns into Marborough House, and upon examining the Leases to those houses from the town, he told the Dutchess of Marlborough that they had encroached eight foot into the breadth of the way to her house; and since this report they have built out several sheds, and made cellars, which does not only make it yet narrower, but from their setting out benches, and drays coming to carry things into the cellars, it is sometimes difficult for two chairs to pass through it; and besides this they let stalls for herbs & stinking things that is a nuisance in the passage to the house. It is not certain that it is in the Treasury's power to pull down all that they have built beyond their grant; but the Dutchess of Marlborough desires no more than to have the passage remain as it was, without encroachments, according to the plan ānexed to her grant from the crown; and if she might humbly propose what would presently be set right & do her justice, it wou'd be only for the Lords of the Treasury to signify that the leases are forfeited by that encroachment of eight foot; but that they will not pull their houses down, if they will themselves pull down those things which they have encroached since this reign."

In the *Minute Book*, vol. 25, p. 82*o*, 22 July 1725, is:—

"Write to the Surveyor acquainting him with the Dutch[s] of Marboroughs complaint about the encroachments and means that

1725. VOL. CCLIII.

people have taken, by building sheds, making cellars and setting out benches, to narrow the way to her House, at least 8 foot, and desire him to examine thereinto and take such measures as may legally be taken for removing the same in case the Crowns Right be concerned therein." 1 *page.*

[? About 9 July.] 15. Complaint of the Under-Keepers of Cranborn Chase, within the Forest of Windsor, to the Earl of Carlisle. Col. Causby has paled in one hundred poles of his own ground, besides three poles which he has encroached in the chase; and there are 7,000 sheep and upwards turned on the chase all the year round, which are much above the number allowed, being only two sheep to an acre. There is no pound to which the distresses may be driven. By reason of the premises, that part of H. M. forest has become much worse, and his Majesty's deer, having no feed there but what is tainted by the sheep, go into the purlieus, where they are destroyed: pray that the feed may be preserved.

In the *Minute Book*, vol. 25, p. 71*q*. 9 July 1725, is:—

"Send the petiĉõn of the Underkeepers of Cranburn Chase" &c. "to the Surveyor of the Woods to consider and report." 1 *page.*

9 July. 16. W. Thompson, Governor of the Bank (of England), to the Lords of the Treasury. Their Lps contract with the Bank for circulating the present Exchequer Bills determines on the 25th inst. Craves to know their Lps sentiments as to a new subscription from their proprietors.

In the *Minute Book*, vol. 25, p. 70*f*, it is mentioned that the above letter was read, "and my Lords, having the terms of the last Contract read to them, do agree that a contract be renewed with the Bank for another year upon the like terms.' [The terms are set out.] 2 *pages.*

15 July. 17. Report of George Turbill [? should be Turvill], "Cust. Recorder" &c., to the Lords of the Treasury. Has inspected the register of the real estates in England, Ireland, and elsewhere (except Scotland) forfeited for treason, and vested in the Commissioners and Trustees, and also the register of the contracts entered into by the Comrs and Trustees with the respective purchasers for the sale of the Estates; and finds that all the estates were contracted for and sold before 29 Sept. 1723. But several estates given or devised to Popish or superstitious uses were seized by the Comrs and Trustees (particulars annexed), which estates pursuant to Act "7" [Geo. I.] have been certified into the Court of Exchequer. Has annexed a state of the account between the public and the York Buildings Company of and for the money contracted by Christian Cole, Esq., on behalf of the Company to be paid for the purchase of part of the late Lord Widdrington's estate, which is all the estate purchased from the Comrs and Trustees acting in England for the Company, &c. No part of the purchase-money contracted to be paid for any other estates sold by the Comrs and Trustees remains unpaid, except 1,620*l.* (being four-fifths of

1725. VOL. CCLIII.

2,025*l.*) contracted to be paid for the purchase of the tythes of Bucklebury, in the co. of Berks ([which are] part of the late Lord Bolingbroke's estate). No profit will accrue to the public from that estate.

Also the two enclosures mentioned, the first of which is entitled:—"Account of Estates of Papists as Registred pursuant to an Act made in the 'First' year of his Majesty's reign."

The minutes in connexion with this report are entered in the *Minute Book*, vol. 25, pp. 68*e* and 72*c*.

A subsequent minute is also entered at p. 75*c*, finishing:—"My Lords order that the said company do attend them on Wednesday next at 11 in the forenoon and bring them an account stated in their way of the purchases made by them, and the debt remaining due thereupon."

And the following minute on the same page marked *c* touching the above paper:—"Write to the Barons of the Exchequer, taking notice of the Estates given to Popish and superstitious uses, which have been certifyed by the Commrs into the Court of Exchequer, and know of them what care is taken about recovering the same for the use of the publique as the Act of Parliament in that case hath directed." 5 *pages*.

15 July. 18. Memorial of Samuel Lynn, Esq., late Muster-Master General of the Marine Forces, to Sir Robert Walpole, K.B., Chancellor of the Exchequer, and the rest of the Lords of the Treasury, for certain warrants to be made effectual to compel Sir Roger Mostyn, formerly Paymaster of Marines, to pay 799*l.* 13*s.* 11*d.* due to memorialist for the contingencies of his office, &c. 1 *page*.

20 July. 19. Memorial of the Comrs of Customs (Scotland) to the Lords of the Treasury. By their memorials of the 23rd of October and 19th of November last they represented the difficulties that attended their officers in doing their duty in this country from the daily insults and abuses of the smugglers and the common people, who are too ready, upon all occasions, to assist the unfair traders and oppose the officers in the execution of their duty. Have received several complaints since from their officers of the continuance of these abuses, and particularly from John Norman, a land-waiter at Irvin, who, on making a seizure of a considerable quantity of goods, had them forcibly taken from him; although he had a small party of the King's forces to assist him, the "rabble were so great" that he and the soldiers were unmercifully beaten and wounded, as their Lordships would observe by the enclosed letter.

The memorial further states:—"the insults which the officers dayly meet with, together with the late behaviour of the people of the Town of Glasgow, give us great reason to apprehend that unless the civil magistrates are more hearty in putting the laws in execution against such as publickly abuse the officers of the revenue, and interpose their authority in protecting them in doing their duty (as the Laird of Blair has done in this case), it will be impossible to

1725. VOL. CCLIII.

levy the King's duties in this country without the assistance of military forces." Custom House, Edinburgh, 20th July 1725.

Accompanied by the letter above referred to, which gives a detailed account as well of the seizure of a considerable quantity of Dutch soap at Pitcon, about six miles from Irvine, and at Crawfield, about two miles further; as of the fight with the rabble, from whom they were obliged to retreat, being greatly outnumbered and beaten. The Laird of Blair rendered them great help and sheltered them in his house. Norman, the writer of the letter, acquainted his Excellency General Wade and the Lord Advocate with the whole affair, seeing they were so near at hand; and at the writer's coming to Glasgow he acquainted Major Gardiner (commanding the Earl of Stair regiment) with the whole, who forthwith introduced him to the General and the Lord Advocate. The General is very pleased at their conduct, though in a passion at what had otherwise happened, and said he would give orders for a whole troop of the Earl of Stair's regiment to be quartered in that country.

In the *Minute Book*, vol. 25, p. 83 (27th July 1725), is:—"Comm[rs] of the Customes in Scotland. Memorial of the 20th instant, representing the insults and abuses their officers meet with from the smugglers; particularly about a quantity of goods clandestinely imported, and forcibly taken from John Norman, Landwaiter at Irvin, after seizure: and intimating the heartiness of the Laird of Blair in putting the laws in execution, is read. Write to the Comm[rs] to prosecute the offenders, and to the Laird of Blair taking notice of his good service, and return him thanks for the same." 4½ *pages*.

[About 22 July.] 20. Certificate of Lord Halifax as to the arrears due and payable at the Receipt of the Exchequer on a rent resolute or corrody of six pounds per ann. out of St. Stephen's, Westminster, due to Anthony Cotton and his heirs. Dated 22 July 1725.

With the above is the following:—

Petition of James Berdoe to the Lords of the Treasury for their Lordships warrant for the payment of the arrears on the above rent resolute or corrody of 6*l.* per ann. This is accompanied by a similar certificate to the above, dated 10 Feb. 1720. 3 *pages*.

[? About 22 July.] 21. Petition of John Hampton to the Lords of the Treasury. Application has been made by sundry persons to the Commissioners of the Customs in Scotland and to the Court of Exchequer there for obtaining debentures for payment of considerable sums for salt remaining in hand in curing fish and flesh exported pursuant to an Act of the 6th year of the reign. As petitioner was acquainted with great frauds committed in running or relanding great quantities of the said salt; as also in weighing and delivering the same over into the hands of the proper officers, he gave information to Mr. Scrope, their Lordships secretary, by means of which 2,000*l.* will be saved to his Majesty. Will have right to the reward provided in such cases, but is at present in very distressed circumstances and

1725. Vol. CCLIII.

prays some allowance for present subsistence. Dated on the back 1725.

In the *Minute Book*, vol. 25, p. 81*f*, 22 July 1725, is:—"John Hampton having been instrumental in discovering frauds committed in the salt dutys in Scotland, is to be paid 20li as his Mats bounty by the hands of Mr Lowther." 1 *page*.

24 July. 22. Lord Lieut. of Ireland (Carteret) to the Duke of Newcastle, sends the petition of Garret Fitz Gerald, of Rathrone, in the Kingdom of Ireland, Esq., referred to him on 24 Nov. last, and the report of his Majesty's Solicitor-General thereupon, viz.:—

Report of Thomas Marlay to the Lord Lieut. of Ireland (John, Lord Carteret) on the petition of Garrot Fitz Gerrald, of Rathrone, Esq., to his Majesty. Finds that the Attorney General filed a bill against the petitioner for a discovery of the effects of Henry Fitz Gerrald, the petitioner's father, and to have a decree for a lease and other chattels, of which the said Henry died possessed. Process of sequestration, &c. issued. Petitioner's uncle, Garrot, was seized of the lands of Rathrone and other lands as an estate for life, &c. In default of issue they were limited to Henry Fitz Gerrald, petitioner's father, for life, with remainders to the first and other sons in tail male; and the said Henry was attainted on account of the Rebellion in 1688, and the remainder vested in the Trustees during the life of the said Henry. Further finds by a claim of Stephen Ludlow, Esq., that the estate was subject to 800*l*. principal money due to him by mortgage and has been discharged by petitioner. Finds that the said Henry though attainted took the profits of the estate till his death in 1715. Such of the Irish forfeitures as are not sold are by Act of Parliament in England invested in the Crown for the use of the public. Is of opinion that his Majesty is only entitled to the profits of the estate received by Henry Fitzgerrald during his life as a Royal Trustee, but that his Majesty is in his own right entitled to all other the assets of the said Henry acquired by him after his attainder. It is his Majesty's undoubted prerogative to order a *noli prosequi* on the bill filed against petitioner: but cannot give an opinion how far it may be proper to stop a proceeding in his Majesty's name wherein his Majesty is a Trustee as to part of what may be recovered.

The petition referred to and memorial from him to H. M. Principal Secretary of State (the Duke of Newcastle) on the same subject, apparently of a little later date. 7½ *pages*.

[? About 24 July.] 23. Memoranda of the nature of a memorial in favour of Mr Simon Jones, who had expended 83*l*. "in matters relating to the late Conspiracy," and of Mr Peter Jolly, who had been very serviceable therein and hoped to have a reward of 50*l*.

Minuted:—"July ye 24 1725, to be payd by Mr Cracherode." ½ *page*.

26 July. 24. Report of the Lord Chief Baron and the rest of the Barons of the Court of Exchequer in Scotland, to the Lords of the Treasury, on the petition to the King of Francis, Lord Napier. Certifies

1725. VOL. CCLIII.

that by the certificate of the Treasurer's Remembrancer, Lord Napier is chargeable with the payment of 227*l.* 4*s.* 7*d.* sterling, as the "Retour duties" due upon his being enfeoffed in the lands and Barony of Edinbillie; and that his Majesty may discharge his Lordship thereof if he pleases.

Also the petition, from which it appears the petitioner was enfeoffed of these and other lands by his grandmother.

His Majesty referred the petition to the Lords of the Treasury, and they referred it to the Barons. 3½ *pages.*

26 July. 25. Report of the same to the same on the petition of Mr Bowles, Deputy Remembrancer of the Court. Certifies that petitioner has kept the accounts of all seizure money paid into the hands of the Receiver General of Customs, as directed by the Privy Seals; and has delivered in controlment Rolls of such moneys as are a charge upon the Receiver General. Advises that he should have 300*l.* for his services and 20*l.* per annum hereafter.

Minuted:—"13th 8br 1725. My Lds agree to the Barons rept."

Also the petition. 2 *pages.*

26 July. 26. Representation from the same of Sir Robert Sinclair's affairs. Have been commanded by their Lordships to call on Sir Robert and examine him touching moneys in his hands (14,179*l.* 18*s.* 7½*d.*) from forfeited estates in Scotland, out of which he has been directed to pay 9,444*l.* 10*s.* 1*d.* for clearing the salaries and incidents of the Comrs of Inquiry and their officers for a year ending Lady day 1725, &c.

Finishes:—"We must acquaint your Lorpps that notwithstanding repeated applications to the Commissioners, for certificates from the proper officer, of moneys paid into the Exchequer, in order to be a charge upon the Receiver General, yet none has been sent of his Receits since the 16th of July 1724; without which the accounts of the said Sir Robert Sinclair cannot be regularly passed." 2½ *pages.*

26 July. 27. Report of the same to the same. Have considered the petition of David Murray, eldest son to Viscount Stormont, and think him an object for the Royal clemency in having a grant passed of his single and life rent escheat.

The petition referred to, from which it appears the petitioner was guilty of contempt of court, but surrendered and suffered a year's imprisonment in the Castle of Edinburgh. Was never possessed of an estate, real or personal, so that nothing came or can come to the crown by his "forfaulture" but is severely affected by the consequences of his sentence. He is thereby deprived of having any settlement from his father, and is in danger of being excluded from the succession to his estates. 2 *pages.*

28 July. 28. Report of F. Fauquier to the Lords of the Treasury, in reply to their Lordships order, to inform them what sum is remaining in Sir Isaac Newton's hands to balance his account of the copper coinage;

1725. VOL. CCLIII.

and by what means the balance has arisen. Annexes a copy of the account from which it appears that the balance is 1,712*l.* 10*s.* 3*d.*

His Majesty's sign manual which directed that coinage has settled the price of the copper fillets or blanks ready to be stamped at 18*d.* per pound; has likewise ordered that it should be coined as near as might be at 23*d.* per pound, and has allowed 3½*d.* per pound for all the charges of receiving, coining, and disposing of the moneys coined; the incidents that attend that coinage having to be defrayed out of the three half-pence remaining (which is the balance that is now resting in his hands) prove very small.

The Sign Manual has ordered that Sir Isaac Newton should account before the Auditors of Imprest, in the same manner as he accounts for the gold and silver coined: as he is now ready to pass that account for seven years past, he craves to have an allowance of 100*l.* for declaring and passing the account through the several offices of the Exchequer, exclusive of the Auditor's Fees, which may be 20*l.* more.

The account referred to.

There is a notice in the *Minute Book*, vol. 25, p. 88*n*, 3 Aug. 1725, that their Lps adjourned the consideration of the report. 3 *pages.*

[About 30 July.] 29. "Copy of petition of the several Brewers in and about Edinburgh to the Lords of Session."

The petitioners complain that they have been cited to "enact themselves" as they are appointed "by an act of sederunt" of the 30th of July, "with certification as effeirs"; that this was a summary act of which there was no example; that they had no intimation as to what purpose or what effect they were to enact themselves, nor so much as a copy of the act of sederunt; that they know of no act of Parliament allowing such citations in any case; that they had never seen or heard of a citation to enact upon the warrant of an Act of Sederunt of their Lordships, or of any court whatever, and could recall very few Acts of Parliament by which any such thing had been done. Must submit it to their Lordships, if Acts of Sederunt of this kind have any privilege by law that give them so much stronger effects than Acts of Parliament themselves. This led them severally to enquire for this Act which was the warrant for the citation, and now they have seen it published, not under the name of an Act of Sederunt, but according to the title "an Act for preventing the want or scarcity of ale or beer and bread in the good town of Edinburgh," wherein there appear several things so extraordinary and touching so very nearly their interest and personal liberty and the liberty of the subject that they hope, since they had no opportunity to be heard before the Act passed, and since it is truly more of the nature of a judgment *parte inauditâ* than of an Act, they are entitled to represent their objections against it, and to desire a reconsideration how far it is consistent with law. In the first place, they apprehend that this Act is directly contrary to the "Claim of Right," one article whereof is "that the charging the lieges with Lawburrows at the King's instance, and imposing of bonds without the

1725. VOL. CCLIII.

authority of Parliament were contrary to law." The Act proceeds upon a memorial at the instance of his Majesty's Advocate in form of complaint that the Brewers are entered into a resolution and confederacy to overthrow all good government; that by law it belongs to their Lordships to prevent the mischief and to take care of the public safety. Upon this, in virtue of their Lordships Act, they (the Brewers) are summarily charged without further evidence to "enact" themselves "not to do what he (His Majesty's Advocate) states as criminal." The facts they are charged with are contrary to no law yet made. Whereas the Lawburrows complained of by the Claim of Right related to crimes that were provided against by express statute.

Again the article of the Claim of Right mentions the imposing of Bonds without the authority of Parliament. Is not the enacting and binding themselves to brew, a bond? Does not this act of Sederunt impose it without the authority of Parliament? They (the Brewers) apprehend the case is very plain. The Claim of Right makes no distinction of causes, and they are not able to discover any distinction that can reconcile this order of their Lps with the articles in the Claim of Right. If the Claim of Right be abolished by the Union, that they must submit to; but at least they would hope to see some law or example for such a proceeding in Great Britain. Believe that none can be mentioned in any free nation. They take other exceptions to the exercise of power not given to their Lordships by Act of Parliament. Find that very strong powers are given to their Lordships, but are entirely ignorant of any powers vested in them to oblige any person to follow any employment one hour or minute longer than he finds convenient. Have looked into this Act of Sederunt. Admit their Lps power to regulate prices, for which, however, there is no express law. The Act proceeds upon a complaint of facts of which there is no evidence and of which there is no truth. They have no privilege to furnish the city with ale any more than any other burgher, and cannot comprehend how they are obliged to furnish the town at their extreme loss. Further put their case in a variety of ways.

Pray their Lordships to repeal the act, or stop its execution, or that they may be heard by counsel against it.

At the foot is:—"Edr 30th July 1725. The Lords having heard this petition read, find that it is false, scandalous and seditious and filled with positions that endeavour to pervert and are flatly contradictory to law, tending to promote opposition and disobedience to his Majesty's Government, and highly reflecting on the authority and justice of this Court, and creating distrusts thereof among the people, and therefore reject the same, and ordain a copy thereof to be forthwith burnt by the hand of the common hangman at the Market Cross of Edinburgh, and appoint and require the Magistrates of the said city to see the same put in execution; and in regard there remains not sufficient time for the Court to proceed fully upon it this Session, ordains Sir John Dalrymple, His Majesty's Clerk, to keep the principal petition, to the end further directions

1725. VOL. CCLIII.

may be given for detecting, prosecuting and punishing, according to law, the authors, advisers, abettors, and subscribers thereof, and discharge the said Clerk to give out any other copy of the same excepting one which he is hereby appointed to give to his Majesty's Advocate attested." 4 *pages.*

31 July. 30. Report of A. Cracherode to the Lords of the Treasury on the petition of William Lock, in which he sets forth that Peter Martin, a pensioner of Chelsea Hospital was robbed and barbarously murdered; that for the discovery of the persons concerned a reward of 100*l.* was offered, and that the petitioner discovered the murderers, who were convicted. Certifies that the reward mentioned was offered, and that William Lock, the petitioner, was committed to Newgate on a strong suspicion of robbing in the streets, and was examined and pressed to make an ingenuous discovery of the murder for some time. At length he confessed that he and four others (specified) murdered the said Peter Martin, one of whom, Daniel Carrol, fled to Ireland, and Valentine Carrick was afterwards executed for highway robbery, but was never tried for the murder. As Lock did not procure the said Carrol to be prosecuted and convicted he never became entitled to his Majesty's pardon, which was promised only on condition of one of the murderers discovering the rest of his accomplices. The petitioner has since been transported. The general words of the advertisement include the petitioner, but it could not be intended that any one of the persons actually concerned in the murder and robbery should be entitled to the reward upon any easier terms than to entitle him to his Majesty's pardon.

The petition, and copy of the London Gazette, Number 6067. Also copy of the sworn information of William Lock and certificate of the Clerk of the Peace, and gaol delivery of the county of Middlesex on the same subject. 10 *pages.*

3 Aug. 31. Report of the Surveyor General (Pulteney) to the Lords of the Treasury on the petition of Bartholomew Wimberley and Henry Binfield, praying their Lordships to grant them a reversionary lease in nineteen messuages or tenements therein mentioned for fifty years. The premises are parcel of the field or close of land formerly called Pall Mall Field alias St James's Field, within the Bailiwick of St James's, and were granted by King Charles II. to, or in trust for, Henry late Earl of St Albans for twenty years, which will expire at Michaelmas 1740. Gives the particulars of the situation of the messuages, &c. and their values. A lease may be granted of them for thirty four years and three quarters, to commence from Michaelmas 1740, for a fine of 1,300*l.*, reserving a ground rent of 2*s.* 6*d.* in the pound, amounting to 90*l.* 15*s.* per ann., which is conformable to the Civil List Act; and the better to ascertain the tenancy of the premises a rent of 12*d.* for each messuage is to be made payable to the Crown during the term in being, but to cease when the rent reserved on the reversionary term shall become payable. Refers their Lordships to other reports

1725. VOL. CCLIII.

which he had made which concern the Dowager Lady Clarges, the Lady Colladon, and Mrs Anne Hawkins.

The petition referred to, and a plan showing the situation of the above properties, their dimensions, &c. 6 *pages and the plan.*

[? About 4 Aug.] 32. Memorial of Sir John Vanbrugh to the Lords of the Treasury. In the year 1705 was appointed Surveyor for the late Duke of Marlborough in designing and conducting the building then begun at Blenheim for the Duke, and acted until the building was stopped in 1712. Received several sums upon account. His account (amongst others) was examined by the late Mr Lowndes, Messrs Craggs & Sloper in 1716, and 2,463*l.* 10*s.* 9*d.* was found to be due to him. Received 800*l.* in part payment out of money remaining of the late Queen's Civil List. A further sum was afterwards issued to Mr Guidott to be applied in the same manner, but the Executors of the late Duke of Marlborough obtained a perpetual injunction against Memorialist, on pretence that he had not been employed in the works of Blenheim by the Duke, but by the Queen, and so had no claim on the Duke's estate. Prays to be paid the remainder (1,663*l.* 10*s.* 9*d.*) from the late Queen's Civil List. Undated, but ? about 4 Aug. 1725 by the following, which is entered in the *Minute Book,* Vol. 25, p. 89*c* (4 Aug. 1725).

"Sr John Vanbrugh is called in, and his peticõn for the residue of an arreare on an account stated by Craggs, Lowndes and Sloper for his service and expences relating to the works at Blenheim is read; and my Lords are pleased to agree to the payment thereof out of the late Queen's arrears: but Sir John is to know whether Mr Guidott, in the case the same be issued to him on the unsatisfyed order in his name for Blenheim debts, will pay the same over to him."

Another paper on the same subject, with the following query at the foot by Sir John Vanbrugh: "Whether the remainder of what is due to me, may not be ordered out of this money." 3 *pages.*

5 Aug. 33. Memorial of the Court of Directors of the Bank of England to the Lords of the Treasury praying that their Lordships will direct their order to the proper officer of the Exchequer to issue to the cashier ten thousand pounds by way of imprest, and upon account to reimburse the Bank the charges about certain annuities granted by the Act of 9 & 10 Anne.

In the *Minute Book,* Vol. 25, p. 90*e,* 10 Aug. 1725, is:—"Issue to the Cashire of the Bank 10000li out of the General Fond upon accot to reimburse charges which he hath or shall be at in passing his accounts and carrying on the business of paying the several annuities chargeable on the said General Fond according to the desire of the Court of Directors in that behalf signifyed by their memorial of the 5th instant." 3 *pages.*

6 Aug. 34. Memorial of Sir Roger Mostyn and Sir Bibye Lake, Barts., to the Lords of the Treasury, praying their Lordships to issue the 11,630*l.* 15*s.* 0*d.* due to Sir Bibye Lake, an agreement having been arrived at by the memorialists as well as upon the release of the decree in Chancery. Signed.

1725. VOL. CCLIII.

In the *Minute Book*, Vol. 25, p. 90*e*, 10 Aug. 1725, is:—"A memorial of the 6th instant signed by Sr Roger Mostyn and Sir Bibye Lake, signifying their agreement with respect to the Decree in Chancery for a Marine clothing debt, unpaid; and both desiring that the money to discharge the principal of the said debt may be paid to Sr Roger. My Lords agree thereto, and order that the money received from Whitfield, when brought into the Exchequer, be issued to the Treasurer of the Navy; with so much more out of other proper money in the Exchequer as shall be sufficient to clear the said cloathing debt; and the Commrs of the Navy are to be directed to make an Imprest Bill on the Treaŕer for paying the said sum over to Sr Roger Mostyn, to discharge the said cloathing debt accordingly." 1 *page*.

10 Aug. 35. Lord Portmore to ———. Asks that the report on his memorial, required by the Treasury and sent by the Comrs of Revenue in Ireland, may be given to him. It relates to money due to him out of quit rents of that kingdom, to which, by virtue of his late wife's grant, he is as rightfully entitled as to anything he stands possessed of. London, 10 Aug. 1725.

In the *Minute Book*, Vol. 25, p. 92*g*, is: "Commrs of the Revenue in Ireland their report of the 20th of May 1724 on the Earl of Portmore's demand of 851li 13s 7¼d alledged to be unpaid on the grant to the Counts of Dorchester is read, and it appearing thereby that the Agents of the said Counts and not the Crown are chargeable with the said debt, if any, My Lords adhere to the Report, but order my Lord Portmore a copy thereof if he desires the same." 2 *pages* (4*to*).

23 Aug. 36. Report of the Surveyor General (Pulteney) to the Lords of the Treasury on the petition of William Hucks, Esq., for a grant of a reversionary lease of certain lands at Wallingford, and of the inward ward of Wallingford Castle. The grant asked for comprised certain acres of meadow called King's mead, which were demised by her late Majesty Catherine, Queen Dowager, and all the premises were parcel of her jointure. The lease of the farm of 23 acres, and the farm of 10 acres lying in King's mead, may be granted for one life after the determination of the two lives now subsisting for a fine of 60*l*. 13*s*. 2*d*., reserving the old rent of 4*l*. 17*s*. 6*d*. per ann. in respect of the 23 acres, and the old rent of 2*l*. 4*s*. 6*d*. per ann. in respect of the other farm of 10 acres, and the farm of the inward ward of Wallingford castle may be granted for two lives, and after the decease of William Trafford for a fine of 209*l*. 17*s*. 5*d*., reserving the old rent of 10*s*. per ann. The better to ascertain the tenancy of the premises a rent of 1*s*. per ann. is to be reserved for each of the farms.

In the *Minute Book*, Vol. 25, p. 100*b*, 1 Sept. 1725, is:—"Mr Surveyor's Report of the 23 of August last on Wm Huck's petition for a lease of lands, and a house in Wallingford and Wallingford Castle is read, and my Lords being informed that a peticõn of the wido Randa for renewing a lease of some part of the premises stands

1725. Vol. CCLIII.

referred to the Surveyor, Mr Hucks is advised to deal with the said Randa for her interest that all hardships on any pretence to a tenants right in her may be avoided." 4 *pages.*

27 Aug. 37. Report of the Surveyor General (Pulteney) to the Lords of the Treasury, on the petition of the Governor and Company of Chelsea Waterworks, praying his Majesty to grant them leave to make a reservoir in the circle of the Walnut Tree Walk, in Hyde Park; that they may, from the height of that ground, supply the Royal Palace and Gardens at Kensington with water (if required), and the upper parts of Westminster. The diameter of the circle in the Walnut Tree Walk is 379 feet, and the petitioners propose that the diameter of their reservoir shall not exceed 200 feet. The main of 4 in. to be laid from Tyburn Lane. Other details of the proposal. Advises that the scheme should be carried out.

The petition referred to; also a plan.

In the *Minute Book,* Vol. 25, p. 100*g*, is:—"Mr Surveyors Report of the 27th August last on the peticõn of Chelsea Water Works Company for leave to make a reservoir in the Circle of the Walnut Tree Walk Hyde Park is read and agreed to." 3 *pages besides the plan.*

27 Aug. 38. Comrs of the Navy to Mr Scrope. Have sent a copy of his letter to Comr Kempthorne at Chatham, and recommended him to see the same exactly complied with. Send a copy of the proceedings he had furnished, and ask that it may be laid before the Lords of the Treasury.

The copy referred to, which states that he went to Queenborough to present the Comrs letter, in order to deliver the well there into the care of the Mayor and Corporation. He applied to Mr Evans (the father of the Mayor), who acts as his deputy, to deliver up to the Mayor and Corporation the care and inspection of the well in the Castle, and tendered a short instrument to him (copy enclosed) for the preservation of his Majesty's right in the well. He replied that he would take care of the well; but treated the instrument with contempt, saying (with some warmth) that the seal of the Corporation should not be put to any such thing, insinuating that his Maty had no right thereto. Asks what the pleasure of the Lords of the Treasury is.

Also the copy of the instrument referred to.

In the *Minute Book,* Vol. 25, p. 91 (10 Aug. 1725), is the following touching this well:—"Write to the Commrs of the Navy acquainting them that my Lords are informed that the inhabitants at Queenborough are debarred the free use of the water in the Well there, because they or some of their officers have shut the Well up, which is a grievance the Corporation complains of, and what their Lordp̃s expect the Commrs should effectually redress." 4 *pages.*

31 Aug. 39. Lord Carpenter, Governor of Minorca, to the Lords of the Treasury. Has examined the enclosed proposal of Mr Joseph Gascoigne, and has been with him in the City to view the material to make bedding, blankets, and sheets for his Majesty's troops at

1725. Vol. CCLIII.

Minorca, and finds the same to be very good. Has put his seal to patterns, and as they are provided will inspect them carefully. Is of opinion that the prices are reasonable, except the freight, which is too high, as they may be sent to Port Mahon for 150*l.* The number of non-commissioned officers and soldiers of the four regiments on the Island is 2,096; shows what bedding will be required for two men to each bed. The cost will amount to 3,464*l.* 8*s.* 0*d.* Concludes—"As to the fund for payment, it is improper for me to propose any, and is submitted to your Lops onely in case your Lops should think fitt to order payment for these goods out of the revenues heretofore belonging to the Bishop and Chapter of Mayorca (which since the Island Minorca has been under the dominion of the British Crowne has been collected and kept in the castle of St Phelip) I take the liberty humbly to pray that it may be kept as private as possible; for if the Courts of Vienna or Madrid or any of their Ministers should hear that any part of those revenues were dispos'd of, they would remonstrate against it in the strongest manner, and give great trouble to his Majesty and his Ministers: for in Feb. last the Spanish Ambassadour writt a very pressing letter to his Grace the Duke of Newcastle by way of memoriall, to have those revenues paid forthwith to the Bishop and Chapter of Mayorca; which letter his Grace enclos'd to me, desiring I would let him know the state of that affair, in order to answere the Ambassadour; and I waited on his Grace with the paper annext."

The following is a copy of the paper referred to:—"The pretention of the Ambassadour of Spain, to recover the Church Revenues in Minorca, for the Bishop of Mayorca, is at present more unjust and unreasonable than ever; for 'tis the same as asking his Britanique Majesty to give so much to the Pope; because Dn Athanacio de Estarripa the late Bishop (who only could pretend to those revenues) is dead, and the Pope is heir to all the Bishops under the Dominion of Spain, in such manner and with such riguor, that the Commissarys of the Apostolique Chamber (which are two Cannons in every Cathedral Church) as soon as the Bishop is dangerously ill, and has taken the sacrament, they secure all he has, and when he dyes they are masters of his effects, which they remit to the Apostolick Comissarys that reside at Madrid, and these send it to the Pope; so that in reality what the Ambassadour of Spain asks is that his Majesty should give so much to the Pope, who will return nothing to his Majesty and his subjects but maledictions in cœna Domini."

Accompanying Lord Carpenter's letter is the proposal of Mr. Joseph Gascoigne for the supply of the bedding; also an order to the Lieut. Governor of Minorca to pay 1,154*l.* 16*s.* out of the above revenues to Mr. Gascoigne; a memorial from the latter and other papers on the same subject.

In the *Minute Book*, vol. 25, p. 98*b*, 31 Aug. 1725, is:—"Lord Carpenter's Report of the 31st instant on Mr. Gascoign's proposal for providing bedding, blankets, and sheets for the troops at Minorca is read and approved, and a contract is to be prepared conformable

1725. VOL. CCLIII.

thereto, and to Mr Gascoigne's proposal to be satisfyed for the same out of the Bishop's revenues and other revenues of Minorca." 11 *pages.*

2 Sept. 40. Memorial to the Lords of the Treasury of the Commrs for managing the duty arising by wine licences laying before their Lordships "the state of the case upon the matter of the special verdict found at Bristoll the 12th of August 1725 relating to the said duty." By Stat. 7 Edw. 6th, cap. 5, no person could keep any tavern or cellar or "utter" by retail "by the gallon or lesser or greater measure" any wines unless enabled by that Act, and unless licenced by the Mayor, Aldermen, &c. of every city, borough, or town corporate: and no person could "retail wine to be drank in their houses." The sole liberty then of keeping taverns for retailing within doors was in the Company of Free Vintners and private hands by particular patents. The law stood thus till the statute of 12 Car. 2, cap. 25, when a revenue from wine licences was raised and there was a general liberty of retailing both within and without doors. The King was authorised by this Act to appoint Commissioners to grant licences to enable persons by payment of a rent [to sell] for any term under 21 years. The Act 15 Car. 2, cap. 14, recites the stat. 12 Car. 2. In pursuance whereof the Comrs have from time to time granted licences to retailers: "except only in the beginning of this establishment, when the Vintners of several corporations insisting upon their corporation licences under the Act of 7 Ed. 6, the Commrs brought actions upon the statute 12 Car. 2, and obtained several judgments against them in the years 1687 and 1688, when the power by the Act of 7 Ed. 6 vested in the corporations as to licencing without doors was declared to be lodged by the Act 12 Car. 2 in the Commrs for granting wine licences, who from that time executed such power." But the retail trade, being chiefly amongst retailing merchants, wine coopers and others (which trade was formerly amongst the Vintners and licenced retailers, who paid much larger rents than they do now) they are consequently liable to the same duty, and this they have acquiesced in until a few years last past. Of late one Mr. Ballard, a retailing merchant in Worcester, set up a wine cellar and supplied the country with wine, but suffered none to be drunk in any place within his possession, and insisted that such retailing was not within the statute, for that the words (to be drunk or spent within his Mansion House, &c. or without his Mansion House) intended no more than within his house or some other place in his possession about his house, as gardens, arbours, and such places. Having taken the Attorney General's opinion, and other wine cellars having been set up which undersold the vintners who took licences, the Comrs brought an action against Ballard, who afterwards submitted to take licence, but dying immediately afterwards no licence was taken. Several merchants at Bristol set up cellars in like manner, and the Comrs gave them notice that actions would be commenced against them: whereupon Mr. Andrews, one of the retailers, wrote by his attorney that if the Comrs would send down a writ he would give an appearance, and try the point

VOL. CCLIII.

1725.

whether he was a retailer within the statute or not. Whereupon an action was tried before Mr. Justice Denton at Bristol. At the trial Mr. Justice Denton spoke to the following purpose, viz.: as it was a matter of law he was willing it should be determined by the Court above; but that he would give his opinion in a few words, and leave it to the jury to do as they thought proper. That he would give his opinion entirely upon the Act 12 Car. 2, he looking upon the other Acts as historical and to be left out of the case, that the Act being said to be for the better ordering the selling of wine by retail in taverns and other places, the words other places must intend places of the like nature, such as inns and alehouses, and that, as to the words to be drunk or spent within, &c. or without, must be intended of some place within the retailers possession and that he wondered the office should be for putting a new construction upon the Act, and endeavouring to bring in retailers of wine that served gentlemen's houses and the like. Upon the prayer of the counsel for the Crown the jury found specially that the defendant was an importer of wines, that he sold by the gallon, and that the wine so sold was drunk in some place out of his possession, and submitted to the Court if he was a retailer within the statute or not. As the present Lord Chief Justice Raymond, when Attorney General, and other counsel were of opinion such retailers were within the Act, the Com^rs submit that the question ought to be argued, and pray their L^ps directions. Wine Licence Office, 2 Sept. 1725.

In the *Minute Book*, vol. 25, p. 107*d*, 21 Sept. 1725, is:—"A memorial from the Com^rs of Wine Lycences dated the 2^d instant, relating to the arguing of a special verdict found at Bristoll, about retailers of wine, which highly concerns the improvement of that revenue, is read; and my Lords order that the same be argued, and that the Comm^rs proceed in this affair as they shall be advised by his Ma^ts Attorney and Sollicitor General with the strictest diligence and application." 2½ *pages*.

15 Sept. 41. Com^rs of the Navy to M^r. Scrope. Have considered the petition of Benjamin Joules, in which he offers to grant a lease of 99 years, with liberty to take clay for the use of his Majesty's Docks at Portsmouth and Plymouth, &c., at the yearly rent of 1*s*. per ann., as an acknowledgment of his title to the place from whence he proposes to supply the clay, upon consideration of their Lordships granting him a lease of some lands, mills, and houses belonging to the Crown near Portsmouth at a reasonable rent. Finds that this Board have constantly been of opinion that Mr Joules has no just claim to the place from whence he proposes to supply the clay, the same being within the flux and reflux of the sea; as is found by the board's letters to Mr Lowndes and Mr Stanhope; and that the service at Portsmouth and Plymouth is in no want of the clay, being well supplied since the year 1718 from other places in Portsmouth harbour, to which neither Mr Joules nor anyone else can lay any claim. Navy Office. 1 *page*.

16 Sept. 42. Petition of George Clarke, Secretary of the Province of New York in America, to the Lords of the Treasury, viz., "for establish-

VOL. CCLIII.

1725.

ing the salary of 50^{li} p ann. on the quit rents, as also the incidents of his office, amounting to about 60^{li} p ann." The prayer of the petition is that their Lordships will allow those sums already received by him on the Governor's warrants for his salary and incidents; and that for the future they may be so established on the quit-rents that the Receiver General of this Province may pay to Petitioner all his arrears of salary and incidents, as well as the salary and incidents for the time to come; and that their Lordships will, in consideration of the loss of his office [of Clerk of the Circuits], give him such further relief out of the quit-rents as may be a suitable support to him.

The petitioner represents "that soon after the glorious and happy Revolution a revenue was given by Act of Assembly of the said Province for support of the Government there, in consequence whereof salarys were established by the Governour and Council, on the officers of the said Government, and the incidents of their offices paid thereout. That the Secretary of the said Province, being likewise Clerk of the Council, and having some other small offices annexed to it (as in other his Maiesty's Provinces in America) for his support, the office of Secretary being rather an expence than a place of profit, the Governour and Council did establish a salary of fifty pounds p anñ on the Secretary as Clerk of the Council, which together with the incidents of this whole office were paid to him during the continuance of the revenue.

"But that Revenue expiring in 1709, the Assembly could not be prevailed on for many years to give any other, so that the Governour and the officers of the Government were without any support, till in 1714 they passed a Bill to pay the debts of the Government; by which means your Lordship's petitioner was paid part of his arrears of salary and incidents, as other the officers were; and the remainder thereof by another bill past in seventeen hundred and seventeen.

"That in the year 1715 this present Assembly being chosen, the Honourable Brigadier Hunter, the then Governour of this Province, by his admirable prudence and dexterity so wrought upon them that they settled a revenue; but at the same time desired the Governour that it might be applyed to such officers, to such uses, and in such proportions only as they themselves had then agreed upon. This the Brigadier was under a necessity to comply with; for from the year 1709 to that time the Assembly had refused to settle a Revenue as formerly, without particular applications of it in the bill; which the Governour could not consent to. By this agreement they gave to their own clerk a salary of eighty pounds a year and all his incidents, to commence the 13th of June, seventeen hundred and fifteen, but to your Lordships' petitioner only thirty pounds a year, without any provision for his incidents; notwithstanding your Lordships' petitioner as Clerk of the Council during the continuance of the first-mentioned revenue had an allowance of salary at least equal to that of the Clerk of the Assembly, and the incidents of his whole office; and notwithstanding that the service of your Lordships' petitioner is every Session of Assembly more

VOL. CCLIII.

1725.

than that of the Clerk of the Assembly; seeing he attends all Committees and draws all their reports, which the other does not. But there was no remedy, the Brigadier being obliged to adhere to his promise," &c.

Under these hard circumstances petitioner was obliged to wait till the quit rents should be more duly collected. Petitioner had fallen under the displeasure of the present Governor, William Burnett, Esq., who had taken from him the office of Clerk of the Circuits, and had given the same to M[r] Morris, son of the present Chief Justice of this Province. Petitioner fled for protection to Horatio Walpole, Esq., H.M. present ambassador at the Court of France, who obtained a letter to the Governor from Lord Carteret, then H.M. principal Secretary of State, signifying H.M. pleasure that the Secretary's office should not be dismembered, and desiring him to reinstate petitioner or recompense him. The Governor having put it out of his power by the Commission granted to M[r] Morris to restore petitioner, offered him 50*l.* per ann. to make his salary equal to that of the Clerk of the Assembly and to pay all the incidents of his office out of the quit-rents. New York, 16 Sept. 1725. 3 *pages.*

20 Sept. 43. Report of the Surveyor-General (Pulteney) to the Lords of the Treasury on the petition of Sarah Renda, widow and relict of Thomas Renda, Esq., for a reversionary lease of Wallingford Castle and the premises therewith holden in the county of Berks. As to the outward ward, in consideration of the great expenses which petitioner's late husband had been at, "and tenant right," if their Lordships pleased to gratify petitioner, he (the Surveyor) thinks a lease of this ward for a term of twenty-six years and a half, from the expiration of the present term, may be worth a fine of 180*l.* reserving the old rent of 50*l.* per ann. and an increased rent of 7*l.* 10*s.* per ann.

He (the Surveyor) says that some gentlemen of credit in the neighbourhood, to whom he had written, certified "that the prison house and some cottages (formerly parcel of that ward) were demolished; that there were no buildings on that part of the said premises, other than an old barn, called the gaol barn, which was out of repair, and a pigeon house, then lately built near the said barn by the said Thomas Renda." The quantity of ground to this ward was about 16 acres, and was valued at about 30*l.* per. ann.

As to the inward ward of the Castle, the gentlemen referred to further certified "that the same consists of a dwelling house, a garden, a small bowling green and two orchards, which they thought a pleasant situation, and believed would then let at thirty or forty pounds per annum." Advises that a lease may be granted for two lives (after the decease of the surviving nominee in the present lease) for a fine of 209*l.* 17*s.* 5*d.*, reserving the old rent of 10*s.* per ann. All which will be conformable to the Civil List Act.

A particular was rated for a lease of the outward ward of Wallingford Castle to be passed to William Hucks for three and twenty and a half years, in reversion of Thomas Renda's term of

1725. VOL. CCLIII.

$7\frac{1}{2}$ years, then to come. On the 23rd of Aug. he (the Surveyor) made a report on the petition of Hucks for a lease of the inward ward. Also refers their Lordships to another report in Nov. 1723, made by him on a memorial of Sir John D'Oyly for a lease of both the forementioned wards. 20 Sept. 1725.

Accompanied by the petition, also an affidavit and a legal opinion on the same subject. 6 *pages.*

21 Sept. 44. Secretary of State (Newcastle) to the Lords of the Treasury. Transmitted by the King's command on 31 May last a copy of a letter received from the Lord-Lieut. and Privy Council of Ireland, wherein they desired that a new gold coinage, which had been made in Portugal, might be current in Ireland; and that a proclamation might be issued for that purpose. The Lord-Lieut. had again written to him to know his Majesty's pleasure upon this matter, and had represented that should this coin be counterfeited in Ireland, great quantities would be sent over hither. Asks their Lordships opinion as to what was proper for the King to do therein. Encloses an extract of a letter from the Collector of Donoghadee to the Com^is^ of Revenue in Ireland, relating to a Commission, said to be given to Sir John Shaw, authorising him to burn all boats that shall bring meal or grain from Ireland to Scotland. The Lord-Lieut. desires to be informed what answer he may give them upon it.

The copy of the letter and the extract referred to.

In the *Minute Book,* vol. 25, p. 108, 22 Sept. 1725, after stating that the above letter was read, it proceeds: "As to the first, my Lords think the Bank should be advised with thereupon, and Mr Jacomb being present, my Lords order to speak to the Bank about making a loane to pay off the deficient tallys on the Land tax anno 1723. He is to take the papers with him about the said Portugal coynage, and desire some of them to be here with my Lords on Tuesday next, between 11 & 12 in the forenoon; and as to the other part, about Irish victuals, let a copy of the warrt for establishing a new General Surveyor in Scotland be transmitted to his Grace, and let him know that the issuing this Commicõn was necessary, to quiet the mighty complaints Scotland had against the importacõn of Irish victual there." 5 *pages.*

30 Sept. 45. Report of A. Cracherode and George Turbill to the Lords of the Treasury on the petition of John Roberts, who says he was employed by several of his Majesty's Deputy-Lieutenants and Justices of the Peace for the county of Lancaster before, at, and after the Rebellion, and who had given to the Commissioners of Forfeited Estates information respecting the estate of Mr Edward Winkley, of Bannister Hall, in that county, which invalidated a fraudulent claim and pretended settlement of the estate. The Comrs soon after sold the estate for 35,000*l.*, and petitioner hoped for one-third of the estate, but never received any reward or consideration. Petitioner was appointed by the Commissioners Steward and Receiver of some of the forfeited estates in that

county, but was now under prosecution for an arrear of 370*l*. The Com[rs] could not pay to him the value of one-third of the estate (1,166*l*. 13*s*. 4*d*.), as petitioner was not strictly speaking the first discoverer, therefore he prays for so much of it as shall be found to remain after the debt due from the petitioner to the public is satisfied, and in the meantime that there should be a stop of proceedings against him and his sureties. The report is generally favourable to the petitioner, and admits the assistance rendered as well in the detection of the fraudulent claim as in other matters, and recommends as a reward for his services that the bond should be given up and cancelled and that all proceedings should be stayed. Dated 30 Sept. 1725.

Minuted:—"12th 8[br] 1725. Stay process for months."

Accompanied by the petition, which has on the second page the reference "to Mess[rs] Cracherode and Turbill, and their Lordships direct M[r] Cracherode to stay proceedings." Dated 21 April 1725.

Also a certificate in favour of the petitioner, who is there described as M[r] John Roberts, of Preston. It has 10 signatures. 6½ *pages*.

30 Sept. 46. Report of the Officers of the Board of Works to the Lords of the Treasury giving an estimate of the charge of the painting the ceilings of the Gallery and Great and little closets, the stair case, &c. at Kensington as demanded by M[r] Kent. Whitehall, 30 Sept. 1725.

This is written on the back of the letter from Lord Grafton, asking by his Majesty's command that their Lordships would give orders to M[r] William Kent to paint the above ceilings, &c.

Accompanied by a letter signed "J. Thornhill" to the Com[rs] of Works stating that he was informed that they had received instructions to employ some improper person to do the gilding on the wainscot in the Gallery at Kensington, &c. As the gilding has always been done by his predecessors and himself, thinks it is a great encroachment on their office as well as on his patent and those who shall succeed him.

The Lords of the Treasury are their immediate directors, and by their authority he is willing to be concluded. Great Piazza, Cov. Garden, Sept. 29, 1725.

In the *Minute Book*, Vol. 25, p. 113 (5 Oct. 1725), is: "Board of Works report of 30th September 1725 about the charge of the painting and gilding at Kensington is read. Write to the Vice Chamberlain to let my Lords know if any agreement has been made with M[r] Kent about the painting, and write to the Board of Works to let them know that the gilding on the wainscot is to be performed by S[r] James Thornhill, the King's painter, whose office it is to perform works of that nature." 3 *pages*.

19 Oct. 47. Report of H. Kelsall to the Lords of the Treasury. Was present by their Lordships' commands at the Assay of the copper money remaining in the Pix in the Tower of London, and attended Sir Isaac Newton, who with the other proper officers opened the Pix, in

1725. VOL. CCLIII.

which several half pence and farthings taken out of heaps promiscuously at the times of the respective coinages were kept, and upon putting forty six half pence into a scale, found the weight to be a pound avoirdupois, wanting a half penny weight, which is within the remedy allowed by his Majesty in the warrant directing the coinage of copper money. Upon putting thirty one half pence and thirty farthings into the scale, found the weight to be a pound avoirdupois and a halfpenny weight over, which ballances the want of so much weight in the 46½ pence.

In order to assay the goodness of the copper, four half pence and eight farthings were put into the fire, and after they had been in an intense heat for half an hour they were laid upon an anvil and beaten with a hammer to a great thinness, which some of them bore without cracking in the least, though the greatest part of them are split at the edges. 19 8[br] 1725.

In the *Minute Book*, Vol. 25, p. 119 (19 Oct. 1725), it is mentioned that M[r] Kelsall's report is read "and it appearing that both weight and fineness answered as they ought to do, my Lords were satisfyed with the tryals made." 1½ *pages.*

10. Nov. 48. "Mint Report on Portugal Coins." The report is made by "W. Cary" and "Is. Newton in pursuance of an order of reference from the Lords of the Treasury, who direct the weight and assay to be taken of the five sorts of Portugal gold moneys mentioned in their Lordships order, and that they should give their opinion at what value "they may reasonably go in Ireland" in case his Majesty, by proclamation, make them current in Ireland. The pieces differ in value, the smallest being of the value of 4*s.* 4*d.*, and the largest 3*l.* 11*s.* 6½*d.* The merchants will be apt to cull out the lightest for Ireland, and send the heaviest to the melting pot, and the pieces will quickly grow lighter, by wearing in Portugal, before they come into Ireland, and the smallest pieces will wear fastest in proportion to their weight & value; and if they are to be made current by proclamation, some abatement of the value must be made for this lightness. Mint Office, Nov. 10, 1725. 1 *page.*

11 Nov. 49. Thomas Clements to ——. Hopes he has received the account of the fees sent to him. Sends copy of his report to the Lord Lieut. about his (the correspondent's) demand on the Treasury at the time Mr. Pratt was removed. Mr. Pratt has left the Treasury affairs in so great confusion that the Committee of Accounts sit five or six hours every day. Dublin, 11 Nov. 1725. 1 *page.*

21 Nov. 50. Report of the Solicitor General (Sir C. Wearg) to the Lords of the Treasury on the petition of Mary, the wife of Charles Cox, Esq., and of Dame Elizabeth Jekyll, wife of Sir Joseph Jekyll, Knight, sisters and co-heirs and also administratixes of John, Lord Somers, deceased. The petition sets forth that Sir William Hayward and Sir John Talbott, Knights, surviving trustees for sale of fee farm and other rents belonging to the Crown, conveyed to Humphrey Hetherington, Esq., in trust for Lord Somers, among other rents, the fee farm rent of 67*l.* 5*s.* 6¼*d.* out of the manor of

1725. VOL. CCLIII.

Bray, in the co. of Berks, and the fee-farm rent of 67*l.* 18*s.* 0¼*d.* out of the manor of Cookham in the same county, and that on the pretence that they are quit-rents, parcel of the said manors and excepted from sale by an Act passed the 22nd of King Charles the Second for sale of fee-farm and other rents, they have since been detained in the hands of the respective reeves or tenants. Has examined into the allegations of the petitioner and an account of the receipts of the rents. Refers to the statute 22 Car. II. chap. 6. By Mr. Jett's state of the rents of the above manors it appears that the rents in question, before the execution of the deed of 6 Jan. 1697, stood charged as rents of assize, payable by the free and customary tenants of the respective manors. Is of opinion that the rents are included in the exception in the Act of Parliament. Apprehends that the rents in question did not pass by the deed of 6 Jan. 1697 for want of a proper description, and that they ought to have been answered to the Crown and stood in charge in the Auditors' office, &c. Finishes :—"In the present case I apprehend there will not be any occasion for a re-conveyance from Mr. Hetherington if it shall be thought proper to make any recompense to the petitioners for the rents in question; because those rents did not vest in the Trustees and consequently could not pass by the grant to Mr Hetherington."

The petition referred to, an affidavit of Mr. Hetherington, and three other documents touching the same matter.

In the *Minute Book*, vol. 25, p. 124*d* (26 Nov. 1725):—"Mr Sollicitor General's Report of the 21st instant on the peticõn of the executors of the Lord Sommers, touching rents evicted out of Lord Sommers's grant of Fee-Farm Rents and not since answered to the Crown is read, and my Lords order that the most speedyest ways and means be taken for the recovery of those rents and the arrears thereof to the Crown." 18 *pages.*

25 Nov. 51. Memorial of the Comrs of Excise to the Lords of the Treasury. The Barons of the Exchequer discharged all further proceedings against Hugh Cleghorn, one of the maltsters in Edinburgh, in relation to a charge of horning, given him on his accepted bill for the duty of his malt stock in hand; in respect there was no bill passed as the warrant for the horning; but immediately, upon other bills presented to the Court, they granted hornings against him and eleven other maltsters in Edinburgh, so that now they hope to give a good account of the malt duty.

Have an account from their collector in the Orkneys, that when their officers attempt to survey any malthouse there, a mob of women immediately arises and will not allow them entrance. Unless some forces are sent there, it is not expected that the malt duty can be made effectual in those islands. Excise Office, Edinb., 25 Nov. 1725.

[Letters of *Horning* are warrants for charging persons in Scotland to pay duties probably being originally proclaimed by horn or trumpet. See *Tomlin's Law Dictionary* under Horning.] 1 *page.*

1725. Vol. CCLIII.

2 Dec. 52. Capt. E. Vernon to John Scroop, Esq., Secretary to the Lords of the Treasury. His Majesty in consideration of his zeal and affection, &c., granted him 1,000*l.*, and directed the Commissioners of the Navy to cause the same to be paid out of the sale of the old stores, but that fund being insufficient he had only received 300*l.* Prays for relief out of other moneys in the hands of the Treasurer of the Navy.

In the *Minute Book*, vol. 25, p. 131*g*, is :—" My Lords order that 700li the remainder of 1000li payable to Capt. Vernon by the Treasurer of the Navy, out of monies arising by sale of old stores be paid, (since the fond of old stores proves deficient) out of imprest money repaid by Sr Thos Littleton. So write to the Exchequer for issuing the 700li to the Treasurer of the Navy for that purpose accordingly." 2 *pages.*

4 Dec. 53. " Copy of Capt. Thos Morphy's peticon to ye Ld High Treasurer for paymt of 480li 10s 8d due to him from the Crown."

The claim was for money expended for repairs and keeping in order " her Majesty's Marshalsea at the Savoy, to make the Marshall Prison fit to secure soldiers and deserters of the Guards, and for the accommodation of the recruits of her Majesty's army in the year 1710, 1711 & 1712 " &c.

There is an abstract of the workmen's bills and a copy of a report by Sir Chr. Wren and two others saying that they might be justly paid.

On the dorse is :—" Whitehall 4th Decr 1725. It doth not appear by the books of the Office of His Majesty's Secry at Warr, that any warrt has been issued for payment of the £480 10 8 within mentioned, or any part thereof. Rd Arnold." 3 *pages.*

7 Dec. 54. Report of A. Cracherode to the Lords of the Treasury. Has considered the annexed petition of Francis Trenley, Agent to the Officers and Company of his Majesty's ship " Lanceston," whereby he sets forth that the Officers and Company were captors of a pirate ship, called the " Vengeance," and that they carried the same into Jamaica, where they caused the whole crew to be convicted. The petitioner prays that the rewards offered by H.M. proclamations may be ordered. The report sets out the effect of the proclamations and gives the names of the pirates captured, and the sums due for their capture, amounting to 1,190*l.* Also the names of the captors and the amounts due to each. Is of opinion that the petitioner should receive the sums which he was appointed by letters of attorney to receive, as well as Captain Bartholomew Candler's share, being altogether 903*l.* 12*s.* 10¾*d.*, and the remainder should be reserved until claimed.

The petition referred to, an Order in Council, certificate of the Governor of Jamaica (Henry, Duke of Portland), certificate of William Cockburn, Esq., Registrar of the High Court of Admiralty at Jamaica, a list of the men and their quality belonging to the ship " Launceston," and four letters of attorney, one of which contains

1725. VOL. CCLIII.

the signatures of such of the crew as appointed Mr Edward Jasper, of London, gent., their attorney. They all relate to the same business. 26 *pages.*

10 Dec. 55. Memorial of Nicholas Paxton to the Lords of the Treasury. The 300*l.* paid to memorialist to carry on proceedings against the deficient Masters of the Court of Chancery has been expended. Prays for a further order for 300*l.* to defray 70*l.* to the officers and clerks of the Bank for their trouble in preparing books of account and for further necessary proceedings. 1¼ *pages.*

11 Dec. 56. Charles Delafaye to the Lords of the Treasury. The Lords Justices have thought fit, in order the more effectually to put in execution the sentence passed by the Court of Justiciary in Scotland, upon James Falconar and four others, for being concerned in the late notorious riots at Glasgow, that they should be brought hither on one of the Custom House sloops in Scotland, under a sufficient guard of soldiers, in order to their being transported to some of H.M. plantations in America. Their excellencies ask their Lordships to give proper orders for that purpose. Whitehall, 11 Dec. 1725. 1 *page.*

13 Dec. 57. Report of the Attorney and Solicitor General to the Lords of the Treasury, viz., on a proclamation of 21 Dec. 1718 annexed. The question was whether certain petitioners who claimed rewards for persons convicted of piracy, "that were not pirates, or so proved to be before 1 July 1719, and for acts of piracy committed by such persons after the first of July 1719," were entitled to the rewards given by the above proclamation; and also whether the rewards on the foot of the proclamation were payable for any other persons than such as are subjects of Great Britain. Their opinion was that no person could be entitled to the rewards promised, unless the persons so discovered, or seized, were subjects of Great Britain, and should be proved to have been pirates before, or upon, the first day of July 1719, and should be brought to justice and convicted of some act of piracy committed before that day.

Also the printed proclamation. 2 *pages.*

14 Dec. 58. Patrick McDowall to ————. Gives him the trouble of the enclosed gift in favour of the Master of Stormont which he asks may be done for him. Sir Robert Walpole promised that it should. "The gift of the vacant tyths in favor of Mr Murray of Broughtoun, which is in Mr Lounds hands for building of a bridge hes bein much wanted this year, that water hes bein soe high that it could not be crosed for severall dayes togither."

Baron Kennedy's life has been despaired of for some days, but he is now in a fair way of recovery. Edinburgh, Dec. 14, 1725. 2 *pages.*

14 Dec. 59. "Copy. Order of Council relating to Col. Moody late Governor of Placentia." The Lords of Trade had reported that certain lands and houses belonging to Col. Moody had been seized to the

1725. Vol. CCLIII.

value of 732*l.*, and a fort was being built on them, and they recommended that satisfaction should be made to the Colonel. The Order of Council is, that the Lords of the Treasury should report upon the subject. There is the following note at the foot:—"14th Decr 1725. Colonel Moody to attend the Board and make good the above allegations. L.S." 2 *pages.*

14 Dec. 60. Report of H. Pelham to the Lords of the Treasury on the petition of Madestard Jordan in respect to a pension of 100*l.* per ann. to Sarah Owen, widow of Captain Michael Owen, given to her husband for the loss of his right hand. Petitioner alleged that he had advanced 200*l.* to Mrs Owen on the strength of the grant of the pension. Possibly he might have conceived it safe to do so. War Office. 14 Dec. 1725. 1 *page.*

20 Dec. 61. Petition of John Denew, merchant, and Edwd Steadman and John Green, gentlemen, to the Lords of the Treasury. Petitioner having discovered a parcel of Low Marsh land in the parish of Long Port, in the co. of Somerset, called Common Moor, containing near 300 acres, belonging to and withheld from the Crown, preferred a petition to their Lordships for a lease and the benefit of their discovery, but their Lordships declined then to come to any determination on the report. Pray that a Commission or letter of inquiry may be issued, and on the return thereof a lease of the lands may be granted to them. 1 *page.*

20 Dec. 62. A scheme or proposal on the part of the Lords of the Treasury for the reduction of the advances from the Treasury to Mr Missing, who contracted to constantly keep up a magazine at Gibraltar of six months' provisions for 1,500 men. The garrison having been increased to upwards of 6,000 men, their Lordships advanced 15,000*l.*, and the whole money now advanced to him is 20,000*l.* As the siege is raised a great part of the forces are brought back, and the present number victualled is about 3,000, and the advanced money has to be reduced in proportion. Dated "20 Dec. 1725," but query after 1727, from the siege of Gibraltar. 1 *page.*

22 Dec. 63. Report to the Lords of the Treasury of Mr A. Cracherode of the costs for law charges of all causes under his "conduct' for the business of the last term. 9 *pages.*

25 Dec. 64. Thomas Clutterbuck to [ ]. The letter from the Lords of the Treasury to the Lord Lieut. did not desire his opinion in what manner the demand might be satisfied, but "whether any public money remains in the hands of the teller which by proper directions may be applicable to discharge the said fees." [It is not clear what the demand was, nor who makes it; but an effort was being made to get a King's letter to discharge it.]—Dublin Castle, Dec. 1725.

On the outside is:—"Mr Clutterbuck the 25th Decer 1725. 6 *pages.*

1725. VOL. CCLIII.

[? 1725 or 1726.] 65. "Proposals for raising 103,480li pr ann. for the use of the crown in a manner that will be beneficiall and not burthensom to ye nation in general."

The proposal was to abolish the duty on hair imported to make periwigs, and to put a duty on periwig ribbon and on the stock of periwigs in hand. The paper also includes reasons for the proposals and "The Calculation." 6 *pages*.

[Perhaps about 1725 or earlier.] 66. Petition of Lieut. Colonel George Howard to the King. The lands, &c. in the town and manor of Clare and Sudbury, also within the borough of Thackstead, Bardfurd [? Bardfield] Magna, and Asham, and divers lands in the hundred of Begglerhill alias Bebberheath, Cotford, Risbridge, Thedwaiter, and Lockford, and other lands in Suffolk granted by King William for 31 years, having fallen into the hands of a popish heir and the profits being converted to superstitious uses, prays for a reversionary grant of the same for 31 years. 1 *page*.

1725. 67. "Petition. Thomas Greig & others, Burgesses ot the Borough of Coupar, to the Lords Commrs of his Majesty's Treasury, 1725." An election for the borough having been carried on illegally, the same was set aside and the borough remained without magistrates, and must so remain until a new election can be had under his Majesty's royal warrant. Have applied to his Majesty for the grant of a warrant. There are no magistrates and counsellors by whom alone "Stentmasters" can be appointed for assessing the land tax. Taking advantage of these unhappy circumstances, the Receivers of the Land Tax have ordered distress by quartering against the petitioners and other burgesses; and they are thus liable to that hardship without being able to disengage themselves, and so they must continue to suffer until an election is had, unless their Lordships would order the quartering to be removed. Pray for relief. 2 *pages*.

1725. 68. Petition (with blanks not filled up) of John, Lord Balmerino and Cowper to the Lords of the Treasury. There is due to his Majesty 204*l*. Scotch, yearly, for blench duties payable for the Lordship of Cowper, and 92*l*. 13*s*. 4*d*. for blench duties for the Lordship of Balmerino. It has been usual for the Sovereign to grant the arrears of blench duties and to make grants of them for some years to come to their vassals. Prays a grant, &c. of these duties. Dated on the back 1725. 2 *pages*.

1725. 69. Petition of William Ross, of Tayn, in North Britain, to the Lords of the Treasury. Was appointed, in conjunction with his father, uncle, and cousin, by the Comrs of Forfeited Estates in North Britain, to collect the rents of several highland forfeited estates; and in the execution of their office they were attacked by some hundred highlanders in arms, who wounded petitioner dangerously in the breast by a musket shot, killed his cousin, and wounded his father in the neck and arm, and robbed them of papers,

1725 VOL. CCLIII.

money, &c. Prays, in consideration of their sufferings, &c., for the the grant of a warrant appointing him surveyor of foreign salt for the Port of Inverness. Dated on the back 1725. 1 *page.*

[? About 1725.] 70. Memorial of Daniel Campbell, Esq., to the Chancellor of the Exchequer. The few duty or quit-rent of 500*l.* sterling payable to the Crown out of the lands and Island of Islay in Scotland, has for several years been granted by the Crown to the family of Lennox and Richmond. Memorialist is proprietor of the lands and Island of Islay, out of which the few duty is payable, and petitioned, in consideration of his services, for a lease or grant of the reserved rent or tack duty of 41*l.* 13*s.* 4*d.* sterling. The petition was referred to the Barons of the Exchequer in Scotland. The Barons by their report of 26 July 1725, certified that the grant or lease of the few duty of 500*l.* per ann. by Queen Anne was made to Edward Hyde, eldest lawful son of Edward, Lord Cornbury, nephew to Charles, late Duke of Lennox, and Lady Katherine Stewart alias "Obrain," the said Duke's sister, and his heirs: but that is determined by the death of her Majesty: his Majesty, however, might, if he pleased, grant the reserved rent of 41*l.* 13*s.* 4*d.* to memorialist during his Majesty's life, and the arrears thereof from 1706. The memorialist's sufferings and losses by the late affair at Glasgow are too "nottour" to be mentioned. Prays a grant of the rent or tack duty of 41*l.* 13*s.* 4*d.* and the arrears. 2 *pages.*

[Perhaps 1724 or 1725.] 71. Abstract of the report of the Barons of the Exchequer in Scotland upon Lady Cromertie's petition that her jointure may be paid her out of her husband's estate. Her Ladyship by her marriage contract was provided with "40 chalders of victual by way of Locality" out of lands lying most convenient to Castle Leod, which with the houses and gardens thereof were given her as a jointure-house. The consideration was 2,000 marks "scots," or 1,111*l.* 2*s.* 2*d.* sterling paid to her husband by way of marriage portion.

"The Barons say that his Majesty may, if he please, grant Lady Cromertie her jointure as if her husband was naturally dead, yet as it cannot operate in prejudice of lawful creditors, they cannot see how far such grant can be available for the relief of her Ladyship or her family. Undated. 1½ *pages.*

[? 1725.] 72. "Prince William's fees of hon^r for Knighthood of the Bath." The above is the outside title to a paper which is headed "A Bill of fees due to the King's Majesty's servants from all persons that receive the Hon^r of Knighthood of the Bath." In *Haydn's Book of Dignities*, p. 394, is a list of knights created on the revival of the order in 1725, amongst whom is "His Royal highness, William Augustus duke of Cumberland." 2 *pages.*

[? 1725.] 73. Memorial of Richard Macgwire and Josiah Poole, merchants and farmers of the Isle of Man, to the Lords of the Treasury. The Earl of Derby by lease of 9 Feb. 1721 let to memorialist the duties and customs on the arrival of all ships and boats at the Isle of Man,

1725. VOL. CCLIII.

and for goods, &c. imported and exported, and all the Earl's storehouses and warehouses in Castletown, Ramsey, Douglas, and Peeletown, and the use of an apartment in the Castle (the customs of the goods exported out of the Isle for the use of the Earl, his heirs, &c. excepted) from 1 March 1721, for 21 years, at a rent of 1,050*l.* payable quarterly at Liverpool; with a proviso for the rent to cease in time of Quarantine, and then only one third of the duties collected, to be paid by memorialists, and they to have the other two thirds for their own use. Are informed that if the customs and trade of the Isle were under the collection and inspection of officers appointed by his Majesty, the Customs of Great Britain would be increased at least 100,000*l.* per annum.

The Crown for several months past has been at great expense for ships to guard the coast and trade of the Island, which would be saved by the Customs being vested in Trustees.

By an Act passed in the last Sessions of Parliament their Lordships are authorized to agree with the Earl of Derby (who has only an estate for life in the Customs, subject to memorialists' lease as they apprehend), and with the Trustees appointed by the said Act for the Hon[ble] Henrietta Bridget Ashburnham, an infant (who has a right to the inheritance subject to the Earl's estate), and also with memorialists for their interest in the Isle or the Customs thereof, for such considerations as their Lordships shall think fit. Propose to assign their interest to such persons and on such terms as their Lordships shall think just.

Undated, but in the *Minute Book*, vol. 25, p. 204*k* (2 Aug. 1726), is:—"Write to the Comm[rs] of Customs to know the precautions they have taken for regulating the trade to & from the Isle of Man since the Act of the last session of parliament passed for improving the Customs, &c." 1½ *pages.*

[? 1724 or 1725.] 74. Petition of John Leverock, yeoman, and Robert Saint Clare, distiller, to the Lords of the Treasury. Petitioners were taken up on 26 Feb. 1724, and close confined in M[r] Chandler's house (being one of H.M. messengers) until 13 Sept. following, by order of the Secretary of State. Their imprisonment was not for any offence, but they were detained as evidences against Sir Alex[r] Anstrother: complain that they were kept short of food and without the decencies of life. Pray for some allowance. Undated. 1 *page.*

[? About 1725.] 75. Memorial of Richard Woollaston, Esq., to ———. Was chosen a member of Parliament for the borough of Witchurch, in Hampshire, in 1696; and served the borough till Lord Oxford dissolved the Ministry, and the Queen the Parliament. Acted also for the following Parliament, when "M[r] Tilny and M[r] Vernon spent about 7,000*l.* to turn M[r] Woollaston out," who had for above 14 years kept up the honest interest there, at an incredible expense. He always brought in a friend, and particularly General Shrimpton, when he was abroad in the army at the usual times of the elections; and was not only at expenses there but at several boroughs and counties at every new election, to bring in honest gentlemen: and

1725. VOL. CCLIII.

though he did not stand himself this parliament he spared for no money, nor pains, to get those chosen that were attached to his Majesty's interest in several counties and boroughs. Has never once swerved from the interest of his country, but has not received the least consideration except a lease of the Abbey of Furnace, in the county of Lancaster, for 29½ years, from the late Queen, obtained by the interest of the late Lord Godolphin: and this cost him 1,500*l*. to maintain the right of the Crown. In this case he was cast on a nicety of law, the question being "whether y[t] estate upon y[e] forfeiture was come back to y[e] King as King, or as Duke of Lancaster."

Since his Majesty's Accession M[r] Preston clandestinely agreed "to pay a 1,000[l] into the Exchequer to resign up y[e] 15 years w[ch] he has recovered to make them 31 years, y[e] king not knowing of any lease M[r] Woollaston had, and thereby he is defeated of his reversion" unless he will enter into a long and chargeable suit. These misfortunes and expenses for the public service have extremely impaired memorialist's fortune. He has besides had a family of 23 children, and neither he, nor any of them, has had the least place under the Government. Undated; but perhaps 1725, as a Richard Woolaston is stated to have received money as of his Majesty's bounty. See *Minute Book*, vol. 25, Index 95*d*, &c. 1 *page*.

[? 1725.] 76. Petition of Samuel Boucher to the Lords of the Treasury. In the year 1721, being bound for Bengal, in the East Indies, discovered that the Captain had put out certain goods and sold them at the Cape of Good Hope. Petitioner and others at great loss caused the Captain to be tried in or about Hilary term 1724, and he was fined 1,000*l*. and the goods condemned at 700*l*. and upwards. Prays for relief. 1 *page*.

[In or after 1725.] 77. Petition of Christopher Popping and divers others, including Jane Rhodes, the widow of Henry Rhodes, who died intestate possessed of 40,000*l*. personalty. Jane Rhodes claimed as his widow letters of administration, together with a moiety of his personal estate under the custom of London, whereof the intestate was a freeman; the petitioners insist that they are entitled to his personalty as next-of-kin. William Rhodes as next-of-kin had entered a caveat and suits ensued. Pray that no new orders shall be made out until their Lordships' further directions therein.

[Sir R. Walpole is described as Knight. The date must be in 1725 or after. *See Beetson's Political Index*, vol. 1, p. 339.] 3 *pages*.

[? 1725.] 78. Opinion of Isaac Jennings and Thomas Mazine addressed to Sir Robert Walpole, K.B., first Lord of the Treasury, as to a duty on malted corn, giving many particulars as to distilling, &c. and how a duty might be collected.

Undated, but Sir R. Walpole was made a Knight of the Bath 1725, and a Knight of the Garter the next year. 1 *page* (*brief size*).

1725.

VOL. CCLIV. 1725. CLASSIFIED, AND DOCUMENTS FOR WHICH A BRIEF DESCRIPTION SUFFICES.

1. Claims sent in to the Treasury from the Treasurer of the Chambers Office in the year 1725, for the charge of the barges and watermen, messengers, stationery, and other bills. 9 *pages*.

2. Lord Chamberlain's warrants or letters to the Lords of the Treasury for various payments for furniture, &c. One is for payment of 324*l*. 2*s*. 7*d*. to Mr Kent for painting the sides of the "Cube Room at Kensington," and another for two silver trumpets for the horse guards; and there are such orders as the following at the foot of some of them:—"Let this warrant be executed," &c. 8 *pages*.

3. Reports, &c. of the Com^rs of Customs. (1) On remission of the King's half of the duty in case of seizure; (2) on allowances paid to officers in the plantations on the continent of America, either by the establishment or by incidents [recommend the offices to be sunk]; (3) on the gross and net produce of the revenue under the Com^rs management, granted for the Civil List; (4) on a reward for apprehending Gib Jarvis, *alias* Tomkin, a notorious owler, returned from transportation; (5) on the embarkation of 26 horses, custom free, for a regiment of dragoons on the Irish establishment; (6) on interest on certain bonds; (7) on the appointment of agents or solicitors to advise and assist the board in the management, and to carry on the prosecutions and the business of the Solicitor of the Customs; (8) on the right to search and seize goods on vessels of war by Custom House officers; (9) on payment for the rebuilding and repair of the first floor of the east wing of the Custom House in Thames Street, and erecting an additional building on Wool Key. 49 *pages or parts*.

4. Reports, &c. of the Com^rs of Excise to the Lords of the Treasury. (1.) Report on the memorial of Edmund Elwill, Esq., Controller of the Accounts of Excise, for an allowance for himself and clerks. Mention that the first grant of the office of Comptroller was, by patent of 3 April 1661, to Elias Ashmole and William Chiffinch, Esq^res, and at the death of Mr Chiffinch, Mr Ashmole became sole Comptroller. At the death of Mr Ashmole in the year 1693 Lord Viscount How succeeded, Col. Sydney was Controller in 1714. In the year 1715 a claim of 300*l*. per ann. additional salary for himself and clerks was made by the present Controller, and was disregarded as unreasonable by the then Lords of the Treasury. The Com^rs conceive that the reason was, that no addition of business was, by the new duties, added to the Controller himself, who does not execute his office in person, nor give any attendance for the performance of that business: and that it was sufficient to pay the hands that were to dispatch the business, which

1725. VOL. CCLIV.

makes the case of the Com^{rs} of Excise to differ from that of the Comptroller, inasmuch as the Com^{rs} execute their office in person, and every new duty brings a real addition of pains and attendance to themselves; recommend 100*l.* per ann. for two additional clerks. The report finishes:—"Upon this occasion we beg leave to observe to your Lord^{ps} that the business in the Comptroller's Office must suffer, since there are clerks imployed in it at large salarys that do no business themselves, but hire deputys to perform it for them at small ones, and we find that one of the clerks now imploy'd by the Comptroll^{r} in the coffee, tea, and chocolate dutys is by no means qualified for it. As this evil has formerly been complained of without redress, we most humbly beg your Lord^{ps} commands that for the future no clerk be admitted into the service of the Comptroller without the approbation of the Comm^{rs} of Excise." [*Minuted*:—"W^{t} signed."] (2.) An account of the gross and clear produce of the branches of the revenue of the Civil List funds, 1699 to 1715 (3.) Memorial enclosing, for perusal and to be laid before the House of Commons, an account of all moneys paid out of the Excise Office for the privy purse, secret service, pensions, &c. without account. (4.) Report on the petition of Alexander Gillinders, bondsman for Alexander Irvine, who was employed as one of the billmen under the Treasurer of the Excise; any loss to the revenue must be made good by Mr Poyntz, the Receiver General [of Excise]. (5.) Gross and net receipts on the hereditary and temporary excise. And (6.) Report on the memorial of William Burroughs, Esq.: recommend additional salary of 50*l.* a year for himself and clerks. 16 *pages.*

5. Reports, &c. of the Com^{rs} of Excise, Scotland, to the Lords of the Treasury. (1) As to the question of 34 gallons, English, being equal to 12 gallons, Scots, recommending a parliamentary remedy, as the accounts were much perplexed by the present method. (2.) Draft of a clause proposed to be brought into an Act of Parliament on the same subject. (3.) On the petition of John Ramsay, late land carriage-waiter at Glasgow town: approving of his dismissal. (4.) As to the maltsters making an entry, upon oath, of malt in stock, giving an account of the opposition the payment of the duty met with. Have an account from their Surveyor General that but one maltster has allowed entrance at Dundee, and that for so doing the mob had got into his house and broke his copper, and would have done other mischief but for the soldiers. Their officers, with a party of soldiers, seized 640 gallons of brandy at Elgin, and put it in a vault there with a sentry to guard it, and sent a vessel to remove it to Leith, and the general ordered a corporal and four privates to go on board and secure the seizure, the soldiers that lay at Elgin being marched to Inverness. The ship no sooner arrived than the next night the mob got up, and notwithstanding that three of the soldiers who went with the ship were posted in the ship where only access was to be had to the vault, the mob got great hammers and broke open the door and fired into the ship, upon which the soldiers discharged their pieces amongst the mob and killed one man; but for all that the mob passed on, disarmed the soldiers, and took away the

1725. VOL. CCLIV.

brandy, and upon a complaint of the father of the man that was killed the magistrates imprisoned the soldiers and made out a warrant against the supervisor and officer; but they made their escape from thence and are come to Edinburgh. This affair was laid before the Lord Advocate and the General and his Lordship wrote to the magistrates to set the soldiers at liberty, and the General says that if it be not done before he comes to Elgin he shall take care to do it himself. The persons were so disguised that the collector cannot discover any of them. At Edinburgh the maltsters have all allowed the officers entrance and made entries of their malt, but have not paid their duty nor given security, and it is understood that they will not pay till compelled by law. His Lordship has acquainted the Com^rs^ that as soon as a sufficient force comes to Edinburgh he will procure a Justice of Peace Court and get judgment for the duty, and the General will give orders to the soldiers to see the "decreets" put in execution. The Advocate will endeavour to prevail with the maltsters to pay the duty without such measures.

In the Lothians, Fife, Firstdale, and the shire of Dumfries the maltsters have made their entries, and allow the officers entrance into their malt-houses, but in few places else; nay, some private gentlemen in those places have actually paid the duty, and they hope by the assistance of the Lord Advocate and the forces that the other parts of Scotland will be brought to a submission. [In the *Minute Book*, vol. 25, p. 83*c* (27 July 1725), is:—"A letter from the Comm^rs^ of Excise in Scotland dated the 20th instant, giving an account of their proceedings about the Malt Duty and the resistance they met therein, as also of the rescuing a great seizure of brandy at Elgin, is read. Write to the Comm^rs^ of Excise approving their proceedings and advising them to pursue with diligence and by all legal methods the bringing the said duty to bear, and to correct the insolence of those who rescued the said seizure by prosecuting them with effect."] (5.) As to further steps taken to make the malt duty effectual. The maltsters at Edinburgh have not paid the duty nor given security; and their discourse is, that if the Justices give judgment against them they will all go to prison and leave off brewing; which can be with no other view than to distress the people and disturb the quiet of the place. The Lords of Session have obliged them, on or before the tenth of Aug., to give security to carry on their trade for three months or to go to prison. By the two Acts of *sederunt* the Lords ordered their petition to be burnt by the common hangman, which was done. No more than one brewer has complied with the Acts, and he is branded with the name of traitor to his country, and the people he served with drink returned it to him, being exasperated at him for what he had done. The generality of the maltsters in Paisley, Renfrew, and Air have (according to the example of Glasgow) made entries and given security; but at Stirling, Perth, and Dundee they will not allow the officers entrance into their malt-houses nor yield any manner of obedience to the law, and the officers meet with the same opposition at Aberdeen and Dundee. Their officers are to note

1725. Vol. CCLIV.

these denials that the delinquents may be prosecuted. The Lord Advocate has exerted himself to the utmost to bring the maltsters in and about Edinburgh to reason, but without success; but when the people here (Edinburgh) are brought to compliance, no doubt the other parts of the country will follow. P.S.—As directed, they will prosecute with the utmost rigour any persons concerned in "any "mobbish tumults, rescues, and disorders." In the *Minute Book*, vol. 25, p. 90*i* (10 Aug. 1725), is:—"Write to the Comm[rs] to acknow-"ledge the receipt of their letter, incite their diligence and direct "them to advise on all proper occasions with the Lord Advocate." (6.) The maltsters in Edinburgh and precincts still refuse to pay their duty, and an information against twelve of them for double duty is to be heard tomorrow, (viz., 25 Aug.). All of them (except Baily Simpson, one of the present magistrates) left off brewing, and only one has been prevailed on to carry on the trade. The maltsters in Stirling, Perth, Dundee, and Aberdeen continue to deny the officers access, and some about Aberdeen that did allow entrance now refuse it. The collectors are to lay informations against them before the Justices of the Peace, and if they refuse to act they will be prosecuted in the Court of Exchequer. In the *Minute Book*, vol. 25, p. 98*c* (31 Aug. 1725), is a notice that this letter was read and acquiesced in. (7.) On summoning the brewers to appear before the Justices (Edinburgh) on the 25th instant, the whole of the brewers in the city and precinct (save two) ceased from brewing, and on the day appointed the Bench of Justices, consisting of the Earl of Lauderdale and sixteen others, gave the penalty desired; but the brewers appealed to the Quarter Sessions, when the Com[rs] doubt not the judgment will be confirmed. By "the prudent management of the Lord Hay, the Lord Advocate, and others the concert of the Brewers is now broke," a good number of them have begun or design to begin to brew, and they (the Com[rs]) doubt not that the opposition to the malt tax will decline apace, the whole country seeming to depend on the behaviour of this place. Inverness has been brought to comply and give security "by the assistance of General Wade and Cullodon, Lord Advocate's brother." Four or five of the ring-leaders of the brewers in Edinburgh were taken up some days ago and are "continued" in separate prisons. (8.) The maltsters at Stirling and Perth still refuse the officers access; those at Dalkeith, Musselburgh, as well as at Preston Pans and Dunbar, have given security for the duty, and many at Haddington have done the like; those at Linlithgow, Barrowstoness, Grangepans, and Falkirk will neither pay nor give security: when informations are laid against the delinquents, the Justices will either oblige them to secure the duty, or give judgment against them for double duty. Of thirty maltsters in Edinburgh and precincts seventeen have complied, and there is an information against the other thirteen before the Justices for double duty. The maltsters in the Isles of Orkney would not allow entrance into their malt-houses. They (the Com[rs]) have procured letters from Lord Morton and Col. Douglas ordering them (the maltsters) to pay strict obedience to the

1725. VOL. CCLIV.

law, but they continue to deny access and have beaten and abused one of the officers, and they (the Comrs) have written to General Wade to order a detachment of troops to Kirkwall to protect the officers. [This letter is referred to in the Minute Book, vol. 25, p. 109*g*. It was read "and to be laid up with other their former letters."] (9.) Mr. Burnet (one of the Comrs) has prevailed with the magistrates of New Aberdeen to promise that upon informations being laid against the maltsters within their jurisdiction, who had incurred penalties, they (the magistrates) would give the full penalties unless entries were made and securities given, &c.

Mr. Burnet likewise ordered an information to be laid before the Justices of the shire of Aberdeen against the maltsters in and about Old Aberdeen for the penalties of denying entrance, but it was thought advisable to let it stand over for a fortnight or they would appeal, which might be of worse consequences to the revenue. The maltsters of New Aberdeen who appealed to the next quarter sessions may understand that the penalties incurred by them may be recovered elsewhere than before the Justices.

At Stirling the maltsters continue to refuse access, and they (the Comrs) have ordered information to be laid before the Justices: if that would not bring them to submission, they would be prosecuted before the Lords of Justiciary.

At Perth the General Supervisor has been allowed entrance into most of the malt-houses, and the maltsters at Haddington who had refused giving security have now complied. (10.) There was a meeting of the Justices at Stirling on the 5th of Oct. in respect to the maltsters entering their stock in hand. It was insisted by the Excise Officers that the entries should be made on oath, but the majority of the Justices were against it and thought that lenity therein would bring the maltsters to more ready compliance. Intend to take the Lord Justice General's advice whether any other prosecutions should be carried on against them before the General Quarter Sessions or not.

The maltsters at Hamilton have at last made entries of their stock and given security.

[This letter was ordered to be laid up with the rest. See *Minute Book*, vol. 25, p. 114*s*.] 27½ *pages*.

6. Various financial papers, including such as relate to Loans on the Land Tax, the National Debt, income of her late Majesty's Civil List, Supplies, State of Mr. Beranger's debt, the Sinking Fund, the Aggregate Fund, Exchequer Bills, the South Sea Company, sums voted by Parliament. 54 *pages*.

7. Papers relating to the affairs of the Trustees and Comrs for the Forfeited Estates in Scotland, viz. :—(1.) List of the certificates from the late Trustees and Commrs for the Forfeited Estates in Scotland dated the 19th, 21st, 23rd, and 26th of January 1724–5, delivered into the Court of Exchequer the 3rd of February following, and (2) six papers entitled :—"Abbreviat by Sir Robert Sinclair, Barrt, Receiver General in Scotland, of receipts, payments and remains of

1725. VOL. CCLIV.

the rents and profites and sale of the forfeited estates in Scotland." The first of the six is on 2 Jan. and the last on 31 May 1725. (3.) "Account of money in the Excheqr of Scotland arising from Forfeited Estates" in Scotland. 9½ *large pages*.

8. Estimates (1) "of several extraordinary expences on account of His Majtys land forces not provided for by Parliament; (2) "of the charge of the six Independent Compies of foot for the security of the Highlands;" (3) of the charge of the Guards, Garrisons, and other his Majesty's land forces in Great Britain; (4) of the charge of His Majesty's forces in the Plantations, Minorca and Gibraltar. 5 *pages*.

9. An estimate of the charge of the Out-Pensioners of Chelsea Hospital. 1 *page*.

10 and 11. Two reports of Charles Harison concerning licences granted by the Court of Exchequer to compound upon penal laws, &c. from the last day of Michaelmas term 1724 to the last day of Michaelmas term 1725. 7 *pages*.

DOCUMENTS for which a brief description suffices.

Date.	Description of Document.	From	To	Purport.
? Beginning of 1725.	12. Petition -	Guy Palmes, Esq. -	Lords of the Treasury.	For relief, his necessities great and his creditors pressing. In the *Minute Book*, vol. 25, p. 4c, 19 Jan. 1724–5: — "Mr. William Palmes to be paid on his pencõn to Xmas last by the hands of Mr. Chetwynd." 1 *page*.
20 Jan.	13. Letter - -	Ch. Delafaye -	—	Asks to be reimbursed the fees at the Treasury on 375*l.*, viz., 20*l.* 3*s.* 9¾*d.* 1 *page*.
22 Jan.	14. Do. - -	"Transport Officers"	John Scrope, Esq., Secretary to the Lords of the Treasury.	Salaries for transport service to cease, but the Chief Clerk and two others to be continued until the books and papers are removed to the Sick and Hurt Office at Deptford, &c. 3 *pages*.
3 Feb.	15. Do. - -	The Judges - -	"My Lords" -	For an order for 200*l.* to Mr. Wm. Townsend as a reward to the persons employed in examining and stating the Accounts of the Masters in Chancery and of the Usher for incidents. 1 *page*.

1725. Vol. CCLIV.

Date.	Description of Document.	From	To	Purport.
15 Feb.	16. Letter - -	Count De La Leppe Shaumbourg.	—	Asks that Mrs. Susanne de Molliens may be put on the list of pensions of Queen Anne now before the Treasury, her pension of 40*l.* being 2½ or 3 years in arrear. 1 *page.*
16 Feb.	17. Report - -	Ordnance Officers -	Rt. Hon. the Earl of Cadogan.	On petition of Mr. Tho. Howard and another for compensation for loss of ship, being a tender on a bomb vessel in the Mediterranean. 1 *page.*
[? About 17 Feb.]	18. Petition -	Henry Harcourt, late Comptroller of the Classis Lottery, anno 1711.	Lords of the Treasury.	For directions to be given in respect to a claim he had upon the executrix of John Dutton Colt, Esq., late Paymaster of the Lottery. *Minuted:* — "17th Febry. 1724–5. He must apply to the Admx. of the Paymar. of the Classis Lottery, ao. 1711, for paymt. of this money; pursuant to my Lords of the Trearys. warrt. in this behalfe." 1 *page.*
17 Feb.	19. Letter - -	Lord Lieut. of Ireland (Carteret).	Do. -	On the petition of Captain William Moore praying to be placed on half pay in Ireland. The Board of General Officers are of opinion that some provision should be made for him. The petition, which states that he raised a company at his own charge and was, with them, beseiged at Londonderry, and the report of the General Officers. In the *Minute Book*, vol. 25, p. 26m, is:—"Write to Lord Lieut. or his Secretary for a more explicit opinion as to the case of Capt. Moore for half pay." 4 *pages.*
20 Feb	20. Report -	P. Medows and Ja. Bruce, Controllers of Army Accounts.	Do. - -	On two victualling lists for Gibraltar of Mr. Missing. 5 *pages.*
26 Feb.	21. Certificate -	Deputy Auditors of Imprests.	—	The pension of 1,000*l.* per ann. to Henry Priestman, Esq., for his services in the Navy has been paid. Also copy of the warrant. 1½ *pages.*
5 Mar.	22. Letter - -	William Corbett -	—	Sends an account of the pension of Mr. Priestman and an affidavit of his death: prays a warrant for the arrears. 1 *page* (*quarto*).

1725. Vol. CCLIV.

Date.	Description of Document.	From	To	Purport.
25 Mar.	23. Account -	—	—	"Debts owing to the Civil Government at the time of her late Majesty's demise and what has been paid towards discharging the same." 1 *page*.
3 April	24. Letter - -	Duke of Newcastle -	Lords of the Treasury.	Sends the petition of Francis Maynard, Esq., praying a pension upon the Irish Establishment, together with the reports and certificates. In the *Minute Book*, vol. 25, p. 39*b*, 13 April 1725 (after stating that the above were read), "MyLords thereupon order a warrant to be prepared for placing him on the establishment of Ireland at 100*l.* per ann. pencõn from Lady Day last." 1 *page*.
5 April	25. Do. - -	Auditor Harley -	John Scrope, Esq., Secretary to His Majesty's Treasury.	As to what forwardness Mr. Hampden's account, as late Treasurer of his Majesty's Navy is in. 1 *page*.
5 April	26. Memorial -	J. Hancock, yeoman of the Robes (in the absence of the Earl of Cadogan).	Lords of the Treasury.	On the state of moneys due to the Office of H.M. Robes. On the back is:—"26 May 1725. Messrs. Mehmet, Mustapha, Lockman and Schroder, four pages of the Bedchamber, are to be paid 20*li.* each by the hands of Mr. Lowther for the Court mourning for the late King of Spain and the late Czar of Muscovy, being 10*li.* a piece for each mourning: so these are not included in the Earl's demand." Also a certificate of the surplusage. 1½ *pages*.
10 April	27. Report -	Comrs. of Stamp Duties.	Do. - -	On the petition of the Searchers and Surveyors of Cards and Dice against the augmentation of their salaries. Also the petition. 2 *pages*.
16 April	28. Memorial -	A. Cracherode -	Do. - -	For payment of the 200 guineas agreed by their Lordships to be paid to Mr. Hughs and his wife for the conveyance of a piece of ground, for widening the passage in St. Margaret's Lane, leading to the House of Lords. 1 *page*.

1725. Vol. CCLIV.

Date.	Description of Document.	From	To	Purport.
28 April	29. Account -	—	—	Net produce of the Civil List Articles from Christmas 1699 to Lady Day 1715. Exchequer Auditor's Office. 1 *page.*
8 May	30. Letter - -	Lord Lieut. of Ireland (Carteret).	Lords of the Treasury.	His income is impaired by the fees on licences for export of wool and falls short by 756*l.* 6*s.* 6*d.* Prays for a warrant to complete his salary. Also abstract of the produce of the wool licences. In the *Minute Book,* vol. 25, p. 46*i,* is a notice that this letter was read and agreed to. 3 *pages.*
[After 12 May.]	31. Account -	Joseph Downing, printer and bookseller.	[Do.] - -	Of the charge of 10,694 "Seaman's Monitor" distributed among the officers and seamen in his Majesty's service, 1723, 1724, and 1725. Also an account of the delivery of the copies. 4 *pages.*
14 May	32. Memorial -	Earl of Lincoln, late Paymaster Genl. of the Forces.	Do. - -	For 1,847*l.* 7*s.* 8*d.* to be paid into his hands out of the contingencies or extraordinaries of the forces to complete the warrant for provisions, &c. for Annapolis Royal furnished by Col. Philips. 1 *page.*
21 May	33. Letter - -	Lord Townshend -	Do. - -	For directions to be given for payment of 24*l.* to Col. Spicer for particular services. In the *Minute Book,* vol. 25, p. 51*b,* is a notice that this is to be paid by the hands of Mr. Lowther. 1 *page.*
27 May	34. Memoranda -	—	—	Certified copy of memoranda made by the Auditors, upon the accounts of the Treasurers, for the Transport service, in the reign of her late Majesty Queen Anne. Signed "Jer. Oakeley, Depty. Auditr." 2 *pages.*

1725. VOL. CCLIV.

Date.	Description of Document.	From	To	Purport.
[? About 27 May.]	35. Petition -	John Dovey -	The Rt. Hon. Sir William Young, one of the Lords of the Treasury.	Asks for the grant of a warrant for Richard Dovey, petitioner's brother, to be sworn in as "one of the Inspectors on Cards and Dice." Petitioner obtained a presentment from the Commissioners of Stamp duties, which he delivered to the Rt. Hon. Sir Robert Walpole, on behalf of his brother, whom Col. Schutz recommended to Sir William. The presentment referred to. In the *Minute Book*, vol. 25, p. 65*e*, is:—"Richard Dovey to be Inspector of Cards and Dice according to the presentment of the Commissioners." 2 *pages*.
[? About 28 May.]	36. Memorial -	William Hamilton -	Lords of the Treasury.	Praying for 36*l*. 5*s*. to make up what is wanting for the expenses for beadmen's gowns and other charities upon His Majesty's birthday. 1 *page*.
31 May	37. Do. - -	Lord Cadogan -	Do. - -	Acknowledges the receipt from the Jewel Office of 7,346 oz. of white plate for part of his equipage as Ambassador Extraordinary and Plenipotentiary to the States General. The employment having determined, asks for a Privy Seal to discharge him of the plate. Certificate relating thereto. 2 *pages*.
1 June	38. Representation	Comrs. for Taxes -	Do. - -	Asking for allowance of 40*l*. for an extraordinary clerk for keeping the accounts of the Receivers' payments on the tax upon Papists, &c. 1 *page*.
5 June	39. Letter - -	W. Sanderson -	The Rt. Hon. Sir Robt. Walpole.	Sends an order of the House of Lords for payment of fees to the Gentleman Usher of Black Rod, and a Bill of fees and charges due to the Black Rod ordered to be paid by the Earl of Suffolk for the custody of Pattrige and Adams, and expenses in seeking after Bishop. 3 *pages*.

1725. VOL. CCLIV.

Date.	Description of Document.	From	To	Purport.
21 June	40. Report - -	General Officers -	Lord Lieut. of Ireland (Carteret).	On the petition of Capt. John Gerbet and others. Finds that they are entitled to half pay. 1 *page*.
[? About 24 June.]	41. Memorial -	—	—	"About the arrears of the late Lady Charlotte de Schulenbourg," and a pension to Nymphe Ehrengard de Schulenbourg, her daughter." 1 *page* (*quarto*).
13 July	42. Copy of an order.	—	—	From the Court of Chancery for the issue of a writ "ne exeat regnum" against William Rhodes in a suit Jane Rhodes widow of Henry Rhodes *v*. Will. Rhodes, John Manby, and Mary his wife. 1 *page*.
23 July	43. Report -	Edward Carteret and Geoffrey Walpole, Esqrs., H.M. Postmasters General.	Lords of the Treasury.	Have considered the petition of Mr. John Lefebore, and think him a very diligent and good officer, and that what he alleges in his petition is true, and that he deserves encouragement. Accompanied by his petition, which states that his whole time is taken up at the Post Office, and that he has to sit up many nights successively. Conceives that he deserves an equal reward of an additional salary to that given to other gentlemen for the discovery of the late plot, viz., 300*l*. a year from Midsummer 1723. *Minuted*: — "Lre writ 29th July to Postmars. to increase his salary in the manner as desired in his peticoñ & to pay the same from Midsr. 1723 out of the monys in the Secrys hands of the Post Office for his Mats. special service. "Altered, being ordered to comence from Lady day 1725." 2 *pages*.
28 July	44. Memorial -	Anthony Cracherode	Do. - -	Asks for 1,000*l*. upon account, to discharge several bills of the Clerks in Court; and to carry on H.M. affairs. 1 *page*.

Date.	Description of Document.	From	To	Purport.
2 Aug.	45. Report -	Controller of the Army Contracts (Ja. Bruce).	Lords of the Treasury.	On the memorial of Thomas Missing, Esq., contractor for Victualling the garrisons of Placentia and Annapolis-Royal. 1 *page.*
7 Sept.	46. Letter - -	Ch. Delafaye -	Do. - -	Encloses extracts of letters from Col. Kane, Lieut. Governor of Minorca, relating to expense on account of three row boats belonging to Tunis that put into that Island. The extracts referred to. 2½ *pages.*
14 Sept.	47. Memorial -	J. Hancock, yeoman of Robes.	Do. - -	For the salaries of the Officers of the Robes. *Minuted:* — "Warrant signed 23 Septembr. 1725." 1 *page.*
21 Sept.	48. Letter - -	Ch. Delafaye - -	—	Has written a letter to the Lords of the Treasury for the determining of Col. Lascelles's salary. In the *Minute Book*, vol. 25, p. 107*b* (21 Sept. 1725), is : — "Mr. Lascells, who was appointed to inspect the demolition of the works at Dunkirk and Mardyke, is to be paid his allowance to the 17th instant, incl., and no further. Mr. Delafaye having by letter of that date signifyed the King's pleasure that his employment should then cease and determine." 1 *page.*
[29 Sept.]	49. Estimates -	—	—	Of the debt of the Navy at Mich. 1725 and comparisons with other years from 1721. 3 *pages.*
27 Mar. and 8 Oct	50. Certificates -	Comrs. of the Office of Alienations.	Lords of the Treasury.	Of the gross and net produce of their office. 2 *pages.*

1725. Vol. CCLIV.

Date.	Description of Document.	From	To	Purport.
13 Oct.	51. Petition -	Thomas Moore -	Lords of the Treasury.	The minute on the paper which explains the nature of it is: —"Thomas Moor's peticõn for 1,000*li.* to be allowed him for his service in the Office of Paymaster of the Forces, after his Commission was superseded, and beyond what their Lordp̃'s have already allowed on the Auditor's Report of his cravings, is read and rejected. "On another memll. of the 7th of January 1728. My Lords are to be informed what has been done on several former applications made by him to this Board for the like service." 1 *page.*
21 Oct.	52. Letter - -	Ch. Delafaye -	Do. - -	Signifying the Lords Justices' orders to subsist till Christmas next Brigadier Bisset's regiment, which was coming from Minorca to Ireland. 2 *pages.*
3 Dec.	53. Petition -	Thomas Kemp, of the Tower of London.	Do. - -	As to payment of Brigadier Munden's salary to his death, viz., 19 Sept. 1725. The following entry in the *Minute Book,* vol. 25, p. 129*l* (7 Dec. 1725), explains the nature of the petition: — "Thomas Kemp's peticõn is read for Brigadier Munden's arrears, as out Ranger of Windsor Forest, to the day of his death; the same being assigned to him by the said Brigadr. My Lords will not enter into the consideracõn or merit of the said assignment; but when the arrears come to be paid, the warrant for the same shall be made to the Executors or Administrators of the said Brigar., subject to what was due and owing, at the time of his death, to the Keepers under him on the salaries which he allowed them." 1 *page.*
[? About 4 Dec.]	54. Do. -	Rice Williams -	The Rt. Hon. Sir Robt. Walpole.	For a warrant to appoint him as a tide-waiter. Also a certificate in his favour, signed by the minister, churchwardens, and inhabitants of St. Margaret's, Westminster. Dated 4 Dec. 1725. 2 *pages.*

1725. VOL. CCLIV.

Date.	Description of Document.	From	To	Purport.
18 Dec.	55. Memorial -	Anthony Cracherode	Lords of the Treasury.	For 1,000*l.* on account to pay 300*l.* by way of imprest to Nicholas Paxton and to carry on his Majesty's causes, &c. In the *Minute Book*, vol. 25, p. 138*d* (22 Dec. 1725), is: — "Mr. Cracherode's memorial of the 18th instant for 1,000*l.* for carrying on law charges is read and agreed to." 1 *page.*
[25 Dec.]	56. Abstract -	—	—	Of produce of H.M. revenue in Ireland for a year. 1 *page.*
[? 1724 or 1725.]	57. Letter - -	Duke of Newcastle -	Lords of the Treasury.	For 120*l.* to be paid to Solomon Negri, employed by his Majesty in the interpretation of the Oriental languages. 1 *page.*
1725.	58. Petition -	Catherine Drummond, spouse to Lieut. Lawrence Drummond.	The Chancellor of the Exchequer (Walpole).	For directions to be given for the speedy payment of the three years' arrears of her husband's pension of 100*l.* per ann. due at Lady day 1725. *Minuted*:—"To be paid to the time that other pensions at the Exchequer are paid. Several are paid to Lady day 1724." 1 *page.*
[? Between 1718 and 1725.]	59. Memorial -	Col. Geo. Fielding -	Lords of the Treasury.	For a warrant to the Great Wardrobe for clothing of the nine trumpeters and a kettle drummer of H.M. regiment of horse guards. 1 *page.*
? 1725.	60. Warrant (draft)	—	—	For "Alexander Abercrombie to receive the balance on the final accounts of the late Receivers and Paymasters of the Equivalent Fond in Scotland." 1 *page.*
? 1725.	61. Certificate -	Tho. Spence -	Lords of the Treasury.	As to the sum necessary to discharge the principal upon the Lottery Ao. 1713 "as far as No. 93 Cour. 34," with interest to Mich. 1725. 1 *page.*

1726.

VOL. CCLV. 1726. JANUARY.

1. A paper with the following titles:—
New Year's Gifts and other annual dues for the Lords.
New Year's Gifts paid and distributed by M[r] Scrope.
New Year's Gifts, or other annual gratuities, for the Secretaries and for the clerks.
There is also a second paper of a similar nature. 4 *pages.*

[? About 4 Jan.] 2. "A caveat humbly layd before the Right Hono[ble] the Lords Com[rs] of his Ma[ties] Treasury, by the Hono[ble] Philip Bertie, Esq., Thomas Hayter & James Bengough, Gent., and their representatives; that noe lease or grant of certaine lands lyeing in Lincolnshire (called derelict lands) be made to any person or persons before the parties above named or their agent has notice thereof and be heard therein."
On the back is:—"4th Jan[ry] 1725–6 caveat entred p order of M[r] Secr[y] Scrope." 1 *page.*

[? About 4 Jan.] 3. "Benj[n] Collier, Esq. Caviat *v.* Combes Savoy Lease. 4 Jan[ry] 1725–6. Caveat entred p order of M[r] Scrope."
A paper thus *docketed*:—The premises situated in the Strand were mortgaged to Collier and were held of the Crown. 1 *page.*

5 Jan. 4. Report of the Com[rs] of Works to the Lords of the Treasury upon the question by what authority M[r] Sympson, one of the Keepers in Hampton Court Park, has been many years employed to inspect the River that feeds the King's park and gardens there with water, their L[ps] having agreed that Thomas Guilliam, a servant of the Earl of Halifax, shall succeed to that business in case M[r] Sympson (who lies dangerously ill) shall happen to die. Find that in 1701, when H.M. gardens were united to this office, M[r] Sympson had 20*l.* per ann. for looking after and inspecting the River; and the allowance has ever since been continued to him for looking after the repairing and cleaning the River; and according to the best enquiry they can make he was appointed by the Superintendent of the Gardens. 1 *page.*

11 Jan. 5. Memorial of A. Cracherode to the Lords of the Treasury praying for half a year's salary for himself and clerks, and for 100*l.* for perusing and marking out the criminal passages in pamphlets and printed papers brought to him by the messenger of the press for that purpose during six months ending 18 Oct. last. 1 *page.*

[? After 15 Jan.] 6. "The Answer of the Governour & Court of Assistants of the York Buildings Company, purchasers of forfeited Estates in England & Scotland, to the memorial and complaint of Abraham Meure, James Peachy, and John Edwin, Esq[rs], &c.," addressed to the R[t] Hon.

1726. VOL. CCLV.

Robert Walpole, Esq., and the rest of the Lords of the Treasury. The Memorialists are not the chief annuitants, nor could they prevail on any considerable number of the annuitants to join them; neither was their purchase money any considerable part of the price agreed for on purchasing the forfeited Estates. The whole body of the annuitants have been punctually paid. By the Act 6 & 7 [Geo. I.] the purchasers of forfeited Estates, being bodies corporate, may grant annuities for life thereon, but are not obliged that such annuities shall affect and charge the land: yet the complainants insist on this. The Respondents lay not any stress upon it that the annuities now possessed by the complainants chiefly arise on prize-tickets purchased by them at second hand 'in the Alley' after they had been depreciated; but that pursuant to the Acts the Governor and Company did grant annuities, and they and the original purchasers had the opinions and advice of Mr Serjt Pengelly & Mr Serjt Comyns, who settled the form of the Annuity Bond. Conceive they are not now to make a new bargain. The Governor and Court of Assistants agreed to a public declaration, which was read at their General Court, touching Annuity Bonds for Lottery Annuity Prizes (the terms of which are quoted); but notwithstanding this treaty was to promote a charitable purpose, yet the good intent is obstructed, and the stockholders discouraged and intimidated, &c. Pray that in consideration of the losses sustained by them by purchasing these Estates they may have their Lps favour in completing their purchase money and granting conveyances. And if to gratify the complainants, the respondents shall be debarred from making Lotteries, the Respondents also pray their Lps will permit, and the annuitants consent, that some part of the Estates may be sold again, for discharging the remainder of the purchase money, and for buying in at higher prices than they cost the complainants or others of the York Buildings Annuitants such of the Company's Annuities as they are willing to part with."

Also the memorial of the complainants, which has the following *minute* on it:—"15th Jan. 1725. The York Buildings Compa to consider this meml & to return it with their answer." 5 *pages.*

19 Jan. 7. J. Scrope to the Attorney and Solicitor General. Under a Royal Proclamation of 21 Jan. 1719, and on the reports of Mr Cracherode, the Lords of the Treasury have paid 5,000*l.* or thereabouts in rewards within these five years, and have great demands not yet satisfied. The offenders seem to increase rather than diminish. Their Lordships ask the Attorney and Solicitor General what can be done to relieve the King of this expense, as it appears from the enclosed list of the value of the things taken that the reward could never have been intended to be thus given. 19 Jan. 1725.

Also a printed copy of the proclamation, and the list referred to. 3 *pages.*

29 Jan. 8. Report of the Comrs for Taxes to the Lords of the Treasury, sending an account of the whole charge of the tax upon Papists,—

1726. VOL. CCLV.

the discharge by certificates and payments into the Exchequer,—how much there is in the receivers' hands,—and how much remains uncollected. Are of opinion that when all the certificates and *insupers* shall be returned the 3,507*l.* 19*s.* 10¾*d.*, paid by the receivers into the Exchequer and the poundage to Commrs, clerks, collectors, and receivers deducted, no considerable sum can be expected out of the 7,879*l.* 8*s.* 7*d.* which remains uncollected.

Also the account referred to. 2 *pages.*

1 Feb. 9. The same to the same. Have caused an account of the net produce of the tax upon Papists to be laid before the House of Commons.

The account referred to. 2 *pages.*

9 Feb. 10. "Memorial and petition" of Hannah Penn, the widow of William Penn, Esq., deceased, "proprietor of Pennsylvania," and of John, Thomas, Margaret, and Richard Penn, her children by the said Wm Penn, to the Lords of the Treasury. William Penn proposed to surrender to her late Majesty his powers of Government, and her Majesty agreed to accept the surrender, and to allow him 12,000*l.*, to be paid in four years. Her Majesty on 9 Sept. 1712, directed 1,000*l.* to be paid to William Penn, but he was soon after incapacitate to complete the sale; but by his will before the sale he devised the same to Trustees to be sold to her Majesty. Petitioners exhibited their Bill in the Court of Exchequer against the heir-at-law to prove the will *per testes*, and have made the Attorney General a party in the suit, and the cause is to be tried after Hilary term; pray that the Attorney General may have instructions on his Majesty's part against the hearing of the cause. 1 *page.*

12 Feb. 11. Comrs of Revenue in Ireland to the Lord Lieut. of Ireland. In reply to an order from the Lords Justices, referring to them a report of the Attorney General and papers relating to a petition of Sir Laurence Esmond for reducing the quit-rents on the lands, and asking if they (the Comrs) had any objection, they enclose copies of (1) the Attorney General's report on the petition, (2) of a report of James Topham, Esq., late Clerk of the Quit-Rents thereon, and (3) copy of an opinion of his Majesty's Solicitor General on the reports of Mr Attorney General and Mr Topham. Custom House, Dublin, Feb. 12, 1725.

The lands referred to were mountainous lands in the county of Wicklow, containing 12,852 acres (Irish Plantation measure), other lands in the co. of Wexford containing 4,166 acres of like measure, lands in the co. of Catherlogh, containing 560 acres. The lands of Aghavanna are also referred to, consisting of 10,079 acres in the co. of Wicklow, besides 1,000 acres thereof granted to Sir Robert Booth. Also 1,288 acres in the same county, and lands of Tausinagh in the co. of Wexford, containing 4,166 acres, and lands of Killdavan and other lands in the co. of Catherlogh, containing 560 acres (probably those above referred to).

"Read 16 July 1727." 11¼ *pages.*

1726. Vol. CCLV.

12 Feb. 12. "A list or certificate of the accompts of the severall Surveyors of his Maties woods remaining in my office undeclared pursuant to the severall signe manuals and warrants hereafter mentioned with the respective summs of money remaining in their hands so far as the same appears to me, and likewise a state of the revenue of the Savoy Hospital to Michas 1722 inclusive."

It also relates to the auditing of the accounts of the Receiver General of the Savoy revenue.

Dated 12 Feb. 1725. 10 pages.

15 Feb. 13. Copy of report of the Barons of the Exchequer of Scotland to the Lords of the Treasury in England respecting the satisfying certain claims for salaries to the late Comrs and Trustees for the Forfeited Estates in Scotland by Sir Robert Sinclair, late Receiver General of the Forfeited Estates. When certain sums were paid there would be a balance of 6,032*l.* 15*s.* $2\frac{5}{12}$*d.* in the Receiver's hands. Advise that the late Receiver should have 3d in the pound on all the money he received. Edinburgh, 15 Feb. 1725–6. 2 *pages.*

16 Feb. 14. Representation of the Barons of the Exchequer in Scotland to the Lords of the Treasury. Upon the establishment of this Court they were allowed for their accommodation the house and rooms where the Exchequer and Treasury of Scotland met before the Union. The Court disposed of the places in the best manner that could be for the conveniency of the several offices and the records belonging to them. By the addition of some new offices and the multiplicity of vouchers and records there is an absolute necessity for some other rooms for the better disposing and securing of them. By the surveys of Mr McGil, an architect, it appears that there may be built a storey over that part of the Exchequer called the Exchequer Chamber, consisting of 40 feet in length and 21 in breadth, at an expense of 500*l.* Advise that the storey should be built. Edinburgh, Exchequer Chamber, 16 Feb. 1725–6.

Also copy of the same with four words additional. 4 *pages.*

16 Feb. 15. Report of the same to the same on the petition of James Cleland, Keeper of the Tolbooth Prison, in the city of Edinburgh. From the year 1689 to 1 Feb. 1707 the Keeper of the prison was paid, as well house dues, as for the necessary aliment of all indigent prisoners committed to his custody, for public crimes, extending to about 94*l.* per annum. In the absence of His Majesty's Advocate, the Solicitor General reports that he has no objection to the payment of that part of the account for alimenting poor criminals, who otherwise must have starved before being brought to justice or discharged. With respect to the house dues for poor criminals, it seems doubtful if the full dues paid by civil prisoners should be insisted on for public criminals. Upon the whole is of opinion in equity he ought to have relief on account of the burthen of prisoners for public crimes; and that it may not be unreasonable to settle an annual sum on the Keeper as an equivalent for such

1726. VOL. CCLV.

aliment and fees. The petitioner's fees for alimenting the poor prisoners and for the house dues from 24 June 1719 to this time amount to 395*l.* 17*s.* 4⅓*d.*, being about 72*l.* per ann. In regard that the accounts were paid before the Union, that the Keeper of the prison gives good security for the faithful discharge of his office, is obliged to keep many servants, has no salary from the City for the same, or other perquisite, but what arises from the house dues and entering prisoners for civil debts, and that all prisoners of any note are brought from all parts of Scotland and committed to this gaol for trial, where the Court of Justiciary sits, they (the Barons) conceive it may be reasonable that the account should be paid. Beg leave to observe that by a clause in the Act of last Sessions for the more effectual disarming of the Highlands in Scotland, the freeholders of every shire, county, or district in Scotland shall at their meetings of the Head Courts yearly assess the several shires or "stewartries" to defray the charges of apprehending and subsisting criminals, &c. Cannot learn that any notice has been yet taken of this power, but are of opinion some such provision is very necessary to be enforced, that the Government may be eased of these expenses. 16 Feb. 1725–6.

Minuted:—" Rd : disagreed to."

Also the petition referred to. 5½ *pages*.

21 Feb. 16. Report of the same to the same on the petition of Archibald Douglas, of Cavers. It appears by the Report of the Treasurer's Remembrancer that Mr Douglas as Sheriff of the county of Roxburgh is accountable to his Majesty for 579*l.* 0*s.* 6½*d.* " as the Blench, Book, Castleward, and Retoured Duties due from the Term of Whitsuntide 1715 and to the said Term 1725." His Majesty may, if he so please, grant his warrant to discharge the petitioner of the 579*l.* 0*s.* 6½*d.* upon passing his accounts of the Sheriffship according to the course of the Exchequer. 21 Feb. 1725–6.

Also the petition.

Minuted:—" Agreed to." 3 *pages*.

22 Feb. 17. Memorial of the South Sea Company to the Lords of the Treasury. In pursuance of the Act of the last Parliament for encouraging a British Greenland Fishery, by taking off the duties on whale fins, oil, and blubber of whales which are caught in Greenland seas in British ships, there is a prospect of success; but the Act takes no notice of seals and other creatures which abound in and upon those frozen seas; which therefore, tho' part of the product of those fishing voyages, are liable to duties subsisting before that Act passed. These amounted to a prohibition, from which they should be exempted. St David's Straits have always been understood to be part of the Greenland Seas, and the Dutch annually send many ships on the Fishery; but as the Straits are not expressly comprehended in the Act, the fins, oil, &c. imported into Great Britain still continue liable to the former high duties. Pray that their Lps would represent the matter to Parliament with expedition, that the necessary directions may be given as the Company's

1726. VOL. CCLV.

ships are to depart in March next, some to Greenland and others to St David's Straits if they are encouraged by Parliament. South Sea House, 22 Feb. 1725. (Signed.)

Minuted:—"23 February 1725. Read and my Lords are of opinion their request is reasonable, and that they should apply to Parliament to be releived therein." 2 *pages*.

25 Feb. 18. The Lord Lieut. of Ireland (Carteret) to the Lords of the Treasury. Yesterday sent his Majesty's answers to the Addresses of both Houses, and the Commons agreed *nemine contradicente* to the enclosed address to which he gave the enclosed answer.

The address related to the arrears of half-pay officers.

There is only one enclosure on the same subject. 7 *pages*.

[After 25 Feb.] 19. Petition to the Lords of the Treasury of the Chapel Wardens of the Chapel of St John the Baptist and other the inhabitants within the precinct of the Savoy in respect to a claim upon them from his Majesty's Exchequer of 51*l.* or thereabouts which Mr Tilson says they have received from the profits of the burial ground and tolling bell of the Chapel "before the death of his late Majesty's lease thereof to them." Represent that in 1718 they preferred their petition to the Treasury, praying that certain repairs might be made by the Crown to their chapel and chapel yard, which was allowed; but the allowance being deficient, the chapel yard still remained in great desolation (more like a dunghill than a Christian burial place), and the tolling bell remained entirely useless; whereupon they preferred a second petition praying for a further allowance of 100*l.* to make good those repairs, or that they might retain the profits of the burial ground and tolling bell. The Surveyor General (Mr Pulteney) reported on this that the profits were worth 14*l.* yearly, and that by their Lordships' warrant they might retain for the repairs such sums as they expended up to 100*l.*, or that petitioners might have an Exchequer lease thereof for 21 years at the rent of 4*l.* 13*s.* 4*d.* Mr Pultney made no allowance for extravagant expense of the lease. Petitioners were directed by their Solicitor, who is Mr Auditer Jett's Deputy, to retain the money due and to become due, which they did, and completed the repairs. Upon these assurances, petitioners laid out 150*l.* and other sums, besides 47*l.* 16*s.* 4*d.* for fees (for the lease, which was not finished till 25 Feb. 1725) to the Surveyor General and others. When the premises were of the value of 14*l.* per ann. they were made use of by the parish of St Mary-le-Strand, which had then no place for the burial of its dead: but before the lease passed the parish was provided with a burial place of its own, which reduced the income to 5*l.* 10*s.* ever since, so that counting the net produce of 5*l.* 10*s.* per ann. at 5*l.* per cent. for 21 years the real value is about 66*l.* Petitioners have taken up money at interest to complete the repairs and are not able to pay the money received: and besides "have a much greater quantity of poor to maintain" by his Majesty's Garrison being kept there than when there was none kept there. Petitioners hope that the re-assumption of their lease may be

1726. VOL. CCLV.

upon payment to them of the money expended, or for a warrant to retain in their hands the profits they and their predecessors have received before the passing the lease, to support them against the threats and menaces of the Deputy Receiver General of the Hospital revenues. (Signed.) 3 *pages.*

[? About Feb. 1725–6.] 20. Petition of John Farquhar, land waiter at Burrowstonness, to the Lords of the Treasury. Petitioner in the month of Jan. 1723–4 secured in the King's warehouse a considerable parcel of goods, entered as ordinary tow, out of two ships from Rotterdam. Upon a reference to the Com[rs] the difference of the duty amounted to above 40*l.* sterling. The owners were so much incensed that they threatened to be revenged, and "they pitched on a Sabbath day to put their malicious design & threatning in execution, when some of their accomplices came to the pet[rs] house in disguise, in time of divine worship, and there being no person in the house but the petitioner's wife, they immediately seized upon her, and after they had stopped her mouth with some of the said tow, which they had brought for that purpose, and blindfolding her, they threw her on a bed, barbarously tied her hands and feet, and then went and rifled the petitioner's house," &c. "And then left her in that sad condition until the pet[r] and the servant came from church and relieved her when near stifled, having no breath but what she drew by her nose, by which treatment and the fear she was put into, she had almost lost her life," &c. The Collector represented to the Com[rs] the above barbarous usage, but as yet petitioner had had no relief: prays for relief.

Undated, but in the *Minute Book,* vol. 25, p. 216*f* (30 Aug. 1726), is:—"Comm[rs] customes in Scotland report of the 25th February last whereby 80[li] is proposed to be paid to John Farquehar, land waiter at Burrowstoness, for loss and damages he sustained by robbers, is read and agreed to." 1 *page.*

3 Mar. 21. Report of the Surveyor General (Pulteney) to the Lords of the Treasury on the Memorial of the Governor and Company of Chelsea Waterworks, praying their Lordships to intercede with his Majesty that they may have leave to dig such a quantity of clay, in an old pit in Hyde Park, as may enable them to finish their reservoir which, by H. M. permission, they have begun. They (the Company) estimate that the quantity required would be 1,400 loads. The object was for a better supply of the Royal Palace at Kensington and the new buildings on the east side of the wall of the park with water. The pit they propose to take the clay from is the same from whence the Surveyors of the Highways within the parish of St. Martin-in-the-Fields were permitted some time since to take gravel, and is situate on the south side of a hill in the park, called Buck Barn Hill, in a very retired place, so that little or no damage can be done by what is proposed, either to the herbage or ornament of the park. Thinks that leave may be granted under certain restrictions; also suggests precautions for the safety of the deer in the park.

The memorial referred to. 4 *pages.*

1726. VOL. CCLV.

10 Mar. 22. Robert Armstrong to Charles Burniston, Esq., Surveyor General of H.M. woods in North America. Respecting claims made by the inhabitants of Townships to cut trees in districts laid out as Townships. Says the townships are large, and are many miles square, and contain thousands of acres of wood land, where the timber most fit for the service of the Crown [is grown]; although the twentieth part thereof is not under any immediate improvement. The inhabitants of the province of Maine since the late Act passed (8 Geo. I.) pretend that the whole of that tract is the property of the Township. Is of opinion that the trees whether standing or felled are the property of His Majesty. In the year 1722 seized 43 pine trees cut by one Lord O'Libbie without licence in the province of Massachusets Bay, from 24 to upwards of 30 inches in diameter, at 12 inches from the earth, which trees grew five miles from any tillage, fenced land, or inclosure, the Judges ruling that they lay within the township of Borwick. Has previously drawn attention to these matters in reports to which he refers. Forty more similar trees fit for masts and bowsprits have been cut without licence. And by the late Act the officer cannot stop the inhabitants as the latter pretend, &c. Has marked with the broad R, in the woods of the province of New Hampshire, about 300 trees from 24 to 34 inches diameter, and about 200 in the province of Maine. Boston, March 10th, 1725. 3 *pages.*

15 Mar. 23. A. Cracherode to the Lords of the Treasury. Has received orders from the Rt Hon. Viscount Townshend to assist Mons. Thom, resident here, from the Duke of Wolfenbuttel, to get his secretary, John Brown, discharged out of custody of the Sheriff's Officer of Middlesex, by whom he is detained at the suit of Edw. Dogan and several others. Has endeavoured to get Brown set at liberty, but fruitlessly. The further execution of the order by petitioning the Lord Chancellor and the two Chief Justices "according to the directions of the Act of Parliament for preserving the privileges of Ambassadors and other public ministers of Foreign Princes and States" will be attended with expense. Asks for their Lordships' commands. 15 Mar. 1725. 1 *page.*

2 April. 24. "Abstract of an agreement between the Dutchess of Buckinghamshire on behalf of her son Edmund, Duke of Buckinghamsh, of the one part and George Prissick, Gent., of the other part. Dated 2 April, 1726." Touching the delivery to the Duchess of such quantity of alum as should be agreed upon, at the alum works at Sunderland in the co. of York, at 9*l.* a ton, and touching a loan by the Duchess to George Prissick, &c.

Also another abstract of the same paper. 7 *pages.*

7 April. 25. "Report from the Board of Works relating to the supplyg His Majesty's Palaces of St James's & Whitehall with water from the Chelsea Company."

Mr Deputy Surveyor has waited on the Board of Greencloth, and reports that there is no contract for water in that office; but the Board finds that there is a verbal contract in the Treasurer of the

VOL. CCLV.

1726.

Chamber's Office with the New River Company, for serving the Palace & stables at St Jameses three times a week wth water at 36*l.* per ann. The Company have frequently complained of this contract, and have often insisted upon 60*l.* per ann. for this service. Have treated with the Chelsea Waterworks, who are willing to furnish his Majesty's palace & stables with a constant service day and night for 36*l.* per ann., whereby the palace will be better served & there will be a greater security against fire.

As to the palace of Whitehall, it has been supplied with so much of the Hyde Park water as could be spared from St Jameses. But the water is now designed for St Jameses only, and the New River Company having taken off the two inch main "from their Trees," which Whitehall was constantly supplied with, the palace will be almost destitute of water. There are in and about Whitehall 104 houses or appartments and 2 in Spring Garden that used to be supplied with water, 29 of which are upon Exchequer leases. The Chelsea Company are willing to supply them with constant service at 100*l.* per ann., which is a reasonable allowance, &c. 2 *pages*.

9 April. 26. Report of the Comrs for Taxes to the Lords of the Treasury returning the names of the present Receivers of the Land Tax and Duties on Houses, with a state of their several accounts. Twelve of the Receivers have cleared their accounts, others are stating their accounts with the Auditor. Arrears of two others will be discharged by over-payments in previous years, and five others are under prosecution. Office for Taxes, 9 April 1726.

Also the list of the present receivers of the Land Tax and Duties on Houses. 2 *pages*.

16 April. 27. Representation of the Comrs of Excise (Scotland) to the Lords of the Treasury. Renew their former representation with regard to the difficulty that attends the management of the revenues of Excise, which they are of opinion requires a parliamentary remedy. [The difficulty relates to the 12 Scots gallons which were said by the 7th Article of the Union to amount to 34 gallons, English. *See* preface to *Calendar of Treasury Papers*, 1702–1707, p. ix.] Conclude that 36 gallons allowed by the Justices is too much notwithstanding the trial made by the English gallon pot; because that particular gallon pot proved to be erroneous. The Brewers have not failed all along to take the benefit of the Justices' sentence, by retaining so much of the duty charged upon them as might answer the difference between 36 gallons, fixed by the Justices, and 34 gallons charged by the Officers. This retention very much perplexes the accounts. Propose that, if it appears reasonable to their Lordships, the Brewers' retention amounting to 40,800*l.* should be allowed by a clause in an Act of Parliament; and that certain alterations should be made which would result in an impost of 2*s.* a barrel containing 34 English gallons. Excise Office, Edinburgh, 16 April 1726. 3 *pages*.

VOL. CCLV.

1726.

30 April. 28. Report of the Surveyor General (Pulteney) to the Lords of the Treasury on two anonymous papers relating to the manor of Winckfield, in Windsor forest, which was on sale. Was required by their Lordships to examine the title, and treat with the seller; but the indisposition of Mr Anthony Meek, the owner, had prevented his entering upon the treaty till the 9th inst. The owner claims to be seized in fee of eight undivided parts of the nine parts of the manor, &c., but he (the Surveyor) has not examined into the validity of Mr Meek's title, presuming their Lordships will think that matter more proper for the consideration of H.M. counsel learned in the law, when the terms of the purchase shall be agreed to. The other ninth part of the manor, Mr Meek says, is in Henry Grey, Esq. He says that the manor is of a very large extent, and a Court Leet and Court Baron belong to it; and within it is another manor, which pays quit-rents to Winkfield, that there are several freehold tenants, copyhold tenants of inheritance, and leasehold tenants, in all near one hundred. Every freehold tenant upon alienation or death pays a relief of a year's quit-rent, and every copyhold tenant upon a mortgage (for a longer term than a year and a day), as also on alienation or death, pays a fine, being a year's quit-rent and a sum certain in lieu of a herriot; all which appears by an ancient presentment of the homage made in the 13th year of James I. The quit-rents, he says, amount to 16*l.* 9*s.* 6*d.* per ann., and for his eight parts he demands forty years' purchase, amounting to 585*l.* 15*s.* 7*d.* For the profits and perquisites of courts he demands thirty years' purchase. Though Mr Meek may have a right to cut timber in the forest, presumes it must be according to forest law, that is, after a writ of *ad quod dampnum*. Mr Meek further says that there is a small farm or warren, within which are the seven water conduits mentioned in the paper annexed marked A, from which Windsor Castle was formerly, and may again be, supplied with very good water; there is also another small farm and several small tenements and other parcels of land. These he demanded 30 years' purchase for. There are several large sluice ponds stocked with carp, valued at 20s an acre, for which 30 years' purchase is claimed; also pits and places for digging and cutting peat and turbary; thirty years' purchase for the value of these was demanded. Observes that Mr Grey having an estate of a ninth part, he presumes it will not answer his Majesty's intention to purchase unless Mr Grey's part be likewise bought. Has perused a copy of an indenture of 10 April, 3 James I., between the then Lord and Lady of the Manor of the one part, and the Copyholders or Customary Tenants of the other part, by which the former grant to the latter very extensive privileges. The inducement for his Majesty to purchase the manor is to obtain power to inclose some parts of the Common within that part of the forest called Swinly Rail, for the better preserving the game: and Mr Meek admits he cannot sell his eight parts of the Common free and discharged from all manner of right which any tenant of the manor or other person whatsoever

1726. Vol. CCLV.

may lawfully claim of commoning or digging any sort of earth in any part of the waste or common. 30 April 1726.

The two papers referred to, and the reference of the matter to Mr Scope.

One of the documents commences:—"The mannor of Winkfield about 3 miles distant from Windsor of a very large extent takes in Winckfield Church, the Common Fields and the inclosures thereabouts and part of the Horse Race on Ashcott Heath reaches within a mile and half of Windsor Great Park & there adjoynes to a mannor belonging to the crown which goes into the said park and extends to the taking part of Bagshott park." 8 *pages.*

5 May. 29. Estimate of the Surveyor of Woods (Wither) for the enlargement of the paddock in Hyde Park, and for the enclosing the same by a brick wall at the cost of 2,201*l.* 14*s.* 5*d.* 1 *page.*

5 May. 30. Report of the same to the Lords of the Treasury, on the petition of the Keepers of the Bailiwick of Surrey, who were appointed by Brigadier Munden, the late Out-Ranger of Windsor forest, and who had to keep horses and hounds to perform their duties in driving the deer back into Windsor forest when they strayed therefrom.

The report is in a very decayed condition, but seems to be in favour of the petitioners. 5 May 1726.

Accompanied by three petitions and a memorandum. 4 *pages.*

[About 9 May.] 31. Petition of Ralph Astley, of Atherton, in the county of Lancaster, to the King. Petitioner (full of zeal for his Majesty and government when the rebels approached Lancashire in the year 1715) got together, with his neighbour Mr Wood, a great number of men (his workmen and others) to oppose and suppress that unnatural Rebellion, and marched with about 300 men, provided with the best arms, from Atherton to Ribble Bridge, about fifteen miles, and took possession of all the passes leading to it, which he kept for many days; so that no rebel could make his escape that way, and took about thirty prisoners whilst the Troops were subduing the rebels, who had taken refuge in the town of Preston. By this he incurred great expense as well as the displeasure of the disaffected gentlemen of the county by his zeal for his Majesty. Prays for speedy relief out of the privy purse to supply the pressing wants of his distressed numerous family, till his Majesty finds a proper opportunity to reward him for his zeal.

Also a certificate in corroboration of the petition.

On the back is:—"100g." Also "Copie of ye original presented unto his Majesty & took into his closet Monday ye 9th of May 1726, my Lord Sussex then in waiting."

In the *Minute Book*, vol. 25, p. 184*c*, 6 June 1726, is—"Prepare a sign manual for 105li bounty to Ralph Astley." 1 *page.*

[After 21 May.] 32. Four papers relating to pensions of Thomas Bludworth, Esq., and John Hampden, Esq., pages of honour to his Majesty. The salary of the former is mentioned as having been 260*l.* per ann.

1726. VOL. CCLV.

and that of the latter 156*l.* per ann., payable on the establishment of the stables. Both had been removed into the army and were losers by the transfer. One of the papers is a copy of a warrant granting to Thomas Bludworth a pension of 150*l.* per ann. till he shall be further provided for by some office or employment whereby his salary shall increase to 260*l.* per ann. at the least. Dated 21 May 1726.

In another of the papers of 28 April 1726, "His Majesty ordered that for the time to come the Master of the Horse shall not lay before his Majesty the name of any person to be placed upon the list of pentions on the Establishment of the Stables unless he be actually in his Majesty's service and become incapable of further service thro' age or misfortune."

In the *Minute Book*, vol. 25, p. 217*l*, 30 Aug. 1726, is:—"Mr. Hampden, heretofore a page of Honour, and now on the Establishment of ½ pay as a Capt of Dragoons, is to have so much paid him p ann. by the hands of Mr Negus as will make his ½ pay equall to the salary or allowances to a page untill he shall be better provided for." 3½ *pages.*

23 May. 33. Report of Mr A. Cracherode to the Lords of the Treasury on the petition of Edward Woodward and three others, who claimed the reward of 40*l.* offered for the apprehension of William Gates, commonly called Vulcan, who was committed for an assault upon Henry Best, one of the keepers of Enfield Chace: in favour of the petitioners. [Gates was required to surrender within 40 days for shooting at the keepers and for killing deer; and not having surrendered was attainted of felony and was apprehended, sentenced to death, and hung.]

The petition, two certificates, and copy of the London Gazette. 7 *pages.*

2 June. 34. Memorial of Joseph Garton, Provost Marshal of the three Regiments of Guards, to His Majesty's Secretary-at-War (the Rt Hon. Henry Pelham, Esq.). When he (memorialist) was appointed Provost Marshal, the Adjutant-General was ordered to take possession of part of a house adjoining the prison in the Savoy, but he found the Rev. Mr Sing, Minister of Somerset House Chapel, lay dangerously ill and in possession of that part of the house, and the Secretary-at-War and Adjutant-General allowed him to continue for life, being a known well-affected person to the Government, and the prison was as safe with his being there as if he (the memorialist) had it in his possession. Has "had 36 prisoners at a time broke into the house & not one of them got away." On the death of Mr Sing, memorialist took possession and put in a servant of Mr Sing's to take care of the same. On the 27th of May "instant" Sir Thomas Moore, a gentleman from the Temple, ordered the house to be clear by that day sevennight, for he was to have a warrant from the Treasury to come into it. Prays that the person in possession may be allowed to remain, and that the liberty of the yard may be continued for the health and preservation of the prisoners, the

1726. VOL. CCLV.

prison being very close, weak, and wanting repair. On the back is "2 June 1726."

In the *Minute Book*, vol. 25, p. 181*q*, is:—"Sr Thomas More s peticõn for a lease of a house in the Savoy, as also the Provost Marshall's peticõn desiring the same house for his habitation for the safety of his prisoners are read, and my Lords do not think fit to grant a lease thereof." 1 *page*.

[About 4 June.] 35. Petition of William Hucks, Esq., to the Lords of the Treasury. Her late Majesty Catherine, Queen Dowager, and her Trustees, by lease dated 28 March 1682, demised a meadow in Wallingford called North Eights, and other lands in the co. of Berks, to Mr John Arnold for 70 years, if his three sons, or either of them, so long live at a rent of 2*l.* 1*s.* per annum. Petitioner is entitled to the premises by purchase, and two of the lives are in being. Prays their Lordships (upon surrender of the two lives) to grant him a new lease for 31 years.

Referred on 4 June 1726 to the Surveyor General (Phillips Gybbon, Esq.) for his report thereon.

In the *Minute Book*, vol. 25, p. 202, 27 July 1726, is a minute that the Report of 23 July 1726 on Wm Hucks petition for a lease of certain lands at Wallingford was read and agreed to. 1 *page*.

[? About 13 June.] 36. Petition of John, Earl of Stair, to the Lords of the Treasury. The Bay of Loch Ryan, in the county of Galloway, lies very convenient for trade, and if a key or harbour were built there it would greatly contribute towards the improvement of the wealth and increase of the numbers of his Majesty's subjects; but the inhabitants are not in any condition to afford the expense, so that the improvement of the wool and other produce will continue to be neglected, unless some encouragement be given by his Majesty towards building a key or harbour in the said Bay: and as there is about sixty or seventy pounds yearly of the rents of the Bishopric of Galloway unappropriated to pious uses, petitioner prays their Lordships to obtain his Majesty's warrant, granting the sum of 60*l.* yearly, during the abolition of Episcopacy, out of the rents of the Bishopric, to be applied by him towards building and supporting a convenient harbour there. Referred 13 June 1726 to the Comrs of Customs, Scotland, to report thereon. 1 *page*.

13 June. 37. The magistrates of the town of Glasgow to ———. Though the Legislature has thought fit to subject this Corporation to the payment of Mr Campbell, of Shawfields, damages, yet it affords some satisfaction to hear from the gentlemen commissioned to attend to their affairs at London during the dependence of the Bill before Parliament, that the person to whom the letter was addressed had signified that it was contrary to his inclination that the Corporation should be liable to these damages. Return their sincere and hearty thanks for these expressions of favour, and hope for his good offices to procure "an ease to this city of that sum, which indeed the Corporation is hardly able to pay." Have the utmost abhorrence

1726. VOL. CCLV.

of the unlawful riots that happened, and nothing shall be wanting to preserve the peace and quiet of the town. Glasgow, 13 June 1726.

In the *Minute Book*, vol. 25, p. 182, 3 June 1726, is:—"Give notice to the Comm^rs of Excise in Scotland that the Excise belonging to the Town of Glasgow is vested in the King after the 24 June 1726 and put under their management until the 6080^li given by Parliament to Daniel Campbell for losses and damages in the Riot at Glasgow shall be satisfied and the interest thereof." 2 *pages.*

20 June. 38. Copy of the Orders and Instructions to the Board of Works, dated 20th June 1726. They consist of 39 items. 13 *pages.*

22 June. 39. Report of the Barons of the Exchequer in Scotland to the Lords of the Treasury. Have examined the warrant annexed prepared for H.M. signature for granting and conveying to William Calderwood of Poltoun, one of the senators of the College of Justice, "and the other heirs of Tailzie," the lands of Poltoun and other lands lying within the Sheriffdom of Edinburgh. Find that this "signature" contains an erection of the lands into a barony, which gives a jurisdiction and some other privileges usually granted by the Crown to subjects, and no casualties are discharged by the same. Exchequer Chamber, Edinb^r, 22 June 1726. 1 *page.*

[? About 24 June.] 40. Petition of John Warner and two others, executors and trustees of the will of Matthew Barton, Esq., deceased, to the Lords of the Treasury. By an instrument of 22 Feb. 1722, the deceased was constituted King's Clerk and Controller of the coinage of half pence and two pences, "for the service of his Maties Island of America;" which coinage was by letters patent granted by the King to William Wood, Esq., and by such letters patent William Wood granted to the King's Clerk and Controller 200*l.* per ann. as long as Matthew Barton continued to execute his office. The deceased discharged his duty until his death, and there was due to him 540*l.* 4*s.* 3*d.* The said William Wood pretends that he has been hindered in the execution of the powers granted to him, and that he cannot pay Matthew Barton's salary; and insists that if he is accountable for the same, it is to his Majesty and not to the petitioners: pray their Lordships to make an order thereon consistent with justice and equity.

Minuted:—"Read 24 June 1726. Write to Mr Wood to know if the coynage for the plantac̄ons under the King's patent was ever proceeded on, if proceeded on, what quantity of metall was coyned, the place where, and whether the Comptroller by himself, clerks or others, was at any trouble charge or expence therein." 3 *pages.*

25 June. 41. The Lord Chamberlain of the Household (Grafton) to the Lords of the Treasury. Signifies the King's pleasure that they should give orders for painting, whitewashing, &c. in Mrs Cressett's lodgings in Somerset House.

On the back is:—"The King in his instructions to ye Board of Works strictly prohibits and forbids that he be at any charge for

1726. VOL. CCLV.

repairing or altering any houses, apartments, or lodgings inhabited by persons of his Mats grace and favour; and directs that no allowce thereof be made in the accots of the works or otherwise. Cockpit, 25 June 1726. 1 *page.*

[? About 29 June.] 42. Petition of Robert Jones, Esq., to the King. Petitioner is the son and executor of Elizabeth Jones, widow of the late Bishop of St. Asaph, deceased, and has, at his own expense, "sped" a commission of enquiry, whereby the estate of Mount Kennedy, in the county of Wicklow, was found to be forfeited to the Crown, by the attainder of Sir William Kennedy, and to be of the value of 720*l.* per annum: and the sheriff in the month of June last seized the estate by a writ of seizure out of the Court of Exchequer; as appears by a certificate of the Remembrancer of that Court. Letters in 1714 and 1725 directed that, when the estate should be seized, a lease or custodiam thereof should be made to the petitioner for 99 years, reserving $\frac{3}{4}$ths of the clear yearly value to his Majesty. Petitioner applied for an order to the Court of Exchequer to have the lease or custodiam passed under the seal of the Court: but the Court declared it had no power to intermeddle. Inasmuch as his Majesty's title is only for the life of Sir William Kennedy, and the prosecution has been very expensive to petitioner, and there is a considerable arrear due to his Majesty from the intruders, prays for directions to be given to the Court of Exchequer that a lease or custodiam be passed to the petitioner for 99 years if the said Sir William Kennedy should so long live, reserving $\frac{3}{4}$ths of the yearly value of 720*l.* to his Majesty.

Also the certificate referred to, dated 29 June 1726. 2 *pages.*

7 July. 43. H. H. to ———. Amongst several others had a design to purchase "those deemed French lands" on the Island of St Christophers, and being well acquainted with them could have made abundantly more of them than any other person. Finds some persons are commissioned to go over and sell them, and is willing to set the value of them in the true light. They may dispose of these lands by a lease or grant from the Crown of 32 years, perhaps, for two or three hundred thousand pounds. Is well assured that the Comrs are not gone because the wind has been contrary for them two months past: so that they might have unerring advantageous directions as to the sale. Is well assured that more than 150,000*l.* would have been laid down for them here. Proposes that he should have 1*s.* in the pound for his method, and asks, "Would not any person give 1s to have nineteen got for him?" July 7, 1726. 1 *page.*

10 July. 44. George Yeates to the Rt Hon. Sir Robert Walpole, M.P., "to be left at the Treasury Office." There is a very great destruction of young timber made in the Bishopric of Winchester, not by the order of the Bishop, but by Ed Forbes, Esq., who is woodward of the Bishopric by patent for life; and by one Cleverley, employed as his deputy. They cut down vast numbers of timber trees, and those not decaying trees, which are the most proper to be cut;

1726. VOL. CCLV.

and they cut all the young growing trees, because they will strip. This they do for the sake of the bark, which the officer Forbes claims as his fee. They have cut a great number of very small young growing trees this spring, which would pay double interest of money for standing. They give the Bishop an account of what number of them they think fit, and the rest they dispose of without acquainting his Lordship. The officer claims and takes as his fee, besides all the bark, all the cordwood and faggots and all the timber from the second bough upwards; which in a vast many of the trees is half the timber. When they have made very large assignments to the tenants (perhaps a great deal more than twice as much as they have occasion for) then truly the said Cleverley takes a great part of the timber so assigned and sells it and the tenants and the two officers share the money, as the writer is told. Is informed that there is no year in which, if the Bishop raises 500*l.* for himself out of the woods, but the officer raises for himself 6*l.*, 7*l.*, or 800*l.* Is a tenant himself and fears there will, in a short time, be little or no timber left for any of the tenants except his honour interposes by laying these things before Parliament. 2 *pages.*

12 July. 45. Report of the Surveyor of the Woods (Ch. Wither) to the Lords of the Treasury concerning Forelands, lying in the parish of Wingfield, in Windsor Forest, which Henry Grey, Esq., has proposed to sell to the Crown. Has surveyed the lands, which lie contiguous to the inclosure called Swinley Rails, and are reputed to contain fifty acres and to be worth about 20*l.* per ann. As his Majesty has given directions for the increase and preservation of the game in that part of Windsor Forest, conceives that it would conduce very much to that end if the Crown were possessed of the lands, because they lie so near the inclosure of Swinley that the game is tempted to resort thither and is in danger of being destroyed by Mr Grey's tenant. 1 *page.*

20 July. 46. Robert Armstrong, Esq., to Charles Burniston, Esq., Surveyor General of His Majesty's Woods in America. Is surprised that nothing has been done for the preservation of H.M. timber, &c., refers to previous letters on this subject in which he had stated that in the province of New Hampshire forty trees, fit for masts and bowsprits, from 24 to 34 inches diameter, had been cut without licence. Messrs Baley and Hawes, merchants, for whom the trees were cut, take no notice of Mr Burniston as if there were no such man as Surveyor General of the King's woods, &c. A contract has come from the Navy Board to Mr Waldo for five years to supply the navy with two ship loads of masts every year. Is told that there is no mention of either his correspondent or himself in the licence. Is quite crazed, considering the care he has taken for the preservation of the King's timber, that he has had no suitable encouragement from home to support him. Has gone so far, that he is in danger of his life, as it is well known at home the barbarous

1726. VOL. CCLV.

treatment officers meet with that do their duty (Attested copy.)

"Red ye 11th of Octobr 1726. 2 *pages.*

21 July. 47. Report of the Surveyor General (Philip Gybbon) to the Lords of the Treasury on the petition of the Minister and Churchwardens of the Lutheran Church in the Savoy, who state that His Majesty by sign manual granted their congregation a chapel with a small piece of ground adjoining, but one James Dorsell had enclosed part of the ground and converted it into a timber yard, and they pray to be put into quiet possession thereof. Sets out the state of the case as shown in (1) the sign manual which granted to the congregation a chapel, a dwelling-house for the minister, a small piece of ground adjoining, and the vestry room and a small house upon it; and (2) the counter part of a lease dated 12 March 1685, from the master and chaplains perpetual of the Hospital of the Savoy to Caleb Hooke, gent., for 40 years, of a house there and a plot of ground, 49½ feet by 13 feet then expired. The report is in favour of the petitioners, and asks their Lordships to give such directions for the enforcing a due compliance with the sign manual and for the asserting his Majesty's right to the ground as they shall think proper. Mr Dorsell also keeps possession of the house without any apparent grant from the Crown or paying any rent for it.

Accompanied by the petition and a coloured plan. 6 *pages.*

22 July. 48. Report of the Comrs of Customs (Scotland) to the Lords of the Treasury on the petition of Mr Andrew Drummond, praying directions to be given to the Comrs to pay him 575*l.* ordered by their Lordships' warrant to be issued to David Graham, Esq., late collector of customs at Port Glasgow, the money having been advanced by petitioner; are of opinion that a balance due from Mr Graham of 440*l.* 2*s.* 7¾*d.* to the Crown should first be satisfied, together with a further sum of 31*l.* 17*s.* 6*d.*

The petition referred to.

In the *Minute Book,* vol. 25, p. 204*m* (2 Aug. 1726), is:—"Write to the Commrs acquainting them that my Lords are of opinion, if any means be, to recover the said balance, they shall not bring the warrant in to aid the same; for it will be an unreasonable hardship in case Mr Drummond's reimbursement be defeated by applying that warrant to Graham's balances." 3 *pages.*

22 July. 49. Report of the Barons of the Exchequer (Scotland) to the Lords of the Treasury on the petition of Sir Harry Innes of Innes, Baronet. It appears by the Certificate of the Treasurer's Remembrancer that the petitioner is chargeable with the payment of 175*l.* sterling, "as the taxtward, relief and marriage duties, due to his Majesty upon his being infeoffed in the lands and barony of Innes: as heir to Sir Harry Innes, his father; in the year 1723." Testify as to his loyalty and that of his predecessors. His Majesty may direct the petitioner to be discharged of the sum specified.

The representation referred to. 2 *pages.*

1726. VOL. CCLV.

25 and 26 July. 50. Com[rs] of Excise (Scotland) to the Lords of the Treasury. One M[r] William Cumming, a merchant in Edinburgh, having obtained payment of a receipt for arms amounting to 85*l.*, which they suspected to be forged, upon enquiry they found that not only that receipt but several others were forgeries. Suspicion is thrown on David Stewart, late collector at Inverness, of being concerned in the forgery, and measures are taken for his arrest. Another of the forged receipts being paid to one Alexander M[c]Cullck, they have the Justice Clerk's warrant to apprehend him likewise. Excise Office, Edinburgh, 25 July 1726.

P.S. David Steuart is secured, and in the Tolbooth of Inverness, and he is to be brought to Edinburgh for examination. 26 July 1726. 4 *pages.*

26 July. 51. Report of the Barons of the Exchequer (Scotland) to the Lords of the Treasury on a warrant for the Royal Signature granting to Sir Arthur Forbes, of Craigievar, the lands of Craigievar, Logiefintry, Oneilcorss Swalland and others lying within the Sheriffdom of Aberdeen, proceeding upon the resignations of Sir John and Sir William Forbes and others. "Find part of the said lands hold simple waird part few & part blench, and the signature contains a *de novo damus* of the whole lands," but "do not find that there are any casualties or forfeitures by recognition or escheat affecting the said lands, or any few or blench duties payable out of the same, that will be discharged by the said *de novo damus*, &c. Such of the rents as are to be taxed are valued at 57*l.* 9*s.* 8½*d.* yearly, &c." 2 *pages.*

26 July. 52. Report of the same to the same on the petition of the Rector, Principals, and Professors in the University of S[t] Andrews. Set out that King Charles II., for the advancement of learning in that University, by Charter of 1 Oct. 1668, "did mortify 200*l.* ster. per annum out of his rents and customs in Scotland, to be divided as therein set out. By the articles of the Union, the Universities and Colleges in Scotland are to continue for ever as then established: but there being no express saving in the articles of the grant, and the rents and customs of Scotland after the Union being thereby put upon a quite different footing, conceive the grant could not affect them, without the consent of the Crown. Her late Majesty, on 31 May, in the 11th year of her reign, granted to the Principals and Professors allowances amounting to 210*l.* in full satisfaction of all claims. His present Majesty on 19 Jan. 1718 approved of the distribution of the 210*l.* among the Principals and Professors. Are of opinion that these annual allowances must be understood to be in satisfaction of the said 'mortification' in 1668. The allowances to the Principals and Professors is small, and they in some measure merit his Majesty's royal favour. 26 July 1726.

The petition referred to. 5 *pages.*

26 July. 53. Report of the same to the same. Have considered that part of the annexed memorial of John Callender of Craigforth, which relates to his claim for a parcel of meal. It appears that M[r]

VOL. CCLV.

1726. Callender had been used, by leave from the Governors of Stirling Castle, to lodge his meal in the girnells or storehouses of the Castle till a market offered for the sale thereof, and in August 1715 he had 400 bolls of good and sufficient meal in the said girnells. Having sold this meal, Major Holbourn, then Deputy Governor of the Castle, was required to allow it to be taken away, but he refused his assent, without a special order from the Government, as a Rebellion was likely to break out, and the garrison might have occasion for it. Mr Callender by such refusal understood the Government to be his debtor for the meal at the current price of 13*s.* 4*d.* per boll. The meal continued in the Castle till the beginning of 1717. By order of the Governor (the late Earl of Rothes) 224 bolls, two firlots, and one peck were sold for 93*l.* 11*s.* 4*d.*, being much spoiled. The rest was spoiled and embezzled by the soldiers during the Rebellion. The value of the whole was 275*l.* sterling. Have directed Col. Blackader, the Deputy Governor, to pay the 93*l.* 11*s.* 4*d.*, and are of opinion that provision should be made for satisfying the remainder.

In the *Minute Book*, vol. 25, p. 295 (10 May 1707), is:—"My Lords having no money in their power applicable to this service, they cannot comply with the opinion of the Barons concerning the same."

Also the memorial. 4 *pages.*

27 July. 54. The Duke of Newcastle to the [Lords of the Treasury]. By his Majesty's command transmits a representation of the Comrs for Trade and Plantations, recommending the employment of Captain William Taverner to make a survey of the west and north-west parts of Newfoundland. It will be very much for the public service by greatly contributing to the increase of the cod fishery, and to the establishing of the salmon fishery; which has of late years been begun there and is daily improving. Asking their Lordships to consider the same and lay the matter before his Majesty. 27 July 1726.

The *Minute Book*, vol. 25, p. 211*k* (17 Aug. 1726), states that this letter and the report were read "and are again to be considered when my Lords shall be informed of a fund out of which the said charge may be defrayed." 1 *page much faded.*

The above letter is accompanied by the representation referred to, which is hereafter fully described, together with the petition of Captain William Taverner, which has on it besides the minute above referred to, another of 18 Jan. 1727–8. "My Lords do not know of any fund out of which this charge may be defrayed." Also copies of two memorials from merchants concerned in the Newfoundland fishery praying that the survey might be completed."

Commissioners of the Board of Trade to the Duke of Newcastle. Have lately had under consideration the memorial from the mayor, merchants, &c. of the town and port of Poole, trading to, or concerned in, the fishery of Newfoundland. The memorial sets forth that there has been for many years a fishing trade carried on, on

1726. VOL. CCLV.

the eastern side of the Island, and that the town of Poole alone employed therein forty ships last year. The fishery on the west and north-west sides of the Island . . . . . . the Crown of Great Britain by the French at the treaty of Utrecht is very good, and great plenty of fish might be taken there were it not for the dangers that attend the voyages; the west and north-west coast never having been surveyed. Therefore they pray that a proper person may be appointed to take soundings of the coast, and to form an exact survey thereof, that charts may be made for the use of all Her Majesty's subjects, to enable them to fish upon the west and north-west coast. Are of opinion that nothing will tend more to the public service than that a survey be made of the west and north-west of Newfoundland as proposed. Think this the more necessary, as it will be the means of establishing the salmon fishery, which has of late years been begun there. Her late Majesty granted a commission, dated 21 July 1713, to Captain William Taverner, constituting him her Surveyor of Newfoundland, at a salary of 20s. a day; and he surveyed the Islands of St Peters and Columba, as also that part of Newfoundland lying between Cape St Maries and Cape. . . . . . . He made a report of his proceedings, and several reports in relation to the trade, which together with the several drafts he has made of these bays, creeks, and harbours surveyed by him, are very distinct and have been of great use. Have received several memorials from the merchants of London and the outports, "in favour of him & his capacity of performing the said service." Inform his Grace that he (Mr Taverner) is going thither with a small sloop of his own of about 50 tons burden, to erect a salmon fishery there; and considering he is willing to undertake the survey, and is in every way capable of this important piece of service, ask his grace to recommend to his Majesty the advantage of the survey. . . . . . . [Send his Grace] an account of what the late survey of part of this Island cost the Crown, that he may judge how far Captain Taverner's proposals are reasonable. Whitehall, March 30, 1726. 8 *pages* (the first two documents injured and much faded).

1 Aug. 55. Report of the Attorney and Solicitor General to the Lords of the Treasury. Received from Mr Scrope their Lordships' commands with a printed copy of his Majesty's proclamation of 21 Jan. 1719, promising rewards for discovering and apprehending persons guilty of robberies in the streets or highways in London and Westminster, or within five miles round the same, and a list of rewards paid pursuant thereto. Mr Scrope informs them that their Lordships have referred the case of persons applying for such rewards to Mr Cracherode, and have been induced by his reports to pay 5,000*l.*, or thereabouts, for such rewards within these five years. Great sums are still demanded for like rewards, and the offenders increase. Are asked what is proper to be done to ease his Majesty from this great expense, it seeming to their Lordships that the rewards are paid for the crafts and doings of pickpockets, &c., for detecting which practices their Lordships conceived the rewards were never intended.

1726 VOL. CCLV.

Mr Cracherode has assured them (the Attorney and Solicitor General) that he never reported any person was entitled to such rewards unless the Judge or Justices before whom the criminal had been tried and convicted had first certified to the Sheriff that such conviction was a conviction for a robbery upon the highway, and had therefore ordered the Sheriff to pay the reward of 40*l.* given by the Act of 4 & 5 Will. and Mar., and that he always annexed to his report an attested copy of the certificate and order of the Judge or Justices, to the end their Lordships might see his opinion as to the crime, &c. It appears to them that by the proclamation whosoever shall discover and apprehend any person guilty of that offence, which the laws deem a robbery within the limits described in the proclamation, will upon conviction of the offender be entitled to receive 100*l.* without regard to the value of the thing taken. As to what is suggested about pickpockets that cannot have happened after Mr Cracherode's reports. What may be proper to be done to ease the King from the burden is a question of prudence rather than law, for whilst the proclamation continues in force any person performing the service will be entitled to the reward; but his Majesty can determine the force of the proclamation whenever he thinks fit by publishing a new one. Whether such repeal may be advisable, or may not rather be taken as an encouragement to the committing of such crimes, seems to deserve great consideration. 6 *pages.*

4 Aug. 56. Comrs of Excise (Scotland) to the Lords of the Treasury, in respect to a representation and petition of David Steuart, lately a collector of Excise and his securities. The petitioner (Steuart) being since detected or suspected of divers frauds and forgeries in his office, has been taken into custody at Inverness, and they presume is (under a strong guard) on his way to Edinburgh to be examined: pray that the consideration of the petition and report may be suspended till further examination is made in the case. Excise Office, Edinburgh, 4 Aug. 1726. 1 *page.*

16 Aug. 57. Memorial of Joseph Gascoigne to the Lords of the Treasury. The Lord Carpenter, Governor of the Island of Minorca, having represented to their Lordships the extreme necessity for benches or bedsteads for the soldiers in garrison in that Island to preserve their health, as they are lying some on uneven pieces of wood, some on the ground, and many on stones, and as his Lordship thinks it absolutely necessary to issue out 1,048 new beds, it is his opinion that these benches or bedsteads will be of such service as to make the bedding last three or four years longer. Is willing to make that number of benches or bedsteads at 18*s.* each, and to receive payment out of the revenues late of the Bishopric and chapter of Majorca. Treasury Chambers, 16 Aug. 1726.

"Read and agreed to." See *Minute Book,* vol. 25, p. 210*c.* 3 *pages.*

23 Aug. 57*a.* George Gray to Sir Robert Walpole, First Comr of the Treasury. Apprehends that no report has been made from the

1726. VOL. CCLV.

Com^rs of Customs to the Treasury in relation to the informations the writer delivered them concerning the frauds in the customs and trade of South and North America. Asks for an opportunity to convince Sir Robert of the truth of what he had advanced, in respect to the methods used in accomplishing the frauds, the deficiency of the officers in their duty, and the proportion of them liable to corruption. Cock Pit, Aug. 23, 1726.

Also another paper on the subject of the frauds. 7 *pages.*

24 Aug. 58. Contract entered into by Joseph Gascoigne, of St Martin's in the Fields, with the Lords of the Treasury for the supply of 1,048 benches for the soldiers in the Island of Minorca. Dated 24 Aug. 1726.

Also a bond entered into for performance of the contract. 2 *pages.*

[? About 30 Aug.] 59. Representation of John Sydenham to the Lords of the Treasury. Was appointed agent to take care of his Majesty's part ($\frac{1}{10}$) of the wrecks granted to Captain Jacob Rowe, between 10 & 53 degrees of North Latitude. Proceeded to the Isle of May on 6 Jan. 1720 and took up treasure, whereof his Majesty's share was 1,940*l.*, since which he has been on several expensive expeditions, particularly one in the Gulf of Florida, &c., where he suffered great hardships without success. Their Lordships on 14 June 1725 ordered him 250*l.*, to make up his expenses out of money due to H. M. on account of wrecks; prays that the same may be paid.

Minuted:—(30 Aug. 1726) "John Sydenham's petic̃on for 250^li to be paid as the King's Agent upon Rows diveing Engine for wrecks is read, and he attending, was called in and my Lords reject his request of being paid in any other manner than is menc̃oned in the Minute of the 14 June 1725, and require him to desist any further applicac̃on unless there be effects of that kind for his satisfaction which he is at liberty to see after." 2 *pages.*

1 Sept. 60. "From the Comm^rs to Mr Scrope ab^t laws necessary to be passed there." [St Christophers.] Have by letter of yesterday's date troubled their Lordships, but in addition address several articles to him (Mr Scrope) to be recommended for his Majesty's service immediately, as regards calling general assemblies of freeholders or planters; ask that the Chief Governor should have an additional instruction requiring him to issue writs with all speed, summoning the freeholders and such as shall have accepted from & signed contracts (for lands of ten acres or more) with the Com^rs for sale of French lands, to meet and choose a number of representatives, equal to the number now chosen for the English part of the Island; the French part being the full half of the Island, and better cultivated; and that such representatives be directed to meet the representatives of the English part of the Island, and with them form one Assembly or House of Representatives, jointly to enact laws for the public weal, &c., and "at their first meeting the following laws be recommended to them & Council," viz.:—

1726. Vol. CCLV.

An Act declaring such Election legal, and appointing all assemblies hereafter to be in like manner elected.

An Act to unite the two parts of this Island & make the whole subject to the following laws, viz. :—

To the Law now in force giving to his Majesty the duty of four and half p cent.

To the Law now in force for regulating the Militia.

To the Law now in force establishing Courts of King's Bench & Common Pleas.

To the Law now in force for better government of slaves.

To the Law now in force for better government of white servants.

And to such other laws now in force as shall be judged fit to remain in force in the whole Island.

The Com^rs also propose a new law to be enacted to divide the French part of the Island into three parishes, &c. St Christophers, 1 Sept. 1726. 4 *pages.*

6 Sept. 61. Petition of John Yates to the R^t Hon. Sir Robert Walpole. Has found out that Sir Charles Yates's estates [of Buckland] in Berkshire and elsewhere, were always entailed upon the heirs male, with the reversion in the Crown; and having laid before Mr Attorney General the first case annexed, he put the annexed queries to petitioner, who begs assistance for the production of the records and papers required.

Accompanied by the "Case," which states that Sir Charles Yates before the outlawry of his son John, went to France and died possessed of estates worth 8,000*l.* per ann. His son John raised a troop of horse and opposed King William and was outlawed for high treason and died in France about 1701, so eight years' profit to the Crown is 64,000*l.* Sir Robert Frogmorton, a papist, also marrying his sister (daughter of Sir Charles) got into possession of the estates and made great waste, and his wife dying, left one son, who fled to France. The estates were entailed upon the heirs male, and the said John Yates is next protestant heir-at-law.

Also Queries of the Attorney General put to Mr Yates, and his answers. 3½ *pages.*

10 Sept. 62. Com^rs of Excise (Scotland) to the Lords of the Treasury. Upon the examination of David Stewart, late Collector of Excise at Inverness, who was charged with making false precepts for arms, he throws all the guilt upon one John Monro, of Navarre, near Inverness, as shown by the copy of a paper enclosed. Have obtained a warrant for Monro's apprehension, and presume he is either skulking in some part of the North or gone beyond the seas, which evidences his guilt, as he is a person of considerable substance. Have in custody one James McCulloch, who they believe to be an amanuensis to Mr Monro in forging the precepts. Have sent to the commander of the troops at Inverness to assist in securing him. Hope to penetrate to the bottom of this villany.

1726. VOL. CCLV.

The paper referred to is headed :—" Information. David Stewart, late Collector of Excise at Inverness, against John Monro, of Navarre, of his being guilty of the frauds found out in the precepts of arms in the county of Ross." 7 *pages.*

14 Sept. 63. Board of Trade to the Lords of the Treasury. The Governor (Captain Pheney) and Council of the Bahama Islands have desired them to beg their Lordships to intercede with his Majesty, that certain bills may be returned to them and applied to discharge the public debts of the Islands, contracted chiefly for the fortifications; are of opinion that it will be of great service to that infant settlement.

Enclose copy of their receipts and payments for the last year.

Minuted :—" 20 Sept[r] 1726. Read and agreed to." 4 *pages.*

17 Sept. 64. Copy of report indorsed :—" The Report of the General Officers on the Petition of Captain Lewis Armand to the Lords of the Treasuy"; but it is addressed "to their Excellencies the Lords Justices Gen[l] and Gen[l] Gov[rs] of Ireland." Captain Armand prayed to be placed for half pay on the Military Establishment of Ireland at 4*s.* 9*d.* per day, instead of his present pension of 3*s.* on the Civil Establishment. In regard that the petitioner never had a commission of captain, nor ever served as such, and does not appear to have distinguished himself for his Majesty's service in the time of the Rebellion, as set forth in his petition, any otherwise than by a certificate from Colonel Cavalier, which seems of so extraordinary a nature that they have annexed it for consideration, are of opinion that petitioner is not entitled to half pay. Dated 17 Sept. 1726.

Also copy of the certificate, the petition, and copy of a warrant.

The petition is *minuted* :—" 13 Dec. 1726. Rep[t] ag[st] him." 6 *pages.*

28 Sept. 65. Representation by the Com[rs] for Taxes to the Lords of the Treasury as to the Insupers standing out upon the accounts of the several Receivers General of Taxes. Are informed, and are very well assured, that great sums are now due and in arrear upon the land revenue and fee-farm rents. Ask for warrants and directions to the King's Remembrancer, the Clerk of the Pipe, and the Auditors of the Land Revenue to make out and deliver a list of such collectors, &c., and of the annual sums wherewith they stand charged, as well as of their arrears, that they (the Com[rs]) may prosecute and recover the same. 2 *pages.*

30 Sept. 66. The Duke of Newcastle to the Lords of the Treasury. Sends a report of the Com[rs] for Trade and Plantations upon the petition of William Toshach, merchant, praying satisfaction for the loss of his house in Placentia, the same having been taken up for his Majesty's use, and comprehended within the New Fortifications there. The King desires their Lordships to do what seems reasonable therein. Sept. 30, 1726.

Also a copy of the letter.

The report is not with the paper. 2 *pages.*

VOL. CCLV.

1726.

[? About 4 Oct.] 67. Petition of Thomas Kemp to the Lords of the Treasury. Has an assignment of the late Brigadier Munden's salary as outranger of Windsor Forest, and received the same until Christmas 1724. The Brigadier died on 19 Sept. 1725 in petitioner's debt 1,700*l.* over and above "the appointm[t] made to him of the said salary." The underkeepers have obtained a warrant for payment of their wages out of the arrears due to the Brigadier, which excludes petitioner from the benefit of his assignment. Prays their Lordships to direct the payment of the Brigadier's salary to him.

There is also another paper containing some further particulars as to the salary and proposals for the distribution of it.

Minuted:—"Read 4th October 1726. My Lords having already order[d] the Under Keepers to be paid their arrears out of the salary granted for Munden and them, which arrears amo[t] to 391[li], they are content that the vacant pay between Munden's death & M[r] King's succeeding to that office be paid the said Kemp towards his great debt from Munden. So prepare a proper w[t] accordingly." 2 *pages.*

18 Oct. 68. Report signed "W. Cary" to the Lords of the Treasury. Is of opinion that Evan Williams is guilty of felony in paying two shillings counterfeit money to Edward Davis, contrary to the 8 & 9 W. 3 cap. 25 ss. 7, &c. The evidence of high treason for coining and for having and hiding coining tools is so loose, that he is doubtful if any jury will convict., &c. Half pence are not the lawful coin nor is the counterfeiting of them a capital offence; but conceives the counterfeiting them is a misdemeanour against the common law of England. The prosecution in this case is not barred, for Williams was apprehended within three months after he committed the offence. A bill of indictment ought to be preferred at the very first assizes or sessions of gaol delivery after the offender is apprehended, or else he has a right to be discharged or bailed by the rules of practice in the Crown Laws. Mint Office, 18 Oct. 1726. 1 *page.*

18 Nov. 69. Com[rs] of Excise (Scotland) to the Lords of the Treasury. Lay before their Lordships the copy of a decree or ordnance made at the quarter sessions for the peace in the county of Fife, which appears to have been made upon the application of the tanners and other traders in leather without any intimation to the Officers of Excise. The decree is in direct opposition to the laws for securing the duty. The quarter sessions consisted of three gentlemen who did not defer the consideration of the matter for a larger attendance of the justices nor enquire into the truth of the allegations in the petition. Communicated the affair to the Earl of Ilay before he set out for London, who expressed a high resentment against their proceedings, and directed the laying them before their Lordships. Can now acquaint their Lordships with the setting aside of that judgment by a numerous meeting of the justices. In order that as little harm might be done to the revenue as possible they despatched the orders contained in a letter to their collector, subjoined.

1726. VOL. CCLV.

Besides the letter referred to there are the decree and the subsequent one setting it aside. The first sets out that the petitioners, &c. "are extremely prejudged and damnaged by the practice of the Officers of Excise appointed to survey & stamp ye leather qch [which] will plainly appear to their honours in ye parlīs following, viz., the saids officers of Excise oblidge their petitioners to draw their hydes and dry the same in order to be stamped before ye hydes are fully lickered; qch takes away the natural substance of the leather & renders ye same so 'friesh' that it does not near half so well as if it were fully lickered, dressed & curried, before drying & stamping: & this is not only an evident damnadge to ye leidges in general, but likewise occasions a great uneasiness to their petitioners, from the outcry and calumny of ye country, y^t they make their shoes of rotten leather." 7 *pages*.

24 Nov. 70. Report of the Barons of the Exchequer of Scotland to the Lords of the Treasury. Have examined the warrant for granting "to Coll. John Arnott all and haill the lands and Barony of Abbotshall, &c. which pertained before to the deceased, Mr Andrew Ramsay of Abbotshall, and proceeds upon a decreit of sale from the Lords of Session in favour of the said John Arnott as the highest offerer for those lands at a public roup." The signature contains a *de novo damus* and erection of the lands into a barony which gives him a jurisdiction and some other privileges, &c. 1 *page*.

7 Dec. 71. Copies of report, petition, and other papers connected with the application of Marianne de Courteille, widow of Abraham de Courteille, sometime a captain in Col. de la Meloniere's regiment, for the continuance of the pension (2*s*. 6*d*. a day) of her late husband. The report dated 7 Dec. 1726. 8 *pages*.

15 Dec. 72. Memorial of the Com^rs of Customs (Scotland) to the Lords of the Treasury, representing the inconvenience and detriment arising to the revenue "from the member ports of Greenock, Kirkudbright & Port Patrick continuing on the foot they now are; for by the returns to the Com^rs issued out of the Court of Exchequer here, for those places to be members of the Ports of Port Glasgow, Dumfries & Stranraer, it has hitherto been the practice to make the collector of each of those head ports answerable for the receipts of his respective member port": the accounts have to be included and are thereby perplexed. It seems an absurdity to join two collections, which can have no connexion with each other. It causes uneasiness to the officers, and was probably the reason that the Ports of Kirkaldy & Anstruther, and also Barrowstoness and Alloa (formerly united), were some years ago separated. Propose that they (the Com^rs) may be authorised to issue their deputations to the respective persons, now acting as Deputy Collectors and Deputy Controllers, to be Collectors and Controllers, in order to their accounting with the Controller General and remitting their receipts to the Receiver General directly, without being answerable to the officers at the head ports. Their Lordships in 1723 directed that the Collector

1726. VOL. CCLV.

& Controller of Port Glasgow shall appoint deputies to execute the offices of Collector & Controller at the Port of Greenock, to be paid out of their salaries (additions being made to that end). Suggest that 50*l*. out of the 200*l*. inserted on the establishment for the Collector of Glasgow be allowed to the Collector of Greenock, and of the 100*l*. on the establishment to the Controller of Port Glasgow 25*l*. be allowed to the Controller of Greenock, &c. 3 *pages*.

17 Dec. 73. Com^rs of Excise (Scotland) to the Lords of the Treasury. Previously acquainted their Lordships of the detection of abuses by fictitious precepts or receipts for arms. David Steuart's information, against John Monro, of Navarr, has been confirmed before the Lord Advocate, by Jonathan Thompson. Give an account of the arrest of Monro (which was effected by John Steuart, a private gentleman in the regiment of Scotch Grays) and of his escape at a Ferry, in the dark. The whole of this ill-conduct has been communicated to Col. Campbell, the present Commander-in-Chief, who has laid the same before General Wade to have his directions, as all the persons concerned are military men. Have a brother of Monro's in custody, one Hugh Monro, for the like practices in other parts of the country, whose trial will soon come on, but the proof is not so clear againt him. 3 *pages*.

20 Dec. 74. Memorial and petition of Sir Bibye Lake, Bart., to the Lords of the Treasury, praying that Charles Mason, Esq., Receiver and Paymaster of the Transport Office, may be directed forthwith to clear and pass his account or produce the tallies mentioned in his memorial to the Auditor; and that petitioner may have liberty to pay into the Receipt of the Exchequer, what shall appear to be due to the Crown from Mr Mason to clear the account; and that thereupon, his extended estate may be granted and assigned to petitioner, to reimburse him what he shall pay on account thereof. 2 *pages*.

5 & 22 Dec. 75. A paper indorsed:—" Case of ye York buildings Comp^a with respect to allowances claimed upon the ballance of their accounts with the Public. With the Solicitor Generall & Councell^r Fane^s opinion upon ye same."

Headed:—" 1726, 26 Octr. Some cases and queries between the Honble Comiss^rs of the Forfeited Estates in Scotland & the Govr & Comp^a of Undertakers for raising the Thames Water in York Buildings, with respect to the estates purchased by the Company, the method of accounting for the same in stating of Interest & the claims, teinds, fews & other deductions chargeable thereon."

The answers to the queries are signed by "Fran. Fane on 5 Decr 1726" and by "C. Talbot, 22 December 1726."

In the *Minute Book*, vol. 25*p*, 299*c* (19 May 1727), is:—" Write to the York Buildings Company to know what progress they have made in settling the ballances to be paid the Crown for the Estates they purchased of the Comm^rs for Forfeitures and to advise the

1726. VOL. CCLV.

hastening and paying in the said ballances to avoid the measures that must be taken in case this affair is further neglected or delayed." 9 *pages.*

13–29 Dec. 76. Various papers relating to proposals made by Samuel Power for duties to be laid on hats, skins, hair, and glue. They contain many particulars as to conies and cony skins, the places where they were bred and from whence they were transported, as well as the manner of dressing the skins. One of the papers is a catalogue or list of furs and skins as charged in the "Book of Rates." Samuel Power proposes that if the Lords of the Treasury approve of the laying on these duties, or any of them, he may be appointed one of the managers. The first is dated 13 Dec. and the last 29 Dec. 1726. 12 *pages.*

31 Dec. 77. Report of Mess[rs] Singleton, Rogerson, and Marlay to the Lords Justices General and General Governors of Ireland. Are required to prepare a draft in form of a letter for the Royal signature to secure the purchasers of M[r] Pratt's estate from any claim of the Crown, on that estate. Have prepared the annexed draft.

The draft referred to. The lands are not specified, but the office of Constable of the Castle of Dublin with the fees and profits appear to have formed part of the estate. 2½ *pages.*

[? End of 1726.] 78. "The Case of Capt[n] Lewis Armand." He prayed to be put on a level with the other Captains in half pay in Ireland at 4*s.* 9*d.* per diem.

A good many of the particulars of his case are previously set out in this calendar. See 17 Sept. 1726. Vol. CCLV., No. 64.

Also "the case of Charles Hooper of London Gent. & Philip Martin wid[o] & executrix of John Martin Esq[re]." During the Rebellion in Ireland James Waller, Lieut.-Governor of Charles Fort and Kinsale expended 2,000[l] in King William's service towards subsisting and transporting French prisoners. His Majesty, by letter of 17 Apr. 1700, directed a yearly pension of 200[l] to be inserted on the Establishment of Ireland, and paid to M[r] Waller and his assigns, until the 2,000[l] should be paid in one entire payment. The pension was, by direction of M[r] Waller's widow, sold to John Asgill, Esq., for 1,500[l], who sold it to James Hooper, Esq., whose executor received it till 1715, and assigned it to John Martin, Esq., in trust for the payment of James Hooper's debts. After the assignment the pension was omitted in the Establishment. The matter was afterwards referred to the Solicitor General, who was of opinion that the pension was granted in satisfaction of money expended for the public service, and that James Hooper was a purchaser thereof for a valuable consideration; but the original charge being created only by a letter under his Majesty's sign manual, the petitioners can have no relief but by his Majesty's grace and favour. Undated. 3 *pages.*

[There are other papers on the same subject arranged with the classified under the Letters of the Lord Lieutenant of Ireland.]

1726. VOL. CCLV.

1726. 79. "Abstract of the accompt of forfeitures, 1726." Showing the names of the Estates, apparently all in Scotland, and the amounts realised for them, amounting to 295,385*l.* 16*s.* $2\frac{2}{12}$*d.* 2 *pages.*

[? 1726.] 80. Petition of Don Joseph de Mellis to the Rt Hon Sir Robert Walpole. Was in hopes that by the late peace between the Courts of Vienna and Madrid he might have disposed of his "State" [? estate] in Valencia in the same manner as those that followed the Emperor into Germany who are unwilling to return to Spain: but has had no other answer to his demands at the Court of Madrid, than that he has taken up arms with the English in the late Expedition of Vigo, and that he is a heretic. Applied to the Emperor to be recommended to the Court of Madrid; but was told "that he must not expect any favour from that ungrateful Court of Vienna, as long as he continues a Protestant and in England." Petitioner went in the late expedition with Sir John Jennings, and at Santona when the Spaniards fired at the fleet, petitioner was sent by the Admiral ashore with a flag of truce, where he got intelligence and did all the services at the hazard of his life, if he had been discovered. Is "sensible afflicted" to be obliged to trouble his Excellency, who in so distinguished a manner, so lately relieved him: but as he is ready at all times to sacrifice his person for his Majesty's government, hopes his Excellency will continue his protection to him, and recommend him to his Majesty for some small matter upon the compassionate list. Undated, but probably 1726, the peace between Vienna and Madrid is referred to under the year 1725 in *Hume and Smollett's History of England*, Vol. VIII., p. 275 (published 1854). 1 *page.*

[? 1726.] 81. Petition of William Newsham of Warwick, Esq., to the Lords of the Treasury. Petitioner and his father before him were Receivers General of the Land-tax for the county of Warwick, "from whence returns of money are not to be had, by reason ye intercourse of trade with Londo is very small." In consideration whereof the Lords of the Treasury made petitioner's father allowances in his accounts of what he expended for the carriage and conduct of money. In 1718 Mitchener, a clerk of petitioner's father, misapplied a considerable sum of the public money, and petitioner's father was unable to make up the yearly balance, without which he could not petition for the yearly allowances. Petitioner accepted the office and took the debt of his father, and made the payments to the satisfaction of the Comrs of Taxes; but was told he could not have any allowances for his own or his father's accounts until the year 1718 should be cleared. Prosecuted an extent in aid for many years against Mitchener's estate, for the recovery of the public money so misapplied, but could not obtain the same until July last. Is ready to clear all accounts for the last eight years, which could not be settled for the above reason Prays to be allowed the sums expended by him. 1 *page.*

1726. VOL. CCLV.

[There is an entry in the *Minute Book*, vol. 25, p. 344, 12 Aug. 1730, on the subject of these claims.]

1726. 82. "Dissent of the representative of the Burgh of Haddington to the resolution of the Hon[ble] the Convention of Royal Burrows that no clause shall be added to the proposals that are to be laid before his Ma[tie] from them for applying the monies appropriated by act of parliament for encouraging the manufactories, fishing, &c. in Scotland, humbly representing the inability of this part of the Kingdom to sustain the burden of a duty upon malt as it is at present imposed by the last Act of parlia[t] made on that behalf." 1726. 3 *pages.*

[? 1726.] 83. Memorial of Daniel Campbell, Esq., to the Lords of the Treasury. There is payable to the Crown out of the lands and Island of Islay in Scotland, a yearly few duty, or quitrent, of 500*l.* sterling. This duty has for several years been granted by the Crown to the family of Lenox and Richmond in Scotland, and their descendants. Queen Anne by charter, dated 28 February 1707, ratified by parliament, granted the same to Edward Hyde, eldest lawful son of Edward, Lord Cornbury, nephew of Charles, late Duke of Lennox, and Lady Catherine Steuart alias Obrain, the said Duke's sister, and to his heirs and "assigneys," and to Henry, Lord Hyde, eldest son of Lawrence, Earl of Rochester, as his trustee "for the space of three nineteen years" from Whitsuntide 1701, the said Edward Hyde being obliged to pay to her Majesty for tack duty 41*l.* 13*s.* 4*d.* sterling. Memorialist being proprietor of the lands and Island of Islay, out of which the few duty of 500*l.* per ann. is payable, petitioned and prayed for a lease or grant of the reserved rent or tack duty of 41*l.* 13*s.* 4*d.* sterling, payable by those claiming under the lease. The Barons of the Exchequer, to whom the matter was referred, reported on 26th July 1725 that the grant or lease determined by the demise of her Majesty, but that his Majesty might renew the same, and grant the reserved rent of 41*l.* 13*s.* 4*d.* to memorialist during his Majesty's life, and the arrears since 1706. The memorialist's sufferings and losses by the late affair at Glasgow "are too nottour to be mentioned." Prays to have the grant in accordance with the report. [The late affair at Glasgow mentioned, arose out of the riots at Glasgow, where the house of Daniel Campbell, Esq. (who was a member of Parliament), was rifled. See *Hume and Smollett's Hist. of England*, Vol. VIII., p. 278 (Edition 1854).]

Also copy of the grant of Queen Anne to Edward Hyde. 5 *pages.*

1726. 84. Memorial of Francis, Earl of Godolphin to the Lords of the Treasury, praying payment of the arrears of 65*l.* per ann., being the allowance of the Deputy Ranger of Windsor Little Park, which was unpaid for five years from Midsummer 1721. Also that the rails, gates, and fences might be repaired. 1 *page.*

1726. VOL. CCLV.

1723–1726. 85. "An account of the ordinary revenue of the University of Glasgow for the crops and years 1723, 1724, 1725 and 1726; including the hundred pound sterling granted to supply the deficiency of the revenue: together with the annual expences of the said University, for these four years; with which the said revenue is burdened, humbly presented to the Right Honourable the Lords of His Majesty's Treasury, according to the directions given by the late Majesty Queen Ann, under the great seal dated at Windsor, the 16th day of December 1713, whereby Her Majesty appropriats one hundred pounds for the supplying the deficiency of the said revenue." Signed: "Neil Campbell, Principal. 1 *double page.*

[1726 or later.] 86. Petition of Ensign James Anderson, formerly a quarter master in Count Nassau's, since Lord Stanhope's regiment of dragoons, to the Rt Hon. Sir Robert Walpole, K.G., Chancellor of the Exchequer and First Lord of H.M. Treasury. Served as quartermaster in 1706, until taken prisoner in the retreat of the army from Madrie [? Madrid], and so continued with many hundreds till 1709. Whilst in confinement his post was given to one Talbott, who was advanced to be a Cornet and then a Lieutenant, which was petitioner's due. Was ordered 122*l.* 2*s.* as the balance of his subsistence, and soon after made Ensign in Col. Munden's regiment of foot. Served till 1712. Arrears of 80*l.* 1*s.* 2*d.* are still due. Armfield his agent had neglected to press for the arrears, which petitioner now prays for. ? 1726 or later, Sir Robert Walpole knighted in that year.

Also a balance sheet of petitioner's pay. 1 *page.*

[? 1726 or 1727.] 87. "Memorandum relating to the pension of 800*l.* per ann. granted to the late Duke of St Albans for life out of the revenue of Ireland."

The present duke had agreed that the pension of 800*l.* per ann. granted to his father should be regranted in trust for Ld Henry, Ld Sidney, Ld George, Ld James, and Ld Aubry Beauclerk, the younger sons of the late Duke unprovided for. [? 1726 or 1727 from the death of the late Duke.] 1 *page.*

[1726 or later.] 88. An opinion (unsigned) respecting the conduct of Mr Wilkins, who was in partnership with Messrs Toovey, Peele, and Woodward as proprietors of the "London Journal," and who concealed from them the profits he made of the paper. The paper came into the Government service in Sept. 1722, and Lord Townshend ordered 650 of the papers to be weekly sent to the Post Office to be dispersed in the country. These seem afterwards to have increased to 2,200 a week, for which Mr Wilkins received 2d each, and only accounted for three halfpence to his partners. The paper states that the stamp was put on papers in 1725, and that there was an allowance of one in 25 of such papers to all retailers. Mr Wilkins owns that the paper sank in value by being taken into the Government service. 2 *pages.*

VOL. CCLV.

1726.

[? 1726.] 89. Petition to the King of Archibald McAulay, His Majesty's "Conservator of the Scots privileges at Camten, and of Beatrix, Ann, and Mary Kennedy lawful daughters to the deceased Sir Andrew Kennedy, of Cloburn," praying for a warrant for 200*l.* [a year] to pay the salary of the said Archibald McAulay, who had been appointed to succeed Andrew Kennedy, deceased, in the above office on condition that he paid regularly 100*l.* to the other petitioners to liquidate their father's debts and relieve their distress. 2 *pages.*

VOL. CCLVI. 1726. CLASSIFIED.

1. Four Papers connected with the affairs of the Bank of England, viz.: —

(1.) "The Bond of the Cashieres of the Bank for their receipt of the Lottery for one million."

(2.) Memorial of the Court of Directors for allowance for their charges of management of the three per cent. annuities.

(3 and 4.) Memoranda as to dividends on Lottery Annuities, &c. 4 *pages.*

2. Warrants of the Lord Chamberlain of the Household (Grafton) to the Master of the Great Wardrobe (Montague) for the supply of various articles and materials 13 *pages.*

3. Memorial and Reports of the Com[rs] of Customs to the Lords of the Treasury as to (1) coals shipped without the over-sea duty to Port Mahon for burning lime and bricks for the fortifications there; also for the use of the forces in the garrisons of Gibraltar and Minorca without paying foreign duty; (2) as to liberty to discharge goods imported at Northam or any other place than the lawful keys at the Port of Southampton. The proprietors of the River Itchin, running from Winchester into Southampton River and the sea, give their reasons why the privilege should be allowed them of not confining themselves to the lawful keys, and cite the case of the river Thames and other parts of the kingdom. It has always been the practice as well in London as other ports to grant liberty to merchants by special sufferances to discharge timber, iron, and other bulky goods at places which are not set out by commission as lawful keys and wharfs under the care of the proper officers upon their being paid by the merchants for their extraordinary expenses and attendance. See no reason why the indulgence should not be continued. Also the petition of the Mayor and Bailiffs of Southampton (3) as to the precautions taken for regulating the trade to and from the Isle of Man since the Act of the last session "for improvement of the revenues of Customs, Excise and Inland Duties." 7 *pages.*

1726. Vol. CCLVI.

4. Reports and other papers of the Com[rs] of Excise on the produce of the inland duties upon coffee, tea, chocolate: and comparisons of the produce of other exciseable articles. 9 *pages.*

5. Various financial papers, including states of the cash in the Exchequer, state of the Exchequer Bills, Income of the Aggregate, General and South Sea Funds, State of the Sinking Fund, Lotteries, Civil List, &c. 43 *pages.*

6. Letters of the Lord Lieut. of Ireland to the Lords of the Treasury (1) as to additional pay to three troops of dragoons; (2) as to the issue of debentures for payment of the officers of the army (Ireland); (3) on the petition of Charles Hooper, of the City of London, gent., and of "Philip" Martin, widow and executrix of John Martin, Esq., deceased. [This is accompanied by several papers, mostly copies touching the same business. The particulars of the case of Charles Hooper and the widow Martin are more fully set out in a previously described undated paper. (*See* vol. CCLV., 78. ? End of 1726. "The case of Charles Hooper," &c.)]; (4) as to a pension of 100*l.* per ann. to John Porter, Esq., alderman of Dublin; (5) as to a ship burnt at Glandore Bay in the time of the late contagion; (6) as to an addition of 200*l.* per ann. to the pension of the Earl of Roscommon; (7.) The same to Richard, Earl of Cavan; (8) as to a pension of 200*l.* per ann. to Henry Barry, Esq., son to the Lord Santry; (9) as to the demand of M[r] Pratt, the Deputy Vice-Treasurer; and (10) as to placing Ensign Hunt Walsh on half pay. 30 *pages.*

7. Applications (chiefly) by the Treasurer of the Navy (Pattee Byng, Esq.) for money for the service of the Navy interspersed with accounts of money and tallies remaining in the hands of the Treasurer of the Navy. 25 *pages.*

8. A collection of papers touching the sale of that part of the Island of St. Christophers called Basse Terre and Cabeçâ Terre, consisting of 16,000 acres. The sale was made pursuant to an Address of the House of Commons and a commission addressed to William Mathew, Esq., Lieut. Governor of the Leeward Charribbee Islands in America, Gilbert Fleming and Edward Mann, Esq. (copy accompanying), and was also in accordance with instructions from the Lords of the Treasury (copy also accompanying). By the instructions no lot or parcel of land was to be sold exceeding 200 acres. One third of the purchase money was to be paid within a month, and five years were allowed for the payment of the other two thirds. Accounts were to be kept of all the proceedings of the Com[rs]. The collection consists mostly of letters to the Secretary of the Treasury (Scrope), describing the proceedings of the Com[rs] in carrying out the sale. In the letter of M[r] Fleming of 3 Aug. he mentions the necessity of determining the present grants, and proposes returning the $\frac{1}{3}$ of the purchase money in bills.

The following shows the opinion of the writer upon the proposal: "Extract of a letter from M[r] Tho. Butler to M[r] John Davy Breholt, merchant in London. Dated at S[t] Christophers the 3[d] August 1726. I have yours by M[r] Fleming who has brought out what may justly be called an Act of Banishment for three parts in four

1726. Vol. CCLVI.

of his Mats subjects in this Island: for certain it is, that not one man in 20 of the present settlers of the French lands are in a condition to purchase them on the terms the Commrs give out they will insist on, so that the rich Autegonians and Barbadians and the Commrs themselves must be the purchasers; in short it is lamentable to see the consternation the people are in, and nothing can now be heard but crying and wringing of hands for the so near approach of this depopulation; the consequence whereof must inevitably be, that first those who are turned out of their habitations and sent adrift, possibly may, and, it's much to be feared, will go to the French and Spanish Islands, where, no doubt, they will be well recĕd and thoroughly encouraged; secondly the British merchants and those here who have given large credit to these settlers, will every one lose their debts, and thirdly, his Maty instead of gaining one subject the more by the bargain will lose 2 or 3,000 very good ones; besides that his revenue of 4 & ½ p ct, and other duties imposed on the comodities of this Island imported to Britain and other his Mats dominions, will be chekt for at least 3 years; for as of course 10,000 negroes will be carried off, the new settlers must purchase as many and make their settlement equal to what they are at present, before his Maty will receive the same revenues as he now does; and all this for such a poor pittance as 100,000li that sum (notwithstanding what may have been given out to the contrary) being the utmost the whole French part of this Island will sell for. Add to all this the unpeopling and ruin of the fine & large town of Bassa Terre, built at a vast expence by the merchants and other Traders & which is in the greatest danger of being once again seen in flames, the people in general not sparing to declare, that no stranger shall be the better for their houses and works, wch they say and with truth cost them no small sums," &c.

In the letter of 6 Aug. the Comrs speak of the complaints going home against them in respect to a plantation formerly granted to president Davis, of which Mr John Willett and Mr John Spooner have actual possession, and they say "that if anything can possibly cast a tincture of partiality or prejudice on what we have done in this affair, it must be that the plantation these gentlemen would purchase is one of those we have desired their Lordships liberty to purchase for ourselves."

In that of 9 Aug. they say:—"We are too well assured a gentleman of this Island has very industriously led the present possessors into combinations to keep us as much as may be in the dark, to depreciate the lands, to cast an odium on the Commission, and have formed themselves into partys to disturb a fair sale to any but themselves." *Again*:—"His Excy, Generall Hart (who is a possessor), the day Mr Mathew and Mr Fleming waited on him at Antigua, proposed to them that he had an arrear of four years of 1,200*l.* a year salary due to him, part of which he would offer in payment. However willing and desirous the Commissioners are to gratify his Excy, they do not think themselves impowerd so to do without your Lordship's directions." The Comrs were desirous of "contracting with all such as are reasonable proposers." And,

VOL. CCLVI.

1726. "'twould be too hard to putt to publick sale a spott of ground of hardly one hundred yards square, to take from the possessor a house he may have built of twenty times its value, if his Majesty can have the full value of his land by contracting with the present inhabitant."

In that of 17 Aug. The Com^rs refer to their Lordships the offer of General Hart to purchase 285 acres at 10*l*. an acre. They also refer to their difficulty about Mr Robert Cuningham, who claimed a "vast tract of three hundred and ninety-eight acres" about which a Chancery suit was progressing.

In that of 27 Aug. Mr Fleming says:—"We have the pleasure of observing that the combinations, threats, complaints, and clamours wch have been made use of to drive the poorer sort to despair, and to interrupt and depreciate our sales have been ineffectual." *Again*:—"While we were treating with the people of Basse Terre town, after declaiming on the hard condition of the poor and other possessors of the French lands, His Excellency was pleased to say it was severe to oblige them to purchase, the English part was given gratis to settlers, and a sale of lands from the Crown to the subject was unknown in the French or any other American colonys." He further said that the affair would be carried into Parliament.

In that of 29 Aug. Mr Fleming says that if their Lordships should favour Mr Hart they (the Com^rs) could not depend upon his assistance.

In that of 31 Aug. the Com^rs say:—"May we presume to recommend to your Lordshipps for His Majesty's approbation that we may confirm to the parishioners of Basse terre parish the church and church yard there, being about three acres. To the French Protestants for their Church and Church Yard a like quantity granted to them in Irish Town, and on which the old French settlers had their hospital. To the Parish of St. Paul Cabeça terre the land of the Old Covent at Covent Gutt for their Church and Church Yard, being to be a like quantity of about three acres, and the same quantity of land and ruins of the Carmelite Church in Upper Basse-terre for the Parish intended there. This will not lessen the value of sale; no one will buy churches or church yards."

In the letter of 1 Sept. the Com^rs suggest various new laws to be made.

In that of 20 Oct. to Mr Scrope, Mr Fleming says that among the contracts that will be laid before their Lordships "is one made with William Wells for a plantation in Cabeça terre Quarter, conteining one hundred & fifty-seven acres of land. This plantation was proposed for by two persons. By one Hilden, who has a grant for it, and within the meaning of our instructions is the possessor; and by one Woodropp who rented it of him, and neither of them in their proposalls offered above ten pounds an acre. I shall endeavour to the end of this affair to act up to the expectations you have of me, and always suppose myself within your view. I therefore own to you, Sir, that this contract is made in trust for myself, and without treating with Mr Hilden the possessor on his proposall, or putting up the land to public sale. But I begg leave to represent that the

1726. VOL. CCLVI.

malice we have raised against us in some people, by a due regard to our duty, has forced us in this respect out of the common road. I give the full value. The possessor has, indeed no other meritt but his possession, and if I understood Sr Robert Walpole right (when I had the honour of being introduced by you to the Lords of the Treasury) that, in his opinion, gives no strong pretensions to a preference, inasmuch as the possessors have hitherto had the lands for nothing. This possessor has injoy'd the plantation above twelve years gratis, and he has besides a very good one on which he lives, and (if I am not partiall to myself) I have the fairer pretensions to favour, since this gentleman was for male practices removed by the Treasury from the collection of the Customs in this Island. He is already provided for, and I don't know where else I can be setled on a tolerable lott." * * * * "It will be two years from my entering on the land before I can reap any proffitts, and 'tis necessary to be prepared for setling. Negros are not allways at market, which putt me under a necessity of buying some which offer'd, who will remain a heavy charge upon me 'till I have land to work y^m on."

In the letter of 1 Nov. they hope to conclude the business of the Commission by February.

In that of 30 Nov. they say:—"The discouragements we have all along mett with here, are chiefly from Generall Hart, His Majesty's Cheif Governor. We have hitherto stifled our complaints to their Lordshipps, but his Excellency's persecutions grow intolerable, and we apprehend bad consequences from his behaviour. He cannot forgive his not being named one of the Commissioners, that in words, he is required '*at his utmost perill*' to support us, which, His Excellency says, is a treatment never used to a Captain Generall, that we did not write their Lordshipps his offer of 10*l.* p acre for his land was a sufficient price, but only a generous first offer. These reasons, at least we know no others, have all along brought his Ex^cys indignation against us, and no means have been wanting to depreciate the lands, to exasperate the poor first, and now, all the inhabitants ag^t us. He publickly in Council, and in all places, stigmatizes the Commission, as an unheard of hardship, to sell lands in the colonys, that the people of the Island are hereby render'd miserable, that he himself is ready, if others will follow him, to go and settle Sancta Cruz, that he can give grants for lands there and spoil our bargains by carrying off our chapmen, that we grind the poor subject, and much more. To which for answer we assure their Lordshipps and you, Sir, we sold the land of equall value to his Excellency's, and adjoyning to it, for 17*l.* sterling p acre. We have not remov'd one single family off the Island, we have introduc'd no strangers. His Excellency himself once form'd a scheme for selling these lands, however barbarous the selling them at all is now. Not a purchaser complains, that we know of, and not one, but if he would part with his bargain, we could dispose of it at the same price, it may be for more; and so far are we from grinding the poor, or the subject, we can prove we have done every thing with utmost tendernesse, as farr as the duty of a trust

1726. VOL. CCLVI.

repos'd in us could admit; and no man living can say we have accepted a present of the value of a single pistole, or acted with any other consideration than of his Majesty's service. The days of driving off familys by thirtys, of extorting hundreds of pistoles from the settlers for grants, and thousands on assurances that the whole disposall of these lands were to be in other hands, ceased with the publishing his Majesty's commission to us. We begg their Lordshipps' and your protection. We shall now dayly gather in great sumes of money, temptation enough to evill-minded people to insult and rob us, without such incouragem[ts] from the Cheif Magistrate among us." * * *

Several of these letters are in duplicate as well as the enclosures to them.

There are also some letters signed "Galfridus Gray," addressed to the R[t] Hon. S[r] Robert Walpole, and one by him to John Scrope, Esq., Secretary to the Lords of the Treasury, as to his proposals for the sale of these lands. 184 *pages.*

9. Four letters (two with enclosures) from H. Pelham to John Scrope, Esq., as to ships taken up for transport of troops from Ireland, army clothing detained in the Custom House at Dublin for custom duties, and for payment of the transport of troops. 8 *pages.*

10. Reports of the Com[rs] of Stamps to the Lords of the Treasury. (1) On a proposed act for the relief of suitors in the Court of Chancery as it affected their department; (2) On the petition of John Walsh as to the construction of the statute 10 Anne c. 19, touching the payment of the duties on ballads and songs and other little books and papers. As musical books and papers are not within any of the exceptions in the act, they apprehend the duties ought to be paid; and (3) On the case of David Thomas who had counterfeited the stamps on parchment and paper and vended the same, and was sentenced to death, but had received a respite. If the twelve penny die and crown die were not delivered up it might be attended with the most dangerous consequence to the revenue. There is also another paper having a few entries which, perhaps, may be a comparison of excise or stamp duties for 1724, 1725, and 1726. 11 *pages.*

1726.

VOL. CCLVII. 1726.

Documents for which a brief description suffices.

Date.	Description of Document.	From	To	Purport.
1726. —	1. Two Estimates	—	—	Of the charge of the Office of Ordnance for the year 1726. Also copy of warrant. 3 *pages.*
3 Jan.	2. Abstract of Account.	—	—	Of the number of men borne and mustered on board H.M. ships in sea pay in the year 1725. 1 *page.*
12 Jan.	3. Petition -	Her Majesty Q. Anne's 24 Musicians and Instrument Keeper.	Lords of the Treasury.	Asking them to order that 300*l.* 7*s.* 3½*d.* due to them for arrears should be paid out of money remaining in the Exchequer to pay such debts. Also a certificate. 2 *pages.*
29 Jan.	4. Order in Council.	Lords of the Council	Do. - -	For the usual allowance of 200*l.* to be distributed among the Under Clerks of the Council. *Minuted:* — "23d Feb. 172⅚. Prepare a warrt. for an allowance to the clerks." 1 *page.*
1 Feb.	5. Certificate - (copy).	Robert Sedgwick, Clerk of the Jewels.	—	As to the delivery of plate to Lord Bingley, Ambassador Extraordinary and Plenipotentiary of Queen Ann, and as to what he now stood charged with. 1 *page.*
2 Feb.	6. Memorial -	Brigadier Bisset -	Lords of the Treasury.	For directions to the Paymaster General to pay the subsistence of his regiment at Gibraltar. 1 *page.*
3 Feb.	7. Do. - -	Comrs. for Hawkers and Pedlars.	Do. - -	For directions as to the payment of fees upon passing the late Comrs. accounts. 1 *page.*
4 Feb.	8. Petition -	Dame Ann FitzHarrey.	The Rt. Hon. Sir Robt. Walpole, Knt., First Comr. and the rest of the Comrs.	Is a prisoner in Newgate for debt in deplorable condition. Petitioner's father advanced 10,000*l.* to the Crown, and was killed after 40 years' service. Was allowed 250*l.* pension, and afterwards only 50*l.*, which was much in arrear. Prays compassion. 1 *page.*

1726. VOL. CCLVII.

Date.	Description of Document.	From	To	Purport.
7 Feb.	9. Certificate -	W. Keene for C. Stanhope, Esq.	—	As to arrears due from her late Majesty to Francis Clerk, Esq., Clerk of the Cheque, to the Yeomen of the Guard. 1 *page.*
8 Feb.	10. Memoranda -	—	—	Of proceedings made by Hatch Moody in the accounts of the late Robert Murray, Esq., formerly paymaster of the 1,400,000*l.* Lottery, 1714. 2 *pages.*
19 Feb.	11. Petition -	Margaret Stanley, widow.	Lords of the Treasury.	Her husband served on sea and land in King William and Queen Anne's time, and was obliged by gout, wounds and old age to quit his Commission. His father was killed in the Dutch wars. Petitioner's brother, Lt.-Col. James Kirke, of Villers' horse, was killed at Athlone. Is in miserable distress. At the foot is this note:—"This poor widow is an object of great charity. J. Guise." 1 *page.*
7 March	12. Memorial -	Lord Cadogan -	Do. - -	For a privy seal to discharge him from the plate impressed to him as ambassador to the States General. Also a certificate of the plate. 2 *pages.*
24 March	13. Report - -	[Comrs. of Works] Fr. Negus, and Ch. Whither.	Do. - -	As to the bridge in Hyde Park in the way to Kensington. Advise the building of a new bridge of brick and a brick wall. Also an estimate. 3 *pages.*
25 March	14. State of Account.	—	—	Rendered by the Rt. Hon. Geo. Earl of Cholmondely, High Steward of the Manor of Richmond *alias* West Sheen. 1 *page.*
28 March	15. Letter - -	Lord Townshend -	Lords of the Treasury.	Signifying the King's directions that Captain Samuel Taylor, master of a sloop, should be paid, according to contract, for bringing over three criminals from Holland concerned in the murder of Thomas Ball. Also he contract. 2 *pages.*

Date.	Description of Document.	From	To	Purport.
[29 March	16. Letter - -	Lord Grafton -	Lords of the Treasury.	For orders to be given for new doors in the galleries at Kensington according to Mr. Kent's design. 1 *page*.
29 March	17. Letter - -	Do. -	Do. - -	For orders to be given for five wainscot presses for keeping the records of the German Chancery at St. Jameses. 1 *page*.
29 March	18. Account -	—	—	Of the produce of the duty on coals by virtue of an Act of the first year of his Majesty's reign for making provision for the ministers of the new churches. 1 *page*.
2 April	19. Certificate -	Wm. Ashburnham, Cor. Cayley, of the Alienation Office.	Lords of the Treasury.	Of the gross and net produce of the Alienation Office. 1 *page*.
[? About 5 April.]	20. Petition -	Lady Fitzharris -	Do. - -	Is now "and for severall reigns past hath been supported by charity of the Crown." Is arrested and imprisoned for 100*l*. debt. Prays for relief. *Minuted*: — "5th April 1726, 20*li*. ordered." 1 *page*.
21 April	21. Petition -	Sir Bibye Lake, Bart.	Do. - -	For the estates of Robert Peter to be invested in petitioner or his nominee to reimburse petitioner's debt. Also a copy of letter to the Attorney and Solicitor General about Mr. Peter's debt. 2 *pages*.
23 April	22. State of Accounts.	—	—	Of the public taxes behind and undeclared within Mr. Auditor Godolphin's division. 3 *pages*.
27 April	23. Report -	A. Cracherode -	—	State of causes under prosecution. 5½ *pages*.
[? About 27 April]	24. Caveat -	—	—	"Richard Woolaston, Esq., against grant of the fee of the dissolved monastery of Furneis com. Lancastr'." 1 *page*.
3 May	25. Copy of Minute	—	—	Touching the employment of under clerks in making up accounts of revenues, &c. See *Minute Book*, Vol. 25, p. 173*n*. 1 *page*.

1726. Vol. CCLVII.

Date.	Description of Document.	From	To	Purport.
3 May	26. Petition -	Thomas Plaisted, of London, merchant.	Lords of the Treasury.	Petitioner was charged with running 1,000*li.* weight of snuff, and gave bond for payment of 200*l.*, the amount of the duty. Prays that the bond may be given up on payment of 33*l.* 6*s.* 8*d.* and for a *nolle prosequi* to be entered. Also a scheme to prevent the running of snuff. 2 *pages.*
11 May	27. Opinion -	—	—	The Attorney and Solicitor General's opinion as to the power of the Comrs. of Customs in regard to compositions with offenders against the custom laws. (Copy.) 2½ *pages.*
13 May	28. Report -	—	—	Of Charles Harrison concerning licences granted by the Court of Exchequer to compound upon penal laws. From the last day of Mich. term 1725 to 13 May 1726. 3 *double pages.*
[29 May]	29. Account -	—	—	Of the "Fieu and Blench duties" payable to the Crown out of lands specified in Scotland. 5½ *pages.*
10 June	30. Report - -	A. Cracherode -	—	As to causes "under prosecution: with the states thereof." 7 *pages.*
7 July	31. Letter - -	Lord Longford -	—	Asks for "that warrant" which he had the goodness to order for his (Lord Longford's) relief. His Majesty's bounty cannot extend to a greater object of compassion. Also Report dated 13 March 1724 of Lord Carteret on the petition of Christopher, Lord Viscount Longford, to be restored to his full pension of 500*l.* per ann, since reduced to 250*l.* The petition and the copy of the warrant. The petition states that he forfeited an estate of 12,000*l.* a year for his adherence to the Prince. 5 *pages.*

1726. VOL. CCLVII.

Date.	Description of Document.	From	To	Purport.
11 July	32. Report - -	A. Cracherode -	Lords of the Treasury.	On petition of John Pratchet and others for the reward of 40*l.* offered for the apprehension of one Thomas James, who assaulted and grievously wounded Henry Best, one of the keepers of Enfield Chase. Also the petition, copy of the London Gazette, a certificate, and an affidavit. 7 *pages.*
12 July	33. Certificate -	Charles Stewart -	—	Testifying that Mr. Abraham Benider was interpreter in the Spanish and Arabick languages during the time Mr. Charles Stewart was Ambassador to the Emperor of Morocco, and recommending him as a qualified person. ½ *page.*
27 July	34. Letter - -	The Duke of Newcastle.	Lords of the Treasury.	Transmits a letter from the Lord Lieut. of Ireland enclosing a report on the petition of Gerald Fitzgerald, Esq., who prays for a *nolle prosequi* to a prosecution against him in the Exchequer for recovery of certain effects alleged to be in his possession. The report referred to, at the end of which is the opinion of the Solicitor General for Ireland thereon. 4 *pages.*
10 Aug.	35. Depositions -	—	—	"Copy Precognition." Touching a charge of 'making counterfeit coin, made at Aberdeen against Isaac Darlington, a soldier in Col. Kirk's regiment. 2 *pages.*
12 Aug.	36. Report - -	A. Cracherode -	Lords of the Treasury.	On petition of John Gedney. In favour of a warrant being granted to H.M. Attorney General to consent to an order of the Court of Exchequer for 94*l.* 3*s.* 8*d.*, which should be paid over to the petitioner for a debt and costs due to him from John Talk *alias* Taulk. Also the petition and three other papers. 6 *pages.*
17 Aug.	37. Copy of Royal Warrant.	—	The Lord Lieut. of Ireland, &c.	For allowing 100*l.* per ann. to Lord Kenmaire for the use of his mansion house, called Ross Castle, and ground thereunto belonging, wherein at the reduction of Ireland a garrison was placed. Forces were still quartered there. 3 *pages.*

Date.	Description of Document.	From	To	Purport.
25 Aug.	38. Report - -	Secretary - at - War (H. Pelham).	Lords of the Treasury.	Mr. Missing, the contractor for salt meat for the soldiers at Minorca, to make a return of the quantity he has shipped, as it was apprehended the continuance of the contract would create a disturbance. 1 *page*.
18 and 30 Aug.	39. Opinion -	—	—	Copy of counsel's opinion "on Mr. Kemp's case in relation to Brigadier Munden's assignment of his salary as out-ranger." 1 *page*.
31 Aug.	40. Receipt -	—	—	For accounts and papers required by the Comrs. appointed to settle the accounts of the York Buildings Co., viz., for estates purchased in Scotland. 1 *page*.
Aug.	41. Account -	—	—	Dr. and Cr. account of fees to the clerks at the Treasury for the month of August 1726. There is also an account of the Deputy Clerk of the Pipe, of fees to be divided for the use of the Lords of the Treasury. 6 *pages*.
[? About Aug.]	42. [Petition] -	Thomas Maynard, Esq., one of the Comrs. of Customs.	Lords of the Treasury.	For their warrant to the Comrs. of Customs at Edinburgh to pay him 200*l*. after his year's residence in the service of H.M. Customs there. Their Lordships always allowed for travelling charges, &c. 400*l*. to a Commissioner thus employed, and 200*l*. had been paid. See *North Britain Book*, Vol 7, p. 408. 1 *page*.
15 Sept.	43. Letter - -	Secretary to the Admiralty (Burchett).	John Scrope, Esq., Secretary to the Treasury.	As to the waste and abuses in cutting trees in New England, whereby there is a difficulty in procuring masts, &c. for the Royal Navy. Also two copies of letters on the same subject. 8 *pages*.
[27 Sept.	44. Proposal -	John Comyns -	Rt. Hon. Sir Robert Walpole.	"For the laying an additional duty of three pence ℘ yard on linnens printed, painted, stain'd or dyed in Great Birtain." 1 *page*.

Date.	Description of Document.	From	To	Purport.
[About 28 Sept.]	45. Account or bill.	—	—	"His Majesty's bill for the servants of his Majesty's Household," from 20 March 1725–6 to 28 Sept. 1726. It is an apothecary's Bill. The names of the patients are given as well as all the items. 27 *pages*.
[About 28 Sept.]	46. Memorandum	—	—	"Gold & silver coined from the end of the year 1714 to the 28 Sepr. 1726." ½ *page*.
[About 29 Sept.]	47. List - -	—	—	Copy of a list of names and amounts for which the warrants of the Lords of the Treasury were required. 24 June to 29 Sept. 1726. 1 *page*.
[? About 29 Sept.]	48. Petition -	James Haye, tailor to the Great Wardrobe.	Rt. Hon. Sir Robert Walpole.	For payment of his bill. 3 *pages*.
5 Oct.	49. Letter - -	Board of Greencloth	Lords of the Treasury.	Encloses two computations of the expense of H.M. Household (1) for three quarters of a year ending at Mich. 1726 and (2) for a year commencing Mich. 1726. 3 *pages*.
6 Oct.	50. Certificate -	Comrs. of the Office of Alienations.	Do. - -	Of the gross and net produce of the office. 1 *page*.
12 Oct.	51. Memorial -	Receiver General of the Deductions of 6*d*. per lib. (Francis Burton).	Do. - -	Encloses copy of a memorial. Has not received any account from the Comrs. of the Admiralty of any deduction upon any payment made by their Lordship's directions. The copy referred to which relates to "deductions upon the rent of the House where the Admiralty Office is now kept," &c. 2 *pages*.
22 Nov.	52. Certificate -	—	—	Of the state of the trial in "Rex *v*. Laugherne." [Julyan Laugherne was convicted for striking a Custom House officer of the Port of Fowey.] Also two letters, one of which is from the Mayor of Fowey and others, pleading for removal of the fine or a mitigation thereof. 4 *pages*.

1726. VOL. CCLVII.

Date.	Description of Document.	From	To	Purport.
28 Nov.	53. Report and opinion.	J. Willes - -	—	That on payment of 2,100*l.* a "non pros." should be entered in the actions commenced against the Executors of Thomas Thruppe; the testator being indebted for duties on run goods amounting to 4,823*l.* 10*s.* 3 *pages.*
6 Dec.	54. Report - -	Secretary - at - War (H. Pelham).	Lords of the Treasury.	For the Lords of the Admiralty to give directions to the Comrs. for Victualling the Navy to furnish provisions for 645 men to be transported to Gibraltar on four of H.M. men-of-war. Also, for the contractor to make an additional supply to the garrison there. 2 *pages.*
15 Dec.	55. Letter - -	J. Burchett - -	John Scrope, Esq.	The Lords of the Admiralty desire him (Mr. Scrope) to inform the Lords of the Treasury of the necessity of paying the wages of the men removed from the "Union" and other ships to ships about to sail on foreign service. 1 *page.*
26 Dec.	56. Do. - -	The Duke of Newcastle.	Lords of the Treasury.	The King has ordered 500*l.* to be issued out of the revenues of Ireland to be distributed among the persons who were losers by the burning of a ship at Glendore in April 1721, on suspicion that she came from Marseilles, which was then infected with the plague. The master having prevaricated is not to participate therein. 2 *pages.*
28 Dec.	57. Representation	The Collector and other Customs officers at Southwold.	[Do.] - -	In favour of John Pugh, a good officer at Dunwich, who was diligent in preventing smuggling. Also seven affidavits. 9 *pages.*
29 Dec.	58. Letter -	George Hathaway -	The Rt. Hon. Sir Robert Walpole.	Encloses two schemes for lotteries, viz., one with nine blanks to a prize, the other four blanks to a prize. Also the enclosure. 2 *pages.*

1726. VOL. CCLVII.

Date.	Description of Document.	From	To	Purport.
1726.	59. Memorial -	William Hamilton, H.M. Almoner in Scotland.	Lords of the Treasury.	For 40*l*. 3*s*. 5*d*. sterling to make up the difference on the allowance upon the Establishment, which was increased according to his Majesty's life. 1 *page*.
[1726 or later.]	60. Do. - -	John Lane, Surveyor of the Horse Guards.	Do. - -	For a warrant for 1,118*l*. 11*s*. 6*d*. for rebuilding and repairing the Office of the Paymaster General, the Office of Commissary General of the Musters, the Office of the Comrs. of Chelsea Hospital, &c. [Thomas Ripley, Esq., is mentioned as Controller of the Works, and he seems to have been appointed 14 April 1726. See *Minute Book*, Vol. 25, p. 168*c*.]
[? 1726.]	61. Petition -	Magdalen Jollyvet, widow of Evert Jollyvet.	Do. - -	For three-quarters of her husband's pension at 50*l*. per ann. 1 *page*.
[1726 or later.]	62. Do. - -	Evan Morgan, Victualler.	The Hon. Richard Arundell, Esq., Surveyor Genl. and the rest of the Comrs. of Works.	For an allowance of 20*l*. He kept a victualling house under the Court of Wards in Westminster, for the use of the footmen of the members of Parliament, and having to move his beer out of the cellar it was spoilt, &c. 1 *page*. [Arundell was appointed 14 April 1726. See *Minute Book*, Vol. 25, p. 168*b*.]
[? 1726 or 1727.]	63. Memorial -	Arthur Van Sittart, of Shottesbrooke, Berks, Esq.	Lords of the Treasury.	Two memorials for rent due from Mote Park, which is laid into the Great Park at Windsor. 2 *pages*.

1727.

VOL. CCLVIII. 1727. JANUARY–MARCH.

[? 1727.] 1. "Proposal relating to the Duties on Wines." States that there is a variation in "the four subsidies according to the Port of importation as London or an out port." Upon a moderate computation the quantity of wine imported into the outports is $\frac{1}{3}$ of what is imported into London. The Crown loses 18,747*l.* 12*s.* 8*d.* annually by what is imported into the outports. Proposes that the outports should be charged the same as London. Also makes other proposals for no other design than to put the wine trade upon the same foundation throughout England. The proposal is followed by various calculations and examples. Undated, but entries for retail for the year 1726 are mentioned, and it is after that date. 7½ *pages*.

[? 1726 or 1727.] 2. Petition to the King of George Berkeley, Doctor of Divinity, Dean of Derry, and President of Saint Paul's College in Bermuda. His Majesty, by letters patent of 3 June 11th year of his reign (1725), founded a college in Bermuda, consisting of a President and nine fellows for the education of American Missionaries and for supplying the British Plantations with clergy. The House of Commons addressed the King to make provision for the same out of the lands in the Island of St Christopher, yielded by France to Great Britain, by the Treaty of Utrecht. Prays his Majesty to direct the passing of [? a warrant for such provi]sion out of the lands, as his Majesty should see fit, for the maintenance of the President and Fellows. Signed. [The date is uncertain, but the scheme for founding the college was unsuccesful, and had entirely failed in 1728 (apparently for want of money) and it would be before that year. See a Biographical Dictionary published 1784, Vol. II., p. 170, under the name "Berkeley."] 1 *page*, 4to.

[After 1726.] 3. "The methods used by the smuglers in the illegal importation of goods and other frauds in the Customs. What further powers and provisions are wanted by law to prevent such frauds with the reasons why it may be adviseable to pass such a law."

The document consists of three columns headed:—

(1) The frauds practised, (2) The remedy proposed, and (3) Why such remedy may be reasonable. 7 *large pages*.

[After 1726.] 4. Several papers (mostly copies) arising from a petition of Valentine Brown, commonly called Lord Viscount Kenmare, whose mansion (Ross Castle) at the reduction of Ireland in 1691 had been used as barracks for quartering soldiers. There was also a good dwelling-house adjoining to the Castle, which was just finished in 1688, and is irreparably damnified. Petitioner resided in England during his minority and his friends did not think fit to complain; but on the death of his father, petitioner came into quiet possession of the estate of the family and he is put to great inconvenience for

1727. VOL. CCLVIII.

want of a proper habitation. Killarney, a market town (whereof petitioner is owner) lies within two miles, is a thoroughfare, and is in all respects more proper for the reception of soldiers. Petitioner's house stands in an island in a lough or lake up in a nook of the country. If it be thought necessary to erect a barrack in that part of the country, petitioner, for a reasonable price, will set out and allow ground for that end in the Town of Killarney. Prays for the restoration of the mansion, or for a sum sufficient to build a suitable house or for an annual pension.

The papers include (1) copy of an Order in Council of 5 May 1722, referring the petition to the Lord Lieut., also the petition; (2) a letter from the Lord Lieut. referring the same to the Lords Justices; (3) a reference by them to the Attorney and Solicitor General; (4) their report which states that Sir Valentine deceased and Nicholas Brown, petitioner's father, were both attainted of treason, and the estate vested in their late Majesties King William and Queen Mary, and the reversion in fee, &c. of the petitioner became vested in trustees for the sale of forfeited estates in Ireland, and were by them sold and conveyed to John Asgill, Esq., for 3,070*l.* 14*s.* 4½*d.* purchase money. On 30th March 1726 Asgill demised the castle, town, and Island of Ross to Richard Hedges and Murtagh Griffin, Esq., for the life of the petitioner. As the petitioner is now become entitled thereto, an order to satisfy him should be made; but he was not entitled to any compensation till his title accrued by the death of his father.

(5.) "Surveyor General's Report on the affair of Val. Brown, commonly called Lord Kenmare," giving a valuation of the buildings, &c.

(6.) "Memorial of Val. Brown, comonly called Lord Kenmare."

There is also an affidavit on the same subject. 26 *pages.*

Another set of most of these papers, some of which are originals. 20 *pages.*

3 and 5 Jan. 5. "Report of the Commissrs of Stamp Dutys relating to the information given by Reay Sabourn touching frauds in the Apprentice Duty" in Scotland. Mr Bowles, the solicitor for the Commissioners, attended Mr Sabourn, but could not prevail with him to give satisfaction to the particulars required. Mr Sabourn and one Samuel Hodgson, concerned in making the discoveries, aim at procuring a commission to inspect registers, &c., proposing thereby to find out many frauds; but the Head Distributor for North Britain, the Comr's solicitor there, and their Distributor for Edinburgh, have each of them a power to inspect public books, registers, &c. It was found that these inspections were not effectual for preventing frauds. Are of opinion that the putting the laws in execution against such as are detected of defrauding the Stamp or Apprentice Duties is a proper expedient for preventing that practice and preserving the revenue: and accordingly directions have been formerly given to Mr Bowles to prosecute offenders, and particularly those against the Apprentice Duties. The produce of the duties on indentures in Scotland, they conceive, is too small to bear the expense of any new officers.

1727. VOL. CCLVIII.

Accompanied by (1) a memorial of Mr Hodgson on the same subject, dated 5 Jan. 1726–7; (2) an interloquitur or sentence of Lord Grange pronounced Decr 21, 1726; and (3) a "scheme" referred to in the memorial. 5 *pages*.

9 Jan. 6. Report of the Surveyor General (Philip Gybbon) to the Lords of the Treasury, on the representation of Mr Evan Lloyd, who offered to become the purchaser of the right of the Crown to the Estate of Mr Morgan Whitley, formerly Receiver General of Taxes for Chester and North Wales, who died greatly indebted to the Crown, against whom an extent issued in A.D. 1700. By Inquisition he was found seised in fee of an Estate called Parkey, in the co. of Denbigh. Several *levaris* have since issued to which no returns have been made. Has perused the Inquisition whereby it is found that Morgan Whitley was seized in fee of a capital messuage called Plas Dio [commonly called Parkey] with appurtenances in Bedwall, Pickhill, and Abingburg Vaur, in the co. of Denbigh, containing 50 acres of arable land, 20 acres of meadow, and 50 of pasture or thereabouts of the annual value of 40*l.* The original debt of the Receiver was 45,007*l.* 19*s.* 11½*d.*, and there has since been paid into the Exchequer 14,342*l.* 9*s.*, and 18,208*l.* 11*s.* 3*d.* was thought by the Comrs and Agents for Taxes reasonable to be allowed him on his several cravings. In an affidavit referred to, the Estate is estimated to be of the annual value of 40*l.* Lands in Denbighshire are estimated to sell for at least twenty years' purchase. The Comrs and Agents for Taxes observe that all estates of Receivers, seized as aforesaid, have been usually sold before the King's Remembrancer, and the money paid into the Exchequer and applied to the proper aids. 9 Jan. 1726.

The representation referred to. 4 *pages*.

10 Jan. 7. Representation by the Excise Comrs, Scotland, to the Lords of the Treasury; as well upon matters previously represented as upon others not hitherto communicated to the Treasury, with a view to a parliamentary remedy. Describe their difficulties with regard to the English barrel, and the difference between it and 12 gallons Scots. Are of opinion that the 34 gallons, English, ought to be the measure of the Brewers' charge, and that the allowance given is of too long a standing to be taken away otherwise than by a declaration of Parliament. It is doubtful whether by the present Malt Act they are empowered to compound with private families otherwise than in England; although the duty be but half as much as in England. Are of opinion that they (the Comrs) should have further power to compound, not only with private families, but even for whole islands, parishes, and districts: the inhabitants are so poor that the duties will scarcely exceed the salaries of the officers. When informations are laid before the Justices of the Peace for frauds, or offences committed against the laws of excise, the judgments given are generally such as rather to encourage these frauds than to deter others from committing the like offences. The officers are extremely discouraged in their duty, as the justices generally reduce the penalty so low that little or nothing comes to the officers' share,

1727 VOL. CCLVIII.

and frequently the Justices acquit the offenders from any penalty, though the proof be never so clear. The remedy has been to prosecute in the Exchequer or some other Court at Edinburgh; but many of the offenders are so poor that the carrying prosecutions through those Courts (where the penalties are never mitigated) would ruin many people, and be very chargeable to the Government, for few of the people would be able to pay the penalties in their full. Would propose a mean between these two extremes by giving them (the Com^rs^) power to compound for penalties upon the desire made to them by the offenders before the Courts had determined the matter. Refer to frauds in connexion with receipts given under the Act 1 [Geo. I.] for arms surrendered, the persons surrendering the same being entitled to receive the full value of the arms from Collectors of the Land Tax or Excise.

Send the clauses which they desire to have added to the Malt Bill or some other Bill. 7 *pages.*

11 Jan. 8. Memorial of Sidney Godolphin, Esq., Auditor of Wales, to the Lords of the Treasury. The Duke and Duchess of Bolton obtained a warrant for the renewal of a lease from the Prince of Wales of the Pre and Post Fines and of the King's silver, &c. within the several counties of South Wales. Their Lordships have lately granted the "same fines" to "one Mr Rock within several counties of North Wales, [and memorialist] was dubious how to act, and had asked their Lordships' directions, but had not yet received their orders: asks directions. 11 Jan. 1726." 1 *page.*

14 Jan. 9. Proposal signed "W. Edgell" and "Robert Bonell" addressed to the Rt Hon. Sir Robert Walpole for raising 2,500,000*l.* No interest was to be paid for this annuity but such as should commence from Midsummer 1734 and continue till Midsummer 1755, and be paid (if the nominees so long live) at the rate of 30*l.* per cent. per annum. The Sinking Fund was to be charged therewith unless the House of Commons provide otherwise. The scheme is set out in figures. 14 Jan. 1726.

Accompanied by a letter from them to Chr. Tilson, Esq., on the same subject. 4½ *pages.*

17 Jan. 10. Report of the Comrs for managing the stamp duties as to the steps taken by them with respect to the prosecution of the Advocates in Scotland since the 2d of August 1714. Having been informed by one of their officers, on 30 Oct. 1724, that some Advocates had lately been admitted in the Court of Session in Scotland without paying the duty of 40*s.* charged on every such admission, they ordered Mr Bowles, their solicitor, to consider what would prevent that practice for the future. He advised that, as prosecutions would be difficult, application should be made to the Court of Session to make an order thereon. Have been informed by their Solicitor that, upon an application to be made by them (the Comrs) to that Court, they would make an order to secure the duty in time coming, and to recover what is past. Have signed the representation of which the enclosed is a copy. 17 Jan. 1726.

The copy referred to. Dated 12 Jan. 1726. 3 *pages.*

VOL. CCLVIII.

1727.

1 Feb. 11. Thomas Tickell to Mr Secretary Clutterbuck. Has laid before the Lords Justices (Ireland) his letter, enclosing the King's warrant for 335*l.* 14*s.* 3¼*d.*, to Lord Shannon, to reimburse him "for so much money paid to the public by his Lordship, on the account of his absence from Ireland in 1720 and 1721." Their Excellencies being apprehensive lest some observations may be made upon the reciting part of the warrant, when it is produced in the House of Commons, have consulted the Prime Serjeant, and the Attorney and Solicitor General, who have all confirmed their Excellencies in their opinion, that notwithstanding Lord Shannon's reasonable claim and his Majesty's undoubted power to order this money by his Royal letter, yet there was reason to fear it would raise a clamour in the House of Commons. Persons might not be wanting there to construe this, his Majesty's favour, as a virtual exemption of a particular person from paying a public tax, and perhaps they might propose a clause in the next money bill for preventing the like for the future. Proposes, on the part of their Excellencies, that another letter should be obtained without alleging the reasons mentioned in the reciting part of the present warrant.

The warrant referred to. 3½ *pages.*

[? About 1 Feb.] 12. Memorial of the Governor and Court of Assistants of the York Buildings Company, on behalf of themselves and the Company, to the Lords of the Treasury. Have attended the Comrs for the forfeited Estates in Scotland, and represented their claims, supported by the opinion of the Solicitor General and of Mr Fane, their counsel. The Comrs have made up the accounts of the four first estates purchased, and also of Fingash, another estate purchased by the Company, and have drawn them to a balance of 9,734*l.* 5*s.* 3½*d.*, without having allowed the Company any consideration for tithes and casual rent of Winton, &c. The Company is overcharged 2,071*l.* 11*s.* The Comrs have issued their precepts for 9,734*l.* 5*s.* 3½*d.*, being the balance without any allowance, &c. What is of great consequence to the Company is, to have the case of the two years' rent, which was given to such of the Company's servants as remained dutiful to the King, fully considered, and relief given. Are advised that their tenants have good right thereto. In that case the amount must be deducted from the Company's debt due to Government.

Since the Comrs closed the accounts, the Company have received another case from their agents in Scotland, showing that the tiends of Winton did not belong to the forfeited Earl, which they ask their Lps to take into consideration. These tiends are charged to the Company by the sales at the same rate as the lands, although tiends upon the best title are never valued above nine years purchase in Scotland, and if redeemable at six or under according to their tenure. The case and circumstances of the Company at this time press very hard for their Lordships' compassion and protection.

"Recd 1 of Feb. 17$\frac{26}{7}$." 1 *large page.*

3 Feb. 13. Memorial of the same to the same. The Company, by the mismanagement of Sir John Meres, their late Governor, being

1727. Vol. CCLVIII.

involved in great debts and difficulties, appointed a Committee to examine into their (the Company's) affairs to discover the unwarrantable measures Sir John had entered into.

The Committee have found that he was guilty of a very great breach of trust in misrepresenting in his speeches at the General Courts the true state of the Company's affairs, by altering the minutes of several General Courts some days after they were adjourned, and thereby quite perverting their sense and intention, and by the misapplication of their money. A narrative of which unwarrantable proceedings is annexed. Lay the case before their Lordships, and hope they will give such remedy by extent or aid, or otherwise, as may be proportioned to their (the Company's) great loss, &c.

The narrative referred to, which consists principally of extracts from the Minute Books of the York Buildings Company, observations thereon, &c. 22 *pages and* 4 *parts of pages.*

3 Feb. 14. The Board of Ordnance to the Lords of the Treasury. Respecting a petition of Col. Moody for 732*l.* 3*s.* 4*d.*, the value alleged of houses and lands purchased by him at Placentia, which have been since taken to erect forts upon; and respecting a petition of William Touchack, merchant, for 80*l.*, being the alleged value of a house, &c. purchased by him at Placentia, taken for the same purpose. Wrote to Mr Horneck, their engineer at Placentia, and to Mr Herbert, who acted as overseer of the fortifications erected there, to give an account of what they knew thereof. Send the report returned by Mr. Horneck and a certificate by Mr Herbert. Dated 3 Feb. 1726.

Accompanied by a copy of the same, and two copies of the papers referred to, viz.:—

(1.) A letter signed Wm Horneck, dated 20 Dec. 1726, relating to Col. Moody's demand of 732*l.*, which, he alleged, was the value of houses and lands purchased by him at Placentia, and taken or seized upon for his Majesty's service to erect fortifications upon. The letter is from William Horneck to the Board of Ordnance He says the area of the Stone Tower is about 100 ft. English (being about a quarter of an English acre), and the value of the land in that country is generally estimated by what the French call *chaloupe de grave,* which signifies as much beach, or other ground, as will serve to cure such a quantity of fish as one chaloupe, or fishing boat will catch in the summer season. The common estimate the French gave there was six fathom in front upon the waterside; and 200 in depth, which contains an English acre. The Stone Tower Mr Herbert erected was upon the ground of one Chevalier. The price of the fee simple was valued at 20*l.* and some small advance for the cabins. If the gentlemen who make these claims can produce any orders from their honors empowering their officers to take the lands and houses for H.M. service, no doubt the sufferers ought to have reparation; but if not, the demand is a very great abuse. All the planters at Placentia would be glad to divide 700*l.* amongst them and think themselves nobly paid.

1727. VOL. CCLVIII.

When he (the writer) lived there these houses and lands, represented as of vast consequence, were pulled down by the soldiers and inhabitants, as things abandoned, and Col. Moody gave them to any one who would possess them. He (the writer) and the officers refused to accept the possession of what has lately arisen to so great a value. Cannot forbear admiring this gentleman's making them (the Board of Ordnance) the purchasers of his land thirteen years after he was willing to give them away for nothing. If Col. Gledhill has taken away the possession of any of these gentlemen, he ought to be regularly sued at law for the same, as other Governors of plantations have been.

(2.) The certificate of Humphrey Herbert, who valued the cabin which he took down occupied by Mr William Touchack at about 12*l.* or 14*l.* 13 *pages.*

4 Feb. 15. Order made by the Lords of the Committee for the affairs of Jersey and Guernsey, to whom a representation of the States of the Island of Jersey, relating to the settling the value of the English and French coin in that Island, &c., had been referred. Ordering the representation and copies of two orders in council to be referred to the Lords of the Treasury to examine and report thereon. Dated, Council Chamber, 4 Feb. 1726.

Accompanied by the papers above referred to, respecting the value, &c. of French crowns, British crowns and Half-crowns, Liards, or small French coins of copper or base metal, and also respecting the pay, &c. of the soldiers. 11 *pages.*

8 Feb. 16. Report of A. Cracherode to the Lords of the Treasury, on the petition of Francis Medlicott, Esq., Deputy Ranger of Enfield Chace, who was indicted for assault and battery by John Cogdall and Wm Harvey, whom he found loaded with poles and furzes which they had cut in the Chace. In endeavouring to arrest them he wounded Cogdall. They are both common notorious trespassers. The petitioner prayed for *nolle prosequi* to be entered. Is of opinion that the suffering such a prosecution to go on would be a great discouragement to all his Majesty's officers in Forests, &c., and that a warrant to the Attorney General for a *nolle prosequi* should be granted.

Accompanied by the petition, two affidavits, copy of the indictments, affidavit of the conviction of Cogdall for the trespass in cutting the furzes, and a summons to William Harvey. 9 *pages.*

8 Feb. 17. "An account of such of the National Debts incurred before the 25th of December 1716 as are redeemable, with the interest or annuity attending the same, and when such interest or annuity will be reduced & when the same are redeemable." *Addressed:*— "To the Honoble the Knights, Citizens & Burgesses in Parliament assembled." In tabular form. Dated 8 Feb. 1726. 1 *large sheet.*

8 Feb. 18. Report of the Barons of the Exchequer of Scotland to the Lords of the Treasury on the petition of Sir David Nairne, Secretary of the Order of the Thistle, appointed by Royal warrant on 29 Jan. 1703-4, for life, with a pension of 300*l.* yearly, the latter

1727. VOL. CCLVIII.

granted by letters of Privy Seal of Scotland. Are of opinion that he has a just title to his salary. Edinburgh, Exchequer Chamber, 8 Feb. 1726–7.

The petition and a copy of the warrant. 8½ *pages.*

8 Feb. 19. Order in Council on the petition of George Eames, Gent., relating to the payment of 140*l.* for convicting Bridstock Weaver and William Ingram of piracy, referring the same to the Lords of the Treasury for their report.

Also the petition and a certificate. 8 Feb. 1726. 4¼ *pages.*

13 Feb. 20. Report of the Barons of the Exchequer of Scotland to the Lords of the Treasury. Have examined the warrant annexed for the royal signature for granting and conveying "to James Ballantine the lands of Hollinglie, and others lying in the parish of Innerleithen, Lordship of Ettrick forest, & Sheriffdom of Selkirk, upon the resignations of Robert & James Rutherfoords." Find this signature contains a taxing of the marriage of the heirs of James Ballantine & successors. The valued rent of these lands is 33*l.* 6*s.* 8*d.* sterl And "though, by taxing the marriage thereof, according to the rules settled by the Privy Seal for taxing of lands holding *few cum marritagio,* the Crown accepts of less than what it would be, by the strict rules of law, entitled to; which is two years' free rent of the heir's whole lands, after discounting of the debts of the said heir: yet because what is taxed is a certainty, & certainly affects the said lands, without the trouble of these processes, which are requisite where the marriage remains untaxed, it hath been, by practise, held a reasonable way for the Crown to exercise its bounty, to such of its vassels as his Majesty is inclined to extend his grace and favour to."

No few duties or other casualties due to the Crown are discharged by this signature. 13 Feb. 1726–7. 1 *page.*

17 Feb. 21. Report of Anthony Cracherode, Esq., Solicitor for the affairs of the Treasury, to the Lords of the Treasury, on the petition of John Powell, of the parish of South Myms, Middlesex, farrier, who was fined 10*l.* for an assault upon Henry Lambeth, and committed to the New Prison at Clerkenwell until the fine was paid, &c. He was also fined 10*l.* for another assault and committed to prison until the fine was paid. Petitioner has been a prisoner since the 11th of Oct. 1725, and prays to have his fines discharged. Affidavits annexed confirm his statement that he is quite unable to pay the fines, and it would be an act of great goodness and charity in their Lordships to grant a warrant to the Attorney General to acknowledge satisfaction.

The petition, two affidavits, and a certificate. 7 *pages.*

[? About 18 Feb.] 22. Petition of Marmaduke Coghill, Esq., Doctor of Laws, and Judge of the Courts of Prerogative and Faculties in the Kingdom of Ireland, to the King. King James I., in his twentieth year, by letters patent under the great seal of Ireland, constituted Christopher, Archbishop of Armagh and his successors forever Judges

1727. Vol. CCLVIII.

or Presidents of the courts above named, with power to appoint any person to execute the office. The King also granted to the Archbishop, for the execution of the office, one moiety of the taxes of Faculties. Michael, Archbishop of Armagh, on 13 June 1699, appointed petitioner as his substitute, and granted him all the fees due. The King is entitled to a moiety of the taxes of all faculties, which moiety (as was conceived) was granted by King James to the Archbishop and his successors. All other fees, except the moiety of the King's moiety, were granted by the Archbishop to petitioner, in like manner as to his predecessors; and the Archbishops have always received a moiety of the moiety of the King's part, and the predecessors of petitioner have received the other moiety. Soon after petitioner was constituted Commissary of the Courts, the moiety of the King's part of the Taxes of Faculties was demanded of petitioner by the Clerk of the Faculties, he alleging that only a moiety of the King's moiety was granted to the Archbishop, and not the whole moiety: and petitioner being unwilling to have a suit with the Crown, paid into the Exchequer, not only what he had received, but also what his father, Sir John Coghill, had received when Commissary; and the King's moiety or proportion of the taxes of Faculties has ever since been paid to the Clerk of the Faculties in Chancery. The office of Commissary of the Courts, or Substitute of his Majesty's Courts of Prerogative and Faculties, is of great consequence and dignity; but no salary or allowance has been settled for its support, except the fees and perquisites, which are so small that they will not support the petitioner. Prays for a grant for life of that part of the taxes of Faculties which was received by his predecessors, amounting to about 25*l.* per annum, and that all the sums paid to the Clerk of the Faculties, since petitioner was made Commissary, may be repaid to him.

On the back is,—"In Lord Lieut's of 28 Jan. 1726."

Two affidavits in support of the petition. Also a certificate, dated 18 Feb. 1726, from the Deputy Auditor General that upon search made in his office he does not find any account passed of the Clerk of the Faculties since the year 1700. 4¾ *pages.*

22 Feb. 23. Return to Parliament indorsed:—"An acco^t^ of the gross produce of the severall branches of the Civil List revenues with all deductions for charges of management or any other acco^t^ whatsoever before the same was paid into the Exchequer. With an acco^t^ of the net produce paid in by the severall officers from ye 1st day of Augt 1714 to Michas. 1725: distinguishing each year. Stated from the acco^t^ thereof collected from the proper offices and herewith delivered into this Hono^ble^ House under the numbers 1, 2, 3, 4, 5, 6, 7, 8." The paper is signed "M. Frecker," and dated 22 Feb. 1726-7.

There is also a duplicate of the first page with some little variation. 4 *pages.*

10 March. 24. The Governor and Assistants of the York Buildings Company to J. Scrope, Esq. If they do not find relief at this time, they will

1727. Vol. CCLVIII.

be inevitably ruined. Have enclosed a short account between the public and the Company. The most considerable article of the Company's credit is left blank, and yet the Company has overpaid for the Scotts' estates. In the account all the controversy about the Scotts' estates is reduced to four heads (specified), which they pray the Lords of the Treasury to take into consideration. The account of Widdington they will prepare and lay before their Lordships on Monday next. Propose a clause to be obtained from Parliament to settle the Company's accounts, and for conveying the estates in Scotland by bargain and sale, to be enrolled in England, in the same manner as Widdington is to be conveyed. The Company have paid the money decreed by the Com[rs] upon the claims of the creditors, and have taken assignments of the "Decrees." It is hoped that the Company will not be obliged to pay the money mentioned in the Decrees into the Exchequer, from whence it must be again issued to them. York Buildings House, 10 March 1726–7.

The account referred to. The names of the places where the property is situate are:—Panmure, Winton, Kilsyth, East Reston, Tingath, Pitcarne, Marishal, Linlithgow, and Southesque. 4 *pages.*

23 March. 25. Copy of letter of the Lord Lieut. of Ireland to the Lords of the Treasury, returning the petition of Marmaduke Coghill, Esq., LL.D., and Judge of the Courts of Prerogative and Faculties in Ireland, praying for a grant, for his life, of that part of the taxes of Faculties which his predecessors in office received, amounting to about 25*l.* per annum. Had referred the petition to the Lords Justices, who had referred it to the Attorney and Solicitor General whose report he encloses. In favour of the petitioner. Arlington Street, March 23, 1726.

The report of the Attorney and Solicitor General on the petition of Marmaduke Coghill, Esq., Doctor of Laws and Judge of His Majesty's Court of Prerogative and Faculties in Ireland, to his Majesty. The Report sets out the effect of the Act of 28 Hen. VIII., viz.: that the King was to have one moiety of the taxes of all Faculties and the other parts of the taxes to be divided between the Archbishop of Canterbury, the Lord Chancellor or Keeper of the Great Seal, the King's Clerk of the Faculties in Chancery, and the Lord Archbishop's Clerk of the Faculties, and that the Act is made of force in Ireland. King James I. by letters patent dated 10 April in the 20th year of his reign appointed Christopher, Archbishop of "Ardmagh" and his successors Judges of the Court of Prerogative and Faculties in Ireland with one moiety of the "Taxes of Faculties" growing to his Majesty out of that Court for the charges of that Commission. Further they find that the Archbishops of Armagh have ever since the grant from King James I. received the moiety of the King's part and that Sir John Coghill, the petitioner's predecessor, received the remaining moiety of the King's part of the Taxes of Faculties, not granted to the Archbishops of Armagh, and that petitioner's predecessors since 1660 have received the moiety without accounting to the Crown, and insisted that the same was granted to the Archbishops of

1727. Vol. CCLVIII.

Armagh and allowed by them to their Commissaries but they (the Attorney and Solicitor) cannot find any such grant. [Some other particulars are given.] The petitioner's office of Judge or Commissary of the Prerogative and Faculties is an office of great dignity and consequence and requires constant attendance, and the security of the greatest part of the personal property of the Kingdom depends upon the execution of the office by a person of great abilities and known integrity. The petitioner has no salary annexed to the office, and the fees amount to no more than 3 or 400*l.* per ann. On the whole, are of opinion that only one fourth of the taxes of Faculties rated above 4*l.* belongs to the Crown since the grant by King James the First, and that his Majesty can recover the sum received on account of the one-fourth part from the Clerk of the Faculties in Chancery or such persons as have received the same, and may grant the same to the petitioner: also his Majesty's share of the Taxes of Faculties to the petitioner for life. 24 Feb. 1726. 7 *pages.*

[*See also* the petition on p. 444, No. 22.]

27 March. 26. "An accompt of the debt which at Lady day last was due and owing in the Treasurer of the Chambers Office, unto His Ma[ts] serv[ts] & others, payable there, distinguished under general heads of expence, and by the several quarters in w[ch] the same became due & payable."

Signed:—"C. Stanhope." March 27, 1727. 8 *pages.*

29 March. 27. The Chevalier Dupetitbois to "Milord." Upon the representation which he (the writer) made to the King of the cause of his coming from France and seeking an asylum in this country, and upon the offer which he made of his services, the King accorded to him a gratuity of 200*l.* sterling. Lord Townshend is charged to speak to his "Excellency" thereon. For five weeks he (the writer) went daily to the house of his Excellency to ask this favour, but on account of his illness he could not give him (the writer) a public audience. Prays him to give orders for a speedy payment of the money. Dated "A Londre, ce 29 Mars 1727." (French.)

In the Minute Book, Vol. 25, p. 290*r*, 19 April 1727, is:—"Write to the Exchequer for the following issues * * * To Marq[s] Pettibour 200[li]." 3 *pages.*

31 March. 28. J. Blenman, Attorney General [? at Barbadoes], to his Excellency.

Has received from M[r] Secretary a warrant from M[r] Lascelles, collector of Bridge Town, to M[r] Lenoir, appointing him collector of the "Hole Town" in the room of M[r] Kempster, deceased; has also received a copy of M[r] Lascelles 49th Instruction from the Com[rs] of Customs and the 18th and 26th Instructions of M[r] Dunbar, Surveyor General of this Island, &c.; together with M[r] Dunbar's letter to M[r] Lascelles, all which papers his Excellency has referred to him (the Attorney General) to give his opinion whether M[r] Dunbar by his Instructions can lawfully depute M[r] Lascelles, or any other person, to grant a warrant there to any officer of the Customs? If he can,—

1727. Vol. CCLVIII.

whether it ought not to be done by a deputation and not by a letter? but if he cannot (as there is now an absolute necessity for a collector of the Hole Town), how the post may be filled at present till Mr. Dunbar shall appoint some fit person for it? Has carefully perused the several papers, and observes, previous to answering the question, that he conceives Mr Lascelles's 49th Instruction gives him no power at all in this respect; for the further Instructions he is to receive from the Surveyor General plainly relate only to his duty in his own employment, &c. To come to Mr Dunbar's Instructions, as he has undoubtedly full power in case of death, absence, or suspension of any officer of the Customs to appoint some fit person in his stead, so it is obvious that he has not thereby any express power of delegating the same to another. Takes it that authorities of this kind, which carry with them a trust, ought not to be extended beyond the plain import of the words in which they are expressed, nor is it likely that the Honourable Board would have omitted to give such a power of delegation had they intended it should be practised, &c.

Heretofore there were two Commissioners of the Customs for this Island who always had this power, but afterwards a Surveyor General and a Collector of the Bridge Town were appointed in their room, and these two "Officers," whilst possessed by Mr Edwards and Mr Perry, who were the first that ever enjoyed them, had, at different times, according to their respective interests at Home, the power now spoken of; but he (the Attorney General) never understood that either of those gentlemen could, or ever did, take upon himself to delegate it to the others.

Taking it, therefore, that Mr Dunbar cannot in strictness give Mr Lascelles a power to appoint an officer of the Customs there, especially by letter only, the question will be: How any vacancy shall be supplied in the absence of the Surveyor General? Apprehends this is easily answered, seeing that it cannot be doubted but his Excellency may for his Majesty's service well appoint a person to act in such an office till the gentleman empowered by the Comrs shall be in the way to do it, or till one be appointed from home. To evince which, he needs only suppose that there were a vacancy of the place of Collector for the Bridge (who is allowed to be the principal officer of the Customs next to the Surveyor), which is a post that must necessarily be forthwith filled, now it is not to be supposed that his Excellency would sit still whilst his Majesty suffered in his revenue without exercising that authority which has been so worthily exerted on all other occasions, and this being the case of a Collector, though of another district, carries with it the same reason and requires the like vigilance.

But, after all, it may not be unworthy of his Excellency's most prudent consideration, that as the officers of the Customs are answerable for their own behaviour, and not so immediately under his care, and as Mr Dunbar seems to insist in his letter to Mr Lascelles, on his Excellency having signified to him his intention not to interfere or concern himself with the customs or officers of it whether his Excellency may not choose to leave them to their own methods

1727. Vol. CCLVIII.

rather than give them an opportunity of interrupting his Excellency in his other more important affairs of Government. 31 March 1727.

The four papers above referred to, and four other papers on the same subject. 14 *pages.*

VOL. CCLIX. April—August.

---

6 April. 1. Memorial of the Court of Directors of the Bank of England to the Lords of the Treasury. As to money imprested to their chief Cashier for charges of management, and the allowance made for fees paid to the Treasury and Exchequer: also as to fees paid to the Auditors. Pray for a further sum to be imprested to the Cashier. Signed: David Le Gros, Secretary. 6 April 1727.

Minuted:—"15 July 1725. Mr Auditor Harley's Report of the 5 December 1722 on the demands of the Bank of England for the charges of the annuity offices there for the 2 years ended at Michas 1719 is again read, and my Lords order a warrant to be prepared for allowing 6,918^l 8^s 3^d conformable thereto: but see the Minute formerly taken about ye Auditor's fees being part of the said allowance and take care that the warrant be adapted thereunto." 1 *page.*

8 April. 2. Report of the Surveyor General (Phil. Gybbon) to the Lords of the Treasury. Has considered the petition of Sir John Guise, Bart., for the lease of the Office of Water-Bailiff or Conservator of the River Severn, "who is willing to decline that part of his petition which relates to the waste grounds upon or near the said river."

Petitioner has produced an attested copy of a grant of 23 Oct., 26 Charles 2, to Sir Thomas Monins, Bart., of the Office of Water-Bailiff of the River Severn, with all fees, &c., at a rent of 10*l.* per ann., which expired in 1708. By a parliamentary survey in 1652, this office was estimated at (communibus annis) 560*l.*, viz., that part of the river above Gloucester Bridge at 200*l.*, and that below the bridge at 300*l.* per ann. Finds by the books in his office that Mr Chomley (one of his predecessors) reported in 1718 on the petition of John Appletree, Esq., that a fine of 3,000*l.* might be a reasonable consideration for a lease of 31 years of this office, at the old rent of 10*l.* per ann.; whereupon the petitioner represented to the Treasury Board that the rent reserved by the former grant had never been "answered" to the Crown, and that the fishery of the River Severn was almost destroyed, and therefore desired that the lease might pass without fine. An affidavit of the same petitioner states that Sir Thomas Monins was, by his suits and expenses, in the execution of that office, rendered incapable of paying the rent, of which his widow was discharged by privy seal, and that since the decay of the Fishery, the fishermen would not pay above 1*s.* per annum for a licence, for which they formerly gave ten. Some gentlemen of note of Gloucester, Worcester, and Salop have informed him that they cannot certainly determine the annual profit, it entirely depending on the power with which the officer shall be invested; that the office may be exercised with great oppression and cannot be of service for the preservation of the Fishery, the like power of conservatorship being vested in the Justices of the Peace of the said counties by several Acts of Parliament.

The petitioner alleges that the Justices do not take proper care for the preservation of the Fishery, which will be totally destroyed unless a water-bailiff is appointed by the Crown, and that he is not willing to pay any fine, nor more than the ancient rent of 10*l.* per ann. As several Acts of Parliament have been made for the preservation of the Fishery, is in doubt whether his Majesty can now appoint a water-bailiff, with the same powers and privileges as were formerly granted, and cannot say whether any, and what, fine is reasonable. Supposes their Lordships will take the opinion of Mr Attorney or Mr Solicitor General on this occasion, and they will be better able to judge on what terms this office may be granted. 8 April 1727.

Also the petition. 4 *pages.*

[? About 11 April.] 3. An application to the Lords of the Treasury to postpone till Christmas the payment of certain sums for which the executors of Nicholas More, Esq., as a surety, had become answerable, in consequence of an embezzlement by one Milns, who was connected with the Wine Licence Office.

Also another paper much to the same effect; and the Gazette in which the sale of More's Estate is announced.

Minuted:—"11 Aprill 1727. My Lords can do nothing in this." 4 *pages.*

12 April. 4. Report of the Surveyor General (Philip Gybbon) to the Lords of the Treasury on the petition of Sir Thomas Frankland, Bart., who desires to set part of his rails four feet into the Park leading from St James's to Hyde Park, for the security of his house; and to make a door into the park, in the middle of his house, instead

1727. Vol. CCLIX.

of one now at the north-west corner of it. The Surveyor General thinks that what is asked for may be granted by a licence during his Majesty's pleasure.

Also the petition. 2 *pages.*

14 April. 5. Report of the Postmasters General (Ed. Carteret and E. Harrison) to the Lords of the Treasury. Having received the King's warrant for settling two packet-boats, for the conveyance of letters and packets between Gibraltar and Lisbon, or some other part of Portugal, for the manning the vessels, &c.; represent that one of the two packet-boats, lately employed on the Groin station, having sailed for Portugal, they gave immediate orders to have her stationed between Lisbon and Gibraltar. Have directed the Commander of the other Groin Packet-boat (which is detained by the Spanish Governor at Corunna) to repair forthwith to Lisbon, with directions for the Agent there to hire for him the most convenient ship for a packet-boat that can be procured, and to put her directly upon the station between Lisbon and Gibraltar. Have directed the strengthening the packet-boats which pass between Great Britain and Lisbon with ten men to each boat, together with guns and other arms and warlike stores. Ask approval for what they have done.

Copy of the warrant referred to. 2 *pages and* 2 *halves.*

19 April. 6. Fr. Negus to Mr Scroope. Finds it impossible by any examination to contradict what Thomas Robinson and George Field charge for provisions, &c. for the tigers, civet-cats, and East Indian birds; but George Field charges 8*l.* for his care and trouble, after the rate of 10*s.* a week, being double the allowance made by their Lordships to Robinson. But Field alleges that since 8 Sept. he had the additional care of two tigers and two civet-cats, and that the tigers are so unruly that he spends much of his time in tending them, and has a man to help him, for whom he asks 10*s.* a week. John Combs has expended in Kensington paddock the quantity of provisions mentioned, and the prices are according to contract. He craves after the rate of 30*l.* per ann. As to the directions for the future maintenance and keeping the foreign beasts and birds, proposes that a daily sum be allowed the gardener for the same, viz., for each tiger 16*d.* per day, each civet-cat 4*d.*, and each Indian bird 2*d.*, for their meat, and 2*s.* 6*d.* to the gardener for his care and necessaries. Further proposes that the keeper of the beasts in the paddock shall make a monthly account of the number under his care, and of the provisions furnished for them; but no certain allowance can be made till such time as the alterations commanded by his Majesty have been made, and it is known what feed they may have from the herbage, for at present they are confined in enclosures which afford very little herbage, &c. The best check the nature of the thing will bear seems to be a frequent examination, &c. 19 April 1727.

Also the directions given by the Treasury to make the above report. Dated 16 Feb. 1726–7. 3 *pages.*

Vol. CCLIX.

1727.

21 April. 7. Report of his Majesty's Advocate and Solicitor General for Scotland (Dun. Forbes and Ch. Areskine) to the Lords of the Treasury on several papers laid before their Lordships by the York Buildings Company, relating to certain demands of allowances claimed by the Company out of the moneys due by them, as the price of forfeited estates purchased by them in Scotland; together with a memorial from the late Commissioners of the forfeited estates there. The chief articles in the allowances demanded are:—

(1.) The value of the tithes of certain estates by them purchased which were sold by the Commissioners at the same rate of purchase as the other parts of the estates, but which the Company affirm belonged to the Crown, and therefore are not alienable by the Commissioners.

(2.) The overcharge in the rental of the "Coalery" and salt works of the estate of Winton, which the Company affirm the Commissioners set up as yielding 1,000*l.* per ann., whereas the Company say these works produce no more than 600*l.* per ann., and they, having bought at five years' purchase, insist they are entitled to retain five years' purchase of the difference.

(3.) Interest of the purchase money of the estates of Panmuir, Winton, Kilsyth, and East Reston, to the value of 2,071*l.* charged by the Com[rs].

(4.) "Two years' rents of such of the tenants of the estates by them purchased, as remained dutiful to his Majesty" during the Rebellion.

On the 1st the opinion of the Advocate and Solicitor General is, that if any of the tithes belonged to the Crown the sale cannot defeat the right of the Crown, and the Company are entitled to a deduction. Cannot determine whether any of the tithes sold belonged to the Crown, but there are some suits touching these before the Court of Session.

As to the second, it does not appear to them that the Commissioners did affirm that the coalery and salt works of Winton had yielded, or might yield, 1,000*l.* per ann. If they rated the value too highly they appear to have made some satisfaction to the Company by selling it at five years' purchase, whereas the usual rate for such casual rent in sales in Scotland is seven years' purchase.

As to the third, it appears that on 4 Aug. 1721 the Company paid 6,600*l.* of 120,963*l.*, the price of the four estates first purchased, and from thence till 19 Oct. in the same year they made several payments till the 120,963*l.* was nearly paid up, &c. The Company agree to be charged with interest for the balance as if it was part of the principal, &c.

As to the last article, viz., the two years' rent of the tenants, the Company have laid nothing before them to countenance this demand. The tenants who remained dutiful had a right by law to detain those rents in their own hands, but as it does not appear

1727. VOL. CCLIX.

that they remained dutiful, or demanded the rents, or had any right to them, it is conceived they had no legal claim.

On the whole subject apprehend that the Company cannot be compelled to pay up the price without the proper allowances being made. London, 21 April 1727.

The memorial referred to.

With these are two balance sheets of the York Buildings Company's accounts between 1721 and 1728, apparently not connected with the above report. 7 *pages* (*some of them double pages*).

In the *Minute Book*, vol. 25, p. 299*c*, 19 May 1727, is:—"Write to the York Buildings Company to know what progress they have made in settling the ballances to be paid the Crown, for the Estates they purchased of the Comm[rs] for Forfeitures, and to advise the hastening and paying in the said ballances to avoid the measures that must be taken in case this affair is further neglected or delayed."

22 April. 8. Representation made by the Directors of the Equivalent Company at their Court held 22 April 1727, to the King, viz., that, as the improvement of manufactures and fisheries in Scotland "is now endeavouring to be promoted" under the King's influence and protection, and that the fund of the Equivalent Company arises there, and is the only one of that nature, in that part of the Kingdom, the Company apprehend it would be a great advantage if they were authorized to borrow and lend money upon securities in Scotland only, and had the power of banking there. Pray his Majesty to grant letters patent under the great seal of Scotland to enable such of the proprietors of that Comany as will subscribe their stock for that purpose, to have the power of banking in Scotland only; and that the proprietors may be erected into a Corporation. 1 *page*.

[? About 22 April.] 9. Memorial of the Governor and Company of the Bank of Scotland. The Bank of Scotland was erected by Act of Parliament Anno 1695, and the act declares it unlawful for any other persons to set up a distinct "Company of Bank" within that Kingdom for 21 years, yet it seems plain from their being erected in a perpetual succession, that it was intended, in case the undertaking did succeed, they should continue the National Bank of Scotland, and that there was no thought that any other bank should be erected, but by the same legislative authority. The Company have executed their trust with very moderate advantage to the adventurers, and to the universal satisfaction of that part of the nation. "The Bank of Scotland has been informed that application hath been made, or is intended to be made," to the King by the Equivalent Company in Scotland for a new Charter, giving to them a power to carry on a trade of banking in Scotland, in manifest emulation and prejudice of the said bank.

1727. VOL. CCLIX.

The Bank of Scotland has never been wanting to give its aid for carrying on the public service; particularly by undertaking the recoinage in Scotland, immediately after the Union, when the Privy Council were under no small difficulty how to get it effectuated; and as oft as invasions have been attempted, or public disturbances, or rebellion raised, has taken care timeously to dispose of what money was in the bank, in such a manner as secured it from the power of the enemy and in the hands of the Government.

If two companies are erected it will occasion continual "justling" and attempts to undermine one another, probably to the ruin of both.

The doing anything, especially at this time, to the prejudice of the Bank, will undoubtedly be attended with the worst consequences to that part of the nation, as it must occasion a general convulsion in matter of credit, if not put an entire stop to it; for that the Bank, of necessity, must stop further loans and must, to prevent the attempts of a new created rival company, make a general demand upon their debitors and proprietors, and, of consequence, these will make the like demand of the private persons indebted to them; and as a great part of Scotland is engaged with the Bank, it is obvious what confusion this must produce.

The grant will be highly prejudicial to Scotland and be very ungrateful to that part of the nation, as two hundred and ten shares of the Equivalent Company's stock are in the hands of others than Scotsmen, and only about thirty-eight in the hands of residents. The profits would be drawn out of Scotland, which would be drained of cash and the inhabitants would be disabled from paying the taxes.

Hope that no power of banking will be granted to the Equivalent Company to the prejudice of the Bank of Scotland. Undated, but see previous entry.

In the *Minute Book*, vol. 26, p. 1*g*, 30 May 1727, is:—"The Report of the Lord Advocate and Solicitor of Scotland, dated the ——day of————, on the memorial of the Bank of Scotland, and on the draught of a Charter for the Equivalent Company to bank there is read, and a Charter ordered to be prepared for the King's hand in the manner it stands amended by the said Report." 2½ *pages*.

17 May. 10. Memorial of the Com^rs^ and Trustees of the Forfeited Estates, "who acted in Scotland," to the Lords of the Treasury. In consequence of two several references from their Lordships, were obliged to bring up several of their officers, with a great number of books and papers, to enable them to settle the affairs between the public and the York Buildings Company; and nothing remains but to pay in the balances and to execute the proper conveyances. But by a late Act it is provided, that the books and writings shall, on or before the 12th of June, be delivered to the Court of Ex-

1727. VOL. CCLIX.

chequer. No method having, by this Act, been provided for the proper defence of the public "relating to the claims & demands which shall be made on the part of the purchasers of the Estates not yet conveyed, as was provided by former Acts," they (the Com^rs^) desire their Lordships to authorize William Kennedy, their Accountant, and Alexander Ross, their Solicitor, to act as their agents.

Send a particular of the moneys due and free to the public out of the Forfeited Estates, which may be soon recovered.

Pray that 650*l.* may be imprested to William Kennedy for rent, salaries, &c. 17 May 1727.

The particular referred to.

In the *Minute Book,* vol. 25, p. 299*d,* 19 May 1727, is :—"My Lords say (Mr Bond and Mr Cuningham, late Comm^rs^ for Forfeitures being present) that out of the first money for forfeitures in their power, they will issue 650^li^ to clear debts in the way of their late office, according to their memorial. But as to the appointing Mr Kennedy and Mr Ross officers for taking care of the Records, and of the estates not yet sold, my Lords suspend the consideration thereof till the Act is printed, which transfers the Records and unsold estates to the Exchequer in Scotland." 3 *pages.*

19 May. 11. "A. Cracherode's Report upon the peticon of John Pulley, relating to money in the hands of the late Sheriff of Bedfordshire upon ye outlawry of Jo^n^ Fincham, 19° Maij 1727."

For reasons given, is of opinion, that a warrant may be properly granted to the Attorney General, empowering him to consent on the King's behalf that the sum of 130*l.* 15*s.* 10*d.* in the hands of the late sheriff, may, by his Majesty's Court of Exchequer, be ordered to be paid to the petitioner, John Pulley, in part of the debt due to him from John Fincham, upon a mortgage and bond, mentioned, whenever petitioner shall apply to the Court of Exchequer for such an order. May 19, 1727.

The petition and five other documents touching the same matter. 10 *pages.*

20 May. 12. Report of the Surveyor of H. M. Woods (Charles Wither, Esq.) to the Lords of the Treasury on a memorandum of the Duchess Dowager of Marlborough. Is of opinion it would increase and preserve the game in Windsor Great Park if 200 acres of the coarsest ground therein were annually ploughed and sown with some sort of grain, provided it was divided into six or more parcels as remote as can well be from each other, and that after three years' tillage they are laid down with proper grass seed.

The memorandum of the Duchess states that it was to remind Sir Robert Walpole that some time ago he was desirous to have some ground ploughed in the park, and she answered, that whatever he would have done of that kind, she should be very glad of, provided his Majesty paid for it. On which Sir Robert wrote from Norfolk that he thought it was reasonable, and that he would pay

1727. Vol. CCLIX.

for it. Since this nothing had been done, because the Duchess expected he would give particular directions. Twenty-five years ago she found the park ploughed in several parts, which, as soon as she could she got rid of, because the bills she had on that account were more than 1,000*l.* a year; which made her think that it was reasonable for the King to pay for any extraordinary charge occasioned by his command. But, having been at the Lodge about six weeks, upon examining into that matter, she finds that what she formerly paid upon that account was a great abuse, and that she can plough any ground that is proper to be ploughed without any expense to the Crown, and with some little advantage to herself. A great part of the ground in the park is overrun with thistles and produces nothing that is of use. She would plough up one or two hundred acres every year at no charge to the Crown if she had an order from the Treasury. For she does not think it proper for her to do anything in this matter without orders. 2 *pages.*

25 May. 13. Report of the Surveyor General (Gybbon) to the Lords of the Treasury on the memorial of Thomas Burdus, Esq., who claimed the remainder of a term of 31 years' lease of the coal mines in Lanton *alias* Lampton Hills, in the common fields of Wickham, in the county of Durham, granted by letters patent of 28 Aug. 1697 to Thomas Neal, Esq., and Michael Thompson, gent. Memorialist prayed for another term of 31 years under the same rents, viz., 1*l.* 6*s.* 8*d.* per annum, and a sixth of the clear yearly value of the collieries.

Has this day made his report on the several memorials of the Lord Viscount Vane and the Lord Barnard for a reversionary lease of the coal mines at Lanton Hills only, in the former of which he has given an account of the ancient as well as the present condition of the mines.

As to the other colliery in the parish of Wickham, finds that King James I. on 28 Apr., in his 21st year, granted it to Alexander Stevenson for three lives, at a rent of 1*l.* 6*s.* 8*d.* per annum, without fines, and no lease appears to have been since made of it by the Crown till that in 1697.

The Parliament surveyors in 1649 valued the colliery at 130*l.* per annum. The surface of the ground contained by estimation 110 acres. There was then yearly paid by the farmers thereof, 3*l.* 6*s.* 8*d.* to the town of Wickham, for free egress and regress, with "way leave and stay leave," for their coals, wood, and other materials. Some gentlemen of note have written that these coal mines have been long wrought out and can be of no value. If their Lordships grant to the memorialist a lease of the two collieries, a lease may be passed to him without fine for 29½ years from 28 Aug. 1728, when the term in being will expire, reserving a rent of 10*l.* per annum (which he now offers) and one full sixth part of the clear yearly value; but if their Lordships grant a reversionary lease of the colliery at Lanton Hills to Lord Vane or Lord Barnard, then a reversionary lease of the other colliery at Wickham may be

Vol. CCLIX.

1727.

passed to the memorialist, without fine, for the term aforesaid, reserving a rent of 1*l.* 6*s.* 8*d.* per annum (which he now offers), and one-sixth part of the clear yearly profits, which will be conformable to the Civil List Act. 25 May 1727.

On the back of the report is a warrant to the Surveyor General approving of that part of the report which relates to Wickham, &c. The signatures to the warrant are scored through. There is also the memorial.

In the *Minute Book*, vol. 26, p. 45*a*, 24 Oct. 1727, is:—"The several Reports of the Surveyor General dated the 25th May 1727 on the peticons hereunder menconed, viz.:—William, Lord Viscot Vane, Gilbert, Lord Barnard, Thomas Burdus for a new lease of certain Collierys in the mannor of Softly, com. Durham, are read, and my Lords are of opinion the reasons are stronger on the side of the Lord Vane than other the peticoners, and do thereupon agree that the same be renewed to him." 5 *pages*.

25 May. 14. Report of the same to the Lords of the Treasury on the memorial of the Rt Hon. Gilbert, Lord Barnard, who represents that Christopher, Lord Barnard, being Lord of the Manor of Raby, was entitled to the wastes of it, within which are the lands called the Manor of Softly. States (as in the last report) the grant of the lease of 28 Aug. 1697 to Neal and Thompson.

The late Lord Barnard claimed the mines at Lanton Hill, and the lessees, on disputes about the same, being unable to support their right, released their interest in them to his Lordship. The Manor of Raby was settled on Memorialist on his marriage. The Memorialist being in possession of Cockfield Colliery, for which he pays a Fee Farm rent of 10*l.* per ann. to the Crown, the grant of a lease of the other Colliery to any other person would be a hardship, and tend to involve him in disputes with the Crown. To avoid which, desires a lease of the Colliery at Lanton Hills for 31 years, or three lives, at a rent of 10*l.* per ann. Refers to reports he has made on the memorials of Viscount Vane and Thomas Burdus, Esq. In the former has given an account of the ancient and present states of the Lanton Hill Colliery, and of leases of it granted by the Crown for at least 96 years, and cannot find, from any writings produced to him, that Christopher, late Lord Barnard, had any legal claim to this Colliery; and consequently neither this Memorialist nor Lord Vane could derive any from him. The Lord Vane acknowledges that the Manor of Raby is settled on the present Lord Barnard and his issue male; but insists that the Colliery does not lie within the Manor, but within the Manor of Softley, and has produced writings whereby the Manor of Softley, and particularly the lands at Lanton Hills, are settled on Lady Vane for life, then to the issue male of the Lord Vane, with a remainder to him in fee. If their Lordships grant the Colliery at Lanton Hills to the Memorialist, a reversionary lease thereof may be passed to him, without fine, for 29½ years, from 29 Aug. 1728, when the term in being will expire, reserving a rent of 10*l.* per

1727. Vol. CCLIX.

ann. (which he offers to pay) and one sixth part of the clear yearly value of the Colliery. 25 May 1727.

See the Minute following the preceding report.

Also the memorial referred to. 3 *pages*.

29 May. 15. W[?] Robinson to the Duke of Newcastle. The Secretary to his Majesty's embassy in France having in Mr Walpole's absence, during 10 months, at several times, made divers journeys to Chantilly, Marly and Versailes for H.M. special service; and having been at other extraordinary expenses, amounting to 300 sterling and upwards, hopes his Grace will represent his case to the King, and that his Majesty will have consideration of him. The late M. Craufurd, secretary to Lord Stair's embassy, has had like allowances by warrants from the King to the Treasury.

Accompanied by copy of warrant in favour of Mr Craufurd for 800*l*., viz., 300*l*. as a present in reward for his journey, &c. in coming from Paris with the Convention treaty, and 500*l*. as of Royal bounty for his good services. London, 29 May 1727. 2 *pages*.

— May. 16. Memorial of James, Duke of Chandos, to the Lords of the Treasury. Lays before their Lordships a state of several sums of money paid by him for the use of the late war, which through the expedition used in preparing and passing his accounts were overseen and not inserted in any of his former accounts. The sums amount to 14,612*l*. 7*s*. 6*d*. Prays that a warrant may be directed to the Auditors of Imprests authorizing them to allow him the same on his final account. May — 1727.

Also the account. 5 *pages*.

1 June. 17. Memorial of the Governor and Court of Assistants of the York Buildings Company to the Lords of the Treasury. Have drawn up an account of Widdrington Estate, purchased by the Company, and have stated the balance, with the several cravings upon the account; and will pay in the balance when directed. By direction of the Comrs of Forfeited Estates in Scotland have delivered all their vouchers to the officers of the Comrs, and "all their conveyances of claims upon those Estates"; which vouchers amount to upwards of 170,000*l*. By an Act of last session may be summoned to produce these vouchers before the Barons of the Exchequer of Scotland to adjust their accounts, and have written two letters to the Secretary of the Commissioners, and a letter to the Commissioners themselves, desiring to have the vouchers again, but can obtain no answer. York Buildings House, 1 June 1727. Signed.

Minuted:—"Directors to attend on Thursday next at 12."

In the *Minute Book*, vol. 26, p. 6c, 8 June 1727, is:—"Gentlemen of the York Buildings Company are called in, and Mr Chancellor acquaints them, that the Lords have inspected the Accots before them, of the purchase money for Widdrington estate, and that, however

1727. Vol. CCLIX.

reasonable the deductions may be, which they desire to be made out of the purchase money, yet their Lordships conceive they have no power over the same, but say it may be proper for the Attorney Generall to exhibit a bill against them in the Exchequer to compleat their contract for the said estate, and that then the equity of their demands will be before the Court, and the Court may order accordingly. So transmit the Acco^ts and papers relating thereto to Mr Cracherode, for him to advise with Mr Attorney Generall and proceed accordingly. The Company at my Lords' request do agree to pay into the Exchequer 2,500^li in further part of the purchase money." 1½ *pages.*

3 June. 18. "Barbados. George Plaxton his account as Treasurer settled by the Honble the Committee of Publick Accounts from the 8th day of Aug^st 1725 excl. to 8th Aug^st 1726 inclusive."

It has the following memorandum at the foot:—"Barbados the 3^d of June 1727 George Plaxton, Esq., did then personally appear before me and was sworn to the truth of this Account. Hen. Horsley." 14 *large pages.*

[Before 11 June.] 19. Petition of Helen Flemming, spinster, to the King. About three years ago the late Lord Viscount Longford, by petition, represented to the King that he was led to bear arms in the Revolution of Ireland, whereby his estate, now worth 12,000*l.* per ann., was seized to the Crown and sold among the Irish forfeitures; that he followed the late King James to France, but after several years' service there (where he bore the rank of Lieut.-General and had a regiment of two battalions) upon the first appearance of her late Majesty's declaration, published at Lisbon, 25 April, in the third year of her reign, by the Duke of Schomberg, Commander-in-Chief of her Majesty's forces in Portugal (inviting home all her subjects of Ireland or Great Britain that had been in the service of France or other her enemies), her father sacrificed all his honours abroad and was the first that returned to his duty and allegiance. His attainder was taken off, and he had a pension of 500*l.* per ann., and a commission to raise a regiment, with which he was commanded to Spain, where he served till the peace. His pension was reduced to 250*l.* per annum, and he petitioned for its restoration to 500*l.* per annum to him and his daughter. The petition was referred to Lord Carteret, the Lord Lieut. of Ireland, who reported on it 13 March 1724, that the bounty would be properly bestowed. The Treasury agreed thereto and ordered a warrant for restoring the pension of 500*l.* per ann. from Lady day 1725. The Lords Justices thought fit to have it respited at the Treasury till his Majesty's return from Hanover, and afterwards it was respited till July last, when the Treasury ordered a new warrant, but before it reached his Majesty he (Lord Longford) died.

Petitioner is his only issue surviving, and by her mother's marriage settlement had a portion of 8,000*l.* payable out of the estate which her father lost, and there was no provision made

1727. VOL. CCLIX.

for her. Has deeply shared in her father's misfortunes, and has sacrificed upwards of 2,000*l.* left to her by her friends, and stands engaged for 960*l.* more for the remainder of her father's debts. Prays to have the benefit of the warrant which was ordered for her father's late augmentation, from the commencement thereof to his death, and such further provision for her future support as shall seem meet to his Majesty. Undated, but before the death of King Geo. I.

In the *Minute Book,* vol. 26, p. 49*e*, 31 Oct. 1727, is:—"Mr Chancellor acquaints my Lords * * * * that it is the King's pleasure also that Helen Flemming, daughter of the late Lord Viscot Longford, be added to the same Establishment [the Civil Establishment of Ireland] for 50li p ann." 1 *page.*

[? Between 1722 and 11 June 1727.] 20. Memorial of the Nobility, Gentlemen, and Inhabitants living in, and near, his Majesty's Castle of Windsor, and the Borough of New Windsor, and the several seats and villages adjacent. Her Majesty Queen Anne, at the expense of the Crown, made a handsome large gravel walk, now called the King's Avenue, leading from the Palace of Windsor into the Park, called Windsor Great Park, and from thence up to a road going across the Park from Egham into the Forest of Windsor, and to the several seats and villages situated therein, which is a great ornament to the Castle, and is of great use and safety for the Royal Family and his Majesty's subjects to go from the Castle and Borough into the Forest to hunt, and to the several seats and villages therein; being the only road in the winter that is passable. The walk or road has been ever since repaired at the expense of the Crown; but by the wet season, and want of gravel, it is now ruinous and dangerous. Pray for orders to be given to repair the same. It has 42 signatures. 1 *page.*

GEORGE II.

[After 11 June.] 21. Abstract of the Accounts of Anthony Cracherode as "Solicitor for the affairs of his late Majesty's Treasury," viz.: "to his late Maty's demise, shewing what his late Maty owed him, and what he must further disburse to get his accots passed. Wth an accot of what was due from his office at his late Maty's death." 3 *pages.*

[After 11 June.] 22. An account of money advanced for secret services by Wm Stanhope, Esqr, his Majty's late Ambassador Extraordry & Plenipotentiary at the Court of Spain, from the 20th May 1720 to the 11th June 1727.

1727. VOL. CCLIX.

By the account there remained due to him 2,939*l.* 10*s.* 9*d.* At the foot is this memorandum:—"That I never charged any other extra-Extraord^{ry} disbursements, nor any thing for my journey home, nor that of my family and equipage, nor for the many expensive ones which I was constantly obliged to make, in following the Court, during the seven years that I remained in Spain. W.S."

In the *Minute Book*, vol. 26, p. 40*l.*, 13 Oct. 1727, is the following, which may refer to the above:—"Write to the Exchequer for satisfying the order for 2,800^{li} in the name of Mr Stanhope." 1½ *pages.*

[Between 11 June and 19 Oct.] 23. The sums for which William Cayley, his Majesty's Consul at Cadiz, craved allowance; viz., for his extraordinary disbursements in his late Majesty's service from 3 Feb. 1725–6 to 20 May 1727.

Minuted:—"19th Oct. 1727. To be layd before the King." 2 *pages.*

[After 11 June.] 24. "An acc^{t} of the sums owing at the time of his late Ma^{ts} demise to sundry persons on allowances payable by the hands of Mr Tilson." There are 12 persons to whom the sums were due. ½ *page.*

[About 13 June.] 25. Report of the Barons of the Exchequer of Scotland to the Lords of the Treasury on the petition of Daniel Campbell, Esq., referred to them on 22 May 1723. Her late Majesty on 28 Feb. 1706 granted to Edward Hyde, eldest son of Edward, Lord Cornberry, his heirs and assigns, the few duties of the lands and Island of "Ilay," lying in Argyleshire, of the yearly value of 500*l.* sterling, for three nineteen years, commencing from Whitsuntide 1701, at a rent of 41*l.* 13*s.* 4*d.* sterling. The grant or lease determined by the death of Her Majesty. His Majesty can renew or confirm the same, and may grant to the petitioner during His Majesty's life the reserved rent of 41*l.* 13*s.* 4*d.* sterling, which has not been accounted for since 1706.

The report is dated 20 July 1725. It was, however, not received until 13 June 1727, as appears by a minute on the back.

Also the petition. 2½ *pages.*

14 June. 26. Report of A. Cracherode, Esq., to the Lords of the Treasury, on the petition of John Barber and James Wrexham, who had caused Anthony Mathieu, late of the parish of St. George, Southwark, hatter, to be outlawed for debt. Is of opinion that a warrant may be properly granted to the Attorney General empowering him to consent that the sum of 70*l.* 2*s.* paid into the Court of Exchequer may be paid to the petitioners as part of the money due to them.

The petition and three other documents relating thereto. 7½ *pages.*

15 June. 27. Representation of the Barons of the Court of Exchequer in Scotland to the Lords of the Treasury. Soon after the constitution

1727. Vol. CCLIX.

of "the court" it was found necessary for the better carrying on of the public service to have an agent or correspondent at London. Upon the death of Mr Richard Lerego in the year 1716, the Barons nominated and appointed Mr Joseph Tudor in his place. "The business incumbent on him" has much increased by the many public affairs put under management of the Court. The Court hitherto has only been enabled to make an allowance to Mr Tudor out of the fund for prosecutions and petty expenses. As their opinion is that Mr Tudor deserves much better encouragement, recommend that he be placed upon the establishment for civil affairs [in Scotland] at the rate of 200*l.* per annum. Edinburgh, Exchequer Chamber, 15 June 1727. 2 *pages.*

19 June. 28. Memorial from the Comrs appointed by His late Majesty for building fifty new churches in and about the cities of London and Westminster and suburbs thereof, and for rebuilding the parish church of St Mary, Woolnoth, in the city of London, addressed to the Lords of the Treasury, desiring their Lordships to direct the further sum of 25,000*l.* to be raised by a loan at the Exchequer at four per cent. upon the credit of the fund of 21,000*l.* per ann. charged upon the duties on coals and culm. Old Palace Yard, Westminster, 19 June 1727. Seven signatures. 1 *page.*

22 June. 29. Report of the same to the same, on the memorial of William Duff, of Bracco. There is due to the Crown upon the enfeoffment of the memorialist in sundry lands in the county of Banff and Regality of Kinloss the sum of 222*l.* 8*s.* 6$\frac{10}{12}$*d.*, of which his Majesty may, if he please, discharge the memorialist. 22 June 1727.

Also the memorial.

In the *Minute Book*, vol. 26, p. 20*d*, 2 Aug. 1727, is a minute that the above report was "read and agreed to." 2 *pages.*

[?3 July.] 30. Certified copy of representation of merchants and owners of ships in London to the Lords of the Treasury. Upon a trial lately had before the Lord Chief Baron upon the seizure of a ship for bringing goods from Holland which were of the growth of the East Indies, judgment was given against the claimant, Mr Van Neck, and the ship forfeited. Set out, that if the law is to be so strictly put in execution, without any regard to innocence, far from answering the intention of the legislature, which intended to encourage and increase shipping and navigation, it will necessarily prove the destruction of it, since the act of any common sailor or passenger by bringing over contraband goods with the view of disposing of them or of becoming informer will subject to forfeiture the property of innocent persons. Hope their Lordships will give directions for the relief of Mr Van Neck, and to prevent further accidents that may befall others who are daily liable to the like misfortune.

The date of the original was 24 June 1727, and it was certified by a notary on 3 [?July] 1727. The name of the notary and the lower part of the document is torn away. 1 *m.* (*parchment*).

1727. Vol. CCLIX.

15 July. 31. J. Scrope to Mr Brucer, late cashier of the Prize Office. Philip Cavendish, Esq., formerly commander of H.M. ship "Tiger," has complained to the Lords of the Treasury of the detention in the hands of the cashier of 175*l.* of prize money. Sends the petition for his answer thereto. Treasury Chambers, 15 July 1727.

Also the petition which states that the money was detained under the pretence that the petitioner had plundered a prize which he sent into Lisbon. The petitioner prayed that Mr Brucer should give an account why he detained the money, and should make it appear that petitioner did plunder the prize, for which, if he could show the least grounds, petitioner would give up all pretensions to the prize money. 2 *pages.*

18 July. 32. Alured Popple to John Scrope, Esq. By command of the Comrs for Trade and Plantations sends, for the information of the Lords of the Treasury, extracts of a letter from Col. Hart, Governor of the Leeward Islands, and of some papers therein referred to, in relation to the seizure of some of the effects belonging to a Spanish vessel lost at Barbuda. Whitehall, July 18, 1727. 44 *pages.*

25 July. 33. Copy of an opinion, signed "Thomas Reeve, 25 July 1727," on the question "Whether the grant of 1696 is not good against the Crown who have now deputed Commrs to sell all the French part of St Kitts yielded thereto by the Treaty of Utricht, or whether the lands in question having by cession at the peace of Reswick leye under the dominion of the French King, the grant to Thauvet is become void?" Thinks (for the reasons given) the grant will survive to Thauvet. 1 *page.*

25 July. 34. Report of the Barons of the Exchequer of Scotland to the Lords of the Treasury, on the report of the Comrs of Customs, made on the petition of the Earl of Stair, for building a "Key" in Lochryan Bay, and for a grant to his Lordship of 60*l.* per ann. out of the rents of the Bishopric of Galloway for building and supporting the same. Certify that no further proof has been offered to them as to the conveniency and advantage of having such a key than the papers annexed to the report. And as to the grant of 60*l.* per annum out of the rents of the Bishopric, they find that the rents and grants made by the King's predecessors to the Universities in Scotland, and other burthens, have so exhausted the revenues of the Bishopric as not to admit of a grant therefrom. But if his Majesty approves of the building the key, there are sufficient Crown rents within the receipt of the Chamberlaincy of Galloway, not particularly appropriated, as to answer the 60*l.* per ann. which his Majesty may grant. Edinburgh, Exchequer Chamber, 25 July 1727.

The report of the Comrs of Customs and copy of the petition referred to; also copy of the above report and copies of two other papers on the same subject. 7 *pages.*

27 July. 35. Papers connected with claims on the States General for damages done to Mr Jeronimy Clifford by the Governor of Surinam.

1727. Vol. CCLIX.

The first is of the nature of a petition to the Lords of the Treasury, and commences as follows:—"27 July 1727. My Lords,—In the year 1718 Mr John Denne, of Littlebourn, in Kent, a near relation of mine, gave me an account of the names of 106 relations of mine then living in Kent who are all descended from two brothers and one sister my late father, Mr Andrew Clifford, had.

"And for these 20 years past I have had neither father nor mother, brother nor sister, wife nor child, living, to leave what God has been pleased to give me in this world. Therefore I though fit to send you the annext list of my relations' names, whom I have at heart to bequeath what I have unto them. Now, without his Majesty's justice in the matter of my complaint against the Dutch, my whole estate will sink into the hands of foreigners, to the great loss of my said poor relations. Now may God and the King, with your Lordships' intercession to his Majesty in their behalf, enable me to feed the hungry and cloath the needy, and to send the rich empty away. And for whatsoever sums of money his Majesty shall come to grant me on this account, your Lordships shall see me give away immediately the one half thereof to my said poor relations, and the other half to them at the day of my death."

Refers to written and printed cases, a list of which he encloses, and says that his case has depended in the Cabinet Council since Queen Anne's reign. Asks their Lordships' interposition with his Majesty for subsistence money, until he is relieved by the King or Parliament. The postscript is:—"I lodge at a bakers next door to the Ship Tavern at Charing Cross."

Accompanied by the list referred to, a declaration by the petitioner (described as a "merchant and sugar planter of the Dutch Colony of Surinam in America") before a notary, that he had appeared and declared that in the year 1718 the account (which is enclosed) of the names of 106 relations of the petitioner, from the first, second, third, and fourth degrees of lineage, who were living in the county of Kent, was delivered to him," &c., and that he intended to make them his heirs.

Also copy of another petition, which petitioner intends to lay before his Majesty in Council, copy of Order in Council of 9 July 1705, an extract from the Resolution of the States General of 16 Feb. 1697 concerning the damages: giving also "a short estimate" of the damages.

Besides these there is another copy of the Order in Council, and copies of the 5th, 6th, and 7th articles of peace made with Holland in 1674.

There is also copy of another Order in Council of 3 May 1705 on the same subject. 19 *pages*.

12 Aug. 36. "Copy Order of Council for Gold work, jewels, &c. for the Coronacõn, with a Schedule of particulars."

The order is dated 12 Aug., and the particulars 11 Aug. 1727.

The "particulars" of what would be required for the coronation are signed:—"Ja: Brudenell," and consisted:—

"For the King:"—The Imperial Crown, a circlet, St Edward's Crown. The sceptre with the dove, the sceptre with the cross and

VOL. CCLIX.

1727. the orb (all to be adorned with jewels), St Edward's staff, the gold spurs, the four swords, the ampulla and spoon for the anointing, paten and chalice, and a ruby ring.

"For the Queen":—A circlet, the crown, the sceptre with the cross, the ivory rod with the dove, and a ruby ring. 2½ *large pages.*

23 Aug. 37. "Copy of an opinion of Sr Philip Yorke dat. 23 Augt 1727 on the power of officers of the Customs to seize East India goods landed in the Isle of Man."

His opinion was that the officers, as officers, could not make a seizure because (as he took it) the Commission of the Commissioners of Customs did not extend to that Island. Aug. 23, 1727. 1 *page.*

VOL. CCLX. 1727. SEPTEMBER—DECEMBER.

4 Sept. 1. "Copy [of] Mr Audr Jett's report on the peticōn of the Admr of Mr Samuel Burton, late Recr Genll of the rents and revenues of the Savoy Hospital."

The account was for nine years ending Mich. 1723; and the petitioner prayed a warrant to the Auditor for allowing the usual fees. This, as shown by the Auditor's Report, would reduce the balance from 353*l.* 7*s.* 3½*d.* to 113*l.* 7*s.* 3½*d.*, which sum he had paid into the Exchequer. 4 Sept. 1727. 3 *pages.*

[? About 5 Sept.] 2. Petition of John Plunkett and George Kelly, prisoners in the Tower of London, to the Lords of the Treasury for a renewal of the warrant for their subsistence, the allowance granted by his late Majesty not having been paid since his Majesty's demise.

On the back are the following minutes, &c.:—

"5 7ber 1727. Mr Cracherode to endorse ye allowances by wh authority granted & to wt time paid.

"Septr 12th 1727. I have pd the petrs 5s a day to the 10th of June last inclusive by warrt of Trea̅ry; wch if my Lords think fit to renew I beg an imprest of 500li having hitherto carryed on his Matys affairs out of my own money. A. Cracherode."——"26 7ber 1727. To be layd before the King."——"30 Novr 1727. Mr Cracherode is to continue to pay the allownces formerly settled for the subsistence of Mr Plunket and Kelley the two prisoners in the Tower." 1 *page* (4to).

7 Sept. 3. Report of Thomas Jett, Auditor, to the Lords of the Treasury, upon the accounts of Samuel Burton, deceased, late receiver of the rents of the Savoy Hospital. His final account, ending Mich. 1723, was examined and stated in order to be engrossed for declaration. Has frequently written to Henry Howarth, Esq., the present Receiver

1727. VOL. CCLX.

of the Savoy rents, to make speedy payment into the receipt of the Exchequer, but as his accounts have not been laid before him (the Auditor), cannot say what the balance is, but believes it may be about 500*l.* His late Majesty demised to the chapel wardens of the Savoy, the profits of breaking up the ground in the chapel and chapel yard, and the tolling of the bell for 21 years, with a clause of reassumption. The chapel wardens have in their hands about 51*l.* of the profits of the ground and bell, before the patent, which they absolutely refuse to pay. If they are threatened with the reassumption it may be a means of getting in the money, "no distress being to be had" 7 Sept. 1727.

Minuted:—"Lrẽs sent to Poworth, Chapell Warden." In the *Minute Book*, vol. 26, p. 28*n*, 13 Sept. 1727, is:—"Mr Auditor Jett's report of the 7th Septr, about the rents of the Savoy Hospital, is read and my Lords order a letter to be writ to the Chapell Wardens of the Savoy to pay 51li in their hands belonging to the Crown of profitts arising by the ground and bell before the comencement of their lease thereof into the Exchequer or Receiver of those Rents forthwith." 2 *pages.*

[? About 12 Sept.] 4. Petition of James Clarke, Esq., to the King. In the late Queen's reign, when the liberties and privileges of the city of Dublin were struck at, and many violent attempts made by the then Government of Ireland to subvert the ancient constitution of that city, in favour of the Pretender, John Forster, Esq., then Recorder (since Lord Chief Justice of the Common Pleas) sent for petitioner, who was at that time in considerable business in the King's Bench in that kingdom, and asked him if he would venture to be concerned as agent or manager for the then lord mayor, aldermen, sheriffs, and citizens in all the prosecutions then carried on and unjustly supported against them in the said Court; which petitioner most readily agreed to, and acted therein with integrity and resolution, and constantly and diligently attended to the same, though he well knew he should thereby incur the displeasure of the judges, and hazard the loss of his business, which happened accordingly.

Soon after the late King's Accession, the petitioner residing at Kilkenny, discovered great disaffection to His Majesty and the Government, in the majority of that Corporation; the petitioner caused a petition to be preferred to the House of Commons of Ireland, which brought their evil and disaffected practices under a strict enquiry, and on full proof thereof before a committee, an Act was passed for regulating that Corporation and strengthening the protestant interest and disfranchising several of the aldermen and common councilmen; the obtaining whereof, &c. was in great measure due to petitioner.

Petitioner removed to England to solicit business from Ireland in the Treasury and other public offices, and fell into such business as was in some measure a support to him and his large family.

Petitioner was set upon and knocked down by street robbers and thereby deprived of his memory and speech, which occasioned

1727. Vol. CCLX.

his loss of business. Prays to be placed on the establishment of Ireland for a pension.

Also certificate in petitioner's favour with 61 signatures. 3 *pages.*

[? About 15 Sept.] 5. Petition of Martin Killigrew, Esq., to the Lords of the Treasury. Petitioner let for 21 years for the use of his Majesty, a parcel of ground called Castle Hill, in the co. of Cornwall, on which Pendennis fort is erected, at a rent of 200*l.*, which has been paid pursuant to the King's warrant by the Paymaster General, who declines to continue the payment by virtue thereof: prays to have his Majesty's warrant for the rent. Undated.

In the Minute Book, Vol. 26, p. 29*b*, 15 Sept. 1727, the petition is referred to as read "and ordered accordingly." 1 *page.*

18 Sept. 6. Three letters signed "Cha: Wager" (1) addressed to the R[t] Hon. Sir R. Walpole, in respect to Mr Consul Russell, and the money to be paid for the present to the King of Morocco. Thinks Mr Russell's account is very low, and he cannot do without his salary. Bashé Kornich's account should be allowed. He is very likely to be Governor of "that province" near Gibraltar. "Admiralty Office, Tuesday morning" [? before 18 Sept.]

Adds this postscript: "I am told Mr Gascoign is dying, his places at Port Mahon are (I presume) too much for me to ask for, being tenable, I suppose, by a Member of Parl[t]. I beg pardon for that hard word, I had no other ready."

(2.) To the same. It has been thought proper that M[r] Russell (who was appointed Consul to Barbary) should go to Tetuan, altho' he has received no new instructions; because the Basha and people there must be kept in good humour if possible, their assistance for provisions and "fascines," &c. being so necessary for this garrison, that they could be put to great difficulties if that should be refused; especially in case the siege should begin again. As it is likely that M[r] Russell will be obliged to go to Maquiness, and he cannot go thither without more money than he had (viz. 100*l.*), advised him to draw a bill upon the Treasury for 200*l.* more. Hopes the bill will be paid without deduction. The Morocco Ambassador chose at last to be sent to Tangier, which made it the more necessary for M[r] Russell to go Tetuan; they being at present under different Bashas, and it is necessary to keep fair with both if possible, as well as with the King of Morocco. Torbay [? ship] at Gibraltar the 18th of Sep[r] 1727.

(3.) To M[r] Delafaye. M[r] Russell has at last gone to Tetuan, as it was thought proper both by Lord Portmore and himself (the writer). It is to the same effect as the last. Asks M[r] Delafaye to speak to the Duke of Newcastle about the bill. Dated as above. 4½ *pages* (4[to]).

In the *Minute Book*, vol. 26, p. 59*k*, 19 Dec. 1727, is:—"The King is pleased to allow 200[li] clear of charges according to Sir Charles Wager's letter of the 18th Sept[r] last paid M[r] Russell to continue his journey to Mequinez with the late King's present."

1727. VOL. CCLX.

Again, p. 86*n*, 14 March 1727–8. "Sir Charles Wager's letter of the 18th September last is read advising and desiring payment of Mr Russell's Bill of Exchange of 200li to Mr Thos Revell or order to enable him to go over to Tetuan, the assistance of the Basha of that place being necessary for provision, fascines, &c. for Gibraltar. My Lords order a warrant for the King's hand for paying of the said bill. Accordingly the fees and charges attending the recept thereof are to be included unless already paid upon a Minute of the 19 Decr 1727." 4½ *pages* (4to).

21 Sept. 7. "Arch. Hutcheson" to the Hon. William Clayton, Esq., one of the Lords of the Treasury. Spoke to Sir Robert Walpole of Mr Cunyngham's affair, and went afterwards to the Treasury and read what Mr Tilson had indorsed "on the bill brought from the Privy Seal." Asks Mr Clayton to remind Sir Robert of it, that he may put it in his bag for the King's signing, and thereupon a new bill will be prepared by the Attorney General. Thought the Order in Council on the hearing between Mr Cunyngham and Mr Spooner, was somewhat hard on the former, who has surrendered his former patent on the faith that a new patent should be passed to him of all the lands in the former grant, excepting those in the possession of Mr Spooner, and the bill was accordingly drawn. Thinks the honour of the Administration is now concerned in the passing of a new grant; and there does not appear to be the least shadow of reason for delay. London, Septr 21, 1727. 1 *page* (4to).

25 Sept. 8. The Officers of Works to the Lords of the Treasury, sending an account of the debt owing at the time of the late King's death, to the officers, servants, and others, payable in the Office of Works. From April 1726 to 11 June 1727. Sept. 25, 1727.

Accompanied by the account. 13 *large pages*.

26 Sept. 9. Articles of agreement made between the Lords of the Treasury and Jonathan Forward, of London, merchant, viz., that in consideration of 5*l*. per head he the said Jonathan Forward will convey to plantations in America the persons in Newgate under sentence of transportation or in the county gaols of Hertford, Bucks, Essex, Kent, Sussex, and Surrey. Dated 26 Sept. 1727. 1 *m. parchment*.

[After 29 Sept.] 10. State of what is due to the Countess of Portland for the expense of their Royal Highnesses officers and servants under her government from Mich. 1726 to Mich. 1727 when the new establishment commenced.

Docketed:—"Countess Portland. Expenses. Young Princesses in the year ended Mich's 1727."

Also "an abstract of what is due on account of ye young princesses family. Michaelmas 1727." "Examin'd M. Portland."

Amongst the persons to whom payments were made was "To Mr. Handell 195[£]. 5 *pages*.

VOL. CCLX.

1727.

1 Oct. 11. The pastors of the Evangelical Churches of the vallies of Piedmont to the King of Great Britain. The Protestant Churches in general, and those in particular which depend on his Majesty's rule, have true cause to bewail the loss of his late Majesty. The Evangelical Churches of the vallies of Piedmont, which have been subsisted by a miracle, have been, as much as any, sensible of the inexpressible loss, and now shed their tears on the Royal ashes. They would, like Rachel, refuse all consolation if Providence had not raised up his Majesty to succeed to the throne.

These Churches have always been an object of extraordinary Christian charity of the King's predecessors since they were brought back from their dispersion in A.D. 1686. Ask his Majesty's protection and for continuation of the charity by which they have hitherto existed. Signed by the Moderator and five of the Pastors. Dated in the Valley of Lucerne in Piedmont "1 8bre 1727."

Indorsed:—"The Minrs of ye Vaudois to his Maty, praying for a continuation of their pensions." 2 *pages.*

2 Oct. 12. Order of Council on a report from the Comrs for executing the office of Lord High Admiral, respecting the case of Dame Margaret Walker, widow of Sir Hovenden Walker, formerly Rear Admiral of the White Squadron of the Fleet, who was in such bad circumstances, that she was unable to support herself and daughters, with the common necessaries of life. His Majesty in Council refers the report to the Lords of the Treasury to consider and report, if they have any objection to apply the money, arising from the rights and perquisites of the Admiralty, as proposed by the report of the Comrs to real objects of charity, not otherwise entitled to pensions or bounties. 2½ *pages.*

14 Oct. 13. Lord Cobham to ——.

Received his correspondent's letter with the report of the Paymaster General of the Forces, on the representation of the States of Jersey, with a letter annexed to the report, from the Captains of the three Independent Companies of Invalids, garrisoned in Jersey. Is surprised to find so much stress laid on the letter, which is sent to him to answer. Would have hoped that such a letter could not have deserved so much countenance in opposition to the united request of the whole States of Jersey. The first reason advanced by the three Captains against the representation is that whatever English money comes to Jersey, goes to France, by reason of its trade and the advantage of the exchange. This, instead of being any objection against, is an unanswerable reason for complying with the request of the States; for it admits the very grievance complained of, and desired to be redressed; for it is undoubtedly true, whilst the French "liards" now current in Jersey bear their present exorbitant price, no English money, nor French neither, but liards, can be kept there, but will be all exported to France, and there laid out in liards to be imported into Jersey, by reason of the advantage of the exchange.

The second reason is that if the money should be lost it would be difficult to subsist the men till the government can be made

VOL. CCLX.

1727.

acquainted therewith. Replies that if the whole subsistence of the three companies be ordered to be paid in England, to a person he will nominate, he will engage that the same shall be duly paid to the soldiers in Jersey, free from charge to the government. The next reason is that French farthings are very convenient change for the soldiers. Replies, he cannot apprehend why English half-pence and farthings will not be as convenient change as French farthings, &c. The last reason assigned is that there is a greater demand for bills of exchange than all the officers, &c., can supply. Replies, the extravagant profits made by bills of exchange, from a want of specie in the Island, will furnish an answer to this objection, as well as discover the true occasion of the whole letter. 3½ *pages.*

[? About 24 Oct.] 14. Memorial of John Montgomerie, Esq., Governor of New York, to the Lords of the Treasury. It has always been the custom, upon his Majesty's appointing a Governor for New York, to send with him several utensils and commodities to be by him presented from his Majesty to the Kings or Chiefs of the Indian Nations in alliance with his Majesty's subjects. It is recommended that some addition be made upon this occasion to the presents usually allowed; to more firmly establish the friendship with the Indian nations already in alliance with these Colonies, and if possible to extend it to others.

Also the list estimated to cost 1,300*l.* 17*s.* 6*d.*

Minuted:—"Read 24th October 1727. The Books are to be searched for presidents of such presents, to whom delivered, how provided, the value and when."

30th December 1709.—Paid to Col. Hunter, Gover^r of New York, for his Ma^t's present to the five Indian Nations, provided by him, 300li.

11th May 1716.—Paid to George Bampfield for his Ma^t's present to the five Indian Nations provided by him and consigned to the Governor of New York, 323*l.* 15*s.* 4*d.*

The aforegoing paid out of the Civil List.

31st March 1721.—Paid to George Bampfeild for his Ma^t's present to the five Indian Nations, provided by him and consigned to the Governor of New York out of the 4½ ℘ cent., 882*l.* 2*s.* 10*d.*

The present now desired amounts to the sum of 1,300*l.* 17*s.* 6*d.*

In the *Minute Book*, vol. 26, p. 49, 31 Oct. 1727, is:—"Prepare a sign manual for issuing to Col^o John Montgomerie, Governor of New York, 800li without acco^t to be laid out by him in suitable presents to be given to the Chiefs of the Indian Nations in alliance with the King, upon his first entring upon that Government." 2 *pages.*

31 Oct. 15. "An account of the charge of their Majestys' coronation in his Majesty's Jewel Office," to which is added "An account of the expense of the late King's coronation." Signed, "Ja. Brudenell," Jewell Office, Oct. 31, 1727.

Also three other papers connected with the expense of the same coronation. 4 *pages and* 2 *halves.*

1727. VOL. CCLX.

[? About Oct.] 16. Memorial of James Bogle to the Rt Hon. Sir Robert Walpole praying him to move his Majesty to grant him a commission as one of the Deputy Auditors of the Exchequer of Scotland in the room of Robert Arbuthnot, deceased. [Sir James Dalrymple claimed the right of naming a deputy in the room of Robert Arbuthnot, but this was disputed by memorialist.] Undated, but ? about Oct. as in the *North Britain Book*, vol. 8, p. 446, is the appointment of John Philip Gent as Deputy Auditor on 2 Nov. 1727 ,so that Bogle appears to have been unsuccessful in his application. 2 *pages*.

9 Nov. 17. "Copy of Mr Atto Genl's opinion about patent officers taking the oaths." The questions submitted to the Attorney General applied to Custom House Officers. 7 *pages*.

17 Nov. 18. Alured Popple to John Scrope, Esq. On the 16th of March 1726–27 enclosed, by order of the Lords of Trade and Plantations, for the opinion of the Lords of the Treasury, the draft of a bill for the more effectual preservation of his Majesty's woods in America, and also the draft of a clause proposed to make the bill more effectual by obliging all the importers of masts, yards, and bowsprits to produce a certificate of their having been cut by licence from the Surveyor of Woods, before the importers can receive any bounty; but as their Lordships do not know whether the bounty given by 3 & 4 Anne is to be renewed, they desire to have the opinion of the Lords of the Treasury how far a clause to that effect may be proper to add to the bill, &c. Whitehall, 17 Nov. 1727. 2 *pages*.

23 Nov. 19. Report of Mr A. Cracherode to the Lords of the Treasury on the petition of Grace Cockcroft, spinster, a natural daughter of John Cockcroft, heretofore of Fort St. George, in the East Indies. Petitioner prayed that the legacy of 100*l*., with the interest thereof, or the South Sea Annuities directed to be set apart to answer the same may be paid to her for the payment of 6*l*. 17*s*. 6*d*. remaining due for the maintenance and burial of John Cockcroft the godson of the testator, and the rest for her use. The report finds that the allegations are true, and that Francis Elde, Esq., one of the Masters of the Court of Chancery, set apart 157*l*. 6*s*. 1*d*. in South Sea Annuities to make good the legacy of 100*l*. given to John Cockcroft, the son. His Majesty, in strictness of law, is well entitled to the same and to the dividends; but as petitioner has greatly suffered by the subscription of 2,500*l*. Lottery Annuities into the South Sea Company, is of opinion that petitioner is an object of compassion, and that the Attorney General should be authorised to consent to an order of the Court of Chancery for the transference of the same to the petitioner. 23 Nov. 1727. 7½ *pages*.

27 Nov. 20. Particulars of causes under prosecution with the States thereof in the terms of Hilary, Easter, Trinity, and Michaelmas 1727. Accompanied by a memorial of Anthony Cracherode to the Lords of the Treasury for an order for 1,000*l*. upon account to carry on his Majesty's causes and business. Dated 27 Nov. 1727.

1727. VOL. CCLX.

In the margin are the minutes of what was to be done as regards the suits.

In the *Minute Book*, vol. 26, p. 51, 28 Nov. 1727*l*, is: "Prepare a warrant for issuing 1,000li to Mr Cracherode on accot of Law charges." 41 *pages and* 3 *halves*.

28 Nov. 21. Memorial of John Conduit to the Lords of the Treasury for payment of 520*l*. The amount was due on his account of the charge of gold and silver medals delivered before and since the Coronation. Mint Office, 28 Nov. 1727.

In the *Minute Book*, vol. 26, p. 51*d*, 28 Nov. 1727, is:—"Mr Conduit's memorial for 520li to clear his accot of the charge of gold and silver medals delivered before and since the Coronacõn is read and a wart ordered to be prepared accordingly."

Also the account referred to. 2 *pages*.

29 Nov. 22. Report signed Ja. Brudenell to the Lords of the Treasury. With regard to the practice of admitting foreign ministers and others to have plate from the Jewel Office, and to bespeak the same after what fashion they please. It is what always has been done, and if it has introduced extravagance it has not been in the power of the office to help it as there are no instructions to forbid the same. If the estimates are made by no rule, and are put so low, there must be exceedings. It appears from the books that estimates have been little regarded; for instance, in the case of Ambassadors their warrants were estimated at 2,500*l*., which is much about 6s 8d per oz. for white and 10s per oz. for gilt plate, which was so far from being sufficient, even in those days that the warrants usually amounted to 2,900lb or 3,000l; and this was before there was any duty on silver or poundage on the Civil List to be paid, and when workmanship was a great deal cheaper. Their Lordships will see by the account that the warrants much exceed their respective estimates, and they have done so from the beginning. To prevent extravagance, is of opinion that a medium should be found out to frame a new estimate, and a limitation should always go with it, and this may be made either when it comes before their Lordships to be countersigned or may be expressed in the body of the warrant, in the same manner as the present Lord Chancellor's warrant under the late King's sign manual for 4,000oz of white plate, wherein though the like liberty is given to him as to others of having it made after what fashion he pleases, there is a proviso that the whole do not exceed 1,700*l*., which is after the rate of 8*s*. 6*d*. per oz. Fears this example will be too straight for a standard, especially for Ambassadors, who will not be contented as his Lordship has been, to receive the better half of his warrant in common plates and dishes, without which it will not do at that price. Jewel Office, Nov. 29, 1727.

The account above referred to taken out of the books of the Jewel Office between 1714 and 1724.

The above report seems to have resulted from the following Minute (Minute Book, vol. 26, p. 46*f*, 26 Oct. 1727). "My Lords observing that the practice of admitting Foreign Ministers and others, having plate from the Jewell Office, to order the fashion in which such plate shall be wrought, hath introduced great extravagancy and increase of expence to the Crown in that office; my Lords order a letter to be writ to the Master, to know the instruccõns (if any) which his office is under, and to certifye what the excess has amounted to, for all plate so fashioned during the late King's reign, and to report what methods may best be pursued for easing this and extravagancies of any other kind in the said Office for the future." 3 *pages.*

29 Nov. 23. Four papers relating to the University of Glasgow, entitled as follows:—

(1.) "In the University of Glasgow the salaries of the following members are" [The names and salaries follow.]

(2.) "The salaries of the Professors and Masters in the University of Glasgow, and the funds from which they are paid." Novr 29 1727.

(3.) "The Officers and Masters of the University of Glasgow are elected or presented as followeth."

(4.) "The humble memorial of the Rector, Principal, Professors and Masters of the University of Glasgow," praying that the funds intended for the gentlemen who should study Divinity in Foreign Universities might be allowed to be received by them for continuing their studies at Glasgow. This last is, perhaps, of a later date than the other papers. 6½ *pages.*

1 Dec. 24. Report of the Postmasters-General (Ed. Carteret and E. Harrison) to the Lords of the Treasury. Recapitulating a former representation of 14 April last, viz., that they had made an addition of two packet-boats to convey letters between Gibraltar and Lisbon, or some other part of Portugal, and an addition of men and ammunition for packets between Great Britain and Lisbon. The addition of 10 men to each packet was since thought insufficient, and at the desire of the merchants trading to Portugal, at the end of May last, they ordered a further addition of 15 men to each of the four Lisbon boats and 10 men to the "Groin Boat" designed for Gibraltar. Mr Dormer, his Majesty's envoy at Lisbon, having thought it unnecessary to send packet boats between Portugal and Gibraltar, they (the postmasters) have dismissed the vessel they hired at Lisbon for that service, and the other boat which was ordered for Gibraltar (belonging before to the Groin Station) they have stationed between Great Britain and Lisbon. Await their Lordships' directions thereon, as well as respecting the additional expense. Annex an account of the annual charge of the packets.

The account referred to, headed:—"The usual charge of the Falmouth Pacquet Boats p annum." 3 *pages.*

5 Dec. 25. The Rev. Sutton Morgan to the Lords of the Treasury. Sends the report of the "Governors of the Post Office" upon his petition praying them to commiserate his hard and unfortunate case. Has expended about 400*l.* upon the [Skerrys] Light House for the

1727. VOL. CCLX.

good of the public, for which he was in continual dread of being arrested and thrown into prison. "The Governors" reported entirely in his favour, only they preferred giving him one entire sum instead of an annuity. This and his arrears might be granted without forming a precedent. Dec. 5, 1727.

Minuted:—"20th Decr. To the Mars & Wardens of Trinity House to consider and give their opinion thereupon."

Accompanied by the report referred to, in which the Postmasters reply to the second allegation in the petition, that it does not appear to them that any packet boat in his Majesty's service has been, or ought to be, charged with payments to the Light Houses anywhere upon the coasts. To the third allegation they say that the Skerrys Light is of great use and benefit to all shipping which pass those seas, and in particular to the packet boats upon the Irish station; as appears not only by certificates of his Grace the Duke of Grafton and several other persons of quality and distinction, but also by the Custom house officers, the captain of the yacht, the captains of the Irish packet boats and many masters of merchant ships. The Lords of the Treasury on 19 Sept. 1723 directed a warrant to the Postmaster-General to pay 200*l.* to Mr Wm Trench, who was then owner of the Skerrys Light House, as the money which the navigation contributed to support the Light House was not sufficient.

The petition is also with the report.

Anterior to the above letter there is the following in the Minute Book, vol. 26, p. 34*c*, 28 Sept. 1727:—"Mr Morgan for whom a warrant was lately obtained for 50li p ann at the Post Office, for maintaining the Light-House on the Skerries is to be writ to, to attend my Lords about the same, their Lordps being of opinion that they have been deceived by him in his applicacon for that allowance."

At p. 59*o* of the Minute Book, vol. 26, 19 Dec. 1727, is:—"Postmasters report of the 29th Novr last, on Sutton Morgan's peticon for an allowance for maintaining the Skerry Light House is read, and Mr Morgan attending, was afterwards called in, and my Lords acquaint him that they have no ground from the said report to bring any further charge upon the King for maintaining the said Lighthouse; but they will transmit the papers to the master and wardens of Trinity House, who are a Corporacon, and invested with the care of many Light-Houses; for them to consider and give their opinion thereupon."

Again, at p. 78*c*, 19 Feb. 1727–[8]. "Mr Chancellor acquaints my Lords that the King is pleased to give Sutton Morgan, in consideration of his maintaining the Skerrie Light-Houses, 300li in full of past & all future pretencons whatsoever. So the warrant formerly signed by the King for 50li p ann. is taken up and cancelled." 4½ *pages.*

[? About 5 Dec.] 26. Petition of John Scott, of Ancrum, Esquire, to the Lords of the Treasury. On the water of Ale, near to the parish church of

1727. Vol. CCLX.

Ancrum, in the co. of Roxburgh, there was of old a stone bridge of four arches and three large pillars, built for a passage to all travellers from the eastern or western parts of the county; so that without that bridge, when the waters were out, they would all be stopped in their journeys. The bridge is very decayed by the floods and by the rapidity of the current. The county is not empowered by law to levy the sum requisite for repairs. Proposes, as an expedient, to repair the same, that as he is now the proprietor of the barony of Langnewton, and pays 27*l.* 15*s.* 6⅔*d.* yearly to the Crown, he should have a gift of the same, and be burthened with the repair of the bridge.

The heritor of the barony of Langnewton used to pay yearly to the minister of Langnewton the sum mentioned, but the fabric of the church is gone to ruin, and the parish is now united to the parish of Ancrum. The Court of Commissioners for plantation of churches appointed the stipend to be paid to the "Diocy of Breichen," and after the abolition of prelacy it was paid to the Crown.

Referred to the Barons of the Exchequer to report thereon, 5 Dec. 1727. [*See also* the *North Britain* Book, vol. 9, p. 2.] 1 *page.*

6 Dec. 27. Order of the House of Lords on the petition of Luke Nettervill, Esq., viz.: that the Bishop of Elphin and the Lord Ferrard attend the Lord Lieutenant with the petition and the resolution of the House, and desire his Excellency to lay them before his Majesty. 6 Dec. 1727.

The petition and resolution referred to:

The petitioner states that his brother is the Lord Viscount Nettervill and enjoys a considerable estate in [Ireland], and that petitioner is in most miserable condition with a numerous family, and the House of Lords twice recommended him to His Majesty for a pension, to enable him to give suitable education to his children. He is the only one that the peers had applied for to the late King in the two last years of his reign, and has been a protestant for many years, and the only one of his family, and educates his children in that faith; for which reason he is abandoned by all his popish relations, and has nothing under heaven to subsist himself and his children.

In the Minute Book, vol. 26, p. 67*l*, 11 Jan. 1727-8, is:—"3 January 1727. For a pencõn of 200li p ann. during pleasure to Luke Nettervillc on the recommendation of the House of Lords of that Kingdom." 3 *pages.*

1725 to 18 Dec. 1727. 28. Several papers as to the personal estate and debts of David, Earl of Northeske. A grant to trustees of the personal estate was proposed for the use of the Earl's wife and children. The Earl was sheriff of Forfar and a Crown debtor. Between 1725 and 1727, but the last date is 18 Dec. 1727. 11 *pages or parts of pages.*

19 Dec. 29. Memorial of Sir John Hobart, Bart., "Treasurer of his Mats Chamber, to the Lords of the Treasury." Transmits account of what is due to his Majesty's servants payable by him, amounting

VOL. CCLX.

1727.

to 9,148*l.* 0*s.* 4¾*d.* Prays an order for payment, and that they may stand on the same footing with those payable by the Cofferer. 19 Dec. 1727.

Accompanied by the account of the debt owing at the time of his late Majesty's decease to the officers, servants, and others, which shows the names as well as the salary due to each of them. 26 *pages.*

19 Dec. 30. A similar account of what is due to his Majesty's servants and others, payable in the Treasurer of the Chamber's Office, from 11 June 1727 to Mich. following. 19 Dec. 1727. 13 *pages.*

[About 19 Dec.] 31. Memorial of John Baird, Alexander Abercromby, Patrick Campbell, and Robert Johnston, Esquires, late Receivers and Paymasters of the interest due to the creditors of the public in Scotland, to the Lords of the Treasury. As appears by the papers united, they are "really super-expended" the sums set out, amounting to 2,111*l.*, and, in the opinion of the Barons of the Exchequer of Scotland, provision should be made for repayment; pray for relief.

Indorsed: "Recẽid from Capt. Abercrombie Dec. y[e] 19th 1727."

The payments were chiefly made to the Equivalent Company.

Accompanied by a former representation of the memorialists and a report of the barons. 10½ *pages.*

20 Dec. 32. Robert Byng to the Hon[ble] M[r] Secretary Scroope. Represents what he presumes is the occasion of the alteration of late years in the Admiralty Droits, so that the money arising from them cannot be depended on, and will be very insufficient to answer any relief to widows of sea officers.

Among the rights and perquisites of the Lord High Admiral, those have proved most beneficial which arose from the tenths of prizes taken by H.M. ships of war, and from the tenths of prizes taken by privateers or such as obtained Letters of Marque, as likewise the goods and effects of pirates; besides all wrecks of the sea, flotsoms, &c., the duties relating to anchorages, all royal fishes, all sea-weeds and minerals, the sand and gravel used for the ballasting of ships, &c. The Commanders of H.M. ships of war never had the entire right to prizes till the Act of 1708 allowed the right in the captors, the prizes being constantly accounted for till that time. From whence it appears this part of the Lord High Admirals rights have been given away by Parliament. In 1720 when there were some differences with Spain, the payment of the tenths of prizes due from privateers was exempted and discharged by an Order in Council. The accounting for the goods of pirates has been most shamefully neglected. The Governors of Plantations and Commanders of ships of war have seized the goods and kept them for their own private benefit.

When the Captains of H.M. ships of war seize goods of pirates they refuse to account for them at home, or to agents, and the greatest part is not accounted for.

1727. VOL. CCLX.

Vice-Admirals of maritime counties have also neglected to account for Admiralty droits. Private persons pretending to the rights of Admiralty unjustly seize them, and detain them by force. "Flotsom" and other goods are concealed and used for private advantage. The country people commit most barbarous and inhuman actions towards persons wrecked.

Though the Solicitor for the affairs of the Navy is likewise appointed Solicitor of the rights and perquisites of the Admiralty, he thinks himself not empowered to disburse any money imprested to him for any service in discharge of his duty as Solicitor of the Droits of Admiralty. Believes these obstructions not to be so great, but that they may be easily removed. Proposes some remedies.

"Treasury Office. For the Navy Decemb^r 20th 1727." 8 *pages.*

30 Dec. 33. [Copy of] "Mr Talbot, the Sollicitor General's opinion, relating to the stamps necessary to be put upon all warrants. 30 December 1727." Signed C. Talbot.

Also [copy of] "Sr Edward Northey's opinion relating to the Stamp Dutys. 20th August 1712." 3 *pages.*

[? About 1727.] 34. Petition of Thomas Hyde, only son and executor to his mother, Elizabeth Hyde, lately deceased. In the year 1688 petitioner's father, Thomas Hyde, being commander of a vessel belonging to Pool, was in Holland at the time of King William's expedition to England. The Princess of Orange and the States of Holland having several packets of the greatest consequence to be delivered to the Prince, who had then landed in the West of England, the masters of several English ships were strenuously solicited to undertake this service with promises of great rewards, but declined on account of the danger in case of discovery. His mother with a messenger went to the Princess of Orange, then at the Hague, with whom she had audience, and the Princess assured her "that as the case was of a precarious nature she and her family should be the better for it as long as they lived. The affair being agreed to, his mother returned to Rotterdam with the packets, and his father sailed to England and arrived at Pool in Dorsetshire." On their arrival, his mother, with the letters quilted in her clothes, set out from Pool, "went thro' several of King James's troops, and about thirty miles from Pool met the Prince of Orange and delivered into his own hands the letters." On the settlement of the Crown an allowance of 50*l.* per annum was settled on his father and mother and the survivor of them, which they enjoyed all the reigns of the King and Queen and Queen Anne and the late King George. On the death of petitioner's mother, he, in the month of July last, petitioned the Board that the allowance should be continued to him in his own name. Upon enquiry, finds it is continued in his mother's name. Prays it may be continued to him in his own name. Undated. 2 *pages.*

[? About 1727.] 35. Petition of Samuel Allen of London, gentleman, attorney-at-law, to the Lords of the Treasury, was employed by the Com^rs and Trustees of the Estates forfeited in the Rebellion, in the beginning of his late Majesty's reign, acting for England, first as their solicitor, and after the death of the secretary, as secretary and

1727. Vol. CCLX.

solicitor. Was summoned by the Committee of the House of Commons (to whom all the books and papers relating to the sale of the estate of the late Earl of Derwentwater were referred) and several times examined, was afterwards summoned by the House and the House of Lords to give evidence on the bill for making void the several contracts for the sale of the late Earl's estate; prays for recompense. 1 *page*.

1727. 36. Memorial of the University of St. Andrews [to the King]. After the union, Queen Anne granted 210*l.* per annum to each of the four Universities in North Britain, King Geo. I. continued the same upon the establishment of the Civil List. Pray his present Majesty to continue the same. 1727. 1 *page*.

[? 1727.] 37. Petition of John Goodwin, master and pilot of H.M yacht Carolina, to the King. Was pilot to the King's father, who took notice of his behavour in a very particular manner and ordered him a pension of 50*l.* per ann., as appears by the copy of warrant annexed. On applying to the Treasury is told that his name is not upon the books. Gives particulars of his services and says that he had been pilot to most of the British Admirals and prays that directions may be given for the continuance of his pension, and that the arrears may be paid.

Also copy of the warrant. Dated 19 May 1727. 2 *pages*.

[? 1727.] 38. Petition of Robert Georges, gent., to the Lords of the Treasury. In 1690 was admitted a clerk in the Pay office, when Mr Fox was made paymaster of the forces in Flanders, was "entertain'd" as accountant and soon after as cashier, till Mr Foxes dismission [afterwards] was controller of customs at Bridgewater, until displaced from a misrepresentation, and when the injustice was made known was minuted for the next patent place vacant in the customs, but Her Majesty's death happening, nothing was done therein. Her Majesty made him Yeoman Sadler and Store Keeper on the establishment of her stables, with a house to it, in the "Green Meuse." This he enjoyed till the new establishment after the Accession of his late Majesty, King George, when his name was left out, and the name of one of the Master of the Horse's domestic servants was placed in his stead. Petitioner had expectation of estates in Gloucestershire and Wiltshire, of at least 500*l.* per ann., which were enjoyed by his ancestors between five and six hundred years; but was defrauded of them by forgery, perjury, and subornation, after 17 years controvercy in the Courts of Chancery, &c.

Prays to be recommended to the King for comfortable maintenance, &c. 1 *page*.

[End of 1727.] 39. "Supplemental" petition of the Rev. Mr Sutton Morgan, to the Lords of the Treasury. Petitioner lately petitioned and set forth his deplorable case, relating to the Skerries Light House, and prayed assistance of the Crown to support the same. Their Lordships referred the petition to the Trinity House to report thereon. Queen Anne granted letters patent to William French, Esq., deceased, petitioner's father [in law], to build the light house, contrary to the report of the Trinity House; as appears in an annexed

1727. report, but Captain Davison and Mr Brown, named therein, finding the difficulty and great expense to be greater than they could surmount, rejected the undertaking, and Wm French at the request of the commanders of H.M. packet boats, merchants and mariners, undertook the work and in a short time finished it, to the great satisfaction of all persons who are preserved by it, though to the ruin of himself and family. Petitioner's counsel advise that their Lordships might have granted the prayer of his petition, without any reference to the Trinity House, in regard to the renewal, with the addition of one half penny per ton and double upon foreigners and remittance of the reserved rent of 5*l.* per annum; and petitioner is advised that their Lordships may grant the 50*l.* per ann., with arrears formerly granted by their Lordships, without any reference to any other board or power whatever. Appended to the petition is a letter signed by three bishops and five others, to the Lords of the Treasury, stating that the foundation for Queen Ann's granting the letters patent to petitioner's father in law was the annexed report.

Undated, but the era of J. Bishop of St. Asaph and W. Bishop of Bangor, as well as the previous petition of 5 December, confine it to the end of 1727.

The report referred to, signed "John Manley Supervizor Genl," which touches upon the opposition of the Trinity House to the grant of letters patent to a private person, and states that they claim "a right to the profit that may arise therefrom when erected: but notwithstanding their pretences conceives it's plain her Majesty is not in the least restrained from granting power to any private person to erect a light-house, where in her royal wisdom she shall think fit." Strongly advises the building of the light-house there, though some would have it erected upon the very head of land at Holyhead in Anglesea; but most, and the best opinion is that that place is so high that the clouds will often render the light invisible. Dated 8 Aug. 1712. 3½ *pages.*

[? End of 1727.] 40. Memorial of Henry Samuel Eyre, Esq., administrator of the Marquis of Navarre, deceased, to the Lords of the Treasury, praying for orders to be given to Mr. Cracherode to pay him 175*l.* 16*s.* 5*d.*, being the amount of the taxed bills of the clerk in court and solicitor concerned in the cause of the Marquis of Navarez, beginning 1 June 1723 and ending Michaelmas term 1727, when the cause was determined by agreement. [The Marquis was in 1715 possessed of effects to the value of 16,000*l.* in Jamaica; and being desirous to go to Carthagena, agreed with the owner of a vessel to transport him, his family, and effects, to Sancta Martha on the coast of Carthagena; but the master landed him at "Tholu" after having robbed him of all his treasure. The vessel some days after was forced into Charlestown in Carolina, by stress of weather, and the master was arrested, and King George I. gave directions that Mr Craven the Governor (who suffered the master to escape) should be prosecuted at the expense of the Crown. A bill was exhibited in Chancery against Mr Craven and others for a discovery and relief. Mr. Craven put in an answer, and set forth an account of the effects,

1727. VOL. CCLX.

amounting to 3,000*l.* Mr Cracherode, out of H.M. treasure, paid the expenses of the suit until 1722, when the Treasury revoked the orders for carrying on the suit, which was afterwards continued at the expense of the complainant.

Two other papers connected therewith. 5½ *pages.*

[? 1727 or later.] 41. The paper of which the following is a copy is perhaps an enclosure to another paper not now forthcoming.

"The method of business at the Treasury on issuing money. As no money is issued at the Exchequer but by the authority of the Great or Privy Seal, therefore on the occasion of anything to the Crown it is usual to pass a Privy Seal, which is called the General Letters of Privy Seal as also Letters Patent under the Great Seal, which is called the General Letters Patent Dormant.

"General Letters of Privy Seal directs the High Treasurer, Chancellor of the Exchequer, or Commissioners of the Treasury, out of any the King's treasure, from time to time, being in the receipt of the Exchequer, to pay all such sum or sums of money for any public or particular uses and service as the King, by warrt under his royal sign manual, shall direct, or appoint to be paid, by way of imprest or otherwise, as the said warrant shall require and direct.

"This Privy Seal bears date the 26th June 1727, and by virtue thereof the King signs a warrant for secret service, for disbursements, for rewards for services, bounties, &c.

"General Letters Patent Dormant directs the High Treasurer, &c., out of any money for the uses of the Civil Government, to pay to the High Treasurer or Commissioners of the Treasury 8,000*l.* a year salary; and all fees, wages and rewards, for services and attendances due to all other the officers, deputies, ministers." ½ *page.*

[? End of 1727.] 42. "Charges of the office baggage from England to Rhenen in Westphalia and back, postage, &c. in June 1727.

Also "Expenses of the office baggage from Rhenen in Westphalia to England after the death of his late Majesty."

The last is signed:—"Geo. Tilson." 2 *pages.*

[? 1727.] 43. "Memorial for the roaprie, soaprie and pinrie of Glasgow and soaprie and pinrie of Leith" to the Barons of the Exchequer [of Scotland] in reply to a memorial presented to their Lordships in summer last, and in obedience to their Lordships commands directing an account to be laid before them of what sums might be a reasonable equivalent for the surrender of their rights of exemption from the duties on materials imported for the use of their manufactories. Apprehend that the annual value of their gifts of exemption ought to be computed at sixteen years purchase, which would amount for each of them to—1,195*l.* 8*s.*

	£	*s.*	*d.*
For the rope work at Glasgow taken from a medium of ye former importation -	1730	0	0
And for the pin work yr at a medium of former years - - - - - -	689	19	8
And for ye pin work at Leith also at a medium - - - - - - -	126	5	4

1727. VOL. CCLX.

The duties on goods imported for manufactures as taken from the Custom House books will differ very much from their account which is defective by being destroyed or carried off in the Rebellion.

Also a copy of the above, in the margin of which is "Anno 1727." $4\frac{3}{4}$ *pages.*

[Probably 1727.] 44. Representation of the Justices of the Peace of the Shires of Haddington and Berwick to the Right Hon. the Lords Com[rs] of Police. Upon application of the Justices of the peace of the two shires, to the Com[rs] of Police, in A.D. 1717, the latter (to whom the business properly belongs) represented to the late King George, the necessity of completing the Bridge of Coldbrandspath, and that the Justices could not impose the sums necessary; but that Sir James Hall, in whose lands the bridge is situated, proposed to build the bridge, and keep it in repair, upon his getting a right to his feu duties payable to His Majesty; and after a representation of the matter to his Majesty, he granted the duties during his life. After this the bridge was built, and the great advantage thereof to His Majesty's forces, and to the common post, as well as to all other travellers to and from England, renders the same an universal concern—so they represent, that the former gift being determined by His Majesty's death, there may be danger of the bridge falling for want of repair. Pray the Com[rs] to apply to His Majesty for a continuance of the gift. Undated. 32 signatures. 1 *large page*

[? 1727.] 45. Petition of Robert, Earl of Morton, to the King, by the infeofments of his estate in Orkney and Zetland is subject to pay a feu duty to the Crown of 100*l.* per ann. In consideration of the singular services of petitioner's ancestors, the duty has never been exacted. For the forwardness of the late Earl and of the petitioner in supporting the Crown, his late Majesty granted the duty by a Commission of Chamberlanrie to John Ewing, Esq., for the behoof of petitioner for 21 years if the King so long lived. This has become void by the demise of the King. Prays relief. Undated, but in the *North Britain Book,* vol. 8, p. 321, a petition from him of an earlier date was referred to the Barons of Scotland for report on 20 May 1727. 1 *page.*

[? End of 1727 or 1728.] 46. A similar petition of the same Earl to the King. In addition to what is above stated the petitioner says that his late brother enjoyed the Admiralty of Orkney and Zetland by Commission from the late King William, Queen Ann, and his late Majesty while the late Earl lived; that upon his demise the Earl of Sutherland obtained a Commission from his late Majesty for the Admiralty, which is now become void; that the Earl of Sutherland having no interest in that country nor so much as a foot of ground there, and unknown to the people, occasions frequent disputes betwixt his deputes and the inhabitants, much to the detriment of the petitioner and his vassals and tenants; and that the petitioner's estate lies in that country with the whole jurisdiction thereof, except the Admiralty. Prays relief. 1 *page.*

1727. VOL. CCLX.

[1727 or later.] 47. Petition of Lieut. Col. John Irwin to the Lords of the Treasury. Was sent to Ireland to be placed on the establishment of half pay as Lieutenant Col. of Foot, and did duty during the Rebellion. Was left out of the establishment in 1720 until replaced, but without retrospect pay. Prays to be allowed the arrears out of a debt due to the Crown from the Collector of Sligo.

Copies of four other documents connected with Irwin's case. 4 *pages*.

[After 1727.] 48. Memorial of Patrick McDowall, of Edinburgh, gentleman. Has a claim on the Government for 910*l*. in right of his father-in-law since the year 1696. The late King George referred his case to Sir Robert Wallpole, who told him that he could not expect England would pay the Scot's debt; and that until he could find out a fund in Scotland undisposed of he could not expect payment. The returned duties or fines payable by the vassals of the Crown in Scotland, upon their being admitted tenants, are not disposed of, and there is no regular account of them brought into the Exchequer. The tenants ordinarily give bonds to the sheriffs of the counties, where the estates lie, to be accountable for these fines when called for, and being small sums and attended with difficulty to bring them in, they are little inquired after, and when Parliament men happen to be admitted tenants they procure gifts from the Treasury of the duties or fines payable by them. The "feu duties" out of the estate of the late Earl of Seaforth, in the north of Scotland, have not been paid since the Rebellion, in regard the lands are not yet sold and the rents cannot be levied but by military force. Prays a warrant to the Barons of the Exchequer in Scotland to grant him a commission for collecting such feu duties as have or shall become due to the Crown and to discover concealed tenants who lie out unentered, and have not attorned to the Crown, &c. 1 *page*.

[1727 or 1728, or later.] 49. Proposition of Charles Whytell and Joseph Robinson to the Lords of the Treasury. Proposers laid before their Lordships a memorial for destroying fraudulent trade, carried on, to, and from the Isle of Man; whereupon an Act of Parliament was passed and the trade is almost destroyed to the great improvement of the revenue in Great Britain and Ireland. The great encouragers of the fraudulent trade were the farmers of Customs of that Island and their collector, who have now sold all their effects and gone out of the Island. The yearly charge of the Island for officers and cruising vessels, stationed about the Island, is 2,008*l*. 8*s*. 8*d*. This they propose to reduce to 1,428*l*. 8*s*. 8*d*. by doing away with the cruisers and by having a new establishment of officers, tidesmen, and boatmen. At each port there would be eight persons, viz., one port officer, one tidesman, and six boatmen. The proposers observe, "that the notoriety of the disaffection of the people of the Island, is scarce to be imagined, but by them who have lived in it; and the same is chiefly owing to the Bisp̃ of the said Isle, admitting all kinds & sorts of persons, from several parts of Britt. & Ireland, as

1727. VOL. CCLX.

well as the natives of the said Isle into orders, without their taking the abjuration oath, and the Reformation 'togather' with its fruits; the rights & doctrines of the Church of England never having been as yet regularly introduced by a proper authority into the said Island, and the Ecclest[l] polity thereof being grounded upon a popish, & builded up after a non-juring plan, the laiety are, and cannot but be, thereby miserably oppressed & deluded; and the Papists in Ireland being prohibited from purchasing land estates in that kingdom, have in general turned their money into stock in trade, & have at all times goods & merchandizes to the value of many thousand pounds in the said Island, and their ships trading frequently & directly from Ostend, & some constantly from the ports of Spain; as matters stand at present in y[e] Island, arms, & ammunition may privately be lodged there (& even foreign military officers concealed) without danger of discovery or of any molestation at the re-shipping of them in favour of any attempt which the Pretender may make upon Ireland or Great Britain: & much larger quantities of gunpowder have been imported from time to time into Island than the use thereof could demand, and in the time of the late war with France, lead brought from Scotland & other warlike ammunitions was wont to be exported from the said Island to the French dominions," &c. 3¼ *pages.*

VOL. CCLXI. 1724. CLASSIFIED. PART I.

1. Letters from the Secretary to the Lords of the Admiralty to John Scrope, Esq.

(1.) The Lords of the Admiralty do not conceive it can be of any service to send the Lords of the Treasury the particular stations of the ships employed the last year: but send the names of the ships and vessels employed, with their complements of men. 10 Jan. 1726–7.

There is the following "Draft of y[e] letter to M[r] Burchett 11th of Jan[ry] 1726–7." In reply, "I am comãnded to acquaint you that the Ld C. of the Treasury are suprised at the answer you sent by order of the Lords Co. of y[e] Admiralty to my letter of [10th] inst. It having been usual for y[e] House of Comõns to call every year for the very same account which I wrote to desire you to move the L[ds] of the Admiralty for. The Lords of the Treasury desired they might see it for their information only, that they might be the better enabled to serve His Majesty in parliament when the several accounts usually laid before the House of Comõns shall come to be considered there & did not expect there would have been any objection to their seeing this week, what everybody will see next week. As for y[e] account you sent, it can be of no possible use to any body, it being as is supposed an account only of y[e] compliments of y[e] severall ships, w[th]out distinguishing the several times when

1727. Vol. CCLXI.

the severall ships were in sea-pay and what number of men were born[e] or muster'd each month on ye several ships."

The following is added, but is scored out:—

"But as an account of this kind is absolutely necessary for his Majesties service, to be laid before the Lords Com̃ of his M's Treasury, their Lordships have sent an order to the Com̃issioners of the Navy to prepare and lay this account before them, from whom they hope they shall receive a civil answer."

A copy of the letter is referred to and entered in the *Minute Book,* vol. 25, p. 266, 11 Jan. 1726. In the notice of the letter before the copy of it is:—"My Lords resent this treatment from the Lords of the Admiralty and agree to Mr Scropes signing the following letter to Mr Burchett thereupon".

(2.) As to the difficulty of furnishing masts from New England. (Two enclosures.)

(3.) As to the raging sickness at Chatham. The workmen prayed to have some part of their wages. (Petition enclosed.)

(4.) As to the waste of his Majesty's woods in New England by the inhabitants cutting them down and using them. (Three enclosures.) 33 *pages or parts of pages.*

2. Reports of the Commissioners of the Office of Alienations to the Lords of the Treasury, certifying the gross and net produce of the office, &c. 4¼ *pages.*

3. Twenty-two certificates of the swearing and admission of various persons to offices in the Household by the Duke of Grafton, Lord Chamberlain of the Household. 22 *pages.*

4. A parcel of bills and memoranda of materials delivered to the Great Wardrobe, &c., connected with the coronation of King George the Second. There are also four other papers of a similar nature connected with the Office of the Robes, one of which relates to materials furnished for the coronation of King Geo. I. 49 *pages or parts of pages.*

1727. 5. Reports of the Com^rs^ of Customs to the Lords of the Treasury respecting (1) the running of East India Goods out of the ship Carnarvon in A.D. 1722: (2.) The proceedings against Wm Bradford of Brighthelmstone, Sussex, mariner, who had a deputation from the Duke of Newcastle as Vice Admiral of the County to seize goods "found floating on the sea for the use of his Grace": (3.) The petition of several merchants, importers of copper from Barbary, for a drawback on copper refined in England: (4.) "The petition of the merchants of Norwich, relating to the 'premios' on stuff manufactures exported on an Act of the 8th of the late King, the debentures for which are stopped by the Custom House officers at Yarmouth." This is accompanied by a copy of the Attorney and Solicitor General's opinion. 27 *pages.*

6. Estimates, viz., of the charge of guards, garrisons and other H.M. land forces in Great Britain; of several extraordinary expenses of H.M. forces incurred and not provided for by Parliament (two):

1727. VOL. CCLXI.

of the Office of Ordnance (two); of the out-pensioners of Chelsea Hospital; of the charge of H.M. forces in the plantations of Minorca and Gibraltar; and of the charge of augmenting H.M. forces in Great Britain. For the year 1717.

Also two accounts of services incurred and not provided for by parliament, and a computation of savings by the reduction and sending back of four regiments of foot from Great Britain to Ireland; in the year 1727. 15 *pages.*

7. Reports of the Com^rs of Excise to the Lords of the Treasury (1) on the produce of the Civil List. (2.) On an account of the gross produce, salaries, incidents and other deductions, and the net produce of the revenues under their management. (3.) On a grievous outrage upon one of their officers at Blackstock, near Snape, in the co. of Suffolk, by the smugglers who cut off the nose of the officer. (4.) As to repayment of 26,428*l.* 11*s.* 5*d.* paid out of his late Majesty's Civil List Revenues. (5.) Concerning the 3,700*l.* per week paid out of the late King William's arrears, and whether the amount was made good or replaced to the late King's account. (6.) As to money, paid into the Exchequer, arising out of that part of the excise which was appropriated to the Civil List. Also as to arrears. 12 *pages.*

VOL. CCLXII. CLASSIFIED. PART II.

1. Various papers of a financial nature, such as accounts of income and issues out of the Civil List revenues, balances from Paymasters of the Lotteries, sums remaining in the Exchequer of Receipt, state of the South Sea Company's funds, produce of duties arising by licencing hawkers and pedlars. State of public debts provided for by Parliament, with a view of the sinking fund, &c. 33 *pages or parts of pages.*

2. Letters of the Lord Lieut. of Ireland (Carteret) to the Lords of the Treasury. (1.) For his Majesty's signature to a letter securing the purchasers of Mr. Pratt's Estate from any claim of the Crown. (2.) For similar signature for granting the profits of the See of Derry during the vacancy to the Right Rev. Dr. Downes, the present Bishop. (3.) For payment of 60*l.* to the Lord John Kerr, Brigadier General of H.M. forces in Ireland, who had received that amount short of his pay as Brigadier General. (Also report enclosed.) (4.) For the proper instruments to be prepared for the augmentation to eleven battalions in Ireland of one serjeant, one corporal, one drummer, and as many privates to each company as can be raised and paid from the savings on the Irish Establishment by the removal of four regiments specified [*Minuted*:—"W^t signed 23 March 1726]. (5.) In favour of the petition of Alexander

1727 Vol. CCLXII.

Cairnes, Baronet, who prayed an addition of two lives to the Grant he has of the Lodges of the Deer Park at Dublin. (6.) For 4,034*l.* 5*s.* from Ireland for arms sent out of Ordnance stores. (7.) About increase of pay to the Deputy Commissaries of the Musters in Ireland. (8.) About new arms for the regiments of horse and dragoons upon the establishment of Ireland. (9.) About the deficiency of fees for licences for exporting wool from Ireland to Great Britain; the fees forming a considerable portion of the Lord Lieut[s] income. (10.) For the proper instrument to be prepared for the Royal signature to place Capt. Edward Columbine upon the establishment of half pay in Ireland as captain of foot. (11.) As to fees due for Public Bills to the Usher of of H.M. Council Chamber in Ireland. (12.) As to a grant of letters patent prayed for by Lawrence Esmond, for reducing the Quit Rents on the lands mentioned in a report of the Com[rs] of H.M. revenue. (13.) As to the balance due to his Majesty, on the Vice-Treasurer's accounts (Ireland). (14.) For H.M. warrant for payment of the charge of providing 400 barrels of gunpowder for Ireland. (15.) Respecting the grant of the rents, &c. of the archbishopric of Cashel, during the vacancy of the see, to D[r] Timothy Goodwin, who was presented thereto. [*Minuted:*—" Ordered."] (16.) Respecting the petition of Major Claudius Testefolle, late of the regiment of horse commanded by Col. Ligonier. The major prayed to be placed on half-pay. (17.) For Captain Edward Columbine to be put on half-pay as captain of foot. (18.) For a sign manual to be obtained for 80*l.* to make up the pay of Lord John Kerr equal to other brigadiers, and for the continuance of the increased allowance, the late King's letter in his favour not having been put in execution by the demise of his Majesty. (19.) For Michael Smith, Esq., Captain of a company in H.M. own Royal regiment of foot in Ireland, to be placed on half-pay, in consequence of his labouring under a disorder which has affected his senses. (20.) Respecting additions to the establishment of Ireland, viz. Theophilus Clements, Esq., & the Marquis of Miremont, and for each of the other brigadiers general on the military establishment of Ireland to have 20*s.* per diem; for Capt. Alexander Guibert de Sissac, Capt. Alexander Duvernier, Capt. John Meissonier, and Capt. Edward Columbine to have half pay as captains of foot at 4*s* 9*d.* per diem each, and Lieut. John la Bastide and Lieut. Joseph Meissoniers as Lieutenants of foot at 2*s.* 3*d.* per diem each.

Several of the above have enclosures, but in others the enclosures are wanting. 44 *pages.*

3. Three papers relating to payments made in the Treasury Office, Dublin; (1) on account of military contingencies; (2) for the use of the barracks; and (3) by several warrants of concordatums. Signed "Lu Gardiner Dep[y] Rec[r] Gen[l]." 18 *pages or parts of pages.*

4. Memorials from the Treasurer of the Navy to the Lords of the Treasury applying for moneys for payment of wages; paying

1727. Vol. CCLXII.

off ships; victualling, &c. Signed by "Pattee Byng" or by William Corbett, his substitute. Many of these have minutes on the back such as "Lr̃e signed," &c.

There are also a few other subordinate papers connected with the navy. *26 pages or parts of pages.*

5. Memorials from the Paymaster General of the Forces to the Lords of the Treasury for payment of subsistence and other moneys for the troops. Signed "S. Compton," or by his deputy.

Many of them have minutes on the back such as "Lr̃e signed," &c. 14 *pages.*

6. Edmund, Bishop of London to the Lords of the Treasury. Asks their Lordships to order the payment of 20*l.* each for his Majesty's bounty for the passage of the following persons:—

The Rev. Mr Matthias, appointed a minister in Jamaica.

The Rev. Mr John Becket, A.M., appointed a minister in Virginia.

The Rev. Mr Richard Watts, do.

The Rev. Mr Henry Caner, A.B., appointed a minister in the Province of Connecticutt in New England.

The Rev. Mr Patric Rose, A.M., appointed a minister in Barbados.

The Rev. Mr John Miln, appointed a minister in Albany in the Province of New York.

The Rev. Mr Joseph Smith, appointed a minister in Virginia.

The Rev. Mr Ebenezer Miller, A.M., appointed a minister in the Province of Massachusetts in New England.

The Rev. Mr Henry Husband, A.M., appointed a minister in Antegoa in America. 9 *pages.*

VOL. CCLXIII. 1727. Classified. Part III.

1. Letters (many being in duplicate) of William Matheu, Gilbert Fleming, and Edward Mann, Commissioners for the sale of the French part of the Island of St Christophers, called Basse Terre and Cabecça Terre, Basse Terre Town and Deep Bay Town, some addressed to the Lords of the Treasury and others to their Secretary, John Scrope, Esq., giving an account of their proceedings in carrying out their Commission, in which they were a good deal involved in disputes with the Governor (General Hart), who had greatly obstructed their proceedings. In the letter of 12 Jan. 1726–7 they say: "We hope sir, from this, that His Excellency's conduct will be alter'd for the future, and be no more an impediment to the service, and in this hope, we humbly offerr there may be an oblivion as to what is past; unlesse Mr Hart should give us fresh occasion of application to you, and then we shall be more perticuler on the foregoing, and send you copys of the above mentioned letters. We

1727. Vol. CCLXIII.

own we are the more inclin'd to this because we have strong reports that M[r] Hart is remov'd from his Governm[t]. His actions, therefore, will hereafter have the lesse influence to the prejudice of our proceedings, and (unlesse we should find it necessary) we would not pursue him under this mortification, and indeed, on the compremising this matter, we were under some engagements of honour not to carry it further."

In another of the same date they say: "We fear at last we shall be distressed in getting ridd of the Salt Pond lands, even at an average of 25*s.* sterl. ꝑ acre. 'Tis a miserable poor barren, dry soil. We have gott into a project, and made a little beginning in it. We find in the good part of the Island many poor settlers on five to fifteen acres of land. These are not able to purchase, and 'tis pity too to weaken the Island by driving them off. We are therefore trying to persuade them to remove to the salt ponds, on lands to be given them gratis, and by selling the lands they quitt to greedy neighbours, we expect to find our account in the price we make them pay, which shall be, at least, equall to the value of the land we pretendedly give att the salt ponds, and these convenient patches too; and both partys pleas'd without hurt to His Majesty's service."

In that for 22 March 1727 they say: "We already grow fearfull that Gen[l] Hart will break with us again. He still seems to decline treating for his plantation, till he can bring us to his terms of purchase and this we cannot gratify him in, without justly incurring their Lordship's displeasure."

In another of 27 March 1727 they say: "We pray leave to observe to you the improvements allready made in the Island since the sales. Instead of little thatched cottages we see handsome buildings rising, substantially built of brick, stone or good timber boarded and shingled, which purchasers now erect with pleasure."

In that of 6 May to M[r] Scrope they say of Governor Hart: "Of late he has been so outragious and especially on our proceeding in a dispute between him and M[r] Boyd, which we formerly mention'd to you that he has made it impossible for us to forbear remonstrating to their Lordships his behaviour, with respect to our Commission, or to treat further with him."

In a second letter to him of the same date they enclose a letter to the Lords of the Treasury, and "Observations on a scheme for sale of the late French Lands in S[t] Christophers." [This latter contains particulars of the produce, &c. of the Island.]

In the letter of 6 May to the Lords of the Treasury are inclosed two Accounts (1) of lands sold, the quantities whereof are ascertained by an actual survey, for which the Com[rs] have signed contracts and (2) of lands similarly sold, for which contracts have not been signed.

In that to M[r] Scrope of 22 June they set out in detail the dispute between Governor Hart and M[r] Boyd, which principally caused the resentment of the Governor to the Com[rs]. It arose from M[r] Boyd proposing to purchase a parcel of land formerly called "Bourks

1727. VOL. CCLXIII.

plantation," and lately belonging to one James Ward, in the possession of the Governor, and of which he claimed the pre-emption.

In that of 27 July to the Lords of the Treasury they enclose duplicates of their last, and of the several accounts therein referred to. They also "send a separate and very candid account" relating to Governor Hart, and an account of some further sales in Basse Terre and Deep Bay towns. Compute that they have yet about 1,646 acres of manurable land to sell besides the salt ponds. (7 enclosures.)

In that of the same date to Mr Scrope encloses duplicate of their last, &c. 101 *pages. Most of the letters are* 4*to.*

2. Another collection of papers connected with the proceedings of the above Commissioners, including the following:—

Memorials of Dame Frances Stapleton.

Articles of agreement between the King on the one part, and Giles Mardenbrough, of the Island of St Christopher [of the other], in respect to a purchase of land in Basse Terre. Dated 23 Jan. 172[7].

On the back is a certificate of the Lords of the Treasury confirming the purchase. Dated 2nd of Nov. 1730.

Letter signed "Galfridus Gray" to John Scrope, Esq., and a paper docketed "Mr Scrope's observations on Gray's scheme."

Certified copy of the report of the Board of Trade on the case of Captain Andrew Thauvet, an inhabitant of St Christopher's.

Copy of articles of agreement between the King and William McDowall, and confirmation similar to those above named, as entered in the books of the Auditor of Plantations.

Depositions of John Willett, Esq. before one of the Justices of the King's Bench and Common Pleas in the above Island.

(These relate to Mr Mann's affairs, hereafter noticed.)

Letter from Governor Hart to Mr Scrope. Had applied to have his salary as Governor, which was payable out of the 4½ per cent. accepted in part payment of what was due to the Com^rs for the purchase of his plantation; but as that could not be complied with, has drawn bills of Exchange. Prays that the warrants for his salary may be signed, there being 3½ years due. It will be ruin to him by not having his bills paid, for want of effects in his agent's hands, at a time when he is superseded in his government by Lord Londonderry. 30 March 1727.

Two dockets for grants of land to Robert Cunningham, Esq.

Another letter of Governor Hart to J. Scroope, Esq., respecting his plantation of 280 acres, on which he had laid out 4,000*l.* in works and buildings, besides double that amount in stocking it with negroes. The Com^rs had not power to sell more than 200 acres to any one person, and a great part of his (the General's) expense would be useless if he could not purchase the whole. A claim to purchase 50 acres had been made, and the matter was considered by the Com^rs, who eventually refused to treat with the writer, and alleged that he had so behaved himself that they would represent his conduct to the Lords of the Treasury. Asks M^r

1727. VOL. CCLXIII.

Scroope to desire their Lps to suspend the matter till he can give them satisfaction. Adds that perhaps some former obligations which he put Mr Mathew under, of doing his duty, as Lieut.-Governor, had contributed to this resentment.

Several papers relating to disputes between Edward Mann, Esq., on the one part, and John Willett and John Spooner, Esq., on the other, concerning a plantation lately belonging to President Davis, deceased.

"A List of Plantations in St. Christopher's which the Commissioners have contracted or agreed for, which will bear an additional price, and how much per acre."

Abraham Meure to —— as to licence to Mr Mathew to come to England, he having been left out of the Council of three of the Islands by Lord Londonderry's instructions. He must think it an insupportable disgrace. Encloses the address of the Assembly of the Island of St Christopher praising his administration.

"Extract [or abstract] of letters from [the] Commrs for sale of French lands in St Christophers to [the Lo]rds of the Treasury" (39 letters in all). 79 *pages*.

3. Papers relating to the collection of, and accounting for, taxes, including "A state of the severall accompts of the Receivers of the publick taxes behind and undeclared;" a report of the Comrs of Taxes on the arrears of the tax upon Papists and on land, and petitions for employment in connexion with the taxes. 12 *pages*.

4. Monthly debtor and creditor accounts of fees of the Treasury officers from Jan. to September (February being wanting). 24 *pages or parts of pages*.

5. Three warrants, two signed by the Duke of Grafton, the other by the Duke of Sussex, to the Master of the Great Wardrobe, for supply of furniture for the House of Peers, &c. (being parts of a series), also a merchant's bill of articles delivered into the wardrobe. 6 *pages*.

6. Several certificates of receipts, payments, and remains of the revenue arising by Wine Licences and two or three other papers connected with the business of the Wine Licence Commissioners. 15 *pages*.

7. Memorials, &c. of the Board of Works to the Lords of the Treasury relating to works at Hampton Court, Kensington Gardens, the Court of requests at Westminster, set apart for keeping the Records of the Court of King's Bench, Essex House in Essex Street, taken for "repositing" his Majesty's and the Cotton Libraries, preparations for the Coronation, the Earl of Leicester's House in Leicester Square, keeping the gardens in order at Windsor, Hampton Court, Kensington, St. James's, and Newmarket.

There is also an attested copy of the establishment of the Office of Works as it stood at the time of the King's demise; also another memorial as to the expense of the Coronation, together with an account of the ordinary expense in the office, which included the Tower of London, Whitehall, St. James's, Westminster, Denmark

1727. VOL. CCLXIII.

House, Winchester, Newmarket, Hampton Court House and Gardens, and Kensington House and Gardens, Windsor Castle, and the Mews. 22 *pages.*

8. Four letters from H. Pelham, Secretary at War, to John Scroope, Esq., Secretary to the Treasury, (1) for the Lords of the Treasury to be moved in respect to an order to Mr Missing, contractor for provisions for the garrison of Gibraltar, to furnish provisions for 1,200 more men; (2) for a warrant for payment of 2,008*l.* 17*s.* 6*d.* for transport of troops from Ireland to England, to be countersigned, and for an order to issue moneys into the hands of the Paymaster General for the remainder, 808*l.* 17*s.* 6*d.*; (3) for directions to be given to the King's printer to send to his office 200 Acts of Parliament for punishing mutiny, desertion, &c., and the like number of printed books of the Articles of War, to be distributed among the land forces; (4) for a warrant of his Majesty to pay 500 men 1,160*l.* 1*s.* 9*d.* to the paymaster of the forces in Minorca, to be countersigned. 16 Dec. 1726 to 14 Sept. 1727. 5 *pages.*

VOL. CCLXIV. 1727.

DOCUMENTS for which a brief description suffices.

Date.	Description of Document.	From	To	Purport.
[After 1726.]	1. List -	—	—	Of offices in Scotland during pleasure. 4 *pages.*
1 Jan.	2. Account -	Francis Burton, Recr. Genl. of Deductions.	—	Of the deductions of 6*d.* in the pound from 30 Nov. to the 31 Dec. 1726. 1 Jan. 1726. 1 *page.*
9 Jan.	3. Letter -	Lord Chamberlain (Grafton).	Lords of the Treasury.	For a present of 500*l.* to the Ambassador from the Emperor of Morocco, who was about to return home, and of 100*l.* to his mufti secretary and kinsman, and 30*l.* to his interpreter, and 100*l.* for clothing to the Ambassador's slaves. 1 *page.*
2 Feb.	4. Account -	The above Francis Burton.	--	Of the receipt, payment, and remains of the deductions of 6*d.* in the pound for Jan. 1726. 1 *page.*
16 Feb.	5. Balance sheet	—	—	The Public Treasury's Account of cash in New Providence. Sworn in Council. 2 *pages.*
21 Feb.	6. Letter -	Excise Comrs., Edinburgh.	Lords [of the Treasury].	As to sums due to their Collectors for salaries, &c. paid by them. 1 *page.*

1727. VOL. CCLXIV.

Date.	Description of Document.	From	To	Purport.
24 Feb.	7. Memorial -	William Moore, Esq., Deputy Muster Master General.	The Lords Justices Genl. and Govrs. of Ireland.	For his Majesty's letters for replacing and continuing several battalions of foot which embarked from Ireland, and which are to be paid on the Irish Establishment. [*Minuted* :—" Wt. Signed. 23 March 1726."] 2 *pages*.
27 Feb.	8. Bills - -	John Harper and Jonas Morris.	—	Made out to the Hon. Col. Jervais Parker, Quartermaster-General of H.M. Forces, for provisions for men, for ship-hire, &c. 5 *pages*.
8 Mar.	9. Memorandum	J. Gilbert, sub-almoner.	The Lords of the Treasury.	For money due "for discretionary and daily alms." *Minuted* :—" Ordered." ½ *page*.
10 Mar.	10. Letter -	Duke of Grafton -	Do. -	For orders to be given for new flooring "with right wainscot all his Majesty's appartment in the lower lodging at Kensington." 1 *page*.
10 Mar.	11. Account -	—	—	Of the charge of the taking and removing the deer from Hampton Court House Park, and delivering them at Portsmouth to John Russell, Esq. His Majesty's Consul by Charles Howard, Keeper of the Duke of Somerset. Referred 11 March 1726. 2 *pages*.
13 Mar.	12. Account -	—	—	Balance sheet of the York Building's Company, in account with the Government in connexion with the Widdrington Estate. 1 *large page*.
14 Mar.	13. Affidavit -	—	—	Of Peter Fowler of Dublin, tobacconist, as to fraudulent shipping of tobacco for the drawback: it being "good for nothing either to smoak or chaw." 1½ *pages*.
18 Mar.	14. Letter -	H. Pelham, Secretary-at-War.	John Scrope, Esq.	Encloses copy of charter party, and desires the Lords of the Treasury may be moved to issue money to the Paymaster-General for transport of troops from Ireland to Gibraltar. 2 *pages*.

1727. VOL. CCLXIV.

Date.	Description of Document.	From	To	Purport.
21 Mar.	15. Letter -	The Earl of Stair -	–	His brother is one of the Barons of the Exchequer in Scotland, and held the place from Queen Ann, of discoverer of concealed rents of the Crown in Scotland, with a salary of 100*l.* per ann., which is unpaid. Reminds his correspondent that he (the correspondent) thought the Baron should have the salary for life. Asks him to give directions thereon. 2 *pages.*
23 Mar.	16. Account -	—	—	Of the gross and net produce of the stamp duties. 1 *page.*
23 Mar.	17. Bill - -	William Smith	Comrs. of the Navy.	For bedding for a detachment of foot guards of Col. Clayton's regiment bound for Gibraltar. 1 *page.*
24 Mar.	18. Certificate -	Lieut. Governor of Gibraltar.	Lords of the Treasury.	Of provisions in store in the garrison. 1 *page.*
29 Mar.	19. Account -	—	Do. -	Of the debt of the Jewel Office. 1 *page.*
30 Mar.	20. Letter -	Duke of Newcastle -	Do. -	For notice to be given to the contractors, &c. for provisions to have the ships ready to carry the same to Gibraltar, to be convoyed by two men-of-war ordered to reinforce Sir Charles Wager. 1 *page.*
3 April	21. Report -	Postmasters (Ed. Carterett and E. Harrison).	Do. -	On the petition of Dorothy Musgrave, who was the widow of Philip Musgrave, late Postmaster of Boston, New England, and was left in indigent condition. Confirms the truth of the petition. Also a certificate. 3 *pages.* In the Minute Book, Vol. 25, p. 291*i*, 19 April 1727 is :—* * * "As the postma'rs report her a proper object of compassion, write to them to know if their officers, like others in the Revenue, have submitted to a deduction out of their salaries to make a fund for age and indigency. 3 *pages.*
8 April	22. Abstract -	—	—	Of land revenue within Auditor Godolphin's division. 2 *pages.*

VOL. CCLXIV.

1727.

Date.	Description of Document.	From	To	Purport.
8 April	23. Account -	—	—	Of produce of the petty branches of the Civil List Revenue. Mich. 1726 to Mich. 1727. Excheqr. Auditrs. Office. 8 April 1727. 1 *page*.
10 April	24. Memorial -	John Robinson, Searcher in the Port of London.	Lords of the Treasury.	On the question of signing debentures for drawbacks for refined copper entered outwards as Barbary copper unwrought. 2 *pages*.
10 April	25. Abstract -	—	—	Of the annual charge of the Receiver General of H.M. land revenue under the audit of Thomas Jett, auditor. 4 *pages*.
28 Sept. 1726 to 19 Apr. 1727.	26. Bill - -	—	—	Of the Apothecary of H.M. Household. 45 *pages*.
19 April	27. Certificate -	—	—	Of moneys paid into the Exchequer between Christmas 1726 and Lady Day 1727, upon the deduction of 6*d*. per pound duty on victuallers, &c. 1 *page*.
26 April	28. Memorial -	Francis Negus, Esq.	Lords of the Treasury.	For the issue of money to complete the repairs of Swinley Lodge in Windsor Forest. 1 *page*.
2 May	29. Report -	—	Lords Justices of Ireland.	Report of the Board of General Officers in relation to new arms for the several regiments of horse and dragoons on the Irish establishment. 2 *pages*.
[? About 10 May.]	30. Petition -	Henry Harcourt, late Controller of "the Classis Lottery, Ao. 1711."	Lords of the Treasury.	For 78*l*. 15*s*. to be paid to him by the representatives of John Dutton Colt, who was paymaster of the Class Lottery anno 1711, pursuant to a warrt. from the Treasury. *Minuted*: — "Read 10th May 1727. My Lords order that the said 10*l*. be satisfyed out of the first money that shall be recovered from the said Colt or his sureties." 1 *page*.
15 May	31. Letter -	Edward Smith -	Do. -	Is appointed by the Admiralty to cruise upon the smugglers on the coasts of Kent and Sussex. Asks to have a Commission from their Lordships. 1 *page*.

1727. VOL. CCLXIV.

Date.	Description of Document.	From	To	Purport.
15 May	32. Memorial	Thomas Missing, Contractor for victualling the Garrison of Gibraltar.	Lords of the Treasury.	That as his lists and vouchers for victualling the garrison cannot now come so regularly by reason of the war, immediate despatch may be given to them by the controllers of the accounts of the army. 1 *page*.
[? About 24 May.]	33. Letters and papers.	—	—	Copies of Lord Lieutenant's letters and other papers, about a demand by the Usher of the Council Chamber [in Ireland] for his fees, &c. A note is added:—"Nothing appears to be due to the petitioner by any of these papers relating to his case." 6 *pages*.
[? About 24 May.]	34. Affidavits and a petition.	—	—	Respecting silks, tea, &c. shipped from Rotterdam to London, and seized as contraband. 7 *pages*.
[? About 25 May.]	35. Letter	—	—	Recommending Mr. Hayes to succeed Mr. Shermer as Receiver General of the county of Berks, the latter having misbehaved himself in his office, being charged with misapplying the public money. *Minuted*:—"25 May 1727. Appointed." 1 *page*.
30 May	36. Do.	Duke of Newcastle	Lords of the Treasury.	The King has ordered that Mr. Theocaris Rali Didichi, a native of Aleppo, should succeed Mr. Solomon Negri lately dead, as interpreter of Oriental languages. 1 *page*.
30 May	37. Account	—	—	Of the gross and net produce of the duties on Hawkers and Pedlars from 1725 to 1727 both inclusive. Dated 30 May 1727. 1 *page*.
31 May	38. [Memorial]	Ch. Wither	Lords of the Treasury.	For payment for the works and repairs in Richmond new park. 1 *page*.
31 May	39. Report	P. Medows	Do.	On Mr. Missing's memorial praying payment of 7,740*l*. in advance for provisions furnished for the garrison of Gibraltar. Controller's Office 31 May 1727. *Minuted*: — "Prepare a warrt. Wt. signed hereupon." 2 *pages*.

1727. VOL. CCLXIV.

Date.	Description of Document.	From	To	Purport.
1 June	40. Do. -	Comrs. for Hackney Coach Licences.	Lords of the Treasury.	Have caused Mr. Wharton, the Receiver of the revenue from hackney coaches and chairs to make an account of the gross produce of the same for 3 years. Account annexed. 3 *pages*.
[? About 8 June.]	41. Petition -	Thomas Kennedy, Esq.	Do. - -	For payment of his claim for serving the office of His Majesty's Advocate in Scotland, also for his services as one of the Solicitors in Scotland. A declaration of Sir "Hew" Dalrymple, Lord President of the Session, which seems to be referred to in the petition. Dated 8 June 1727. Also draft of a warrant. 3 *pages*.
[After 11 June.]	42. Statement -	—	—	"State of some remains of Civil List moneys in Scotland incurr'd preceding the 11th of June 1727, unapplyed." 1 *page*.
12 June	43. Account -	—	—	Of expenses of his late Majesty's Household, Chambers, Chapels, and Stables from 1 July 1726 to 11 June 1727 exclusive, being the day of His Majesty's demise. Board of Green cloth. 1 *page*.
6 July	44. Memorial -	Thomas Cornwallis and others.	Lords of the Treasury.	For reward for their services in taking the lottery tickets for 1726 and signing and delivering certificates in exchange. Lottery office. 1 *page*.
12 July	45. Petition -	John Chubb, Surveyor of the Port of Loo in Cornwall.	Do. - -	Prays to be established at his former salary of 60*l*. per ann. 1 *page*.
19 July	46. Letter -	Comrs. of the Navy -	Mr. Scrope -	Send copies of letter received, of the progress in taking up shipping to transport soldiers to Ireland. Also the copies. 4 *pages*.
[After 2 Aug.]	47. Memorial -	C. Stanhope, Treasurer of the Chamber.	Lords of the Treasury.	For a warrant for the salary of Mr. William Keene, his Chief Clerk. 1 *page*.
15 Aug.	48. Warrant -	[Lord Chamberlain of the Household], (Grafton.)	The Hon. James Brudnall, Esq., Master of H.M. Jewel Office.	For delivery of 1,000 oz. of white plate to the Rt. Hon. the Earl of Godolphin, Groom of the Stole. 1 *page*.

1727. VOL. CCLXIV.

Date.	Description of Document.	From	To	Purport.
29 Aug.	49. List - -	—	—	Of provisions sent to Gibraltar by Thomas Missing for the use of the garrison from June to 23 Aug. 1727. 1 *page.*
4 Sept.	50. Memorial -	Thomas Missing, Contractor for Victualling.	Lords of the Treasury.	For an estimate to be given of the number of men to be provided for in the Garrisons of Gibraltar, Placentia, and Annapolis Royal in America. *Minuted:*—"The contract subsisting is for 2,000 men at 10*d.* per man a week, dated 2d June 1726, and to continue for 6/m. certain and afterwards untill 6/m. warning on either side." 1 *page.*
15 Sept.	51. Letter -	James Brudenell [Master of H.M. Jewel Office].	Do. - -	For a warrant for Mr. Robert Sedgwick, Clerk of H. M. Jewel Office to renew his patent for holding that place. In the Minute Book, Vol. 26, p. 31, 21 Sept. 1727*k*, is: — "Prepare a warrant likewise for renewing the patent to Robert Sedgwick the present Clerk of the Jewel Office." 1 *page.*
18 Sept.	52. Letter -	Master of the Horse (Earl of Scarborough).	Do. - -	For 3,000*l.* to be issued to him at the Receipt of the Exchequer upon an unsatisfied order for 10,000*l.* for the Stables. 1 *page.*
29 Sept.	53. Account -	—	—	Of the sums wanting for three months course of the Victualling ending 31 Dec. 1725. 1 *page.*
[After 29 Sept.]	54. Do. -	—	—	Entitled "An abstract of what is to be paid." *Docketed:* — "Princess's expences, Mich'mas 1727." ½ *page.*
30 Sept.	55. Letter -	T. Plumptre, Deputy Treasurer [? Ordnance].	Lords of the Treasury.	Sends copy of a letter and account from the Principal Officers of the Ordnance, applying for money to carry on the service. 4 *pages.*

1727. Vol. CCLXIV.

Date.	Description of Document.	From	To	Purport.
[? About 18 Oct.]	56. Petition -	Michael Baker, Gent. and St. Lo Baker, his son.	Lords of the Treasury.	Held the office of Marshal of the Marshalsea of the Court of Exchequer, at Westminster, which devolved upon the above Michael, the son of Michael, for the last seven years by the death of his father, and St. Lo acted for the last 12 years as his grandfather's and father's deputy. Pray that the grant may be renewed to both petitioners. Also two certificates. *Minuted*—"18th Octobr. 1727 Patent to be renewed.' 3 *pages*.
19 Oct.	57. Letter -	Lord Kilmallock -	—	200*l*. was ordered to him, but owing to his late Majesty's death no settlement was made. Prays his correspondent's intercession with his present Majesty. *Minuted :* — "19th Octr. 1727. To be layd before the King." 2 *pages*.
[? About 28 Oct.]	58. Petition -	William Hall, Controller of Customs, Milford.	Lords of the Treasury.	For the grant of a fiat for renewing his patent. *Minuted :*—"28 October 1727. Fiant renewed." 1 *page*.
[? About 14 Nov.]	59. Memorial -	Alicia Hyde -	Robert Walpole, Esq., and the other Lords of the Treasury.	For payment of his debt of 18*l*. 5*s*. for chocolate due from the late Queen. *Minuted :* — "14 Novr. 1727. No such pson. on ye acct. of arrs." 1 *page*.
11 Dec.	60. Letter -	Master of the Horse (Earl of Scarborough).	Lords of the Treasury.	For the further sum of 3,000*l*. to be issued to him out of an unsatisfied order for 10,000*l*. In the Minute Book, Vol. 26, p. 57, 12 Dec. 1727*c*, is:—"Issue to the Earl of Scarborough 3,000li. upon account of the Extraordinary expence of the stables." 1 *page*.
15 Dec.	61. Letter -	Comrs. of the Navy -	Mr. Scrope -	Send estimate of the debt of the Navy. 1 *page*.
20 Dec.	62. King's Warrant	—	—	Appointing Edmund Gooch Gamekeeper within ten miles round Richmond and Hampton Court Palaces in the room of James Stevens. (Countersigned and entered in three offices.) 1 *m*. (*parchment*.)

1727. Vol. CCLXIV.

Date.	Description of Document.	From	To	Purport.
21 Dec.	63. Memorial -	Treasurer of Greenwich Hospital (Philip Cavendish).	Lords of the Treasury.	4,448*l.* 19*s.* 11*d.* is due to the Royal Hospital at Greenwich for abatements of seamen's six pences. Asks that the remaining arrears may be ordered to be paid into his hands. 1 *page.*
[? About 23 Dec.]	64. Petition -	John Smith and William Leslie, Deputy Chamberlains, for joining tallies in the Court of Exchequer.	Do. - -	Praying for a warrant to the Rt. Hon. George, Earl of Halifax, Auditor of the Receipt of the Exchequer, to cause an order to be drawn for payment of 44*l.* 16*s.* 9*d.* for discharging the duties of their office. Also the Earl's certificate. Dated 23 Dec. 1727. 1 *page.*
[? After 23 Dec.]	65. Do. - -	Doctor William Neilson, late Director of H.M. Hospital at Gibraltar.	Do. - -	Prays for stop of process issued against him for 1,680*l.* by the Sheriff of Middlesex. Produces his account and copy of a letter dated 23 Dec. 1727 O.S. On the back is "This petition recomended by Mr. Heron." 2 *pages.*
[? About 25 Dec.]	66. Statement -	—	—	State of the fund belonging to the invalids of Scotland in the hands of Archibald Douglas, of Cavers. Brought down to Christmas, 1727. 1 *page.*
27 Dec.	67. Letter -	Lord Chamberlain (Grafton).	Lords of the Treasury.	The King's pleasure is that 300*l.* be paid to Sir Clement Cotterell, Master of the Ceremonies, to be presented to Count Gravenitz, Plenipotentiary from the Duke of Wirtemberg, about to return home. 1 *page.*
Jan.—Dec.	68. Account -	—	—	Of the sums received [for fees?] from various officers and persons: made up monthly. The object is not apparent. 18 *pages.*
[? 1727.]	69. Memorial -	Arthur Vansittart, of Shottesbrook, Berks, Esq.	Lords of the Treasury.	Prays payment of 900*l.*, viz., for three years rent of Mote Park, which is laid into the Great Park at Windsor, besides fees. 1 *page.*
[? 1727 or 1728.]	70. Petition -	Ann Pugh - -	Do. - -	Is only surviving child of Captain Richard Pugh, commander of the "Norwich" man-of-war, who was drowned in a hurricane. At the Accession of his "immediate Majesty" petitioner "was struck out." Prays to be put on the list again. 1 *page.*

1727. VOL. CCLXIV.

Date.	Description of Document.	From	To	Purport.
[? 1727.]	71. Petition -	Richard Evans, the younger, of Great Torrington, Devon, woolcomber.	The Rt. Hon. Sir Robert Walpole, Knt.	In consideration of his trouble and expense in prosecuting Joseph Beale, of Bristol, a tradesman, for sedition. Prays to be made a tide-waiter. Also two certificates, dated 1726–7. 3 *pages.*
[? End of 1727.]	72. Memorial -	Mary Marshall, widow of Richd. Marshall.	The Rt. Hon. Sir Robert Walpole, Chancellor of H. M. Exchequer.	For payment of the arrears due to her late husband for his late Majesty's stud [amounting to 2,207*l.* 0*s.* 10*d.*] 1 *page.*
[? 1727 or 1728.]	73. Do. - -	Michael Aiskew, Clerk-Assistant of the House of Commons.	Lords of the Treasury.	Attends all Committees of the House as clerk; keeps Minute Books, &c. There are no fees but the usual salary out of the Royal Bounty. For the session ended 15 May 1727 received no allowance. Prays relief. 1 *page.*
[? 1727 or 1728.]	74. Petition -	Christopher Key, Bailiff and Collector of the rents, &c. of the Bailiwick and Manor of St. James, Middlesex.	Do. - -	For a warrant to the Auditor to give allowance in his account of 15*l.* per ann. for the fees payable to the Auditor, the salary of petitioner being only 18*l.* 15*s.* per ann. 2 *pages.*
[? About 1727.]	75. Do. -	Thomas Robe and John Matthews, Esqrs.	Do. - -	By letters patent of 1 Aug. 1726, petitioners are constituted Clerks of the Market of the King's Household with a salary of 20*l.* per ann. Have set and estreated fines, and have been ordered to pay them into the Court of Exchequer to the amount of 300*l.* Pray for payment of the salary. Also an extract from the patent. 3 *pages.*
[? 1727.]	76. Do. -	Henry Lowman, and Mary his wife.	Do. - -	For the warrant, dated 12 May 1727, for their salary as Housekeeper of the palace of Kensington to be satisfied. 1 *page.*
[? 1727.]	77. Address -	House of Commons, Ireland.	The King -	Conveying their thanks to his Majesty for his answer to their address. Pray for 10,000*l.* to clear the Army for a year commencing 1 July 1724 and ending 30 June 1725. Also for the Half Pay Officers. 2 *pages.*

1727. VOL. CCLXIV.

Date.	Description of Document.	From	To	Purport.
[? 1727.]	78. Memoranda -	—	—	The officer who kept the Council Books of the Prince, when Prince of Wales, says that there is no order entered for the continuance of patents, nor any order relating to Sir Humphrey Howarth till 1725, &c. ½ *page.*
[? 1727 or later.]	79. Petition -	William Winde -	Lords of the Treasury.	Was appointed (1 Geo. I.) Inspector of Prosecutions in the Court of Exchequer for uncustomed goods, with fees of 12*d.* in the pound on moneys paid into court. By a recent Act forfeitures are allowed to be prosecuted before the justices of the peace. Apprehends that he has a a right to the forfeitures. Prays that the Comrs. of Customs may be ordered to pay him his allowance of 12*d.* in the pound. 1 *page.*
[1727 or later.]	80. Account -	—	—	" Arrears of salary due to the Livery Servants of the late King from 1st July 1726 to the 10th of June 1727, and who are not provided for by his present Majesty nor the Queen nor the Prince of Wales' Establishments." 2 *pages.*
[? 1727 or later.]	81. Memorial -	Major-General Wroth	Lords of the Treasury.	For relief as to a debt long since due. 1 *page.*

VOL. CCLXV. 1728. JANUARY—JULY.

[? About 1728.] 1. " A List of the several Governours of his Majesty's Plantaĉons whose salaries are paid out of the 4 & ½ per cent." Undated, but ? 1728, as Henry Worseley, Esq., was Governor of Barbadoes until 1728, and John Pitt, Governor of Bermuda, was appointed in 1727, and both are mentioned.

With it is also a similar list. 2 *pages.*

1727–8. VOL. CCLXV.

[After 1727.] 2. Petition of Anna Reynolds, widow, to the Lords of the Treasury. Petitioner's husband was a lieutenant in the Hon. Col. Thomas Harrison's regiment, and served all the late war in Spain, where he received several wounds, particularly at the battle of Almanza, and died after 30 years' service in 1720. Petitioner was put on the pension [list] of officers' widows in Ireland, but on the late examination by Lord Carteret was objected against by reason of her absence and the want of friends to appear for her. Prays to be a partaker of the Royal bounty. Undated. [The pension had not been paid for seven years.] 1 *page.*

[? After 1727.] 3. Memorial of James, Duke of Hamilton and Brandon, Keeper of the Palace of Holy-rood House, to the King. The palace has fallen into ruinous condition for want of repair. His late Majesty gave orders for 1,000*l.* to be employed by the direction of the Barons of the Exchequer in Scotland to prevent it from falling. The money was employed for repair of the roof of the chapel and a part of the roof of the palace, but is far short of what is absolutely necessary. Prays for orders to be given for the repairs. 1 *page.*

4 Jan. 4. Memorial of the Com[rs] for Licencing and regulating Hackney Coaches and Chairs to the Lords of the Treasury. The salaries, upon the first creation of this Commission in the reign of Will. III., were 200*l.* per ann. to the Commissioners. The produce of the office being only 2,800*l.*, the salaries were reduced to 100*l.* 600 chairmen have been added to their management and 100 hackney coaches; and the revenue has advanced to 10,550*l.* per ann., but the salaries continue the same. On the one hand they are pressed by a multitude of recommendations from persons of quality and distinction, some of whom they must disoblige; and on the other they have to do with a rude and unreasonable sort of people. Receive almost daily affronts in the execution of their office (perhaps the more from the meanness of their salaries.) Pray an augmentation of their salaries.

On the back is a warrant for an additional 50*l.* to the salaries, which was confirmed by the Lords of the Treasury on 4 Jan. 1727–8. 3 *pages.*

6 Jan. 5. Com[rs] of Land Tax to the Lords of the Treasury. Lay before their Lordships the difficulties they lie under for the present year for the Palaces of Whitehall, S[t] James, &c. If the entire sum should be expected to be raised, the greatest hardship must fall on his Majesty's family, and others there being two months and ten days on his late Majesty's account unpaid to his servants, and in the pensions half a year. Make suggestions thereon. S[t] James's, 6 Jan. 1727. 1 *page.*

9 Jan. 6. "A List of the several Receivers of the Land Tax and duties on houses within my division who have not passed their accompts for the years hereafter mentioned. Signed:—Ex[r] p S. Godolphin Aud[r] 9 die Jan. 1727." 2 *pages.*

1727-8. VOL. CCLXV.

10 Jan. 7. "Resolutions of the [Irish] House of Commons in favour of Eliazer Peirson and Samuel Peirson," who had been at great expense and trouble in endeavouring to promote a better method of tillage and husbandry in Ireland. Two hundred pounds was awarded to them. 1 *page*.

10 and 11 Jan. 8. Similar resolution of the House for the payment of 2,000*l*. to the Hon. Richard Stewart, Esq., and his partners, as an encouragement to them to better enable them to carry on the Colliery of Ballycastle in the co. of Antrim.

Accompanied by Stewart's petition. 3 *pages*.

14 Jan. 9. "Case of the teinds of Winton, advised by Lawyers in Scotland."

Memorial of the Governor and Company for raising the Thames water in York Buildings. The Company in 1719 purchased the forfeited estate of Wintone at 19 years' purchase, and paid to the receipt of the Exchequer in Scotland 50,208*l*. 18*s*. 4½*d*. As the Earl [of Winton] stood enfeoffed in the teinds as well as the lands the company paid the same price for the teinds as for the lands. H. M. Solicitor General has entered a claim in behalf of the Crown, in place of the Bishop of Edinburgh, before the Lords Com^rs^ for Plantations of Kirks and valuation of teinds. Memorialists claim a deduction [from the purchase money]. The Bishop's right is established as follows, viz., the teinds of the parish of Tranent belonged before the Reformation to the Abbey of Holyrood-house, which by the abolition of popery fell into the King's hands, and was erected into a temporal Lordship in favour of John Bothwell, son to the Bishop of Orkney. [Gives other details as to the title.]

It is plain these teinds belong to the Bishop of Edinburgh, and the Earl of Winton could have no other right but as the Bishop's tacksman. 14 Jan. 1727. 4 *pages*.

15 Jan. 10. Memorial of the Master and Worker of the Mint, (signed John Conduit,) addressed to the Lords of the Treasury, praying for new standard trial pieces, by which the gold and silver moneys are tried, the existing pieces being quite used up by the several trials of the pix. The Jury of Goldsmiths have represented to the Privy Council the necessity of having new pieces. Mint Office, 15 Jan. 1727-8.

Accompanied by another paper, headed:—

"The method observed when the last standard trial piece was made." The Wardens of the Goldsmiths Company returned a Jury of 26 persons, who were sworn before the Lord High Treasurer, on 6 June 1707, to prepare two several standard trial pieces of such quantities that each might be divided into seven pieces: and by warrant, 150*l*. was allowed to the Master and Worker, to pay to the Wardens for their charges. 2 *pages*.

16 Jan. 11. Report of the Attorney and Solicitor General to the Lords of the Treasury on the memorial of the Right Hon. the Lord William

1727–8. VOL. CCLXV.

Powlett, one of the four Tellers in the receipt of the Exchequer. The memorial sets forth that the cash room of the office was broken into through the roof, and one of the locks of the strong chests was forced off, and 4,191*l.* 14*s.* 6*d.* was taken out. The locks were all locked according to the Act of Parliament of 8 & 9 King William. The money remains a charge upon the Lord William Powlett. It does not appear to them that the loss was occasioned by any wilful default or neglect. The question in the present case is, whether any felonious taking will be a discharge to a Teller in his accounts, for the money lost thereby; which never having been judicially determined, seems to be a point of considerable difficulty.

If the bailiff or receiver of a private person is robbed of money received for the use of his master without his own default, he is by law entitled to an allowance upon his account for the money so lost; but in the cases of a common carrier, master of a ship, and innkeeper, by the Common Law, robbery is no discharge to them for the money or things with which they are entrusted, notwithstanding it happened without their concurrence or privity. It has been held that a Receiver General of Taxes is not entitled to any allowance upon his account for money lost by robbery. The case of the Tellers of the Exchequer seems to be within the reason of the cases last mentioned, the King being, by law, under the necessity of intrusting them with the receipt of his revenue. Wherefore, and in regard that the Tellers of the Exchequer have a reward for receiving and keeping the money paid into their offices, it doth not appear that the memorialist, according to the ordinary course of the Exchequer, is entitled to have an allowance in his account for the sum claimed, or that he can be discharged from the same otherwise than by the aid of the legislature. But if their Lordships should be of opinion that, as the case is new and the point of law not free from doubt, this matter should undergo any further examination, the proper method of having it determined is by bringing it regularly in judgment before the Court of Exchequer. 16 Jan. 1727.

The memorial dated 24 Jan. 1726; also eight affidavits.

In the *Minute Book*, vol. 26, page 73*i* (24 Jan. 1727–8), is:—

"Mr Attorney and Soll^rs^ report of the 16 instant, on the Lord Powlets peticõn, to be relieved against the loss of 4,191*l.* 14*s.* 6*d.* by a robbery, in his office, as one of the Tellers of the Exchequer, is read: and my Lords agree in opinion with the Attorney and Sollicitor, that it cannot be discharged, otherwise than by the aid of the legislature, and think it reasonable that a clause should be prepared to be passed in some act this Sessions for discharging the same." 17 *pages.*

19 Jan. 12. Report of the Controllers of the Accounts of the Army (Medows and Bruce) to the Lords of the Treasury on the quantity and species of provisions in store at Gibraltar.

Accompanied by two "states" of the provisions. 3 *pages.*

19 Jan. 13. Report of the same Controllers of Army Accounts (Medows and Bruce) to the Lords of the Treasury on two lists of the numbers of

1727-8. VOL. CCLXV.

persons victualled in the Garrison of Gilbraltar, between 3 July 1727 and 27 Aug. following, by Thomas Missing, Esq., the contractor. 7,878*l.* 6*s.* 1*d.* are due.

Also a computation of the persons victualled. 2 *pages.*

19 Jan. 14. "Abstract of the state of the funds destined for improvements in Scotland and of the proceedings and proposals of the Commissioners and Trustees for fisheries and manufactures in that country." Undated, but by comparison with a warrant entered in the *North Britain Book,* vol. 9, p. 104, the date is 19 Jan. 2½ *pages.*

20 Jan. 15. Henry Lowman to ——. Sends the butcher's bill of meat delivered for feeding the leopard, tiger, and lion, from 17 June to 9 Dec. 1727, at Kensington Palace, before they were sent to the Tower. The quantity is less than what Sir John Eyles said he gave them, which was six lb. of meat per diem each. His Majesty has seen the bill and gave directions to have it sent on to the Treasury. "There is owing to this poor man from his late Majesty for 18 months the like service." Kensington, 20 Jan. [1727-8?].

Accompanied by the bill. 2 *pages and two lines.*

23 Jan. 16. Representation to the King of Lord Carpenter, governor of the Island of Minorca. When the late Lord Stanhope took the island in 1708 it was left to the choice of the people whether they would remain there under obedience to King Charles the Third, or quit the island and adhere to Philip the Vth, and all who chose the latter had their estates confiscated: but by the treaty of Utrecht they were to be restored to their estates and other rights.

Col. Kane, Lieut.-Governor, was applied to, and he (Lord Carpenter) was lately applied to by several of the proprietors of the estates to restore them, which they could not do without his Majesty's order; but Col. Kane having written on the subject, he (Lord Carpenter) offers his opinion, viz., that such persons as by the treaty of Utrecht have a right to be restored to their estates will be forthwith put into possession of them, before the meeting of a congress in order to avoid difficulties, and it might give them a pretence to demand again the dominion of that island for the non-performance of the articles of cession.

If his Majesty give such orders, they should be directed to Lieut-Governor Kane and the Court of his Royal patrimony to examine well into the pretensions of such as demand to be restored to their estates and then restore them.

The estates are of trifling value to his Majesty, as when the fees of the court there are paid little remains, and such estates ought to have been restored to the proprietors when the peace was concluded in 1713.

When the war was begun again in 1718, by the hostilities of Sicily, the officers of the Royal revenue seized on the estates of all persons who resided in any of the dominions of Spain, as confiscated: and whether such estates ought to be restored or not

1727–8. VOL. CCLXV.

should be inquired into. These are very few, for he (the Governor) knows but of . . . . . One of them should have been restored long since, the case being thus:—There is one Doña Maria Louiça Vela, a native of Minorca, who had a small censo or rent-charge upon four different estates, and a small house, the value of the whole being 40 dollars per ann., and this gentlewoman having lived in the Island of Sardinia when the Spaniards took it in the year 1717, her censo and house were confiscated, as well as the estates of those who resided in Spain: and although the Island of Sardinia was soon after delivered to the Emperor, and put into possession of the King of Sardinia, yet the confiscation has not been taken off, but though Col. Kane would not annul a confiscation made by the King's officers, yet he directed that the produce of the house and censo should neither be passed to account of the Crown nor to the account of the gentlewoman, but kept in deposit in the Royal treasury till the King's pleasure be known; which affair he represented to the Minister, but never had any answer to it. The Vice-Roy of Sardinia has often written to Col. Kane in her favour, and very lately again. It is to be observed that she dwelt in Sardinia before, when the Spaniards took it, and has continued to live there ever since. On the back is Jan. 23, 1727–8. 1 *page.*

23 Jan. 17. "Hilary Term, 1727. A. Cracherodes particular of the causes now under prosecution, with States thereof. Dat. 23th Janry 1727." 13 *pages.*

26 Jan. 18. Geo. Tilson to Mr Scrope. Sends enclosed a list of his Majesty's Ministers employed at Foreign Courts in the department of Lord Townshend. Whitehall, 26 Jan. 1727–8. [There are thirteen names.] 2½ *pages.*

31 Jan. 19. Memorial of his Majesty's servants the King's Heralds and Pursuivants-of-Arms to the Lords of the Treasury. According to ancient custom the fee of 100*l.* is due to them for their services at the coronation and 100 marks for the coronation of her Majesty and for several robes upon those occasions; 167*l.* for his Majesty's assuming his stall, as sovereign of the Order of the Garter 40*l.* and for largesses due to them upon the creation of two peers, the Lords Percy and King, 5*l.* for each, in all 183*l.* 13*s.* 4*d.* By the demise of his late Majesty the warrant to the Treasurer of the Chamber for the yearly payment of largesses to the petitioners for their attendances upon great festivals amounting to 40*l.* is become void: pray payment.

Minuted:—"Read 11 Janry 1727. My Lords observe that the Lord Percey becomes a peer by descent; but order a warrant to be prepared in case their demands be according to usage. Upon inspecting the books all their demands are as usual, except as follows:—

"100 marks are demanded for the Queen's Coronation, but no such sum is found to have been paid either on the Coronation of King James's Queen, or of Queen Mary, though the last was a sovereign by descent.

"10li is demanded for largesses on the creating two peers, such largesses upon creations are of ancient usage & have been always paid, but where the peerage comes by descent no such precedent appears in the books."

United to the above is the following paper in reply to the above remarks. It is in Anstis' hand and signed by him and nine other heralds.

"To the Right Honble the Lords Comrs of his Majesties Treasury.

The Representation of the officers of arms sheweth—

That these officers finding an endorsement entred by your Lpps order upon their memorial for largesses relating to two articles of it, conceive it to be their duty to state the facts & rights in both cases.

The first observation is made upon the fee claimed for largesses for the Lord Percy (which amounts to five pounds only) which is thought not to be due in regard his Lpp (as it is worded) became a peer by descent, but that in case it should appear to be according to usage, then a warrant should be prepared for payment of it.

They therefore crave leave to represent, that the Barony of Percy for several ages was conjoined with the Earldome of Northumberland and that by the severanse, whenever any writ of summons issued to any Baron Percy, it became the Duty of the Heralds to proclaime the largesse; thus in the very last Bill entred in the Treasury Books, it will appear, they were paid for largesses upon the severance of the Barony of Lynn from the Viscounty Townshend of Rainham, & upon the severance & revival of the Barony of Clinton out of the Earldome of Lincoln, & they are ready to show that those payments were according to precedents, if your Lpps please to demand them.

The other observation endorsed is, that the summe of one hundred marks now claimed for largesse upon her Majesties coronation was not paid for the coronation of King James, or that of Queen Mary though the last was a sovereign by descent.

If it had been specified, whether this relates to the consort of King James the first, or the second, or of the first or second Queen Mary, they should have been enabled to have returned a more determinate answer; However they own, that though largesse was demanded for the coronation of King James the seconds consort, yet they believe the same was not paid; but humbly submit to your Lpps whether that payment might not have been ordered, in case the Heralds at that time had produced the authorities, which will be inserted in this paper.

But then Queen Mary was a sovereign by descent & yet no largesse was paid; It is certain that Queens, sovereigns, Mary the first & Elizabeth, paid largesses for their coronations, but the case of Queen Mary the second crowned with King William according to the Act of Parliament was very different, and no largesse could be due for her, separate from King William; the very ceremonial of that solemnity shews it, for the largesse for both of them was single, or joint, as both made one sovereign, and they were crowned with equal rites belonging to sovereignty. This was the true reason why no largesse money was claimed for Her, distinct from King William, and not upon the account here mentioned, for her sister Queen Anne paid her largesse.

But the instance of a Queen Consort is very different, for at her Coronation (whether the solemnity be performed at the same time that the King is crowned, or at a different time) the rites are distinct, the regalia distinct, the prayers, the unctions and the whole formularies distinct, and the actions performed separately.

1727–8. VOL. CCLXV.

Upon such Coronations of Queen Consorts, these officers claime their largesses & in proof of that right will not tyre your Lpps with citations from the books in their own Library, which would be very numerous, (though their books are allowed evidence at law in relation to other persons) but omitting them as domestick witnesses, shall at present refer to other undeniable authorities.

Garter assures your Lpps that some years since he transcribed the copy of an original privy seal dated in June 5 Edward IV. commanding the Treasurer & Chamberlains of the Exchequer to pay the largesse for the Coronation of his Queen Consort, and if yr Lpps will be pleased to direct a clerk to search the *Exitus Pellis* with him, he doubts not but the payment will be found as well as that original privy seal; upon which he will readily put the issue of this claim.

But this is a modern proof comparatively with the following ones. It goes no further back than two hundred sixty two years. Richard the second came to the throne in 1377, and in his reign there is a rolle with this title *Ces sont les droicts & largesses appurtenans & d'aunci-entie accustomez aux Roys d'armes selonc le usance en royaulme d'Engleterre*, which is printed in a collection of *Discourses upon Antiquities*, published at Oxford in 1720, in p. 245, where after the largesse for the King's Coronation, and several other particulars, follows the articles relating to the Queen, & among them largesse for her Coronation.

The Original chances to be preserved in the Cotton Library with the same title prefixed, where indeed the words are *Quant la Royne est novelment coroné, appartient aux ditz Roys d'armes et Heraldes notable largesse de cent marcs, ou 40li.* Titus C. 1., p. 457.

It was therefore so long since the antient usage of England to pay the Heralds largesse for the Coronation of a Queen Consort, at some Coronations preceding that time one hundred marks, at others only forty pounds.

It farther happens that there are several other exemplars of this Rolle still extant in the Libraries in Oxford, in the Harleyan Library, & in private hands wrote in the reigns of the three Henries & of Edw. IV., whereof attested copies with the ages of the originals shall be laid before your Lordshipps if required, after the following proofs of the continuance of this antient usage shall be considered.

Henry the Seventh was a Prince very serious in the issuing his money, and had the claims of his several officers laid before him, among others the demands of the Heralds upon several occasional articles were confirmed by him under his sign manual, in which this largesse for the Coronation of a Queen Consort is expressly mentioned; and it is not to be omitted that notwithstanding his parsimony in his own Coronation, which did not exceed the charge of 4,000li, yet he allowed 100li thereof to the Heralds, & what is more applicable to the present subject, that largesse was paid the Heralds upon the Coronation of his Queen, as it is entered in the Cotton Library Julius B. 12. This sign manual is entered & attested in the Heralds Office, being the proper Repository for it.

But it chances likewise that there was a book marked B × laid by order in his Majesties Paper Office containing the rights of the Heralds, which they presume is still in that place, by which they will be decided in this and all other cases, and they humbly request your Lpps, that upon the producing it, you will be pleased to order all such payments to be regularly made, as shall appear by it to be their antient just rights, and parcell of their Freeholds.

1727–8. VOL. CCLXV.

They have not as yet examined the payments in the Pelle Office of the first year of Hen. VIII., but it appears from Hall, a contemporary author, that the largesse upon the Coronation of Queen Anne Bullein was paid: but least a distinction should be offered, that this was a Coronation, not performed at the same time with that of the Sovereign himself, it must be owned to have been transacted with the same rites & ceremonies, and that such a dyference in the times of performing these rites makes no real distinction in the right of fees. they appeal to the judicial determinations made in the Court of Claims relating to the cupps demanded by the Lord Mayor of London.

Most of the authorities here cited are in the French language but there is also a very antient Tract in Latin, whereof one copy remains in the Harleyan Library, and another in the Museum at Oxford, entitled, *Jura, debita et largitates appertineñ de antiqua consuetudine armorum officialibus, secundum morem et consuetudinem Angliæ.* After the first article of one hundred pounds for the King's Coronation follows immediately this paragraph. *Item in Coronatione Reginæ pertinet largitas centum marcarum, aliquando quadraginta librarum sterlingorum.*

By this short state (to which large additions may be easily made) it is hoped, that the antiquity & right of this largesse fee is sufficiently asserted, and that the Officers of Arms (who consist of thirteen persons) acquiesce in the fees received many centuries since, by their predecessors, which probably is the singular instance among all his Majesties officers.

And as these officers performed their respective duties at her Majesties Coronation, so they humbly hope, that a warrant will be ordered for their largesse upon that occasion." Herald's Office, last of January, 1727–8. 5 *pages.*

Jan. 20. Petition of John Rotherham of Barnet in Hertfordshire, gentleman, to the King. Was the author of the burning the damaged and corrupt tobaccos in 1714, whereby the revenue is increased 100,000*l.* per ann. Was promised a pension of 2,000*l.* per ann., but has not obtained a penny. Offered a proposal for preventing counterfeiting, and to produce a fund upon the distillery of Great Britain sufficient to support the charge thereof, which will bring into the Exchequer 200,000li per ann. free of all charges of recoining. Was, in 1721, referred to the Lords of the Treasury, and by them to Sir Isaac Newton, Knt and the principal officers of the Mint, but could obtain no report from them except he would disclose the whole secret, which he refused to do unless assured of a suitable reward. Will impart the secret or invention to Sir Andrew Fountayn or to any single person if suitably provided for. Prays for a post or a pension. Janry 1727.

Also his proposal. 2 *pages.*

7 Feb. 21. Report of Mr Auditor Harley to the Lords of the Treasury on the memorial of Charles Shales, of London, goldsmith, son and executor of John Shales, Esq., formerly Commissary of Provisions for the land forces encamped on Hounslow Heath in the years 1687 and 1688, and on other occasions, and services therein mentioned in the years 1689, 1690, and 1691. It was agreed in 1710 on the part of the Crown that the Accountant should be discharged of all

1727-8. VOL. CCLXV.

the *insupers* standing out in the Exchequer against his father in consideration of his giving up demands amounting to 6,221*l.* 9*s.* 2¾*d.*, &c. Finds these allegations true. Also as to another sum of 4,117*l.* 10*s.* 6*d.* set insuper on the said Commissary Shales. Advises that it cannot be allowed. 7 Feb. 1727.

Minuted:—"Read and agreed to."

Also the memorial. 4 *pages.*

15 Feb. 22. Report of A. Cracherode to the Lords of the Treasury on the memorial of John Markham, of Winslowe in the county of Bucks, Attorney-at-Law. One of the Justices of the Peace having required, by his warrant, that Bennett Tompkins, petty constable of Newton Longueville, should provide two able teams to draw part of the baggage of the Duke of Argyle's regiment from Winslowe to Chipping Wycombe, he positively refused to obey. Upon a distress of 40s being levied for his refusal, Tompkins and nine others rescued the distress in a riotous manner. After being indicted they humbly submitted themselves and were discharged, paying the fees of the court. The Justice of the Peace employed the memorialist to prosecute the affair, and he was still unpaid. Certifies that the contents of the memorial appear to be true, and is of opinion that the memorialist should be paid. Dated 15 Feb. 1727.

Accompanied by the memorial and a list of the charges of the prosecution.

Minuted:—"18 ejusdm. Ordered." 4 *pages.*

[? About 19 Feb.] 23. Debtor and creditor account of Consul John Russell "on account of the Journey to & from Mequinez."

This includes expenses of subsisting the captives.

"An account of money given at the Court of Mequinez and whilst I was in Barbary and for necessary things to add to his Majesty's present." The account is brought down to 19 Feb. 1727.

There is also the following:—

"An account of the receipt and disposal of his Majesty's present to the Emperor of Morocco & his Ministers."

Further, "An accompt of medicines expended during my stay at Mequinez and other parts of Barbary &c." This was an account of Mr Knight "surgeon" of his Majesty's ship "Success" and was paid by the Consul. 18 *pages.*

27 Feb. 24. "Auditor Foley's representation of his expences in answering precepts of the Commrs for stating the debts of the army" addressed to the Lords of the Treasury. Asks their Lordships to obtain his Majesty's warrant for an allowance of five hundred and fifty pounds for him, in like manner as Mr Auditor Harley was allowed by his late Majesty's warrant of 7 Sept. 1726. Febry 27, 1727. 1 *page.*

6 March. 25. "Copy of a letter from the Lord Lieutt & Privy Councill of Ireland, to the Duke of Newcastle, with a bill for preventg frauds and abuses in the Customs & Excise."

1727–8. VOL. CCLXV.

The articles of "Bay and Woollen Yarn" have been rated by the Commons at 15^s and 8^s per stone. This would be a loss to the Hereditary revenue of 286*l.* 14*s.* 2*d.* per ann. Have raised the former from 15^s to 16^s 8^d, which, together with the duty upon woollen yarn, rated at 8 shillings, will produce 3,772*l.* 5*s.* 6*d.* per ann., which is something more than it now produces. If his Majesty condescended to the prayer of the Commons for the rates at 15^s and 8^s, it would be a signal mark of the Royal goodness. Council Chamber, Dublin, 6 March 1727. 3 *pages.*

9 March. 26. Report of the Attorney and Solicitor General for Ireland (Tho. Marlay and Robert Jocelyn) to the Lord Lieut. (Carteret) on the petition of Catherine O'Brien, and on the report of the Auditor General thereon as to the scope of the annuities of 200*l.* per ann., and an additional 200*l.* per ann., granted to Lady Frances Keightly and Thomas Keightley, and the survivor, and as to a later grant to Thomas Keightley and Catherine, his daughter. 4 *pages.*

13 March. 27. Memorial of the Postmasters General (Ed. Carteret and E. Harrison) to the Lords [of the Treasury], asking for directions on a memorial of the merchants trading to the north parts of Spain and Portugal, who proposed that two packet boats should be again appointed to go between Falmouth and the Groin, as it was till the Vice-Roy of Galicia seized one of the packets about a year since. Also to know their Lordships' pleasure whether the additional seamen entered some time ago upon the Lisbon packet boats should be discharged or continued.

In the *Minute Book*, vol. 26, p. 96*a* (1 May 1728), is :—"Write to the Postmasters to put an immediate end to the increased charge, and acquaint them that the pacquet boats whose stations were altered are to be put upon their former stations." 1 *page.*

15 March. 28. Gilbert Elliot to John Scrope, Esq. Made application to the Executors of Alexander Stevenson, Esq., the late agent to the Two Independent Companies in Jamaica, who had delivered to him an account of balances. Is under great concern for the many hardships that the want of their pay has occasioned to the companies in general and to the several officers, but most particularly to Lieut. Dodd, who commands the Governor's Company, and to Col. De Launay, Captain of the other Company, who have taken up money in Jamaica for their subsistence and drawn bills for the same which are yet unpaid, &c. Begs that the enclosed "state" may be laid before the Lords of the Treasury for them to give directions for issuing the balance to the two Companies. 2 *pages.*

19 March. 29. "Mr. Cracherode's state of the proceedings ag^t the late $Comm^{rs}$ of Hawkers & Pedlars." 19 Mar. 1727–8.

Procured writs of extent against all the late $Comm^{rs}$ out of the Court of Exchequer (who were indebted on their final account 36,668*l.* 13*s.* 5*d.*) where he could learn that the Commissioners had estates, &c. or where their persons might be found. None of them

1727–8. VOL. CCLXV.

could be taken. Could not hear that three of them had any visible estate. In Norfolk the sheriff seized the several estates of Mr John Attwood and Mr John Burton. In the counties of Middlesex and Gloucester the sheriffs seized the lands, &c. of Mr George Townshend and his goods in his chambers in Lincoln's Inn. It is apprehended that the rents, &c. of the surplus of the estate of George Townshend, Esq., late father of the late Commr, will belong to the Crown towards the discharge of the debt. 2 *pages.*

23 March. 30. Gilbert Elliot to John Scrope, Esq., as to claims on the Executors of Mr Stevenson, agent to the two Independent Companies in Jamaica. Application had to be made to the Treasury to issue money to discharge the Bills of Exchange drawn by the officers for the two Independent Companies in Jamaica and for themselves, and all demands due to them by the late agent, he having been appointed by warrant from the King, whereupon it was supposed that the Treasury would of course order an extent to be issued against his effects to reimburse as much of the money as could be recovered thereby, and would make a demand in Parliament for any deficiency. The executors at a meeting before General Hunter went away, acquainted him that they did not know when the effects might come to their hands; but that there was an estate which might be more easily recovered by the "Prerogative process." Asks Mr Scrope to move the Lords of the Treasury to order the balance to be paid in advance upon account of the pay of the companies, and to direct the prosecution of an extent.

On the back are copies of minutes or memoranda touching the same matter of a previous date to the letter. 2 *pages.*

28 March. 31. Memorial of William Sanderson, clerk to the Rt Hon. Sir Robert Walpole, K.G. Says he was the author of an expedient to prevent the Bristol and other mails from being robbed. The scheme seems to have been to write with red ink on the foreside of all bank notes and other notes the name of the Post Town, where they put in their letters, the day of the month and also the addition of these words (viz.) from London to Bristol or from Bristol to London, and the same method to be used with the Cross Posts. These services have been attended with a great deal of expense and loss of time, and no mail robberies have since been committed. Asks for compensation. March 28, 1728.

Also copy of the Gazette relating to the same.

In the Minute Book, Vol. 26, p. 94*h* (11 Apr. 1728) "Send the petition of William Saunderson, clerk, to be rewarded for a scheme which he alledges to have projected and now used as an expedient to prevent the robbing of mails, to the Postmars to report what they know concerning the said scheme with their opinion as to the peticõner's services therein." 2 *pages.*

30 March. 32. Report of Phil. Gybbon, Surveyor-General, to the Lords of the Treasury on the petition of Richard Webster, who represents

1728. Vol. CCLXV.

that John Webster, his father, assigned the remainder of his lease from the Crown of certain land called Salthillhays, in the county of Lancaster, for securing a small sum to William Banks, who, about 15 years before, took possession of the land which his executor still keeps. As petitioner's ancestors have been tenants to the Crown, time immemorial, prays a reversionary lease of the premises. By affidavit produced it is alleged that John Webster built a barn and enclosed and improved the premises, but was bound for a sum of money to William Banks, who called up the principal (about 50*l.*), but offered to make it up 100*l.* if petitioner and his brother (executors to their father) would assign to him the lease, promising never to claim the tenant right thereto. [Mentions other evidence produced.] Has also made a report on the petition of James Haldane, Esq., for a new lease of the premises for one Edward Gelderd.

If their Lordships grant the petitioner's request in consideration of his father's improvements, by which the value of the premises has been considerably raised, and because his ancestors have been so long tenants of the Crown, a lease may be passed to him for 31 years, for a fine of 60*l.*, with the ancient reserved rent of 10*l.* per ann.

Also the petition.

In the *Minute Book,* Vol. 26*n*, p. 99 (3 May 1728) * * * "It appearing to my Lords that all tenant right to the premises had been long since assigned by Webster to Haldane, their Lordships agree to the report in favour of Haldane." 4 *pages.*

[? About March.] 33. Memoranda of various sums between the years 1715 and 1728 allowed to the envoys from Tripoli and Tunis and to the ambassadors from the Emperor of Morocco. 3 *pages.*

2 April. 34. R. Edgcumbe to ———. Sends a paper signed by all the Trustees and Capt. Prat himself, which he hopes will be evidence enough for his correspondent to proceed regularly in the affair of Col. Hatton.

Accompanied by the paper:—The Trustees were empowered to sell Capt. Prat's estate and effects, and his "employment of Constable of the Castle of Dublin to discharge his debt to the Crown and Col. Thomas Hatton offered 3,000*l.* (Irish money) for the Office and the Trustees gave their assent to an application to be made by the Col. to his Majesty for a patent constituting him Constable." 3 *pages.*

5 April. 35. "A state of the severall accots of the revenues of the public taxes which are behind and undeclared within the division of Mr Auditor Jett in the year 1726 inclusive."

"Exam. p Tho. Jett Audr 5 Aprill 1728." 11 *pages.*

8 April. 36. Memorial of the Cofferer to the Lords of the Treasury asking for the issue of money to meet the expenses of his Majesty's household, chambers, and chapel, and for the Princess Amelia. Dated, Cofferer's Office, 8 April 1728. Also an application from

1728. VOL. CCLXV.

the Board of Greencloth to the Cofferer, referred to in the above memorial. 3 *pages*.

1 May. 37. Report of the Surveyor of the Woods (Wyther) to the Lords of the Treasury on the memorial of Francis, Earl of Godolphin, relating to what was due on "the establishment of Windsor Little Park, amounting to 65*l*. per ann." The same is in arrear from Midsummer 1721. The surveyor never has any money in his hands, but what is by warrant appropriated to particular uses. Is not surprised that Windsor Little Park is in so ruinous a condition, since very little money has been expended there since his late Majesty's Accession. According to the particulars given, the repairs would amount to 1,342*l*. 2*s*. 10*d*. Proposes to raise it out of the Manor of Rosedale (co. York), Chertsea and Hardwick (co. Surrey), the Manor of Cawood (co. York), where all the timber is reserved to the Crown, but much spoiled by the tenants and out of the forest of Whichwood (co. Oxon).

Also the memorial.

Minuted:—"1st of October 1728. Read and agreed to, and woodfalls are to be made in the severall places mentioned in this report: except only the mannor of Cawood Com. York, which is to remain untouched untill the question between the Archbishop of York and the Crown touching the timber within the said mannor is determined." 3 *pages*.

2 May. 38. Copy of the Resolutions of the House of Lords, Ireland, recommending the payment of the officers and servants of the House for their services during the Sessions. The sums are put in the margin. 2 *pages*.

4 May. 39. Report of the Board of General Officers to the Lord Lieut. of Ireland on the petition of Lettice Campbell, widow. Find that her late husband, Lieut.-Col. Josias Campbell, served the Crown above thirty years. In the late war in Spain he expended 310*l*. in the public service which was not repaid, and 190*l*. was due to him for loss of his baggage. Recommend her for the Royal bounty.

Also the petition and a report on the case in 1710. 6 *pages*.

[? About 17 May.] 40. Report of the Rt Hon. Charles, Earl of Carlisle, Governor and Captain of the Castle of Windsor, on the petition of Baptist Nunn, Janitor of Windsor Castle; who complained that he was deprived of the fees due to him as Janitor of the Castle and that his lodgings have been detained from him. Has examined an old and almost illegible table of fees, setting forth the fees due to every officer of the honour and Castle of Windsor. Believes that, of late years, the orders contained therein have not been duly observed. Has directed the table of fees to be transcribed and hung up in the Court Room; and that the persons concerned should observe the orders. Gives an account of the occupation of the lodgings which were then in the occupation of Mr. Owen the Steward of the Court. It appears that the Constable had the disposal of several lodgings in the out parts and towers of the Castle which he

1728. Vol. CCLXV.

appointed as he thought fit. Does not think that the Steward, the Janitor, the Secretary, or any other officer under the jurisdiction of the Constable, has any right to lodgings by virtue of his office; but as they are appointed by the Constable. Is of opinion that Mr Owen has no right whatever to the lodgings.

"Recd May 17th 1728." 4 *pages.*

23 May. 41. Robert Byng to the Hon. Mr Secretary Scroope. The rights of Admiralty have to be paid to him. Has applied to Samuel Shute, Esq., late Governor of New England, to comply with his Majesty's orders during the time he was in that government; but as he knows not that his predecessor gave any such account, he excuses himself, unless their Lordships give the necessary orders. Asks that orders may be given for Mr Shute to account with him for the Admiralty Droits received during his government of New England.

Minuted:—"6th June 1728. Prepare a proper warrt to Mr Shute." 2 *pages.*

23 May. 42. Affidavit of W. Sanderson, Receiver of Holford, in the co. of Somerset, to the effect, viz.: that he sent a letter subscribed A.Z. to the Post-master General offering an expedient to prevent the robbery of the Bristol and other mails and of the subsequent negotiations with the Post Office, and that he never received any reward for his scheme. Mr Carteret, however, claimed the contrivance of the scheme wholly to himself. When he (Sanderson) applied to the Treasury did not the least doubt but that he should be well rewarded. Sworn 23 May 1728.

In the *Minute Book*, Vol. 26, p. 106*d*, 29 May 1728, is:—"Postmaster's Report of the 17th of Aprill last on Wm Sanderson's memorial is read, to be rewarded for a scheme which he, as alleged, invented, and was put in practice by the Postmars to prevent the robbing of the mails; and my Lords being satisfyed by the said report; that the said Sanderson has no pretence to any reward for such service, the scheme made use of appearing to have been entirely formed in the said Office, without the assistance of Sanderson, or any other person whatsoever. The said Sanderson attending, was called in, and my Lords acquainted him that they adhere to the Postmaster's report, and advise him to desist giving himself or their Lordships any further trouble; for that nothing more will be ordered therein." 3 *pages* (*quarto*).

29 May. 43. Sir John Fortescue to [ ]. Hopes he will take the case of his (Sir John's) arrears of salary under his consideration. Everybody agrees 'tis his right, and Sir Robert Walpole promised it should be paid, and the question is only upon the method. His claim is from the last day of Trinity term last (21 June) to the day of his *supersedeas* being 27 Sept. at 2*l*. 6*s*. 10½*d*. per diem, amounting to 229*l*. 13*s*. 3*d*. 'Tis said Mr Justice Cowper received not only for the days above, but for the residue of the time, "home to the last day of Mich. term," which was the whole 375l; as tho' he had been a judge from the 21st of

1728. VOL. CCLXV.

June to the last day of Mich. term. If this payment was made entire to him with a view that he (Sir John) should share it with him and be paid his 229*l.* 13*s.* 3*d.* it was right; but if paid as Michas. term's whole salary, it could not be his due, because his salary appointed by the King's grant was said expressly to commence and to be made payable from the 24th of October, the date of his patent. In this computation he will be paid about 60l more than is strictly due. The King's grant was drawn by Mr Attorney General with a view not to hurt him (Sir John) in the receipt of his arrears, more especially when he had gone a circuit and expended above 100*l.* in the King's service. It is very strange to talk of premiums for leaving practice; it was paid to him with one of these views (for, *quicquid solvitur, solvitur ad modum solventis*) either that he should share with him (Sir John) for his proportion; (then 'tis money received for his use) or else as a salary wholly due to him, then the surplus, is money received to the use of the Crown, because the grant does not warrant the payment; in which case he (Sir John) does not see but it is in the power of the Crown to set matters right another time by recouping what is overpaid. Serjts Inn, 29 May 1728.

Minuted:—"7th June 1728. Prepare a warrt for this sum."

In the *Minute Book* for that date (vol. 26, p. 110*f*) is:—"Prepare a warrant for paying to the late Mr Justice Fortescue his salary as a judge from the time he was last paid the same to the day he was superseded, notwithstanding Mr Justice Cowper was paid for that intermediate time." 3 *pages*.

4 June. 44. Alured Popple (for the Lords of Trade) to John Scrope, Esq. The Lords of Trade have prepared a draft (enclosed) of instructions for David Dunbar, Esq., appointed Surveyor of H. M. Woods in America. By an article in Col. Philips's instructions for the Government of Nova Scotia, he is restrained from granting any land to people that would become settlers there, until the Surveyor of the Woods has set out a certain tract of land as a nursery of trees for the use of the Royal Navy. It will be for his Majesty's service that the Surveyor General be despatched as soon as possible, that the settlement of Nova Scotia may be no longer delayed.

In the *Minute Book*, vol. 26, p. 132*c*, 13 Aug. 1728, is:—"Mr David Dunbar, Surveyor of the woods in North America, informing my Lords by letter of the 8th instant that he is to set out very soon for America, and being under their Lordps orders, desires to know their commands or further instructions for him, and he, being present, is acquainted that their Lordships have no further instructions than what he hath already received and is advised to proceed to his post without delay." 1½ *pages*.

5 June. 45. An imperfect paper containing the Establishment of his Majesty's Civil List in Scotland. Dated 5 June 1728.

Entered in *North Britain Book*, vol. 9, pp. 96–99. 3 *pages*.

VOL. CCLXV.

1728.
7 June. 46. Report of A. Cracherode to the Lords of the Treasury on the petition of Thomas Benson, Esq., who prosecuted at the sessions of gaol delivery at Newgate one Eccles Russell for conspiring with William Cunningham, Esq., and several other disorderly persons, to take away Anne, the wife of the petitioner, with divers goods of petitioner's to the value of 300*l.* Russell was found guilty and received sentence to pay a fine of 300*l.* to his Majesty. Petitioner prays that the fine may be granted to him. The Report substantially confirms the particulars in the petition. He was in addition to be imprisoned until the fine or rather two fines of 200*l.* and 100*l.* were paid. Russell still remained in prison. Mr Cracherode recommends that the fines should he paid to petitioner.

The petition and three certificates.

Minuted:—"Read and Mr Chancellor of the Exchequer will lay the same before the King and receive his Maj^ts pleasure thereupon." 6 *pages.*

[? About 7 June.] 47. Petition of John Lawton appointed to methodize and abstract the Records in the Chapter House and other places in the Receipt of the Exchequer at Westminster, addressed to the Lords of the Treasury. Has constantly performed their Lordships' constitution, dated 3 July 1724. Prays for a new constitution. The Chapter House (wherein most of the Records are reposited) being a large capacious building, and so near the east end of Westminster Abbey, where masons daily work, is affected very much by their dust. Asks to have a person allowed him, to dust the Records and clean the office, which he finds by experience would be the means of very much preserving them (nothing being more detrimental than dust). Also asks for a consideration for parchment, paper, pens, ink, books, and other necessaries, which will be very much wanted now he has nearly finished the sorting the King's Bench and Common Pleas Rolls under his care "in order to abstract those" and cover great numbers of others.

Minuted:—"7th June 1720. See what his appointments are."

Lower down:—"200^li ℘ ann. for himself.
222 „ for 3 clerks.
———
420."

In the *Minute Book*, vol. 26, p. 124*l*, 19 July 1728, is:—"John Lawton's memorial representing the great addition of Records ordered by the House of Lords to be removed to the Chapter House, under his care, and for a further allowance in respect thereof, is read. My Lords thereupon consider the allowance he at present receives for himself and clerks and the services performed for the same, and are of opinion there is no foundation for augmenting the allowance." 1 *page.*

12 June. 48. Report of John Conduit, Esq., Master and Worker of the Mint, on the petition of John Dassier, Engraver and Medallist to the Republic of Geneva, offering to assist at His Majesty's Mint,

1728. VOL. CCLXV.

and desiring permission to make medals within the Tower of London. Advises that it may be for his Majesty's service to encourage Mr. Dassier (who is a Protestant, an able artist, and bears a good character) to stay in England, where so few are skilled in that business. It seems advisable to give him leave to coin, at his own expense, and for his own advantage, within his Majesty's mint, such medals as do not interfere with those made by Mr. Croker and such as are approved by the master and worker; and to employ him in making puncheons or dies for the coinage of money, when there shall be occasion, and to pay him out of the coinage duty, he not being a natural born subject nor consequently capable of enjoying any certain salary. This was not to interfere with Mr Croker, the Chief Engraver, who had, besides his salary, the profit he made by the medals he coined at his own expense, upon extraordinary public occasions, which he well deserved; having served the Crown upwards of thirty years.

Also the petition.

In the *Minute Book*, vol. 29, p. 119*a*, 26 June 1728, is :—* * * "Agreed subject to such restrictions as shall not deprive the King's Engraver of any [of] his advantages." 4 *pages*.

26 June. 49. A paper indorsed :—"A case in relacõn to the settlemt made on the mar. of Mr Wilkinson, Junr. For Mr Sollr Generall's opinion." The point was whether the estate was liable to answer a debt due to the Crown. Signed "P. Yorke & C. Talbot, 26th June 1728." 3 *pages*.

26 June. 50. "The demand of Henry, Lord Viscount Lonsdale, Constable of his late Majesty's Tower of London, for safe keeping prisoners there, according to the retrenchment made by King Charles the 2d, &c." From 8 Oct. 1726 to 10 June 1727, dated June 26, 1728. 1 *page*.

29 June. 51. Ro. Hunter [Governor of Jamaica] to the Right Hon. the Lords of Trade. Sends "His Matys Acct of Imposts, Fortifications and Acct Currt from the 7th of April 1725 to ye 25th of March, 1728." The assembly meets on "Tuesday next, the 2nd of June." Will send their Lps an account of what they shall do. Jamaica, June 29, 1728.

The letter is accompanied by 17 accounts. *Each of* 2 *or* 3 *pages*.

16 July. 52. Thomas Matthew to Mr Scrope. Mr Man has brought an ejectment against Mr Willett and Mr Spooner, and if they are evicted all their buildings, improvements, and crop must fall into his hands. "In the case of King, Hart and others with Thauvet," is advised, that on moving the Chancellor of the Leeward Islands for a writ "de domino Rege inconsulto" in order to stay proceedings against these persons, as occupiers of the King's lands, till directions could be had from the Lords of the Treasury, such writ was denied; so that the expense of this matter lies wholly on these poor people, at whose charge the Plantations have been settled. Hopes that their Lordships will order his Majesty's proper

1728. VOL. CCLXV.

officers in the Island to assist in the defence of H. M. title. Had applied to the Governor (M^{r} [or ? General] Mathew) and the other Com^{rs} without effect. The memorials of Mr Heldens, Mr Lowndes, Mr Bridgewater, Mr Griffes, Mr Johnson, M^{r} O'Neals, and Mr Buller are before their Lordships and show how necessary it is that some directions should be given to the Commissioners not to alter the possessions of the possessors till a full examination and their Lordships' determination has been had concerning them. 2 *pages.*

25 July. 53. Report of the Barons of the Exchequer of Scotland to the Lords of the Treasury. Have examined the Warrant for the Royal signature for granting and conveying the "five merk land of old extent of Auchenreoch and others, lying in the parish of Urr & Stewartry of Kirkcudbright, to William & Thomas McGeorges, proceeding upon the resignations of John Hamilton of Auchenreoch, senior, and John Hamilton his son, and John McGeorge."

"The signature contains only a taxing of the Ward holding of these lands; so that no non-entry dutys, or casualties and forfeitures by recognition, or escheat, affecting the said lands, can be discharged by the taxing of the Ward holding."

The valued rent of the lands appears to be 18*l.* 6*s.* 8*d.* By taxing the "Ward holding" according to the rules settled by the privy seal, the Crown accepts a fifth of what it would be entitled to, where dower or tenancy by the courtesy or maintenance of the heir doth not fall in. The real rent of the lands is always more than the valued rent; yet because what is taxed is a certainty, it hath been by long practice held to be reasonable and legal for the Crown to exercise its bounty to such of its vassals as his Majesty is inclined. Signed. 2 *pages.*

26 July. 54. Representation of the Barons of the Exchequer of Scotland to the Lords of the Treasury. By the Act of 6 Anne for settling and establishing a Court of Exchequer in Scotland it is provided that there shall be the following offices in that Court, viz., Queen's Remembrancer, Treasurer's Remembrancer, Clerk of the Pipe, and such other offices as are in being in the Court of Exchequer in England, or are in being in Scotland "relating to signatures, gifts & Tutorys" as the Queen and her successors shall constitute. The offices of King's Remembrancer, Lord Treasurer's Remembrancer, and Clerk of the Pipe were established. No office of Pleas was then constituted, as there did not appear an immediate occasion for it, but now the office appears absolutely necessary; for the want of the office has occasioned the Officers of the Revenue to be frequently pursued before other courts. To prevent this inconvenience, actions of law against the Officers of Customs have been brought in the King's Remembrancer's Office, contrary to the course of practice of the Exchequer in England. "The Court does not intend to hold plea or admit of any suits in the said office which do not concern the revenue and the officers of it." Signed. 2 *pages.*

1728. Vol. CCLXV.

[Between June 1727 and 30 July 1728.] 55. A memorial and a petition of "Don Manuel Mercader, son of the Marquis De la Vega, sometime Arch Deacon and Chancellor of the Kingdom of Valencia and Vicar General of his Majesty's Island of Minorca." The memorial is addressed to Sir Robert Walpole, and states that the King, in 1715, granted to memorialist 300*l.* per ann. for subsistence, during his residence here, which had been regularly issued to the 5th of March 1726. Since that time he has been in great difficulties for want of the allowance and is in danger of imprisonment.

The petition states that Queen Anne, by the treaty of Utrecht, stipulated that the inhabitants of Minorca should enjoy all their liberties, honours, and estates, with the free exercise of the Roman Catholic religion as formerly, so far as should not be inconsistent with the laws of Great Britain, and her Majesty promised to fulfil the same. Her Majesty despatched an order to Col. Kane, Lieut.-Governor of Minorca, to assemble the principal inhabitants, and to signify her pleasure for sending to England two or three able persons to settle the Government, both ecclesiastical and civil, of that Island; and her Majesty promised to defray the expenses of the persons coming over, attending here and going back to Minorca. The Col. complied with the order, and the inhabitants deputed Don "Manual" Mercader, then Vicar General of the Island, and Doctor Francis Sancha, Assessor General, to come over to England; the expense of whose voyage was paid by Mr Gascoigne, Receiver General of the Island. The Deputies arrived in England on the 1st of September, a month after the late Queen died, and having attended the arrival of his Majesty and his Royal father at the Court of Great Britain, they were introduced to his Majesty by the Duke of Argyle, then Governor of Minorca, and to his late Majesty by General Stanhope, then Secretary of State, when they presented "sixty-seven several articles for his Majesty's service," and his Majesty by several warrants ordered the Deputies to be supported. The assessor, after a year, returned to Minorca owing to ill-health and advancing years, and the King ordered his expenses to be paid and that memorialist should remain till further order, and that the Lords of the Treasury should allow him 300*l.* per annum. This sum has been allowed to the 5th of March 1725–6. Petitioner's long stay in England, "and appearing always a good subject to his Majesty, warm in his publick and private conversation for his Majesty's interest and glory of the British nation, moderate and charitable in religious affairs, his enemies have thence taken occasion to accuse him at the Court of Rome of being married, and that he is turned Protestant, for which reason and because he gave four churches in Minorca for the use of the English troops in the year 1714, when Vicar General there, the late Pope deprived him of his Dignitys of Archdeacon of Valencia, worth six hundred pounds stirling p. ann., and the Inquisition of Spain has received several informations against him," so that he has lost all that he had in the world, and even the liberty of returning with safety of

1728. VOL. CCLXV.

his life to his native country. Prays to be paid the arrears due to him of 375 pounds or that he may be otherwise supported.

In the *Minute Book*, vol. 26, p. 128*f*, 30 July, 1728, is :—"Don Emanuel Mercador is to be paid 300*l.* as his Ma[ts] bounty." 2 *pages.*

VOL. CCLXVI. 1728. AUGUST—DECEMBER.

2 Aug. 1. Charles Wager to the "Hon[ble] John Scrope, Esq." Has, with Mr. Consul Russell, perused the particulars of the present intended for the Emperor of Morocco. Cannot find that any thing can well be reduced, except the musical clock, guns, and pistols, amounting to 327*l.* 15*s.* Believes the chariot should be lined with "Cafoy," which with the lace will come to 15*l.* more than the present estimates. But as there is a bill for Basha Hamet which appears not to be part of the Emperor's present, and that Basha is said to be out of favour, this might be deducted : viz., two silver teapots, a silver watch, and an air gun, amounting to 63*l.* 2*s.*, and then there will be room to add a "glass scrutore" to the Emperor's present, and to make the addition to the chariot. M[r] Knight the Surgeon's account of expenses in Barbary seems to me very reasonable.

Admiralty Office, 2 August 1728.

Also "An account of the cost of Bashaw Hammett's things, sent by Consul Russell to get mended, and what the Bashaw and his brother, the Governor of Tangier, desires may be brought them." 3 *pages.*

5 Aug. 2. Report of Ch. Wither, surveyor of the woods, to the Lords [of the Treasury], on the return of the Verderers and Regarders of the New Forest concerning the state of the fences and enclosures therein. By the statute 9 & 10 Will. III., the King and his successors were empowered to enclose 2,000 acres of the waste lands of the Forest (the whole containing 85,454 acres); and after the enclosure of the 2,000 acres they were empowered annually, for 20 years to enclose 200 acres. When the wood grown thereon becomes past danger of browsing of cattle, &c., and the same is laid open, the King and his successors may enclose the like quantity. The Com[rs] who were appointed, enclosed 1,000 acres and no more, and there is a very great and promising growth of young timber; insomuch that in the enclosure called Rhinfield only, there are 370,000 young oak and beech trees, out of danger from abuse of the cattle. The forest officers have represented that if Burley, Rhinfield, and Woodfidly enclosures are out of danger of the browsing of cattle, and may safely be laid open, that Brinley Coppices, Castle of Mall-wood, and Bugg-pits, ought to be kept well

VOL. CCLXVI.

1728.

fenced from cattle. The damage done by the colliers and other trespassers is very great. Is of opinion that it would be well worth while to cause all trespassers to be prosecuted severely by the Attorney General. Advises that Burley, Rhinfield, and Woodfilly enclosures should be laid open to the waste of the forest, and that enclosures completing the 2,000 acres should be made.

Accompanied by memorial of the Verderers and Regarders of the New Forest, relating to the fences there. 4 *pages.*

[? About 6 Aug.] 3. Memorial of the late Com[rs] and Trustees for the Forfeited Estates in England to the Lords of the Treasury.

Christopher Cole for the Governor and Company of Undertakers for raising the Thames Water in York Buildings in the year 1720 contracted with memorialists for the purchase of part of the late Lord Widdrington's Estate, in the co. of Northumberland, for 57,100*l.* Several sums were paid into the Exchequer on account of the purchase thereof; but a considerable part remained unpaid, and the Attorney General has filed an information in the Exchequer against the Governor and Company to compel them to perform the contract. Memorialists have no interest in the contract except as trustees. Pray that their L[ps] solicitor may be directed to defend memorialists and pay the expenses of the suit.

In the *Minute Book*, Vol. 26, p. 130*e*, 6 Aug. 1728, is:—"Write to M[r] Cracherode to appear for and defray the expence, if any, that the late Comm[rs] and Trustees for Forfeited Estates in England may be put to on acco[t] of the informacon now in the Excheq[r] against the York Buildings Company relating to their contract with the said Comm[rs] for the purchase of the late Lord Widdrington's Estate, according to their memorial in that behalf." 1 *page.*

[? About 6 Aug.] 4. Memorial of M[rs] Ruperta Howe, Chief Rangeress of Alice Holt and Woolmer Forests, in the co. of Southampton, to the Lords of the Treasury. Desires that the true state of the case as regards the allowance for repairs and payments of Keepers may be presented to his Majesty so that orders may be given according to the former precedents. The repairs of the lodges in Alice Holt and Woolmer Forests will amount to 643*l.* 8*s.* Hopes the repairs will be ordered. Asks for two years and three quarters of the salaries of the Keepers due at Midsummer, to be paid "12th Aug. 1728" [but ? 2 Aug.].

Also estimates of the repairs.

In the *Minute Book*, Vol. 26, p. 131*p*, 6 Aug. 1728, is:—"M[r] Chancellor says that the King consents to the making repairs and paying keepers' wages in Holt Forest notwithstanding the restrictive clause in the grant under which M[rs] How holds the rangership thereof. So prepare a warrant for the said repairs and paying the said keepers upon M[r] Wither's report made in that behalf." Again, at p. 132*d*, 13 Aug. 1728, "Mrs. Ruperta Howe's peticon for repairs in Holt Forest and keepers' wages is read and order[d] to be dispatched conformable to the Minute of the 6th instant." 3 *pages.*

VOL. CCLXVI.

1728.

12 Aug. 5. John Lawton to the Honble Mr Scrope. Has searched out and copied "come precedents of the ordinary and extraordinary methods practiced for innovating tallies," which he sets out. [The precedents go back to the reign of Edw. I.] Observes that it may reasonably be imagined that there has been always a power, *virtute officii*, in the Chancellor and Barons of the Exchequer to remedy any casual loss of tallies by their warrant, as is now used; for the practice of innovating tallies appears by the rolls too frequent, to suppose the King was applied to on all those occasions. "Innovates" have been constantly granted, but all the authorities on which they were grounded formerly are not to be had in the Receipt side of the Exchequer. It is submitted whether an inquiry into this matter on the law side would not be proper, especially as it rather seems to have been, and does so now continue to be, the province of the Chancellor and Barons to grant their warrants in those cases, than of the Lords of the Treasury. Exchequer, 12 Aug. 1728.

Accompanied by copies of the precedents. 12 *pages*.

13 Aug. 6. Memorial of Thomas Missing, contractor for Victualling the Garrison of Gibraltar, to the Lords of the Treasury. The Victualling Office at Gibraltar is so damnified and demolished by bombs, &c. in the last siege, that the contractor hath not room or shelter for the provisions; insomuch that large quantities have been, and still are, obliged to be exposed to the inclemencies of the weather. The Government have to provide sufficient storehouses. Prays that orders may be given to put the same in proper condition. 530 casks of beef and pork are exposed to the open air.

In the *Minute Book*, vol. 26, p. 139*b*, 22 Aug. 1728, is:— * * * "Ordered that the Agent Victualer there do take care all necessary repairs be performed, so as the publique may be freed from any demands of the Contractor for damage he may sustain for want thereof. Write to the Com^rs^ of Victualling to order accordingly." 1 *page*.

15 Aug. 7. Memorial of the Com^rs^ of Customs, Scotland, to the Lords of the Treasury. The old Bank of Scotland, some time ago, stopped payment of its notes, and immediately issued new notes, which are now called Cash or Specie notes; while the Bank refuses to pay its old notes. Upon a question of law, before the Lords of Session, for recovering payment of the old notes, they adjudged that no summary execution could pass thereupon, as in other cases, by which the possessor of such notes is subject to a long and expensive process before any recovery can be had. These notes have ever since the Union been received by all the officers of the revenue as cash, and lest the revenue should suffer they ask that some directions may be given. "Custom h^o^, Edinb^r^, 15 August 1728."

In the *Minute Book*, vol. 26, p. 164*f*, 23 Oct. 1728, is:— * * * "My Lords are of opinion that the publique money in the hands of any of the King's Receivers should not be suffered to remain with persons who refuse paying their notes, but suspend the

1728. VOL. CCLXVI.

issuing any orders about the same till this day sevennight in expectation of my Lord Isla's being then in town for their Lordps to discourse him thereupon."

Again:—p. 181*b*, 31 Dec. 1728, "Write to the Commrs and Excise in Scotland acquainting them that my Lords have considered their respective memorials relating to the cash notes of the old Bank, and for the reasons therein mencõned their Lordps are of opinion that the notes of the said old Bank ought not to be received in the revenue, and direct them to govern themselves accordingly. 1 *page*.

27 Aug. 8. Letter. Sir C. Wager to Rt Hon. Sir R. Walpole. Besides the money for the "Rescrit" he will want for Bashe Hamet's account and on two other accounts 524*l*. 0*s*. 11*d*. In the *Minute Book*, vol. 26, p. 140*f*, 27 Aug. 1728, is:—"Sr Charles Wager having certified my Lords that Consul Russel's accot of his journey to and from Mequinez is reasonable, prepare a sign manual for paying to the Consul the ballance due thereupon and 300li for his intended journey." 1 *page*.

29 Aug. 9. The Duke of Newcastle to the Lords of the Treasury. "The French Ambassador having, by order from his Court, made application to the King in behalf of the Dowager Lady Teynham, who is administratrix of the late Earl of Sussex, petitions for the payment of a sum of 20,000*l*. alledged to be due from the Crown to that family, as also for an arrear of interest on the said sum," the Duke sends, by the King's command, the enclosed papers, which the Ambassador put into his (the Duke's) hands for their Lps' consideration and report thereon. Hampton Court, Aug. 29, 1728.

Accompanied by the petition of the above Dowager and translation thereof, which states that the 20,000*l*. was granted to the Earl of Sussex by King Charles II. on his marriage with the King's daughter, and that there was 11,800*l*. interest due on the death of Queen Anne. King George promised the Earl that he should be reckoned as one of the creditors of the late Queen for the interest, and that he should receive his quota of her effects and the principal sum of 20,000*l*. and interest accrued since. Prays that the interest may be paid to her, and that her case may be represented to the King for the payment of the principal and interest during the reign of his Majesty.

Also four other documents. 18 *pages*.

July to August. 10. Thirteen papers, consisting of contracts, estimates, and tradesmen's bills, together with "An abstract of the different Tradesmen's Bills, who have agreed with Consul John Russell to furnish a present for the Emperor of Morocco, pursuant to the order of the Rt Honble the Lords Comrs of his Majesties Treasury."

The bills amounted to 1,497*l*. 8*s*. 5*d*., and the following minute relates to them. See *Minute Book*, vol. 26, p. 131, 6 Aug. 1728. "Sr Charles Wager's letter of the 2dinstant, about abatements to be made, on Mr Russell's accot of the tradesmen's bills, for the present to be sent to the Emperour of Morocco, is read, and my Lords say the particulars must be so accommodated as not to exceed 1,500li.

1728. VOL. CCLXVI.

So let Sr Charles Wager's letter and reducements be considered by Mr Russell; and he is thereupon to bring the whole within that sum, and then prepare a sign manual for issuing the 1,500^li to Mr Russell for that purpose, in manner the money for the former present was issued, and under the same inspection." 14 *pages.*

6 Sept. 11. Copy of an attested copy of "Mr Attorney & Mr Solicitor Genl's report in relation to the King's right to the woods in the Massa. Bay, &c. Dated Decr 23^d, 1726." The copy was attested 6 Sept., 1728.

The opinion relates to the construction to be put on the Act of 8 Will. III., entitled "An Act giving further encouragement for the importation of Naval Stores," &c. The Attorney and Solicitor General hold that the Act does not take away the right reserved to the Crown by the Charter of Massachusetts Bay in the 3rd of Will. and Mary, as to cutting trees of the diameter of 24 inches at 12 inches from the ground, whether the same are growing within or without any township. 3 *pages.*

18 Sept. 12. Charles Corkyse to Christopher Tilson, Esq., at the Treasury Chambers, as to certain wax candles, wine, &c. imported by Count Broglio. All Foreign Ministers at their first coming have their baggage and what belongs to their equipage, with an allowance of wine, without duty, pursuant to the Treasury warrant relating to Foreign Ministers, but on their having new credentials to his present Majesty the Foreign Ministers have constantly paid duties for all the goods they have imported, except on their allowance of wine. Custom House, London, 18 Sept. 1728.

Accompanied by copy of a letter from the Com^rs of Customs to Sir Robert Walpole on the same subject. 3 *pages.*

23 Sept. 13. Thomas Tomkyns to the Lords of the Treasury. Brings to their Lordships' notice Mr Wood's proceedings, who claims to be able to make sow or pig metal with pit coal, and to furnish from thence bar-iron equally cheap with that made by the writer's method. Makes various strictures upon Mr Wood's invention, and says that what he has hitherto dispersed abroad, and declared to be metal of an extraordinary purity, is really far short in purity to pig metal, long since made with pit coal fire, and nothing superior to the ore itself. Hopes he may be at liberty to obstruct Mr Wood in his present request.

In the *Minute Book*, vol. 26, p. 151*g*, 24 Sept. 1728, is:—"Thomas Tonkyns' letter of the 23rd instant touching Mr Wood's proceedings in suing for a patent for melting iron with pit coal, which interferes with a patent before obtained by him, is read: But as the application to my Lords in this case is very improper, the matter in dispute being for the Secretary of State to consider, and not their Lordps, they return no answer thereto."

Again, p. 239*g*, 23 July 1729, is:—"Order of Council dated the 16 of June last, referring to my Lords the peticõn of Thomas Tomkyns, late cashire to the hawkers & pedlars, praying liberty from his present imprisonment, under an extent for a debt to the

1728. VOL. CCLXVI.

Crown; so as he may prosecute an undertaking, which is his by patent, of making iron malleable with sea or pit coal fire, is read. My Lords say that this debt is inexcusable, and that the publique affairs in Parliament have suffered by means thereof; and that his pretence of being the inventor of making iron malleable, in manner aforesaid, is no sufficient cause for his enlargement, nor can he, in their Lordps opinion, be inabled by means of the said undertaking to make any satisfaction to the publique for the said debt." 3 *pages.*

24 Sept. 14. Petition of Robert Knaplock, Jacob Tonson, John Pemberton, and Richard Williamson to the Lords of the Treasury. Have been appointed by the Speaker of the House of Commons to print the several reports, "representation," and votes mentioned in the account annexed. Have delivered as usual for the service of the House 658 of each of the same on each day of the Sessions; and by further order have delivered 5,600 more of the "Representation," amounting to 591*l.* 1*s.* 10*d.*; pray for payment "as the like demands have been usually paid out of ye contingent expences of his Majesty's Civil Government."

The account referred to.

The minute on the back on 29 July 1729 states that "My Lords understanding that the Votes delivered for the service of the House itself were not used heretofore to be paid for by the Crown, their Lordps order that fact to be inquired into and stated, and enquire also whether the printed Reports for the House about the South Sea Directors' Estates, dated 6th Febry 1721 and 25 April 1726, and for which 32*l.* 18*s.* is charged in the said accot, were printed and delivered in this King's or the late King's time."

In the *Minute Book,* vol. 26, p. 283, 7 Jan. 1729–30, is:—"My Lords reconsider Mr Tonson and Mr Knaplock's petition which was read 29 July last for 591*l.* 10*s.* for printing reports, votes, and representacons of proceedings in the House of Commons, and do thereupon agree that they be paid for all extrary papers and proceedings that the House may order to be printed; but their Lordps cannot advise that the King should be at the charge of paying them for the Votes dayly delivered to the House of Commons." 3 *pages.*

27 Sept. 15. The Attorney General (Yorke) to the Rt Hon. Sir R. Walpole. Has perused the Acts of Parliament which appear to concern a question submitted to him, and is of opinion that the 16,400*l.* 8*s.* per ann. "being now determined, falls into the Civil List, as a temporary incumbrance discharged; unless there be some Act subsequent to the South Sea Act, 6 Geo I., that makes any particular appropriation of it," &c. Linc. Inn, Sept. 27, 1728.

Also six other papers apparently connected with the above. 16 *pages or parts of pages.*

1 Oct. 16. Report of Nicholas Paxton (in the absence of Mr Cracherode) to the Lords of the Treasury on the petition of Charles Townsend in behalf of George Townsend, Montague Bacon, John Atwood, and

1728. Vol. CCLXVI.

John Burton, late Com^{rs} for licencing hawkers, pedlars, and petty chapmen. The debt due from the Com^{rs} is 36,663*l.* 13*s.* 6*d.*, towards recovery whereof several writs of extent have been issued out of the Court of Exchequer into the several counties where the Com^{rs} had estates or effects, or where their persons might be taken. By the inquisitions taken upon such writs it appears that George Townesend was seized of goods to the value of 7*l.*, and that George Townesend, late of Lincoln's Inn, Esq. (father of the said George), by will directed his Trustees and Executors to pay the rents, &c. of his estate in such manner as his eldest son (the said George) shall direct. Conceives that the Crown will stand in his place, and be entitled to the rents during his life, or until the debt is satisfied. The Trustees have filed a Bill in the Exchequer against the creditors to oblige them to prove their debts. By an inquisition taken 7 April 1727 it appears that John Atwood was, in the 12th year of his late Majesty, seized for life of the manors of Saxlingham . . . Saxlingham Nether-hall, Saxlingham, Verdens, Thorpe Hall, and . . . and messuages, &c., situate therein, of the yearly value of 312*l.* 16*s.* 6*d.*, which were seized by the sheriff of the co. of Norfolk. By an inquisition taken by the said sheriff, in the 13th year, it appears that John Burton was seised of messuages in Great Yarmouth of the annual value of 163*l.*, besides some goods and chattels, which were also seized unto the King's hands. The said John Burton conveyed by deed, dated about 1712, divers messuages and premises in Great Yarmouth, Thurne, Oby, and Ashby, alias Askeby, to Trustees. Could not discover that Montague Bacon had any estate whatsoever. Has received proposals from Mr Robert Atwood for purchasing the estate of John Atwood, and from John Burton on behalf of William Burton. Makes suggestions as to the purchase money. The friends of Montague Bacon are willing to pay 100*l.* as a composition for his debt. He is maintained by his friends and is sometimes disordered in his senses.

Accompanied by the petition, three proposals and four affidavits.

By the petition it seems that an Act of Parliament was passed to enable the Lords of the Treasury to compound the debt.

Minuted:—" 1st of October 1728. Read, and My Lords come to no determination thereupon, untill they shall be informed whether upon compositions of the like nature, yearly provisions have been allowed to the compounders out of their estates, for the maintenance of themselves and familyes, and order inquiry to be made accordingly.

" 8th October 1728. My Lords resume the consideration of Mr Paxton's report of the 1st instant, touching the composition to be made with the late Comm^{rs} for licencing hawkers and pedlars, and having precedents laid before them, by which it appears that sums of money in gross have been usually accepted and taken for compositions, and no mention made of any allowance or defalcation for the maintenance of the compounders and their familyes, their Lordships are pleased to accept from the undernamed as a com-

1728. VOL. CCLXVI.

position from them respectively, for the debt to the Crown, the following sums, viz.: from Montague Bacon 100li. From John Atwood 2000li. From John Burton 234li. So prepare a warrt on the Act of Parliament for making the composition with the aforenamed persons accordingly. And then there will remain on the said Act only George Townsend one of the said late Cōmmrs to be compounded with." 12 *pages*.

1 Oct. 17. Report of the Comrs of the Revenue in Ireland to the Lords of the Treasury on the petition of Matthew Palin, gent. In the month of Jan. 1714, the petitioner, by a memorial to the Comrs of Revenue, Ireland, made discovery of the Crown's title to the lands, in the petition mentioned, lying in Westmeath, late the forfeiture of Henry Fitzgerald, who was indicted and outlawed for high treason. If the lands were not recovered it was to be at the expense of the petitioner, and he was to have a fourth part should they be recovered. This was agreed to. The title was tried in the Court of Exchequer in Easter term 1716, and a verdict found for the Crown. After great expense this was set aside. By a new trial a second verdict was found for the Crown and possession ordered. A lease was made by the Comrs of the said lands to Richard Berry, Esq., since deceased; but a writ of error was brought by the defendants in last Easter term to reverse the judgment. The petitioner was reimbursed all his costs, and has received a fourth part of the profits since the recovery. The Comrs of Revenue are of opinion that the petitioner has no just pretension to a custodiam thereof, to the prejudice of the heir of Mr Berry, or to any further gratification. Custom House, Dublin, Oct. 1, 1728.

In the *Minute Book*, vol. 26, p. 161s, 15 Oct., is:—* * * "My Lords agree with the Comrs that the peticōner hath no just pretencōns to a custodiam of the forfeited lands of Henry Fitzgerald therein mencōned, or any further gratification for his discoveries relating thereto other than the ¼ part of the profitts which he hath already received." 3 *pages*.

22 July–7 Oct. 18. Three letters from Thomas Tomkyns, one addressed to — Paxton, Esq., Solicitor to the Lords of the Treasury, a second unaddressed, and the third to the Lords of the Treasury, pressing to be liberated from the Poultry Comptor Prison, in order that he might superintend some ironwork apparently at "Oka-Moore" over which their Lordships had some control, and to prevent the men being dispersed, as they had now twelve months' experience. The work has always been intended as a school for the instruction of workmen who were to be drawn off from time to time and employed at other places.

One of the letters encloses a letter signed Rupert Hurst, addressed to Mr Tomkyns. The writer was employed at the works at Oka-Moore. The letter is dated at Cheadle, July 15, 1728. There is also a petition from Mr Tomkyns to the Lords of the Treasury, begging to be transferred to the Fleet Prison, as he was threatened to be turned over to the common side of the prison, and was in ill-health. It is *minuted* :—

1728. VOL. CCLXVI.

"Read 6 Augt 1728. My Lords say that in this case the liberty of his person entirely depends upon the sufficiency of the security which he sometime since proposed to give, but no such security having been reported to their Lordp̃s by Mr Cracherode, who was appointed to enquire into their sufficiency, their Lordp̃s can do nothing therein."

In the letter to the Lords of the Treasury Mr Tomkyns says that he is advised that his confinement cannot be strictly legal, and gives the reasons, which he sums up thus;—either he must be accountable to the Crown or to the Commissioners; but as he is undeniably accountable to the Com^{rs} he must not be to the Crown. His patent is his only dependence, and is seized, and it was esteemed to be worth a million to the nation. The letter is *minuted*:— "15 Octr 1728. My Lords say his confinement is by Excheq^{r} process, and if he has reasons, he may apply to the Court of Excheq^{r} to hear the same." Dated between 22 July and 7 Oct. 1728. 9 *pages*.

May–8 Oct. 19. Papers relating to expenses of Cossum Choja the Tripoli Ambassador, including a number of receipts for moneys paid for hotel bills, &c. by Jezreel Jones on his Excellency's account. Dated between May and 8 Oct. 1728.

There is also a petition of Jezreel Jones to the R^{t} Hon. Sir Robert Wallpole for allowance of money disbursed by him for "My ben Moosa Zeph Zeph, the Basha of Tangiers friend."

Minuted:—"Read 18 June 1728. My Lords order 40^{li} to be paid him to recompense his trouble in attending an African Officer from the Governor of Tangier whilst here, clear of all charges at the Excheq^{r}." 69 *pages and small scraps*.

13 Oct. 20. Lord Townsend to the Lords of the Treasury. By his Majesty's command sends copy of a letter received from the Duke of Argyle relating to the fortifications which are to be carried on at Gibraltar. Asks for the money to be provided. Windsor, Oct. 13, 1728.

In the enclosure it appears that 1,000^{l} per month was to be expended, and that the money given by Parliament would be wholly expended before the order could arrive.

In the *Minute Book*, vol. 26, p. 159*c*, 15 Oct. 1728, is:— * * * "Their Lordp̃s do agree to issue to the Treasurer of the Ordnance 8,000^{li} by 1,000^{li} a month to answer bills of Exchange as they shall be drawn from thence for that service with which my Lord Townshend is to be acquainted." 3 *pages*.

14 Oct. 21. Report of Edmund, Bishop of London, unaddressed—in respect to the right of appointment of a minister to the Savoy Church. Since the dissolution of the hospital it has been uncertain to whom the right of appointing belongs. During this uncertainty Mr Parry performed the duty for some time, and he (the Bishop) gave a certificate thereof, and obtained an order from the Treasury to receive the salary (20*l*. a year). In the same manner Mr Wilkinson applied for a certificate and this he (the Bishop) gave, believing that Mr Parry had relinquished the cure. Does not know that M^{r}

1728. VOL. CCLXVI.

Parry had any title besides bare possession. If his title is found to be valid, he is not injured by the payment made to Mr Wilkinson, &c. Supposes the thing he chiefly aims at, in presenting the petition, is to establish his title. It is much to be wished that full inquiry were made in whom the right of nomination rests, in order to settle a known legal minister. There has been great disorder and confusion among the inhabitants for some time past. It seems fit that the minister should be accommodated with a house or lodging.

Accompanied by the "petition of the Minister and Chapel wardens of the Precinct of the Savoy."

In the *Minute Book*, vol. 26, p. 160, 15 Oct. 1728, is:—"Bishop of London's representacõn of the case between Mr Wilkinson and Mr Parry, touching their respective pretensions to the office of preacher at the Savoy Church, is read, and my Lords find no cause to remove, or dispossess Mr Wilkinson; and are of opinion that the house or lodging, if any, which Mr Parry had, as minister there, should be put into the said Mr Wilkinson's possession. And if no such house or lodging was possessed by Parry, that then Mr Wilkinson be admitted into those lodgings lately possessed by one Mr Synge, deceased, according to the desire of the Chappel Wardens and inhabitants in that behalf."

[There is a further entry in the *Minute Book* at p. 329*c*, in relation to a dwelling for the minister, but it would seem to be the answer to another petition.] 3 *pages*.

18 Oct. 22. Copy of the opinions of the Solicitor General (Talbot) and of "Jo. Chesshyre" as to what duty was leviable by the Collector at Whitehaven upon corn imported. Reference is made to "the Act for improvement of Tillage and the breed of cattle," and it is stated that by that Act the rates to be paid for custom and poundage were for every quarter of wheat, when the same should not exceed the price of 2*l.* 13*s.* 4*d.* per quarter, 16s, and when the quarter exceeded 2*l.* 13*s.* 4*d.*, then 8s should be paid, &c. 6 *pages*.

29 Oct. 23. Lord Townshend to the Lords of the Treasury. The King having continued to William Finch, Esq., the same pay he received when Envoy Extraordinary to the States General, his Majesty desired their Lordships to give directions for paying him 8*l.* by the day until further orders: and to Brigadier Dubourgay, Envoy Extraordinary to the King of Prussia, 5*l.* by the day; and to Robert Jackson, Esq., 3*l.* by the day as Resident from his Majesty at the Court of Sweden, as well as bills of extraordinaries to the two last. 1½ *pages*.

23 Nov. 24. Report of the Surveyor General (Philip Gybbon) to the Lords of the Treasury, on a memorial of the Lord Bishop of Oxford, who represented that the tenants of Stow Wood and Shotover Wood (on the surrender of a lease from the Crown for 60 years from 1636) were each bound to pay to the Bishop of Oxford 50*l.* a year, and that King William on 16 June 1696 granted to the late Duke of Leeds a reversionary interest for 31 years of the same woods

from the decease of Queen Catherine without any notice of those pensions, so that they have now determined. King George I. in the 4th year of his reign also granted a lease in reversion of Shotover Forest "at the two yearly rents of fifty pounds and fifty pounds payable at the Exchequer without any notice of the fifty pounds payable as a pension to the Bishop. The lease will take effect from 5 Dec. 1736. The Bishop prays relief. The surveyor reports fully upon the effect of these leases, and concludes that from Lady day 1727 till the expiration of the grant to the Duke of Leeds in 1736, there is no rent payable to the Crown for all the above lands except part of 3*l.* 18s. 4¼*d.* per ann.; so that, during that lease, it seems impracticable for any pension out of these lands to be granted to the Bishop.

Accompanied by the petition. 5 *pages.*

28 Nov. 25. Mr Auditor Harley to the Rt Hon. William Clayton, Esq. Has searched all the accounts of the Great Wardrobe from Queen Elizabeth to Queen Anne, but "cannot find that the particular vouchers, to maintain the actual payment of the sums expressed in these warrants, have been delivered to the Auditors, who pass these accounts upon the authority of the warrants. In King Charles the Second's time a Comptroller was established, who, together with the Surveyor, the Clerk of the Robes and the Clerk of the Wardrobe, signed the accounts. This method was continued during that reign, but from that time was discontinued by Lord Montague, who only signed the accounts. Has looked over many of the old accounts, but cannot find what fees were taken for "measurage and poundage, which surely were very considerable; because Earl Montague, upon the supersedure of his allowance of 2,200*l.* per annum, which was granted to him in lieu of these fees, insisted upon his enjoying the same, and that the supersedure of his salary could not deprive him of the ancient profits of the office." Has been informed that an eighth of a yard and an eighth of a pound were formerly taken, when this office was far more extensive than it now is.

In the docket it is called a "copy," but it seems doubtful if it is not the original.

With this is an official copy of part of a royal warrant previous to the year 1719 with some variations in the warrants made thereto relating to the duties of the officers of the Great Wardrobe. 6 *pages.*

30 Nov. 26. "Representation about the Great Wardrobe made by Wm Clayton, Esqre, one of the Lords of the Treasury." [This is a copy of an elaborate report from which may be gathered that] the demands of the Master of the Wardrobe amounted to 19,411*l.* 14*s.* 8½*d.* (as appears by the enclosure "A.") His demands for his own salary and allowances and that of his Deputy, the Clerk of the Wardrobe and for incident charges and also for divers salaries and allowances to officers and to tailors, arras workers and others amounted to 5,056*l.* 5*s.* 0½*d.* being part of the above sum. The whole state and condition of the office has been enquired into, viz., as to passing the accounts before the Auditors of Imprests, the buying of goods, &c.

VOL. CCLXVI.

1728.

The authority of the Master of the Great Wardrobe to buy goods, &c. is founded upon a warrant of the Lord Chamberlain of the Household (copy enclosed, marked "C.") Whether the goods, when furnished, cost more, or less, than the estimate; or whether the estimate is well considered, is not examined by any body at the Treasury; but left wholly to the Master or his Deputy.

Mr Dummer, the Deputy Master, was examined at the Treasury. [Gives the particulars of his examination.] There is no contract in writing with any of the tradesmen, but merely by word of mouth when parcels are brought into the office, he sometimes makes an entry of the quantities, and sometimes does not. The Master of the Great Wardrobe and the clerk are the only patent officers. Mr Bumpstead, Clerk of the Robes, makes up the accounts of the wardrobe, but makes no abatements in the bills. He is appointed by the Lord Chamberlain and engrosses the account on parchment. The parchment warrant, the Latin Book, the Imprest Roll, and Dormant Warrants are all that are delivered to the auditors to pass the master's account. There is no person to check the workmen belonging to the Wardrobe; or to see that the work is well performed in the several palaces, &c. Upon finding no satisfaction from Mr Dummer's examination, the several tradesmen were examined. Most of them admit that if the goods were sold in their shops, for ready money, they could afford them a little cheaper. Some of them say they know of no allowance of poundage "except the 6*d.* p £ duty." As no abatement of the demands was likely to be obtained, a skilled person was shown the patterns produced of silks, laces and "Haratines," and gave the prices at which he could furnish them, and the difference was from 4½*d.* to 4*s.* 6*d.* a yard less than those supplied. Recommends that some person should repair to the respective palaces, and see whether the goods contained in the bills and work done, answered in quantity, quality, and price, to those set down in the book transcribed from the bills. The packer who furnishes cloth and stuff voluntarily offers to abate about 7½ per cent. on his bill, &c. There are some items paid by the Wardrobe, connected with the army and navy that seem unreasonable to be charged to the Civil Government. Conceives it would be fully as reasonable to bring the pay of the army upon the Civil Government, since the Civil List has been separated from the Military Establishment, ever since the Revolution. [Gives the salaries, fees, &c. of the different officers.] The certain annual expense in the office, besides goods and work done, amounts to 6,126*l.* 0*s.* 8*d.* [Gives the manner and method of receiving the money at the Exchequer for the expense of the office, and of passing the accounts.] The Auditor passes the account without any alteration, or seeing any voucher, for any payment contained therein; and "this appears to have been the ancient method in which the accounts of this office have been passed. Steps had been taken to amend this method. From the year 1667 enquiries had been made by the Treasury, and Instructions were signed by King Charles II. for regulating the expense and passing the accounts, and some alterations were made in Queen Anne's reign and in that

VOL. CCLXVI.

1728.

of King Geo. I., as contained in an enclosure (B). Nothing was done therein except that the annual expense in the reign of King Geo. I. was limited to 13,000*l.*; but the limitation was of no advantage for the expenses continued in the usual way ever since, and have far exceeded the limitation.

The enclosures are copied at the end of the report.

In the *Minute Book*, Vol. 26, p. 172*a*, 6 Dec. 1728, is:—"The King having layd his commands on Mr Clayton to make a thorough examination into the state, method, practice and condition of the office of the Great Wardrobe, he accordingly lays before my Lords a full and ample representation thereupon in writing, which is read and approved. And it is agreed that a copy thereof be made to be transmitted to the Duke of Montague, which representation is entered in the Warrant Book not relating to money No—pag.—" 17 *pages*.

3 Aug. and 3 Dec. 27. Memorial of Mr A. Cracherode to the Lords of the Treasury "praying payment of 391li 6s 10d due at his late Maty's decease for arrrs of his salary &c." 3 Dec. 1728. [He had an allowance of 200*l.* per ann. for perusing and observing upon pamphlets and newspapers.]

It is accompanied by another memorial from him, dated 3 Aug. 1728, setting out a list of bills that had been demanded of him by various persons for moneys expended or for business done for his late Majesty's service. 5½ *pages*.

23 Nov. to 5 Dec. 28. Letter signed "Jer. Dunbar to David Dunbar Esq. Surveyor General of His Majesty's Woods in America at his house in Clargys Street, Piccadilly, London." Had written that he had sent Mr Armstrong and Mr Slade into the woods in New Hampshire and the province of Maine, where they were both taking care of the timber that is to be cut for the King's use. Designs to set out to-morrow morning to meet Mr Armstrong at Piscataqua, and to go with him from thence to Casco Bay, where the Contractors are at work, and after that to make a tour with him thro' the provinces. Sends two letters (copies), one from Mr Auchmuty, who is Advocate General, the other from Mr Armstrong, as to the state of the woods there and the laws relating unto them. Messrs Haley and Hamilton will set out for Anapolis as soon as the season permits. P.S. Has been informed that the General Assembly have within these two years granted several townships, on purpose to evade the Act of Parliament, whereby they are prohibited from cutting timber without townships.

Accompanied by the letters referred to. The first relates to the King's rights and the law in respect to the woods, and the second to the claims to cut trees within townships. There are also copies of two other letters which the Surveyor had received, viz., from Mr Robert Armstrong as to false representations sent home respecting him; and from Thomas Haley as to expected difficulties in their survey. 9 *pages*.

10 Dec. 29. Report of the Barons of the Exchequer of Scotland to the Lords of the Treasury on the petition of the Legatees, &c. of Major

1728. VOL. CCLXVI.

James Le Blanc, deceased, respecting the disposition of the property of the latter. As no heir appears who can by the laws of Scotland succeed to the property, [his relations being Roman Catholics and debarred from the succession of heritable subjects] the same devolves upon his Majesty. The remains of the personal estate, when the debts are paid, will be inconsiderable. It having been usual for the Crown to grant gifts of "ultimus hæres," they are of opinion that it will be a proper act of the Royal bounty to pass a signature for granting to Dr Thomas Young the real estate of the Major.

Also the petition. 4 *pages*.

16 Dec. 30. An original Royal Warrant addressed to Edmund Bishop of London for publication of a notice in all the parish churches, of a collection of the benevolence to be made at the respective dwellings of charitable and well-disposed people, in each parish, to alleviate the distress in and about the city of London. The sums collected to be paid into the chamber of London, and to be distributed by the Lord Mayor. The Bishop was also instructed to call upon the Treasury for a sum directed by his Majesty to be paid as an example. 16 Dec. 1728.

On the outside besides the address is:—26 March 1728. Paid 1,000li Becher Mayor." 2 *pages*.

[? About 24 Dec.] 31. Petition of Phillips Farewell and Richard Moore, Wharfingers, at Scotland Yard, Whitehall. Are undertenants of a parcel of ground in Middle Scotland Yard, Whitehall, adjoining the River Thames, which was granted to the Duke of Chandos and his heirs with free liberty of making a wharf for landing and carriage of goods. In October last the wharf was broken up, to make a drain, whereby petitioners have been prevented from doing any work. They have not only lost their business but have entirely lost their customers, and must be ruined unless relieved.

Minuted:—"It is a common sewer. The inconvenience must be submitted to."

The Minute is also entered in the *Minute Book*, Vol. 26, p. 180*e*, 24 Dec. 1728, with this difference, that the words "if any" are added after the word "inconvenience." 1 *page*.

26 Dec. 32. Copy of the Attorney and Solicitor General's Report (P. Yorke and C. Talbot) to the Lords of the Treasury in respect to the preparation of the necessary instruments for perfecting his Majesty's contract, with the Lords Proprietors of Carolina, for the purchase and surrender of their title and interest in that province. Have considered the report of a Committee of the Lords of the Privy Council, of 26 March 1728, stating the proposals of several of the Lords Proprietors, "which were appointed by Order in Council, of 28 March 1728, and have inspected titles of the Lords Proprietors. It appears there are eight Lords Proprietors, of whom the Right Hon. Lord Carteret is one, who is no party to the contract. The other seven parts are alleged to be vested in the following persons, viz., one part in James Bertie and Dodington Greville, Esqres, as

1728. VOL. CCLXVI.

surviving Trustees under the will of Henry, late Duke of Beaufort; and the remaining six parts severally in the Right Hon. the Lord Craven, the said James Bertie in his own right, Henry Bertie, Esq., Sir John Colleton, Archibald Hutchinson and Joseph Blake, Esq. [State the difficulties as to the titles.] Conceive that a good title to these seven proprietorships cannot be made to his Majesty without an Act of Parliament, &c. As some progress must be made immediately, have prepared a draft of conveyance, with certain covenants. [The consideration money was 17,500*l.*, and other matters are set forth in connexion with the same proprietorships.] 26 Dec. 1728.

With the above are (1.) "Alterations proposed to the draught by tho Proprietors' agents." (2.) The Order in Council of 28 March above referred to. (3 to 8.) Copies of other papers relating to the same business. 27 *pages.*

27 Dec. 33. Opinion of the Attorney General (Sir P. Yorke) on the case submitted to him, as to a proposed reversionary grant in perpetuity to Greenwich Hospital, of the North and South Foreland Lighthouses and Lights, previously vested in Robert Osboldstone, but then held by Greenwich Hospital for an unexpired term of 5 years, "which it is presumed His Majesty may so grant, notwithstanding the Acts of 12th, & 13th Wm 3d, c. 12th, s. 6, & 1st Ane, c. 7th, s. 7th, as was done in the case of the grant of the Lights at Milford, 1714, at Portland, 1716, at St Beshead, 1717, at Foulness, 1719, and of the Cashett Lights, 1723, 9o Georgii to Trinity House. And of sevl grants of Lights, since the said statutes, to private persons for terms of years exceeding the terms submitted by those statutes, viz.: of the Skerry Lights to Mr French, 1714, for 60y: of the Harwch to Sr Is. Rebow 1707 for 31ys, to commence 1725 to determine 1756: & of the same lights to Sr Is. Rebow 1716 for 60y, to commence from 1756." 27 Dec. 1723. 2½ *pages* (*brief size*).

[? End of 1728.] 34. Petition of Richard Shelton, Secretary to the Lords Proprietors of Carolina, to the Lords of the Treasury. Has been Secretary above 20 years to the Lords Proprietors of Carolina without receiving any constant payment for his regular salary or disbursement. In the late treaty between His Majesty and the Lords Proprietors for the sale and surrender of the Province to the Crown, there was an estimate made of the arrears due from the inhabitants, amounting to 9,500*l.* with an account of the claims of their officers, amounting to 4,824*l.* 7*s.* 1*d.*, which ought to be answered out of the arrears. His Majesty granted 5,000*l.* to satisfy this demand. Claims payment of 1,039*l.* 7*s.* 1*d.* and 400*l.* rent for an office. Some of the proprietors who lately purchased their titles and signed an account which acknowledged the claims now refuse to allow and pay several of the articles and thereby reduce the petitioner to one-half. Prays for direction how to proceed for the full payment of his demands.

Also copy of the memorial of the Proprietors of Carolina to the Lords of the Treasury, and "an Estimate of Arrears due to the

1728. VOL. CCLXVI.

Proprietors of South and North Carolina" together with "An Account of the several Claims upon the Proprietors not yet adjusted."

In the *Minute Book*, vol. 26, p. 238*f*, 22 July 1729, is:—"Mr Paxton attending is called in, and also Major Horsey and Mr Shelton's petition, Secretary to the Lords Proprietors of Carolina, complaining of the reductions of his demands on the said proprietors, and that they be desired to take care that when the 5,000li be paid to them to satisfye the debts and demands which by the accot given in amounted to no more than 4,824*l*. 7*s*. 1*d*., whereof Shelton's is part, that the persons having such demands be satisfyed so as his Maty or their Lordps may be effectually secured from all importunities about the same, and the arrears meant to be purchased for the said 5,000li may be no waies incumbred therewith." *Again*, at p. 241*a*, 24 July 1729, is:—"My Lords at Mr Shelton's request order a letter to be writ to Major Horsey desiring him, together with Mr Lehuep to Inspect the books and accots belonging to the Lords Proprietors of Carolina and to state what is now due and owing from them to the said Mr Shelton as their Secretary." 6 *pages*.

[? End of 1728.] 35. Memorial of Sidney Godolphin and Thomas Jett, Esquires, Auditors of his Majesty's Land Revenues, in the several counties of England and Wales, to the Lords of the Treasury. Are obliged to send receipts and proclamations into the several counties of England and Wales, directed to the Sheriffs thereof, to give notice to tenants of the times and places of the several audits, where to pay the rents due to the Crown. The Comrs of the Treasury in the late reign granted their warrant to the Postmaster General, to pass the parcels from the Auditors, post free. For want of such warrant being renewed at Michaelmas last, 1728, most of the Sheriffs returned the parcels, so that the tenants had no notice where to pay their rent.

Pray a warrant for free postage of the same for the future 1 *page*.

1728. 36. Memorial of Thomas Greig, Provost of Coupar, and the other magistrates and community of that burgh. During the time of episcopacy in Scotland, the Archbishop of St Andrews had right to the teinds of certain borough acres, lying in and about the town of Coupar, belonging partly to the town itself (as being a part of the town's patrimony) and partly to the inhabitants, the heritors thereof. The Archbishop, and afterwards the Crown, used to grant tacks or leases of the teinds, but the tacksman was never allowed by these tacks, or used to draw the teinds *ipsa corpora*, but only to exact two marks and a half, Scots, for each acre of the town's patrimonial lands, and two pounds money, as aforesaid, for each acre belonging to the inhabitants "holding burgage in name of Teind duty." About the year 1676 the then Archbishop of St Andrews gave a tack of these teinds to the Duke of Rothes, then Provost of Coupar, and the Crown, as coming in place of the Archbishop, has from time to time renewed these tacks to the Earls of

Rothes, who, till of late, were from the year 1676 almost constantly elected Provosts of Coupar. The above duties amount yearly to 500*l.*, Scots, whereof the tacksman was bound to pay 35*l.*, Scots, to the first minister of the town of Coupar, and 165*l.* "money foresaid" to the second minister, in all 200*l.*, Scots; so that there is a free remainder to the tacksman of 300*l.*, Scots, yearly. The stipend paid to the town's second minister is but about 800 marks yearly, which is by far too little, &c., and as the Earl of Rothes' tack is nearly expiring Provost Greig requests the advice and assistance of the town's friends, and specially of his Majesty's Advocate for Scotland, that a new tack may be obtained from the Crown, burthened with 200*l.*, Scots, additional to the second minister. 1728. 1½ *page.*

[? 1728.] 37. Petition of George Fitzgerald, of London, merchant, and James Smith, of London, refiner, assignees in a Commission of Bankruptcy awarded against Gilbert Langley, goldsmith, in behalf of themselves and other creditors, to the Lords of the Treasury. In June last the bankrupt took up several of his creditors' diamonds and a gold repeating watch set with diamonds, to the value of nearly 10,000*l.* He ran away into Holland and carried the goods with him. Through the Earl of Chesterfield [Ambassador to Holland] the effects were seized in Holland, and the jewels are in a merchant's hands there for the use of the creditors. These very jewels have been negotiated for several years past in London, and have paid his Majesty's duty when first brought into England. The bankrupt trusted several goods, &c. of great value to one John Gadbury at Rotterdam, who by virtue of a protection of the States General refuses to account with the petitioners. Pray for a warrant to bring over the jewels and watch, custom free; and that their Lordships will recommend the petitioner's case to Lord Chesterfield to make instances to the States General that Gadbury's protection may be superseded.

Minuted:—"The Comm^rs^ Customes to permit the pet^rs^ to bring over these diamonds & watch, & to be lodged in their warehouse, till their Lordp̄s determine whether the duty should be paid or not." 1 *page (brief size).*

[Perhaps about 1728?] 38. "A particular account of the orders past by the Governour and Council for which there is at present no fund." The last date is in April 1728. There is nothing to show that the above is connected with the following document except that it is found with it.

Memorial of the Governor of Barbadoes to the Lords of the Treasury praying them to send directions to the Com^rs^ of Customs for granting him a "Bill of Store" for his household goods and necessary provision which he is to carry with him to Barbados, viz., 50 tons of goods, two coaches and 10 horses.

Minuted:—"Upon affidavit made that they are for the use of his own family the L^ds^ do agree to this." 3 *pages.*

1728. VOL. CCLXVI.

[? 1728 or a little later.] 39. "An acco^{t} of the unavoidable charge and the meanes to prevent it, with safety, in case of a warr with France, which otherwise the nation must be at, in sending forces to the Island of Barbadoes for its security, which cannot be less than 2,000 men; if they resolve to preserve the same: on which Island (besides it's own importance) depend the safety of the Leward Islands and consequently the sugar trade to the Kingdom of England."

The duty of 4½ per cent. towards the repair of the forts, &c. had been collected, but misapplied by order from England, and of late was made one of the funds for the Civil List. 1 *page*.

[1728 or later.] 40. Memorial of John Philp, one of the Auditors of the Accounts of his Majesty's revenues in Scotland under Sir James Dalrymple, General Auditor of the same [to the Lords of the Treasury] setting forth his claims to the office, and applying for a new commission.

At the foot is a note that his Majesty, upon the memorial, had appointed him by letters patent of 2 Nov. 1727 (Robert Arbuthnot being dead) to be deputy auditor of all accounts of the revenue in Scotland at a salary of 200*l*. per ann. "which office he has ever since executed."

"With copys of Sr Dav^{d} Dalrymple and James Dalrymple's patents as auditors." 12 *pages*.

VOL. CCLXVII. 1728. CLASSIFIED. PART I.

---

1. Warrants of the Lord Chamberlain of the Household to the Lords of the Treasury, the Master of the Great Wardrobe and the Treasurer of the Chamber for the payment of moneys or delivery of articles to various persons.

Among the persons in whose favour the warrants were issued were:—The Marquis Rangoni, first Minister and Envoy Extraordinary from the Duke of Modena, Count Welderen and Monsr Sylvius, Ambassadors Extraordinary from Holland, Signior Giacinto Fiorelli, Secretary from Venice, and the Envoy from Tripoli. Dated between 21 May and 10 Dec. 1728. 19 *pages*.

2. Reports, &c. of the Com^{rs} of Customs to the Lords of the Treasury, viz.:—

(1.) Recommending the payment into the Exchequer of money arising from East India goods seized coming from Rotterdam to London, about which there had been a trial.

Minuted:—"The Lords agree with ye Comm^{rs} in opinion."

(2.) For a sufficient reward to be offered for the apprehension of a gang of 30 or 40 smugglers, who had violently beaten and

1728. VOL. CCLXVII.

wounded the Riding Officer and Constable of the port of London, when discharging their duty on the coast, at Clackton.

Minuted:—"To be layd before ye King. To be done."

(3.) Recommending Thomas Hammond of London, merchant, who was a considerable trader for twenty years, but by misfortunes owed the Crown 6,987*l.* 8*s.* 9½*d.*, viz., that he and his sureties should be permitted to apply to Parliament for relief.

(4.) On the petition of the Rt Hon. James Earl of Derby, respecting a wreck in the Isle of Man, viz., as to timber belonging to the Earl being brought into England for his own use.

The opinion seems to be adverse.

Minuted:—"April 1728. Lords agree to this rept."

(5.) "Memorial of the Comrs of the Customs concerning the accompting for enumerated goods, after they are disposed of." (Copy.)

(6.) Presentment by the Comrs as to the promotion of two landing waiters in the port of London.

(7.) Report on the petition of the above said Thomas Hammond praying their Lps to accept the composition of 300*l.*, for the debt of himself and securities, in pursuance of the power given by the late Act. (2,509*l.* 7*s.* 7½*d.* had been recovered.) Advising that the offer should be accepted.

Minuted:—"Agreed to."

(8.) Report of the Commissioners of Customs, with an account of the revenues under their management, applicable to His Majesty's Civil List, from 10 June 1727 to Midsummer 1728, and the arrears standing out at that time. 22 Oct. 1728.

Also petitions and other subordinate documents connected with the above. 83 *pages.*

3. Four papers, three of which are addressed to the Lords of the Treasury, and all connected with the affairs of the Comrs of Excise, viz.:—

(1.) Copy of warrant from the Lords of the Treasury empowering the Comrs of Excise to pay 330*l.* 14*s.* out of the Excise revenues to themselves, on account of the increased expense of passing their commission occasioned by several additional duties being put under their management.

Also copies of two other documents connected therewith.

(2.) Memorial of the Comrs enclosing an account of the quantity of silver wrought plate upon which duty had been paid from 1 June 1720 to 25 March 1728.

(3.) Presentment of the Comrs, with an account of the gross and net receipts on the temporary and hereditary excise from 10 June 1727 to Midsummer 1728.

(4.) Letter of the Comrs laying before their Lordships an estimate of the gross and net produce of the arrears (Excise) standing out at Midsummer 1728. 8 *pages.*

1728. VOL. CCLXVII.

4. Three papers docketed as follows:—

"Establishment of Half Pay to the Reduced Officers of the Additional Companys of the Four Regiments sent to Ireland from the 25th of July 1727. Dated 24 Jan. 1727/8."

"Establishment for six Regimts of Foot, commencing the 25th day of December 1727. Dated 1 May 1728.

"Ao 1727. Civil List Estabt, Scotland." Dated 5 June 1728 (Copy). 10 *pages.*

5. A series of estimates, numbered on the back 1 to 5, for the year 1728.

(1.) Of the charge of H.M. forces in the Plantations, Minorca and Gibraltar.

(2.) Of the charge of guards, garrisons and other His Majesty's Land Forces in Great Britain.

(3.) Of the charge of 2,224 horse, 1,836 dragoons, and 8,034 foot, of the troops of His Highness the Landgrave of Hesse Cassell.

(4.) Of several extraordinary expenses of His Majesty's Forces incurred and not provided for by Parliament.

(5.) Of the charge of the Out Pensioners of Chelsea Hospital.

Also an estimate of the charge of the Office of Ordnance for the year 1728. 9 *pages.*

6. Various Financial papers such as an account of National Debts contracted before 25 Oct. 1716 and since discharged, and an account of those since that date; a state of pensions payable by Mr Steuart; a state of the 35,000*l.* per ann. granted out of the Civil List Revenues in the 12th of Queen Anne. (Year uncertain, but after the beginning of Geo. II.); and produce of the several branches of H.M. Civil List from 10 June 1727 included, to Midsummer 1728. 38 *pages.*

7. Letters from the Lord Lieutenant of Ireland (Carteret) to the Lords of the Treasury.

(1.) "For a pension of 200li p ann. during pleasure to Luke Netterville on the recommendation of the House of Lords." The Lord Lieut. recommends him "as a person zealously attached to his Majesty's Royal family and Government, and desirous to give a liberal education to his eldest son, who is next in remainder to the present Viscount Netterville, and to continue to breed his whole family in the Protestant religion, which he, himself, professes.

In the *Minute Book,* Vol. 26, pp. 66 and 67, this letter is referred to amongst others, and "My Lords order that proper warrants be prepared, and will lay the same with the letters before the King."

(2.) On the memorial of Henry, Lord Bishop of Cloyne, concerning the lands and manor of Donoughmore. The memorial has been referred to the Lords Justices, who further referred it to the Attorney and Solicitor General. Is of opinion that no part of the undisposed forfeitures, in that kingdom, can be sold. Recommends that the present Bishop should obtain an Act of Parliament in Great Britain to charge his immediate successors with three-fourths

1728. Vol. CCLXVII.

of 1,340*l.* due to the late Bishop. This would be a proper relief to the present Bishop, and is the method established in Ireland when encumbrances are left upon Bishoprics on account of improvements made upon the sees.

(3.) On the memorial of Col. Clement Nevill and Col. Phineas Bowles in behalf of their own and the rest of the Regiments of Dragoons in Ireland, praying for an addition of 2[d] per day to the pay of each Corporal of Dragoons. Recommending the same, and asking for a Royal letter for that purpose.

Minuted:—"3[d] May, 1728 then read; but dispatched p.w. dated 27 Mar. 1728."

(4.) Transmitting the Resolution of the House of Commons of Ireland, that 2,000*l.* may be paid to the Hon. Richard Stewart, Esq., and his partners, to enable them to carry on the Colliery of Bellycastle, in the co. of Antrim, asking for a Royal letter to direct the payment.

(5.) Transmitting similar Resolution on the petition of Eleazer Peirson and Samuel Peirson, who had been at great expense and trouble in endeavouring to promote a better method of tillage and husbandry: in favour of the payment to them of 200*l.* as a reward for their expense and trouble: asking for a Royal Letter to direct the payment.

(6.) On the petition of Sir Alexander Cairnes, Bart., asking leave to resign the patent for his life as Keeper of Phœnix Park, near Dublin, and to obtain a new one, during the lives of three other persons. Has been asked by several persons of distinction to recommend this petition to his Majesty. It would be very agreeable in Ireland, where petitioner is a Member of Parliament.

(7.) Transmitting Resolution of the House of Commons in favour of 200*l.* being given to William Maple as an encouragement for discovering a new method of tanning leather by vegetable of the growth of Ireland: asking for a Royal Letter to direct the payment.

In the *Minute Book*, Vol. 26, p. 90*c*, after stating that the letter was read, it goes on to say that "the necessary warrants [were] ordered to be prepared thereupon."

(8.) For his Majesty's Royal letter for paying 1,145*l.* 13*s.* 4$\frac{3}{4}$*d.* for 300*l.* barrels of gunpowder contracted to be provided by Nicholas Grueber, to make good the last year's consumption in Ireland.

(9.) In favour of the grant to Simon Audouin and Isaac Audouin of the city of Dublin, brothers of John Audouin, lately executed for murder there, viz., of the forfeitures of the latter.

(10.) For placing Robert Campbell on half pay as Quarter Master of dragoons.

(11.) On the petition of Alderman John Porter and James Stevenson, of the city of Dublin, merchants, on behalf of persons interested in a cargo of a ship burnt on Glendore (Cork) to prevent infection: recommending that 500*l.* should be paid to the freighters.

1728. VOL. CCLXVII.

(12.) Signifying his approval of a new establishment, whereby the battalions of foot are placed upon an equality as to numbers and pay.

(13.) For an additional salary of 300*l.* per annum to be inserted in the new military Establishment of Ireland for the Master General of the Ordnance.

(14.) Sends report of the Attorney and Solicitor General upon the memorial of Benjamin Parry, Esq., relating to the proposal which he laid, the last session of Parliament, before the Committee of the House of Commons, appointed to consider of the building of a new Parliament House, viz., for making a lease to the use of the Crown, of all his right and title in and to the ground described in a Survey of Chichester House and its appurtenances, in Dublin, for the term of 9,000 years, at the yearly rent of 240*l.*, clear of all fees and taxes. Has directed the old Parliament House to be pulled down, and the new Parliament House to be erected as approved by his Majesty.

The Governors of the Blue-coat Hospital have agreed to spare a sufficient number of rooms in the Hospital for holding the next sessions of Parliament.

With the above are the petitions and various subordinate documents. 46 *pages.*

VOL. CCLXVIII. 1728. CLASSIFIED. PART II.

1. Three accounts of plate received in the Jewel Office addressed to the Lords of the Treasury, signed at the foot as allowed "Ja: Brudenell." 3 *pages.*

2. Two letters from Edmund, Bishop of London, to the Lords of the Treasury, for the bounty of 20*l.* to be ordered to be paid respectively to Mr Joseph Horton, A.B., appointed a Minister in the Island of "Bermudas" in America, and to the Rev. Mr William White, Master of Arts, appointed a Minister in Jamaica, as his Majesty's bounty for their passage. 2 *pages.*

3. Papers relating to the affairs of Sir Bibye Lake, Sir Roger Mostyn, Bart., late Paymaster of Marines, and General Wills, whose affairs had been in litigation, as well as those of Robert Peters, a Receiver of Hertfordshire, who was a debtor to the Crown. [These affairs have been repeatedly referred to in preceding portions of this Calendar. *See* Vol. CCXXII., No. 45, &c.]

The papers include extracts from the *Minute Books*, from 15 Dec. 1714 to 17 July 1728, touching this business.

These affairs were fully considered on 9 May 1728, and a previous order to Sir Roger Mostyn to pay to Sir Bibye Lake 7,806*l.* 3*s.* 2¾*d.* was confirmed. See *Minute Book*, vol. 26, p. 100*a*. 36 *pages.*

4. Two applications on behalf of the Navy Board to the Lords of the Treasury for moneys required to carry on the service and another paper as to the debt of the Navy.

1728. VOL. CCLXVIII.

Also a printed copy of Instructions to Captains, &c. of Vessels, relating to Volunteers and the payment of Seamen's wages. 14 *pages*.

5. Memorials from the Paymaster General of the Forces to the Lords of the Treasury, asking them to direct the payment of moneys for subsistence of the forces, &c.

Some of them have a brief minute on the back, such as "Letter signed" or, "To be satisfyd out of effects in the Paym^rs^ hands." 6 *pages*.

6. Letters and papers relating to the proceedings of William Mathew, Gilbert Fleming, and Edward Mann, Esq^res^, Commissioners, appointed 14 June 1726 to contract with such persons (possessors or others) as would become purchasers of the French part of the Island of St Christopher. By their Commission they were appointed Receivers of the one third part of the purchase money, which they were to receive upon signing the contracts; and the other two thirds were to be paid at the end of five years from the dates of the contracts. The purchasers were to pay 10 per cent. interest. The power to the Com^rs^ was only to contract subject to the approbation or disallowance of the Treasury; and in case the contracts were confirmed, the Com^rs^ covenant to grant to the purchasers the fee-simple. The King on 1 May 1728 renewed the powers and added Lord Londonderry to the Commissioners.

The papers include a debtor and creditor account of the sale of lands "late French" to William Mathew amounting to 26,226*l*. 18*s*. 1¼*d*.; a memorial of John Hart, Esq., late H.M. Governor of the Leeward Islands (received 28 May 1728) setting forth his services and his claims, and complaining of hardships from the Com^rs^. He prays that in consideration of what is set out in the memorial, and on account of his long services, and more particularly because he prevailed on the Assembly to pass the Act for the duty of 4½ per cent. &c. that he might continue in possession of the whole of his plantation, &c., or might be allowed to purchase the same for his son Thomas: and for a warrant to be prepared to pay his arrears of salary as governor. Also petition from him of a little later date on the same subject.

In the *Minute Book*, vol. 26, p. 165*b*, 24 Oct. 1728, is:—"Mr Hart late Governor of the Leeward Islands, attending, is called in, and his peticõn for a grant of 85 acres of surplus lands is read, and he is heard thereupon. My Lords acquaint him that they are determined strictly to adhere to the instruction of permitting none to be purchasers in their own right of more than 200 acres; and as they believed the surplus lands he desires may be already sold, but if not sold, the making the grant he desires, would evade and break through the said instructions, they cannot admitt thereof. Mr Hart hereupon submitted, and said he would accept the 200 acres in manner as the Comm^rs^ for sale of St Christopher's lands have conveyed the same."

1728. Vol. CCLXVIII.

Memorial of John Willett of St. Christopher's, Esq. Has been many years an inhabitant of the island and serves his Majesty in his Council and as Vice-Judge of the Admiralty there. Obtained a grant of 200 acres of land which formerly belonged to the French. Sets out what had been done therewith, and prays to be allowed to purchase 100 acres the other 100 acres being enjoyed by Col. Abraham Payne (who married memorialist's sister) and which memorialist was willing to purchase.

Petition of Augustus Boyd of the same island, esquire. A grant of 160 acres of land, belonging to the French, was made to James Ward in 1704. It has since been reduced to 92 acres, and a grant made to him and his son James Ward, jun^{r}, Esq., by John Hart, Esq., the present Governor. The land was leased to one Shepherd, who assigned it to petitioner. It adjoins the plantation of the said John Hart, who prevailed with Shepherd to assign his lease to him and pretends that he ought to be permitted to purchase. The Com^{rs} refused to allow petitioner to purchase. Prays to be admitted to purchase.

Memorial of John Willett and John Spooner of St Christopher's, Esq^{res}. Were jointly possessed of a plantation in the part of the Island which belonged to the French, containing 200 acres. Have served his Majesty ten years in public stations. The Com^{rs} refused to treat with them for the purchase thereof. Pray that their agents in London may be admitted to treat for the same.

Also the case of John Willett and John Spooner, Esq^{res} [more fully set out]. See *Minute Book*, vol. 26, p. 113*b*, where the case is ordered to be drawn out.

There is also an account of lands sold to Edward Mann. 23 Nov. 1728.

The last document is a letter (duplicate) from the three Commissioners to the Hon. John Scrope, Esq. Have had a recess from the business of the Commission, occasioned by Lord Londonderry's arrival, since which have had four meetings. Send copy of minutes, which will show the business done. Think he, Mr Scrope, will discover by the letters that his Lordship takes his province to be, not the completing the commission, but to make insinuation into their (the Com^{rs}) conduct. This would be very irksome to them; "even if they were accountable to him, or his menial servants." However, they are silent on this matter to the Lords of the Treasury. Are in hopes that my Lord (on the resolution the Board came to, on the last meeting, of voting by the judgment of the majority), will think better of it, and treat them as not unworthy of being inserted in the same commission with him. At Antegoa, Nevis, and this Island have promoted "his Lordship's settlements or additional salarys" and done everything to merit his favour, but more is expected of them. After reading their Commission and Instructions his Lordship made some remarks that carried menace with them. He demanded whether the surplusage of the College plantations was sold. They answered, it was, and to Col. Morris. He disbelieved them, but being convinced, he said he expected it had been reserved for him. Told him they

1728. Vol. CCLXVIII.

had for some time been apologising to their Lordships of the Treasury, and to him (Mr Scrope) for not having concluded, and did not know he intended to be a purchaser. He objected to the validity of the sale, and to all the sales made to themselves, because not put up publicly to the best bidders. To this they could only say that they had not made one of these for an undervalue, and they had not got their Lordships correction for these sales. Are persuaded that had this plantation, sold to Col. Morris, been sold for his Lordship, there would have been no objection for any defect in the form of contracting. [Show further how they had proceeded with the sales. Relate various other altercations which they had with his Lordship.] State also the price at which land was sold to the Executors of Holmes as well as to Col. Morris. Doubt not but among their opponents they will raise any sum to oust them (the Comrs), but hope, as they paid "a full candid price" that they, and their fortunes, will be protected against all attempts of malice. His Lordship has surmised that if not otherwise provided for, as a Commissioner, he will come in for an equal share with them (the three Commissioners) in their purchases; but this is impracticable, &c. 25 Nov. 59 *pages.*

7. Four letters of the Lords Comrs of Trade and Plantations to the Lords of the Treasury, enclosing accounts of the Incidental Charges of the Office, and one as to the preservation of the woods in America addressed to John Scrope, Esq. 35 *pages.*

8. Various papers relating to supplies to the Great Wardrobe, also to liveries, salaries, wages, debts, &c. One of the papers includes an account of the bibles and prayer-books supplied to the Chapel Royal at St James's. 42 *pages.*

9. Three papers relating to carpenters' and other work at Hampton Court House Park and at the Paddock at Kensington, apparently connected with the Surveyor General of Woods' Account (Charles Wither). 5 *pages.*

10. Papers connected with the affairs of the Office of His Majesty's Works, viz.—

An account of the annual expense, &c. of the office.

A report on a memorial of Charles, Duke of Richmond and Lenox and other inhabitants in the Privy Garden, within H. M. Palace of Whitehall, as to the work of repaving. *Minuted:*—"Read and Agreed to."

Memorial from the Board of Works to the Lords of the Treasury. Have agreed that the Civil List tax of 6d per pound shall be made good to the Artificers belonging to the Office of Works and pray for a warrant to the Auditor to allow the same.

Memoranda as to certain dormant warrants.

Two accounts as to Carpenters' work at Hampton Court House. 11 *pages.*

Vol. CCLXIX. 1728.

Documents for which a brief description suffices.

Date.	Description of Document.	From	To	Purport.
2 Jan.	1. Certificate -	Lord Halifax -	—	As to the amount at the Receipt of the Exchequer as surplusage of the funds granted to the South Sea Company. 1 *page.*
3 Jan.	2. Memorial -	Sir John Hobart, Bart., "Treasurer of his Majesty's Chambers."	Lords of the Treasury.	For a new privy seal and order thereon to be made in his name for 60,000*l.* 1 *page.*
8 Jan.	3. Letter - -	John Eckersall -	"My Lord" -	Asking him to remind Sir Robert Walpole of his promise that he should have his letters free. *Minuted:* — "Prepare a King's Wart. for allowing to John Eckersall Esqre. as Secretary to the Queen the privilege of sending and receiving his letters free of postage." 1 *page.*
[? About 9 Jan.]	4. Lists of warrants	—	—	For repaying the sheriffs sums disbursed, signed and not signed, before the King's demise.
	also List of Certificates.	—	—	Delivered into the Treasury since the Accession. On the back is :—"List of the sums unpaid to Sheriffs upon the rewards granted by Parliament for apprehending highwaymen, &c. Memorandum. Justice Vaughan for 75 [pounds] expended in the late King's time for taking examinacōns abt. a ryot." *Minuted:* — "9th Jan. 1727–8. To be paid by Mr. Lowther 75*li.*" 2 *pages.*
10 Jan.	5. Warrant -	Privy Council -	Lords of the Treasury.	For allowances to the Under Clerks of the Privy Council. 1 *page.*
16 Jan.	6. Account -	Treasurer of the Chamber (Sir John Hobart, Bart.)	—	Of sums paid for the Christmas quarter 1727. *Minuted* 31 [Jan.] :— "Order'd." 5 *pages.*

1728. VOL. CCLXIX.

Date.	Description of Document.	From	To	Purport.
3 Feb.	7. Certificate -	Noblemen and gentlemen of the co. Lincoln.	Chancellor of the Exchequer.	On behalf of Carr Brackenbury of Spilsby, co. Lincoln, gent. recommending him to be Receiver of Land Tax and other taxes for Lindsey. *Minuted* :—"To be brought in when the Commissions are renew'd." 14 June 1727 (*sic*) appointed. 1 *page*.
Jan. and Feb.	8. Certificates -	[Comrs.] for Wine Licences.	Lords of the Treasury.	Payments and remains of the revenues arising by wine licences. 2 *pages*.
21 Feb.	9. Memorial -	Officers of Ordnance (by J. Plumptre).	Do. - -	For a supply of money to their Office (particular annexed). 4½ *pages*.
23 and 29 Feb.	10. Two Letters -	H. Pelham - -	John Scrope, Esq.	As to 2*d*. a day additional to corporals of dragoons in Ireland. One is minuted :—"Prepare a letter for the King's hand to Lord Lieut. to establish the addl. pay accordingly." (27 Feb. 1727.) 3 *pages*.
5 March	11. Letter - -	G. Medcalfe (Custom House).	Do. - -	As to money seized by Custom House officers at Yarmouth. 2 *pages*.
12 March	12. Do. - -	The Duke of Newcastle.	Lords of the Treasury.	Notifying the continuance of Mr. Theocaris Rali Didichi as Interpreter of the Oriental languages for directions to be given for his having his allowance of 80*l*. per ann. *Minuted* : — "Prepare a warrt." 1 *page*.
19 March	13. Petition -	Thomas Hammond, of London, merchant, for himself and sureties.	The King -	For leave to apply to Parliament to compound with him and his sureties for his debt, each paying 100*l*. In the *Minute Book*, vol. 26, p. 123*f*, 19 July 1728, is : —(After stating that the report on this case had been read and pursuant to a late Act) "The composicõn agreed to, to wit, 300*li*. in case it be paid on or before the 29th of September next, according to the Report." 1 *page*.

1728. VOL. CCLXIX.

Date.	Description of Document.	From	To	Purport.
24 March	14. Tender -	A. Elton and George Caswell.	—	For the delivery at the Mint in the Tower of London, of 40 tons of malliable British copper in fillets to be cut into blanks for half-pence and farthings. 1 *page.*
25 March	15. Account -	Luke Gardiner, "Deputy Recr. Genl."	—	Payments made in the Treasury Office, Dublin, on account of military contingencies for year ending Lady day 1728. 3 *pages.*
25 March	16. Similar account.	Do. - -	—	On account of the Concordatum, same period. 3 *pages.*
25 March	17. Do. - -	Do. - -	—	On account of barracks (Dublin, &c.). 3 *pages.*
25 March	18. Account -	—	—	Money due to Richard Marshall, his Majesty's studmaster, for keeping the stud at Hampton Court. 1 *page.*
26 March	19. Letter - -	Rd. Arnold - -	Christopher Tilson, Esq.	The additional pay of 2*d.* per diem to the corporals of dragoons, to commence on 1 March last. *Minuted:* — "Wt. signed & filled up," &c. 1 *page (quarto).*
6 April	20. Account -	—	—	Of expenses of prosecutions for penalties and duties in the Western Ports. "Pr. Mr. Wyat, Sollr." 1 *page.*
8 April	21. Do. - -	—	—	Of compositions made by persons who were prosecuted for duties or penalties for run goods "since 25 Dec. 1723 to Lady day 1728." 6 *pages.*
8 April	22. Memorial -	Anthony Cracherode	Lords of the Treasury.	For 1,000*l.* to be imprested to him to carry on his Majesty's causes. 1 *page.*
13 April	23. Return -	—	—	Of arrears of land taxes and duties on houses standing out. 4 *pages.*
30 April	24. Account -	—	—	Of expenses of prosecutions for run goods and duties from Mich. 1723 to Lady day 1728 (Custom House, London). 4 *pages.*

1728. Vol. CCLXIX.

Date.	Description of Document.	From	To	Purport.
30 April	25. List - -	—	—	Alphabetical lists of the names of such persons as are now under prosecution for the duties or penalties for run goods. For the port of London and the Northern ports. Also for the Western ports. 22 *pages*.
30 April	26. Warrant (copy).	The King - -	Lord Wilmington	For making out debentures for the pay of the Four Regiments at Minorca. 1 *page*.
7 May	27. Account -	—	—	Of money due from the Exchequer to the Ordnance Office. 1 *double page*.
10 May	28. Warrant (copy).	The King - -	—	Appointing Gilbert Fleming, Esq., Receiver of moneys arising by the sale of the French lands in St. Christophers. 3 *pages*.
30 May	29. Letter - -	John Plumptre for the Officers of Ordnance.	Lords of the Treasury.	Encloses copy of a letter from the Officers of the Ordnance, asking to make renewed solicitations to the Treasury for money to carry on the service. Also an account of money immediately wanted. 3 *pages*.
[? About May.]	30. Petition and other papers.	John Macarell, of the city of Dublin, merchant.	Lord Lieut. of Ireland.	As to his claims as contractor for transporting the troops lately sent to Gibraltar. 20 *pages or parts of pages*.
6 June	31. Letter - -	Lord Carpenter -	Rt. Hon. Sir Robt. Walpole.	As to a Treasury Minute for 20*s*. per diem to be paid him out of the Royal revenues and patrimony of the Island of Minorca. In the *Minute Book*, vol. 26, p. 110 *c*, is :—" Prepare a warrant to be signed by the King for paying to my Lord Carpenter 20*s*. ꝑ diem from Xmas last out of the Royal revenues and patrimonies on his Mats. Island of Minorca by the hands of Joseph Gaiscoign, Receiver General thereof." 1 *page*.
11 June	32. Memorial -	Anthony Cracherode	Lords of the Treasury.	For a half year's salary (250*l*.) and allowance for clerks; and for a further sum of 100*l*. upon his allowance of 200*l*. per ann. for perusing and observing upon newspapers and pamphlets, 1 *page*.

1728. VOL. CCLXIX.

Date.	Description of Document.	From	To	Purport.
15 June	33. Letter - -	Thomas Clutterbuck	Mr. Scrope -	For the payment by the Deputy Vice-Treasurer of Ireland of arrears due from that kingdom for the pay of the regiments on the Irish Establishment which have been subsisted by Great Britain. 1 *page.*
22 June	34. Petition -	Nathaniel Halhed, of Petersham, Surrey, gentleman.	The King -	For a *noli prosequi* to stay proceedings in a case of seizure of 3,700*l.* by the Custom house officers: the owners satisfying the officers. Also an inventory of things seized. 2 *pages.*
24 June	35. Account -	—	—	Of all moneys arising from Crown rents and casualties payable to his Majesty in Scotland; paid in to the Honble. Charles Cathcart, Esq., Recr. Genl. 1 *page.*
24 June	36. Account (copy).	—	—	Of the net receipt of the Post Office revenue, Midsummer 1727 to Midsummer 1728. ½ *page.*
29 June	37. Report -	A. Cracherode -	Lords of the Treasury.	In favour of the Attorney-General acknowledging satisfaction for a fine of 50*l.* due to the Crown from John Ash, a poor prisoner, who had remained in Newgate five years for forging and counterfeiting a promissory note. Is obliged in charity to make this report over again, for one who appeared to be a solicitor for prisoner detains a former report and other papers unless paid a sum of money not due to him. In the *Minute Book*, vol. 26, p. 133*h*, is :—"Mr. Cracherode's Report * * * is read and agreed to according to the report." 2 *pages.*
1 July	38. Account -	—	—	Of [? Francis Burton, Recr. Genl. of Deductions] of the receipts, payments, and remains of the deductions of 6*d.* in the pound from 1 May 1728 to 30 June inclusive. ½ *page.*

1728. VOL. CCLXIX.

Date.	Description of Document.	From	To	Purport.
5 July	39. Certificate -	—	—	Of Thomas Sanderson, Deputy Receiver, viz., of receipts in the Alienation Office. Midsummer 1727 to 29 June 1728. 1 *page*.
11 July	40. Extract from Report.	—	Lords of the Treasury.	Viz., the report rendered by the Auditors of Imprests relating to the arrear of the General Accounts of Customs. ($4\frac{1}{2}$ per cent. upon the Leeward Islands, &c.) 1 *page*.
17 July	41. Account -	Comrs. for Wine Licences.	Do. - -	Of net receipts of the revenue from wine licences. 1 *page*.
22 July	42. Memorial -	Officers of Ordnance (by J. Plumptre).	Do. - -	For a supply of money for their office. (Particulars annexed.) 3 *pages*.
24 July	43. Certificate (copy).	Lords of the Treasury.	—	Of their approval of indentures respecting purchases of lands in St. Christophers. 1 *page*.
30 Aug.	44. Letter - -	Comrs. of Victualling	Secretaries of the Treasury.	As to the preparation of storehouses for the use of Mr. Missing, Contractor for victualling the Garrison of Gibraltar, by the Office of Ordnance. 2 *pages*.
May to Aug.	45. Accounts -	—	—	*Docketed*:—"Lowes Accot." Apparently memoranda of the fees paid or charged on the issue of warrants and other documents in the months of May, July, and August.
25 June to 29 Sept.	46. List - -	—	—	Of ships entered inwards at the Port of New Providence. 1 *page*.
29 Sept. 1727 to 29 Sept. 1728.	47. Account -	—	—	Of revenue from fines and forfeitures upon prohibited and uncustomed goods in North Britain. 1 *page*.
[? About 14 Oct.]	48. Petition -	Francis Elcock, one of his late Majesty's Messengers.	Lords of the Treasury.	There is due to him from her late Majesty Queen Anne 121*l*.7*s*. 2*d*. for salary and service performed. Prays payment having been out of employment for 12 or 13 years. Payment out of money in the Exchequer applicable thereto was ordered 22 Oct. 1728. See *Minute Book*, Vol. 26, p. 163*k*. Also an account of the particulars. 2 *pages*.

Date.	Description of Document.	From	To	Purport.
17 Oct.	49. Certificate -	Comrs. of Wine Licences.	Lords of the Treasury.	Estimating the amount of arrears due to the Exchequer at 1,500*l*. 1 *page*.
[After 21 Oct.]	50. Memorial -	Governor and Court of Assistants of the York Buildings Company.	Do. - -	By Act of 12 Anne premiums were granted to persons who brought any trees fit for masts, &c. from North Britain into South Britain. The time limited by the Act has expired. Prays that a bill or clause may be brought in to encourage the importation of naval stores. Also printed copy of the above Act. 6 *pages*.
22 Oct.	51. Report -	Comrs. for Taxes -	Do. - -	On the petition of Richard Lanham, formerly Receiver General of the Taxes for part of the county of Wilts, for allowances to him of expenses in returning the taxes, &c. Also the petition and two other papers. In the *Minute Book*, Vol. 26, p. 166*f*, is:—"My Lords say that the allowing of such rewards has been, for many years, discontinued, and as arrears of Land Taxes are taken by Parliament tnto the publique supplys of each year they will not revive or give way to these demands." 4 *pages*.
26 Oct.	52. Memorial -	Anthony Cracherode	Do. - -	For 1,000*l*. to be ordered, on account, to carry on his Majesty's affairs. 1 *page*.
[? About 31 Oct.]	53. Petition -	Mary Brown -	[Lords of the Treasury]	Is widow of the Rev. Robert Brown, late Rector of Horsington, in the co. of Lincoln. Lives in the house situate in the Strand, on the south side of the way, in the precinct of the Savoy, late in the possession of Mr. Thomas Churchill, bookinder; has laid out money in repairs, &c. Asks for permission to continue in the house. *Minuted:* — "31st. Oct. 1728. Rd. The Lords don't think proper to grant any lease for ye present; but are willing to let ye petitioner continue in possession till further order from their Lordships." 1 *page*.

1728. VOL. CCLXIX.

Date.	Description of Document.	From	To	Purport.
1 Nov.	54. Report -	"Lu. Gardiner, Depty. Recr. Genl."	Lords Justices of Ireland.	"About arrears from the late Duke of Ormond," due to regiments abroad, and to the Exchequer in England. Further as to demands "on account of the Earl of Arran" &c. 2 *pages*.
[? About 16 Nov.]	55. Letter - -	Thomas Jones -	The Rt. Hon. Sir Robert Walpole.	Represents his service in the Customs in South and North Wales. Annexes a letter as to one Hughes being beaten. Dated 16 Nov. 1728. 2 *pages*.
2 Dec.	56. Account -	—	—	Of deductions of 6*d*. in the pound for Nov. 1728. Signed Francis Burton, Recr. Genl. of the deductions. ¼ *page*.
Dec.	57. Petition -	Susanna Milward	Lords of the Treasury.	The case of Susanna Milward, late of the parish of St. Margarett's Westm[inster], widow of Thomas Milward, Cornett in Sir John Lancer's troop of Horse. Her husband having sold out before he died she has no pension. Has a charge of children and is in great straights. Prays for assistance. 1 *page*.
1 July to 31 Dec.	58. Bill - -	—	—	For the King's most excellent Majesty for provisions delivered for the foreign beasts kept in Kensington paddock. 1 *page*.
[After 1727.]	59. Petition -	John Turner -	Lords of the Treasury.	Is keeper of the Privy Lodgings and standing wardrobe at Hampton Court in ordinary. Hopes that the salary of 12*d*. a day paid to his predecessor may be continued to him (the petitioner). 1 *page*.
[After 1727.]	60. Memorial -	Isaac Jennings and Tho. Mazine.	Do. -	Drew up a scheme as to unmalted corn which was presented to the Treasury in Dec. 1727. The same has been so well approved that a Bill is brought into the House of Commons for granting an aid by laying a duty of 6*d*. a bushel upon all unmalted corn used for distilling. Pray for consideration. 1 *page*.

1728. VOL. CCLXIX.

Date.	Description of Document.	From	To	Purport.
[? End of 1728.]	61. Petition -	John Gill and John Sawyer, Keepers of H.M. Home Park at Windsor.	Sir Robert Walpole.	For payment of their arrears of salary, viz., six years in the late reign and one and a quarter years in the present. 1 *page* (*quarto*).
[After 1727.]	62. Memorandum	—	—	Of the deficiency of the law in relation to trade [and of proposed remedies]. Date uncertain. It chiefly relates to clandestine trade in brandy and horses. 5 *pages*.
[? About 1728.]	63. Memorial	James Cockburn -	Lords of the Treasury.	As to a debt of 1,605*l*. 19*s*. 5*d*. due in connexion with his accounts for his late Majesty's Household. Prays for relief. 1 *page*.
1727 and 1728.	64. Account -	—	—	"A state of the deductions of 6*d*. per pound out of the pay of the Hessians for the years 1727 and 1728 and how much thereof hath been applyed." 1 *page*.
[? 1728.]	65. Do. - -	—	—	"A particular account of the orders passed by the Governour and Council [of Barbadoes] for which there is at present no fund." Various years between 1714 and 1728. 1 *double page*.

GENERAL INDEX.

A

B.

C.

D.

E.

F.

H.

I.

J.

K.

L.

M.

N.

O.

P.

Q.

R.

S.

T.

U.

V.

W.

Y.

Z.

ERRATA.

In Vol. CCXXVII.,	No. 16, *for* "Mr. Lownrds" *read* "Mr. Lownds."
„ CCXXVIII.,	„ 38, "Port of Toy," in the original, but query "Foy" (Fowey).
„ CCXXXIV.,	„ 52, *for* "E. Welcomb" *read* "D. Wescomb."
„ CCXXXVIII.,	„ 21, *for* "Canons" *read* "Cantons."
„ „	„ 97, *for* "T. Fauquier" *read* "F. Fauquier."
	Page 176, Heading : *for* "Vol. CCXLI." *read* "Vol. CCXL."
In Vol. CCXLIV	No. 23, *for* "Trench" *read* "French."
„ CCXLVIII.	„ 15, *for* "Jebb" *read* "Jett."

LONDON: Printed by EYRE and SPOTTISWOODE,
Printers to the Queen's most Excellent Majesty
For Her Majesty's Stationery Office.
[10307.—400.—2/89.]

CATALOGUE

OF

ENGLISH, SCOTCH, AND IRISH RECORD PUBLICATIONS,

REPORTS OF THE HISTORICAL MANUSCRIPTS COMMISSION,

AND

ANNUAL REPORTS OF THE DEPUTY KEEPER OF THE PUBLIC RECORDS,

Printed for

HER MAJESTY'S STATIONERY OFFICE,

And to be purchased,

Either directly or through any Bookseller, from
EYRE AND SPOTTISWOODE, EAST HARDING STREET, FLEET STREET, E.C., or
ADAM AND CHARLES BLACK, 6, NORTH BRIDGE, EDINBURGH; or
HODGES, FIGGIS, & Co., 104, GRAFTON STREET, DUBLIN.

CONTENTS.

ENGLAND.

CALENDARS OF STATE PAPERS, &c.

[IMPERIAL 8vo., boards. *Price* 15*s.* each Volume or Part.]

As far back as the year 1800, a Committee of the House of Commons recommended that Indexes and Calendars should be made to the Public Records, and thirty-six years afterwards another Committee of the House of Commons reiterated that recommendation in more forcible words; but it was not until the incorporation of the State Paper Office with the Public Record Office that the Master of the Rolls found himself in a position to take the necessary steps for carrying out the wishes of the House of Commons.

On 7 December 1855, he stated to the Lords of the Treasury that although "the Records, State Papers, and Documents in his charge constitute the most "complete and perfect series of their kind in the civilized world," and although "they are of the greatest value in a historical and constitutional point of view, "yet they are comparatively useless to the public, from the want of proper "Calendars and Indexes." Acting upon the recommendations of the Committees of the House of Commons above referred to, he suggested to the Lords of the Treasury that to effect the object he had in view it would be necessary for him to employ a few Persons fully qualified to perform the work which he contemplated.

Their Lordships assented to the necessity of having Calendars prepared and printed, and empowered the Master of the Rolls to take such steps as might be necessary for this purpose.

The following Works have been already published in this Series:—

CALENDARIUM GENEALOGICUM; for the Reigns of Henry III. and Edward I. *Edited by* CHARLES ROBERTS, Esq., Secretary of the Public Record Office, 2 Vols. 1865.

This is a work of great value for elucidating the early history of our nobility and landed gentry.

CALENDAR OF STATE PAPERS, DOMESTIC SERIES, OF THE REIGNS OF EDWARD VI., MARY, ELIZABETH, and JAMES I., preserved in Her Majesty's Public Record Office. *Edited by* ROBERT LEMON, Esq., F.S.A. (Vols. I. and II.), *and by* MARY ANNE EVERETT GREEN, (Vols. III.-XII.). 1856-1872.

Vol. I.— 1547-1580.	Vol. VII.— Addenda, 1566-1579.
Vol. II.— 1581-1590.	Vol. VIII.—1603-1610.
Vol. III.—1591-1594.	Vol. IX.— 1611-1618.
Vol. IV.—1595-1597.	Vol. X.— 1619-1623.
Vol. V.— 1598-1601.	Vol. XI.— 1623-1625, with Addenda, 1603-1625.
Vol. VI.—1601-1603. with Addenda, 1547-1565.	Vol. XII.— Addenda, 1580-1625.

These Calendars render accessible to investigation a large and important mass of historical materials concerning the Northern Rebellion of 1566-67; the plots of the Catholic fugitives in the Low Countries; numerous designs against Queen Elizabeth and in favour of a Catholic succession; the Gunpowder-plot; the rise and fall of Somerset; the Overbury murder; the disgrace of Sir Edward Coke; the rise of the Duke of Buckingham, and numerous other subjects.

CALENDAR OF STATE PAPERS, DOMESTIC SERIES, OF THE REIGN OF CHARLES I., preserved in Her Majesty's Public Record Office. *Edited by* JOHN BRUCE, Esq., F.S.A., (Vols. I.-XII.); *by* JOHN BRUCE, Esq., F.S.A., and WILLIAM DOUGLAS HAMILTON, Esq., F.S.A., (Vol. XIII.); and *by* WILLIAM DOUGLAS HAMILTON, Esq., F.S.A., (Vols. XIV.-XVII.). 1858-1888.

Vol. I.— 1625-1626.
Vol. II.— 1627-1628.
Vol. III.— 1628-1629.
Vol. IV.— 1629-1631.
Vol. V.— 1631-1633.
Vol. VI.— 1633-1634.
Vol. VII.— 1634-1635.
Vol. VIII.—1635.
Vol. IX.— 1635-1636.
Vol. X.— 1636-1637.
Vol. XI.— 1637.
Vol. XII.— 1637-1638.
Vol. XIII.— 1638-1639.
Vol. XIV.— 1639.
Vol. XV.— 1639-1640.
Vol. XVI.— 1640.
Vol. XVII.— 1640-41.
Vol. XVIII.—1641-43.
Vol. XIX.— 1644.

This Calendar presents notices of a large number of original documents of great value to all inquirers relative to the history of the period to which it refers, many hitherto unknown.

CALENDAR OF STATE PAPERS, DOMESTIC SERIES, DURING THE COMMONWEALTH, preserved in Her Majesty's Public Record Office. *Edited by* MARY ANNE EVERETT GREEN. 1875-1885.

Vol. I.— 1649-1649.
Vol. II.— 1650.
Vol. III.—1651.
Vol. IV.— 1651-1652.
Vol. V.— 1652-1653.
Vol. VI.— 1653-1654.
Vol. VII.—1654.
Vol. VIII.—1655.
Vol. IX.— 1655-1656.
Vol. X.— 1656-1657.
Vol. XI.— 1657-1658.
Vol. XII.— 1658-1659.
Vol. XIII.— 1659-1660.

This Calendar is in continuation of those during the reigns from Edward VI. to Charles I.

CALENDAR OF THE COMMITTEE FOR THE ADVANCE OF MONEY, A.D. 1642-1656. *Edited by* MARY ANNE EVERETT GREEN. In three parts. 1888.

CALENDAR OF STATE PAPERS, DOMESTIC SERIES, OF THE REIGN OF CHARLES II., preserved in Her Majesty's Public Record Office. *Edited by* MARY ANNE EVERETT GREEN. 1860-1866.

Vol. I.— 1660-1661.
Vol. II.— 1661-1662.
Vol. III.—1663-1664.
Vol. IV.—1664-1665.
Vol. V.— 1665-1666.
Vol. VI.— 1666-1667.
Vol. VII.—1667.

CALENDAR OF HOME OFFICE PAPERS OF THE REIGN OF GEORGE III., preserved in Her Majesty's Public Record Office. Vols. I. and II. *Edited by* JOSEPH REDINGTON, Esq. 1878-1879. Vol. III. *Edited by* RICHARD ARTHUR ROBERTS, Esq., Barrister-at-Law. 1881.

Vol. I.—1760 (25 Oct.)-1765.
Vol. II.—1766-1769.
Vol. III.—1770-1772.

These are the first three volumes of the modern series of Domestic Papers, commencing with the accession of George III.

CALENDAR OF STATE PAPERS relating to SCOTLAND, preserved in Her Majesty's Public Record Office. *Edited by* MARKHAM JOHN THORPE, Esq., of St. Edmund Hall, Oxford. 1858.

Vol. I., the Scottish Series, of the Reigns of Henry VIII., Edward VI., Mary, and Elizabeth, 1509-1589.
Vol. II., the Scottish Series, of the Reign of Elizabeth, 1589-1603; an Appendix to the Scottish Series, 1543-1592; and the State Papers relating to Mary Queen of Scots.

CALENDAR OF DOCUMENTS relating to IRELAND, in Her Majesty's Public Record Office, London. *Edited by* HENRY SAVAGE SWEETMAN, Esq., B.A., Trinity College, Dublin, Barrister-at-Law (Ireland); *continued by* GUSTAVUS FREDERICK HANDCOCK, Esq. 1875–1886.

Vol. I.— 1171–1251.	Vol. IV.—1293–1301.
Vol. II.— 1252–1284.	Vol. V.— 1302–1307.
Vol. III.—1285–1292.	

CALENDAR OF STATE PAPERS relating to IRELAND, OF THE REIGNS OF HENRY VIII., EDWARD VI., MARY, AND ELIZABETH, preserved in Her Majesty's Public Record Office. *Edited by* HANS CLAUDE HAMILTON, Esq., F.S.A. 1860–1885.

Vol. I.— 1509–1573.	Vol. III.—1586–1588.
Vol. II.—1574–1585.	Vol. IV.— 1588–1592.

CALENDAR OF STATE PAPERS relating to IRELAND, OF THE REIGN OF JAMES I., preserved in Her Majesty's Public Record Office, and elsewhere. *Edited by* the Rev. C. W. RUSSELL, D.D., and JOHN P. PRENDERGAST, Esq., Barrister-at-Law. 1872–1880.

Vol. I.— 1603–1606.	Vol. IV.—1611–1614.
Vol. II.— 1606–1608.	Vol. V.— 1615–1625.
Vol. III.—1608–1610.	

This series is in continuation of the Irish State Papers commencing with the reign of Henry VIII.; but for the reign of James I., the Papers are not confined to those in the Public Record Office, London.

CALENDAR OF STATE PAPERS, COLONIAL SERIES, preserved in Her Majesty's Public Record Office, and elsewhere. *Edited by* W. NOEL SAINSBURY, Esq. 1860–1884.

Vol. I.—America and West Indies, 1574–1660.
Vol. II.—East Indies, China, and Japan, 1513–1616.
Vol. III.—East Indies, China, and Japan 1617–1621.
Vol. IV.—East Indies, China, and Japan, 1622–1624.
Vol. V.—America and West Indies, 1661–1668.
Vol. VI.—East Indies, 1625–1629.

These volumes include an analysis of early Colonial Papers in the Public Record Office, the India Office, and the British Museum.

CALENDAR OF LETTERS AND PAPERS, FOREIGN AND DOMESTIC, OF THE REIGN OF HENRY VIII., preserved in Her Majesty's Public Record Office, the British Museum, &c. *Edited by* J. S. BREWER, M.A., Professor of English Literature, King's College, London (Vols. I.–IV.); and *by* JAMES GAIRDNER, Esq., (Vols. V., VI., VII., VIII., and IX.) 1862–1888.

Vol. I.—1509–1514.	Vol. IV., Part 3.—1529–1530.
Vol. II. (in Two Parts)—1515–1518.	Vol. V.—1531–1532.
Vol. III. (in Two Parts)—1519–1523.	Vol. VI.—1533.
Vol. IV.—Introduction.	Vol. VII.—1534.
Vol. IV., Part 1.—1524–1526.	Vol. VIII.—1535, to July.
Vol. IV., Part 2.—1526–1528.	Vol. IX.—1535, Aug. to Dec.
	Vol. X.—1536, Jan. to June.
	Vol. XI.—1536, July to Dec.

These volumes contain summaries of all State Papers and Correspondence relating to the reign of Henry VIII., in the Public Record Office, of those formerly in the State Paper Office, in the British Museum, the Libraries of Oxford and Cambridge, and other Public Libraries; and of all letters that have appeared in print in the works of Burnet, Strype, and others. Whatever authentic original material exists in England relative to the religious, political, parliamentary, or social history of the country during the reign of Henry VIII., whether despatches of ambassadors, or proceedings of the army, navy, treasury, or ordnance, or records of Parliament, appointments of officers, grants from the Crown, &c., will be found calendared in these volumes.

CALENDAR OF STATE PAPERS, FOREIGN SERIES, OF THE REIGN OF EDWARD VI., preserved in Her Majesty's Public Record Office. 1547–1553. *Edited by* W. B. TURNBULL, Esq., of Lincoln's Inn, Barrister-at-Law, &c. 1861.

CALENDAR OF STATE PAPERS, FOREIGN SERIES, OF THE REIGN OF MARY, preserved in Her Majesty's Public Record Office. 1553-1558. *Edited by* W. B. TURNBULL, Esq., of Lincoln's Inn, Barrister-at-Law, &c. 1861.

The two preceding volumes exhibit the negotiations of the English ambassadors with the courts of the Emperor Charles V. of Germany, of Henry II. of France, and of Philip II. of Spain. The affairs of several of the minor continental states also find various incidental illustrations of much interest. The Papers descriptive of the circumstances which attended the loss of Calais merit a special notice; while the progress of the wars in the north of France, into which England was dragged by her union with Spain, is narrated at some length. These volumes treat only of the relations of England with foreign powers.

CALENDAR OF STATE PAPERS, FOREIGN SERIES, OF THE REIGN OF ELIZABETH, preserved in Her Majesty's Public Record Office, &c. *Edited by* the Rev. JOSEPH STEVENSON, M.A., of University College, Durham, (Vols. I.-VII.), and ALLAN JAMES CROSBY, Esq., M.A., Barrister-at-Law, (Vols. VIII.-XI.) 1863-1880.

Vol. I.— 1558-1559.
Vol. II.— 1559-1560.
Vol. III.—1560-1561.
Vol. IV.—1561-1562.
Vol. V.— 1562.
Vol. VI.— 1563.
Vol. VII.— 1564-1565.
Vol. VIII.—1566-1568.
Vol. IX.— 1569-1571.
Vol. X.— 1572-1574.
Vol. XI.— 1575-1577.

These volumes contain a Calendar of the Foreign Correspondence during the early portion of the reign of Elizabeth. They illustrate not only the external but also the domestic affairs of Foreign Countries during that period.

CALENDAR OF TREASURY PAPERS, preserved in Her Majesty's Public Record Office. *Edited by* JOSEPH REDINGTON, Esq. 1868-1883.

Vol. I.— 1557-1696.
Vol. II.— 1697-1702.
Vol. III.—1702-1707.
Vol. IV.—1708-1714.
Vol. V.— 1714-1719.

The above Papers connected with the affairs of the Treasury comprise, petitions, reports, and other documents relating to services rendered to the State, grants of money and pensions, appointments to offices, remissions of fines and duties, &c. They illustrate civil and military events, finance, the administration in Ireland and the Colonies, &c., and afford information nowhere else recorded.

CALENDAR OF THE CAREW PAPERS, preserved in the Lambeth Library. *Edited by* J. S. BREWER, M.A., Professor of English Literature, King's College, London; and WILLIAM BULLEN, Esq. 1867-1873.

Vol. I.— 1515-1574.
Vol. II.— 1575-1588.
Vol. III.—1589-1600.
Vol. IV.—1601-1603.
Vol. V.—Book of Howth; Miscellaneous.
Vol. VI.—1603-1624.

The Carew Papers relating to Ireland, in the Lambeth Library, are unique and of great importance to all students of Irish history.

CALENDAR OF LETTERS, DESPATCHES, AND STATE PAPERS, relating to the Negotiations between England and Spain, preserved in the Archives at Simancas, and elsewhere. *Edited by* G. A. BERGENROTH, (Vols. I. and II.) 1862-1868, *and* DON PASCUAL DE GAYANGOS (Vols. III. to V.) 1873-1888.

Vol. I.—Hen. VII.—1485-1509.
Vol. II.—Hen. VIII.—1509-1525.
Supplement to Vol. I. and Vol. II.
Vol. III., Part 1.—Hen. VIII.—1525-1526.
Vol. III., Part 2.—Hen. VIII.—1527-1529.
Vol. IV., Part 1.—Hen. VIII.—1529-1530.
Vol. IV., Part 2.—Hen. VIII.—1531-1533.
Vol. IV., Part 2.—*continued.*—Hen. VIII.—1531-1533.
Vol. V., Part 1.—Hen. VIII.—1534-1536.
Vol. V., Part 2.—Hen. VIII.—1536-1538.

Mr. Bergenroth was engaged in compiling a Calendar of the Papers relating to England preserved in the archives of Spain. The Supplement contains new information relating to the private life of Queen Katherine of England; and to the projected marriage of Henry VII. with Queen Juana, widow of King Philip of Castile, and mother of the Emperor Charles V.

Upon the death of Mr. Bergenroth, Don Pascual de Gayangos was appointed to continue the Calendar, and he has been able to add much valuable matter from Brussels and Vienna, with which Mr. Bergenroth was unacquainted.

Calendar of State Papers and Manuscripts, relating to English Affairs, preserved in the Archives of Venice, &c. *Edited by* Rawdon Brown, Esq. 1864–1884.

Vol. I.— 1202–1509.	Vol. V.— 1534–1554.
Vol. II.— 1509–1519.	Vol. VI., Part I.— 1555–1556.
Vol. III.—1520–1526.	Vol. VI., Part II.— 1556–1557.
Vol. IV.—1527–1533.	Vol. VI., Part III.—1557–1558.

Mr. Rawdon Brown's researches have brought to light a number of valuable documents relating to various periods of English history; his contributions to historical literature are of the most interesting and important character.

Syllabus, in English, of Rymer's Fœdera. *By* Sir Thomas Duffus Hardy, D.C.L., Deputy Keeper of the Public Records. Vol. I.—Will. I.–Edw. III. 1066–1377. Vol. II.—Ric. II.–Chas. II. 1377–1654. Vol. III., Appendix and Index. 1869–1885.

Rymer's "Fœdera," is a collection of miscellaneous documents illustrative of the History of Great Britain and Ireland, from the Norman Conquest to the reign of Charles II. Several editions of the "Fœdera" have been published, and the present Syllabus was undertaken to make the contents of this great national work more generally known.

Report of the Deputy Keeper of the Public Records and the Rev. J. S. Brewer to the Master of the Rolls, upon the Carte and Carew Papers in the Bodleian and Lambeth Libraries. 1864. *Price* 2*s*. 6*d*.

Report of the Deputy Keeper of the Public Records to the Master of th Rolls, upon the Documents in the Archives and Public Libraries of Venice. 1866. *Price* 2*s*. 6*d*.

In the Press.

Calendar of State Papers and Manuscripts, relating to English Affairs, preserved in the Archives of Venice, &c. Vol. VII.—1559, &c.

Calendar of Letters, Despatches, and State Papers, relating to the Negotiations between England and Spain, preserved in the Archives at Simancas, and elsewhere. *Edited by* Don Pascual de Gayangos. Vol. V. Part 2.—1537, &c.

Calendar of State Papers, Domestic Series, during the Commonwealth, preserved in Her Majesty's Public Record Office. *Edited by* Mary Anne Everett Green. Vol. XV.

Calendar of State Papers relating to Ireland, of the Reign of Elizabeth, preserved in Her Majesty's Public Record Office. *Edited by* Hans Claude Hamilton, Esq., F.S A. Vol. V.—1592–1596.

Calendar of State Papers, Colonial Series, preserved in Her Majesty's Public Record Office, and elsewhere. *Edited by* W. Noel Sainsbury, Esq. Vol. VII.—America and West Indies, 1669, &c.

Calendar of Treasury Papers, preserved in Her Majesty's Public Record Office. *Edited by* Joseph Redington, Esq. Vol. VI.—1720, &c.

Descriptive Catalogue of Ancient Deeds, preserved in Her Majesty's Public Record Office. Vol. I.

Calendar of State Papers, Domestic Series, of the Reign of Charles I., preserved in Her Majesty's Public Record Office. *Edited by* William Douglas Hamilton, Esq., F.S.A. Vol. XX. 1645, &c.

In Progress.

Calendar of Letters and Papers, Foreign and Domestic, of the Reign of Henry VIII., preserved in Her Majesty's Public Record Office, the British Museum, &c. *Edited by* James Gairdner, Esq. Vol. XII.—1537.

Calendar of State Papers, Colonial Series, preserved in Her Majesty's Public Record Office, and elsewhere. *Edited by* W. Noel Sainsbury, Esq. Vol. VIII.—East Indies, 1630, &c.

Calendar of Treasury Papers, preserved in Her Majesty's Public Record Office. *Edited by* Joseph Redington, Esq. Vol. VII.

Calendar of the Patent Rolls, of the Reigns of Edward II. and Edward III.

Calendar of Ancient Correspondence, Diplomatic Documents, Papal Bulls, and the like, preserved in Her Majesty's Public Record Office. *Edited by* C. T. Martin, Esq., B.A., F.S.A.

THE CHRONICLES AND MEMORIALS OF GREAT BRITAIN AND IRELAND DURING THE MIDDLE AGES.

[ROYAL 8vo. *Price* 10*s*. each Volume or Part.]

On 25 July 1822, the House of Commons presented an address to the Crown, stating that the editions of the works of our ancient historians were inconvenient and defective; that many of their writings still remained in manuscript, and, in some cases, in a single copy only. They added, "that an uniform and con- "venient edition of the whole, published under His Majesty's royal sanction, "would be an undertaking honourable to His Majesty's reign, and conducive to "the advancement of historical and constitutional knowledge; that the House "therefore humbly besought His Majesty, that He would be graciously pleased "to give such directions as His Majesty, in His wisdom, might think fit, for "the publication of a complete edition of the ancient historians of this realm, "and assured His Majesty that whatever expense might be necessary for this "purpose would be made good."

The Master of the Rolls, being very desirous that effect should be given to the resolution of the House of Commons, submitted to Her Majesty's Treasury in 1857 a plan for the publication of the ancient chronicles and memorials of the United Kingdom, and it was adopted accordingly. In selecting these works, it was considered right, in the first instance, to give preference to those of which the manuscripts were unique, or the materials of which would help to fill up blanks in English history for which no satisfactory and authentic information hitherto existed in any accessible form. One great object the Master of the Rolls had in view was to form a *corpus historicum* within reasonable limits, and which should be as complete as possible. In a subject of so vast a range, it was important that the historical student should be able to select such volumes as conformed with his own peculiar tastes and studies, and not be put to the expense of purchasing the whole collection; an inconvenience inseparable from any other plan than that which has been in this instance adopted.

Of the Chronicles and Memorials, the following volumes have been published. They embrace the period from the earliest time of British history down to the end of the reign of Henry VII.

---

1. THE CHRONICLE OF ENGLAND, by JOHN CAPGRAVE. *Edited by* the Rev. F. C. HINGESTON, M.A., of Exeter College, Oxford. 1858.

   Capgrave was prior of Lynn, in Norfolk, and provincial of the order of the Friars Hermits of England shortly before the year 1464. His Chronicle extends from the creation of the world to the year 1417. As a record of the language spoken in Norfolk (being written in English), it is of considerable value.

2. CHRONICON MONASTERII DE ABINGDON. Vols. I. and II. *Edited by* the Rev. JOSEPH STEVENSON, M.A., of University College, Durham, and Vicar of Leighton Buzzard. 1858.

   This Chronicle traces the history of the great Benedictine monastery of Abingdon in Berkshire, from its foundation by King Ina of Wessex, to the reign of Richard I., shortly after which period the present narrative was drawn up by an inmate of the establishment. The author had access to the title-deeds of the house; and incorporates into his history various charters of the Saxon kings, of great importance as illustrating not only the history of the locality but that of the kingdom. The work is printed for the first time.

3. LIVES OF EDWARD THE CONFESSOR. I.—La Estoire de Seint Aedward le Rei II.—Vita Beati Edvardi Regis et Confessoris. III.—Vita Æduuardi Regis qui apud Westmonasterium requiescit. *Edited by* HENRY RICHARDS LUARD, M.A., Fellow and Assistant Tutor of Trinity College, Cambridge. 1858.

   The first is a poem in Norman French, containing 4,686 lines, addressed to Alianor, Queen of Henry III., probably written in 1245, on the restoration of the church of Westminster. Nothing is known of the author. The second is an anonymous poem, containing 536 lines, written between 1440 and 1450, by command of Henry VI., to whom it is dedicated. It does not throw any new light on the reign of Edward the Confessor, but is valuable as a specimen of the Latin poetry of the time. The third, also by an anonymous author, was apparently written for Queen Edith, between 1066 and 1074, during the pressure of the suffering brought on the Saxons by the Norman conquest. It notices many acts not found in other writers, and some which differ considerably from the usual accounts.

4. MONUMENTA FRANCISCANA. Vol. I.—Thomas de Eccleston de Adventu Fratrum Minorum in Angliam. Adæ de Marisco Epistolæ. Registrum Fratrum Minorum Londoniæ. *Edited by* J. S. BREWER, M.A., Professor of English Literature, King's College, London. Vol. II.—De Adventu Minorum; re-edited, with additions. Chronicle of the Grey Friars. The ancient English version of the Rule of St. Francis. Abbreviatio Statutorum, 1451, &c. *Edited by* RICHARD HOWLETT, Esq., of the Middle Temple, Barrister-at-Law. 1858, 1882.

The first volume contains original materials for the history of the settlement of the order of Saint Francis in England, the letters of Adam de Marisco, and other papers connected with the foundation and diffusion of this great body. None of these have been before printed. The second volume contains materials found, since the first volume was published, among the MSS. of Sir Charles Isham, and in various libraries.

5. FASCICULI ZIZANIORUM MAGISTRI JOHANNIS WYCLIF CUM TRITICO. Ascribed to THOMAS NETTER, of WALDEN, Provincial of the Carmelite Order in England, and Confessor to King Henry the Fifth. *Edited by* the Rev. W. W. SHIRLEY, M.A., Tutor and late Fellow of Wadham College, Oxford. 1858.

This work derives its principal value from being the only contemporaneous account of the rise of the Lollards. When written, the disputes of the schoolmen had been extended to the field of theology, and they appear both in the writings of Wycliff and in those of his adversaries. Wycliff's little bundles of tares are not less metaphysical than theological, and the conflict between Nominalists and Realists rages side by side with the conflict between the different interpreters of Scripture. The work gives a good idea of the controversies at the end of the 14th and the beginning of the 15th centuries.

6. THE BUIK OF THE CRONICLIS OF SCOTLAND; or, A Metrical Version of the History of Hector Boece; by WILLIAM STEWART. Vols. I., II., and III. *Edited by* W. B. TURNBULL, Esq., of Lincoln's Inn, Barrister-at-Law, 1858.

This is a metrical translation of a Latin Prose Chronicle, written in the first half of the 16th century. The narrative begins with the earliest legends and ends with the death of James I. of Scotland, and the "evil ending of the traitors that slew him." Strict accuracy of statement is not to be looked for; but the stories of the colonization of Spain, Ireland, and Scotland are interesting if not true; and the chronicle reflects the manners, sentiments, and character of the age in which it was composed. The peculiarities of the Scottish dialect are well illustrated in this version, and the student of language will find ample materials for comparison with the English dialects of the same period, and with modern lowland Scotch.

7. JOHANNIS CAPGRAVE LIBER DE ILLUSTRIBUS HENRICIS. *Edited by* the Rev. F. C. HINGESTON, M.A., of Exeter College, Oxford. 1858.

This work is dedicated to Henry VI. of England, who appears to have been, in the author's estimation, the greatest of all the Henries. It is divided into three parts, each having a separate dedication. The first part relates only to the history of the Empire, from the election of Henry I. the Fowler, to the end of the reign of the Emperor Henry VI. The second part is devoted to English history, from the accession of Henry I. in 1100, to 1446, which was the twenty-fourth year of the reign of Henry VI. The third part contains the lives of illustrious men who have borne the name of Henry in various parts of the world. Capgrave was born in 1393, in the reign of Richard II., and lived during the Wars of the Roses, for which period his work is of some value.

8. HISTORIA MONASTERII S. AUGUSTINI CANTUARIENSIS, by THOMAS OF ELMHAM, formerly Monk and Treasurer of that Foundation. *Edited by* CHARLES HARDWICK, M.A., Fellow of St. Catharine's Hall, and Christian Advocate in the University of Cambridge. 1858.

This history extends from the arrival of St. Augustine in Kent until 1191. Prefixed is a chronology as far as 1418, which shows in outline what was to have been the character of the work when completed. The author was connected with Norfolk, and most probably with Elmham.

9. EULOGIUM (HISTORIARUM SIVE TEMPORIS): Chronicon ab Orbe condito usque ad Annum Domini 1366; a Monacho quodam Malmesbiriensi exaratum. Vols. I., II., and III. *Edited by* F. S. HAYDON, Esq., B.A. 1858–1863.

This is a Latin Chronicle extending from the Creation to the latter part of the reign of Edward III., and written by a monk of the Abbey of Malmesbury, in Wiltshire, about the year 1367. A continuation, carrying the history of England down to the year 1413, was added in the former half of the fifteenth century by an author whose name is not known. The original Chronicle contains a history of the world generally, but more especially of England to the year 1366. The continuation extends the history down to the coronation of Henry V. The Eulogium itself is chiefly valuable as containing a history, by a contemporary, of the period between 1356 and 1366. Among other interesting matter, the Chronicle contains a diary of the Poitiers campaign, evidently furnished by some person who accompanied the army of the Black Prince. The continuation of the Chronicle is also the work of a contemporary, and gives a very interesting account of the reigns of Richard II. and Henry IV.

10. MEMORIALS OF HENRY THE SEVENTH: Bernardi Andreæ Tholosatis Vita Regis Henrici Septimi; necnon alia quædam ad eundem Regem spectantia. *Edited by* JAMES GAIRDNER, Esq. 1858.

The contents of this volume are—(1) a life of Henry VII., by his poet laureate and historiographer, Bernard André, of Toulouse, with some compositions in verse, of which he is supposed to have been the author; (2) the journals of Roger Machado during certain embassies on which he was sent by Henry VII. to Spain and Brittany, the first of which had reference to the marriage of the King's son, Arthur, with Catharine of Arragon; (3) two curious reports by envoys sent to Spain in 1505 touching the succession to the Crown of Castile, and a project of marriage between Henry VII. and the Queen of Naples; and (4) an account of Philip of Castile's reception in England in 1506. Other documents of interest are given in an appendix.

11. Memorials of Henry the Fifth. I.—Vita Henrici Quinti, Roberto Redmanno auctore. II.—Versus Rhythmici in laudem Regis Henrici Quinti. III.—Elmhami Liber Metricus de Henrico V. *Edited by* Charles A. Cole, Esq. 1858.

This volume contains three treatises which more or less illustrate the history of the reign of Henry V., viz.: A life by Robert Redman; a Metrical Chronicle by Thomas Elmham, prior of Lenton, a contemporary author; Versus Rhythmici, written apparently by a monk of Westminster Abbey, who was also a contemporary of Henry V. These works are printed for the first time.

12. Munimenta Gildhallæ Londoniensis; Liber Albus, Liber Custumarum, et Liber Horn, in archivis Gildhallæ asservati. Vol. I., Liber Albus. Vol. II. (in Two Parts), Liber Custumarum. Vol. III., Translation of the Anglo-Norman Passages in Liber Albus, Glossaries, Appendices, and Index. *Edited by* Henry Thomas Riley, Esq., M.A., Barrister-at-Law. 1859–1862.

The manuscript of the *Liber Albus*, compiled by John Carpenter, Common Clerk of the City of London in the year 1419, gives an account of the laws, regulations, and institutions of that City in the 12th, 13th, 14th, and early part of the 15th centuries. The *Liber Custumarum* was compiled probably by various hands in the early part of the 14th century during the reign of Edward II. The manuscript, a folio volume, is preserved in the Record Room of the City of London, though some portion in its original state, borrowed from the City in the reign of Queen Elizabeth and never returned, forms part of the Cottonian MS. Claudius D. II. in the British Museum. It also gives an account of the laws, regulations, and institutions of the City of London in the 12th, 13th, and early part of the 14th centuries.

13. Chronica Johannis de Oxenedes. *Edited by* Sir Henry Ellis, K.H. 1859.

Although this Chronicle tells of the arrival of Hengist and Horsa in England in 449, yet it substantially begins with the reign of King Alfred, and comes down to 1292, where it ends abruptly. The history is particularly valuable for notices of events in the eastern portions of the Kingdom, not to be elsewhere obtained. Some curious facts are mentioned relative to the floods in that part of England, which are confirmed in the Friesland Chronicle of Anthony Heinrich, pastor of the Island of Mohr.

14. A Collection of Political Poems and Songs relating to English History, from the Accession of Edward III. to the Reign of Henry VIII. Vols. I. and II. *Edited by* Thomas Wright, Esq., M.A. 1859–1861.

These Poems are perhaps the most interesting of all the historical writings of the period, though they cannot be relied on for accuracy of statement. They are various in character; some are upon religious subjects, some may be called satires, and some give no more than a court scandal; but as a whole they present a very fair picture of society, and of the relations of the different classes to one another. The period comprised is in itself interesting, and brings us through the decline of the feudal system, to the beginning of our modern history. The songs in old English are of considerable value to the philologist.

15. The "Opus Tertium," "Opus Minus," &c., of Roger Bacon. *Edited by* J. S. Brewer, M.A., Professor of English Literature, King's College, London. 1859.

This is the celebrated treatise—never before printed—so frequently referred to by the great philosopher in his works. It contains the fullest details we possess of the life and labours of Roger Bacon: also a fragment by the same author, supposed to be unique, the "*Compendium Studii Theologiæ.*"

16. Bartholomæi de Cotton, Monachi Norwicensis, Historia Anglicana; 449–1298: necnon ejusdem Liber de Achiepiscopis et Episcopis Angliæ. *Edited by* Henry Richards Luard, M.A., Fellow and Assistant Tutor of Trinity College, Cambridge. 1859.

The author, a monk of Norwich, has here given us a Chronicle of England from the arrival of the Saxons in 449 to the year 1298, in or about which year it appears that he died. The latter portion of this history (the whole of the reign of Edward I. more especially) is of great value, as the writer was contemporary with the events which he records. An Appendix contains several illustrative documents connected with the previous narrative.

17. Brut y Tywysogion; or, The Chronicle of the Princes of Wales. *Edited by* the Rev. John Williams ab Ithel, M.A. 1860.

This work, also known as "The Chronicle of the Princes of Wales," has been attributed to Caradoc of Llancarvan, who flourished about the middle of the twelfth century. It is written in the ancient Welsh language, begins with the abdication and death of Caedwala at Rome, in the year 681, and continues the history down to the subjugation of Wales by Edward I., about the year 1282.

18. A Collection of Royal and Historical Letters during the Reign of Henry IV. 1399–1404. *Edited by* the Rev. F. C. Hingeston, M.A., of Exeter College, Oxford. 1860.

This volume, like all the others in the series containing a miscellaneous selection of letters, is valuable on account of the light it throws upon biographical history, and the familiar view it presents of characters, manners, and events.

19. THE REPRESSOR OF OVER MUCH BLAMING OF THE CLERGY. By REGINALD PECOCK, sometime Bishop of Chichester. Vols. I. and II. *Edited by* CHURCHILL BABINGTON, B.D., Fellow of St. John's College, Cambridge. 1860.

The "Repressor" may be considered the earliest piece of good theological disquisition of which our English prose literature can boast. The author was born about the end of the fourteenth century, consecrated Bishop of St. Asaph in the year 1444, and translated to the see of Chichester in 1450. While Bishop of St. Asaph, he zealously defended his brother prelates from the attacks of those who censured the bishops for their neglect of duty. He maintained that it was no part of a bishop's functions to appear in the pulpit, and that his time might be more profitably spent, and his dignity better maintained, in the performance of works of a higher character. Among those who thought differently were the Lollards, and against their general doctrines the "Repressor" is directed. Pecock took up a position midway between that of the Roman Church and that of the modern Anglican Church; but his work is interesting chiefly because it gives a full account of the views of the Lollards and of the arguments by which they were supported, and because it assists us to ascertain the state of feeling which ultimately led to the Reformation. Apart from religious matters, the light thrown upon contemporaneous history is very small, but the "Repressor" has great value for the philologist, as it tells us what were the characteristics of the language in use among the cultivated Englishmen of the fifteenth century.

20. ANNALES CAMBRIÆ. *Edited by* the Rev. JOHN WILLIAMS AB ITHEL, M.A. 1860.

These annals, which are in Latin, commence in 447, and come down to 1288. The earlier portion appears to be taken from an Irish Chronicle used by Tigernach, and by the compiler of the Annals of Ulster. During its first century it contains scarcely anything relating to Britain, the earliest direct concurrence with English history is relative to the mission of Augustine. Its notices throughout, though brief, are valuable. The annals were probably written at St. Davids, by Blegewryd, Archdeacon of Llandaff, the most learned man in his day in all Cymru.

21. THE WORKS OF GIRALDUS CAMBRENSIS. Vols. I., II., III., and IV. *Edited by* J. S. BREWER, M.A., Professor of English Literature, King's College, London. Vols. V., VI., and VII. *Edited by* the Rev. JAMES F. DIMOCK, M.A., Rector of Barnburgh, Yorkshire. 1861–1877.

These volumes contain the historical works of Gerald du Barry, who lived in the reigns of Henry II., Richard I., and John, and attempted to re-establish the independence of Wales by restoring the see of St. Davids to its ancient primacy. His works are of a very miscellaneous nature, both in prose and verse, and are remarkable chiefly for the racy and original anecdotes which they contain relating to contemporaries. He is the only Welsh writer of any importance who has contributed so much to the mediæval literature of this country, or assumed, in consequence of his nationality, so free and independent a tone. His frequent travels in Italy, in France, in Ireland, and in Wales, gave him opportunities for observation which did not generally fall to the lot of mediæval writers in the twelfth and thirteenth centuries, and of these observations Giraldus has made due use. Only extracts from these treatises have been printed before and almost all of them are taken from unique manuscripts.

The Topographia Hibernica (in Vol. V.) is the result of Giraldus' two visits to Ireland. The first in 1183, the second in 1185-6, when he accompanied Prince John into that country. A very interesting portion of this treatise is devoted to the animals of Ireland. It shows that he was a very accurate and acute observer, and his descriptions are given in a way that a scientific naturalist of the present day could hardly improve upon. The Expugnatio Hibernica was written about 1188 and may be regarded rather as a great epic than a sober relation of acts occurring in his own days. Vol. VI. contains the Itinerarium Kambriæ et Descriptio Kambriæ: and Vol. VII., the lives of S. Remigius and S. Hugh.

22. LETTERS AND PAPERS ILLUSTRATIVE OF THE WARS OF THE ENGLISH IN FRANCE DURING THE REIGN OF HENRY THE SIXTH, KING OF ENGLAND. Vol. I., and Vol. II. (in Two Parts). *Edited by* the Rev. JOSEPH STEVENSON, M.A., of University College, Durham, and Vicar of Leighton Buzzard. 1861–1864.

These letters and papers are derived chiefly from originals or contemporary copies extant in the Bibliothèque Impériale, and the Depôt des Archives, in Paris. They illustrate the policy adopted by John Duke of Bedford and his successors during their government of Normandy, and other provinces of France acquired by Henry V. Here may be traced, step by step, the gradual declension of the English power, until we are prepared for its final overthrow.

23. THE ANGLO-SAXON CHRONICLE, ACCORDING TO THE SEVERAL ORIGINAL AUTHORITIES. Vol. I., Original Texts. Vol II., Translation. *Edited and translated by* BENJAMIN THORPE, Esq., Member of the Royal Academy of Sciences at Munich, and of the Society of Netherlandish Literature at Leyden. 1861.

This chronicle, extending from the earliest history of Britain to 1154, is justly the boast of England; no other nation can produce any history, written in its own vernacular, at all approaching it, in antiquity, truthfulness, or extent, the historical books of the Bible alone excepted. There are at present six independent manuscripts of the Saxon Chronicle, ending in different years, and written in different parts of the country. In this edition, the text of each manuscript is printed in columns on the same page, so that the student may see at a glance the various changes which occur in orthography, whether arising from locality or age.

24. LETTERS AND PAPERS ILLUSTRATIVE OF THE REIGNS OF RICHARD III. AND HENRY VII. Vols. I. and II. *Edited by* JAMES GAIRDNER, Esq. 1861–1863.

The papers are derived from the MSS. in Public Record Office, the British Museum, and other repositories. The period to which they refer is unusually destitute of chronicles and other sources of historical information, so that the light obtained from them is of special importance. The principal contents of the volumes are some diplomatic Papers of Richard III.; correspondence between Henry VII. and Ferdinand and Isabella of Spain; documents relating to Edmund de la Pole, Earl of Suffolk; and a portion of the correspondence of James IV. of Scotland.

25. LETTERS OF BISHOP GROSSETESTE, illustrative of the Social Condition of his Time. *Edited by* HENRY RICHARDS LUARD, M.A., Fellow and Assistant Tutor of Trinity College, Cambridge. 1861.

The Letters of Robert Grosseteste (131 in number) are here collected from various sources, and a large portion of them is printed for the first time. They range in date from about 1210 to 1253, and relate to various matters connected not only with the political history of England during the reign of Henry III. but with its ecclesiastical condition. They refer especially to the diocese of Lincoln, of which Grosseteste wa bishop.

26. DESCRIPTIVE CATALOGUE OF MANUSCRIPTS RELATING TO THE HISTORY OF GREAT BRITAIN AND IRELAND. Vol. I. (in Two Parts); Anterior to the Norman Invasion. Vol. II.; 1066-1200. Vol. III.; 1200-1327. *By* Sir THOMAS DUFFUS HARDY, D.C.L., Deputy Keeper of the Public Records. 1862-1871.

The object of this work is to publish notices of all known sources of British history, both printed and unprinted, in one continued sequence. The materials, when historical (as distinguished from biographical), are arranged under the year in which the latest event is recorded in the chronicle or history, and not under the period in which its author, real or supposed, flourished. Biographies are enumerated under the year in which the person commemorated died, and not under the year in which the life was written. A brief analysis of each work has been added when deserving it, in which original portions are distinguished from mere compilations. If possible, the sources are indicated from which compilations have been derived. A biographical sketch of the author of each piece has been added, and a brief notice of such British authors as have written on historical subjects.

27. ROYAL AND OTHER HISTORICAL LETTERS ILLUSTRATIVE OF THE REIGN OF HENRY III. Vol. I., 1216-1235. Vol. II., 1236-1272. *Selected and edited by* the Rev. W. W. SHIRLEY, D.D., Regius Professor of Ecclesiastical History, and Canon of Christ Church, Oxford. 1862-1866.

The letters contained in these volumes are derived chiefly from the ancient correspondence formerly in the Tower of London, and now in the Public Record Office. They illustrate the political history of England during the growth of its liberties, and throw considerable light upon the personal history of Simon de Montfort. The affairs of France form the subject of many of them, especially in regard to the province of Gascony. The entire collection consists of nearly 700 documents, the greater portion of which is printed for the first time.

28. CHRONICA MONASTERII S. ALBANI.—1. THOMÆ WALSINGHAM HISTORIA ANGLICANA; Vol. I., 1272-1381: Vol. II., 1381-1422. 2. WILLELMI RISHANGER CHRONICA ET ANNALES, 1259-1307. 3. JOHANNIS DE TROKELOWE ET HENRICI DE BLANEFORDE CHRONICA ET ANNALES, 1259-1296; 1307-1324; 1392-1406. 4. GESTA ABBATUM MONASTERII S. ALBANI, A THOMA WALSINGHAM, REGNANTE RICARDO SECUNDO, EJUSDEM ECCLESIÆ PRÆCENTORE, COMPILATA; Vol. I., 793-1290: Vol. II., 1290-1349: Vol. III., 1349-1411. 5. JOHANNIS AMUNDESHAM, MONACHI MONASTERII S. ALBANI, UT VIDETUR, ANNALES; Vols. I. and II. 6. REGISTRA QUORUNDAM ABBATUM MONASTERII S. ALBANI, QUI SÆCULO XV^mo^ FLORUERE; Vol. I., REGISTRUM ABBATIÆ JOHANNIS WHETHAMSTEDE, ABBATIS MONASTERII SANCTI ALBANI, ITERUM SUSCEPTÆ; ROBERTO BLAKENEY, CAPELLANO, QUONDAM ADSCRIPTUM: Vol. II., REGISTRA JOHANNIS WHETHAMSTEDE, WILLELMI ALBON, ET WILLELMI WALINGFORDE, ABBATUM MONASTERII SANCTI ALBANI, CUM APPENDICE, CONTINENTE QUASDAM EPISTOLAS, A JOHANNE WHETHAMSTEDE CONSCRIPTAS. 7. YPODIGMA NEUSTRIÆ A THOMA WALSINGHAM, QUONDAM MONACHO MONASTERII S. ALBANI, CONSCRIPTUM. *Edited by* HENRY THOMAS RILEY, Esq., M.A., Cambridge and Oxford; and of the Inner Temple, Barrister-at-Law. 1863-1876.

In the first two volumes is a History of England, from the death of Henry III. to the death of Henry V., by Thomas Walsingham, Precentor of St. Albans.

In the 3rd volume is a Chronicle of English History, attributed to William Rishanger, who lived in the reign of Edward I.: an account of transactions attending the award of the kingdom of Scotland to John Balliol, 1291-1292, also attributed to William Rishanger, but on no sufficient ground: a short Chronicle of English History, 1292 to 1300, by an unknown hand: a short Chronicle Willelmi Rishanger Gesta Edwardi Primi, Regis Angliæ, with Annales Regum Angliæ, probably by the same hand: and fragments of three Chronicles of English History, 1285 to 1307.

In the 4th volume is a Chronicle of English History, 1259 to 1296: Annals of Edward II., 1307 to 1323, by John de Trokelowe, a monk of St. Albans, and a continuation of Trokelowe's Annals, 1323, 1324, by Henry de Blaneforde: a full Chronicle of English History, 1392 to 1406: and an account of the Benefactors of St. Albans, written in the early part of the 15th century.

The 5th, 6th, and 7th volumes contain a history of the Abbots of St. Albans, 793 to 1411, mainly compiled by Thomas Walsingham: with a Continuation, from the closing pages of Parker MS. VII., in the Library of Corpus Christi College, Cambridge.

The 8th and 9th volumes, in continuation of the Annals, contain a Chronicle, probably by John Amundesham, a monk of St. Albans.

The 10th and 11th volumes relate especially to the acts and proceedings of Abbots Whethamstede, Albon, and Wallingford, and may be considered as a memorial of the chief historical and domestic events during those periods.

The 12th volume contains a compendious History of England to the reign of Henry V., and of Normandy in early times, also by Thomas Walsingham, and dedicated to Henry V. The compiler has often substituted other authorities in place of those consulted in the preparation of his larger work.

29. Chronicon Abbatiæ Eveshamensis, Auctoribus Dominico Priore Eveshamiæ et Thoma de Marleberge Abbate, a Fundatione ad Annum 1213, una cum Continuatione ad Annum 1418. *Edited by* the Rev. W. D. Macray, Bodleian Library, Oxford. 1863.

The Chronicle of Evesham illustrates the history of that important monastery from its foundation by Egwin, about 690, to the year 1418. Its chief feature is an autobiography, which makes us acquainted with the inner daily life of a great abbey, such as but rarely has been recorded. Interspersed are many notices of general, personal, and local history which will be read with much interest. This work exists in a single MS., and is for the first time printed.

30. Ricardi de Cirencestria Speculum Historiale de Gestis Regum Angliæ. Vol. I., 447–871. Vol. II., 872–1066. *Edited by* John E. B. Mayor, M.A., Fellow of St. John's College, Cambridge. 1863–1869.

The compiler, Richard of Cirencester, was a monk of Westminster, 1355–1400. In 1391 he obtained a licence to make a pilgrimage to Rome. His history, in four books, extends from 447 to 1066. He announces his intention of continuing it, but there is no evidence that he completed any more. This chronicle gives many charters in favour of Westminster Abbey, and a very full account of the lives and miracles of the saints, especially of Edward the Confessor, whose reign occupies the fourth book. A treatise on the Coronation, by William of Sudbury, a monk of Westminster, fills book ii. c. 3. It was on this author that C. J. Bertram fathered his forgery, *De Situ Brittaniæ* in 1747.

31. Year Books of the Reign of Edward the First. Years 20–21, 21–22, 30–31, 32–33, and 33–35 Edw. I.; and 11–12 Edw. III. *Edited and translated by* Alfred John Horwood, Esq., of the Middle Temple Barrister-at-Law. Years 12–13, 13–14, and 14 Edward III. *Edited and translated by* Luke Owen Pike, Esq., M.A., of Lincoln's Inn, Barrister-at-Law. 1863–1886.

The "Year Books" are the earliest of our Law Reports. They contain matter not only of practical utility to lawyers in the present day, but also illustrative of almost every branch of history, while for certain philological purposes they hold a position absolutely unique. The history of the constitution and of the law, of procedure, and of practice, the jurisdiction of the various Courts, and their relation to one another, as well as to the Sovereign and Council, cannot be known without the aid of the Year Books.

32. Narratives of the Expulsion of the English from Normandy 1449–1450. —Robertus Blondelli de Reductione Normanniæ: Le Recouvrement de Normendie, par Berry, Hérault du Roy: Conferences between the Ambassadors of France and England. *Edited, from MSS. in the Imperial Library at Paris, by* the Rev. Joseph Stevenson, M.A., of University College, Durham. 1863.

This volume contains the narrative of an eye-witness who details with considerable power and minuteness the circumstances which attended the final expulsion of the English from Normandy in 1450. Commencing with the infringement of the truce by the capture of Fougères, and ending with the battle of Formigny and the embarkation of the Duke of Somerset. The period embraced is less than two years.

33. Historia et Cartularium Monasterii S. Petri Gloucestriæ. Vols. I., II., and III. *Edited by* W. H. Hart, Esq., F.S.A., Membre correspondant de la Société des Antiquaires de Normandie. 1863–1867.

This work consists of two parts, the History and the Cartulary of the Monastery of St. Peter, Gloucester. The history furnishes an account of the monastery from its foundation, in the year 681, to the early part of the reign of Richard II., together with a calendar of donations and benefactions. It treats principally of the affairs of the monastery, but occasionally matters of general history are introduced. Its authorship has generally been assigned to Walter Froucester the twentieth abbot, but without any foundation.

34. Alexandri Neckam de Naturis Rerum libri duo; with Neckam's Poem, De Laudibus Divinæ Sapientiæ. *Edited by* Thomas Wright, Esq., M.A., 1863.

Neckam was a man who devoted himself to science, such as it was in the twelfth century. In the "De Naturis Rerum" are to be found what may be called the rudiments of many sciences mixed up with much error and ignorance. Neckam was not thought infallible, even by his contemporaries, for Roger Bacon remarks of him, "This Alexander in many things wrote what was "true and useful; but he neither can nor ought by just title to be reckoned among authorities." Neckam, however, had sufficient independence of thought to differ from some of the schoolmen who in his time considered themselves the only judges of literature. He had his own views in morals, and in giving us a glimpse of them, as well as of his other opinions, he throws much light upon the manners, customs, and general tone of thought prevalent in the twelfth century. The poem entitled "De Laudibus Divinæ Sapientiæ" appears to be a metrical paraphrase or abridgment of the "De Naturis Rerum." It is written in the elegiac metre, and it is, as a whole, above the ordinary standard of mediæval Latin.

35. Leechdoms, Wortcunning, and Starcraft of Early England; being a Collection of Documents illustrating the History of Science in this Country before the Norman Conquest. Vols. I., II., and III. *Collected and edited*

by the Rev. T. OSWALD COCKAYNE, M.A., of St. John's College, Cambridge, 1864–1866.

This work illustrates not only the history of science, but the history of superstition. In addition to the information bearing directly upon the medical skill and medical faith of the times, there are many passages which incidentally throw light upon the general mode of life and ordinary diet. The volumes are interesting not only in their scientific, but also in their social aspect.

36. ANNALES MONASTICI. Vol. I.:—Annales de Margan, 1066–1232; Annales de Theokesberia, 1066–1263; Annales de Burton, 1004–1263. Vol. II.:—Annales Monasterii de Wintonia, 519–1277; Annales Monasterii de Waverleia, 1–1291. Vol. III.:—Annales Prioratus de Dunstaplia, 1–1297. Annales Monasterii de Bermundeseia, 1042–1432. Vol. IV.:—Annales Monasterii de Oseneia, 1016–1347; Chronicon vulgo dictum Chronicon Thomæ Wykes, 1066–1289; Annales Prioratus de Wigornia, 1–1377. Vol. V.:—Index and Glossary. *Edited by* HENRY RICHARDS LUARD, M.A., Fellow and Assistant Tutor of Trinity College, and Registrary of the University, Cambridge. 1864–1869.

The present collection of Monastic Annals embraces all the more important chronicles compiled in religious houses in England during the thirteenth century. These distinct works are ten in number. The extreme period which they embrace ranges from the year 1 to 1432, although they refer more especially to the reigns of John, Henry III., and Edward I. Some of these narratives have already appeared in print, but others are printed for the first time.

37. MAGNA VITA S. HUGONIS EPISCOPI LINCOLNIENSIS. From MSS. in the Bodleian Library, Oxford, and the Imperial Library, Paris. *Edited by* the Rev. JAMES F. DIMOCK, M.A., Rector of Barnburgh, Yorkshire. 1864.

This work contains a number of very curious and interesting incidents, and being the work of a contemporary, is very valuable, not only as a truthful biography of a celebrated ecclesiastic but as the work of a man, who, from personal knowledge, gives notices of passing events, as well as of individuals who were then taking active part in public affairs. The author, in all probability, was Adam Abbot of Evesham. He was domestic chaplain and private confessor of Bishop Hugh, and in these capacities was admitted to the closest intimacy. Bishop Hugh was Prior of Witham for 11 years before he became Bishop of Lincoln. His consecration took place on the 21st September 1186; he died on the 16th of November 1200; and was canonized in 1220.

38. CHRONICLES AND MEMORIALS OF THE REIGN OF RICHARD THE FIRST. Vol. I.:—ITINERARIUM PEREGRINORUM ET GESTA REGIS RICARDI. Vol. II.:—EPISTOLÆ CANTUARIENSES; the Letters of the Prior and Convent of Christ Church, Canterbury; 1187 to 1199. *Edited by* WILLIAM STUBBS, M.A., Vicar of Navestock, Essex, and Lambeth Librarian. 1864–1865.

The authorship of the Chronicle in Vol. I., hitherto ascribed to Geoffrey Vinesauf, is now more correctly ascribed to Richard, Canon of the Holy Trinity of London. The narrative extends from 1187 to 1199; but its chief interest consists in the minute and authentic narrative which it furnishes of the exploits of Richard I., from his departure from England in December 1189 to his death in 1199. The author states in his prologue that he was an eye-witness of much that he records; and various incidental circumstances which occur in the course of the narrative confirm this assertion.

The letters in Vol. II., written between 1187 and 1199, are of value as furnishing authentic materials for the history of the ecclesiastical condition of England during the reign of Richard I. They had their origin in a dispute which arose from the attempts of Baldwin and Hubert, archbishops of Canterbury, to found a college of secular canons, a project which gave great umbrage to the monks of Canterbury, who saw in it a design to supplant them in their function of metropolitan chapter. These letters are printed, for the first time, from a MS. belonging to the archiepiscopal library at Lambeth.

39. RECUEIL DES CRONIQUES ET ANCHIENNES ISTORIES DE LA GRANT BRETAIGNE A PRESENT NOMME ENGLETERRE, par JEHAN DE WAURIN. Vol. I. Albina to 688. Vol. II., 1399–1422. Vol. III., 1422–1431. *Edited by* Sir WILLIAM HARDY, F.S.A. 1864–1879. Vol. IV. 1431–1443. *Edited by* Sir WILLIAM HARDY, F.S.A., and EDWARD L. C. P. HARDY, Esq., F.S.A. 1884.

40. A COLLECTION OF THE CHRONICLES AND ANCIENT HISTORIES OF GREAT BRITAIN, NOW CALLED ENGLAND, by JOHN DE WAVRIN. Albina to 688. (Translation of the preceding Vols. I. and II.) *Edited and translated by* Sir WILLIAM HARDY, F.S.A., and EDWARD L. C. P. HARDY, Esq., F.S.A. 1864–1887.

This curious chronicle extends from the fabulous period of history down to the return of Edward IV. to England in the year 1471 after the second deposition of Henry VI. The manuscript from which the text of the work is taken is preserved in the Imperial Library at Paris, and is believed to be the only complete and nearly contemporary copy in existence. It is illustrated with exquisite miniatures, vignettes, and initial letters. It was written towards the end of the fifteenth century, having been expressly executed for Louis de Bruges, Seigneur de la Gruthuyse and Earl of Winchester, from whose cabinet it passed into the library of Louis XII. at Blois.

41. Polychronicon Ranulphi Higden, with Trevisa's Translation. Vols. I. and II. *Edited by* Churchill Babington, B.D., Senior Fellow of St. John's College, Cambridge. Vols. III., IV., V., VI., VII., VIII., and IX. *Edited by* the Rev. Joseph Rawson Lumby, D.D., Norrisian Professor of Divinity, Vicar of St. Edward's, Fellow of St. Catharine's College, and late Fellow of Magdalene College, Cambridge. 1865–1886.

This is one of the many mediæval chronicles which assume the character of a history of the world. It begins with the creation, and is brought down to the author's own time, the reign of Edward III. Prefixed to the historical portion, is a chapter devoted to geography, in which is given a description of every known land. To say that the Polychronicon was written in the fourteenth century is to say that it is not free from inaccuracies. It has, however, a value apart from its intrinsic merits. It enables us to form a very fair estimate of the knowledge of history and geography which well-informed readers of the fourteenth and fifteenth centuries possessed, for it was then the standard work on general history.

The two English translations, which are printed with the original Latin, afford interesting illustrations of the gradual change of our language, for one was made in the fourteenth century, the other in the fifteenth. The differences between Trevisa's version and that of the unknown writer are often considerable.

42. Le Livere de Reis de Brittanie e Le Livere de Reis de Engletere. *Edited by* John Glover, M.A., Vicar of Brading, Isle of Wight, formerly Librarian of Trinity College, Cambridge. 1865.

These two treatises, though they cannot rank as independent narratives, are nevertheless valuable as careful abstracts of previous historians, especially "Le Livere de Reis de Engletere." Some various readings are given which are interesting to the philologist as instances of semi-Saxonized French. It is supposed that Peter of Ickham was the supposed author.

43. Chronica Monasterii de Melsa ab Anno 1150 usque ad Annum 1406. Vols. I., II., and III. *Edited by* Edward Augustus Bond, Esq., Assistant-Keeper of Manuscripts, and Egerton Librarian, British Museum. 1866–1868.

The Abbey of Meaux was a Cistercian house, and the work of its abbot is both curious and valuable. It is a faithful and often minute record of the establishment of a religious community, of its progress in forming an ample revenue, of its struggles to maintain its acquisitions, and of its relations to the governing institutions of the country. In addition to the private affairs of the monastery, some light is thrown upon the public events of the time, which are however kept distinct, and appear at the end of the history of each abbot's administration. The text has been printed from what is said to be the autograph of the original compiler, Thomas de Burton, the nineteenth abbot.

44. Matthæi Parisiensis Historia Anglorum, sive, ut vulgo dicitur, Historia Minor. Vols. I., II., and III. 1067–1253. *Edited by* Sir Frederic Madden, K.H., Keeper of the Manuscript Department of British Museum. 1866–1869.

The exact date at which this work was written is, according to the chronicler, 1250. The history is of considerable value as an illustration of the period during which the author lived, and contains a good summary of the events which followed the Conquest. This minor chronicle is, however, based on another work (also written by Matthew Paris) giving fuller details, which has been called the "Historia Major." The chronicle here published, nevertheless, gives some information not to be found in the greater history.

45. Liber Monasterii de Hyda: a Chronicle and Chartulary of Hyde Abbey, Winchester, 455–1023. *Edited, from a Manuscript in the Library of the Earl of Macclesfield, by* Edward Edwards, Esq. 1866.

The "Book of Hyde" is a compilation from much earlier sources which are usually indicated with considerable care and precision. In many cases, however, the Hyde Chronicler appears to correct, to qualify, or to amplify—either from tradition or from sources of information not now discoverable—the statements, which, in substance, he adopts. He also mentions, and frequently quotes from writers whose works are either entirely lost or at present known only by fragments.

There is to be found, in the "Book of Hyde," much information relating to the reign of King Alfred which is not known to exist elsewhere. The volume contains some curious specimens of Anglo-Saxon and Mediæval English.

46. Chronicon Scotorum: a Chronicle of Irish Affairs, from the Earliest Times to 1135; and Supplement, containing the Events from 1141 to 1150. *Edited, with Translation, by* William Maunsell Hennessy, Esq. M.R.I.A. 1866.

There is, in this volume, a legendary account of the peopling of Ireland and of the adventures which befell the various heroes who are said to have been connected with Irish history. The details are, however, very meagre both for this period and for the time when history becomes more authentic. The plan adopted in the chronicle gives the appearance of an accuracy to which the earlier portions of the work cannot have any claim. The succession of events is marked year by year, from A.M. 1599 to A.D. 1150. The principal events narrated in the later portion of the work are, the invasions of foreigners, and the wars of the Irish among themselves. The text has been printed from a MS. preserved in the library of Trinity College, Dublin, written partly in Latin, partly in Irish.

47. THE CHRONICLE OF PIERRE DE LANGTOFT, IN FRENCH VERSE, FROM THE EARLIEST PERIOD TO THE DEATH OF EDWARD I. Vols. I. and II. *Edited by* THOMAS WRIGHT, Esq., M.A. 1866–1868.

It is probable that Pierre de Langtoft was a canon of Bridlington, in Yorkshire, and lived in the reign of Edward I., and during a portion of the reign of Edward II. This chronicle is divided into three parts; in the first, is an abridgment of Geoffrey of Monmouth's "Historia Britonum;" in the second, a history of the Anglo-Saxon and Norman kings, to the death of Henry III.; in the third, a history of the reign of Edward I. The principal object of the work was apparently to show the justice of Edward's Scottish wars. The language is singularly corrupt, and a curious specimen of the French of Yorkshire.

48. THE WAR OF THE GAEDHIL WITH THE GAILL, or THE INVASIONS OF IRELAND BY THE DANES AND OTHER NORSEMEN. *Edited, with a Translation, by* JAMES HENTHORN TODD, D.D., Senior Fellow of Trinity College, and Regius Professor of Hebrew in the University, Dublin. 1867.

The work in its present form, in the editor's opinion, is a comparatively modern version of an undoubtedly ancient original. That it was compiled from contemporary materials has been proved by curious incidental evidence. It is stated in the account given of the battle of Clontarf that the full tide in Dublin Bay on the day of the battle (23 April 1014) coincided with sunrise; and that the returning tide in the evening aided considerably in the defeat of the Danes. The fact has been verified by astronomical calculations, and the inference is that the author of the chronicle, if not an eye-witness, must have derived his information from eye-witnesses. The contents of the work are sufficiently described in its title. The story is told after the manner of the Scandinavian Sagas, with poems and fragments of poems introduced into the prose narrative.

49. GESTA REGIS HENRICI SECUNDI BENEDICTI ABBATIS. CHRONICLE OF THE REIGNS OF HENRY II. AND RICHARD I., 1169–1192, known under the name of BENEDICT OF PETERBOROUGH. Vols. I. and II. *Edited by* WILLIAM STUBBS, M.A., Regius Professor of Modern History, Oxford, and Lambeth Librarian. 1867.

This chronicle of the reigns of Henry II. and Richard I., known commonly under the name of Benedict of Peterborough, is one of the best existing specimens of a class of historical compositions of the first importance to the student.

50. MUNIMENTA ACADEMICA, OR, DOCUMENTS ILLUSTRATIVE OF ACADEMICAL LIFE AND STUDIES AT OXFORD (in Two Parts). *Edited by* the Rev. HENRY ANSTEY, M.A., Vicar of St. Wendron, Cornwall, and lately Vice-Principal of St. Mary Hall, Oxford. 1868.

This work will supply materials for a History of Academical Life and Studies in the University of Oxford during the 13th, 14th, and 15th centuries.

51. CHRONICA MAGISTRI ROGERI DE HOUEDENE. Vols. I., II., III., and IV. *Edited by* WILLIAM STUBBS, M.A., Regius Professor of Modern History, and Fellow of Oriel College, Oxford. 1868–1871.

This work has long been justly celebrated, but not thoroughly understood until Mr. Stubbs' edition. The earlier portion, extending from 732 to 1148, appears to be a copy of a compilation made in Northumbria about 1161, to which Hoveden added little. From 1148 to 1169—a very valuable portion of this work—the matter is derived from another source, to which Hoveden appears to have supplied little, and not always judiciously. From 1170 to 1192 is the portion which corresponds with the Chronicle known under the name of Benedict of Peterborough (*see* No. 49): but it is not a copy, being sometimes an abridgment, at others a paraphrase; occasionally the two works entirely agree; showing that both writers had access to the same materials, but dealt with them differently. From 1192 to 1201 may be said to be wholly Hoveden's work; it is extremely valuable, and an authority of the first importance.

52. WILLELMI MALMESBIRIENSIS MONACHI DE GESTIS PONTIFICUM ANGLORUM LIBRI QUINQUE. *Edited by* N. E. S. A. HAMILTON, Esq., of the Department of Manuscripts, British Museum. 1870.

William of Malmesbury's "Gesta Pontificum" is the principal foundation of English Ecclesiastical Biography, down to the year 1122. The manuscript which has been followed in this Edition is supposed by Mr. Hamilton to be the author's autograph, containing his latest additions and amendments.

53. HISTORIC AND MUNICIPAL DOCUMENTS OF IRELAND, FROM THE ARCHIVES OF THE CITY OF DUBLIN, &c. 1172–1320. *Edited by* JOHN T. GILBERT, Esq., F.S.A., Secretary of the Public Record Office of Ireland. 1870.

A collection of original documents, elucidating mainly the history and condition of the municipal, middle, and trading classes under or in relation with the rule of England in Ireland,—a subject hitherto in almost total obscurity. Extending over the first hundred and fifty years of the Anglo-Norman settlement, the series includes charters, municipal laws and regulations, rolls of names of citizens and members of merchant-guilds, lists of commodities with their rates, correspondence, illustrations of relations between ecclesiastics and laity; together with many documents exhibiting the state of Ireland during the presence there of the Scots under Robert and Edward Bruce.

54. THE ANNALS OF LOCH CÉ. A CHRONICLE OF IRISH AFFAIRS, FROM 1041 to 1590. Vols. I. and II. *Edited, with a Translation, by* WILLIAM MAUNSELL HENNESSY, Esq., M.R.I.A. 1871.

The original of this chronicle has passed under various names. The title of "Annals of Loch Cé" was given to it by Professor O'Curry, on the ground that it was transcribed for Brian Mac Dermot, an Irish chieftain, who resided on the island in Loch Cé, in the county of Roscommon. It adds much to the materials for the civil and ecclesiastical history of Ireland; and contains many curious references to English and foreign affairs, not noticed in any other chronicle.

55. MONUMENTA JURIDICA. THE BLACK BOOK OF THE ADMIRALTY, WITH APPENDICES. Vols. I., II., III., and IV. *Edited by* SIR TRAVERS TWISS, Q.C., D.C.L. 1871–1876.

This book contains the ancient ordinances and laws relating to the navy, and was probably compiled for the use of the Lord High Admiral of England. Selden calls it the "jewel of the Admiralty Records." Prynne ascribes to the Black Book the same authority in the Admiralty as the Black and Red Books have in the Court of Exchequer, and most English writers on maritime law recognize its importance.

56. MEMORIALS OF THE REIGN OF HENRY VI.:—OFFICIAL CORRESPONDENCE OF THOMAS BEKYNTON, SECRETARY TO HENRY VI., AND BISHOP OF BATH AND WELLS. *Edited, from a MS. in the Archiepiscopal Library at Lambeth, with an Appendix of Illustrative Documents, by* the Rev. GEORGE WILLIAMS, B.D., Vicar of Ringwood, late Fellow of King's College, Cambridge. Vols. I. and II. 1872.

These curious volumes are of a miscellaneous character, and were probably compiled under the immediate direction of Beckynton before he had attained to the Episcopate. They contain many of the Bishop's own letters, and several written by him in the King's name; also letters to himself while Royal Secretary, and others addressed to the King.

57. MATTHÆI PARISIENSIS, MONACHI SANCTI ALBANI, CHRONICA MAJORA. Vol. I. The Creation to A.D. 1066. Vol. II. A.D. 1067 to A.D. 1216. Vol. III. A.D. 1216 to A.D. 1239. Vol. IV. A.D. 1240 to A.D. 1247. Vol. V. A.D. 1248 to A.D. 1259. Vol. VI. Additamenta. Vol. VII. Index. *Edited by* HENRY RICHARDS LUARD, D.D., Fellow of Trinity College, Registrary of the University, and Vicar of Great St. Mary's, Cambridge. 1872–1884.

This work contains the "Chronica Majora" of Matthew Paris, one of the most valuable and frequently consulted of the ancient English Chronicles. It is published from its commencement, for the first time. The editions by Archbishop Parker, and William Watts, severally begin at the Norman Conquest.

58. MEMORIALE FRATRIS WALTERI DE COVENTRIA.—THE HISTORICAL COLLECTIONS OF WALTER OF COVENTRY. Vols. I. and II. *Edited, from the MS. in the Library of Corpus Christi College, Cambridge, by* WILLIAM STUBBS, M.A., Regius Professor of Modern History, and Fellow of Oriel College, Oxford. 1872–1873.

This work, now printed in full for the first time, has long been a desideratum by Historical Scholars. The first portion, however, is not of much importance, being only a compilation from earlier writers. The part relating to the first quarter of the thirteenth century is the most valuable and interesting.

59. THE ANGLO-LATIN SATIRICAL POETS AND EPIGRAMMATISTS OF THE TWELFTH CENTURY. Vols. I. and II. *Collected and edited by* THOMAS WRIGHT, Esq., M.A., Corresponding Member of the National Institute of France (Académie des Inscriptions et Belles-Lettres). 1872.

The Poems contained in these volumes have long been known and appreciated as the best satires of the age in which their authors flourished, and were deservedly popular during the 13th and 14th centuries.

60. MATERIALS FOR A HISTORY OF THE REIGN OF HENRY VII., FROM ORIGINAL DOCUMENTS PRESERVED IN THE PUBLIC RECORD OFFICE. Vols. I. and II. *Edited by* the Rev. WILLIAM CAMPBELL, M.A., one of Her Majesty's Inspectors of Schools. 1873–1877.

These volumes are valuable as illustrating the acts and proceedings of Henry VII. on ascending the throne, and shadow out the policy he afterwards adopted.

61. HISTORICAL PAPERS AND LETTERS FROM THE NORTHERN REGISTERS. *Edited by* JAMES RAINE, M.A., Canon of York, and Secretary of the Surtees Society. 1873.

The documents in this volume illustrate, for the most part, the general history of the north of England, particularly in its relation to Scotland.

62. REGISTRUM PALATINUM DUNELMENSE. THE REGISTER OF RICHARD DE KELLAWE, LORD PALATINE AND BISHOP OF DURHAM; 1311–1316. Vols. I., II., III., and IV. *Edited by* Sir THOMAS DUFFUS HARDY, D.C.L., Deputy Keeper of the Public Records. 1873–1878.

Bishop Kellawe's Register contains the proceedings of his prelacy, both lay and ecclesiastical, and is the earliest Register of the Palatinate of Durham.

63. Memorials of Saint Dunstan, Archbishop of Canterbury. *Edited by* William Stubbs, M.A., Regius Professor of Modern History, and Fellow of Oriel College, Oxford. 1874.

This volume contains several lives of Archbishop Dunstan, opening various points of Historical and Literary interest.

64. Chronicon Angliæ, ab Anno Domini 1328 usque ad Annum 1388, Auctore Monacho quodam Sancti Albani. *Edited by* Edward Maunde Thompson, Esq., Barrister-at-Law, and Assistant-Keeper of the Manuscripts in the British Museum. 1874.

This chronicle gives a circumstantial history of the close of the reign of Edward III.

65. Thómas Saga Erkibyskups. A Life of Archbishop Thomas Becket, in Icelandic. Vols. I. and II. *Edited, with English Translation, Notes, and Glossary by* M. Eiríkr Magnússon, M.A., Sub-Librarian of the University Library, Cambridge. 1875–1884.

This work is derived from the Life of Becket written by Benedict of Peterborough, and apparently supplies the missing portions in Benedict's biography.

66. Radulphi de Coggeshall Chronicon Anglicanum *Edited by* the Rev. Joseph Stevenson, M.A. 1875.

This volume contains the "Chronicon Anglicanum," by Ralph of Coggleshall, the "Libellus de Expugnatione Terræ Sanctæ per Saladinum," usually ascribed to the same author, and other pieces of an interesting character.

67. Materials for the History of Thomas Becket, Archbishop of Canterbury. Vols. I., II., III., IV., V., and VI. *Edited by* the Rev. James Craigie Robertson, M.A., Canon of Canterbury. 1875–1883. Vol. VII. *Edited by* Joseph Brigstocke Sheppard, Esq., LL.D. 1885.

This publication comprises all contemporary materials for the history of Archbishop Thomas Becket. The first volume contains the life of that celebrated man, and the miracles after his death, by William, a monk of Canterbury. The second, the life by Benedict of Peterborough; John of Salisbury; Alan of Tewkesbury; and Edward Grim. The third, the life by William Fitzstephen; and Herbert of Bosham. The fourth, anonymous lives, Quadrilogus, &c. The fifth, sixth, and seventh, the Epistles, and known letters.

68. Radulfi de Diceto Decani Lundoniensis Opera Historica. The Historical Works of Master Ralph de Diceto, Dean of London. Vols. I. and II. *Edited, from the Original Manuscripts, by* William Stubbs, M.A., Regius Professor of Modern History, and Fellow of Oriel College, Oxford. 1876.

The Historical Works of Ralph de Diceto are some of the most valuable materials for British History. The Abbreviationes Chronicorum extend from the Creation to 1147, and the Ymagines Historiarum to 1201.

69. Roll of the Proceedings of the King's Council in Ireland, for a Portion of the 16th Year of the Reign of Richard II. 1392–93. *Edited by* the Rev. James Graves, A.B. 1877.

This Roll throws considerable light on the History of Ireland at a period little known. It seems the only document of the kind extant.

70. Henrici de Bracton de Legibus et Consuetudinibus Angliæ Libri Quinque in Varios Tractatus Distincti. Ad Diversorum et Vetustissimorum Codicum Collationem Typis Vulgati. Vols. I., II., III., IV., V., and VI. *Edited by* Sir Travers Twiss, Q.C., D.C.L. 1878–1883.

This is a new edition of Bracton's celebrated work, collated with MSS. in the British Museum; the Libraries of Lincoln's Inn, Middle Temple, and Gray's Inn; Bodleian Library, Oxford; the Bibliothèque Nationale, Paris; &c.

71. The Historians of the Church of York, and its Archbishops. Vols. I. and II. *Edited by* James Raine, M.A., Canon of York, and Secretary of the Surtees Society. 1879–1886.

This will form a complete "Corpus Historicum Eboracense," a work very much needed.

72. Registrum Malmesburiense. The Register of Malmesbury Abbey; Preserved in the Public Record Office. Vols. I. and II. *Edited by* J. S. Brewer, M.A., Preacher at the Rolls, and Rector of Toppesfield; *and* Charles Trice Martin, Esq., B.A. 1879, 1880.

This work illustrates many curious points of history, the growth of society, the distribution of land, the relations of landlord and tenant, national customs, &c.

73. Historical Works of Gervase of Canterbury. Vols. I. and II. The Chronicle of the Reigns of Stephen, Henry II., and Richard I., by Gervase, the Monk of Canterbury. *Edited by* William Stubbs, D.D.; Canon Residentiary of St. Paul's, London; Regius Professor of Modern History and Fellow of Oriel College, Oxford; &c. 1879, 1880.

The Historical Works of Gervase of Canterbury are of great importance as regards the questions of Church and State, during the period in which he wrote. This work was printed by Twysden, in the "Historiæ Anglicanæ Scriptores X.," more than two centuries ago.

74. Henrici Archidiaconi Huntendunensis Historia Anglorum. The History of the English, by Henry, Archdeacon of Huntingdon, from A.D. 55 to A.D. 1154, in Eight Books. *Edited by* Thomas Arnold, Esq., M.A., of University College, Oxford. 1879.

Henry of Huntingdon's work was first printed by Sir Henry Savile, in 1596, in his "Scriptores post Bedam," and reprinted at Frankfort in 1601. Both editions are very rare and inaccurate. The first five books of the History were published in 1848 in the "Monumenta Historica Britannica," which is out of print. The present volume contains the whole of the manuscript of Huntingdon's History in eight books, collated with a manuscript lately discovered at Paris.

75. The Historical Works of Symeon of Durham. Vols. I. and II. *Edited by* Thomas Arnold, Esq., M.A., of University College, Oxford 1882–1885.

The first volume of this edition of the Historical Works of Symeon of Durham, contains the "Historia Dunelmensis Ecclesiæ," and other Works. The second volume contains the "Historia Regum," &c.

76. Chronicles of the Reigns of Edward I. and Edward II. Vols. I. and II. *Edited by* William Stubbs, D.D., Canon Residentiary of St. Paul's, London; Regius Professor of Modern History, and Fellow of Oriel College, Oxford, &c. 1882, 1883.

The first volume of these Chronicles contains the "Annales Londonienses" and the "Annales Paulini:" the second, I.—Commendatio Lamentabilis in Transitu magni Regis Edwardi. II.—Gesta Edwardi de Carnarvan Auctore Canonico Bridlingtoniensi. III.—Monachi cujusdam Malmesberiensis Vita, Edwardi II. IV.—Vita et Mors Edwardi II. Conscripta a Thoma de la Moore.

77. Registrum Epistolarum Fratris Johannis Peckham, Archiepiscopi Cantuariensis. Vols. I., II., and III. *Edited by* Charles Trice Martin, Esq., B.A., F.S.A., 1882–1886.

These Letters are of great value for illustrating English Ecclesiastical History.

78. Register of S. Osmund. *Edited by* the Rev. W. H. Rich Jones, M.A., F.S.A., Canon of Salisbury, Vicar of Bradford-on-Avon. Vols. I. and II. 1883, 1884.

This Register, of which a complete copy is here printed for the first time, is among the most ancient of the muniments of the Bishops of Salisbury. It derives its name from containing the statutes, rules, and orders made or compiled by S. Osmund, to be observed in the Cathedral and diocese of Salisbury. The first 19 folios contain the "Consuetudinary," the exposition, as regards ritual, of the "Use of Sarum."

79. Chartulary of the Abbey of Ramsey. Vols. I. and II. *Edited by* William Henry Hart, Esq., F.S.A., and the Rev. Ponsonby Annesley Lyons. 1884, 1886.

This Chartulary of the Ancient Benedictine Monastery of Ramsey, Huntingdonshire, came to the Crown on the Dissolution of Monasteries, was afterwards preserved in the Stone Tower, Westminster Hall, and thence transferred to the Public Record Office.

80. Chartularies of St. Mary's Abbey, Dublin, with the Register of its house at Dunbrody, County of Wexford, and Annals of Ireland, 1162–1370. *Edited by* John Thomas Gilbert, Esq., F.S.A., M.R.I.A. Vols. I. & II. 1884, 1885.

The Chartularies and register, here printed for the first time, are the only surviving manuscripts of their class in connexion with the Cistercians in Ireland. With them are included accounts of the other establishments of the Cistercian Order in Ireland. together with the earliest body of Anglo-Irish Annals extant.

81. Eadmeri Historia Novorum in Anglia, et opuscula duo de Vita Sancti Anselmi et quibusdam Miraculis ejus. *Edited by* the Rev. Martin Rule, M.A. 1884.

This volume contains the "Historiæ Novorum in Anglia," of Eadmer; his treatise "De Vita et conversatione Anselmi Archiepiscopi Cantuariensis," and a Tract entitled "Quaedam Parva Descriptio Miraculorum gloriosi Patris Anselmi Cantuariensis."

82. Chronicles of the Reigns of Stephen, Henry II., and Richard I. Vols. I. II., and III., *Edited by* Richard Howlett, Esq., of the Middle Temple, Barrister-at-law. 1884–1886.

Vol. I. contains Books I.–IV. of the "Historia Rerum Anglicarum" of William of Newburgh. Vol. II. contains Book V. of that work, the continuation of the same to A.D. 1298, and the "Draco Normannicus" of Etienne de Rouen.

Vol. III. contains the "Gesta Stephani Regis," the Chronicle of Richard of Hexham, the "Relatio de Standardo" of St. Aelred of Rievaulx, the poem of Jordan Fantosme, and the Chronicle of Richard of Devizes.

83. CHRONICLE OF THE ABBEY OF RAMSEY. *Edited by* the Rev. WILLIAM DUNN MACRAY, M.A., F.S.A., Rector of Ducklington, Oxon. 1886.

This Chronicle forms part of the Chartulary of the Abbey of Ramsey, preserved in the Public Record Office (*see* No. 79).

84. CHRONICA ROGERI DE WENDOVER, SIVE FLORES HISTORIARUM. Vols. I. and II. *Edited by* HENRY GAY HEWLETT, Esq., Keeper of the Records of the Land Revenue. 1886–1887.

This edition gives that portion only of Roger of Wendover's Chronicle which can be accounted an original authority.

85. THE LETTER BOOKS OF THE MONASTERY OF CHRIST CHURCH, CANTERBURY. *Edited by* JOSEPH BRIGSTOCKE SHEPPARD, Esq., LL.D. Vols. I. and II., 1887, 1888.

The Letters printed in these volumes were chiefly written between the years 1296 and 1333. Among the most notable writers were Prior Henry of Eastry, Prior Richard Oxenden, and the Archbishops Raynold and Meopham.

86. THE METRICAL CHRONICLE OF ROBERT OF GLOUCESTER. *Edited by* WILLIAM ALDIS WRIGHT, Esq., M.A. Parts I. and II., 1887.

The date of the composition of this Chronicle is placed about the year 1300. The writer appears to have been an eye witness of many events which he describes. The language in which it is written was the dialect of Gloucestershire at that time.

87. CHRONICLE OF ROBERT OF BRUNNE. *Edited by* FREDERICK JAMES FURNIVALL, Esq., M.A., of Trinity Hall, Cambridge, Barrister-at-Law. Parts I and II. 1887.

Robert of Brunne, or Bourne, co. Lincoln, was a member of the Gilbertine Order established at Sempringham. His Chronicle is described by its editor as a work of fiction, a contribution not to English history, but to the history of English.

88. ICELANDIC SAGAS AND OTHER HISTORICAL DOCUMENTS relating to the Settlements and Descents of the Northmen on the British Isles. Vol. 1. Orkneyinga Saga, and Magnus Saga. Vol. II. Hakonar Saga, and Magnus Saga. *Edited by* M. GUDBRAND VIGFUSSON, M.A. 1887.

89. THE TRIPARTITE LIFE OF ST. PATRICK, with other documents relating to that Saint. *Edited by* WHITLEY STOKES, Esq., LL.D., D.C.L., Honorary Fellow of Jesus College, Oxford; and Corresponding Member of the Institute of France. Parts I. and II. 1887.

90. WILLELMI MONACHI MALMESBIRIENSIS DE REGUM GESTIS ANGLORUM, LIBRI V.; ET HISTORIÆ NOVELLÆ, LIBRI III. *Edited by* WILLIAM STUBBS, D.D., Bishop of Chester. Vol. I. 1887.

91. LESTORIE DES ENGLES SOLUM GEFFREI GAIMAR. *Edited by* the late Sir THOMAS DUFFUS HARDY, D.C.L., Deputy Keeper of the Public Records; *continued and translated by* CHARLES TRICE MARTIN, Esq., B.A., F.S.A. Vols. I. and II. 1888, 1889,

In the Press.

ICELANDIC SAGAS, AND OTHER HISTORICAL DOCUMENTS relating to the Settlements and Descents of the Northmen on the British Isles. Vols. III.—IV. *Translated by* Sir GEORGE WEBBE DASENT, D.C.L.

WILLELMI MONACHI MALMESBIRIENSIS DE REGUM GESTIS ANGLORUM, LIBRI V.; ET HISTORIÆ NOVELLÆ, LIBRI III. *Edited by* WILLIAM STUBBS, D.D., Bishop of Oxford. Vol. II.

CHARTULARY OF THE ANCIENT BENEDICTINE ABBEY OF RAMSEY, from the MS. in the Public Record Office. Vol. III. *Edited by* the late WILLIAM HENRY HART, Esq., F.S.A., and the Rev. PONSONBY ANNESLEY LYONS.

CHARTERS AND DOCUMENTS, ILLUSTRATING THE HISTORY OF THE CATHEDRAL AND CITY OF SARUM, 1100–1300; forming an Appendix to the Register of S. Osmund. Vol. III. *Edited by* the late Rev. W. H. RICH JONES, M.A., F.S.A., *and* the Rev. W. D. MACRAY, M.A., F.S.A., Rector of Ducklington.

In the Press—(continued).

FLORES HISTORIARUM, PER MATTHÆUM WESTMONASTERIENSEM COLLECTI. *Edited by* HENRY RICHARDS LUARD, D.D., Fellow of Trinity College, Registrary of the University, and Vicar of Great St. Mary's, Cambridge.

RANULF DE GLANVILL; TRACTATUS DE LEGIBUS ET CONSUETUDINIBUS ANGLIÆ, &c. *Edited and translated by* Sir TRAVERS TWISS, Q.C., D.C.L.

CHRONICLE OF ADAM MURIMUTH, with the CHRONICLE OF ROBERT OF AVESBURY. *Edited by* EDWARD MAUNDE THOMPSON, ESQ., Principal Librarian and Secretary of the British Museum.

YEAR BOOKS OF THE REIGN OF EDWARD III. *Edited and translated by* LUKE OWEN PIKE, Esq., M.A., of Lincoln's Inn, Barrister-at-Law.

CHRONICLE OF HENRY KNIGHTON, Canon of Leicester, to the death of RICHARD II. *Edited by* the Rev. JOSEPH RAWSON LUMBY, D.D.

THE LETTER BOOKS OF THE MONASTERY OF CHRIST CHURCH, CANTERBURY. *Edited by* JOSEPH BRIGSTOCKE SHEPPARD, ESQ., LL.D. Vol. III.

ANNALS OR MEMORIALS OF ST. EDMONDSBURY. *Edited by* THOMAS ARNOLD, ESQ., M.A., of University College, Oxford.

RECUEIL DES CRONIQUES ET ANCHIENNES ISTORIES DE LA GRANT BRETAIGNE A PRESENT NOMME ENGLETERRE, par JEHAN DE WAURIN. Vol. V. 1443–1461. *Edited by* the late Sir WILLIAM HARDY, F.S.A., and EDWARD L. C. P. HARDY, Esq., F.S.A., of Lincoln's Inn, Barrister-at-Law.

CHRONICLES OF THE REIGNS OF STEPHEN, HENRY II., AND RICHARD I. Vol. IV. *Edited by* RICHARD HOWLETT, Esq., of the Middle Temple, Barrister-at-Law.

CHRONICA ROGERI DE WENDOVER, SIVE FLORES HISTORIARUM. *Edited by* HENRY GAY HEWLETT, Esq., Keeper of the Records of the Land Revenue. Vol. III.

CHARTULARY OF THE ABBEY OF ST. THOMAS THE MARTYR, DUBLIN. *Edited by* JOHN THOMAS GILBERT, Esq., F.S.A., M.I.R.A.

In Progress.

DESCRIPTIVE CATALOGUE OF MANUSCRIPTS RELATING TO THE HISTORY OF GREAT BRITAIN AND IRELAND. Vol. IV.; 1327, &c. *Edited by* the late Sir THOMAS DUFFUS HARDY, D.C.L., Deputy Keeper of the Records, and C. TRICE MARTIN, Esq., B.A., F.S.A.

THE TREATISE "DE PRINCIPUM INSTRUCTIONE," of GIRALDUS CAMBRENSIS; with an Index to the first four volumes of the "Works of Giraldus Cambrensis," edited by the Rev. J. S. Brewer. *Edited by* GEORGE F. WARNER, Esq., of the Department of MSS., British Museum.

THE RED BOOK OF THE EXCHEQUER, preserved in the Public Record Office. *Edited by* WALFORD DAKING SELBY, Esq., of the Public Record Office.

THE HISTORIANS OF THE CHURCH OF YORK AND ITS ARCHBISHOPS, Vol. III. *Edited by* JAMES RAINE, M.A., Canon of York, and Secretary of the Surtees Society.

PUBLICATIONS OF THE RECORD COMMISSIONERS, &c.

[In boards or cloth.]

ROTULORUM ORIGINALIUM IN CURIÂ SCACCARII ABBREVIATIO. Hen. III.—Edw. III. *Edited by* HENRY PLAYFORD, Esq. 2 Vols. folio (1805—1810). 12*s.* 6*d.* each.

CALENDARIUM INQUISITIONUM POST MORTEM SIVE ESCAETARUM. Hen. III.—Ric. III. *Edited by* JOHN CALEY and JOHN BAYLEY, Esqrs. Folio (1821—1828): Vol. 3, 21*s.*; Vol. 4, 24*s.*

LIBRORUM MANUSCRIPTORUM BIBLIOTHECÆ HARLEIANÆ CATALOGUS. Vol. 4. *Edited by* the Rev. T. HARTWELL HORNE. Folio (1812), 18*s.*

ABBREVIATIO PLACITORUM. Richard I.—Edward II. *Edited by* the Right Hon. GEORGE ROSE and W. ILLINGWORTH, Esq. 1 Vol. folio (1811), 18*s.*

LIBRI CENSUALIS vocati DOMESDAY-BOOK, INDICES. *Edited by* Sir HENRY ELLIS. Folio (1816), (Domesday-Book, Vol. 3). 21*s.*

LIBRI CENSUALIS vocati DOMESDAY-BOOK, ADDITAMENTA EX CODIC. ANTIQUISS. *Edited by* Sir HENRY ELLIS. Folio (1816), (Domesday-Book, Vol. 4). 21*s.*

STATUTES OF THE REALM. *Edited by* Sir T. E. TOMLINS, JOHN RAITHBY, JOHN CALEY, and WM. ELLIOTT, Esqrs. Vols. 7, 8, 9, 10, and 11, folio (1819—1828). 31*s.* 6*d.* each; Indices, 30*s.* each.

VALOR ECCLESIASTICUS, temp. Hen. VIII., Auctoritate Regia institutus. *Edited by* JOHN CALEY, Esq., and the Rev. JOSEPH HUNTER. Vols. 3 to 6, folio (1817-1834). 25*s.* each. The Introduction, separately, 8vo. 2*s.* 6*d.*

ROTULI SCOTIÆ IN TURRI LONDINENSI ET IN DOMO CAPITULARI WESTMONASTERIENS ASSERVATI. 19 Edw. I.—Hen. VIII. *Edited by* D. MACPHERSON, J. CALEY, W. ILLINGWORTH, Esqrs., and Rev. T. H. HORNE. Vol. 2. folio (1818). 21*s.*

FŒDERA, CONVENTIONES, LITTERÆ, &c.; or, RYMER'S FŒDERA, New Edition, folio Vol. 3, Part 2. 1361—1377 (1830): Vol. 4, 1377—1383 (1869). *Edited by* JOHN CALEY and FRED. HOLBROOKE, Esqrs. Vol. 3, Part 2, 21*s.*; Vol. 4. 6*s.*

DUCATUS LANCASTRIÆ CALENDARIUM INQUISITIONUM POST MORTEM, &c. Part 3, Calendar to Pleadings, &c., Hen. VII.—13 Eliz. Part 4, Calendar to Pleadings, to end of Eliz. (1827—1834). *Edited by* R. J. HARPER, JOHN CALEY, and WM. MINCHIN, Esqrs. Folio. Part 3 (or Vol. 2), 31*s.* 6*d.*; Part 4 (or Vol. 3), 21*s.*

CALENDARS OF THE PROCEEDINGS IN CHANCERY, ELIZ.; with Examples of Proceedings from Ric. II. *Edited by* JOHN BAYLEY, Esq. Vol. 3 (1832), folio, 21*s.*

PARLIAMENTARY WRITS AND WRITS OF MILITARY SUMMONS, with Records and Muniments relating to Suit and Service to Parliament, &c. *Edited by* SIR FRANCIS PALGRAVE. (1830—1834.) Folio. Vol. 2, Div. 1, Edw. II., 21*s.*; Vol. 2, Div. 2, 21*s.*; Vol. 2, Div. 3, 42*s.*

ROTULI LITTERARUM CLAUSARUM IN TURRI LONDINENSI ASSERVATI. 2 Vols. folio (1833, 1844). Vol. 1, 1204-1224. Vol. 2, 1224—1227. *Edited by* THOMAS DUFFUS HARDY, Esq. Vol. 1, 63*s.*; Vol. 2, 18*s.*

PROCEEDINGS AND ORDINANCES OF THE PRIVY COUNCIL OF ENGLAND. 10 Ric. II.—33 Hen. VIII. *Edited by* Sir NICHOLAS HARRIS NICOLAS. 7 Vols. royal 8vo. (1834—1837). 14*s.* each.

ROTULI LITTERARUM PATENTIUM IN TURRI LOND. ASSERVATI. 1201—1216. *Edited by* T. DUFFUS HARDY, Esq. 1 Vol. folio (1835), 31*s.* 6*d.* The Introduction, separately, 8vo. 9*s.*

ROTULI CURIÆ REGIS. Rolls and Records of the Court held before the King's Justiciars or Justices. 6 Richard I.—1 John. *Edited by* Sir FRANCIS PALGRAVE. 2 Vols. royal 8vo. (1835). 28*s.*

ROTULI NORMANNIÆ IN TURRI LOND. ASSERVATI. 1200—1205; 1417—1418. *Edited by* THOMAS DUFFUS HARDY, Esq. 1 Vol. royal 8vo. (1835). 12*s.* 6*d.*

ROTULI DE OBLATIS ET FINIBUS IN TURRI LOND. ASSERVATI, temp Regis Johannis. *Edited by* THOMAS DUFFUS HARDY, Esq. 1 Vol. royal 8vo. (1835). 18*s.*

EXCERPTA E ROTULIS FINIUM IN TURRI LONDINENSI ASSERVATIS. Henry III., 1216—1272. *Edited by* CHARLES ROBERTS, Esq. 2 Vols. royal 8vo. (1835, 1836); Vol. 1, 14*s.*; Vol. 2, 18*s.*

FINES, SIVE PEDES FINIUM; SIVE FINALES CONCORDIÆ IN CURIÂ DOMINI REGIS. 7 Richard I.—16 John, 1195—1214. *Edited by* the Rev. JOSEPH HUNTER. In Counties. 2 vols. royal 8vo. (1835—1844); Vol. 1, 8*s.* 6*d.*; Vol. 2, 2*s.* 6*d.*

ANCIENT KALENDARS AND INVENTORIES OF THE TREASURY OF HIS MAJESTY'S EXCHEQUER; with Documents illustrating its History. *Edited by* Sir FRANCIS PALGRAVE. 3 Vols. royal 8vo. (1836). 42*s.*

DOCUMENTS AND RECORDS illustrating the History of Scotland, and Transactions between Scotland and England; preserved in the Treasury of Her Majesty's Exchequer. *Edited by* Sir FRANCIS PALGRAVE. 1 Vol. royal 8vo. (1837). 18*s*.

ROTULI CHARTARUM IN TURRI LONDINENSI ASSERVATI. 1199—1216. *Edited by* THOMAS DUFFUS HARDY, Esq. 1 Vol. folio (1837). 30*s*.

REPORT OF THE PROCEEDINGS OF THE RECORD COMMISSIONERS, 1831—1837. 1 Vol. fol. (1837). 8*s*.

REGISTRUM vulgariter nuncupatum "The Record of Caernarvon," e codice MS. Harleiano, 696, descriptum. *Edited by* Sir HENRY ELLIS. 1 Vol. folio (1838), 31*s*. 6*d*.

ANCIENT LAWS AND INSTITUTES OF ENGLAND; comprising Laws enacted under the Anglo-Saxon Kings, with Translation of the Saxon; the Laws called Edward the Confessor's; the Laws of William the Conqueror, and those ascribed to Henry I.; Monumenta Ecclesiastica Anglicana, from 7th to 10th century; and Ancient Latin Version of the Anglo-Saxon Laws. *Edited by* BENJAMIN THORPE, Esq. 1 Vol. folio (1840), 40*s*. 2 Vols. royal 8vo., 30*s*.

ANCIENT LAWS AND INSTITUTES OF WALES; comprising Laws supposed to be enacted by Howel the Good, modified by Regulations prior to the Conquest by Edward I.; and anomalous Laws, principally of Institutions which continued in force. With translation. Also, Latin Transcripts, containing Digests of Laws, principally of the Dimetian Code. *Edited by* ANEURIN OWEN, Esq. 1 Vol. folio (1841), 44*s*. 2 vols. royal 8vo., 36*s*.

ROTULI DE LIBERATE AC DE MISIS ET PRÆSTITIS, Regnante Johanne. *Edited by* THOMAS DUFFUS HARDY, Esq. 1 Vol. royal 8vo. (1844). 6*s*.

THE GREAT ROLLS OF THE PIPE, 2, 3, 4 HEN. II., 1155—1158. *Edited by* the Rev. JOSEPH HUNTER. 1 Vol. royal 8vo. (1844). 4*s*. 6*d*.

THE GREAT ROLL OF THE PIPE, 1 RIC. I., 1189—1190. *Edited by* the Rev. JOSEPH HUNTER. 1 Vol. royal 8vo. (1844). 6*s*.

DOCUMENTS ILLUSTRATIVE OF ENGLISH HISTORY in the 13th and 14th centuries, from the Records of the Queen's Remembrancer in the Exchequer. *Edited by* HENRY COLE, Esq. 1 Vol. fcp. folio (1844). 45*s*. 6*d*.

MODUS TENENDI PARLIAMENTUM. An Ancient Treatise on the Mode of holding the Parliament in England. *Edited by* THOMAS DUFFUS HARDY, Esq. 1 Vol. 8vo. (1846). 2*s*. 6*d*.

REGISTRUM MAGNI SIGILLI REG. SCOT. in Archivis Publicis asservatum. 1306—1424. *Edited by* THOMAS THOMSON, Esq. Folio (1814). 10*s*. 6*d*.

ACTS OF THE PARLIAMENTS OF SCOTLAND. Folio (1814—1875). *Edited by* THOMAS THOMSON and COSMO INNES, Esqrs. Vol. 1, 42*s*. Vols. 5 and 6 (in three Parts), 21*s*. each Part; Vols. 4, 7, 8, 9, 10, and 11, 10*s*. 6*d*. each; Vol. 12 (Index), 63*s*. Or, 12 Volumes in 13, 12*l*. 12*s*.

ACTS OF THE LORDS AUDITORS OF CAUSES AND COMPLAINTS (ACTA DOMINORUM AUDITORUM). 1466—1494. *Edited by* THOMAS THOMSON, Esq. Fol. (1839). 10*s*. 6*d*.

ACTS OF THE LORDS OF COUNCIL IN CIVIL CAUSES (ACTA DOMINORUM CONCILII), 1478—1495. *Edited by* THOMAS THOMSON, Esq. Folio (1839). 10*s*. 6*d*.

ISSUE ROLL OF THOMAS DE BRANTINGHAM, Bishop of Exeter, Lord High Treasurer, containing Payments out of the Revenue, 44 Edw. III., 1370. *Edited by* FREDERICK DEVON, Esq. 1 Vol. 4to. (1835), 35*s*. Or, royal 8vo., 25*s*.

ISSUES OF THE EXCHEQUER, James I.; from the Pell Records. *Edited by* FREDERICK DEVON, Esq. 1 Vol. 4to. (1836), 30*s*. Or, royal 8vo., 21*s*.

ISSUES OF THE EXCHEQUER, Henry III.—Henry VI.; from the Pell Records. *Edited by* FREDERICK DEVON, Esq. 1 Vol. 4to. (1837), 40*s*. Or, royal 8vo., 30*s*.

HANDBOOK TO THE PUBLIC RECORDS. *By* F. S. THOMAS, Esq., Secretary of the Public Record Office. 1 Vol. royal 8vo. (1853). 12*s*.

HISTORICAL NOTES RELATIVE TO THE HISTORY OF ENGLAND. Henry VIII. — Anne (1509-1714). A Book of Reference for ascertaining the Dates of Events. *By* F. S. THOMAS, Esq. 3 Vols. 8vo. (1856). 40*s*.

STATE PAPERS, DURING THE REIGN OF HENRY THE EIGHTH: with Indices of Persons and Places. 11 Vols. 4to. (1830—1852), 10*s*. 6*d*. each.

Vol. I.—Domestic Correspondence.
Vols. II. & III.—Correspondence relating to Ireland.
Vols. IV. & V.—Correspondence relating to Scotland.
Vols. VI. to XI.—Correspondence between England and Foreign Courts.

WORKS PUBLISHED IN PHOTOZINCOGRAPHY.

DOMESDAY BOOK, or the GREAT SURVEY OF ENGLAND OF WILLIAM THE CONQUEROR, 1086; fac-simile of the Part relating to each county, separately (with a few exceptions of double counties). Photozincographed, by Her Majesty's Command, at the Ordnance Survey Office, Southampton, Colonel Sir HENRY JAMES, R.E., F.R.S., &c., DIRECTOR-GENERAL of the ORDNANCE SURVEY, under the Superintendence of W. BASEVI SANDERS, Esq., Assistant Keeper of Her Majesty's Records. 35 Parts, imperial quarto and demy quarto (1861-1863), boards. *Price* 8*s*. to 1*l*. 3*s*. each Part, according to size; or, bound in 2 Vols., 20*l*. (*The edition in two volumes is out of print.*)

This important and unique survey of the greater portion of England* is the oldest and most valuable record in the national archives. It was commenced about the year 1084 and finished in 1086. Its compilation was determined upon at Gloucester by William the Conqueror, in council, in order that he might know what was due to him, in the way of tax, from his subjects, and that each at the same time might know what he had to pay. It was compiled as much for their protection as for the benefit of the sovereign. The nobility and people had been grievously distressed at the time by the king bringing over large numbers of French and Bretons, and quartering them on his subjects, "each "according to the measure of his land," for the purpose of resisting the invasion of Cnut, King of Denmark, which was apprehended. The Commissioners appointed to make the survey were to inquire the name of each place; who held it in the time of King Edward the Confessor; the present possessor; how many hides were in the manor; how many ploughs were in the demesne; how many homagers; how many villeins; how many cottars; how many serving men; how many free tenants; how many tenants in soccage; how much wood, meadow, and pasture; the number of mills and fish ponds; what had been added or taken away from the place; what was the gross value in the time of Edward the Confessor; the present value; and how much each free man or soc-man had, and whether any advance could be made in the value. Thus could be ascertained who held the estate in the time of King Edward; who then held it; its value in the time of the late King; and its value as it stood at the formation of the survey. So minute was the survey, that the writer of the contemporary portion of the Saxon Chronicle records, with some asperity—"So very narrowly he caused it to be "traced out, that there was not a single hide, nor one virgate of land, nor even, "it is shame to tell, though it seemed to him no shame to do, an ox, nor a cow, "nor a swine was left, that was not set down."

Domesday Survey is in two parts or volumes. The first, in folio, contains the counties of Bedford, Berks, Bucks, Cambridge, Chester, and Lancaster, Cornwall, Derby, Devon, Dorset, Gloucester, Hants, Hereford, Herts, Huntingdon, Kent, Leicester and Rutland, Lincoln, Middlesex, Northampton, Nottingham, Oxford, Salop, Somerset, Stafford, Surrey, Sussex, Warwick, Wilts, Worcester, and York. The second volume, in quarto, contains the counties of Essex, Norfolk and Suffolk.

Domesday Book was printed *verbatim et literatim* during the last century, in consequence of an address of the House of Lords to King George III. in 1767. It was not, however, commenced until 1773, and was completed early in 1783. In 1860, Her Majesty's Government, with the concurrence of the Master of the Rolls, determined to apply the art of photozincography to the production of a fac-simile of Domesday Book, under the superintendence of Colonel Sir Henry James, R.E., Director-General of the Ordnance Survey, Southampton. The fac-simile was completed in 1863.

---

* For some reason left unexplained, many parts were left unsurveyed; Northumberland, Cumberland, Westmoreland, and Durham, are not described in the survey; nor does Lancashire appear under its proper name; but Furness, and the northern part of Lancashire, as well as the south of Westmoreland, with a part of Cumberland, are included within the West Riding of Yorkshire. That part of Lancashire which lies between the Ribble and Mersey, and which at the time of the survey comprehended 688 manors, is joined to Cheshire. Part of Rutland is described in the counties of Northampton and Lincoln.

Fac-similes of National Manuscripts, from **William the Conqueror** to **Queen Anne**, selected under the direction of the Master of the Rolls, and Photozincographed, by Command of Her Majesty, by Colonel Sir Henry James, R.E., F.R.S., Director-General of the Ordnance Survey, and edited by W. Basevi Sanders, Assistant Keeper of Her Majesty's Records. *Price*, each Part, with translations and notes, double foolscap folio, 16*s*.

Part I. (William the Conqueror to Henry VII.). 1865. (*Out of print.*)
Part II. (Henry VIII. and Edward VI.) 1866.
Part III. (Mary and Elizabeth). 1867.
Part IV. (James I. to Anne). 1868.

The first Part extends from William the Conqueror to Henry VII., and contains autographs of the kings of England, as well as of many other illustrious personages famous in history, and some interesting charters, letters patent, and state papers. The second Part, for the reigns of Henry VIII. and Edward VI., consists principally of holograph letters, and autographs of kings, princes, statesmen, and other persons of great historical interest, who lived during those reigns. The third Part contains similar documents for the reigns of Mary and Elizabeth, including a signed bill of Lady Jane Grey. The fourth Part concludes the series, and comprises a number of documents taken from the originals belonging to the Constable of the Tower of London; also several records illustrative of the Gunpowder Plot, and a woodcut containing portraits of Mary Queen of Scots and James VI., circulated by their adherents in England, 1580–3.

Fac-similes of Anglo-Saxon Manuscripts. Photozincographed, by Command of Her Majesty, upon the recommendation of the Master of the Rolls, by the Director-General of the Ordnance Survey, Lieut.-General J. Cameron, R.E., C.B., F.R.S., and edited by W. Basevi Sanders, Assistant Keeper of Her Majesty's Records. Part I. *Price* 2*l*. 10*s*.

The Anglo-Saxon MSS. represented in this volume form the earlier portions of the collection of archives belonging to the Dean and Chapter of Canterbury, and consist of a series of 25 charters, deeds, and wills, commencing with a record of proceedings at the first Synodal Council of Clovestho in 742, and terminating with the first part of a tripartite cheirograph, whereby Thurston conveyed to the Church of Canterbury land at Wimbish in Essex, in 1049, the sixth year of the reign of Edward the Confessor.

Fac-similes of Anglo-Saxon Manuscripts. Photozincographed, by Command of Her Majesty, upon the recommendation of the Master of the Rolls, by the Director-General of the Ordnance Survey, Major-General A. Cooke, R.E., C.B., and collected and edited by W. Basevi Sanders, Assistant Keeper of Her Majesty's Records. Part II. *Price* 3*l*. 10*s*.

(Also, separately. Edward the Confessor's Charter. *Price* 2*s*.)

The originals of the Fac-similes contained in this volume belong to the Deans and Chapters of Westminster, Exeter, Wells, Winchester, and Worcester; the Marquis of Bath, the Earl of Ilchester, Winchester College, Her Majesty's Public Record Office, Bodleian Library, Somersetshire Archæological and National History Society's Museum in Taunton Castle, and William Salt Library at Stafford. They consist of charters and other documents granted by, or during the reigns of, Baldred, Æthelred, Offa, and Burgred, Kings of Mercia; Uhtred of the Huiccas, Ceadwalla and Ini of Wessex; Æthelwulf, Eadward the Elder, Æthelstan, Eadmund the First, Eadred, Eadwig, Eadgar, Eadward the Second, Æthelred the Second, Cnut, Eadward the Confessor, and William the Conqueror, embracing altogether a period of nearly four hundred years.

Fac-similes of Anglo-Saxon Manuscripts. Photozincographed, by Command of Her Majesty, upon the recommendation of the Master of the Rolls, by the Director-General of the Ordnance Survey, Colonel R. H. Stotherd, R.E., C.B., and collected and edited by W. Basevi Sanders, Assistant Keeper of Her Majesty's Records. Part III. Price 6*l*. 6*s*.

This volume contains fac-similes of the Ashburnham collection of Anglo-Saxon Charters, &c., including King Alfred's Will. The MSS. represented in it, range from A.D. 697 to A.D. 1161, being charters, wills, deeds, and reports of Synodal transactions during the reigns of Kings Wihtred of Kent, Offa, Eardwulf, Coenwulf, Cuthred, Beornwulf, Æthelwulf, Ælfred, Eadward the Elder, Eadmund, Eadred, Queen Eadgifu, and Kings Eadgar, Æthelred the Second, Cnut, Henry the First, and Henry the Second. In addition to these are two belonging to the Marquis of Anglesey, one of them being the Foundation Charter of Burton Abbey by Æthelred the Second with the testament of its great benefactor Wulfric.

Public Record Office,
January 1889.

HISTORICAL MANUSCRIPTS COMMISSION.

REPORTS OF THE ROYAL COMMISSIONERS APPOINTED TO INQUIRE WHAT PAPERS AND MANUSCRIPTS BELONGING TO PRIVATE FAMILIES AND INSTITUTIONS ARE EXTANT WHICH WOULD BE OF UTILITY IN THE ILLUSTRATION OF HISTORY, CONSTITUTIONAL LAW, SCIENCE, AND GENERAL LITERATURE.

Date.	—	Size.	Sessional Paper.	Price.
				s. *d.*
1870 (Reprinted 1874.)	FIRST REPORT, WITH APPENDIX - Contents :— ENGLAND. House of Lords; Cambridge Colleges; Abingdon, and other Corporations, &c. SCOTLAND. Advocates' Library, Glasgow Corporation, &c. IRELAND. Dublin, Cork, and other Corporations, &c.	f'cap	C. 55	1 6
1871	SECOND REPORT, WITH APPENDIX, AND INDEX TO THE FIRST AND SECOND REPORTS - - - - - - Contents :— ENGLAND. House of Lords; Cambridge Colleges; Oxford Colleges; Monastery of Dominican Friars at Woodchester, Duke of Bedford, Earl Spencer, &c. SCOTLAND. Aberdeen and St. Andrew's Universities, &c. IRELAND. Marquis of Ormonde; Dr. Lyons, &c.	"	C. 441	3 10
1872	THIRD REPORT, WITH APPENDIX AND INDEX - - - - - - Contents :— ENGLAND. House of Lords; Cambridge Colleges; Stonyhurst College; Bridgewater and other Corporations; Duke of Northumberland, Marquis of Lansdowne, Marquis of Bath, &c. SCOTLAND. University of Glasgow; Duke of Montrose, &c. IRELAND. Marquis of Ormonde; Black Book of Limerick, &c.	"	C. 673	6 0

Date.	——	Size.	Sessional Paper.	Price.
1873	FOURTH REPORT, WITH APPENDIX. PART I. - - - - - - Contents :— ENGLAND. House of Lords; Westminster Abbey; Cambridge and Oxford Colleges; Cinque Ports, Hythe, and other Corporations, Marquis of Bath, Earl of Denbigh, &c. SCOTLAND. Duke of Argyll, &c. IRELAND. Trinity College, Dublin; Marquis of Ormonde.	f'cap	. 857	s. d. 6 8
"	DITTO. PART II. INDEX - - -	"	C. 857 i.	2 6
1876	FIFTH REPORT, WITH APPENDIX. PART I. - Contents :— ENGLAND. House of Lords; Oxford and Cambridge Colleges; Dean and Chapter of Canterbury; Rye, Lydd, and other Corporations, Duke of Sutherland, Marquis of Lansdowne, Reginald Cholmondeley, Esq., &c. SCOTLAND. Earl of Aberdeen, &c.	"	C. 1432	7 0
"	DITTO. PART II. INDEX - - -	"	C. 1432 i.	3 6
1877	SIXTH REPORT, WITH APPENDIX. PART I. - Contents :— ENGLAND. House of Lords; Oxford and Cambridge Colleges; Lambeth Palace; Black Book of the Archdeacon of Canterbury; Bridport, Wallingford, and other Corporations; Lord Leconfield, Sir Reginald Graham, Sir Henry Ingilby, &c. SCOTLAND. Duke of Argyll, Earl of Moray, &c. IRELAND. Marquis of Ormonde.	"	C. 1745	8 6
"	DITTO. PART II. INDEX - - -	"	C. 2102	1 10
1879	SEVENTH REPORT, WITH APPENDIX. PART I. - - - - - - Contents :— House of Lords; County of Somerset; Earl of Egmont, Sir Frederick Graham, Sir Harry Verney, &c.	"	C. 2340	7 6
	DITTO. PART II. APPENDIX AND INDEX - Contents :— Duke of Athole, Marquis of Ormonde, S. F. Livingstone, Esq., &c.	"	C. 2340 i.	3 6
1881	EIGHTH REPORT, WITH APPENDIX AND INDEX. PART I. - - - - Contents :— List of collections examined, 1869–1880. ENGLAND. House of Lords; Duke of Marlborough; Magdalen College, Oxford; Royal College of Physicians; Queen Anne's Bounty Office; Corporations of Chester, Leicester, &c. IRELAND. Marquis of Ormonde, Lord Emly, The O'Conor Don, Trinity College, Dublin, &c.	"	C. 3040	8 6

Date.	—	Size.	Sessional Paper.	Price.
				s. d.
1881	DITTO. PART II. APPENDIX AND INDEX - Contents :— Duke of Manchester.	f'cap	C. 3040 i.	1 9
1881	DITTO. PART III. APPENDIX AND INDEX - Contents :— Earl of Ashburnham.	"	C.3040ii.	1 4
1883	NINTH REPORT, WITH APPENDIX AND INDEX. PART I. - - - - Contents :— St. Paul's and Canterbury Cathedrals; Eton College; Carlisle, Yarmouth, Canterbury, and Barnstaple Corporations, &c.	"	C. 3773	5 2
1884	DITTO. PART II. APPENDIX AND INDEX - Contents :— ENGLAND. House of Lords; Earl of Leicester; C. Pole Gell, Alfred Morrison, Esquires, &c. SCOTLAND. Lord Elphinstone, H. C. Maxwell Stuart, Esq., &c. IRELAND. Duke of Leinster, Marquis of Drogheda, &c.	"	C. 3773 i.	6 3
1884	DITTO. PART III. APPENDIX AND INDEX - - - - - Contents :— Mrs. Stopford Sackville.	"	C.3773ii.	1 7
1883	CALENDAR OF THE MANUSCRIPTS OF THE MARQUIS OF SALISBURY, K.G. (or CECIL MSS.). PART I. - - - -	8vo.	C. 3777	3 5
1885	TENTH REPORT - - - - - This is introductory to the following :—	"	C. 4548	0 3½
1885	(1.) APPENDIX AND INDEX - - The Earl of Eglinton, Sir J. S. Maxwell, Bart., and C. S. H. D. Moray, C. F. Weston Underwood, G. W. Digby, Esquires.	"	C. 4575	3 7
1885	(2.) APPENDIX AND INDEX - - The Family of Gawdy, formerly of Norfolk.	"	C.4576iii.	1 4
1885	(3.) APPENDIX AND INDEX - - Wells Cathedral.	"	C.4576 ii.	2 0
1885	(4.) APPENDIX AND INDEX - - Earl of Westmorland; Captain Stewart; Lord Stafford; Sir N. W. Throckmorton, Bart., Stonyhurst College; Sir P. T. Mainwaring, Bart., Misses Boycott, Lord Muncaster, M.P., Captain J. F. Bagot, Earl of Kilmorey, Earl of Powis, A. Salwey, L. Parkinson, G. Browne, Z. Lloyd, Esquires, Revs. T. S. Hill, C. R. Manning, W. H. Sewell, and others, the Corporations of Kendal, Bishop's Castle, Wenlock, Bridgnorth, Eye, Plymouth, and the County of Essex.	"	C. 4576	3 6

Date.	—	Size.	Sessional Paper.	Price.
				s. d.
1885	(5.) APPENDIX AND INDEX - - - The Marquis of Ormonde, Earl of Fingall, Corporations of Galway, Waterford, the Sees of Dublin and of Ossory, Archives of the Jesuits in Ireland.	8vo.	4576 i.	2 10
1887	(6.) APPENDIX AND INDEX - - - Marquis of Abergavenny, Lord Braye, G. F. Luttrell, P. P. Bouverie, W. B. Davenport, M.P., R. T. Balfour, Esquires.	"	C. 5242	1 7
1887	ELEVENTH REPORT - - - - This is introductory to the following :—	"	C. 5060 vi.	0 3
1887	(1.) APPENDIX AND INDEX - - - H. D. Skrine, Esq., Salvetti Correspondence.	"	C. 5060	1 1
1887	(2.) APPENDIX AND INDEX - - - The House of Lords. 1678–1688.	"	C. 5060 i.	2 0
1887	(3.) APPENDIX AND INDEX - - - The Corporations of Southampton and Lynn.	"	C. 5060 ii.	1 8
1887	(4.) APPENDIX AND INDEX - - - The Marquess Townshend.	"	C. 5060 iii.	2 6
1887	(5.) APPENDIX AND INDEX - - - The Earl of Dartmouth.	"	C. 5060 iv.	2 8
1887	(6.) APPENDIX AND INDEX - - - The Duke of Hamilton.	"	C. 5060 v.	1 6
1888	(7.) APPENDIX AND INDEX - - - The Duke of Leeds, Lord Hothfield, Mr. le Strange; Mr. A. W. Savile; Corporation of Reading, Inner Temple Library, &c. *In the Press.*	"	C. 5060 vii.	—
1888	CALENDAR OF THE MANUSCRIPTS OF THE MARQUIS OF SALISBURY, K.G. (or CECIL MSS.). Part II. - - -	"	C. 5463	3 5
	TWELFTH REPORT.			
	This will be introductory to the following :—			
1888	(1.) APPENDIX. PART I. - - - The Earl Cowper, K.G. (Coke MSS., at Melbourne Hall, Derby), Vol. I.	"	C. 5472	2 7
	Other Appendixes in the Press.			

Stationery Office,
January 1889.

ANNUAL REPORTS OF THE DEPUTY KEEPER OF THE PUBLIC RECORDS.

REPORTS Nos. 1-22, IN FOLIO, PUBLISHED BETWEEN 1840 AND 1861, ARE NO LONGER ON SALE. SUBSEQUENT REPORTS ARE IN OCTAVO.

Date.	Number of Report.	Chief Contents of Appendices.	Sessional No.	Price.
				s. *d.*
1862	23	Subjects of Research by Literary Inquirers, 1852-1861.—Attendances at the various Record Offices, previously to the passing of the Public Record Act.	C. 2970	0 4
1863	24	List of Calendars, Indexes, &c., in the Public Record Office.	C. 3142	0 7½
1864	25	Calendar of Crown Leases, 33-38 Hen. VIII.—Calendar of Bills and Answers, &c., Hen. VIII.-Ph. & Mary, for Cheshire and Flintshire.—List of Lords High Treasurers and Chief Commissioners of the Treasury, from Hen. VII.	C. 3318	0 8
1865	26	List of Plans annexed to Inclosure Awards, 31 Geo. II.-7 Will. IV.—Calendar of Privy Seals, &c., Hen. VI.-Eliz., for Cheshire and Flintshire.—Calendar of Writs of General Livery, &c., for Cheshire, Eliz.-Charles I.—Calendar of Deeds, &c., on the Chester Plea Rolls, Hen. III. and Edw. I.—List of Documents photozincographed, Will. I.-Hen. VII.	C. 3492	0 7
1866	27	List of Awards of Inclosure Commissioners.—References to Charters in the Cartæ Antiquæ and the Confirmation Rolls of Chancery, Ethelbert of Kent-James I.—Calendar of Deeds, &c., on the Chester Plea Rolls, Edw. II.—List of Documents photozincographed, Hen. VIII. and Edw. VI.	C. 3717	1 6
1867	28	Fees in the Public Record Office.—Calendar of Fines, Cheshire and Flintshire, Edw. I.—Calendar of Deeds, &c., on the Chester Plea Rolls, Edw. III.—List of Documents photozincographed,	C. 3839	0 10½

Date.	Number of Report.	Chief Contents of Appendices.	Sessional No.	Price.
				s. d.
		Mary and Eliz., and Scottish, Part I. —Table of Law Terms, from the Norman Conquest to 1 Will IV.		
1868	29	Calendar of Royal Charters.—Calendar of Deeds, &c., on the Chester Plea Rolls, Richard II.-Hen. VII.—Durham Records, Letter and Report.	C. 4012	0 9
1869	30	Duchy of Lancaster Records, Inventory. —Durham Records, Inventory, Indexes to Kellawe's Register. — Calendar of Deeds, &c., on the Chester Plea Rolls, Hen. VIII.—Calendar of Decrees of Court of General Surveyors, 34–38 Hen. VIII.—Calendar of Royal Charters.—State Paper Office, Calendar of Documents relating to the History of, to 1800.—List of Documents photozincographed, Eliz.-Anne.—Tower of London. Index to Documents in custody of the Constable of.—Calendar of Dockets, &c., for Privy Seals, 1634–1711, in the British Museum. Report of the Commissioners on Carte Papers.—Venetian Ciphers.	C. 4165	3 0
1870	31	Duchy of Lancaster Records, Calendar of Royal Charters, Will. II.-Ric. II.—Durham Records, Calendar of Chancery Enrolments; Cursitor's Records.—List of Officers of Palatinate of Chester, in Cheshire and Flintshire, and North Wales.—List of Sheriffs of England, 31 Hen. I. to 4 Edw. III.—List of Documents photozincographed, Scottish, Part II.	[C. 187]	2 3
1871	32	Part I.—Report of the Commissioners on Carte Papers. — Calendarium Genealogicum, 1 & 2 Edw. II.—Durham Records, Calendar of Cursitor's Records, Chancery Enrolments.—Duchy of Lancaster Records, Calendar of Rolls of the Chancery of the County Palatine.	[C. 374]	2 2
1871	--	Part II.—Charities; Calendar of Trust Deeds enrolled on the Close Rolls of Chancery, subsequent to 9 Geo. II. c. xxxvi.	[C. 374] I.	5 6
1872	33	Duchy of Lancaster Records, Calendar of Rolls of the Chancery of the County Palatine.—Durham Records, Calendar of the Cursitor's Records, Chancery Enrolments.—Report on the Shaftesbury Papers.—Venetian Transcripts.—Greek copies of the Athanasian Creed.	[C. 620]	1 10
1873	34	Parliamentary Petitions; Index to the Petitions to the King in Council. –	[C. 728]	1 9

Date.	Number of Report.	Chief Contents of Appendices.	Sessional No.	Price.
				s. *d.*
		Durham Records, Calendar of the Cursitor's Records, Chancery Enrolments.—List of Documents photozincographed. Scottish, Part III.—Supplementary Report on the Shaftesbury Papers.		
1874	35	Duchy of Lancaster Records, Calendar of Ancient Charters or Grants.—Palatinate of Lancaster; Inventory and Lists of Documents transferred to the Public Record Office. — Durham Records, Calendar of Cursitor's Records, Chancery Enrolments.—List of Documents photozincographed, Irish, Part I.—Second Supplementary Report on the Shaftesbury Papers.	[C. 1043]	1 6
1875	36	Durham Records, Calendar of the Cursitor's Records, Chancery Enrolments.—Duchy of Lancaster Records; Calendar of Ancient Charters or Grants.—List of Documents photozincographed; Irish, Part II.—M. Armand Baschet's Report upon Documents in French Archives relating to British History.—Calendar of Recognizance Rolls of the Palatinate of Chester, to end of reign of Hen. IV.	[C. 1301]	4 4
1876	37	Part I.—Durham Records, Calendar of the Cursitor's Records, Chancery Enrolments.—Duchy of Lancaster Records, Calendar of Ancient Rolls of the Chancery of the County Palatine.—M. Baschet's list of French Ambassadors, &c., in England, 1509–1714.	[C. 1544]	1 2
1876	—	Part II.—Calendar of Recognizance Rolls of the Palatinate of Chester; Hen. V.–Hen. VII.	[C. 1544] I.	4 4
1877	38	Exchequer Records, Catalogue of Special Commissions, 1 Eliz. to 10 Vict., Calendar of Depositions taken by Commission, 1 Eliz. to end of James I.—List of Representative Peers for Scotland and Ireland.	[C. 1747]	4 3
1878	39	Calendar of Recognizance Rolls of the Palatinate of Chester, 1 Hen. VIII.–11 Geo. IV. — Exchequer Records, Calendar of Depositions taken by Commission, Charles I.—Duchy of Lancaster Records; Calendar of Lancashire Inquisitions post Mortem, &c.—Third Supplementary Report on the Shaftesbury Papers.—Anglo-Saxon Charters photozincographed.—M. Baschet's List of Despatches of French Ambassadors to England, 1509–1714.	[C. 2123]	4 6

Date.	Number of Report.	Chief Contents of Appendices.	Sessional No.	Price.
				s. d.
1879	40	Calendar of Depositions taken by Commission, Commonwealth-James II.—Miscellaneous Records of Queen's Remembrancer in the Exchequer.—Durham Records, Calendar of the Cursitor's Records, Chancery Enrolments.—Duchy of Lancaster Records, Calendar of Patent Rolls, 5 Ric. II.–21 Hen. VII.—Rules and Regulations respecting the public use of the Records.	[C. 2377]	3 0
1880	41	Calendar of Depositions taken by Commission, William and Mary to George I.—Calendar of Norman Rolls, Hen. V., Part I.—Anglo-Saxon Charters photozincographed.—Report from Rome.—List of Calendars, Indexes, &c. in the Public Record Office on 31st December 1879.	[C. 2658]	4 8
1881	42	Calendar of Depositions taken by Commission, George II.—Calendar of Norman Rolls, Hen. V., Part II. and Glossary.—Calendar of Patent Rolls, 1 Edw. I.—Anglo-Saxon Charters photozincographed.—Transcripts from Paris.	[C. 2972]	4 0
1882	43	Calendar of Privy Seals, &c., 1–7 Charles I.—Duchy of Lancaster Records, Inventory of Court Rolls, Hen. III.–Geo. IV., Calendar of Privy Seals, Ric. II.—Calendar of Patent Rolls, 2 Edw. I.—Anglo-Saxon Charters photozincographed.—Fourth Supplementary Report on the Shaftesbury Papers.—Transcripts from Paris.—Report on Libraries in Sweden.—Report on Papers relating to English History in the State Archives, Stockholm.—Report on Canadian Archives.	[C. 3425]	3 10
1883	44	Calendar of Patent Rolls, 3 Edw. I.—Durham Records, Cursitor's Records, Inquisitions post Mortem, &c.—Calendar of French Rolls, 1–10 Hen. V.—Anglo-Saxon Charters photozincographed.—Report from Venice.—Transcripts from Paris.—Report from Rome.	[C. 3771]	3 6
1884	45	Duchy of Lancaster Records, Inventory of Ministers' and Receivers' Accounts, Edw. I.–Geo. III.—Durham Records, Cursitor's Records, Inquisitions post Mortem, &c.—Treasury of the Receipt of the Exchequer, Calendar of Diplomatic Documents. — Anglo-Saxon Charters photozincographed. — Transcripts from Paris. — Reports from Rome and Stockholm. — Report on Archives of Denmark, &c.—Tran-	[C. 4425]	4 3

Date.	Number of Report.	Chief Contents of Appendices.	Sessional No.	Price.
				s. d.
		scripts from Venice. — Calendar of Patent Rolls, 4 Edw. I.		
1885	46	Presentations to Offices on the Patent Rolls, Charles II. — Anglo-Saxon Charters, &c., photozincographed.—Transcripts from Paris.—Reports from Rome.—Second Report on Archives of Denmark, &c. — Calendar of Patent Rolls, 5 Edw. I.—Catalogue of Venetian Manuscripts bequeathed by Mr. Rawdon Brown to the Public Record Office.	[C. 4746]	2 10
1886	47	Transcripts from Paris.—Reports from Rome.—Third Report on Archives of Denmark, &c.—List of Creations of Peers and Baronets, 1483-1646.—Calendar of Patent Rolls, 6 Edw. I.	[C. 4888]	2 2
1887	48	Calendar of Patent Rolls, 7 Edw. I.—Calendar of French Rolls, Henry VI.—Calendar of Privy Seals, &c., 8-11 Charles I. — Calendar of Diplomatic Documents.—Schedules of Valueless Documents.	[C. 5234]	3 6
1888	49	Calendar of Patent Rolls, 8 Edw. I.—Calendar of Early Chancery Proceedings.—Index to Leases and Pensions (Augmentation Office).—Calendar of Star Chamber Proceedings. *In the Press.*	[C. 5596]	3 3
		Indexes to Printed Reports, viz.:		
		Reports 1-22 (1840-1861) - -	—	4 0
		„ 23-39 (1862-1878) - -	—	2 0

Public Record Office,
Januar 1889.

SCOTLAND.

CATALOGUE OF SCOTCH RECORD PUBLICATIONS

PUBLISHED UNDER THE DIRECTION OF

THE LORD CLERK REGISTER OF SCOTLAND.

[OTHER WORKS RELATING TO SCOTLAND WILL BE FOUND AMONG THE PUBLICATIONS OF THE RECORD COMMISSIONERS, *see* pp. 26–28.]

1. CHRONICLES OF THE PICTS AND SCOTS, AND OTHER EARLY MEMORIALS OF SCOTTISH HISTORY. Royal 8vo., half bound (1867). *Edited by* WILLIAM F. SKENE, LL.D. *Price* 10*s*. *Out of print.*
2. LEDGER OF ANDREW HALYBURTON, CONSERVATOR OF THE PRIVILEGES OF THE SCOTCH NATION IN THE NETHERLANDS (1492–1503); TOGETHER WITH THE BOOKS OF CUSTOMS AND VALUATION OF MERCHANDISES IN SCOTLAND. *Edited by* COSMO INNES. Royal 8vo., half bound (1867). *Price* 10*s*.
3. DOCUMENTS ILLUSTRATIVE OF THE HISTORY OF SCOTLAND FROM THE DEATH OF KING ALEXANDER THE THIRD TO THE ACCESSION OF ROBERT BRUCE, from original and authentic copies in London, Paris, Brussels, Lille, and Ghent. In 2 Vols. royal 8vo., half bound (1870). *Edited by* Rev. JOSEPH STEVENSON. *Price* 10*s*. *each.*
4. ACCOUNTS OF THE LORD HIGH TREASURER OF SCOTLAND. Vol. 1, A.D. 1473–1498. *Edited by* THOMAS DICKSON. 1877. *Price* 10*s*.
5. REGISTER OF THE PRIVY COUNCIL OF SCOTLAND. *Edited and arranged by* J. H. BURTON, LL.D. Vol. 1, 1545–1569. Vol. 2, 1569–1578. Vol. 3, A.D. 1578–1585. Vol. 4, A.D. 1585–1592. Vol. 5, 1592–1599. Vol. 6, 1599–1604. Vol. 7, 1604–1607. Vol. 8, 1607–1610. Vol. 9 in progress. *Edited by* DAVID MASSON, LL.D. 1877–1887. *Price* 15*s*. *each.*
6. ROTULI SCACCARII REGUM SCOTORUM. THE EXCHEQUER ROLLS OF SCOTLAND Vol. 1, A.D. 1264–1359. Vol. 2, A.D. 1359–1379. *Edited by* JOHN STUART, LL.D., and GEORGE BURNETT, Lyon King of Arms. 1878–1880. Vol. 3, A.D. 1379–1406. Vol. 4, A.D. 1406–1436 (1880). Vol. 5, A.D. 1437–1454 (1882). Vol. 6, 1455–1460 (1883). Vol. 7, 1460–1469 (1884). Vol. 8, A.D. 1470–1479 (1885). Vol. 9, 1480–1487. Addenda, 1437–1487 (1886). Vol. 10, 1488–1496 (1887). Vol. 11, 1497–1591 (1888). Vol. 12 in progress. *Edited by* GEORGE BURNETT. *Price* 10*s*. *each.*
7. CALENDAR OF DOCUMENTS RELATING TO SCOTLAND. *Edited by* JOSEPH BAIN. Vol. 1 (1881). Vol. II. 1272–1307 (1884). Vol. III. 1307–1357 (1887). Vol. IV., 1357–1509 (1888). *Price* 15*s*. *each.*
8. REGISTER OF THE GREAT SEAL OF SCOTLAND. A.D. 1424–1513 (1882). A.D. 1513–1546 (1883). A.D. 1546–1580 (1886). A.D. 1580–1593 (1888). *Edited by* JAMES BALFOUR PAUL and J. M. THOMSON. *Price* 15*s*. *each.*

FAC-SIMILES OF THE NATIONAL MSS. OF SCOTLAND. (*Out of print.*)
Parts I., II., and III. *Price* 21*s*. *each.*

Stationery Office,
November 1888.

IRELAND.

CATALOGUE OF IRISH RECORD PUBLICATIONS.

1. Calendar of the Patent and Close Rolls of Chancery in Ireland. Henry VIII., Edward VI., Mary, and Elizabeth, and for the 1st to the 7th year of Charles I. *Edited by* James Morrin, Royal 8vo. (1861–3). Vols. 1, 2, and 3. *Price* 11*s*. each.

2. Ancient Laws and Institutes of Ireland.
   Senchus Mor. (1865–1880.) Vols. 1, 2, 3, and 4. *Price* 10*s*. each. Vol. 5 in progress.

4. Abstracts of the Irish Patent Rolls of James I. Unbound. *Price* 25*s*.
   Abstracts of the Irish Patent Rolls of James I. With Supplement. *Price* 35*s*

5. Ulster, Annals of. Otherwise Annals of Senat; a Chronicle of Irish Affairs from A.D. 431 to A.D. 1540. With a translation and Notes. Vol. 1, A.D. 431–1056. 600 pp. Half morocco. *Price* 10*s*.

Fac-similes of National Manuscripts of Ireland, from the earliest extant specimens to A.D. 1719. *Edited by* John T. Gilbert, F.S.A., M.R.I.A. *Part* 1 *is out of print*. Parts II. and III. *Price* 42*s*. each. *Part IV*. 1. *Price* 5*l*. 5*s*. *Part IV*. 2. *Price* 4*l*. 10*s*.

This work forms a comprehensive Palæographic Series for Ireland. I furnishes characteristic specimens of the documents which have come down from each of the classes which, in past ages, formed principal elements in the population of Ireland, or exercised an influence in her affairs. With these reproductions are combined fac-similes of writings connected with eminent personages or transactions of importance in the annals of the country to the early part of the eighteenth century.

The specimens have been reproduced as nearly as possible in accordance with the originals, in dimensions, colouring, and general appearance. Characteristic examples of styles of writing and caligraphic ornamentation are, so far as practicable, associated with subjects of historic and linguistic interest. Descriptions of the various manuscripts are given by the Editor in the Introduction. The contents of the specimens are fully elucidated and printed in the original languages, opposite to the Fac-similes—line for line—without contractions—thus facilitating reference and aiding effectively those interested in palæographic studies.

In the work are also printed in full, for the first time, many original and important historical documents.

Part 1. commences with the earliest Irish MSS. extant.
Part II.: From the Twelfth Century to A.D. 1299.
Part III.: From A.D. 1300 to end of reign of Henry VIII.
Part IV. 1.: From reign of Edward VI. to that of James I.
In Part IV. 2.—the work is carried down to the early part of the eighteenth century, with Index to the entire publication.

Account of Fac-similes of National Manuscripts of Ireland. In one Volume; 8vo., with Index. *Price* 10*s*. Parts I. and II. together. *Price* 2*s*. 6*d*. Part II. *Price* 1*s*. 6*d*. Part III. *Price* 1*s*. Part IV. 1. *Price* 2*s*. Part IV. 2. *Price* 2*s*. 6*d*.

Stationery Office,
November 1888.

ANNUAL REPORTS OF THE DEPUTY KEEPER OF THE PUBLIC RECORDS, IRELAND.

Date.	Number of Report.	Chief Contents of Appendices.	Sessional No.	Price.
				s. d.
1869	1	Contents of the principal Record Repositories of Ireland in 1864.—Notices of Records transferred from Chancery Offices.—Irish State Papers presented by Philadelphia Library Company.	C. 4157	2 3
1870	2	Notices of Records transferred from Chancery, Queen's Bench, and Exchequer Offices.—Index to Original Deeds received from Master Litton's Office.	[C. 137]	1 0
1871	3	Notices of Records transferred from Queen's Bench, Common Pleas, and Exchequer Offices.—Report on J. F. Ferguson's MSS.—Exchequer Indices, &c.	[C. 329]	2 0
1872	4	Records of Probate Registries - -	[C. 515]	0 2½
1873	5	Notices of Records from Queen's Bench Calendar of Fines and Recoveries of the Palatinate of Tipperary, 1664–1715.—Index to Reports to date.	[C. 760]	0 8
1874	6	Notices of Records transferred from Chancery, Queen's Bench, and Common Pleas Offices.—Report respecting "Facsimiles of National MSS. of Ireland."—List of Chancery Pleadings (1662–1690) and Calendar to Chancery Rolls (1662–1713) of Palatinate of Tipperary.	[C. 963]	0 7½
1875	7	Notices of Records from Exchequer and Admiralty Offices.—Calendar and Index to Fiants of Henry VIII.	[C. 1175]	0 7
1876	8	Calendar and Index to Fiants of Edward VI.	[C. 1469]	1 3
1877	9	Index to the Liber Munerum Publicorum Hiberniæ.—Calendar and Index to Fiants of Philip and Mary.	[C. 1702]	0 8
1878	10	Schedule of Parochial Registers deposited.—Index to Deputy Keeper's 6th, 7th, 8th, 9th, and 10th Reports.	[C. 2034]	0 3½
1879	11	Calendar to Fiants of Elizabeth (1558–1570)	[C. 2311]	1 4
1880	12	Calendar to Fiants of Elizabeth, continued (1570–1576).—Schedule of Parish Registers of Ireland.	[C. 2583]	1 3

Date.	Number of Report.	Chief Contents of Appendices.	Sessional No.	Price.
				s. d.
1881	13	Calendar to Fiants of Elizabeth, continued (1576–1583).	[C. 2929]	1 5
1882	14	Report of Keeper of State Papers containing Catalogue of Commonwealth Books transferred from Bermingham Tower.	[C. 3215]	0 6½
1883	15	Calendar to Fiants of Elizabeth, continued (1583–1586).—Index to Deputy Keeper's 11th, 12th, 13th ,14th, and 15th Reports.	[C. 3676]	1 0
1884	16	Calendar to Fiants of Elizabeth, continued (1586–1595).	[C. 4062]	1 6
1885	17	Report on Iron Chest of attainders following after 1641 and 1688.—Queen's Bench Calendar to Fiants of Elizabeth, continued (1596–1601).	[C. 4487]	1 6
1886	18	Calendar to Fiants of Elizabeth, continued (1601–1603).—Memorandum on Statements (1702) and Declarations (1713–14) of Huguenot Pensioners.—Schedule of present places of Custody of Parish Registers.	[C. 4755]	1 1
1887	19	Notice of Records of Incumbered and Landed Estates Courts.—Report of Keeper of State Papers, containing Table of Abstracts of Decrees of Innocence (1663), with Index.	[C. 5185]	0 6
1888	20	Calendar to Christ Church Deeds in Novum Registrum, 1174–1684. Index to Deputy Keeper's 16th, 17th, 18th, 19th, and 20th Reports.	C. 5535	0 8½

Public Record Office of Ireland,
November 1888.

Lightning Source UK Ltd.
Milton Keynes UK
UKOW05f1854250716

279216UK00012B/199/P